GERIATRICS *At Your* FINGERTIPS®

2016, 18th EDITION

GERIATRICS *At Your* FINGERTIPS®

2016, 18th EDITION

AUTHORS

David B. Reuben, MD

Keela A. Herr, PhD, RN

James T. Pacala, MD, MS

Bruce G. Pollock, MD, PhD

Jane F. Potter, MD

Todd P. Semla, MS, PharmD

Geriatrics At Your Fingertips® is published by the American Geriatrics Society as a service to healthcare providers involved in the care of older adults.

Although *Geriatrics At Your Fingertips*® is distributed by various companies in the healthcare field, it is independently prepared and published. All decisions regarding its content are solely the responsibility of the authors. Their decisions are not subject to any form of approval by other interests or organizations.

Some recommendations in this publication suggest the use of agents for purposes or in dosages other than those recommended in product labeling. Such recommendations are based on reports in peer-reviewed publications and are not based on or influenced by any material or advice from pharmaceutical or healthcare product manufacturers.

No responsibility is assumed by the authors or the American Geriatrics Society for any injury or damage to persons or property, as a matter of product liability, negligence, warranty, or otherwise, arising out of the use or application of any methods, products, instructions, or ideas contained herein. No guarantee, endorsement, or warranty of any kind, express or implied (including specifically no warrant of merchantability or of fitness for a particular purpose) is given by the Society in connection with any information contained herein. Independent verification of any diagnosis, treatment, or drug use or dosage should be obtained. No test or procedure should be performed unless, in the judgment of an independent, qualified physician, it is justified in the light of the risk involved.

Citation: Reuben DB, Herr KA, Pacala JT, et al. *Geriatrics At Your Fingertips: 2016, 18th Edition.* New York: The American Geriatrics Society; 2016.

ISSN 1553-152X
ISBN 978-1-886775-40-4

TABLE OF CONTENTS

Abbreviations and Symbols iii
Drug Prescribing and Elimination.. viii
Introduction xi
Formulas and Reference Information 1
Assessment and Approach.. 4
Appropriate Prescribing, Drug Interactions, and Adverse Events................ 16
Antithrombotic Therapy and Thromboembolic Disease 26
Anxiety 36
Cardiovascular Diseases... 39
Delirium... 66
Dementia 70
Depression.. 78
Dermatologic Conditions.. 84
Endocrine Disorders.. 92
Eye Disorders... 105
Fall Prevention and Falls 113
Gastrointestinal Diseases 120
Hearing Impairment 133
Hematologic Disorders... 138
Incontinence—Urinary and Fecal 146
Infectious Diseases 157
Kidney Disorders... 177
Malnutrition 187
Musculoskeletal Disorders 194
Neurologic Disorders... 216
Osteoporosis 229
Pain 234
Palliative Care and Hospice 253
Preoperative and Perioperative Care 264
Prevention 270
Prostate Disorders 275
Psychotic Disorders 281
Respiratory Diseases 285
Sexual Dysfunction... 301
Skin Ulcers... 306
Sleep Disorders... 316
Substance Use Disorders 323
Women's Health 330
Appendixes
  Assessment Instruments... 335
    Mini-Cog Screen for Dementia 335
    Physical Self-Maintenance Scale (Activities of Daily Living, or ADLs) 336
    Instrumental Activities of Daily Living Scale (IADLs)..................... 337
    PHQ-9 and PHQ-2 Quick Depression Assessment 338
    Rapid Estimate of Adult Literacy in Medicine—Short Form (REALM-SF) 340
    Karnofsky Scale 341
    Palliative Performance Scale (PPS) 342
    Reisberg Functional Assessment Staging (FAST) Scale................... 343
    AUA Symptom Index for BPH... 344
    Opioid Risk Tool... 345
Coding in Geriatrics.. 346
Important Telephone Numbers and Web Sites.............................. 348
Index 350

AUTHORS

David B. Reuben, MD
Director, Multicampus Program in Geriatric Medicine and Gerontology
Chief, Division of Geriatrics
Archstone Foundation Chair
Professor of Medicine
David Geffen School of Medicine at UCLA, Los Angeles, CA

Keela A. Herr, PhD, RN
Professor and Associate Dean for Faculty
Co-Director, Csomay Center for Gerontological Excellence
College of Nursing
The University of Iowa, Iowa City, IA

James T. Pacala, MD, MS
Professor and Associate Head
Distinguished University Teaching Professor
Department of Family Medicine and Community Health
University of Minnesota Medical School, Minneapolis, MN

Bruce G. Pollock, MD, PhD, FRCPC, DFAPA
Vice President, Research
Director, Campbell Family Mental Health Research Institute
Centre for Addiction and Mental Health
Professor of Psychiatry and Pharmacology
Director, Division of Geriatric Psychiatry
University of Toronto, Toronto, Ontario, Canada

Jane F. Potter, MD
Chief, Division of Geriatrics and Gerontology
Director, Home Instead Center for Successful Aging
University of Nebraska Medical Center, Omaha, NE

Todd P. Semla, MS, PharmD
National PBM Clinical Pharmacy Program Manager
Department of Veterans Affairs
Pharmacy Benefits Management Services
Associate Professor, Clinical
Departments of Medicine and Psychiatry & Behavioral Sciences
The Feinberg School of Medicine
Northwestern University, Chicago, IL

ABBREVIATIONS AND SYMBOLS

AAA	abdominal aortic aneurysm
AAOS	American Academy of Orthopaedic Surgeons
ABG	arterial blood gas
ABI	ankle-brachial index
ACC	American College of Cardiology
ACEI	angiotensin-converting enzyme inhibitor
ACI	anemia of chronic inflammation
ACIP	Advisory Committee on Immunization Practices
ACOG	American College of Obstetrics and Gynecology
ACR	American College of Rheumatology
ACS	acute coronary syndrome
ACTH	adrenocorticotropic hormone
AD	Alzheimer disease
ADA	American Diabetes Association
ADLs	activities of daily living
ADT	androgen deprivation therapy
AE	adverse event
AF	atrial fibrillation
AGS	American Geriatrics Society
AHA	American Heart Association
AHI	Apnea-Hypopnea Index
AHRQ	Agency for Healthcare Research and Quality
AIDS	acquired immune deficiency syndrome
AIMS	Abnormal Involuntary Movement Scale
ALS	amyotrophic lateral sclerosis
ALT	alanine aminotransferase
AMD	age-related macular degeneration
APAP	acetaminophen
ARB	angiotensin receptor blocker
AREDS	Age-Related Eye Disease Study (by National Eye Institute)
AS	aortic stenosis
ASA	acetylsalicylic acid or aspirin
ASA Class	American Society of Anesthesiologists grading scale for surgical patients
AST	aspartate aminotransferase
ATA	American Thyroid Association
ATS	American Thoracic Society
AUA	American Urological Association
AUD	alcohol use disorder
BC	Beers Criteria
BMD	bone mineral density
BMI	body mass index
BP	blood pressure
BPH	benign prostatic hyperplasia
bpm	beats per minute
BUN	blood urea nitrogen
C&S	culture and sensitivity
CABG	coronary artery bypass graft

CAD	coronary artery disease
CBC	complete blood cell count
CBT	cognitive behavioral therapy
CCB	calcium-channel blocker
CCP	cyclic citrullinated peptide (antibody test)
CDC	US Centers for Disease Control and Prevention
CDR	Clinical Dementia Rating Scale
cfu	colony-forming unit
$CHADS_2$	Congestive heart failure, Hypertension, Age ≥75, Diabetes, Stroke (doubled) (score)
CHA_2DS_2-VASc	Congestive heart failure, Hypertension, Age ≥75 (doubled), Diabetes, Stroke (doubled), Vascular disease, Age 65–74, and Sex (female) (score)
CHD	coronary heart disease
CKD	chronic kidney disease
CMS	Centers for Medicare and Medicaid Services
CNS	central nervous system
COPD	chronic obstructive pulmonary disease
CPAP	continuous positive airway pressure
Cr	creatinine
CrCl	creatinine clearance
CRP	C-reactive protein
CT	computed tomography
CW	Choosing Wisely recommendation
CXR	chest x-ray
CYP	cytochrome P-450
D&C	dilation and curettage
D5W	dextrose 5% in water
DBP	diastolic blood pressure
D/C	discontinue
DHIC	detrusor hyperactivity with impaired contractility
DM	diabetes mellitus
DMARD	disease-modifying antirheumatoid drug
DPP-4	dipeptidyl peptidase 4
DSM-5	Diagnostic and Statistical Manual of Mental Disorders, 5th ed. (Arlington, VA: American Psychiatric Association; 2013)
DVT	deep-vein thrombosis
ECF	extracellular fluid
ECG	electrocardiogram, electrocardiography
EEG	electroencephalogram
EF	ejection fraction
eGFR	estimated glomerular filtration rate
EPS	extrapyramidal symptoms
ESR	erythrocyte sedimentation rate
EULAR	European League Against Rheumatism
FAST	Reisberg Functional Assessment Staging Scale
FDA	Food and Drug Administration
FEV_1	forced expiratory volume in 1 sec
FI	fecal incontinence
FOBT	fecal occult blood test
FRAX	WHO Fracture Risk Assessment Tool
FTD	frontotemporal dementia

FVC	forced vital capacity
GAD	generalized anxiety disorder
GDS	Geriatric Depression Scale
GERD	gastroesophageal reflux disease
GFR	glomerular filtration rate
GI	gastrointestinal
GLP–1	glucagon-like peptide–1
GnRH	gonadotropin-releasing hormone
GU	genitourinary
Hb	hemoglobin
HbA_{1c}	glycosylated hemoglobin
HCTZ	hydrochlorothiazide
HDL	high-density lipoprotein
HF	heart failure
HR	heart rate
HT	hormone therapy
HTN	hypertension
hx	history
IADLs	instrumental activities of daily living
IBS	irritable bowel syndrome
IBW	ideal body weight
ICD	implantable cardiac defibrillator
ICU	intensive care unit
IgE	immunoglobulin E
IL	interleukin (eg, IL-1, IL-6)
INH	isoniazid
INR	international normalized ratio
IOP	intraocular pressure
iPTH	intact parathyroid hormone
JNC 7	Seventh Joint National Committee on Prevention, Detection, Evaluation, and Treatment of High Blood Pressure
JNC 8	Eighth Joint National Committee on Prevention, Detection, Evaluation, and Treatment of High Blood Pressure
K^+	potassium ion
LBD	Lewy body dementia
LBW	lean body weight
LDL	low-density lipoprotein
L-dopa	levodopa
LFT	liver function test
LMWH	low-molecular-weight heparin
LVEF	left ventricular ejection fraction
LVH	left ventricular hypertrophy
MAOI	monoamine oxidase inhibitor
MCV	mean corpuscular volume
MDI	metered-dose inhaler
MDRD	Modification of Diet in Renal Disease
MDS	myelodysplastic syndromes
MI	myocardial infarction
MMA	methylmalonic acid
MMSE	Mini-Mental State Examination (Folstein's)

MoCA	Montreal Cognitive Assessment
MRA	magnetic resonance angiography
MRI	magnetic resonance imaging
MRSA	methicillin-resistant *Staphylococcus aureus*
MSE	mental status examination
NICE	National Institute for Health and Clinical Excellence (for the United Kingdom)
NNRTI	non-nucleoside reverse transcriptase inhibitor
NRTI	nucleoside reverse transcriptase inhibitor
NSAID	nonsteroidal anti-inflammatory drug
NPH	neutral protamine Hagedorn (insulin)
NYHA	New York Heart Association
OCD	obsessive-compulsive disorder
OGTT	oral glucose tolerance test
OSA	obstructive sleep apnea
OT	occupational therapy
PAD	peripheral arterial disease
PAH	pulmonary arterial hypertension
PCA	patient-controlled analgesia
PCSK9	proprotein convertase subtilisin/kexin type 9
PDE5	phosphodiesterase type 5
PE	pulmonary embolism
POLST	Physician Orders for Life-Sustaining Treatment
PONV	postoperative nausea and vomiting
PPD	purified protein derivative (of tuberculin)
PPI	proton-pump inhibitor
PSA	prostate-specific antigen
PT	prothrombin time *or* physical therapy
PTH	parathyroid hormone
PTT	partial thromboplastin time
PTSD	post-traumatic stress disorder
PUVA	psoralen plus ultraviolet light of A wavelength
QT_c	QT (cardiac output) corrected for heart rate
RA	rheumatoid arthritis
RBC	red blood cells *or* ranitidine bismuth citrate
RCT	randomized controlled trial
RF	rheumatoid factor
RLS	restless legs syndrome
RR	respiratory rate
sats	saturations
SBP	systolic blood pressure
SD	standard deviation
SGLT2	sodium glucose co-transporter 2
SIADH	syndrome of inappropriate secretion of antidiuretic hormone
SLUMS	St Louis University Mental Status (examination)
SNRI	serotonin norepinephrine-reuptake inhibitor
SPEP	serum protein electrophoresis
SSRI	selective serotonin-reuptake inhibitor
sTfR	soluble transferrin receptor
TBW	total body weight
TCA	tricyclic antidepressant
TD	tardive dyskinesia
TG	triglycerides

TIA	transient ischemic attack
TIBC	total iron-binding capacity
TNF	tumor necrosis factor
TSH	thyroid-stimulating hormone
TURP	transurethral resection of the prostate
tx	treatment(s), therapy (-ies)
U	unit(s)
UA	urinalysis
UFH	unfractionated heparin
UI	urinary incontinence
USPSTF	US Preventive Services Task Force
UTI	urinary tract infection
UV	ultraviolet
VF	ventricular fibrillation
VIN	vulvar intraepithelial neoplasia
VT	ventricular tachycardia
VTE	venous thromboembolism
WBC	white blood cell(s)
WHO	World Health Organization

Drug Prescribing and Elimination

Drugs are listed by generic names; trade names are in *italics*. An asterisk (*) indicates that the drug is available OTC. Check marks (✓) indicate drugs preferred for treating older adults. A triangle (▲) after the drug name indicates that the drug is available as a generic formulation. A triangle after a combination medication indicates that the combination is available as a generic, not the individual drugs (ie, even though individual drugs in a combination medication are available as generics, the combination may not be).

Formulations in text are bracketed and expressed in milligrams (mg) unless otherwise specified. Information in parentheses after dose ranges indicate the number of doses into which the daily dose can be split. Abbreviations for dosing, formulations, and route of elimination are defined below.

ac	before meals	OU	both eyes
C	capsule, caplet	pc	after meals
ChT	chewable tablet	pch	patch
conc	concentrate	pk	pack, packet
CR	controlled release	po	by mouth
crm	cream	pr	per rectum
d	day(s)	prn	as needed
ER	extended release	pwd	powder
F	fecal elimination	qam	every morning
fl	fluid	qhs	each bedtime
g	gram(s)	S	liquid (includes concentrate,
gran	granules		elixir, solution, suspension,
gtt	drop(s)		syrup, tincture)
h	hour(s)	SC	subcutaneous(ly)
hs	at bedtime	sec	second(s)
IM	intramuscular(ly)	shp	shampoo
inj	injectable(s)	sl	sublingual
IT	intrathecal(ly)	sol	solution
IV	intravenous(ly)	Sp	suppository
K	renal elimination	spr	spray(s)
L	hepatic elimination	SR	sustained release
lot	lotion	sus	suspension
max	maximum	syr	syrup
mcg	microgram(s)	T	tablet
min	minute(s)	tab(s)	tablet(s)
mo	month(s)	tbsp	tablespoon(s)
npo	nothing by mouth	tinc	tincture
NS	normal saline	TR	timed release
ODT	oral disintegrating tablet	tsp	teaspoon(s)
oint	ointment	wk	week(s)
OL	off-label use	XR	extended release
OTC	over-the-counter	yr	year(s)

INTRODUCTION

Providing high-quality healthcare for older adults requires special knowledge and skills. *Geriatrics At Your Fingertips*® *(GAYF)* is an annually updated, pocket-sized reference that provides quick, easy access to the specific information clinicians need to make decisions about the care of older adults. Since its initial publication in 1998, *GAYF's* up-to-date content and portable format quickly made it the American Geriatrics Society's (AGS) best-selling publication.

In response to the increased use of electronic media in clinical settings, the AGS has also developed *GAYF* for the Web and for mobile devices. Schools can acquire licenses to provide mobile device access for all their faculty and trainees. More information on these formats can be found at www.geriatricscareonline.org.

In this updated 18th edition, we added a new section on the diagnosis and treatment of hypercalcemia and a section on the systemic inflammatory response syndrome (SIRS). We also created tables of commonly used medications that should be avoided or dosage reduced with kidney disease and common clinically important drug-drug interactions. In addition, we have reorganized and expanded the section on medical marijuana. The text and tables contain updated and newly recommended diagnostic tests and management strategies. Among the many updates included in this edition are recommendations about tests and procedures that follow the American Board of Internal Medicine Foundation's Choosing Wisely® Campaign (indicated by a [CW]) and the updated 2015 Beers Criteria for Medications. Medication tables were updated shortly before publication and include specific caveats and cautions to facilitate appropriate prescribing in older adults. Medications available as generic formulations are indicated, because these are often less expensive.

Given its portable size, *GAYF* does not explain in detail the rationale underlying the strategies presented. Many of these strategies have been derived from guidelines published by the Agency for Healthcare Research and Quality and various medical societies (see the National Guideline Clearinghouse at www.guidelines.gov). When no such guidelines exist, the strategies recommended represent the best opinions of the authors and reviewers, based on clinical experience and the most recent medical literature. References are provided sparingly, but many others are available from the organizations listed below, as well as from the current edition of the AGS *Geriatrics Review Syllabus*.

The authors welcome comments about *GAYF*, which should be addressed to the AGS at info. amger@americangeriatrics.org or 40 Fulton Street, 18th Floor, New York, NY 10038.

The authors are particularly grateful to the following organizations and individuals: the John A. Hartford Foundation, for generously supporting the initial development and distribution of *GAYF* and its PDA version; AGS staff, Nancy Lundebjerg, Carol Goodwin, and Elvy Ickowicz, who have served a vital role in *GAYF's* development and its continued distribution and expansion; and the following experts who reviewed portions of this edition:

Daniel Blumberger, MD
Patricia Bruckenthal, PhD, APRN-BC, APN
Catherine E. DuBeau, MD
Gail Greendale, MD
Gerald C. Groggel, MD
Peter Hollmann, MD

Jason M. Johanning, MD
Jerry C. Johnson, MD
James Judge, MD
Helen W. Lach, PhD, RN, GCNS-BC
Andrew Lee, MD
Patrick E. McBride, MD, MPH

Guidelines of the following organizations are the basis of parts of specific chapters:

Advisory Committee on Immunization Practices
Agency for Healthcare Research and Quality
Alzheimer's Association
American Academy of Neurology
American Academy of Orthopaedic Surgeons
American Association for Geriatric Psychiatry
American College of Cardiology
American College of Chest Physicians
American College of Gastroenterology
American College of Obstetrics and Gynecology
American College of Rheumatology
American Diabetes Association
American Geriatrics Society
American Heart Association
American Lung Association
American Pain Society
American Psychiatric Association
American Society of Anesthesiologists
American Thyroid Association
American Urological Association
The Endocrine Society
Ethnogeriatrics Committee, American Geriatrics Society
National Cholesterol Education Program
National Heart, Lung and Blood Institute
National Osteoporosis Foundation
U.S. Preventive Services Task Force
World Health Organization

Editorial Staff

Hope J. Lafferty, AM, ELS, Medical Editor
Joseph Douglas, Managing Editor
Pilar Wyman, Medical Indexer

Technical development and production of print and electronic versions:

Fry Communications, Inc.
Melissa Durborow, Group Manager
Rhonda Liddick, Composition Manager
William F. Adams, Compositor
Jason Hughes, Technical Services Manager
Julie Stevens, Project Manager

Atmosphere Apps
Eric Poirier, Chief Operations Officer

Table 1. Conversions

Temperature	Liquid	Weight
F = (1.8)C + 32	1 fl oz = 30 mL	1 lb = 0.453 kg
C = (F − 32) / (1.8)	1 tsp = 5 mL	1 kg = 2.2 lb
	1 tbsp = 15 mL	1 oz = 30 g

Alveolar-Arterial Oxygen Gradient

$A - a = 148 - 1.2(PaCO_2) - PaO_2$ [normal = 10–20 mmHg, breathing room air at sea level]

Calculated Osmolality

$Osm = 2Na + glucose / 18 + BUN / 2.8$ [normal = 280–295]

Golden Rules of Arterial Blood Gases

• $PaCO_2$ change of 10 corresponds to a pH change of 0.08.
• pH change of 0.15 corresponds to base excess change of 10 mEq/L.

Creatinine Clearance

See Appropriate Prescribing, p 16.

For renally eliminated drugs, dosage adjustments may be necessary if CrCl <60 mL/min.

Cockcroft-Gault formula:

$$\frac{IBW(140 - age) (0.85 \text{ if female})}{(72) (\text{stable serum Cr})}$$

Many laboratories are reporting MDRD as an estimate of GFR (eGFR). This measure is used for staging CKD. The MDRD has not been validated in adults >70 yr old.

GFR should not be equated to CrCl. The use of the MDRD eGFR to adjust drug dosages overestimates renal function in many older adults. The use of Cockcroft-Gault is more accurate to adjust drug dosages. FDA package insert dosing recommendations are almost entirely based on the Cockcroft-Gault estimate of CrCl.

The validity of the Cockcroft-Gault estimate of CrCl in obese patients has been questioned because total body weight (TBW) tends to overestimate CrCl in obese patients, while lean body weight (LBW) tends to underestimate CrCl. In obese patients, use of adjusted body weight (ABW) with correction of 0.3 [ABW(0.3)=(TWB − IBW)0.3 + IBW] or 0.4 [ABW(0.4)=(TBW − IBW)0.4 + IBW] and actual serum Cr in Cockcroft-Gault formula is recommended.

Ideal Body Weight

• Men = 50 kg + (2.3 kg) (each inch of height >5 feet)
• Women = 45.5 kg + (2.3 kg) (each inch of height >5 feet)

Body Mass Index

$$\frac{\text{weight in kg}}{(\text{height in meters})^2} \quad or \quad \frac{\text{weight in lb}}{(\text{height in inches})^2} \quad \times \quad 704.5$$

Age-adjusted Erythrocyte Sedimentation Rate

Westergren:
women = (age + 10) / 2
men = age / 2

Age-adjusted D-dimer

patient age in yr × 10 mcg/L

Partial Pressure of Oxygen, Arterial (PaO$_2$) While Breathing Room Air

100 – (age/3) estimates decline

Table 2. Motor Function by Nerve Roots			
Level	**Motor Function**	**Level**	**Motor Function**
C4	Spontaneous breathing	L1–L2	Hip flexion
C5	Shoulder shrug	L3	Hip adduction
C6	Elbow flexion	L4	Hip abduction
C7	Elbow extension	L5	Great toe dorsiflexion
C8/T1	Finger flexion	S1–S2	Foot plantar flexion
T1–T12	Intercostal abdominal muscles	S2–S4	Rectal tone

Table 3. Lumbosacral Nerve Root Compression			
Root	**Motor**	**Sensory**	**Reflex**
L4	Quadriceps	Medial foot	Knee jerk
	Dorsiflexors	Dorsum of foot	Medial hamstring
L5	Great toe dorsiflexors	Dorsum of foot	Medial hamstring
S1	Plantar flexors	Lateral foot	Ankle jerk

Figure 1. Dermatomes

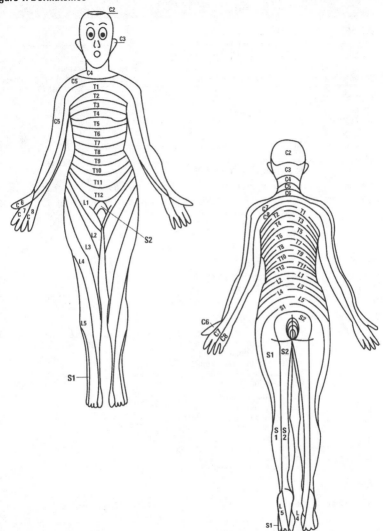

Source: Hamilton, RJ, ed. *The Tarascon Pocket Pharmacopoeia*, 2014 classic shirt-pocket edition. Jones and Bartlett Learning, 2014:143. Sudbury, MA. www.jblearning.com. Reprinted with permission.

ASSESSMENT

Table 4. Assessing Older Adults*

Assessment Domain	Screening Methods	Further Assessments (if screen is positive)	See Page(s)
Medical			
Medical illnesses[a,b]	Hx, screening physical examination	Additional targeted physical examination, laboratory and imaging tests	—
Medications[a,b]	Medications review/reconciliation	Pharmacy referral	16
Nutrition[a,b]	Inquire about weight loss (>10 lb in past 6 mo), calculate BMI	Dietary hx, malnutrition evaluation	187
Dentition	Oral examination	Dentistry referral	—
Hearing[a]	Handheld audioscope, Brief Hearing Loss Screener, whisper test	Ear examination, audiology referral	133
Vision[a]	Inquire about vision changes, Snellen chart testing	Eye examination, ophthalmology referral	105
Pain	Inquire about pain	Pain inventory	234
Urinary incontinence	Inquire if patient has lost urine >5 times in past year	UI evaluation	146
Mental			
Cognitive status[a,b]	3-item recall, Mini-Cog	MSE, dementia evaluation	335
Emotional status[a]	PHQ-2: "Over the past month, have you often had little interest or pleasure in doing things? Over the past month, have you often been bothered by feeling down, depressed, or hopeless?"	PHQ-9 or other depression screen, in-depth interview	338
	GAD-2: "Over the last 2 weeks, how often have you been bothered by the following problems: Feeling nervous, anxious, or on edge? Not being able to stop or control worrying?" (Scoring for each item: not at all = 0, several days = 1, more than half the days = 2, nearly every day = 3; total score of 3 or more is a positive screen)	GAD-7	36
Spiritual status	Spiritual hx	In-depth interview, chaplain or spiritual advisor referral	—
Physical			
Functional status[a]	ADLs, IADLs	PT/OT referral	336–337

(cont.)

Table 4. Assessing Older Adults* (cont.)			
Assessment Domain	**Screening Methods**	**Further Assessments (if screen is positive)**	**See Page(s)**
Balance and gait[a]	Observe patient getting up and walking, orthostatic BP and HR, Romberg test, semitandem stand	Formal gait evaluation, measurement of gait speed, 6-minute walk test	
Falls	Inquire if patient has had ≥2 falls in past year or is afraid of falling due to balance and/or walking problem	Falls evaluation	118
Environmental			
Social, financial status[a]	Social hx, assess risk factors for mistreatment	In-depth interview, social work referral	10–12
Environmental hazards[a]	Inquire about living situation, home safety checklist	Home evaluation	117
Care Preferences			
Life-sustaining tx[a,b]	Inquire about preferences; complete POLST form		10

*See also Assessment Instruments, p 335.

[a]Required elements of the Medicare Initial Annual Wellness Visit

[b]Required elements of Medicare Subsequent Annual Wellness Visits

Medicare Annual Wellness Visit (AWV)
- Can be performed by a physician, physician assistant, nurse practitioner, clinical nurse specialist, or a health professional (eg, health educator, dietitian) under the direct supervision of a physician.
- Initial and subsequent AWVs must include documentation of elements indicated in **Table 4**, plus the following items that are to be established at the initial AWV and updated at subsequent AWVs:
  - A family hx
  - A list of current providers caring for the patient
  - A written 5- to 10-yr schedule of screening activities based on USPSTF/CDC recommendations (Prevention, p 270)
  - A list of risk factors and conditions for which primary, secondary, and tertiary preventive interventions are being applied

INTERPROFESSIONAL GERIATRIC TEAM CARE
- Most effective for care of frail older adults with multiple comorbidities
- Also appropriate for management of complex geriatric syndromes (eg, falls, confusion, dementia, depression, incontinence, weight loss, persistent pain, immobility)
- Common features of team care include:
  - Proactive assessment of multiple domains (**Table 4**)
  - Care coordination, usually performed by an advanced practice nurse or social worker
  - Care planning performed by team members (**Table 5**)

Table 5. Interprofessional Team Members[a]

Profession	Degree	Training	Team Role
Advance practice nurse	APRN	2–4 yr PB	Disease management, care coordination, patient education, primary care, skin and pain assessment
Nurse	RN/LPN (LVN)	2–4 yr B/1–2 yr B	Care coordination, patient education, skin and pain assessment, ADL/IADL screening
Occupational therapist	OTR	2–4 yr PB	ADL/IADL assessment and improvement (including driving and home safety assessments)
Pharmacist	PharmD	4 yr PB ± 1–2 yr PG	Medication review/reconciliation, patient education, drug monitoring
Physical therapist	PT	2–3 yr PB	Mobility, strength, upper extremity assessment and improvement
Physician	MD, DO	4 yr PB + 3 or more yr PG	Diagnosis and management of medical problems, primary care
Social worker	MSW, DSW	2–4 yr PB	Complete psychosocial assessment and improvement, individual and family counseling

Notes: B = baccalaureate (post-high school), PB = post-baccalaureate, PG = post-graduate (ie, residency training)

[a] This is not an exhaustive list. Other common team members include audiologists, dentists, dietitians, physician assistants, speech therapists, and spiritual care professionals.

Table 6. Sites of Care[a]		
Site	**Patient Needs and Services**	**Principal Funding Source**
Home	ADL or IADL assistance	PP for caregiving services
	Skilled nursing and/or rehabilitation services when patient can only occasionally leave the home at great effort	Medicare Part A for nonphysician homecare services (eg, nursing, OT, PT); Part B for outpatient PT/ST/OT services independent of a home care agency;[b] PP for caregiving services
Senior citizen housing	Housing	PP[c]
Assisted living, residential care, board-and-care facilities	IADL assistance, primarily with meals, housekeeping, and medication management	PP, Medicaid for some facilities
Hospital		
Acute care	Acute hospital care	Medicare Part A
Chronic care/ long–term acute care (LTAC facility)	Chronic skilled care (eg, chronic ventilator)	Medicare Part A, PP, Medicaid
Inpatient rehabilitation	Intensive multidisciplinary team rehabilitation	Medicare Part A[d]
Skilled nursing facility		
Transitional care unit	Skilled nursing care and/or intensive multidisciplinary team rehabilitation	Medicare Part A[d]
Short stay/ Rehabilitation	Skilled nursing care and/or straight-forward rehabilitation	Medicare Part A[d]
Long-term care	ADL assistance and/or skilled nursing care	PP, Medicaid
Continuing care retirement communities	Variety of living arrangements ranging from independent to skilled	PP
Hospice (home or facility-based)	Palliative/comfort care for life expectancy <6 mo	Medicare Part A

Note: PP = private pay (may include long-term care insurance).

[a] For useful information about sites of care for patients and families, see www.payingforseniorcare.com.

[b] A yearly cap of $1940 for these services can be exceeded if the therapist documents a "medically reasonable and necessary" exception.

[c] May be subsidized for older adults spending over one-third of income for rent. Some facilities may have access to a social worker or caregiving services for hire.

[d] Medicare Part A pays for 20 d after a hospital stay of ≥3 d, patient or co-insurance pays $161/d (in 2016) for days 21–100 with Part A covering the rest; patient or co-insurance pays 100% after day 100.

HOSPITAL CARE
Common Problems to Monitor

- Delirium (p 66)
- Intra- and postoperative coronary events: postoperative ECG to check
- Malnutrition (p 187)
- Pain (p 234)

- Polypharmacy: review medications daily
- Pulmonary complications: minimized by incentive spirometry, coughing, early ambulation after surgery
- Rehabilitation: encourage early mobility
- Skin breakdown (p 306)

Discharge Planning

- Ideally, all team members should participate in discharge planning, beginning early in the hospitalization.
- Site of care after discharge should be determined by patient's needs (**Table 6**).
- Evidence-based procedures for preventing hospital readmissions include:
  ○ A discharge coordinator (usually a specially trained nurse) who oversees appropriate patient and caregiver education regarding diagnoses and self-care, arrangement of post-hospital care, reconciliation of medications, and follow-up with the patient within 72 h of discharge
  ○ Clearly written discharge plans geared toward the patient, caregivers, and healthcare team members
  ○ Medication reconciliation at the time of discharge and within 1 wk of discharge by a clinical pharmacist
- Tools for achieving effective transitions of care out of the hospital are available through the RED: Re-Engineered Discharge project (www.ahrq.gov/professionals/systems/hospital/red/toolkit/), the Transitional Care Model (www.transitionalcare.info/), and the Care Transitions Program (www.caretransitions.org/caregiver_resources.asp).
- For a safe and effective transfer from the hospital to the nursing home, the following should be completed by the time the patient arrives at the nursing home:
  ○ Interfacility transfer form (the medication administration record is inadequate) that includes a discharge medication list noting new and discontinued medications, discontinuation dates for short-term medications, and any dosage changes in all medications
  ○ Discharge summary (performed by physician) that includes the patient's baseline functional status, "red flags" for rare but potentially serious complications of conditions or tx, orders including medications, important tests for which results are pending, and needed next steps
  ○ Verbal physician-to-physician sign-out

SCHEDULED NURSING-HOME VISIT CHECKLIST

1. Evaluate patient for interval functional change
2. Check vital signs, weight, laboratory tests, consultant reports since last visit
3. Review medications (correlate to active diagnoses)
4. Sign orders
5. Address nursing staff concerns
6. Write a SOAP note (subjective data, objective data, assessment, plan)
7. Revise problem list as needed
8. Update advance directives at least yearly
9. Update resident; update family member(s) as needed

GOAL-ORIENTED CARE, LIFE EXPECTANCY, AND MEDICAL DECISION MAKING

- Goals of care should be established for individual patients
- Goals of care should be based on:
  - Disease-specific care processes and outcomes (eg, HbA$_{1c}$ and retinopathy for patients with DM)—useful for healthier patients with isolated conditions.
  - Goal-oriented outcomes (an individual's goals potentially encompassing a variety of dimensions, including symptoms, functional status, social engagement, etc)—useful for patients with multiple conditions or who are frail.
- Many medical decisions are predicated on estimated life expectancy of the patient. **Table 7** shows life expectancy by age and sex.
- Life expectancy is associated with a number of factors in addition to age and sex, including health behaviors, presence of disease, nutritional status, race/ethnicity, and educational and financial status.
- Conditions commonly leading to death are frailty, cancer, organ failure (heart, lung, kidney, liver), and advanced dementia.
- Active life expectancy reflects the remaining years of disability-free existence. At age 65, active life expectancy is about 90% of total life expectancy; this percentage decreases with further aging.
- Estimated life expectancy can aid individualized medical decision making, particularly when considering preventive tests. A clinician can judge the patient's health status as being above (75th percentile), at (50th percentile), or below average (25th percentile) for age and sex, and then roughly determine life expectancy using **Table 7**. Another way to estimate individual life expectancy is by comorbidity; no comorbidity will add 3–4 yr to average life expectancy (the 50th percentile in **Table 7**) while high comorbidity will decrease life expectancy by 3–4 yr.

	25th percentile		50th percentile		75th percentile	
Age	**Men**	**Women**	**Men**	**Women**	**Men**	**Women**
65	11	14	17	20	24	27
70	8	10	14	16	19	22
75	6	7	11	13	15	17
80	4	5	8	10	12	13
85	2	3	6	7	8	10
90	2	2	4	5	6	7
95	1	1	3	3	4	5

Table 7. Life Expectancy (yr) by Age (United States)*

*Figures indicate the number of years in which a percentage of the corresponding age and sex cohort will die. For example, in a cohort of 65-yr-old men, 25% will be dead in 11 yr (by age 76), 50% will be dead in 17 yr, and 75% will be dead in 24 yr.

Source: Data from Arias E. United States Life Tables, 2008. National Vital Statistics Reports, vol 61, no 3, Sept 24, 2012.

- After individual life expectancy is estimated, the period of time needed for the tx to result in a positive clinical outcome is estimated and compared with the life expectancy of the patient.
  - If estimated life expectancy is longer than the time needed to achieve a positive outcome, the tx is encouraged.
  - If estimated life expectancy is shorter than the time needed to achieve a positive outcome, the tx is discouraged.
  - If estimated life expectancy is about the same as the time needed to achieve a positive outcome, the potential risks and benefits of the tx should be discussed neutrally with the patient.

For example, the benefit of many cancer screening tests is not realized for ~10 yr after detection of asymptomatic malignancies. If a patient's life expectancy is significantly less than 10 yr based only on age and sex, and the patient has poor overall health status compared with age-matched peers, cancer screening would be discouraged because the likelihood of benefit from having the test is low.

INFORMED DECISION MAKING AND PATIENT PREFERENCES FOR LIFE-SUSTAINING CARE

Physicians have no ethical obligation to offer care that is judged to be futile.

Three elements are needed for a patient's choices to be legally and ethically valid:

- A capable decision maker: Capacity is for the decision being made; patient may be capable of making some but not all decisions. If a person is sufficiently impaired, a surrogate decision maker must be involved (**Figure 2**).
- Patient's voluntary participation in the decision-making process.
- Sufficient information: Patient must be sufficiently informed; items to disclose in informed consent include:
  - Diagnosis
  - Nature, risks, costs, and benefits of possible interventions
  - Alternative tx; relative benefits, risks, and costs
  - Likely results of no tx
  - Likelihood of success
  - Advice or recommendation of the clinician

Ideally, patient preferences for life-sustaining care should be established before the patient is critically ill.

- Preferences should be established for use of the following interventions and the conditions under which they would be used: cardiopulmonary resuscitation, hospitalization, IV hydration, antibiotics, artificially administered nutrition, other life-extending medical tx, and palliative/comfort care (Palliative Care, p 253).
- Patients should be encouraged to complete a living will and/or to establish a durable power of attorney for healthcare decision making.
- Use of a POLST form can be very useful in formalizing patient preferences (www.polst.org).

MISTREATMENT OF OLDER ADULTS
Risk Factors for Inadequate or Abusive Caregiving
- Cognitive impairment in patient, caregiver, or both
- Dependency (financial, psychological, etc) of caregiver on elderly patient, or vice versa
- Family conflict
- Family hx of abusive behavior, alcohol or drug problems, mental illness, or mental retardation

- Financial stress
- Isolation of patient or caregiver, or both
- Depression or malnutrition in the patient
- Living arrangements inadequate for needs of the patient
- Stressful events in the family, such as death of a loved one or loss of employment

Figure 2. Informed Decision Making

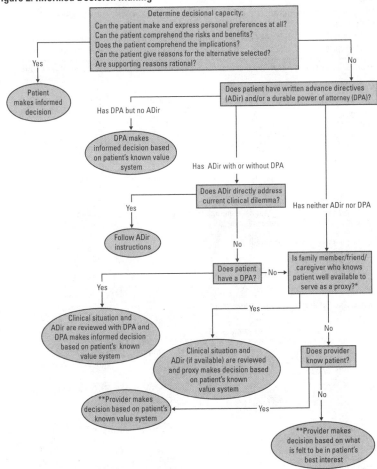

* Most states have laws specifying who should serve as proxy when no ADir or DPA exists. For most of these states, the specified hierarchy of decision makers is (in order): legal guardian, spouse or domestic partner, adult children, parents, adult siblings, closest living relative, close friend.

** Or court-appointed decision maker; laws vary by state.

Assessment and Management

- Interview patient and caregiver separately.
- Ask patient some general screening questions, such as, "Are there any problems with family or household members that you would like to tell me about?" Follow up a positive response with more direct questions such as those suggested in **Table 8**.
- On physical examination, look for any unusual marks, signs of injury, or conditions listed in **Table 8**.
- If mistreatment is suspected, report case to Adult Protective Services (most states have mandatory reporting laws).
- If patient is in immediate danger of harm, create and implement plan to remove patient from danger (hospital admission, court protective order, placement in safe environment, etc).

Table 8. Determining Suspicion and Clinical Signs of Possible Mistreatment of Older Adults

Abandonment

Question to Ask Patient: Is there anyone you can call to come and take care of you?

Clinical Signs:
- Evidence that patient is left alone unsafely
- Evidence of sudden withdrawal of care by caregiver
- Statements by patient about abandonment

Physical Abuse

Question to Ask Patient: Has anyone at home ever hit you or hurt you?

Clinical Signs:
- Anxiety, nervousness, especially toward caregiver
- Bruising, in various healing stages, especially bilateral or on inner arms or thighs
- Fractures, especially in various healing stages
- Lacerations
- Repeated emergency department visits
- Repeated falls
- Signs of sexual abuse
- Statements by patient about physical abuse

Exploitation

Question to Ask Patient: Has anyone taken your things?

Clinical Signs:
- Evidence of misuse of patient's assets
- Inability of patient to account for money and property or to pay for essential care
- Reports of demands for money or goods in exchange for caregiving or services
- Unexplained loss of Social Security or pension checks
- Statements by patient about exploitation

Neglect

Question to Ask Patient: Are you receiving enough care at home?

Clinical Signs:
- Contractures
- Dehydration
- Depression
- Diarrhea
- Fecal impaction
- Malnutrition
- Failure to respond to warning of obvious disease
- Inappropriate use of medications
- Poor hygiene
- Pressure ulcers
- Repeated falls
- Repeated hospital admissions
- Urine burns
- Statements by patient about neglect

(cont.)

Psychological Abuse

Questions to Ask Patient: Has anyone ever scolded or threatened you? Has anyone made fun of you?

Clinical Signs:
- Observed impatience, irritability, or demeaning behavior toward patient by caregiver
- Anxiety, fearfulness, ambivalence, or anger shown by patient about caregiver
- Statements by patient about psychological abuse

CROSS-CULTURAL GERIATRICS

Clinicians should remember that:
- Individuals within every ethnic group can differ widely.
- Familiarity with a patient's background is useful only if his or her preferences are linked to the cultural heritage.
- Ethnic groups differ widely in
  - approach to decision making (eg, involvement of family and friends)
  - disclosure of medical information (eg, cancer diagnosis)
  - end-of-life care (eg, advance directives and resuscitation preferences)

In caring for older adults of any ethnicity:
- Use the patient's preferred terminology for his or her cultural identity in conversation and in health records.
- Determine whether interpretation services are needed; if possible, use professional interpreter rather than family member. When interpreters are not available, online translation services (eg, www.babelfish.com or translate.google.com) or telephone translation services can be useful.
- Recognize that the patient may not conceive of illness in Western terms.
- Determine whether the patient is a refugee or survivor of violence or genocide.
- Explore early on the patient's preferences for disclosure of serious clinical findings, and reconfirm at intervals.
- Ask if the patient prefers to involve or defer to others in the decision-making process.
- Follow the patient's preferences regarding gender roles.

For further information, see *Doorway Thoughts: Cross Cultural Health Care for Older Adults Series* (www.americangeriatrics.org/publications/shop_publications/).

COMPLETING A DEATH CERTIFICATE
- The **Cause of Death** statement in Section 32 of a Death Certificate indicates the provider's opinion, with reasonable probability, of the immediate, intermediate, and underlying causes of death and other significant contributing conditions. See below for details on completing this section.
- The **Manner of Death** statement in Section 37 indicates the provider's opinion of whether the death was natural or unnatural. Unnatural deaths will be reviewed by the coroner or medical examiner; the specific criteria for triggering a review vary by county and state.
- If a patient is on hospice care, the hospice provider will usually complete the death certificate.

Immediate Cause of Death Statement (Section 32.Part I.a)

- Indicates the final disease, injury, or complication causing death (eg, aspiration pneumonia, pulmonary embolism, aortic rupture)
- The approximate interval between the onset of the immediate cause and death is estimated (eg, 4 weeks, minutes, 1 hour for the above examples)
- If the cause of death is not apparent (eg, a very elderly man without clinically apparent major illnesses is found by his daughter to have died in his sleep), some states allow the clinician to indicate "Undetermined natural causes"
- Mechanistic terminal events such as asystole, electromechanical dissociation, cardiac arrest, and respiratory arrest should not be listed in this or any other cause-of-death section

Intermediate/Underlying Causes of Death "Due to/Consequence of" Statement (Section 32.Part I.b–d)

- Indicates conditions and their sequence leading to the immediate cause of death, listed in reverse chronologic order.
- The last of these conditions listed is the **underlying** cause—the disease or injury that initiated the events leading to the patient's death.
- Examples:
  ○ A patient with osteoporosis fractures her hip, develops a DVT in the hospital, and dies of a pulmonary embolus. Pulmonary embolus would be cited as the immediate cause in Section 32.I.a., DVT would be cited as an intermediate ("due to/consequence of") cause in Section 32.I.b., hip fracture would be cited as another intermediate cause in Section 32.I.c., and osteoporosis would be entered in Section 32.I.d. as the underlying cause.
  ○ A patient with late-state Alzheimer disease (AD) dies from apparent aspiration pneumonia. Aspiration pneumonia would be listed as the immediate cause in Section 32.I.a, and AD would be entered as the intermediate/underlying cause in Section 32.I.b.
- The approximate intervals between the onset of the intermediate/underlying causes and death is estimated.

Other Significant Conditions Leading to Death Statement (Section 32.Part II)

- Indicates conditions that likely contributed to death but did not result in underlying causes.
- Risk factors for underlying causes are often listed in this section, eg, hypertension for cerebrovascular disease (the underlying condition) leading to a massive hemorrhagic stroke (the immediate cause of death).

MULTIMORBIDITY

- More than 50% of older adults have ≥3 chronic conditions.
- Management of patients with multimorbidity involves balancing issues of patient preferences and tx goals, prognosis, the evidence of outcomes for tx strategies of individual conditions, interactions among conditions and tx, and feasibility of tx (**Figure 3**).

Figure 3. Approach to the Evaluation and Management of the Older Adult with Multimorbidity

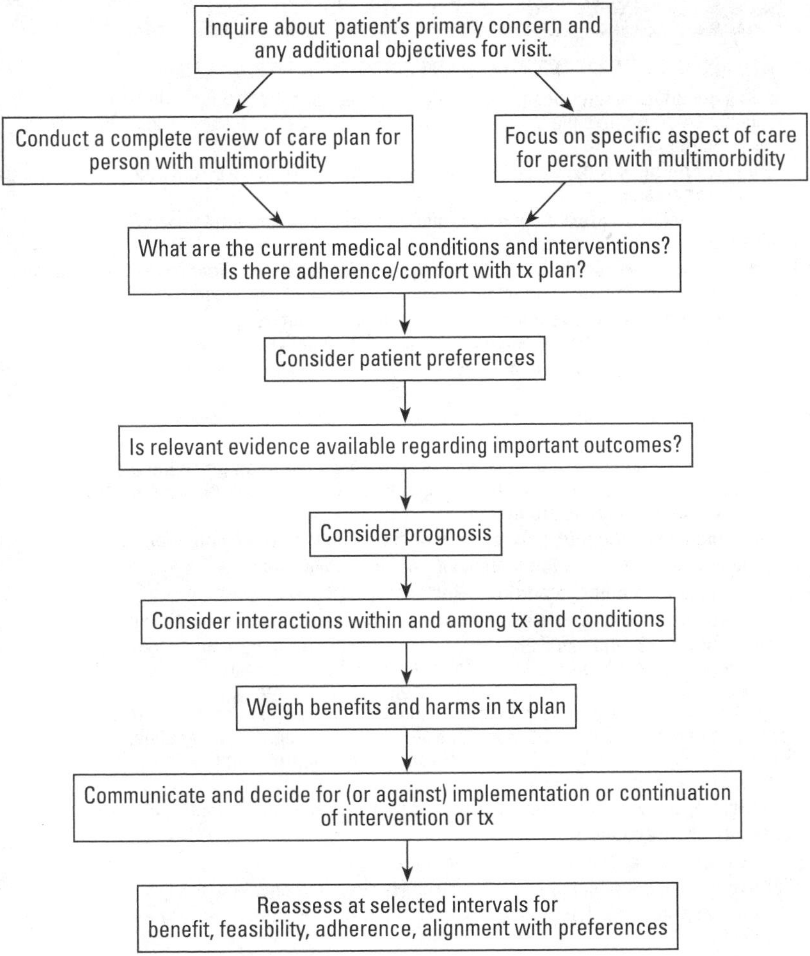

Source: AGS Expert Panel on the Care of Older Adults with Multimorbidity. *J Am Geriatr Soc* 2012;60(10):1957–1968.

APPROPRIATE PRESCRIBING, DRUG INTERACTIONS, AND ADVERSE EVENTS

HOW TO PRESCRIBE APPROPRIATELY AND REDUCE MEDICATION ERRORS

- **Obtain a complete medication history.** Ask about allergies, OTC drugs, nutritional supplements, alternative medications, alcohol, tobacco, caffeine, recreational drugs, and other prescribers.
- **Use e-prescribing to reduce risk of transcription and medication errors and to check insurance coverage.**
- **Avoid prescribing before a diagnosis is made except in severe acute pain.** Consider nondrug tx.
- **Review medications regularly and before prescribing a new medication.** D/C medications that are no longer needed, ineffective, or do not have a corresponding diagnosis.
- **Know the actions, adverse events, drug interactions, monitoring requirements, and toxicity profiles of prescribed medications.** Avoid duplicative effects.
- **Consider the following for new medications:** Is the dosing regimen practical? Is the new medication affordable?
- **Start long-term medications at a low dose and titrate dose on the basis of tolerability and response.** Use drug concentration monitoring when available.
- **Attempt to reach a therapeutic dose before switching to or adding another medication.** Use combinations cautiously: titrate each medication to a therapeutic dose before switching to a combination product.
- **Avoid using one medication to treat the adverse events caused by another.**
- **Attempt to use one medication to treat two or more conditions.**
- **Communicate with other prescribers.** Don't assume patients do—they assume you do!
- **Avoid using drugs from the same class or with similar actions** (eg, multiple opioids).
- **Avoid confusion:** Brand name products can contain different ingredients depending on their indication, eg, *Mylanta Ultimate Strength* liquid contains aluminum and magnesium hydroxide, *Mylanta* maximum and regular strength liquid contains aluminum and magnesium hydroxide plus simethicone, while *Mylanta Supreme* contain calcium carbonate and magnesium hydroxide; *Lotrimin Ultra* crm contains butenafine, while *Lotrimin AF for Her* and *Gyne-Lotrimin* crm contain clotrimazole, and *Lotrimin AF* deodorant powder contains miconazole.
- **Write legibly** to avoid misreading of the drug name (eg, *Lamictal* vs *Lamisil*).
- **Write out the directions:**
    (1) Strength, route, quantity, and number of refills.
    (2) Avoid using abbreviations, especially easily confused ones (qd and qid).
    (3) Always precede a decimal expression of <1 with a zero (0); never use a zero after a decimal.
    (4) Do not use ambiguous directions (eg, as directed [ud] or as needed [prn]).
    (5) Include the medication's purpose in the directions (eg, for high blood pressure).
    (6) Write dosages for thyroid replacement tx in mcg, not mg.
    (7) Always re-read what you've written.

Medication errors associated with e-prescribing:
  (1) Prescribing the wrong drug; look-alike errors (eg, metoprolol succinate instead of tartrate)
  (2) Choosing wrong dosage form (eg, tsp instead of tab)
  (3) Choosing wrong strength (1 mg for 10 mg)
  (4) Choosing wrong directions, quantity, or days of tx
  (5) To avoid delays and server errors, send e-prescriptions after seeing each patient instead of in batches.
- **Educate patient and/or caregiver about each medication.** Include the regimen, therapeutic goal, cost, and potential AEs or drug interactions. Provide written instructions. Assess health literacy using the Rapid Estimate of Adult Literacy in Medicine - Short Form (REALM-SF) tool. See appendix or www.ahrq.gov/populations/sahlsatool.htm
- **Create a pill card for patients** or encourage them to create their own. See AHRQ's software program online at www.ahrq.gov/qual/pillcard/pillcard.htm. For more information, see www.fda.gov/Drugs/DrugSafety/MedicationErrors/default.htm or www.ismp.org/tools/abbreviations/

Medications listed as AVOID or Use with Caution in the 2015 AGS Beers Criteria are indicated in GAYF by [BC]. Some recommendations state to AVOID the drug without exceptions and others apply only to patients with a specific disease or syndrome, or for a specific duration of use or a specific dose. A detailed description of the 2015 AGS Beers Criteria including evidence tables, useful clinical tools, and patient education materials are available at the AGS website: GeriatricsCareOnline.org.

DE-PRESCRIBING: WHEN AND HOW TO DISCONTINUE MEDICATIONS
- Recognize opportunities to stop a medication:
  ○ Care transitions
  ○ Annual/semiannual medication review (eg, annual wellness visit)
  ○ Review existing medications before starting a new medication
  ○ Presentation or identification of a new problem or complaint
- D/C medication if:
  ○ Harms outweigh benefits
  ○ Minimal or no effectiveness
  ○ No indication
  ○ Not being taken, and adherence is not critical
- Plan, communicate, and coordinate:
  ○ Include patient, caregiver, and other healthcare providers
  ○ What to expect/intent
  ○ Instructions, eg, how to taper (if indicated)
- Monitor and follow-up:
  ○ Withdrawal reactions
  ○ Exacerbation of underlying conditions

Examples of medications eligible for de-prescribing: bisphosphonates, antiallergy (seasonal), PPIs and H_2 antagonists, cholinesterase inhibitors, memantine, iron, antipsychotics, and antidepressants.

Source: Adapted from Bain KT et al. *JAGS.*2008;56:1946–1952.

CMS GUIDANCE ON UNNECESSARY DRUGS IN THE NURSING HOME

See the complete guidance at www.cms.hhs.gov/transmittals/downloads/R22SOMA.pdf or Appendix PP of the CMS State Operations Manual. Updated survey guidelines for antipsychotic drugs in dementia are at www.cms.gov/Medicare/Provider-Enrollment-and-Certification/SurveyCertificationGenInfo/Downloads/Survey-and-Cert-Letter-13-35.pdf.

PHARMACOLOGIC THERAPY AND AGE-ASSOCIATED CHANGES

Table 9. Age-associated Changes in Pharmacokinetics and Pharmacodynamics

Parameter	Age Effect	Disease, Factor Effect	Prescribing Implications
Absorption	Rate and extent are usually unaffected	Achlorhydria, concurrent medications, tube feedings	Drug-drug and drug-food interactions are more likely to alter absorption
Distribution	Increase in fat:water ratio; decreased plasma protein, particularly albumin	HF, ascites, and other conditions increase body water	Fat-soluble drugs have a larger volume of distribution; highly protein-bound drugs have a greater (active) free concentration
Metabolism	Decreases in liver mass and liver blood flow decrease drug clearance; may be age-related changes in CYP2C19, while CYP3A4 and CYP2D6 are not affected	Smoking, genotype, concurrent drug tx, alcohol and caffeine intake may have more effect than aging	Lower dosages may be therapeutic
Elimination	Primarily renal; age-related decrease in GFR	Kidney impairment with acute and chronic diseases; decreased muscle mass results in less Cr production	Serum Cr not a reliable measure of kidney function; best to estimate CrCl using formula (see p 1)
Pharmaco-dynamics	Less predictable and often altered drug response at usual or lower concentrations	Drug-drug and drug-disease interactions may alter responses	Prolonged pain relief with opioids at lower dosages; increased sedation and postural instability to benzodiazepines; altered sensitivity to β-blockers

Table 10. Non-Antiinfective Medications That Should Be Avoided or Dosage Reduced With Varying Levels of Kidney Function in Older Adults

Medication Class/ Medication	CrCl (mL/min) When Action Required	Rationale	Recommendation
Amiloride	<30	↑ potassium and ↓ sodium	Avoid
Apixaban	<25	↑ bleeding	Avoid
Cimetidine	<50	Mental status changes	Reduce dose
Colchicine	<30	Gastrointestinal, neuromuscular, bone marrow toxicity	Reduce dose, monitor for adverse effects
Dabigatran	<30	↑ bleeding	Avoid
Duloxetine	<30	↑ GI adverse effects (nausea, diarrhea)	Avoid
Edoxaban	30–50	↑ bleeding	Reduce dose
	<30 or >95		Avoid
Enoxaparin	<30	↑ bleeding	Reduce dose
Extended release: avoid			
Famotidine	<50	Mental status changes	Reduce dose
Fondaparinux	<30	↑ bleeding	Avoid
Gabapentin	<60	CNS adverse effects	Reduce dose
Levetiracetam	≤80	CNS adverse effects	Reduce dose
Nizatidine	<50	Mental status changes	Reduce dose
Pregabalin	<60	CNS adverse effects	Reduce dose
Probenecid	<30	Loss of effectiveness	Avoid
Ranitidine	<50	Mental status changes	Reduce dose
Rivaroxaban	30–50	↑ bleeding	Reduce dose
	<30		Avoid
Spironolactone	<30	↑ potassium	Avoid
Tramadol	<30	CNS adverse effects	Immediate release: reduce dose

COMPLICATING FACTORS

Drug-Food or -Nutrient Interactions

Physical Interactions: Mg++, Ca++, Fe++, Al++, or zinc can lower oral absorption of levothyroxine and some quinolone antibiotics. Tube feedings decrease absorption of oral phenytoin and levothyroxine.

Decreased Drug Effect: Warfarin and vitamin K-containing foods

Decreased Oral Intake or Appetite: Medications can alter the taste of food (dysgeusia) or decrease saliva production (xerostomia), making mastication and swallowing difficult.

Medications associated with dysgeusia include captopril and clarithromycin. Medications that can cause xerostomia include antihistamines, antidepressants, antipsychotics, clonidine, and diuretics.

Drug-Drug Interactions

A drug's effect can be altered, displacement from protein-binding sites, inhibition or induction of metabolic enzymes, or because two or more drugs have a similar pharmacologic effect. For more information, consult a drug-drug interaction text, software, or Internet resource (eg, www.fda.gov/Drugs/DevelopmentApprovalProcess/DevelopmentResources/DrugInteractionsLabeling/ucm093664.htm#classInhibit and medicine.iupui.edu/clinpharm/ddis/), and **Table 11**.

Drug-induced Changes in Cardiac Conduction (Table 12)

- Intrinsic changes associated with aging in cardiac pacemaker cells and conduction system
- Increased sensitivity to drug-induced conduction disorders, eg, bradycardia and tachyarrhythmias
- Electrolyte abnormalities
- QT_c prolongation exacerbated by drugs alone, drug interactions, and altered pharmacokinetics
- A comprehensive list of drugs associated with QT_c prolongation, increase the risk of Torsades de Pointes, or should be avoided by patients with congenital long QT syndrome is available at www.crediblemeds.org.

Table 11. Potentially Clinically Important Non-Antiinfective Drug-Drug Interactions That Should Be Avoided in Older Adults

Object Drug/Class	Interacting Drug/Class	Rationale	Recommendation
ACEIs	Amiloride or triamterene	Hyperkalemia	Avoid routine use; reserve for patients with demonstrated hypokalemia while on an ACEI
Anticholinergic	Anticholinergic	Cognitive decline	Avoid, minimize the number of anticholinergic drugs (**Table 37**).
Antidepressant	≥2 other CNS-active drugs	Falls	Avoid totals of ≥3 CNS-active drugs, minimize the number of CNS-active drugs.
Antipsychotic	≥2 other CNS-active drugs	Falls	Avoid totals of ≥3 CNS-active drugs, minimize the number of CNS-active drugs.
Benzodiazepines and nonbenzodiazepine receptor agonist hypnotics	≥2 other CNS-active drugs	Falls and fractures	Avoid totals ≥3 CNS-active drugs, minimize the number of CNS-active drugs.
Corticosteroids	NSAIDs	Peptic ulcer disease and GI bleeding	Avoid; if not possible, provide GI protection.
Lithium	ACEIs	Lithium toxicity	Avoid, monitor lithium concentrations.

(cont.)

Table 11. Potentially Clinically Important Non-Antiinfective Drug-Drug Interactions That Should Be Avoided in Older Adults (cont.)

Object Drug/Class	Interacting Drug/Class	Rationale	Recommendation
Lithium	Loop diuretics	Lithium toxicity	Avoid, monitor lithium concentrations.
Opioid receptor agonist analgesics	≥2 other CNS-active drugs*	Falls	Avoid, minimize the number of CNS drugs.
Peripheral α-1 blockers	Loop diuretics	Urinary incontinence in older women	Avoid in older women, unless conditions warrant both drugs.
Theophylline	Cimetidine	Theophylline toxicity	Avoid.
Warfarin	Amiodarone	Bleeding	Avoid when possible, monitor INR closely.
Warfarin	NSAIDs	Bleeding	Avoid when possible, monitor INR closely.

*CNS-active drugs: antipsychotics, benzodiazepines, nonbenzodiazepines, benzodiazepine receptor agonist hypnotics, TCAs, SSRIs, and opioids.

Table 12. Examples of Medications With Known Risk to Prolong the QT_c Interval Alone*†

Analgesics
  Methadone
Antidepressants
  Citalopram
  Escitalopram
Antiemetics
  Ondansetron

Anti-infectives
  Azithromycin
  Ciprofloxacin
  Clarithromycin
  Erythromycin
  Fluconazole
  Levofloxacin
  Moxifloxacin
Antipsychotics
  Haloperidol
  Chlorpormazine
  Pimozide
  Thioridazine

Cardiovascular
  Amiodarone
  Cilostazol
  Dispyramide
  Dofetilide
  Dronederone
  Quinidine
  Soltaolol
Cholinesterase Inhibitors
  Donepezil

*Level of risk depends on dosage, baseline QT_c (mild risk if <450 millisec), other patient characteristics, and comorbidity.

†For a comprehensive list, see www.crediblemeds.org.

COMMONLY USED HERBAL AND ALTERNATIVE MEDICATIONS

Note: Herbal and dietary supplements are not subject to the same regulatory process by the FDA as prescription and OTC medications. Product and lot-to-lot variations can occur in composition and concentration of active ingredient(s), or be tainted with heavy metals or prescription medications (eg, sildenafil). Consumers are advised to purchase products by reputable manufacturers who follow good manufacturing procedures that contain the United States Pharmacopeia (USP) seal.

Chondroitin/Glucosamine

Common Uses: Osteoarthritis, RA

Adverse Events: Chondroitin: Nausea, dyspepsia, changes in IOP; Glucosamine: anorexia, insomnia, painful and itchy skin, peripheral edema, tachycardia.

Comments: Meta-analyses have reached mixed conclusions of chondroitin's effectiveness in osteoarthritis of the knee. Neither the AAOS (2010) nor the ACR (2012) recommend chondroitin/glucosamine for knee arthritis. In one trial, knee pain did not respond better to chondroitin alone or in combination with glucosamine compared with placebo in >1500 patients with osteoarthritis. If patients choose a trial of chondroitin plus glucosamine, it should be glucosamine sulfate.

Coenzyme Q$_{10}$

Common Uses: Cardiovascular diseases (angina, HF, HTN), musculoskeletal disorders, periodontal diseases, DM, obesity, AD, Parkinson disease; may lessen toxic effects of doxorubicin and daunorubicin; reversal of statin myopathy.

Adverse Events: Abdominal discomfort, headache, nausea, vomiting

Comments: May increase risk of bleeding; use with caution in patients with hepatic impairment, may decrease response to warfarin; may further decrease BP if taking antihypertensives or other medications that decrease BP; ubiquinol is a reduced form of coenzyme Q$_{10}$

Echinacea

Common Uses: Immune stimulant

Adverse Events: Hepatotoxicity, allergic reactions, GI upset, rash

Drug Interactions: Immunosuppressants; reportedly inhibits CYP1A2, –3A4, induces CYP3A4

Comments: D/C ≥2 wk before surgery; cross-sensitivity with chrysanthemum, ragweed, daisy, and aster allergies; kidney disease; immunosuppression; mixed results regarding effectiveness to shorten duration, reduce severity, or prevent colds; should not be taken for >10 d because of concern about immunosuppression

Feverfew

Common Uses: Anti-inflammatory, migraine prophylaxis

Adverse Events: Platelet inhibition, bleeding, GI upset, swelling of the lips, tongue, and oral mucosa; allergic contact dermatitis from handling fresh leaves

Drug Interactions: NSAIDs, antiplatelet agents, anticoagulants

Comments: D/C 7 d before surgery, active bleeding; cross-sensitivity with chrysanthemum and daisy; evidence lacking for either indication; minimum of 1-mo trial for migraine prophylaxis suggested

Fish oil (omega-3 fatty acids, *Lovaza*)

Common Uses: Decrease risk of CAD and CHD, hypertriglyceridemia, symptomatic tx of RA, inflammatory bowel disease, asthma, bipolar disorder, schizophrenia, and in cases of immunosuppression

Adverse Events: GI upset, dyspepsia, diarrhea, nausea, bleeding, increased ALT and LDL-C

Drug Interactions: Anticoagulants, antiplatelet agents

Comments: Use with caution if allergic to seafood; monitor LFTS, TG, and LDL-C at baseline, then periodically; a 2-mo trial is adequate for hypertriglyceridemia; not proven effective for primary prevention

Flaxseed and flaxseed oil

Common Uses: RA, asthma, constipation, DM, hyperlipidemia, menopausal symptoms, prevention of stroke and CHD, BPH, laxative

Adverse Events: Bleeding, hypoglycemia, hypotension, allergy; Flaxseed only: abdominal pain and bloating, flatulence, diarrhea

Drug Interactions: NSAIDs, antiplatelet agents, anticoagulants, insulin and hypoglycemic agents, lithium (mania)

Garlic

Common Uses: HTN, hypercholesterolemia, platelet inhibitor

Adverse Events: Bleeding, GI upset, hypoglycemia

Drug Interactions: NSAIDs, antiplatelet agents, anticoagulants, INH, NNRTIs, protease inhibitors

Comments: D/C 7 d before surgery; effect on lipid lowering modest and of questionable clinical value

Ginger

Common Uses: Antiemetic, anti-inflammatory, dyspepsia

Adverse Events: GI upset, heartburn, diarrhea, irritation of the mouth and throat

Drug Interactions: NSAIDs, antiplatelet agents, anticoagulants

Comments: D/C 7 d before surgery

Ginkgo biloba

Common Uses: AD, memory, migraine, cardiovascular disease and stroke prophylaxis

Adverse Events: Bleeding, nausea, headache, GI upset, diarrhea, dizziness, heart palpitations

Drug Interactions: MAOIs (increased effect and toxicity), antiplatelet agents, anticoagulants, NSAIDs, midazolam

Comments: D/C 36 h before surgery; mixed results in dementia trials; recent trials tend to have negative results

Ginseng

Common Uses: Physical and mental performance enhancer, digestive, diuretic, immunomodulator, antineoplastic, cardiovascular, CNS, and endocrine effects

Adverse Events: HTN, tachycardia, insomnia, diarrhea, confusion, depression

Drug Interactions: Antiplatelet agents, anticoagulants, NSAIDs, imatinib

Comments: D/C 7 d before surgery, kidney failure

Glucosamine (see **Chondroitin**)

Kava kava

Common Uses: Anxiety, sedative

Adverse Events: Sedation, hepatotoxicity, GI upset, headache, dizziness, EPS, scaly skin rash, urinary retention, exacerbation of PD, rhabdomyolysis

Drug Interactions: Anticonvulsants (increased effect), benzodiazepines, CNS depressants, L-dopa

Comments: D/C 24 h before surgery; compared with placebo, kava kava has demonstrated antianxiety efficacy, but effect small and not robust

Melatonin

Common Uses: Sleep disorders, insomnia, jet lag

Adverse Events: Daytime drowsiness, headache, dizziness, enuresis, nausea, transient depression

Drug Interactions: Warfarin, ASA, clopidogrel, ticlopidine, dipyridamole (loss of hemostasis), antidiabetic agents (decreased glucose tolerance and insulin sensitivity), CNS depressants

Methyl sulfonylmethane (MSM)

Common Uses: Anti-inflammatory, analgesia, osteoarthritis, chronic pain, GI upset

Adverse Events: Nausea, diarrhea, fatigue, bloating, insomnia, headache

Comments: A derivative of dimethyl sulfoxide (DMSO) that produces less odor

Red yeast rice (*Monascus purpureus*, Xue Zhi Kang, natural source of mevinolin the active ingredient of lovastatin)

Common Uses: CHD, DM, hypercholesterolemia

Adverse Events: Nausea, vomiting, GI upset, hepatic disorders, myopathy, rhabdomyolysis

Drug Interactions (theoretical): Cyclosporine, CYP3A4 substrates, digoxin, statins, niacin

Comments: Use with caution in patients taking other lipid-lowering agents

Rhodiola rosea (*Arctic Root*, golden root)

Common Uses: Energy, stamina, strength, enhanced cognitive capacity, stress, improved sexual function, mood and anxiety

Adverse Events: Dizziness, dry mouth

Drug Interactions: Antidiabetic drugs (hypoglycemia), antihypertensives (hypotension), moderate CYP3A4 inhibitor, immunosuppresants (may be an immunostimulant)

SAMe (S-adenosyl-methionine)

Common Uses: Depression, fibromyalgia, insomnia, osteoarthritis, RA

Adverse Events: GI distress, insomnia, dizziness, dry mouth, headache, restlessness

Drug Interactions: Antidepressants, St. John's wort, NSAIDs, antiplatelet agents, anticoagulants, other drugs affecting serotonin (serotonin syndrome)

Comments: Not effective for bipolar depression, hyperhomocysteinemia (theoretical), D/C ≥14 d before surgery

Saw palmetto

Common Uses: BPH

Adverse Events: Headache, nausea, GI distress, erectile dysfunction, dizziness

Drug Interactions: Finasteride, α_1-adrenergic agonist properties in vitro may decrease efficacy; may prolong bleeding time so use with caution with antiplatelet agents, anticoagulants, NSAIDs

Comments: Efficacy in BPH did not differ from placebo in an adequately powered, randomized clinical trial

St. John's wort *(Hypericum perforatum)*

Common Uses: Depression, anxiety

Adverse Events: Photosensitivity, hypomania, insomnia, GI upset, dry mouth, itching, fatigue, dizziness, headache

Drug Interactions: Potent CYP3A4 inducer, finasteride (decreased finasteride concentration and possible effectiveness)

Comments: Wear sunscreen with UVA and UVB coverage; avoid in fair-skinned patients; D/C 5 d before surgery; not effective in severe depression; effects reported to vary from those of conventional antidepressants, yet no more effective than placebo; evaluation of effectiveness may be complicated by product, extraction process, and composition

Valerian

Common Uses: Anxiety, insomnia

Adverse Events: Sedation, benzodiazepine-like withdrawal, headache, GI upset, insomnia

Drug Interactions: Benzodiazepines, CNS depressants

Comments: Taper dose several weeks before surgery

NON-VTE INDICATIONS FOR ANTITHROMBOTIC MEDICATIONS

Table 13. Antithrombotic Medications for Selected Conditions

Indication	Antiplatelet (Table 18)	Anticoagulant (Table 19)					
		VK Antagonist	Heparin	LMWH	Factor Xa Inhibitor	Direct Thrombin Inhibitor	Glycoprotein IIb/IIIa Inhibitor
Atrial fibrillation	ASA	**Warfarin**	—	—	**Apixaban Rivaroxaban Edoxaban**	Dabigatran	—
Valvular disease	ASA	**Warfarin**	—	—	—	—	—
Acute coronary syndrome	**ASA Clopidogrel** Prasugrel **Ticagrelor**	—	UFH	**Enoxaparin** Dalteparin	**Fondaparinux**	**Bivalirudin**	**Abciximab Eptifibatide Tirofiban**
Cardio-vascular disease prevention	**ASA**	—	—	—	—	—	—
Prior TIA/ Stroke	**ASA** Clopidogrel Dipiridamole/ ASA	—	—	—	—	—	—
Peripheral arterial disease	**ASA Clopidogrel**	—	—	—	—	—	—
Heparin-induced thrombo-cytopenia	—	—	—	—	—	**Argatroban Lepirudin**	—

Notes: **First choice in bold text**; Secondary or alternate choice in regular text; LMWH = low-molecular-weight heparin; UFH = unfractionated heparin; VK = vitamin K.

VTE PROPHYLAXIS, DIAGNOSIS, AND MANAGEMENT
Prophylaxis
- Prophylaxis of medical and surgical inpatients is based on patient risk factors and type of surgery.
- See **Tables 18** and **19** for choice of antithrombotic strategy.
- See **Tables 18** and **19** for dosages of antithrombotic medications.

Table 14. DVT/PE Prophylaxis Strategies in Older Medical and Surgical Inpatients

DVT/PE Risk	Surgery Type or Medical Condition	Thromboprophylactic Options
Low	Healthy and mobile patients undergoing minor surgery Brief (<45 min) laparoscopic procedures Transurethral or other low-risk urologic procedures Joint arthroscopy Spine surgery	Aggressive early ambulation after procedure +/– intermittent pneumatic compression
Medium	Immobile (>72 h) patients Inpatients at bed rest with active malignancy, prior VTE, or sepsis Most general surgeries Open abdominopelvic surgeries Thoracic surgery Vascular surgery	Antithrombotic **(Table 15 and Table 19)** +/– intermittent pneumatic compression
High	Acute stroke Hip or knee arthroplasty Hip, pelvic, or leg fracture Acute spinal cord injury	**Table 15**

Table 15. Antithrombotic Medications for VTE Prophylaxis

Indication	Antiplatelet (Table 18)	Anticoagulant (Table 19)					
		VK Antagonist	Heparin	LMWH	Heparinoid	Factor Xa Inhibitor	Direct Thrombin Inhibitor
Medical inpatients at moderate–high risk for VTE; patients with acute stroke or spinal cord injury	—	—	UFH	Enoxaparin Dalteparin	—	Fondaparinux	—
Knee or hip replacement	ASA	Warfarin	UFH	**Enoxaparin Dalteparin**	Danaproid	Apixaban, Fondaparinux Rivaroxaban	Dabigatran Desirudin
Hip fracture surgery	ASA	Warfarin	UFH	**Enoxaparin Dalteparin**	Danaproid	Fondaparinux	—
Nonorthopedic surgery patients at moderate–high risk of VTE	ASA	**Warfarin**	**UFH**	**Enoxaparin Dalteparin**	—	Fondaparinux Rivaroxaban	—

Notes: **First choice(s) in bold text**; Secondary or alternate choice(s) in regular text; LMWH, low-molecular-weight heparin, UFH = unfractionated heparin, VK = vitamin K; VTE = venous thromboembolism (DVT/PE).

DVT Diagnosis

DVT diagnosis is directed by risk score, D-dimer testing, and duplex ultrasound imaging.
- Determine risk score
  - 1 point for each of the following:
    - active cancer
    - paralysis, paresis, or plaster immobilization of lower limb
    - bedridden for 3 d or major surgery in past 12 wk
    - localized tenderness along distribution of deep venous system
    - entire leg swelling
    - calf swelling ≥3 cm over diameter of contralateral calf
    - pitting edema confined to symptomatic leg
    - collateral superficial veins
    - prior DVT
  - −2 points for alternative diagnosis as likely as DVT
- Interpret risk score and further testing
  - ≤0 points = low risk: Obtain moderately or highly sensitive D-dimer test. If negative (D-dimer ≤ patient age × 10), DVT is excluded. If positive, obtain ultrasound of proximal veins for diagnosis. Don't obtain imaging studies as the initial diagnostic test in patients with low pretest probability (low risk) of VTE.[CW]
  - 1–2 points = moderate risk: Obtain highly sensitive D-dimer. If negative, (D-dimer ≤ patient age × 10), DVT is excluded. If positive, obtain ultrasound of either proximal veins or whole leg for diagnosis.
  - ≥3 points = high risk: Obtain ultrasound of either proximal veins or whole leg. If proximal leg ultrasound is negative, repeat proximal ultrasound in 1 wk, obtain immediate highly sensitive D-dimer test, or obtain whole leg ultrasound; negative results of any of these rules out DVT.

PE Diagnosis

- Consider PE with any of the following (classic triad of dyspnea, chest pain, and hemoptysis seen in only ≤20% of cases):
  - Chest pain
  - Hemoptysis
  - Hypotension
  - Hypoxia
  - Shortness of breath
  - Syncope
  - Tachycardia
- Calculate clinical probability of PE using clinical decision rule (**Table 16**), then follow evaluation of PE algorithm (**Figure 4**). Clinical probability of PE unlikely: total ≤4 points; clinical probability of PE likely: total >4 points.

Table 16. Clinical Decision Rule for PE Probability

Variable	Points
Clinical signs and symptoms of DVT (minimal leg swelling and pain with palpation of the 3 deep veins)	3
Alternative diagnosis less likely than PE	3
Heart rate >100/min	1.5
Immobilization (>3 d) or surgery in the previous 4 wk	1.5
Previous PE or DVT	1.5
Hemoptysis	1
Malignancy (receiving tx, treated in last 6 mo, or palliative)	1
Total	

Source: Wells PS et al. *Thromb Haemost* 2000;83(3):416–420. Reprinted with permission.

Figure 4. Evaluation of Suspected Pulmonary Embolism

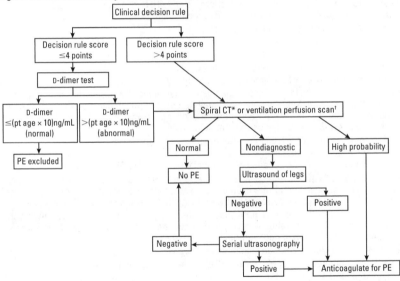

* Multidetector-row CT more sensitive than single-detector CT. Patient must be able to hold breath for 10 sec.

† When unable to use contrast (eg, renal dysfunction), need to avoid ionizing radiation.

Table 17. Antithrombotic Medications for VTE Management

Indication	Antiplatelet (Table 18)	VK Antagonist	Heparin	LMWH	Heparinoid	Factor Xa Inhibitor	Direct Thrombin Inhibitor
				Anticoagulant (Table 19)			
Acute VTE tx	—	—	UFH	**Enoxaparin** **Dalteparin** **Tinzaparin**	—	**Apixaban** **Fondaparinux** **Rivaroxaban**	—
Long-term VTE tx	—	**Warfarin**	—	Enoxaparin Dalteparin Tinzaparin	—	Apixaban Rivaroxaban Edoxaban	Dabigatran

Notes: **First choice(s) in bold text**; Secondary or alternate choice(s) in regular text; LMWH = low-molecular-weight heparin; UFH = unfractionated heparin; VK = vitamin K; VTE = venous thromboembolism (DVT/PE).

- For acute VTE, LMWH or fondaparinux is preferred to UFH in most patients because of lower risk of hemorrhage and mortality. Reduce dosage when CrCl <30 mL/min.
- Length of long-term tx is based on cause:
  ○ Provoked VTE from transient cause (eg, surgery, trauma, prolonged immobility that has resolved): anticoagulate for 3 mo
  ○ Unprovoked VTE: anticoagulate for 3–6 mo or more
  ○ Second unprovoked VTE: anticoagulate indefinitely
- If warfarin is part of a long-term anticoagulation plan, it may be started the same day as acute anticoagulant. Specific conditions may require a period of overlap when both agents should be used (eg, for DVT or PE, heparin or similar products should be used a minimum of 5 d, including 1–3 d of overlap with therapeutic INR).
- Consider low-dose ASA (100 mg/d) after completion of long-term VTE tx (at least 3 mo of warfarin or other anticoagulant)
- Don't reimage DVT in the absence of a clinical change during DVT tx.[CW]
- Acute massive PE (filling defects in ≥2 lobar arteries or the equivalent by angiogram; about 5% of PE cases) associated with hypotension, severe hypoxia, or high pulmonary pressures on echocardiogram should usually be treated with thrombolytic tx within 48 h of onset.
- Submassive PE (about 20–25% of PE cases) is defined as PE with normotension and right ventricular failure; if present, thrombolytic tx should be considered. Submassive PE can be diagnosed by detection of right ventricular failure through:
  ○ Physical exam (eg, increased jugular venous pressure)
  ○ ECG (eg, right bundle branch block [RBBB] or t-wave inversions in leads V_1–V_4)
  ○ Elevated cardiac troponins
  ○ Echocardiography (eg, right ventricular hypokinesis and dilatation)
  ○ Chest CT showing right ventricular enlargement
- Don't perform workup for clotting disorder (order hypercoagulable testing) for patients who develop a first episode of DVT in the setting of a known cause.[CW]

ANTITHROMBOTIC MEDICATIONS
Antiplatelet Agents

Agent	Dosage	Formulations	Comments
Aspirin *(ASA)*[▲][BC]	AF, KR, HR, HFS, SP: 75–325 mg/d Valvular Disease: 50–100 mg/d ACS: 162–325 mg initially, followed by 75–160 mg/d CVDP, PAD: 75–100 mg/d	T: 81, 162, 325, 500, 650, 975	Risk of GI bleeding is dose-dependent. Use with caution in adults ≥80 yr old for primary prevention of cardiovascular disease.[BC] (L,K)
Dipyridamole/ASA *(Aggrenox)*	SP: 1 tablet q12h	T: 200/25	Headache a common side effect. May decrease effectiveness of cholinesterase inhibitors. (L)
Thienopyridines			Class effect: increased bleeding risk when given with ASA
Clopidogrel *(Plavix)*[▲]	ACS: 300–600 mg initially, followed by 75 mg/d SP, PAD: 75 mg/d	T: 75, 300	Some patients may be poor metabolizers due to low activity of the CYP2C19 liver enzyme; unclear if testing for this enzyme activity is effective for guiding dosage; unclear if PPIs inhibit activity (L,K)
Prasugrel *(Effient)*	ACS: 60 mg initially, followed by 10 mg/d	T: 5, 10	Use with caution in adults ≥75 yr old.[BC] Consider maintenance dose of 5 mg/d in patients <60 kg (L,K)
Ticagrelor *(Brilinta)*	ACS: 180 mg initially, followed by 90 mg twice daily	T: 90	Should be used with ASA dosage of 75–100 mg/d (K)

Table 18. Antiplatelet Agents

Notes: ACS = acute coronary syndrome; CVDP = cardiovascular disease prevention; HFS = hip fracture surgery; HR = hip replacement; KR = knee replacement; SP = secondary stroke prevention after TIA/stroke.

Table 19. Anticoagulant Agents

Class, Agent	Dose	Oral Formulation	Comments
Heparin			
Unfractionated heparin *(Hep-Lock)*	VTE prophylaxis: 5000 U SC 2h preop and q12h postop; Acute VTE tx: 5000 U/kg IV bolus followed by 15 mg/kg/h IV; ACS: 60–70 U/kg (max 5000 U) IV bolus, followed by 12–15 U/kg/h IV	NA	Bleeding, anemia, thrombocytopenia, hypertransaminasemia, urticaria (L,K)
LMWH			
Enoxaparin *(Lovenox)*	MP, HR, HFS, NOS: 30 mg SC q12h or 40 mg SC once daily; KR: 30 mg SC q12h; MHS: 40 mg SC once daily; Inpatient VTE tx: 1 mg/kg SC q12h or 1.5 mg/kg SC once daily; outpatient DVT tx: 1 mg/kg SC q12h ACS: 30 mg IV bolus, followed by 1 mg/kg SC q12h	NA	Bleeding, anemia, hyperkalemia, hypertransaminasemia, thrombocytopenia, thrombocytosis, urticaria, angioedema (K)
Dalteparin *(Fragmin)*	HR: 2500–5000 U SC preop, 5000 U SC once daily postop; MP, NOS: 2500–5000 U SC preop and postop; LT VTE tx in cancer patients: 200 U/kg SC q24h × 30 d, followed by 150 U/kg SC q24g for the next 5 mo; ACS: 120 IU/kg SC q12h	NA	Same as above (K)
Tinzaparin *(Innohep)*	Acute VTE tx: 175 anti-Xa IU/kg SC once daily	NA	Same as above; contraindicated in older patients with CrCl <30 mL/min (K)
Heparinoid			
Danaparoid *(Orgaran)*	HR, HFS: 750 anti-Xa U SC twice daily	NA	Same: also used for heparin-induced thrombocytopenia (K)
Direct Factor Xa Inhibitors			Class effect: no antidote for reversal of bleeding. In 1 trial of healthy young subjects, prothrombin complex concentration reversed the anticoagulant effect of rivaroxaban.
Apixaban *(Eliquis)*	AF: 5 mg po q12h HR, KR: 2.5 mg po q12h Acute VTE tx: 10 mg po q12h for 7 d, followed by 5 mg po q12h Secondary prevention of VTE recurrence: 2.5 mg po q12h	T: 2.5, 5	Lower dose to 2.5 mg po q12h if patient has two of the following: age ≥80, weight ≤60 kg, Cr ≥1.5 mg/dL; not recommended in patients with mechanical heart valves (L, K)

(cont.)

Table 19. Anticoagulant Agents (cont.)

Class, Agent	Dose	Oral Formulation	Comments
Edoxaban *(Savaysa)*	AF: 60 mg po once daily VTE after patient has been treated for 5–10 d with a parenteral anticoagulant: weight ≤60 kg: 30 mg po once daily weight >60 kg: 60 mg po once daily	T: 15, 30, 60	Reduce dose to 30 mg/d if CrCl 15–50 mL/min; do not use if CrCl >95 mL/min (K)
Indirect Factor Xa Inhibitors			
Fondaparinux *(Arixtra)*	ACS: 2.5 mg SC once daily MP, KR, HR, NOS: 2.5 mg SC once daily beginning 6–8h postop; Acute VTE tx: weight <50 kg: 5 mg SC once daily, weight 50–100 kg: 7.5 mg SC once daily, weight >100 kg: 10 mg SC once daily	NA	Lower dosage in renal impairment; contraindicated if CrCl <30 mL/min (K)
Rivaroxaban *(Xarelto)*	KR, HR, NOS: 10 mg/d po, begin 6–10 h after surgery; AF: 20 mg/d po with evening meal VTE: 15 mg po q12h for first 21 d, followed by 20 mg/d po	T: 10, 15, 20	Lower dosage to 15 mg/d in AF patients with CrCl 15–50 mL/min; contraindicated if CrCl <15 mL/min; not recommended in patients with mechanical heart valves (L,K)
Direct Thrombin Inhibitors			
Argatroban	HIT + VTE prophylaxis or tx: 2 mcg/kg/min IV infusion	NA	Lower dosage if hepatic impairment (L)
Bivalirudin *(Angiomax)*	ACS: 0.75 mg/kg bolus, followed by 1.75 mg/kg/h IV	NA	(L,K)
Dabigatran *(Pradaxa)*	AF, HR[OL], KR[OL], VTE after patient has been treated for 5–10 d with a parenteral anticoagulant, secondary prevention of VTE recurrence: 150 mg po q12h	T: 75, 150	Reduce dosage to 75 mg po q12h if CrCl = 15–30 mL/min; contraindicated in patients with mechanical heart valves; use with caution in adults aged >75 yr old or if CrCl <30 mL/min[BC]; in cases of severe uncontrolled bleeding or emergency surgery, anticoagulant effect can be acutely reversed with idarucizumab *(Praxbind)* 5 g IV [sol: 2.5 g/50 mL] (K)
Desirudin *(Iprivask)*	HR: 15 mg SC q12h starting 5–15 min before surgery	NA	If CrCl = 31–60 mL/min, starting dose is 5 mg; if CrCl <31 mL/min, starting dose is 1.7 mg
Lepirudin *(Refludan)*	HIT + VTE prophylaxis or tx: 4 mcg/kg bolus, then 0.15 mg/kg/h	NA	Lower bolus to 0.2 mg/kg if CrCl <60 mL/min

(cont.)

Table 19. Anticoagulant Agents (cont.)

Class, Agent	Dose	Oral Formulation	Comments
Glycoprotein IIb/IIIa Inhibitors			
Abciximab (ReoPro)	ACS: 0.25 mg/kg IV bolus, followed by 0.125 mcg/kg/min (max 10 mcg/min)	NA	
Eptifibatide (Integrilin)	ACS: 180 mcg/kg IV bolus, followed by 2 mcg/kg/min IV	NA	
Tirofiban (Aggrastat)	ACS: 0.4 mcg/kg/min IV over 30 min, followed by 0.1 mcg/kg/min	NA	

Notes: ACS = acute coronary syndrome; HFS = hip fracture surgery; HIT = heparin-induced thrombocytopenia; HR = hip replacement; KR = knee replacement; LT = long-term; MP = medical inpatients at moderate-high risk for VTE; NA = not available; NOS = nonorthopedic surgery at moderate–high risk of VTE; VTE = venous thromboembolism (DVT/PE).

Warfarin Therapy

- For anticoagulation in nonacute conditions, initiate tx by giving warfarin▲ *(Coumadin)* 2–10 mg/d as fixed dose [T: 1, 2, 2.5, 3, 4, 5, 6, 7.5, 10]. The usual starting dose for patient >70 yr old is 5 mg/d, adjusted up or down depending on body size, comorbidities, and age.
- INR should be checked every 2–3 d until INR is stable. Reduce dose if INR >2.5 on day 3.
- Half-life is 31–51 h; steady state is achieved on day 5–7 of fixed state. Genetic tests for VKORC1 (modulates sensitivity to warfarin) and CYP2C9 (modulates metabolism of warfarin) are available to help guide dosing for initiation of warfarin tx; it is unknown if their routine use significantly improves outcomes. Medicare does not cover genetic testing.
- For stable outpatients with INRs in the therapeutic range, routine INR monitoring every 12 wk is reasonable.
- Home INR testing results in similar outcomes (rates of stroke, death, or severe bleeding episodes) compared with monthly testing in an anticoagulation clinic.
- Warfarin tx is implicated in **many** adverse drug-drug interactions.
- Some drugs that **increase** INR in conjunction with warfarin (type in *italics* = major interaction):

  - alcohol (with concurrent liver disease)
  - amiodarone
  - many antibiotics*
  - APAP (>1.3 g/d for >1 wk)
  - celecoxib
  - *cilostazol*
  - *clofibrate*
  - *duloxetine*
  - flu vaccine
  - INH
  - *ketoprofen*
  - *naproxen*
  - sulindac
  - *tamoxifen*

  * especially fluconazole, itraconazole, ketoconazole, miconazole, ciprofloxacin, erythromycin, *moxifloxacin*, metronidazole, *sulfamethoxazole, trimethoprim*

- Some drugs that **decrease** INR in conjunction with warfarin:

  - carbamazepine
  - cholestyramine
  - dicloxacillin
  - nafcillin
  - rifampin
  - vitamin K

Table 20. Indications for Warfarin Anticoagulation in the Absence of Active Bleeding or Severe Bleeding Risk

Condition	Target INR	Duration of Therapy
Hip fracture or replacement surgery, major knee surgery	2–3	10–35 d
VTE secondary to reversible risk factor	2–3	3 mo
Idiopathic VTE	2–3	At least 3 mo
Recurrent VTE	2–3	Indefinitely
AF with CHADS$_2$ or CHA$_2$DS$_2$–VASc score ≥2[a]	2–3	Indefinitely
Rheumatic mitral valvular disease with hx of systemic embolization, left atrial thrombus, or left atrial diameter >5.5 cm	2–3	Indefinitely
Mitral valve prolapse with documented systemic embolism or recurrent TIAs despite ASA tx	2–3	Indefinitely
Mechanical aortic valve	2–3	Indefinitely
Mechanical mitral valve	2.5–3.5	Indefinitely
Mechanical heart valve with AF, anterior-apical STEMI, left atrial enlargement, hypercoagulable state, or low EF	2.5–3.5	Indefinitely
Bioprosthetic mitral valve	2–3	3 mo
Peripheral arterial embolectomy	2–3	Indefinitely
Cerebral venous sinus thrombosis	2–3	12 mo
MI with large anterior involvement, significant HF, intracardiac thrombosis, or hx of thromboembolic event	2–3	At least 3 mo

[a] See the Atrial Fibrillation section (**Table 32**, p 58) in the chapter on Cardiovascular Diseases for CHADS$_2$ and CHA$_2$DS$_2$–VASc scoring. Apixaban, dabigatran, edoxaban, and rivaroxaban are alternate options to warfarin. Patients with CHADS$_2$ or CHA$_2$DS$_2$–VASc score = 1 or in whom anticoagulation is contraindicated or not tolerated can be treated with ASA 75–325 mg/d; patients with CHADS$_2$ or CHA$_2$DS$_2$–VASc score = 0 should be treated with ASA 75–325 mg/d or receive no tx.

Table 21. Treatment of Warfarin Overdose

INR	Clinical Situation	Action
3.6–10	No bleeding	Omit next 1–2 doses and recheck INR
>10	No bleeding	Omit next 1–2 doses and give Vitamin K 2.5 mg po, recheck INR
Any	Major bleeding	D/C warfarin; give Vitamin K 5–10 mg by slow IV infusion plus 4-factor prothrombin complex concentrate

DIAGNOSIS

Anxiety disorders as a whole are the most common mental disorders in older adults. Some anxiety disorders (panic disorder, social phobia) appear to be less prevalent in older than in younger adults. Generalized anxiety disorder (GAD) and new-onset anxiety in older adults are often secondary to physical illness, poorer health-related quality of life, depression, or AEs of or withdrawal from medications.

DSM-5 Criteria for GAD

- Generalized Anxiety Disorder 7-item scale (GAD-7) is a self-reported questionnaire for screening and measuring severity of GAD (Spitzer RL et al. *Arch Intern Med* 2006;166:1092–1097).
- Excessive anxiety and worry on more days than not for ≥6 mo, about a number of events or activities
- Difficulty controlling the worry
- The anxiety and worry are associated with 3 or more of the following symptoms:
  - restlessness or feeling keyed up or on the edge
  - muscle tension
  - being easily fatigued
  - difficulty concentrating
  - irritability
  - sleep disturbance
- Focus of anxiety and worry not confined to features of another primary psychiatric disorder; often, about routine life circumstances; may shift from one concern to another
- Anxiety, worry, or physical symptoms cause clinically significant distress or impairment in social, occupational, or other important areas of functioning
- Disturbance not due to the direct physiologic effects of a drug of abuse or a medication or to a medical condition; does not occur exclusively during a mood disorder, psychotic disorder, or a pervasive development disorder

DSM-5 recognizes several other anxiety disorders:
(Italicized type indicates the most common anxiety disorders in older adults.)
- Agoraphobia
- *Anxiety disorder due to a general medical condition*
- OCD
- Panic attack
- Social anxiety disorder (social phobia)
- Substance-induced anxiety disorder

DSM-5 Criteria for Panic Attack

An abrupt surge of intense fear or discomfort with ≥4 of the following (also, must peak within minutes):

- Palpitations, pounding heart, or accelerated HR
- Sweating
- Trembling or shaking
- Sensations of shortness of breath or smothering
- Feelings of choking
- Chest pain or discomfort
- Nausea or abdominal distress
- Feeling dizzy, unsteady, lightheaded, or faint
- Chills or heat sensations
- Paresthesias (numbness or tingling sensations)
- Derealization (feelings of unreality) or depersonalization (being detached from oneself)
- Fear of losing your mind or going crazy
- Fear of dying

Differential Diagnosis

- Panic disorder: recurrent, unexpected panic attacks
- Physical conditions producing anxiety
  - Cardiovascular: arrhythmias, angina, MI, HF
  - Endocrine: hyperthyroidism, hypoglycemia, pheochromocytoma
  - Neurologic: movement disorders, temporal lobe epilepsy, AD, stroke
  - Respiratory: COPD, asthma, PE
- Medications producing anxiety
  - Caffeine
  - Corticosteroids
  - Nicotine
  - Psychotropics: antidepressants, antipsychotics, stimulants
  - Sympathomimetics: pseudoephedrine, β-agonists
  - Thyroid hormones: overreplacement
- Withdrawal states: alcohol, sedatives, hypnotics, benzodiazepines, SSRIs
- Depression

EVALUATION

- Past psychiatric hx
- Drug review: prescribed, OTC, alcohol, caffeine
- MSE
- Physical examination: Focus on signs and symptoms of anxiety (eg, tachycardia, tachypnea, sweating, tremor).
- Laboratory tests: Consider CBC, blood glucose, TSH, B_{12}, ECG, oxygen saturation, drug and alcohol screening.

MANAGEMENT

Nonpharmacologic

- CBT may be useful for GAD, panic disorder, and post-tramatic stress disorder (PTSD); efficacy in both individual and group formats.
- Graded desensitization used in panic and phobia relies on gradual exposure with learning to manage resultant anxiety.
- May be effective alone but mostly used in conjunction with pharmacotherapy.
- Requires a cognitively intact, motivated patient.

Pharmacologic (**Table 41** for dosing of antidepressants and indication of generic status)
- Panic: sertraline; secondary choices include β-blockers and second-generation antipsychotics
- Social phobia: sertraline, venlafaxine XR
- Generalized anxiety:
  ○ Suggested order: SNRIs/SSRIs, (duloxetine, escitalopram, sertraline, venlafaxine XR), buspirone, pregabalin, benzodiazepines
- PTSD: sertraline
  ○ Avoid benzodiazepines.[CW]
  ○ For nightmares, prazosin may be helpful (initiate at 1 mg qhs and titrate slowly to avoid orthostatic syncope).

Buspirone[▲] (BuSpar):
- Serotonin 1A partial agonist effective in GAD and anxiety symptoms accompanying general medical illness (although geriatric evidence is limited)
- Not effective for acute anxiety or panic disorder
- May take 2–4 wk for therapeutic response
- Recommended starting dosage: 7.5–10 mg q12h [T: 5, 10, 15, 30], up to max 60 mg/d
- No dependence, tolerance, withdrawal, or CNS depression
- Risk of serotonin syndrome with SSRIs, MAOIs, TCAs, 5-hydroxytryptamine 1 receptor agonists, ergot alkaloids, lithium, St. John's wort, opioids, dextromethorphan

Pregabalin:
- Although pregabalin is not FDA-approved for the tx of GAD, there is evidence to support its use as both single and adjunctive tx, including in older adults
- Onset of therapeutic response may be longer than that observed in younger adults
- Adverse effects are predominantly somnolence and dizziness
- Risk of dependence or withdrawal appears minimal but is Schedule V medication in the US

Benzodiazepines: (Avoid if hx of falls or fractures.[BC])
- Restrict use to severe GAD unresponsive to other tx[CW] (**Table 22**)
- Preferred: intermediate–half-life drugs inactivated by direct conjugation in liver and therefore less affected by aging (**Table 22**)
- Avoid long-acting benzodiazepines (eg, flurazepam, diazepam, chlordiazepoxide)
- Linked to cognitive impairment, falls, sedation, psychomotor impairment, delirium
- Problems: dependence, misuse (p 327), tolerance, withdrawal, more so with short-acting benzodiazepines; seizure risk with alprazolam withdrawal
- Potentially fatal if combined with alcohol or other CNS depressants
- Only short-term (60–90 d) use recommended

Table 22. Benzodiazepines for Anxiety Recommended for Older Adults

Drug	Dosage	Formulations
Lorazepam[▲] (Ativan)	0.5–2 mg in 2–3 divided doses	T: 0.5, 1, 2; S: 2 mg/mL; inj: 2 mg/mL
Oxazepam[▲] (Serax)	10–15 mg q8–12h	T: 10, 15, 30

Nonbenzodiazepine Hypnotics:
Zolpidem (Ambien),[BC] zaleplon (Sonata),[BC] eszopiclone (Lunesta),[BC] and ramelteon (Rozerem) should not be used for tx of anxiety disorders (Sleep Disorders, **Table 128**).

CORONARY ARTERY DISEASE

Screening/Calculating Risk in Persons Without Hx of CVD (2013 ACC/AHA Guidelines)

- Quantify CVD risk: every 4–6 yr in persons up to age 79 without hx of CVD by assessing traditional risk factors
  - Traditional risk factors for quantifying risk are: increasing age, male sex, African American race, total cholesterol >170, HDL-cholesterol <50, SBP >110, tx for high blood pressure, DM, and current smoking
  - 10-yr risk of CVD can be calculated using a downloadable spreadsheet available at my.americanheart.org/cvriskcalculator or www.cardiosource.org/science-and-quality/practice-guidelines-and-quality-standards/2013-prevention-guideline-tools.aspx
  - If 10-yr risk of CVD is elevated (≥7.5%), patient should be considered for intensive lipid management (p 47), lifestyle alteration, and assessment and tx for obesity
- If tx decision based on 10-yr CVD risk is uncertain, the presence of one or more of the following other risk factors would suggest further increased risk: first degree relative with hx of premature CVD (male <55, female <65), high-sensitivity CRP >2 mg/L, coronary artery calcium >30 Agatson units or >75th percentile, ABI <0.9.
- Don't order coronary artery calcium scoring for screening purposes on low-risk asymptomatic individuals except those with a family hx of premature CAD.[CW]
- Don't routinely order coronary CT angiography for screening asymptomatic individuals.[CW]

Diagnostic Cardiac Tests

- Cardiac catheterization is the gold standard; cardiac CT angiography is a less invasive, but less accurate, alternative.
- Stress testing: The heart is stressed either through exercise (treadmill, stationary bicycle) or, if the patient cannot exercise or the ECG is markedly abnormal, with pharmacologic agents (dipyridamole, adenosine, dobutamine). Exercise stress tests can be performed with or without cardiac imaging, while pharmacologic stress tests always include imaging. Imaging can be accomplished by echocardiography or single-photon-emission computed tomography (SPECT).
- Don't perform stress cardiac imaging or advanced noninvasive imaging in the initial evaluation of patients without cardiac symptoms unless high-risk markers are present.[CW]
- Don't use coronary artery calcium scoring for patients with known CAD (including stents and bypass grafts).[CW]
- Don't obtain screening exercise ECG testing in individuals who are asymptomatic and at low risk for coronary heart disease.[CW]

Acute Coronary Syndrome (ACS)

- ACS encompasses diagnoses of ST segment MI (STEMI), non-ST segment MI (NSTEMI), and unstable angina.
- Suspect ACS with anginal chest pain or anginal equivalent: arm, jaw, or abdominal pain (with or without nausea); acute functional decline.
- Diagnosis is based on symptoms along with cardiac serum markers and ECG findings:
  - STEMI: elevated serum markers, elevated ST segments
  - NSTEMI: elevated serum markers, depressed ST segments or inverted T-waves
  - Unstable angina: nonelevated serum markers, normal or depressed ST segments, normal or inverted T-waves

- Measuring cardiac serum markers:
  - Most protocols call for checking troponins T or I at presentation and 2 h later.
  - A single negative enzyme measurement, particularly within 6 h of symptom onset, does not exclude MI; 2 negative measurements exclude MI.
  - Sensitivity of troponins is improved with use of sensitive or ultrasensitive assays.
  - Troponins are not useful for detecting reinfarction within first wk of an MI. CK-MB is the preferred marker for early reinfarction.
  - Both CK-MB and cardiac troponins can have false-positive results due to subclinical ischemic myocardial injury or nonischemic myocardial injury.
- Troponin levels can be transiently or persistently minimally elevated by many non-ACS causes, including severe HTN, tachyarrhythmias, coronary spasm, HF, viral myocarditis, endocarditis, myocarditis, pericarditis, malignancy, cancer chemotherapy, trauma, PE, sepsis, renal failure, and stroke. Evaluation (hx, physical exam, assessment of renal function, ECG, echocardiography) should focus on finding and treating the underlying cause. Elevated troponin in the face of normal CK-MB can indicate increased risk of MI in the ensuing 6 mo.

Initial Management of ACS (at presentation)

- ASA 162–325 mg initially, followed by 81–325 mg/d
- Chair/bed rest with continuous ECG monitoring
- Oxygen to maintain saturation >90%
- D/C NSAIDs
- If ischemia is ongoing (based on symptoms or ECG changes), give nitroglycerin▲ 0.4 mg sl q5min for a total of 3 doses.
- Nitroglycerin IV is indicated for persistent ischemia, HTN, large anterior infarction, or HF. Begin at 5–10 mcg/min IV and titrate to pain relief, SBP >90 mmHg, or resolution of ECG abnormalities.
- If chest pain persists on nitroglycerin tx, give morphine sulfate 2–4 mg IV with increments of 2–8 mg IV repeated q5–15 min prn.
- Administer antiplatelet agents, anticoagulants, and glycoprotein IIb/IIIa inhibitors according to reperfusion strategy (**Tables 13, 18,** and **19**):
  - Thrombolytic tx: ASA, clopidogrel or ticagrelor, and an anticoagulant
  - Early invasive tx with planned percutaneous cardiac intervention: ASA, clopidogrel or prasugrel or ticagrelor, an anticoagulant, and a glycoprotein IIb/IIIa inhibitor
  - Medical management: ASA, clopidogrel or ticagrelor, and an anticoagulant; consider adding a glycoprotein IIb/IIIa inhibitor
  - CABG: ASA and UFH

Ongoing Hospital Management of ACS (first 24-48 h)

- An oral β-blocker should be started within 24 h of symptom onset and continued long term unless there is acute HF, evidence of a low-output state, pronounced bradycardia, or cardiogenic shock.
- An oral ACEI should be started within 24 h of symptom onset for STEMI patients, for NSTEMI patients with clinical HF or EF <40%, and for NSTEMI patients with HTN, DM, or stable chronic kidney disease (**Table 25**). If patient cannot tolerate ACEIs for reasons other than hypotension, give oral ARB.
- An aldosterone antagonist (spironolactone or eplerenone, p 45) should be added to the above medications in post-MI patients without significant renal disease (Cr ≤2.5 mg/dL in men and ≤2.0 mg/dL in women), without hyperkalemia (serum potassium ≤5.0 mEq/L), and who have LVEF <40%, DM, or HF.

- A high-intensity statin should be started if there are no contraindications. (Dyslipidemia Management, p 47).
- Anticoagulation with warfarin▲ (p 34), apixaban (**Table 19**), edoxaban (**Table 19**), rivaroxaban (**Table 19**), or dabigatran (**Table 19**) is indicated in post-MI patients with AF (2014 ACC/AHA AF Guidelines, p 58–60 and **Table 33**). Warfarin is indicated in post-MI patients with left ventricular thrombosis or large anterior infarction (**Table 20**).
- At time of discharge, prescribe rapid-acting nitrates prn: sl nitroglycerin▲ or nitroglycerin spr q5min for max of 3 doses in 15 min (**Table 23**).
- Longer-acting nitrates should be prescribed if symptomatic angina and tx will be medical rather than surgical or angioplasty. May be combined with β-blockers or calcium channel blockers, or both (**Table 23**).
- Calcium channel blockers should be used cautiously for management of angina only in non-Q-wave infarctions without systolic dysfunction and a contraindication to β-blockers.

Table 23. Nitrate Dosages and Formulations		
Medication	**Dosage**	**Formulations (mg)**
Oral		
Isosorbide dinitrate▲ (*Isordil, Sorbitrate*)	10–40 mg 3 ×/d (6 h apart)	T: 5, 10, 20, 30, 40; ChT: 5, 10
Isosorbide dinitrate SR (*Dilatrate SR*)	40–80 mg q8–12h	T: 40
Isosorbide mononitrate▲ (*ISMO, Monoket*)	20 mg q12h (8 am and 3 pm)	T: 10, 20
Isosorbide mononitrate SR▲ (*Imdur*)	start 30–60 mg/d; max 240 mg/d	T: 30, 60, 120
Nitroglycerin▲ (*Nitro-Bid*)	2.5–9 mg q8–12h	T: 2.5, 6.5, 9
Sublingual		
Isosorbide dinitrate▲ (*Isordil, Sorbitrate*)	1 tab prn	T: 2.5, 5, 10
Nitroglycerin (*Nitrostat*)	0.4 mg prn	T: 0.15, 0.3, 0.4, 0.6
Oral spray		
Nitroglycerin (*Nitrolingual, NitroMist*)	1–2 spr prn; max 3/15 min	0.4 mg/spr
Ointment		
Nitroglycerin 2%▲ (*Nitro-Bid, Nitrol*)	start 0.5–4 inches q4–8h	2%
Transdermal		
Nitroglycerin▲	1 pch 12–14 h/d	0.1, 0.2, 0.3, 0.4, 0.6, 0.8

POST-MI AND CHRONIC STABLE ANGINA CARE
- Unless contraindicated, all post-MI patients should be on ASA, a β-blocker, and an ACEI.
- Give clopidogrel or ticagrelor (**Table 18**) for up to 12 mo in patients receiving stents. Prasugrel (**Table 18**) can be given as an alternative to clopidogrel. Prasugrel should be considered only in patients <75 yr old without hx of TIA or stroke. When using ticagrelor, concomitant ASA dosage should not exceed 100 mg/d.
- If β-blockers are contraindicated, use long-acting nitrates or long-acting calcium channel blockers for chronic angina.
- For refractory chronic angina despite tx with β-blocker, calcium channel blocker, or nitrates, consider addition of ranolazine *(Ranexa)* 500–1,000 mg po q12h [T:500];

contraindicated in patients with QT prolongation or on QT-prolonging drugs, with hepatic impairment, or on CYP3A inhibitors, including diltiazem (p 54).

- Use sl or spr nitroglycerin for acute angina.
- Treat HTN (p 50).
- Treat dyslipidemia with high-intensity statin dose (p 47).
- Treat DM; see p 96 for target goals.
- Weight reduction in obese individuals; goal BMI <25 kg/m^2.
- Aerobic exercise 30–60 min/d, at least intermediate intensity (eg, brisk walking).
- Smoking cessation.
- Encourage adoption of DASH (Dietary Approaches to Stop Hypertension) or Mediterranean diet.
- Consider placement of ICD (p 65) in patients with LVEF ≤30% at least 40 d after MI or 3 mo after CABG.
- Don't perform routine annual stress testing after coronary artery revascularization.[CW]
- Avoid NSAIDs other than ASA.

HEART FAILURE (HF)

Evaluation and Assessment

- All patients initially presenting with HF should have an echocardiogram to evaluate left ventricular function. An EF of ≤40% indicates systolic dysfunction and a diagnosis of HF with reduced EF (HFrEF). An EF ≥50% indicates diastolic dysfunction and a diagnosis of HF with preserved EF (HFpEF). An EF of 41–49% is a borderline classification but patients usually resemble those with HFpEF.
  - Echocardiography can also evaluate cardiac dyssynchrony (**Table 24**) in patients with a wide QRS complex on ECG.
  - Echocardiography with tissue doppler imaging may be helpful in diagnosing diastolic dysfunction.

Table 24. Heart Failure Staging and Management

Clinical Profile	ACC/AHA Staging	NYHA Staging	Management
Asymptomatic but at high risk of developing HF (eg, HTN, DM, CAD present)	Stage A	—	RFR, E
Asymptomatic with structural disease: LVH, low EF, prior MI, or valvular disease	Stage B	Class I	RFR, E, ACEI (or ARB if unable to tolerate ACEI), BB
Normal EF; current or prior symptoms (HFpEF)	Stage C	Class I-IV	RFR, drug tx for symptomatic HF, control of ventricular rate
Low EF[a]; currently asymptomatic but with hx of symptoms	Stage C	Class I	RFR, E, DW, SR, ACEI (or ARB if unable to tolerate ACEI), BB
Low EF[a]; patient comfortable at rest but symptomatic on normal physical activity	Stage C	Class II	Class II–IV: RFR, E, DW, SR, drug tx for symptomatic HF (below), consider biventricular pacing if cardiac dyssynchrony is present, consider placement of ICD if LVEF ≤35% (see p 65)
Low EF[a]; patient comfortable at rest but symptomatic on slight physical activity	Stage C	Class III	
Low EF[a]; patient symptomatic at rest	Stage C	Class IV	
Refractory symptoms at rest in hospitalized patient requiring specialized interventions (eg, transplant) or hospice care	Stage D	Class IV	Decide on care preference; above measures or hospice as appropriate

Notes: RFR = cardiac risk factor reduction; E = exercise (regular walking or cycling); BB = β-blocker, DW = measurement of daily weight; SR = salt restriction (≤3 g/d if severe HF).

[a] Low EF = EF ≤40%

- Other routine initial assessment: orthostatic BPs, height, weight, BMI calculation, ECG, CXR, CBC, UA, electrolytes, calcium, magnesium, Cr, BUN, lipid profile, fasting glucose, LFTs, TSH, functional status.
- Measurement of plasma brain natriuretic peptide (BNP) or N-terminal prohormone brain natriuretic peptide (NT-proBNP) can aid in diagnosis of HF in patients presenting with acute dyspnea.
  - BNP and NT-proBNP levels increase with age.
  - In dyspneic patients >70 yr old:
    - HF very unlikely (likelihood ratio negative = 0.1) if BNP <100 pg/mL (22 mmol/L) or if NT-proBNP <300 pg/mL (35 mmol/L)
    - HF very likely (likelihood ratio positive = 6) if BNP >500 pg/mL (110 mmol/L) or if NT-proBNP >1,200 pg/mL (140 mmol/L)
  - Other conditions causing increased BNP or NT-proBNP levels include impaired renal function, pulmonary disease, HTN, hyperthyroidism, hepatic cirrhosis with ascites, paraneoplastic syndrome, glucocorticoid use, and sepsis.
- Optional: Radionuclide ventriculography, which measures EF more precisely, provides a better evaluation of right ventricular function, and is more expensive than echocardiography.
- If HF is accompanied by angina or signs of ischemia, coronary angiography should be strongly considered.
- Consider coronary angiography if HF presents with atypical chest pain or in patients who have known or suspected CAD.

- Consider stress testing if HF presents in patients at high risk (ie, numerous risk factors) for CAD.
- Avoid thiazolidinediones (**Table 47**), NSAIDs, and COX-2 inhibitors in patients with HF.[BC]

Drug Therapy for Symptomatic HFrEF (AHA Stage C and D, NYHA Class II–IV)

For information on drug dosages and AEs not listed below, see **Table 29**. Efficacy of different medications may vary significantly across racial and ethnic groups; eg, blacks may require higher doses of ACEIs and β-blockers and may benefit from isosorbide dinitrate combined with hydralazine tx.

- Diuretics if volume overload
- ARBs or ACEIs to target doses (**Table 25**). ARBs have been shown to improve HFrEF outcomes in older adults, while ACEIs have been found to improve outcomes in subjects <75 yr old but not in those older than 75.
- β-blockers to target doses (**Table 25**) once volume status is stabilized

Table 25. Target Dosages of ACEIs, Angiotensin II Receptor Blockers, and β-Blockers in Patients with HFrEF

Agent	Starting Dosage	Target Dosage
ACEIs[a]		
Benazepril▲	2.5 mg/d	40 mg/d
Captopril▲	6.25 mg q8h	50 mg q8h
Enalapril▲	2.5 mg q12h	10 mg q12h
Fosinopril▲	5 mg/d	40 mg/d
Lisinopril▲	2.5 mg/d	20 mg/d
Perindopril	2 mg/d	8 mg/d
Quinapril▲	5 mg q12h	20 mg q12h
Ramipril▲	1.25 mg/d	10 mg/d
Trandolapril▲	1 mg/d	4 mg/d
Angiotensin II Receptor Blockers[a]		
Candesartan	4 mg/d	32 mg/d
Losartan▲	12.5 mg/d	50 mg q12h
Valsartan	20 mg q12h	160 mg q12h
β-Blockers		
Bisoprolol▲	1.25 mg/d	10 mg/d
Carvedilol▲	3.125 mg q12h	25 mg q12h
Carvedilol ER	10 mg/d	80 mg/d
Metoprolol XR▲	12.5–25 mg/d	200 mg/d
Nebivolol	1.25 mg/d	10 mg/d

[a] Check Cr and electrolytes 1–2 wk after initiating tx. Titrate to target dosage by gradually increasing or doubling the dose every 2 wk as tolerated.

- Adding an aldosterone antagonist can reduce mortality in patients with NYHA Class II–IV failure. Use either spironolactone▲ *(Aldactone)* 25 mg/d (Avoid doses >25 mg/d[BC] po [T: 25] or eplerenone *(Inspra)* 25–50 mg/d po [T: 25, 50, 100]). Monitor serum potassium carefully and avoid these medications if Cr >2.5 mg/dL in men or >2 mg/dL in women, or serum K+≥5.0 mEq/L.
- Add low-dose digoxin▲ *(Lanoxin)* [T: 0.125, 0.25; S: 0.05 mg/mL]; *(Lanoxicaps)* [T: 0.05, 0.1, 0.2], 0.0625–0.125 mg/d (target serum levels 0.5–0.8 mg/dL) if HF is not controlled on diuretics and ACEIs, with or without an aldosterone antagonist. Avoid doses >0.125 mg/d.[BC] Digoxin may be less effective and even harmful in women and has been associated with increased mortality in patients with AF.
  - Digoxin concentration must be monitored with concomitant administration of many other medications.
    - The following **increase** digoxin concentration or effect, or both:

amiodarone	esmolol	tetracycline
diltiazem	ibuprofen	verapamil
erythromycin	spironolactone	

    - The following **decrease** digoxin concentration or effect, or both:

aminosalicylic acid	colestipol	sulfasalazine
antacids	kaolin pectin	St. John's wort
antineoplastics	metoclopramide	
cholestyramine	psyllium	

- Adding a combination of isosorbide dinitrate and hydralazine (**Table 23** and **Table 29**; also available as a single preparation: *BiDil* 1–2 tabs po q8h [T: 20/37.5]) can be helpful for patients, particularly African Americans, with persistent symptoms. Use vasodilators with caution in patients with hx of syncope.[BC]
- For patients with EF ≤35%, stable symptoms, in sinus rhythm who are taking maximally tolerated doses of β-blockers or intolerant to β-blockers, consider adding ivabradine *(Corlanor)* [T: 5, 7.5] to reduce risk of hospitalization for HF.
- Omega-3 polyunsaturated fatty acid supplements can be added as adjunctive tx for symptomatic patients.
- Correct iron deficiency using IV iron (**Table 65**) with or without anemia.
- Avoid nondihydropyridine CCBs in HFrEF.[BC]
- Class I antiarrhythmics are not indicated.

Drug Therapy for Symptomatic HFpEF

- For acute HFpEF with volume overload, loop diuretics and vasodilation with nitroglycerin are indicated. Parenteral nitroglycerin can cause hypotension in HFpEF patients without elevated BP, so use it cautiously if BP is normal or low.
- For HFpEF without volume overload, pharmacologic management focuses on control of HTN; rate control, especially in patients with AF; and avoidance of digoxin.

Source: Yancy CW et al. *Circulation* 2013;128:e240–e327.

LEG EDEMA

Differential

- Acute (<72 h) unilateral: DVT (by far most common and must be ruled out), ruptured Baker's cyst, ruptured medial head of the gastrocnemius
- Acute bilateral: acute worsening of HF, renal disease

- Chronic unilateral: venous insufficiency, secondary lymphedema (from tumor, radiation tx, surgery), cellulitis, reflex sympathetic dystrophy
- Chronic bilateral: venous insufficiency (most common of all causes), HF, pulmonary HTN, drugs (see below), idiopathic edema, obesity, renal disease, liver disease, primary lymphedema, secondary lymphedema (from tumor, radiation tx, surgery)
- Drugs commonly causing edema include:
  - Antihypertensives: calcium channel blockers, β-blockers, clonidine, hydralazine
  - Hormones: corticosteroids, sex hormones
  - NSAIDs

Evaluation

- History: duration and location of edema; overnight improvement (less likely in lymphedema), presence of pain (more likely in DVT, reflex sympathetic dystrophy); medication review; hx of heart, kidney, or liver disease; hx of cancer and/or radiation tx; sleep apnea (increases likelihood of pulmonary HTN)
- Physical exam: BMI; location of edema; tenderness (more likely in DVT); skin changes; signs of heart, kidney, or liver disease; pelvic exam if suspect pelvic tumor
- Diagnostic studies: CBC, UA, electrolytes, Cr, BUN, glucose, TSH, albumin. See p 28 for workup of possible DVT. Other tests obtained according to hx and physical exam findings.

Treatment

- Venous insufficiency: leg elevation, skin care (daily mild soap and moisturizers), and compression stockings worn during the day (**Table 26**).
  - Below-the-knee stockings are usually sufficient. Above-the-knee stockings are appropriate for more extensive edema and for patients with orthostatic hypotension.
  - ABI measurement should precede use of compression stockings.
  - Compression stockings are not covered under traditional Medicare Part B unless an ulcer is present. Other insurance plans may cover them and require a doctor's prescription for coverage.
  - Anti-embolism stockings (eg, T.E.D.™) are not designed for managing venous insufficiency.
  - Intermittent pneumatic compression pumps can be tried for recalcitrant edema.
  - Compression wraps can be used in patients who have difficulty donning compression stockings.
  - Diuretics should be used only for short-term tx of severe cases; chronic use can lead to intravascular dehydration and electrolyte imbalances.

Table 26. Prescribing Compression Stockings

Stocking Class (Compression Grade)	Pressure Delivered (mmHg)	Indications	Appropriate ABI Range
1 (mild)	10–20	Mild edema Varicose veins	> 0.5[a]
2 (moderate-firm)	20–30	Moderate edema Pigmentation	> 0.8
3 (firm-extra firm)	30–50	Severe edema Lymphedema	> 0.8

[a] Use with great caution in patients with ABI of 0.5–0.8.

- Complex decompression physiotherapy is an intensive multiweek intervention that is covered by Medicare for lymphedema.
- See **Table 17** and p 30 for DVT tx.
- Other tx should be directed at the underlying cause.

DYSLIPIDEMIA MANAGEMENT

Nonpharmacologic

A cholesterol-lowering diet should be considered initial tx for dyslipidemia and should be used as follows:

- The patient should be at low risk of malnutrition.
- The diet should be nutritionally adequate, with sufficient total calories, protein, calcium, iron, and vitamins, and low in saturated fats (<7% of total calories), trans-fatty acids, and cholesterol.
- The diet should be easily understood and affordable (a dietitian can be very helpful).
- Plant stanol/sterols (2 g/d), found in many fruits, vegetables, vegetable oils, nuts, seeds, cereals, and legumes, can lower LDL.
- Cholesterol-lowering margarines can lower LDL cholesterol by 10% to 15% *(Take Control 1–2 tbsp/d, 45 calories/tbsp; Benecol 3 servings of 1.5 tsp each/d, 70 calories/tbsp)*.

Pharmacologic

- 2013 ACC/AHA indications for evidence-based statin tx to reduce cardiovascular risk:
  - Statins are dosed according to intensity of lipid lowering: high-intensity (usually lowers LDL ≥50%), moderate-intensity (usually lowers LDL 30–49%), and low-intensity (usually lowers LDL <30%). See **Table 28** for dosages. The LDL-lowering target should be the percentage of lowering rather than an absolute LDL target value.
  - Patients over 75 yr old:
    - For those with CVD (prior MI, angina, ACS, coronary revascularization, stroke, TIA, or PAD), a moderate-intensity statin is recommended.
    - There are no data for those without CVD. Consider potential risk/benefit of primary prevention based on individual CVD risk, comorbidities, and goals of care.
  - Patients 40–75 yr old:
    - For those with CVD or LDL ≥190, a high-intensity statin is recommended.
    - For those with DM, a moderate-intensity statin is recommended unless they also have a 10-yr CVD risk of ≥7.5% (risk calculator at my.americanheart.org/cvriskcalculator), in which case a high-intensity statin is recommended.
    - For those with a 10-yr CVD risk of ≥7.5%, clinicians should have a discussion with patient about statin tx, assessing CVD risk factors, adverse effects of tx, and patient preferences. If statin tx is elected, a moderate- or high-intensity statin is recommended.
  - Some experts are concerned that the risk calculator designates many more older adults as being eligible for primary prevention with statin tx than previous guidelines. For example, the calculator assesses a 10-yr CVD risk of ≥7.5% in all men aged 63–75 yr old and all women aged 71–75 yr old with optimal values for other risk factors.
- Prescribing statins:
  - Tx is focused more on choice of statin intensity and percentage of LDL lowering rather than targeting a specific LDL level.
  - Check fasting lipids, measure ALT, and screen for DM before initiating tx. If ALT is normal, there is no need to recheck LFTs unless hyperbilirubinemia, jaundice, or clinically apparent hepatic disease occurs.
  - Statins should be taken in the evening.

- Check fasting lipid profile 4–12 wk after statin initiation to assess adherence and response (see above for expected percentage of LDL lowering by intensity).
- If severe muscle pain develops after initiation, D/C statin immediately and check creatine kinase, Cr, and a UA for myoglobinuria.
- Statin tx has been uncommonly associated with increases in HbA_{1c} and fasting glucose.
- A PCSK9 inhibitor (**Table 28**) can be added to statin tx to further lower LDL and cardiovascular risk.
- There are no updated guidelines regarding management of hypertriglyceridemia or mixed dyslipidemia. **Table 27** lists suggested tx choices for these conditions.

Table 27. Treatment Choices for Dyslipidemia

Agent	Type of Dyslipidemia		
	↑LDL	↑TG	↑ LDL + ↑TG + ↓HDL
Statin	1	3	1
Fibrate		1	2
Ezetimibe	3		2, C
Niacin	2	2, C	
Bile Acid Sequestrant	2		2, C
Omega-3 Fatty Acid		2, 3, C	
PCSK9 Inhibitor	C		C

1 = First-line tx; 2 = Second-line tx; 3 = Third-line tx; C = appropriate for combined tx with another agent.

Table 28. Medications for Dyslipidemia

Class	Medication	Dosage[a]	Formulations
Statin (HMG-CoA reductase inhibitor)[b]	Atorvastatin▲ *(Lipitor)*	H: 40–80 mg/d; M: 10–20 mg/d	T: 10, 20, 40, 80
	Fluvastatin▲ *(Lescol, Lescol XL)*	M: 40 mg q12h or 80 mg XL/d; L: 20–40 mg/d	C: 20, 40; T: ER 80
	Lovastatin▲c *(Mevacor, Altoprev)*	M: 40 mg/d; L: 10–20 mg/d	T: 10, 20, 40; T: ER 10, 20, 40, 60
	Pitavastatin *(Livalo)*	M: 2–4 mg/d; L: 1 mg/d	T: 1, 2, 4
	Pravastatin▲ *(Pravachol)*	M: 40–80 mg/d; L: 10–20 mg/d	T: 10, 20, 40, 80
	ASA/pravastatin *(Pravigard PAC)*	1 tab/d	T: 81/20, 81/40, 81/80, 325/20, 325/40, 325/80
	Rosuvastatin *(Crestor)*	H: 20–40 mg/d; M: 5–10 mg/d	T: 5, 10, 20, 40
	Simvastatin▲ *(Zocor)*	M: 20–40 mg/d; L: 10 mg/d	T: 5, 10, 20, 40, 80
Fibrate (fibric acid derivative)	Fenofibrate▲d *(Tricor, Lofibra, Antara)*	48–200 mg/d	T: 48, 54, 145, 160 C: 43, 67, 130, 134, 200
	Fenofibrate delayed release *(Trilipix)*	45–135 mg/d	C: 45, 135
	Gemfibrozil▲e *(Lopid)*	300–600 mg po q12h	T: 600
Cholesterol absorption inhibitor	Ezetimibe *(Zetia)*f	10 mg/d	T: 10

(cont.)

Class	Medication	Dosage[a]	Formulations
Nicotinic acid	Niacin ▲[g]	100 mg q8h to start; increase to 500–1000 mg q8h; ER 150 mg qhs to start, increase to 2000 mg qhs prn	T: 25, 50, 100, 250, 500; ER: 150, 250, 500, 750, 1000 C: TR 125, 250, 400, 500
	Niacin ER ▲[g] *(Niaspan)*	500–2000 mg/d	T: 500, 750, 1000
Bile acid sequestrant[h]	Colesevelam *(Welchol)*	Monotherapy: 1850 mg po q12h; combination tx: 2500–3750 mg/d in single or divided doses	T: 625
	Colestipol ▲ *(Colestid, Colestid Tablets)*	5–30 g mixed with liquid in 1 or more divided doses	Pks or scoops: 5 g, 7.5 g T: 1 g
Fatty acid	Omega-3-acid ethyl esters *(Omacor, Lovaza)*	4 g/d in single or divided doses	C: 1 g
Combination preparations	*Ezetimibe/simvastatin combination*[b] *(Vytorin)*[b,f] Lovastatin/niacin combination[b,c,g] *(Advicor)*	10 mg/10 mg to 10 mg/40 mg qhs 20 mg/500 mg qhs to start; max dose 40 mg/2000 mg	T: 10/10, 10/20, 10/40, 10/80 T: 20/500, 20/750, 20/1000, 40/1000
	Simvastatin/niacin combination[b,g] *(Simcor)*	20 mg/500 mg qhs to start; max dose 40 mg/2000 mg	T: 20/500, 20/750, 20/1000
PCSK9 (Proprotein convertase subtilisin kexin type 9) inhibitor[i]	Alirocumab *(Praluent)*	75–150 mg SC q2wk	Inj: 75 mg/mL, 150 mg/mL
	Evolocumab *(Repatha)*	140 mg SC q2wk or 420 mg SC q1mo	Inj: 140 mg/mL

Table 28. Medications for Dyslipidemia (cont.)

H = high-intensity statin dose, M = moderate-intensity statin dose, L = low-intensity statin dose

[a] Dosage ranges for statins are listed as high-intensity (usually lowers LDL ≥50%), moderate-intensity (usually lowers LDL 30–49%), and low-intensity (usually lowers LDL <30%)

[b] See p 47 for prescribing information.

[c] Numerous drug interactions warranting contraindication or dose adjustment of lovastatin; see package insert for details.

[d] Measure Cr level at baseline, within 3 mo of initiating tx, and q6 mo thereafter. Reduce dose if CrCl <60 mL/min; do not use if CrCl <30 mL/min.

[e] Contraindicated with concomitant statin tx.

[f] Use as monotherapy only in patients unable to tolerate statins, niacin, or a bile acid sequestrant (colesevelam, colestipol) and who have not reached LDL lowering goal.

[g] Obtain baseline and q6 mo LFTs, fasting blood glucose, or HbA$_{1c}$, and uric acid. Monitor for flushing, pruritus, nausea, gastritis, ulcer. Dosage increases should be spaced 1 mo apart. ASA 325 mg po 30 min before first niacin dose of the day is effective in preventing AEs.

[h] Do not use if fasting TG >300 mg/dL. Use with caution if fasting TG is 250–299 mg/dL.

[i] Adjunctive tx for LDL lowering in patients with homozygous familial hypercholesterolemia and in patients with atherosclerotic vascular disease on maximally tolerated doses of a statin.

HYPERTENSION

The following recommendations are combined from JNC 7 and JNC 8, since JNC 8 was not a comprehensive revision of prior guidelines.

Goal BP

JNC 8 recommends a goal BP of:

- SBP <150 mmHg or DBP <90 mmHg in persons aged 60 and over without DM or CKD.
- SBP <140 mmHg or DBP <90 mmHg in adults of all ages with DM.
- SBP <140 mmHg or DBP <90 mmHg in adults of all ages with CKD and GFR ≥60 mL/min/1.73m^2.

In persons aged 70 and over with CKD and GFR <60 mL/min/1.73m^2, there are little data to guide a goal recommendation; tx goals should be individualized according to health status, comorbidities, albuminuria (would suggest lower BP goal), and patient preferences.

Evaluation and Assessment

- Measure both standing and sitting BP after 5 min of rest.
- Base diagnosis on 2 or more readings at each of 2 or more visits. Once diagnosis is made, evaluation includes:
  - Assessment of cardiac risk factors: smoking, dyslipidemia, obesity, and DM are important in older adults.
  - Assessment of end-organ damage: LVH, angina, prior MI, prior coronary revascularization, HF, stroke or TIA, nephropathy, PAD, retinopathy.
  - Routine laboratory tests: CBC, UA, electrolytes, Cr, HbA$_{1c}$, total cholesterol, HDL cholesterol, and ECG
  - Consider renal artery stenosis (RAS) if new onset of diastolic HTN, sudden rise in BP in previously well controlled HTN, HTN despite tx with maximal dosages of 3 antihypertensive agents, or azotemia induced by ACEI/ARB tx.
    - RAS diagnostic test options include renal artery duplex ultrasonography, CT angiography, or MRA.
    - Don't screen for RAS in patients without resistant HTN and with normal renal function, even if known atherosclerosis present.[CW]
    - Medical tx for RAS includes aggressive management of vascular risk factors and antihypertensive regimens that include an ACEI or ARB (monitor Cr closely).
    - Renal artery stenting has not been shown to be superior to medical management of RAS in cases of mild to moderately severe disease (mean stenosis of 73%). Consider stenting only in cases of very severe stenosis in which medical management has failed.

Aggravating Factors

- Emotional stress
- Excessive alcohol intake
- Excessive salt intake
- Lack of aerobic exercise
- Low potassium intake
- Low calcium intake
- Nicotine
- Obesity

Management

- Initiate pharmacologic tx if goal BP (see above) has not been attained using nonpharmacologic methods.
- Lowering BP below 120/80 mmHg is not recommended.
- For patients with suspected "white coat" HTN, 24-h ambulatory blood pressure monitoring (covered by Medicare if office-based BP is >140/90 mmHg) can produce more reliable readings than office-based measurements.

Nonpharmacologic:

- Adequate calcium and magnesium intake as well as a low-fat diet for optimizing general health.
- Adequate dietary potassium intake; fruits and vegetables are the best sources.
- Aerobic exercise: 30–45 min most days of the week.
- Moderation of alcohol intake: limit to 1 oz of ethanol/d.
- Moderation of dietary sodium: watch for volume depletion with diuretic use. Goal: ≤2.4 g Na+/d, optimal ≤1.5 g Na+/d.
- Smoking cessation
- Weight reduction if obese: even a 10-lb weight loss can significantly lower BP. Goal: BMI <25 kg/m².

Pharmacologic: **Table 29** lists commonly used antihypertensives.

- Use antihypertensives carefully in patients with orthostatic BP drop.
- Base tx decisions on standing BP.
- First-line drugs: a thiazide diuretic, an ACEI, an ARB, or a calcium channel blocker.
- Follow-up BP measurements monthly until target BP is attained.
  ○ If BP is not at target, clinician has the option of increasing the dose of the intial drug or adding a second drug from the first-line list above.
  ○ Many patients require 2 or more drugs to achieve goal BP.
- Visits may be q3–6mo if BP is stable at target goal.
- If coexisting conditions, tx can be individualized (**Table 30**).
- Available dose formulations of oral potassium supplements▲: [T (mEq): 6, 7, 8, 10, 20; S (mEq/15 mL): 20, 40; pwd (mEq/pk): 15, 20, 25]

Hypertensive Emergencies and Urgencies:

- Elevated BP alone without symptoms or target end-organ damage does not require emergent BP lowering.
- Conditions requiring emergent BP lowering include hypertensive encephalopathy, intracranial hemorrhage, unstable angina, acute MI, acute left ventricular failure with pulmonary edema, dissecting aortic aneurysm.
- Most common initial tx for emergent BP lowering is IV sodium nitroprusside▲ *(Nipride)* 0.25–10 mg/kg/min.
- Nonemergent (ie, urgent) BP lowering is indicated only in cases in which BP needs to be lowered for procedures or tx (such as β blockade before surgery, p 264) or in asymptomatic people with SBP >210 mmHg or DBP >120 mmHg.
  ○ Administer standard dose of a recommended antihypertensive orally (**Table 29**) or an extra dose of patient's usual antihypertensive.
  ○ If the patient is npo, give **low** dose antihypertensive IV, titrating upward **slowly**. Options include β-blocker (eg, labetalol 20 mg), ACEI (eg, enalapril at 0.625 mg over 5 min), or diuretic (eg, furosemide 10 mg).

Table 29. Oral Antihypertensive Agents

Class, Medication	Geriatric Dosage Range, Total mg/d (times/d)	Formulations	Comments (Metabolism, Excretion)
Diuretics			↓ potassium, Na, magnesium levels; ↑ uric acid, calcium, cholesterol (mild), and glucose (mild) levels
Thiazides			
✓Chlorothiazide▲ *(Diuril)*	125–500 (1)	T: 250, 500	
✓Chlorthalidone▲ *(Hygroton)*	12.5–25 (1)	T: 15, 25, 50, 100	↑ AEs at >25 mg/d (L)
✓HCTZ▲	12.5–25 (1)	T: 25, 50, 100; S: 50 mg/mL; C: 12.5	↑ AEs at >25 mg/d (L)
✓Indapamide▲ *(Lozol)*	0.625–2.5 (1)	T: 1.25, 2.5	Less or no hypercholesterolemia (L)
✓Metolazone *(Mykrox)*	0.25–0.5 (1)	T rapid: 0.5	Monitor electrolytes carefully (L)
✓Metolazone▲ *(Zaroxolyn)*	2.5–5 (1)	T: 2.5, 5, 10	Monitor electrolytes carefully (L)
✓Polythiazide *(Renese)*	1–4 (1)	T: 1, 2, 4	
Loop diuretics			
♥Bumetanide▲ *(Bumex)*	0.5–4 (1–3)	T: 0.5, 1, 2	Short duration of action, no hypercalcemia (K)
♥Furosemide▲ *(Lasix)*	20–160 (1–2)	T: 20, 40, 80; S: 10, 40 mg/5 mL	Short duration of action, no hypercalcemia (K)
♥Torsemide▲ *(Demadex)*	2.5–50 (1–2)	T: 5, 10, 20, 100	Short duration of action, no hypercalcemia (K)
Potassium-sparing drugs			
Amiloride▲ *(Midamor)*	2.5–10 (1)	T: 5	(L, K)
Triamterene▲ *(Dyrenium)*	25–100 (1–2)	T: 50, 100	Avoid in patients with CKD Stage 4 or 5.[BC] (L, K)
Aldosterone receptor-blockers			
♥Eplerenone *(Inspra)*	25–100 (1)	T: 25, 50, 100	(L, K)
♥Spironolactone▲ *(Aldactone)*	12.5–50 (1–2)	T: 25, 50, 100	Gynecomastia; Avoid doses >25 mg/d and avoid if CrCl <30 mL/min.[BC] (L, K)

(cont.)

✓ = preferred for treating older adults; ♥ = useful in treating HFrEF

*See **Table 25** for target dosages in treating HF.

Note: Listing of AEs is not exhaustive, and AEs are for the drug class except when noted for individual drugs.

Table 29. Oral Antihypertensive Agents (cont.)

Class, Medication	Geriatric Dosage Range, Total mg/d (times/d)	Formulations	Comments (Metabolism, Excretion)
Adrenergic Inhibitors			
α_1-Blockers[BC]			Avoid as antihypertensive unless patient has BPH; avoid in patients with syncope; avoid in patients with HF.
Doxazosin▲ *(Cardura)*	1–16 (1)	T: 1, 2, 4, 8	(L)
Prazosin▲ *(Minipress)*	1–20 (2–3)	T: 1, 2, 5	(L)
Terazosin▲ *(Hytrin)*	1–20 (1–2)	T: 1, 2, 5, 10; C: 1, 2, 5, 10	(L, K)
Central α2-agonists and other centrally acting drugs[BC]			Sedation, dry mouth, bradycardia, withdrawal HTN
Clonidine▲ *(Catapres, CatapresTTS)*	0.1–1.2 (2–3) *or* 1 pch/wk	T: 0.1, 0.2, 0.3▲; pch: 0.1, 0.2, 0.3 mg/d	Avoid as first-line antihypertensive. Continue oral for 1–2 d when converting to patch (L, K)
Guanfacine▲ *(Tenex)*	0.5–2 (1)	T: 1, 2	Avoid. (K)
Methyldopa▲ *(Aldomet)*	250–2500 (2)	T: 125, 250, 500; S: 250 mg/5 mL	Avoid. (L, K)
Reserpine▲ *(Serpasil)*	0.05–0.25 (1)	T: 0.1, 0.25	Avoid. Depression, nasal congestion, activation of peptic ulcer (L, K)
β-Blockers*			Bronchospasm, bradycardia, acute HF, may mask insulin-induced hypoglycemia; less effective for reducing HTN-related endpoints in older vs younger patients; lipid solubility is a risk factor for delirium
✓Acebutolol▲ *(Sectral)*	200–800 (1)	C: 200, 400	β_1, low lipid solubility, intrinsic sympathomimetic activity (L, K)
✓Atenolol▲ *(Tenormin)*	12.5–100 (1)	T: 25, 50, 100	β_1, low lipid solubility (K)
✓Betaxolol▲ *(Kerlone)*	5–20 (1)	T: 10, 20	β_1, low lipid solubility (L, K)
✓♥Bisoprolol▲ *(Zebeta)*	2.5–10 (1)	T: 5, 10	β_1, low lipid solubility (L, K)
✓Metoprolol▲ *(Lopressor)*	25–400 (2)	T: 25, 50, 100	β_1, moderate lipid solubility (L)
✓♥Long-acting▲ *(Toprol XL)*	50–400 (1)	T: 25, 50, 100, 200	(L)
Nadolol▲ *(Corgard)*	20–160 (1)	T: 20, 40, 80, 120, 160	β_1, β_2, low lipid solubility (K)
✓♥Nebivolol *(Bystolic)*	2.5–40 (1)	T: 2.5, 5, 10	β_1, low lipid solubility (L, K)

(cont.)

✓ = preferred for treating older adults; ♥ = useful in treating HFrEF

*See **Table 25** for target dosages in treating HF.

Note: Listing of AEs is not exhaustive, and AEs are for the drug class except when noted for individual drugs.

Class, Medication	Geriatric Dosage Range, Total mg/d (times/d)	Formulations	Comments (Metabolism, Excretion)
Table 29. Oral Antihypertensive Agents (cont.)			
Penbutolol *(Levatol)*	10–40 (1)	T: 20	β_1, β_2, high lipid solubility, intrinsic sympathomimetic activity (L, K)
Pindolol▲ *(Visken)*	5–40 (2)	T: 5, 10	β_1, β_2, moderate lipid solubility, intrinsic sympathomimetic activity (K)
Propranolol▲ *(Inderal)*	20–160 (2)	T: 10, 20, 40, 60, 80, 90; S: 4, 8, 80 mg/mL	β_1, β_2, high lipid solubility (L)
Long-acting▲ *(Inderal LA)*	60–180 (1)	C: 60, 80, 120, 160	β_1, β_2, high lipid solubility (L)
Timolol▲ *(Blocadren)*	10–40 (2)	T: 5, 10, 20	β_1, β_2, low to moderate lipid solubility (L, K)
Combined α- and β-blockers*			Postural hypotension, bronchospasm
✓♥Carvedilol▲ *(Coreg)*	3.125–25 (2)	T: 3.125, 6.25, 12.5, 25	β_1, β_2, high lipid solubility (L)
✓♥Extended-release *(Coreg CR)*	10–80 (1)	C: 10, 20, 40, 80	Multiply regular daily dose of carvedilol by 1.6 to convert to CR dose; do not take within 2 h of alcohol ingestion
✓Labetalol▲ *(Normodyne, Trandate)*	100–600 (2)	T: 100, 200, 300	β_1, β_2, moderate lipid solubility (L, K)
Direct Vasodilators			Headaches, fluid retention, tachycardia
♥Hydralazine▲ *(Apresoline)*	25–100 (2–4)	T: 10, 25, 50, 100	Lupus syndrome; used in combination with isosorbide dinitrate for HF in blacks (L, K)
Minoxidil▲ *(Loniten)*	2.5–50 (1)	T: 2.5, 10	Hirsutism (K)
Calcium Antagonists			
Nondihydropyridines			Conduction defects, worsening of systolic dysfunction, gingival hyperplasia
✓Diltiazem SR▲ *(Cardizem CD, Cardizem SR, Dilacor XR, Tiazac)*	120–360, max 480	C: 120, 180, 240, 300, 360, 420; T: 120, 180, 240, 300, 360	Nausea, headache (L)

(cont.)

✓ = preferred for treating older adults; ♥ = useful in treating HFrEF

*See **Table 25** for target dosages in treating HF.

Note: Listing of AEs is not exhaustive, and AEs are for the drug class except when noted for individual drugs.

Table 29. Oral Antihypertensive Agents (cont.)

Class, Medication	Geriatric Dosage Range, Total mg/d (times/d)	Formulations	Comments (Metabolism, Excretion)
✓Verapamil SR▲ (Calan SR, Covera-HS, Isoptin SR, Verelan PM)	120–360 (1–2)	T: 120, 180, 240; C: 100, 120, 180, 200, 240, 300, 360	Constipation, bradycardia (L)
Dihydropyridines			Ankle edema, flushing, headache, gingival hypertrophy
✓Amlodipine▲ (Norvasc)	2.5–10 (1)	T: 2.5, 5, 10	(L)
✓Felodipine▲ (Plendil)	2.5–20 (1)	T: 2.5, 5, 10	(L)
✓Isradipine SR (DynaCirc CR)	2.5–10 (1)	T: 5, 10	(L)
✓Nicardipine▲ (Cardene)	60–120 (3)	C: 20, 30	(L)
✓Sustained release (Cardene SR)	60–120 (2)	T: 30, 45, 60	(L)
✓Nifedipine SR▲ (Adalat CC, Procardia XL)	30–60 (1)	T: 30, 60, 90	(L)
✓Nisoldipine▲ (Sular)	10–40 (1)	T: ER 10, 20, 30, 40	(L)
ACEIs*			Cough (common), angioedema (rare), hyperkalemia, rash, loss of taste, leukopenia
✓♥Benazepril▲ (Lotensin)	2.5–40 (1–2)	T: 5, 10, 20, 40	(L, K)
✓♥Captopril▲ (Capoten)	12.5–150 (2–3)	T: 12.5, 25, 50, 100	(L, K)
✓♥Enalapril▲ (Vasotec)	2.5–40 (1–2)	T: 2.5, 5, 10, 20	(L, K)
✓♥Fosinopril▲ (Monopril)	5–40 (1–2)	T: 10, 20, 40	(L, K)
✓♥Lisinopril▲ (Prinivil, Zestril)	2.5–40 (1)	T: 2.5, 5, 10, 20, 30, 40	(K)
✓Moexipril▲ (Univasc)	3.75–30 (1)	T: 7.5, 15	(L, K)
✓♥Perindopril▲ (Aceon)	4–8 (1–2)	T: 2, 4, 8	(L, K)
✓♥Quinapril▲ (Accupril)	5–40 (1)	T: 5, 10, 20, 40	(L, K)
✓♥Ramipril▲ (Altace)	1.25–20 (1)	T: 1.25, 2.5, 5, 10	(L, K)
✓♥Trandolapril▲ (Mavik)	1–4 (1)	T: 1, 2, 4	(L, K)

(cont.)

✓ = preferred for treating older adults; ♥ = useful in treating HFrEF

*See **Table 25** for target dosages in treating HF.

Note: Listing of AEs is not exhaustive, and AEs are for the drug class except when noted for individual drugs.

Table 29. Oral Antihypertensive Agents (cont.)

Class, Medication	Geriatric Dosage Range, Total mg/d (times/d)	Formulations	Comments (Metabolism, Excretion)
Angiotensin II Receptor Blockers (ARBs)*			Angioedema (very rare), hyperkalemia
✓Azilsartan *(Edarbi)*	20–80 (1)	T:40, 80	(L, K)
✓♥Candesartan *(Atacand)*	4–32 (1)	T: 4, 8, 16, 32	(K)
✓Eprosartan *(Teveten)*	400–800 (1–2)	T: 400, 600	(biliary, K)
✓Irbesartan *(Avapro)*	75–300 (1)	T: 75, 150, 300	(L)
✓♥Losartan▲ *(Cozaar)*	12.5–100 (1–2)	T: 25, 50, 100	(L, K)
✓Olmesartan *(Benicar)*	20–40 (1)	T: 5, 20, 40	Severe GI symptoms (rare) (L, K)
✓Telmisartan *(Micardis)*	20–80 (1)	T: 20, 40, 80	(L)
✓♥Valsartan *(Diovan)*	40–320 (1)	T: 40, 80, 160, 320; C: 80, 160	(L, K)
Renin Inhibitor			
Aliskiren *(Tekturna)*	150–300 (1)	T: 150, 300	Monitor electrolytes in patients with renal disease; contraindicated in patients with DM who are also taking an ACEI or ARB

✓ = preferred for treating older adults; ♥ = useful in treating HFrEF

*See **Table 25** for target dosages in treating HF.

Note: Listing of AEs is not exhaustive, and AEs are for the drug class except when noted for individual drugs.

Source: Data in part from The seventh report of the Joint National Committee on Prevention, Detection, Evaluation, and Treatment of High Blood Pressure: The JNC 7 report. *JAMA* 2003;289:2560–2572.

Table 30. Choosing Antihypertensive Therapy on the Basis of Coexisting Conditions

Condition	Appropriate for Use	Avoid or Contraindicated
Angina	β, CA	
Atrial tachycardia and fibrillation	β, NDCA	
Bronchospasm		β, αβ
CKD	AA, ACEI[a], ARB[a]	
DM	ACEI, ARB, β, T[b]	T[b]
Dyslipidemia		β, T[c]
Essential tremor	β	
Gout		L, T
HFrEF	AA, ACEI, ARB, β, αβ, L	CA
Hyperthyroidism	β	

(cont.)

Table 30. Choosing Antihypertensive Therapy on the Basis of Coexisting Conditions (cont.)		
Condition	Appropriate for Use	Avoid or Contraindicated
MI	β, AA, ACEI, ARB	CA
Osteoporosis	T	
Prostatism (BPH)	α	
Urge UI	CA	L, T

Notes: AA = aldosterone antagonist; α = α-blocker; β = β-blocker; αβ = combined α- and β-blocker; CA = calcium antagonist; NDCA = nondihydropyridine calcium antagonist; L = loop diuretic; T = thiazide diuretic.

[a] Use with great caution in renovascular disease.

[b] Low-dose diuretics probably beneficial in type 2 DM; high-dose diuretics relatively contraindicated in types 1 and 2.

[c] Low-dose diuretics have a minimal effect on lipids.

PULMONARY ARTERIAL HYPERTENSION (PAH)

Evaluation and Assessment
- PAH can be primary (unexplained) or secondary to underlying conditions.
- Almost all cases in older adults are secondary, most commonly associated with chronic pulmonary and/or cardiac disease, including COPD, interstitial lung disease, obstructive sleep apnea, pulmonary emboli, HF, and mitral valvular disease.
- Early symptoms are often nonspecific and include dyspnea on exertion, fatigue, and vague chest discomfort.
- Late symptoms include severe dyspnea on exertion, cyanosis, syncope, chest pain, HF, arrhythmias.
- Physical examination findings relate to manifestations of the associated conditions mentioned above.
- Diagnostic tests:
  - ECG may show right-axis deviation, right atrial and ventricular hypertrophy, T-wave changes
  - CXR may show large right ventricle, dilated pulmonary arteries
  - Echocardiography estimates pulmonary arterial pressure and evaluates possible valvular disease
  - Right heart catheterization is gold standard, with PAH defined as mean pulmonary arterial pressure >25 mmHg at rest or >30 mmHg during exercise.
- Additional tests (eg, pulmonary function tests, sleep study) may clarify severity of coexisting conditions.

Management
- Correct/optimize underlying conditions.
- Supplemental oxygen for chronic hypoxemia
- Diuretics for volume overload from HF
- Avoid calcium channel blockers unless they have been shown to be of benefit from a right heart catheterization vasodilator challenge study.
- Other agents have been studied mainly in primary PAH and are of uncertain effectiveness and safety in secondary PAH:
  - Warfarin (p 26)
  - Prostacyclins: epoprostenol *(Flolan)* by continuous IV infusion, treprostinil *(Remodulin)* by continuous SC infusion, treprostinil or iloprost *(Ventavis)* by inhalation

- Endothelial receptor antagonists: ambrisentan *(Letairis)* 5–10 mg/d; bosentan *(Tracleer)* 62.5 mg q12h × 4 wk, then 125 mg q12h; macitentan *(Opsumit)* 10 mg/d
- Guanylate cyclase stimulator: riociguat *(Adempas)*, 0.5 mg q8h, increase dose gradually to maximum of 2.5 mg q8h
- Sildenafil *(Revatio, Viagra)* po 20–25 mg q8h

ATRIAL FIBRILLATION (AF)

Evaluation and Assessment

Causes:
- Cardiac disease: cardiac surgery, cardiomyopathy, HF, hypertensive heart disease, ischemic disease, pericarditis, valvular disease
- Noncardiac disease: alcoholism, chronic pulmonary disease, infections, pulmonary emboli, thyrotoxicosis

Standard testing: ECG, CBC, electrolytes, Cr, BUN, TSH, echocardiogram

Management (2014 ACC/AHA Guidelines)
- Correct precipitating cause.
- Patients presenting with AF and hypotension, severe angina, or advanced HF should be strongly considered for acute direct-current cardioversion.
- For acute management of AF with rapid ventricular response in patients who do not receive or respond to cardioversion, ventricular rate should be acutely lowered with one or more of the following medications:
  - β-Blockers, eg, metoprolol▲ 2.5–5 mg IV bolus over 2 min; may repeat twice
  - Diltiazem▲, 0.25 mg/kg IV over 2 min
  - Verapamil▲, 0.075–0.15 mg/kg IV over 2 min
- For patients with minimal symptoms or in whom sinus rhythm cannot be easily achieved, rate control (target <110 bpm in asymptomatic patients with normal EF, <80 bpm for symptomatic patients or reduced EF) plus antithrombotic tx is the preferred tx strategy.
  - In patients without left ventricular dysfunction or without HFrEF, rate control can be achieved with oral metoprolol or other β-blocker, diltiazem, or verapamil.
  - In patients with left ventricular dysfunction or with HFrEF, first-line tx for rate control is a β-blocker after fluid status is stabilized; digoxin▲BC or amiodarone BC (**Table 31**) can be used as alternatives for rate control. Digoxin has been associated with increased mortality in observational studies of patients with AF.
  - In patients with preexcitation and AF, digoxin, nondihydropyridine calcium antagonists, and amiodarone are contraindicated.
  - For symptomatic patients in whom ventricular rate does not respond to pharmacologic tx, AV node ablation with pacemaker placement can effectively control rate. Anticoagulation should continue for at least 2 mo post-ablation; long-term post-ablation anticoagulation decisions should be based on stroke risk, bleeding risk, and patient preference (see below).
  - Antithrombotic tx (**Tables 32** and **33**) should be individualized to balance reduced stroke risk vs increased bleeding risk. Two risk scoring instruments are commonly used for assessing stroke risk while bleeding risk can be assessed using the HAS-BLED score (**Table 32**). The CHA_2DS_2-VASc classifies many more older adults as warranting anticoagulant tx than the $CHADS_2$.

○ If anticoagulation is contraindicated or not tolerated in patients with $CHADS_2$ or CHA_2DS_2–VASc scores ≥1, use ASA 81–325 mg/d. Addition of clopidogrel 75 mg/d to ASA lowers stroke risk but also increases risk of major hemorrhage. Both ASA and clopidogrel are less effective for stroke prevention in patients ≥75 yr of age.

Table 31. Selected Medications for Rhythm Control in AF

Medication	Maintenance Dosage	Formulations	Comments (Metabolism)
Amiodarone[▲BC] (Cordarone, Pacerone)	100–200 mg/d	T: 200, 400	Most effective antifibrillatory agent; avoid as first-line tx for AF unless patient has HF or LVH; numerous AEs, including pulmonary and hepatic toxic effects, neurologic and dermatologic AEs, hypothyroidism, hyperthyroidism, corneal deposits, warfarin[▲] interaction (L)
Propafenone[▲] Immediate Release (Rythmol)	150–300 mg q8h	T: 150, 225, 300	Contraindicated in patients with ischemic and structural heart disease; AEs include VT and HF (L)
Sustained release (Rythmol SR)	225–425 q12h	C: 225, 325, 425	
Sotalol[▲] (Betapace, Betapace AF, Sorine)	40–160 mg q12h	T: 80, 120, 160, 240	Prolongs QT interval; AEs include torsades de pointes, HF, exacerbation of COPD/bronchospasm (K)

[a] pretx (30 min before antiarrhythmic administration) with β-blocker, diltiazem, or verapamil is recommended.

Table 32. Risk Instruments to Guide Antithrombotic Treatment in AF

Instrument	What is Assessed	Score Calculation	Antithrombotic Tx by Score 0	1	≥2
$CHADS_2$	Stroke risk	1 point each for HF, HTN, age ≥75 yr, DM; 2 points for hx of stroke	ASA	ASA or Anticoagulant[a]	Anticoagulant[a]
CHA_2DS_2–VASc	Stroke risk	1 point each for HF, HTN, DM, vascular disease, age ≥65 yr, female sex; 2 points each for age ≥75 yr, hx of stroke	ASA or no tx	ASA or Anticoagulant[a] or no tx	Anticoagulant[a]
HAS–BLED	Bleeding risk of anticoagulant tx	1 point each for HTN, abnormal renal function, abnormal liver function, prior stroke, prior major bleeding, labile INRs, age ≥65 yr, alcohol use, drug use		If $CHADS_2$ or CHA_2DS_2–VASc score is 1, the risk of bleeding with anticoagulant tx may outweigh the risk of stroke if the HAS-BLED score is >2. If $CHADS_2$ or CHA_2DS_2–VASc score is ≥2, the risk of bleeding from anticoagulant tx may outweigh the risk of stroke if the HAS-BLED score exceeds the $CHADS_2$ or CHA_2DS_2–VASc score.	

[a] Apixaban, dabigatran, edoxaban, rivaroxaban, or warfarin; see **Tables 19** and **20** for dosing, **Table 33** for selection of anticoagulant.

Outcome	Effect of NOAC Compared to Warfarin			
	Apixaban	Dabigatran	Edoxaban	Rivaroxaban
All-cause mortality	Lower	Lower	Lower	Trend lower[a]
Ischemic stroke	Lower	Lower	Trend lower[a]	Trend lower[a]
Hemorrhagic stroke	Lower	Lower	Lower	Lower
Major bleeding	Lower	Trend higher	Lower	Same
GI bleeding	Same	Higher	Same	Higher

[a] Trend lower means that data are at borderline statistical significance.

Sources: Ruff CT et al. Lancet 2014;383(9921):955–962; Sharma MS et al. *Circulation* 2015;132:194–204.

- For patients with unpleasant symptoms or decreased exercise tolerance on rate control tx, rhythm control via direct-current or pharmacologic cardioversion is the preferred tx strategy.
  - For direct-current cardioversion, 3 methods may be used:
    - Early cardioversion (<48 h from onset): proceed with cardioversion; use adjunctive anticoagulation based on risk of thromboembolism (eg, CHA_2DS_2–VASc score).
    - Delayed cardioversion (≥48 h from onset or unknown duration) with transesophageal echocardiography (TEE): perform TEE to exclude intracardiac thrombus; if no thrombus, begin anticoagulation and cardiovert.
    - Delayed cardioversion (≥48 h from onset or unknown duration) without TEE: anticoagulate for at least 3 wk with INR ≥2 before cardioversion; continue anticoagulation after cardioversion.
  - For pharmacologic cardioversion and rhythm maintenance (recommended only if AF produces symptoms significantly impairing quality of life), rhythm control drugs may be tried (**Table 31**).
  - Stroke risk should be assessed (**Table 32**), and if indicated, antithrombotic tx should be continued indefinitely after cardioversion due to the high risk for recurrent AF.
  - In selected patients with symptomatic AF refractory to antiarrhythmic drugs, catheter or surgical AF ablation may be considered.

AORTIC STENOSIS (AS)

Evaluation and Assessment

- Presence of symptoms—angina, syncope, HF (frequently HFpEF)—indicates severe disease and a life expectancy without surgery of <2 yr.
- Echocardiography is essential to measure mean aortic valve gradient (AVG) and aortic valve area (AVA).
  - Moderate AS is indicated by an AVG of 20–39 mmHg and by an AVA of 1–1.5 cm^2.
  - Severe AS is indicated by an AVG ≥40 mmHg and by an AVA ≤1 cm^2.
- For asymptomatic cases, echocardiography should be repeated annually for moderate AS and q6–12 mo for severe AS.
- Don't perform echocardiography as routine follow-up for mild, asymptomatic native valve disease in adult patients with no change in signs or symptoms.[CW]
- ECG and CXR should be obtained initially to look for conduction defects, LVH, and pulmonary congestion.

Treatment

- Aortic valve replacement (AVR)
  - ○ AVR alleviates symptoms and improves ventricular functioning.
  - ○ In most cases, perform AVR promptly *after* symptoms have appeared.
  - ○ Surgical AVR vs transcatheter AVR (TAVR; a percutaneous procedure in the catheterization lab in which an artificial valve is implanted via a catheter):
    - ▪ In low-risk patients (young, no other heart problems or significant comorbidities), AVR surgery is superior to TAVR.
    - ▪ In high-risk surgical patients (older, cardiac and/or other significant comorbidities), TAVR is preferred, with lower 30-d mortality, major bleeding episodes, and new-onset AF, but higher stroke rate compared to surgical AVR.
- Avoid vasodilators if possible, unless used with invasive hemodynamic monitoring in patients with acute decompensated severe AS and NYHA class IV HF.

ABDOMINAL AORTIC ANEURYSM (AAA)

- Ultrasound should be performed if aortic diameter is felt to be >3 cm on physical examination.
- Ultrasonographic screening for AAA is recommended once for men between age 65 and 75 if former or current smoker.
- Management is based on diameter of AAA
  - ○ <4.5 cm: ultrasound q12mo
  - ○ 4.5–5.4 cm: ultrasound q3–6mo
  - ○ >5.4 cm: surgical referral
- Endovascular repair is associated with significantly less perioperative morbidity and mortality up to 3 yr.

PERIPHERAL ARTERIAL DISEASE (PAD)

Evaluation

Hx should include inquiry regarding the following:
- Lower extremity exertional fatigue or pain, or pain at rest
- Poorly healing or nonhealing wounds
- Cardiac risk factors

Physical examination should include the following:
- Palpation of pulses (brachial, radial, ulnar, femoral, popliteal, posterior tibial, and dorsalis pedis)
- Auscultation for abdominal, flank, and femoral bruits
- Inspection of feet
- Skin inspection for distal hair loss, trophic skin changes, and/or hypertrophic nails

Diagnosis established by ABI <0.9 or other test (**Table 34**).

Table 34. Management of PAD

Signs and Symptoms	Useful Tests	Treatment (see below)
Asymptomatic; diminished or absent peripheral pulses	ABI[a]	Risk factor reduction[b]
Atypical leg pain	ABI, EABI	Risk factor reduction, antiplatelet tx[b]
Claudication: exertional fatigue, discomfort, pain relieved by rest	ABI, EABI, Doppler ultrasound, pulse volume recording, segmental pressure measurement	Risk factor reduction, antiplatelet tx, claudication tx; consider endovascular or surgical revascularization if symptoms persist[b]
Rest pain, nonhealing wound (see also p 306), gangrene	ABI, Doppler ultrasound, angiography (MRI, CT, or contrast)	Risk factor reduction, antiplatelet tx, claudication tx, endovascular or surgical revascularization[b]

Note: EABI = exercise treadmill test with ABI measurement.

[a] Abnormal is <0.9; <0.4 is critical.

[b] Refrain from percutaneous or surgical revascularization of peripheral artery stenosis in patients without claudication or critical limb ischemia.**[CW]**

Treatment

Risk Factor Reduction

• Smoking cessation
• Lipid-lowering tx (Dyslipidemia Management, p 47)
• BP control (goal <140/90 mmHg)
• DM tx (Endocrine chapter, p 92)

Antiplatelet Therapy

• ASA▲ 75–325 mg/d
• Clopidogrel *(Plavix)* 75 mg/d (T: 75] if no response or intolerant of ASA

Claudication Therapy

• Walking program (goal: 50 min of intermittent walking 3–5 ×/wk)
• Cilostazol▲ *(Pletal)* 100 mg q12h, 1 h before or 2 h pc (contraindicated in patients with Class III or IV HFrEF); second-line alternative tx is pentoxifylline▲ *(Trental)* 400 mg q8h [T: 400]
• If ACEI not contraindicated, routine use is recommended to prevent adverse cardiovascular events in patients with claudication.

	Frequency		Increased Risk
Cause	(%)	Features	of Death
Vasovagal	21	Preceded by lightheadedness, nausea, diaphoresis; recovery gradual, frequently with fatigue	No
Cardiac	10	Little or no warning before blackout, rapid and complete recovery	Yes
Orthostatic	9	Lightheaded prodrome after standing, recovery gradual	No
Medication-induced	7	Lightheaded prodrome, recovery gradual	No
Seizure	5	No warning, may have neurologic deficits, slow recovery	Yes
Stroke, TIA	4	Little or no warning, neurologic deficits	Yes
Other causes	8	Preceded by cough, micturition, or specific situation	No
Unknown	37	Any of the above	Yes

Table 35. Classification of Syncope

Source: Adapted from Soteriades ES et al. *N Engl J Med* 2002;347:878–885.

Evaluation

- Focus hx on events before, during, and after loss of consciousness; hx of cardiac disease (significantly worsens prognosis of syncope of all causes); careful medication review.
- Focus on cardiovascular and neurologic systems in physical examination.
- ECG and orthostatic BP or pulse check for all patients.
- Characteristics associated with serious outcomes and likely to require urgent/emergent further testing and monitoring include:
  - age >90 yr
  - male sex
  - abnormal ECG
  - hx of arrhythmia (VT, symptomatic supraventricular tachycardia, third-degree or Mobitz II AV block, sinus pause >3 sec, symptomatic bradycardia)
  - hx of HF
  - dyspnea
  - abnormal troponin I
  - SBP <90 mmHg or >160 mmHg
- Additional testing as suggested by initial evaluation:
  - Ambulatory ECG monitoring for further evaluation of arrhythmia
  - Stress testing to investigate ischemic heart disease
  - Echocardiography to investigate structural heart disease
  - Electrophysiologic studies in patients with prior MI or structural heart disease
  - Tilt-table testing for suspected vasovagal cause
  - Head imaging, EEG for suspected neurologic cause
  - Don't perform imaging of the carotid arteries for simple syncope without other neurologic symptoms.[CW]
  - In the evaluation of simple syncope and a normal neurological examination, don't obtain brain imaging studies (CT or MRI).[CW]
  - If suspected orthostatic cause, evaluation for Parkinson disease, autonomic neuropathy, DM, hypovolemia.

Management

- Patients with cardiac syncope require immediate hospitalization on telemetry; exclude MI and PE.
- Strongly consider hospital admission for patients with syncope due to neurologic or unknown causes, particularly if concurrent heart disease.
- Patients with syncope due to vasovagal, orthostatic, medication-induced, or other causes can usually be managed as outpatients, particularly if there is no hx of heart disease.
- Tx is correction of underlying cause.

ORTHOSTATIC (POSTURAL) HYPOTENSION

See also **Table 55**.

Evaluation and Assessment

- Associated with following symptoms usually after standing: lightheadedness, dizziness, syncope, blurred vision, diaphoresis, head or neck pain, decreased hearing
- Diagnosis: ≥20 mmHg drop in SBP or ≥10 mmHg in DBP within 3 min of rising from lying to standing
- Causes
  - Medications, including antihypertensives, phenothiazines, TCAs, MAOIs, acetylcholinesterase inhibitors, SGLT2 inhibitors, anti-Parkinsonian drugs, PDE5 inhibitors (for erectile dysfunction)
  - Autonomic dysregulation (suggested by lack of compensatory rise in HR with postural hypotension): age-related decreased baroreceptor sensitivity, Parkinson disease and related disorders, peripheral neuropathy, prolonged bed rest
  - Hypovolemia
  - Anemia

Management

- Correct underlying disorder, particularly by discontinuing medications that could exacerbate hypotension
- Alter movement behavior: educate patients to rise slowly, flex calf and forearm muscles when standing, stand with one foot in front of other, avoid straining, and elevate head of bed
- Dietary changes: avoid alcohol, maintain adequate fluid intake, increase salt and caffeine intake
- Above-the-knee compression stockings (at least medium compression strength, eg, Jobst)
- Pharmacologic interventions:
  - First-line: fludrocortisone[▲]: 0.1–0.2 mg q8–24h [T: 0.1]; use with caution in patients with HF, cardiac disease, HTN, renal disease, esophagitis, peptic ulcer disease, or ulcerative colitis; watch for fluid overload and hypokalemia.
  - Midodrine[▲] *(ProAmatine):* 2.5–10 mg q8–24h [T: 2.5, 5]; use with caution in patients with HTN, DM, urinary retention, renal disease, hepatic disease, glaucoma, BPH.
  - Pyridostigmine[▲] *(Mestinon):* 60 mg q24h [T: 60]; can be used in combination with midodrine 2.5–5 mg/d.
  - Caffeine: 1 cup of caffeinated coffee q8–12h; alternatively, caffeine tabs 100–200 mg q8–12h; useful for postprandial hypotension when taken with meals. Avoid in patients with insomnia.[BC]
  - Droxidopa *(Northera):* 100–600 mg q8h [T: 100, 200, 300]; use with caution in patients with HTN, cardiac disease, HF, mild cognitive impairment, dementia, Parkinson disease on carbidopa tx.

∘ Erythropoietin (**Table 67**) can be useful for hypotension secondary to anemia if Hb <10 mg/dL.

IMPLANTABLE CARDIAC DEFIBRILLATOR (ICD) PLACEMENT

Indications
- Carefully consider age, life expectancy, and comorbid status for deciding ICD placement. Data are limited in patients >65 yr old and suggest no all-cause mortality benefit in patients >75 yr old.
- Established indications:
  ∘ Cardiac arrest due to VF or VT
  ∘ Spontaneous sustained VT with structural heart disease
  ∘ Spontaneous sustained VT without structural heart disease not alleviated by other tx
  ∘ Unexplained syncope with hemodynamically significant VF or VT inducible by electrophysiologic study when drug tx is ineffective, not tolerated, or not preferred
  ∘ Nonsustained VT, CAD, and inducible VF by electrophysiologic study that is not suppressed by Class I antiarrhythmic
  ∘ LVEF ≤30%, NYHA Class II or III HF, and CAD >40 d after MI
  ∘ ICD + biventricular pacing for advanced HF (NYHA Class III or IV), LVEF ≤35%, and QRS interval ≥120 millisec or mild HF (NYHA Class I or II), LVEF <30%, and QRS interval ≥130 millisec
- Less established: Nonischemic cardiomyopathy with LVEF <35% and either premature ventricular complexes or nonsustained VT

Contraindications
- Terminal illness with life expectancy <6 mo
- Unexplained syncope without inducible VT or VF and without structural heart disease
- VT or VF due to transient or easily reversible disorder
- End-stage HF (ACC/AHA Stage D) not awaiting cardiac transplant

Complications
- Surgical: infection (1–2%), hematoma, pneumothorax
- Device-related: lead dislodgement or malfunction, connection problems, inadequate defibrillation threshold
- Tx-related: frequent shocks (appropriate or inappropriate), acceleration of VT, anxiety and other psychological stress
- End-of-life planning: discuss and document the circumstances in which the patient would desire the ICD to be turned off. ICDs can be turned off by the cardiologist or the device manufacturer's representative. Don't leave an ICD activated when it is inconsistent with the patient/family goals of care.[CW]

DIAGNOSIS

Diagnostic Criteria—Adapted from *DSM-5*

- Core symptom: disturbed consciousness (ie, decreased attention, environmental awareness)
- Cognitive change (eg, memory deficit, disorientation, language disturbance) or perceptual disturbance (eg, visual illusions, hallucinations)
- Three subtypes: hyperactive, hypoactive, and apparently normal alertness but cannot attend
- Rapid onset (hours to days) and fluctuating daily course
- Evidence of a causal physical condition

Risk Factors

- Dementia greatly increases risk of delirium.
- Advanced age, comorbid physical problems (especially sleep deprivation, immobility, dehydration, pain, sensory impairment).
- Hospitalization and/or surgery (Postoperative Delirium, p 268)

Prediction of Delirium Risk in Hospitalized Older Patients

- Physical restraints; >3 new medications; Foley catheter; malnutrition; any iatrogenic event
- 1 point each for any, likelihood of delirium based on total: 0 points: 4%; 1–2 points: 20%; ≥3 points: 35%

Evaluation

- Assume reversibility unless proven otherwise.
- Thoroughly review prescription and OTC medications, and alcohol usage.
- Exclude infection and other medical causes.
- 4AT (www.the4AT.com) is a screening instrument for rapid initial assessment of delirium and cognitive impairment, but is not diagnostic.
- Confusion Assessment Method (CAM): Both acute onset and fluctuating course and inattention and either disorganized thinking or altered level of consciousness. CAM–S allows for scoring of delirium severity. (Inouye SK. *Ann Intern Med* 2014;160[8]:526–533). For nonverbal patients, use CAM-ICU to assess attention and level of consciousness (Ely EW. *JAMA* 2001;286[21]:2703–2710).
- Laboratory studies may include CBC, electrolytes, LFTs, ammonia, thyroid function tests, renal function tests, serum albumin, B_{12}, serum calcium, serum glucose, UA, oxygen saturation, ABG levels, CXR, and ECG.
- Brain imaging and EEG typically not helpful unless there is evidence of cerebral trauma, possible stroke, focal neurologic signs, or seizure activity.

CAUSES

(Italicized type indicates the most common causes in older adults.)

Medications (Table 36 and Table 37)

- *Anticholinergics* (Avoid[BC])
- Anti-inflammatory agents, including prednisone
- Benzodiazepines or alcohol—acute toxicity or withdrawal

- Cardiovascular (eg, digoxin, antihypertensives, diuretics)
- Lithium
- Opioid analgesics, especially meperidine (Avoid[BC])

Table 36. Potentially Differentiating Features of Medication-induced Delirium

Medication type	Early	Late
Anticholinergic	Visual impairment, dry mouth, constipation, urinary retention	↑ HR, mydriasis, ↓ bowel sounds
Serotonin syndrome	Tremor, diarrhea	Hyperreflexia, clonus, myoclonic jerks, ↑ bowel sounds, diaphoresis
Neuroleptic malignant syndrome	↑ EPS	Marked rigidity, bradyreflexia, hyperthermia

* The use of urinary catecholamines and/or metabolics as diagnostic aids require further evaluation.

Table 37. Some Drugs with Anticholinergic Properties[BC]

Antidepressants

Amitriptyline	Doxepin	Protriptyline
Amoxapine	Imipramine	Trimipramine
Clomipramine	Nortriptyline	
Desipramine	Paroxetine	

Antihistamines

Brompheniramine	Clemastine	Diphenhydramine
Carbinoxamine	Cyproheptadine	Hydroxyzine
Chlorpheniramine	Dimenhydrinate	Loratadine

Antimuscarinics (urinary incontinence)

Darifenacin	Oxybutynin	Trospium
Fesoterodine	Solifenacin	
Flavoxate	Tolterodine	

Antiparkinson agents

Benztropine	Trihexyphenidyl

Antipsychotics

Chlorpromazine	Olanzapine	Promethazine
Clozapine	Perphenazine	Thioridazine
Fluphenazine	Pimozide	Thiothixene
Loxapine	Prochlorperazine	Trifluoperazine

Antispasmodics

Atropine products	Homatropine	Scopolamine
Belladonna alkaloids	Hyoscyamine products	
Dicyclomine	Propantheline	

Skeletal Muscle Relaxants

Carisoprodol	Orphenadrine
Cyclobenzaprine	Tizanidine

* AGS updated Beers Criteria for potentially inappropriate medication use in older adults.[BC] American Geriatrics Society 2012 Beers Criteria Update Expert Panel. *J Am Geriatr Soc.* 2012;60(4):616–631.

Infections

Respiratory, skin, urinary tract, others

Metabolic Disorders

Acute blood loss, *dehydration, electrolyte imbalance*, end-organ failure (hepatic, renal), hyperglycemia, *hypoglycemia, hypoxia*

Cardiovascular

Arrhythmia, *HF, MI*, shock

Neurologic

CNS infections, head trauma, seizures, stroke, subdural hematoma, TIAs, tumors

Miscellaneous

Fecal impaction, *postoperative state*, sleep deprivation, urinary retention

PREVENTIVE MEASURES

Table 38. Preventive Measures for Delirium[a]	
Target for Prevention	**Intervention**
Cognitive impairment	Orientation protocol: board with names, daily schedule, and reorienting communication Therapeutic activities: stimulating activities 3 times/d
Sleep deprivation	Nonpharmacologic: warm milk/herbal tea, music, massage Noise reduction: schedule adjustments and unit-wide noise reduction 0.5 mg melatonin or 8 mg ramelteon may prevent delirium in acute care
Immobility	Early mobilization: ambulation or range of motion 3 times/d, minimal immobilizing equipment
Visual impairment	Visual aids and adaptive equipment
Hearing impairment	Amplification, cerumen disimpaction, special communication techniques
Dehydration	Early recognition and volume repletion
Infection, HF, hypoxia, pain	Identify and treat medical conditions

[a] May also be valuable for management

MANAGEMENT

Nonpharmacologic

- Ensure safety.
- Use families or sitters as first line.
- Physical restraints can lead to serious injury or death and may worsen agitation and delirium.[CW] Use soft physical restraints or mitts only as last resort to maintain patient safety (eg, to prevent patient from pulling out tubes or catheters).

Pharmacologic

Avoid antipsychotics for behavioral problems unless nonpharmacological options (eg, behavioral interventions) have failed or are not possible, and the older adult is threatening substantial harm to self or others.[BC]

For acute agitation or aggression that impairs care or safety (other than delirium due to alcohol or benzodiazepine withdrawal), choose from one of the following:

- Haloperidol (the most often recommended and studied agent; controls symptoms and may reduce duration and severity of delirium)

- Because of risk of QT$_c$ prolongation, the IV route is not recommended. *Caution:* If the patient is taking other medications that prolong QT$_c$ (**Table 12**), D/C all if possible. Even oral or IM dosing may prolong QT$_c$. Obtain an ECG before the first dose (if possible) or as soon as the patient is calm enough to tolerate the procedure. If QT$_c$ exceeds 500 ms, ***do not*** administer any antipsychotic; all may prolong QT$_c$. If QT$_c$ >460 ms, correct any deficiency of Mg^{++} and K$^+$ and recheck.
- Haloperidol *(Haldol)* 0.5–1 mg po [T: 0.5, 1, 2, 5, 10, 20; S: 2 mg/mL]; evaluate effect in 1–2 h.
- If patient is not able to take medications po, haloperidol 0.5–1 mg IM [5 mg/mL] (twice as potent as po, peak effect 20–40 min). Reevaluate q30–60min for continued troublesome agitation.
- Double the dosage if initial dose is ineffective. Administer additional doses (IM dose q30min or oral dose q60min) until agitation is controlled. Rarely, additional doubling of the dosage is necessary. Most older patients respond to 1–2 mg total dose.
- Calculate the total dose administered to achieve control of symptoms, and give half the equivalent oral dose the next day, divided for q12h administration. Hold a dose if sedation occurs.
- Maintain effective dose for 2–3 d.
- Slowly taper and D/C haloperidol over 3–5 d while monitoring for recurrence of symptoms. If necessary, continue the minimal dose necessary to control symptoms.
- EPS will develop with prolonged use. If use exceeds 1 wk, switch to a second-generation antipsychotic agent.
- Quetiapine is the drug of choice for patients with LBD, Parkinson disease, AIDS-related dementia, or EPS. Initial dosage 12.5–25 mg po daily or q12h, increase q2d prn to a max of 100 mg/d (50 mg/d in frail older adults). Once symptoms are controlled, administer half the dose needed to control symptoms for 2–3 d; then taper as described above.

Delirium due to alcohol or benzodiazepine withdrawal, use a benzodiazepine, eg, lorazepam in dosages of 0.5–2 mg IV q30–q60min or po q1–2h and titrated to effect. Validated scales are used to guide dosing of benzodiazepines in alcohol withdrawal (www.chce.research.va.gov/PAWS/content/1.htm). Because these agents themselves may cause delirium, gradual withdrawal and discontinuation are desirable. If delirium is secondary to alcohol, also use thiamine at 100 mg/d (po, IM, or IV).

PROGNOSIS

- Weeks or months to resolve
- Waxing and waning mental status continues as patient improves, but there will be a general trend toward improvement.
- Persistent symptoms at discharge: 44.7%; at 1 mo: 32.8%; at 3 mo: 25.6%; at 6 mo: 21%.
- Accelerated cognitive decline: Patients with AD may experience a faster rate of cognitive decline after an episode of delirium.
- Prolonged delirium is associated with higher risk of death (2.5 times more likely within 1 yr compared to those whose delirium has resolved).

DEMENTIA SYNDROME (*DSM–5:* MAJOR NEUROCOGNITIVE DISORDER)
Definition

Chronic acquired decline in one or more cognitive domains (learning and memory, complex attention, language, visual-spatial, executive) sufficient to affect daily life.

Estimated Frequencies of Causes of Dementia

- AD: 60–70%
- Other progressive disorders: 15–30% (eg, vascular, Lewy body [LBD], frontotemporal [FTD])
- Completely reversible dementia (eg, drug toxicity, metabolic changes, thyroid disease, subdural hematoma, normal-pressure hydrocephalus): 2–5%

Screening

- Dementia is largely unrecognized and underdiagnosed. Clinicians should have a low threshold for triggering an investigation for possible cognitive impairment.
- The value of dementia screening in older adults is controversial. Some professional organizations strongly endorse screening while others do not recommend it, citing lack of evidence of benefit. USPSTF 2014 concluded that evidence was insufficient to recommend either for or against dementia screening.
- Screening for cognitive impairment is a required element of the initial and subsequent Medicare Annual Wellness Visit.
- Suitable screening tests in primary care include the Mini-Cog (p 335) the Memory Impairment Screen (MIS), General Practitioner Assessment of Cognition (GPCOG), and the Informant Questionnaire on Cognitive Decline in the Elderly (IQCODE).

EVALUATION

Although completely reversible dementia (eg, drug toxicity) is rare, identifying and treating secondary physical conditions may improve function.

- Hx: Obtain from family or other caregiver
- Physical and neurologic examination
- Assess functional status (p 336–337)
- Assess for depression (PHQ-9 [p 338], GDS)
- Evaluate mental status for attention, immediate and delayed recall, remote memory, and executive function. Useful assessment instruments include MoCA (www.mocatest.org) and SLUMS (medschool.slu.edu/agingsuccessfully/pdfsurveys/slumsexam_05.pdf) to evaluate attention, immediate and delayed recall, remote memory, and executive function. Use MMSE, CDR, or FAST for staging.

Clinical Features Distinguishing AD and Other Types of Dementia

- AD: Memory, language, visual-spatial disturbances, indifference, delusions, agitation
- FTD: Personality change, executive dysfunction, hyperorality, relative preservation of visual-spatial skills
- LBD: visual hallucinations, delusions, EPS, fluctuating mental status, sensitivity to antipsychotic medications
- Vascular dementia: abrupt onset, stepwise deterioration, prominent aphasia, motor signs

Laboratory Testing

CBC, TSH, homocysteine, MMA, serum calcium, liver and kidney function tests, electrolytes; HIV, and serologic test for syphilis (selectively); genetic testing and commercial "Alzheimer blood tests" are not currently recommended for clinical use.

Neuroimaging

The likelihood of detecting structural lesions is increased with:
- Onset age <60 yr
- Focal (unexplained) neurologic signs or symptoms
- Abrupt onset or rapid decline (weeks to months)
- Predisposing conditions (eg, metastatic cancer or anticoagulants)

Neuroimaging may detect the 5% of cases with clinically significant structural lesions that would otherwise be missed.

FDG-PET scans approved by Medicare for atypical presentation or course of AD in which FTD is suspected. See www.petscaninfo.com/portals/pat/medicare_guidelines_alzheimers.

Florbetapir F18 *(Amyvid)* has been approved by the FDA for the detection of amyloid plaques. A positive scan does not establish diagnosis. Medicare will not cover.

PROGRESSION OF AD

- 2011 National Institute on Aging/Alzheimer's Association research criteria identify preclinical stages using PET and CSF biomarkers of Aβ or neuronal injury.
- Mild cognitive impairment (MCI) requires "modest" cognitive decline that does not interfere with "capacity for independence in everyday activities" (eg, paying bills or taking medications correctly).
- 6–15% annual conversion of MCI to dementia syndrome; some cases may not progress.
- Treating vascular risk factors (HTN, DM, high cholesterol) may reduce risk of progression to AD.
- Cognitive decline meets the "major" criteria (ie, dementia syndrome) when "significant" impairment is evident or reported and when it does interfere with a patient's independence to the point that assistance is required.

Mild Cognitive Impairment (preclinical)   *MMSE 26–30; CDR 0.5; FAST 3; MoCA <26 (more sensitive)

- Report by patient or caregiver of memory loss
- Objective signs of memory impairment
- No functional impairment
- Mild construction, language, or executive dysfunction

Early, Mild Impairment (yr 1–3 from onset of symptoms)   *MMSE 21–25; CDR 1; FAST 4

Functional impairments	• Managing finances
	• Driving
	• Managing medications
Cognitive changes	• Decreased insight
	• Short term memory deficits
	• Poor judgment

Behavioral issues	• Social withdrawal • Mood changes: apathy/depression
Complications	• Poor financial decisions • AEs due to medication errors
Middle, Moderate Impairment (yr 2–8)	***MMSE 11–20; CDR 2; FAST 5–6**
Functional impairments	• IADL • Difficulty with some ADLs • Gait and balance
Cognitive changes	• Disoriented to date and place • Worse memory • Getting lost in familiar areas • Repeating questions
Behavioral issues	• Delusions/agitation/aggression • Apathy/depression • Restlessness/anxiety/wandering
Complications	• Inability to remain at home/ALF • Falls
Late, Severe Impairment (yr 6–12)	***MMSE 0–10; CDR 3; FAST 7**
Functional impairments	• ADLs including continence • Mobility • Swallowing
Cognitive changes	• Little or unintelligible verbal output • Loss of remote memory • Inability to recognize family/friends
Behavioral issues	• Motor or verbal agitation/aggression • Apathy/depression • Sundowning
Complications	• Pressure sores • Contractures • Aspiration/pneumonia

*MMSE = Mini-Mental State Examination; CDR = Clinical Dementia Rating Scale; FAST = Reisberg Functional Assessment Staging Scale (p 343); MoCA = Montreal Cognitive Assessment.

Prognosis

• Among nursing-home residents with advanced dementia, 71% die within 6 mo of admission.
• Distressing conditions common in advanced dementia include pressure ulcers, constipation, pain, and shortness of breath.

NONCOGNITIVE SYMPTOMS

Psychotic Symptoms (eg, delusions, hallucinations)

• Seen in about 20% of AD patients
• Delusions may be paranoid (eg, people stealing things, spouse unfaithful)

- Hallucinations (~11% of patients) are more commonly visual

Depressive Symptoms
- Seen in up to 40% of AD patients; may precede onset of AD
- May cause acceleration of decline if untreated
- Suspect if patient stops eating or withdraws

Apathy
- High prevalence and persistence throughout course of AD
- Causes more impairment in ADL than expected for cognitive status
- High overlap with depressive symptoms but lacks depressive mood, guilt, and hopelessness

Agitation or Aggression
- Seen in up to 80% of patients with AD
- A leading cause of nursing-home admission
- Consider superimposed delirium
- Consider pain as a cause in moderate or severe dementia and possible trial of analgesics (Pain chapter, p 234)

RISK AND PROTECTIVE FACTORS FOR DEMENTIA

Definite Risks	Possible Risks	Possible Protections
Age	Delirium	Mediterranean diet
APOE-E4 (whites)	Head trauma	Physical activity
Atrial fibrillation	Heavy smoking	
Depression	Hypercholesterolemia	
Down syndrome	HTN	
Family hx	Lower educational level	
	Other genes	
	Postmenopausal HT	

TREATMENT

Primary goals of tx are to improve quality of life and maximize functional performance by enhancing cognition, mood, and behavior.

General Treatment Principles
- Identify and treat comorbid physical illnesses (eg, HTN, DM)
- Promote brain health by exercise, balanced diet, stress reduction
- Supervised exercise, whether individual or group, slows disability and prevent falls
- A 2-yr randomized controlled trial (FINGER) of diet, exercise, cognitive training, and vasular risk monitoring was shown to prevent cognitive decline in at-risk older people.
- Vitamin E at 2000 IU/d found to delay functional decline in mild to moderate AD
- Avoid anticholinergic medications (eg, benztropine, diphenhydramine, hydroxyzine, oxybutynin, TCAs, clozapine, thioridazine)
- Set realistic goals
- Limit prn psychotropic medication use
- Maximize and maintain functioning

- Identify, quantify, and examine context of any problematic behaviors (is it harmful to patient or others) and environmental triggers (eg, overstimulation, unfamiliar surroundings, frustrating interactions); exclude underlying physical discomfort (eg, illnesses or medication); consider nonpharmacologic strategies
- Consider referral to hospice (FAST=7; diminished speech, movement, and consciousness)

Caregiver Issues
- Establish and maintain alliance with patient
- Discuss with patient and family concerns (eg, driving)
- Intervene to decrease hazards of wandering
- Advise family about sources of care and support, financial and legal issues
- Information about clinical studies can be found at www.alz.org/research.

Nonpharmacologic Approaches for Problem Behaviors

To improve function:
- Behavior modification, scheduled toileting, and prompted toileting (p 152) for UI
- Graded assistance (as little help as possible to perform ADLs), practice, and positive reinforcement to increase independence

For problem behaviors:
- Music during meals, bathing
- Walking or light exercise
- Simulate family presence with video or audio tapes
- Pet tx
- Speak at patient's comprehension level
- Bright light, "white" noise (ie, low-level, background noise)

Approaches for assessment and management of dementia can be found on the UCLA Alzheimers and Dementia Care Program Web site (dementia.ucla.health.org/body.cfm?id=68)

The evidence base for specific nonpharmacological approaches using a person-centered approach to care is growing. A nonpharmacological toolkit for reducing antipsychotic use in older adults by promoting positive behavioral health, developed by investigators at Pennsylvania State University can be found at: nursinghometoolkit.com. Nonpharmacological strategies for hospitalized older adults and their caregivers can also be accessed at hospitalelderlifeprogram.org.[BC]

Pharmacologic Treatment of Cognitive Dysfunction
- Patients with a diagnosis of mild or moderate AD should receive a trial of a cholinesterase inhibitor; donepezil also approved for severe AD (**Table 39**).
  - Cholinesterase inhibitors should be prescribed with periodic assessment for cognitive benefits and adverse gastrointestinal effects.[CW] In particular, patients should be monitored for weight loss.
  - Only 10–25% of patients taking cholinesterase inhibitors show modest global improvement, but many more have less rapid cognitive decline.
  - Initial studies show benefits of cholinesterase inhibitors for patients with dementia associated with LBD, Parkinson disease, and vascular dementia. May worsen behavioral variant FTD.
  - Cholinesterase inhibitors may attenuate noncognitive symptoms and delay nursing-home placement.

- AEs increase with higher dosing. Possible AEs include nausea, vomiting, diarrhea, dyspepsia, anorexia, weight loss, leg cramps, bradycardia, syncope, insomnia, and agitation.
- Patients with moderate to severe AD may benefit from trial of memantine *(Namenda)*
  - Side effects minimal (confusion, dizziness, constipation, headache)
  - Recent controlled trial did not demonstrate significant advantage to the combination of memantine and donepezil compared with donepezil alone in patients with severe dementia.
  - To evaluate response:
    - Elicit caregiver observations of patient's behavior (alertness, initiative) and follow functional status (ADLs [p 336] and IADLs [p 337]).
    - Follow cognitive status (eg, improved or stabilized) by caregiver's report or serial ratings of cognition (eg, Mini-Cog [p 335]; MMSE).
- D/C cognitive enhancers when FAST = 7 (p 343).

Table 39. Cognitive Enhancers		
Medication	**Formulations**	**Dosing (Metabolism)**
Cholinesterase Inhibitors		
Donepezil *(Aricept)*[a,b]	T: 5▲, 10▲, 23; ODT: 5, 10; S: 5 mg/mL	Start at 5 mg/d, increase to 10 mg/d after 1 mo (CYP2D6, -3A4); must be on 10 mg/d ≥3 mo to consider increasing to 23 mg/d in moderate to severe AD. Avoid if hx of syncope.[BC] (L)
Galantamine▲ *(Razadyne)*[a,c]	T: 4, 8, 12; S: 4 mg/mL	Start at 4 mg q12h, increase to 8 mg q12h after 4 wk; recommended dosage 8 or 12 mg q12h (CYP2D6, -3A4). Avoid if hx of syncope.[BC] (L)
(Razadyne ER)	C: 8, 16, 24	Start at 1 capsule daily, preferably with food; titrate as above. Rare complication: Stevens-Johnson syndrome
Rivastigmine▲ *(Exelon)*[a]	C: 1.5, 3, 4.5, 6; S: 2 mg/mL; pch: 4.6, 9.5, 13.3	Start at 1.5 mg q12h and gradually titrate up to minimally effective dosage of 3 mg q12h; continue up to 6 mg q12h as tolerated; for pch, start at 4.6 mg/d, may be increased after ≥4 wk to 9.5 mg/d (recommended effective dosage; value of increase to 13.3 mg/d is not established): retitrate if drug is stopped. Avoid if hx of syncope.[BC] (K)
NMDA antagonist		
Memantine *(Namenda)*[b,d]	T: 5, 10 S: 2 mg/mL	Start at 5 mg/d, increase by 5 mg at weekly intervals to max of 10 mg q12h; if CrCl <30 mL/min, max of 5 mg q12h (K)
(Namenda XR)	C: 7, 14, 21, 28	Start at 7 mg/d, increase by 7 mg at weekly intervals to max of 28 mg; if severe renal impairment, max of 14 mg daily (L)
(Namzaric)	C: 28/10, 14/10	Fixed-dose combination of donepezil and memantine for patients previously stabilized on combination tx of both individual drugs

[a] Cholinesterase inhibitors. Continue if improvement or stabilization occurs; stopping medications can lead to rapid decline.

[b] Approved by FDA for moderate to severe AD.

[c] Increased mortality found in controlled studies of mild cognitive impairment.

[d] Patients can switch directly from *Namenda* IR 20 mg (10 mg tabs twice daily) to *Namenda* XR capsules 28 mg once daily on the day after the last dose of a 10-mg IR tab. Patients with severe renal impairment on *Namenda* IR 5 mg twice-daily tablets can be switched to *Namenda* XR 14 mg once-daily capsule.

- Ginkgo biloba is not generally recommended (p 23).

- *Axona* (medium-chain TG) has insufficient evidence to support its value in preventing or treating AD, and long-term effects are uncertain.

Treatment of Agitation

- Consider nonpharmacologic approaches first before pharmacologic tx (**Table 40**).
- Steps to reduce nonverbalized pain (p 235).
- Cognitive enhancers may slow deterioration, and agitation may worsen if discontinued.
- Low doses of antipsychotic medications have limited role but may be necessary.[CW] Note that this use is off-label and increases risk of death compared with placebo in patients with AD. CATIE-AD trial (*NEJM* 2006;355:1525–1538) showed modest tx benefit compared with placebo for olanzapine and risperidone that was mitigated by greater EPS, sedation, and confusion. In this trial, quetiapine did not appear to be efficacious compared with placebo but caused greater sedation (**Table 107** and **Table 108**).
- CATIE-AD reported second-generation antipsychotics cause weight gain, particularly in women treated with olanzapine or quetiapine; olanzapine tx was also associated with decreased HDL cholesterol.
- Behavioral variant FTD: consider memantine or SSRI.

Treatment of Apathy

- Assess and treat underlying depression.
- Cholinesterase inhibitors help.
- Methylphenidate (5–20 mg/d), very limited data, may cause agitation and psychosis.

Table 40. Pharmacologic Treatment of Agitation			
Symptom	Medication	Dosage	Formulations
Agitation in context of psychosis	Aripiprazole[a,b,BC] *(Abilify)*	2.5–12.5 mg/d	T: 5, 10, 15, 20, 30
	Olanzapine[a,b,BC] *(Zyprexa)* *(Zydis)*	2.5–10 mg/d	T: 2.5, 5, 7.5, 10, 15, 20; ODT: 5, 10, 15, 20
	Quetiapine[a,b,BC] *(Seroquel)*	12.5–100 mg/d	T: 25, 100, 200, 300
	Risperidone[▲a,b] *(Risperdal)*	0.25–3 mg/d	T: 0.25, 0.5, 1, 2, 3, 4; S: 1 mg/mL
Agitation in context of depression	SSRI, eg, citalopram[▲] *(Celexa)*	10–20 mg/d	T: 20, 40; S: 2 mg/mL
Anxiety, mild to moderate irritability	Buspirone[▲] *(BuSpar)* Trazodone[▲] *(Desyrel)*	15–60 mg/d[c] 50–100 mg/d[d]	T: 5, 7.5, 10, 15, 30 T: 50, 100, 150, 300
Agitation or aggression unresponsive to first-line tx	Carbamazepine[▲] *(Tegretol)*	300–600 mg/d[e]	T: 200; ChT: 100; S: sus 100/5 mL
	Divalproex sodium[▲] *(Depakote, Epival)*	500–1500 mg/d[f]	T: 125, 250, 500; S: syr 250 mg/mL; sprinkle capsule: 125

(cont)

Table 40. Pharmacologic Treatment of Agitation (cont.)			
Symptom	**Medication**	**Dosage**	**Formulations**
	Olanzapine[b,g] *(Zyprexa IntraMuscular)*	2.5–5 mg IM	Inj
Sexual aggression, impulse-control symptoms in men	SSRIs, Second-generation antipsychotic or divalproex[▲]	See dosages above	
	If no response, estrogen[▲] *(Premarin)*	0.625–1.25 mg/d	T: 0.3, 0.625, 0.9, 1.25, 2.5
	medroxyprogesterone[▲] *(Depo-Provera)*	100 mg IM/wk	Inj
	or		
	Leuprolide acetate *(Lupron Depot)*	**Table 106**	

[a] Avoid.[BC]

[b] Increased risk of mortality and cerebrovascular events compared with placebo; use with particular caution in patients with cerebrovascular disease or hypovolemia.

[c] Can be given q12h; allow 2–4 wk for adequate trial.

[d] Small divided daytime dosage and larger bedtime dosage; watch for sedation and orthostasis.

[e] Monitor serum levels; periodic CBCs, platelet counts secondary to agranulocytosis risk. Beware of drug-drug interactions.

[f] Can monitor serum levels; usually well tolerated; check CBC, platelets for agranulocytosis, thrombocytopenia risk in older adults.

[g] For acute use only; initial dose 2.5–5 mg, second dose (2.5–5 mg) can be given after 2 h, max of 3 injections in 24 h (max daily dose 20 mg); should not be administered for >3 consecutive d.

CAREGIVER ISSUES

- Over 50% develop depression.
- Physical illness, isolation, anxiety, and burnout are common.
- Intensive education and support of caregivers may delay institutionalization.
- Adult day care for patients and respite services may help.
- Alzheimer's Association offers support, education services (eg, Safe Return); chapters are located in major cities throughout US (p 348 for telephone, Web site).
- Family Caregiver Alliance offers support, education, information for caregivers (p 348 for telephone, Web site).

EVALUATION AND ASSESSMENT

Recognizing and diagnosing late-life depression can be difficult. Older adults may complain of lack of energy or other somatic symptoms, attribute symptoms to old age or other physical conditions, or neglect to mention them to a healthcare professional.

Consider screening with Patient Health Questionnaire 2 (PHQ-2):

• Over the past 2 wk, have you often had little interest or pleasure in doing things?

• Over the past 2 wk, have you often been bothered by feeling down, depressed, or hopeless?

Score each item: 0 = not at all, 1 = several days, 2 = more than half the days, 3 = nearly every day; a score ≥3 indicates high probability of depressive disorder.

Follow-up and/or assess tx with structured self-assessment scale such as the GDS or the PHQ-9 (p 338).

Medical Evaluation

TSH, B_{12}, calcium, liver and kidney function tests, electrolytes, UA, CBC

DSM-5 Criteria for Major Depressive Disorder (Abbreviated)

Five or more of the following criteria have been present during the same 2-wk period and represent a change from previous functioning; at least one of the symptoms is either depressed mood *or* loss of interest or pleasure. Do not include symptoms that are clearly due to a medical condition.

• Depressed mood

• Loss of interest or pleasure in activities

• Significant weight loss or gain (not intentional), or decrease or increase in appetite

• Insomnia or hypersomnia

• Psychomotor agitation or retardation

• Fatigue or loss of energy

• Feelings of worthlessness or excessive or inappropriate guilt

• Diminished ability to think or concentrate, or indecisiveness

• Recurrent thoughts of death; suicidal ideation, attempt, or plan

The *DSM-5* criteria are not specific for older adults; cognitive symptoms may be more prominent.

Subsyndromal Depression

Subsyndromal depression does not meet full criteria for major depressive disorder and may include adjustment disorders and milder depression with anxiety symptoms but can be serious and associated with functional impairment. In older adults, subsyndromal depression may actually reflect major depression not diagnosed by current diagnostic criteria and may require pharmacologic and nonpharmacologic intervention.

MANAGEMENT

Tx should be individualized on the basis of hx, past response, and severity of illness as well as concurrent illnesses.

Nonpharmacologic

For mild to moderate depression (PHQ-9 scores 4–9) or in combination with pharmacotherapy: CBT, mindfulness-based CBT, interpersonal tx, problem-solving tx, or repetitive transcranial magnetic stimulation (rTMS) (p 82), bright light tx in morning for seasonal depression.

For patients with major depression with mild to moderate dementia, problem adaptive therapy (PATH) may be helpful. PATH is a home-based tx that integrates problem-solving approaches with alternate strategies, environmental adaptations, and caregiver participation to improve the regulation of emotion. Supportive tx for cognitively impaired patients focuses on expression of affect, understanding, and empathy (Kiosses DN et al. *JAMA Psychiatry* 2015;72[1]:22–30).

For severe pharmacological-resistant or psychotic depression, consider electroconvulsive tx (ECT) (p 81).

Pharmacologic

For mild, moderate, or severe depression: the duration of tx should be at least 6–12 mo after remission for patients experiencing their first depressive episode. Most older adults with major depression require maintenance antidepressant tx. Ensure adequate initial trial of 4–6 wk after titrating up to therapeutic dosage; if inadequate response, consider switching to a different first-line agent or second-line tx or psychiatric referral/consult. Combining antidepressants can lead to significant adverse effects. SSRIs may increase hemorrhagic stroke risk; low initial dosages and monitoring are recommended, especially in patients at risk of stroke. Check sodium before starting SSRI and after a few weeks of tx; high index of suspicion for hyponatremia. SSRIs are also associated with increased risk of GI and postsurgical bleeding.

Choosing an Antidepressant (Table 41 and list on p 81)

First-line Therapy: SSRI; consider sertraline.

Second-line Therapy: Consider venlafaxine▲, duloxetine, mirtazapine▲, or bupropion▲.

Third-line Therapy: Consider augmentation of first- or second-line antidepressants with aripiprazole or quetiapine, or SSRI with buspirone▲ or bupropion▲.

Table 41. Antidepressants Used for Older Adults				
Class, Medication	**Initial Dosage**	**Usual Dosage**	**Formulations**	**Comments (Metabolism, Excretion)**
SSRIs	*Class AEs:* EPS, hyponatremia, increased risk of upper GI bleeding, suicide (early in tx), lower BMD and fragility fractures, risk of toxicity if methylene blue or linezolid co-administered. Avoid if hx of falls or fracture; caution if hx of SIADH.[BC] (L, K [10%])			
Citalopram▲ *(Celexa)*	10–20 mg qam	20 mg/d	T: 20, 40, 60; S: 5 mg/10 mL	20 mg/d is max dosage in adults >60 yr old; risk of QT_c prolongation
Escitalopram *(Lexapro)*	10 mg/d	10 mg/d	T: 10, 20	10 mg/d is max dosage in adults >60 yr old; risk of QT_c prolongation

(cont.)

Table 41. Antidepressants Used for Older Adults (cont.)

Class, Medication	Initial Dosage	Usual Dosage	Formulations	Comments (Metabolism, Excretion)
Fluoxetine▲ (Prozac)	5 mg qam	5–60 mg/d	T: 10; C: 10, 20, 40; S: 20 mg/5 mL; C: SR 90 (weekly dose)	Long half-lives of parent and active metabolite may allow for less frequent dosing; may cause more insomnia than other SSRIs; CYP2D6, -2C9, -3A4 inhibitor (L)
Fluvoxamine▲ (Luvox)	25 mg qhs	100–300 mg/d	T: 25, 50, 100	Not approved as an antidepressant in US; greater likelihood of GI AEs; CYP1A2, -3A4 inhibitor (L)
Paroxetine▲ (Paxil)	5 mg	10–40 mg/d	T: 10, 20, 30, 40	Increased risk of withdrawal symptoms (dizziness); anticholinergic AEs; CYP2D6 inhibitor (L)
(Paxil CR)	12.5 mg/d	12.5–37.5 mg/d	T: ER 12.5, 25, 37.5; S: 10 mg/5 mL	Increase by 12.5 mg/d no faster than once/wk (L)
Sertraline▲ (Zoloft)	25 mg qam	50–200 mg/d	T: 25, 50, 100; S: 20 mg/mL	Greater likelihood of GI AEs (L)
Additional Medications				
Bupropion▲ (Wellbutrin)	37.5–50 mg q12h	75–150 mg q12h	T: 75, 100	Consider for SSRI, TCA nonresponders; safe in HF; may be stimulating; can lower seizure threshold. Avoid.[BC] (L)
(Wellbutrin SR▲, Zyban▲)	100 mg q12h or q24h	100–150 mg q12h	T:100, 150, 200	
(Wellbutrin XL▲)	150 mg/d	300 mg/d	T: 150, 300	
Levomilnacipran (Fetzima)	20 mg q24h × 2 d	40 mg q24hmax; 120 mg/d	C: ER 20, 40, 80	SNRI (L, K 58%)
Methylphenidate▲BC (Ritalin)	2.5–5 mg at 7 AM and noon	5–10 mg at 7 AM and noon	T: 5, 10, 20	Short-term tx of depression or apathy in physically ill older adults; used as an adjunct. Avoid if insomia.[BC] (L)
Mirtazapine▲ (Remeron)	15 mg qhs	15–45 mg/d	T: 15, 30, 45	May increase appetite; sedating; ODT (SolTab) available (L)
Vilazodone (Viibryd)	10 mg/d for 7 d, then 20 mg/d	40 mg/d	T: 10, 20, 40	Metabolized by CYP3A4; limited geriatric data; AEs: diarrhea and nausea
Vortioxetine (Brintellix)		5–10 mg q24h max; 20 mg/d	T: 5, 10, 20	SSRI with 5-HT1A agonist and 5-HT3 antagonist activity (L)

(cont.)

Table 41. Antidepressants Used for Older Adults (cont.)

Class, Medication	Initial Dosage	Usual Dosage	Formulations	Comments (Metabolism, Excretion)
TCAs				Avoid.[BC]
◆Desipramine▲ (Norpramin)	10–25 mg qhs	50–150 mg/d	T: 10, 25, 50, 75, 100, 150	Therapeutic serum level >115 ng/mL (L)
◆Nortriptyline▲ (Aventyl, Pamelor)	10–25 mg qhs	75–150 mg/d	C: 10, 25, 50, 75; S: 10 mg/5 mL	Therapeutic window (50–150 ng/mL) (L)
SNRIs				Caution if hx of SIADH.[BC]
◆Duloxetine (Cymbalta)	20 mg/d, then 20 mg q12h	40–60 mg q24h or 30 mg q12h	C: 20, 30, 60	Most common AEs: nausea, dry mouth, constipation, diarrhea, urinary hesitancy; reduce dosage if CrCl 30–60 mL/min; contra-indicated if CrCl <30 mL/min (L)
Venlafaxine▲ (Effexor)	25–50 mg q12h	75–225 mg/d in divided doses	T: 25, 37.5, 50, 75, 100	Low anticholinergic activity; minimal sedation and hypotension; may increase BP and QT_c; may be useful when somatic pain present; EPS, withdrawal symptoms, hyponatremia (L)
(Effexor XR)	75 mg qam	75–225 mg/d	C: 37.5, 75, 150	Same as above
Desvenlafaxine (Pristiq)	50 mg/d	50 mg; max 400 mg	SR tab: 50, 100	Active metabolite of venlafaxine; adjust dosage when CrCl <30 mL/min (L, K 45%)

◆ = Also has primary indication for neuropathic pain.

Antidepressants to Avoid in Older Adults

- Amitriptyline▲ (eg, *Elavil):* anticholinergic, sedating, hypotensive[BC]
- Amoxapine▲ *(Asendin):* anticholinergic, sedating, hypotensive; also associated with EPS, TD, and neuroleptic malignant syndrome[BC]
- Doxepin▲ (eg, *Sinequan):* anticholinergic, sedating, hypotensive[BC]
- Imipramine▲ *(Tofranil):* anticholinergic, sedating, hypotensive[BC]
- Maprotiline▲ *(Ludiomil):* seizures, rashes[BC]
- Protriptyline▲ *(Vivactil):* very anticholinergic; can be stimulating[BC]
- St. John's wort: drug interactions, photosensitivity, hypomania[BC]
- Trimipramine *(Surmontil):* anticholinergic, sedating, hypotensive[BC]

Electroconvulsive Therapy (ECT)

Generally safe and very effective. Potential complications include temporary confusion, anterograde and retrograde amnesia, arrhythmias, aspiration, falls.

Indications: Severe depression when a rapid onset of response is necessary; when depression is resistant to drug tx; for patients who are unable to tolerate antidepressants, have previous response to ECT, have psychotic depression, severe catatonia, or depression with Parkinson disease.

Evaluation: Before ECT, perform CXR, ECG, serum electrolytes, and cardiac examination. Additional tests (eg, stress test, neuroimaging, EEG) are used selectively.

Contraindications:
- Increased intracranial pressure
- Intracranial tumor
- MI within 3 mo (relative)
- Stroke within 1 mo (relative)

Consider Maintenance ECT:
- Hx of ECT-responsive illness
- Resistance or intolerance to medications alone
- Serious medical comorbidity
- More effective than pharmacotherapy after successful ECT

Repetitive Transcranial Magnetic Stimulation (rTMS)
- Series of magnetic pulses directed to brain at frequency of 1–20 stimulations per sec. Each tx session lasts ~30 min, and a full course of tx may be as long as 30 sessions.
- Placebo-controlled studies have demonstrated moderate effect sizes for tx-resistant depression in younger adults and appears safe with minimal adverse effects.
- Limited experience with rTMS in tx-resistant late-life depression; rTMS tx parameters may need to be optimized to address age-related changes such as prefrontal cortical atrophy.

Depression and Parkinson Disease
Patients with Parkinson disease and depression may benefit more from nortriptyline than SSRIs. Pramipexole may also reduce depressive symptoms independent of effect on motor symptoms (also p 223).

Psychotic Depression
- Psychosis accompanying major depression; increased disability and mortality
- ECT is the tx of choice
- Olanzapine 15–20 mg/d added to sertraline 150–200 mg/d significantly improves remission rate vs placebo.

BIPOLAR DISORDER
See **Table 43**.
- 5–19% of mood disorders in older adults.
- Usually begins in early adulthood, family hx.
- 10% may develop after age 50.
- Distinct period of abnormally and persistently elevated, expansive, or irritable mood for longer than 1 wk.
- Symptoms may include racing thoughts, pressured speech, decreased need for sleep, distractibility, grandiose delusions.
- A single manic episode is sufficient for a diagnosis if secondary causes are excluded.
- Late-onset mania may be secondary to head trauma, stroke, delirium, other neurologic disorders, alcohol abuse, or medications (eg, corticosteroids, L-dopa, thyroxine).
- Use aripiprazole, lurasidone, olanzapine, quetiapine, risperidone▲, or ziprasidone for acute mania (**Table 107**) and D/C antidepressants if taking.
- If depression emerges in bipolar disorder, lamotrigine▲ may be helpful.
- Initiate long-term tx (**Table 43**) as soon as patient is able to comply with oral tx.

Table 42. Medications for Management of Bipolar Disorders

Medication	Mania		Depression	
	Acute	*Maintenance*	*Acute*	*Maintenance*
Atypical antipsychotics	All +	Aripiprazole + Olanzapine +/–	Quetiapine + Olanzapine +/– Lurisadone+	Olanzapine +/–
Mood stabilizers				
Lithium ▲	+	+	+	+
Valproate ▲	+	+/–	–	+/–
Lamotrigine ▲	–	+/–	+	+
Carbamazepine ▲	+	+/–	?	+/–
Antidepressants				
SSRIs	Avoid	Avoid	+	+
TCAs	Avoid	Avoid	–	–

Note: + = evidence to support use; +/– = some evidence to support use; – = evidence does not support use; ? = has not been studied.

Table 43. Long-term Treatment of Bipolar Disorders*

Medication	Initial Dosage	Usual Dosage	Formulation	Comments
Lithium ▲ *(Eskalith, Eskalith CR, Lithobid)*	150 mg/d	300–900 mg/d Levels 0.4–0.8 mEq/L	T: 300; T: ER 300; T: CR 450; C: 150, 300, 600; syr 300 mg/mL	Risk of CNS toxicity; cognitive impairment; hypothyroidism; interactions with diuretics, ACEIs, calcium channel blockers, NSAIDs
Carbamazepine ▲ *(Tegretol, Tegretol XR)*	100 mg q12h	800–1200 mg/d Levels 4–12 mcg/L	T: 100, 200, 400	Many drug interactions; may cause SIADH; risk of leukopenia, neutropenia, agranulocytosis, thrombocytopenia; monitor CBC; drowsiness, dizziness
Valproic acid ▲ *(Depacon, Depakene, Depakote)*	125 mg q12h	750 mg/d in divided doses Levels 50–125 mcg/L	T: 125, 250, 500	Can cause weight gain, tremor, several drug interactions; risk of hepatotoxicity, pancreatitis, neutropenia, thrombocytopenia; monitor LFTs and platelets
Lamotrigine ▲ *(Lamictal)*	25 mg/d	100–200 mg/d	T: 25, 100, 150, 200	D/C if rash; interaction with valproate (when used together, begin at 25 mg q48h, titrate to 25–100 mg q12h); prolongs PR interval; somnolence, headache common

*Limited evidence base in older adults. See www.healthquality.va.gov (also **Table 92**).

DERMATOLOGIC CONDITIONS COMMON IN OLDER ADULTS

For numerous dermatologic images, see hardinmd.lib.uiowa.edu/dermpictures.html.

Actinic Keratosis (hardinmd.lib.uiowa.edu/dermnet/mouthcancer5.html)

Erythematous, flat, rough, scaly papules 2–6 mm; may be easier felt than seen; precancerous (can develop into squamous or basal cell carcinoma); cutaneous horn may develop; affects sun-exposed areas, including lips (actinic cheilitis)

Risk Factors: UV light exposure (amount and intensity), increased age, fair coloring, immunosuppression

Prevention: Limit UV light exposure, use sunscreen with UVA and UVB coverage, wear protective clothing

Treatment

- Topical 5-fluorouracil *(Carac* crm 0.5% daily × 4 wk, *Efudex* crm 5% q12h × 2–4 wk, *Fluoroplex* crm 1% to face, 5% elsewhere, q12h × 2–6 wk) to entire area affected
- Imiquimod 3.75% pk *(Zyclara).* Apply 1 or 2 pk to face or scalp (not both) qhs × 14 d, wash off with soap and water after 8 h. Rest 14 d, then repeat another 14 d. Max 56 pk/2 cycles
- Imiquimod 5% pk *(Aldara).* Apply 1 or 2 pk to face or scalp (not both) qhs × 16 d, wash off with soap and water after 8 h. Rest 14 d, then repeat another 14 d. Max 56 pk/2 cycles
- Cryosurgery
- Aminolevulinic acid *(Levulan Kerastick* 20%) applied to lesions with blue light illumination after 14–18 h, repeat in 8 wk
- Ingenol mebutate 0.015% gel *(Picato).* Face and scalp: apply q24h × 3 d; trunk and extremities: apply q24h × 2 d. Allow gel to dry × 15 min, do not wash or touch for 6 h
- Curettage with or without electrosurgery
- Chemical peels, dermabrasion, laser tx

Basal Cell Carcinoma (hardinmd.lib.uiowa.edu/skincancerbasal.html)

Can affect any body surface exposed to the sun, most often head and neck

Types

- Nodular: pearly papule or nodule over telangiectases with a rolled border; may contain melanin; most common type
- Superficial: scaly erythematous patch or plaque, may contain melanin
- Morpheaform: indurated, whitish, scar-like plaque with indistinct margins

Risk Factors

- Exposure to UV radiation, especially intense intermittent exposure during childhood or adolescence
- Physical factors: fair skin, light eye color, red or blonde hair
- Exposure to ionizing radiation, arsenic, psoralen, UVA radiation, smoking
- Immunosuppression (eg, after solid-organ transplant)

Prevention: Avoid sun exposure, use sunscreen with UVA and UVB coverage, wear protective clothing

Treatment: (localized control)

- Surgical: Mohs micrographic surgery, cryosurgery, excision, curettage and electrodessication
- Nonsurgical: radiotherapy, imiquimod 5% crm *(Aldara)* applied daily 5 d/wk × 6 wk (not for use on face, hands, or feet); photodynamic tx; 5-fluorouracil 0.5% crm or sol q12h × 3–6 wk or longer; vismodegib *(Erivedge)* 150 mg q24h until disease progresses or unacceptable toxicity (L, F 92% [C:150])

Candidiasis (hardinmd.lib.uiowa.edu/yeastinfectionpictures.html)

Erythema, pustules, or cheesy, whitish matter in body folds; satellite lesions

Treatment: See intertrigo; antifungal powders (**Table 44**)

Cellulitis (hardinmd.lib.uiowa.edu/cellulitis.html)

Ill-defined erythema, pain, blisters and exudates; most often affects lower dermis and subcutaneous tissue, commonly the legs; group A streptococci and *Staphylococcus aureus* most frequent pathogens

Treatment

- Antistaphylococcal penicillin, amoxicillin-clavulanate▲ × 10 d
- Macrolide (eg, erythromycin▲), 1st-generation cephalosporin (eg, cephalexin▲), or tetracycline▲ if penicillin allergy
- MRSA suspected or known
  - ○ Oral empiric options: clindamycin, TMP/SMX, doxycycline, minocycline, or linezolid
  - ○ Tailor tx to culture and sensitivity results when available

Erysipelas (hardinmd.lib.uiowa.edu/cellulitispictures.html#pics3)

Bright red, edematous, and tender with unilateral distribution; orange peel appearance; well-demarcated border with vesicles and bullae; affects lower dermis and subcutaneous tissue, face and legs

Treatment: Penicillin; erythromycin, clindamycin, linezolid, or cephalosporin if penicillin allergy

Folliculitis (hardinmd.lib.uiowa.edu/folliculitis.html)

Multiple small, erythematous papules and pustules surrounding a hair; most often affects areas with coarse, short hair (ie, neck, beard, buttocks, thighs)

Treatment

- Mild localized cases—topical antibiotic: mupirocin 2%▲ *(Bactroban)*, erythromycin, or clindamycin
- Extensive or severe cases—oral antistaphylococcal penicillin, amoxicillin-clavulanate, or erythromycin

Impetigo (hardinmd.lib.uiowa.edu/impetigopictures.html)

Very contagious; nonbullous and bullous variants; honey-colored crusts on face around nose and mouth

Treatment

- Small, localized lesions: topical mupirocin 2%▲ *(Bactroban)* q8h × 7–10 d, topical retapamulin 1% oint *(Altabax)* q12h × 5 d
- Widespread: oral antistaphylococcal penicillin, erythromycin, or a cephalosporin × 10 d

Intertrigo

Moist, erythematous lesions with local superficial skin loss; satellite lesions caused by *Candida*; can affect any place two skin surfaces rest against one another (eg, under breasts, between toes)

Treatment
• Keep area dry.
• Topical antifungals (**Table 44**), absorbent pwd, 1–2% hydrocortisone▲ or 0.1% triamcinolone▲ crm q12h × 1–2 d if inflamed

Melanoma (hardinmd.lib.uiowa.edu/melanomapictures.html)

Less common than nonmelanoma lesions; usually asymptomatic

Clinical Features

Asymmetry: a line down the center of the lesions does not create a mirror image

Border: irregular, ragged, fuzzy, or scalloped

Color: nonuniform throughout the lesion

Diameter: >6 mm (considered relatively insensitive as an independent factor)

Types
• Lentigo maligna: most often located on atrophic, sun-damaged skin; irregular-shaped tan or brown macule; slow growing
• Superficial spreading: occur anywhere; irregular-shaped macule, papule, or plaque; coloration varies
• Nodular: a rapidly growing, often black or gray papule or nodule
• Acral lentiginous: located on the palms, soles, or nail beds; dark brown or black patch; more common in Hispanic, black, and Asian individuals

Risk Factors
• Very fair skin type
• Family hx
• Dysplastic or numerous nevi
• Sun exposure; blistering sunburns as a child

Prevention: Avoid sun exposure, use sunscreen with UVA and UVB coverage, wear protective clothing

Treatment: Surgical excision

Neurodermatitis

Generalized or localized itching, redness, scaling; can affect any skin surface

Treatment: Mid- to higher-potency topical corticosteroids (**Table 45**); exclude other causes, (eg, allergies, irritants, xerosis)

Onychomycosis (hardinmd.lib.uiowa.edu/toenailfungus.html)

Thickening and discoloration; affects nails *(Tinea unguium)*

Treatment: Obtain nail specimens for laboratory culture to confirm diagnosis before prescribing itraconazole or terbinafine.
• Itraconazole▲ *(Sporanox* [C: 100; S: 100 mg/mL]), contraindicated in HF (L), mycologic cure rate on pulse tx 63%

- Toenails: 200 mg po q24h × 3 mo—23% complete cure rate (negative mycologic analysis and normal nail) reported with this regimen, or 200 mg po q12h × 1 wk/mo × 3 mo
  - Fingernails: 200 mg po q12h × 1 wk/mo × 2 mo ("Pulse Therapy") or 200 mg q24h × 12 wk
- Fluconazole▲ *(Diflucan* [T: 50, 100, 150, 200; S: 10, 40 mg/mL]) (L), mycologic cure rate 48%
  - Toenails: 150 or 300 mg po/wk × 6–12 mo
  - Fingernails: 150 or 300 mg po/wk × 3–6 mo
- Efinaconazole (*Jublia* [Sol: 10%])
  - Toenails: apply q24h × 48 wk
- Terbinafine▲ (*Lamisil* [T: 250]), avoid if CrCl <50 mL/min, mycologic cure rate 76%
  - Toenails: 250 mg po q24h × 12 wk—48% complete cure rate reported with this regimen
  - Fingernails: 250 mg po q24h × 6 wk
- Ciclopirox▲ *(Loprox, Penlac):* Toenails and fingernails—apply lacquer q12h to nails and adjacent skin; remove with alcohol q7d—8% complete cure rate reported with this regimen
- Mentholatum (eg, *Vicks VapoRub*) applied 2–3 ×/d for several months has been reported as a tx for fungal infections of the nail but has not been compared with marketed tx or placebo
- OTC lacquers (eg, *Fungi-Nail*) treat the fungus around the nail but do not penetrate the nail
- Laser tx: improves appearance; not covered by insurance

Psoriasis (hardinmd.lib.uiowa.edu/psoriasis.html)

Well-defined, erythematous plaques covered with silver scales; severity varies; can affect all skin areas, nails (pitting)

Treatment
- Topical corticosteroids, UV light, PUVA, methotrexate, cyclosporine, etretinate, sulfasalazine, tacrolimus, pimecrolimus *(Elidel)*, tazarotene gel 0.05%, 0.1%, anthralin preparations, and tar + 1–4% salicylic acid
- Calcipotriene for nonfacial areas
- Cyclosporine, methotrexate, and biological agents for extensive and recalcitrant disease

Rosacea (hardinmd.lib.uiowa.edu/rosaceapictures.html)

Vascular and follicular dilatation; mild to moderate; can accompany seborrhea; can affect face (nose, chin, cheeks, forehead) or eyes (dryness, blepharitis, conjunctivitis)

Prevention: Avoid triggers (stress, prolonged sun exposure and exercise, hot and humid environment, alcohol, hot drinks, spicy foods); may be worsened by vasodilators, niacin, or topical corticosteroids. Wear sunscreen with UVA and UVB coverage (SPF ≥15) or sunblock with titanium and zinc oxide. See www.rosacea.org.

Treatment
- Topical (for mild cases and maintenance)
  - Azelaic acid 15% gel *(Finacea)* q12–24 h or 20% crm *(Azelex, Finevin)* q12h
  - Brimonidine 0.5% gel *(Mirvaso)* q24h
  - Benzoyl peroxide 2.5, 5, 10% crm, gel, wash, soap q12–24h
  - Ivermectin 1% crm *(Soolantra)* q24h
  - Metronidazole 0.75% crm▲ *(MetroCream)* q12h or 1% crm or gel *(Noritate, MetroGel)* q24h
  - Sodium sulfacetamide 10% + sulfa 5% (*Rosula* aqueous gel, *Clenia* crm, foaming wash) q12–24h, avoid if sulfa allergy or kidney disease (K)
  - Erythromycin 2% sol▲ q12h
  - Tretinoin▲ 0.025% crm or liq, 0.01% gel qhs

- Oral (for moderate to severe papular-pustular rosacea)
  - Tetracycline▲ 250–500 mg q8–12h × 6–12 wk
  - Doxycycline▲ 50–100 mg q12–24h × 6–12 wk
  - Minocycline▲ 50–100 mg q12h × 6–12 wk
  - Clarithromycin▲ 250–500 mg q12h × 6–12 wk
  - Metronidazole▲ 200 mg q12–24h × 4–6 wk
  - Erythromycin▲ 250–500 mg q12–24h × 6–12 wk
  - Azithromycin▲ 250–500 mg q24h × 6–12 wk

Scabies (hardinmd.lib.uiowa.edu/scabiespictures.html)

Burrows, erythematous papules or rash, dry or scaly skin, pruritus (worse at night); spread by close, skin-to-skin or sexual contact; can affect interdigital webs, flexor aspects of wrists, axillae, umbilicus, nipples, genitalia. Diagnostic confirmation by microscopic exam of skin scrapings in mineral oil.

Treatment

- Infestation can result in epidemics; treat all contacts and treat environment
- Oatmeal baths, topical corticosteroids, or emollient creams for symptom relief
- Apply topical products from head to toe:
  - Permethrin 5% crm▲ (Elimite), wash off after 8–14 h, repeat in 7–10 d if symptomatic or if live mites were found
  - Lindane 1% crm▲ (K-well, Scabene), wash off after 8–12 h
  - Crotamiton 10% crm (Eurax), less effective, leave on 48 h, repeat in 7–10 d if necessary
  - Ivermectin (Stromectol) 200 mcg/kg po, may repeat once in 1 or 2 wk [T: 3, 6]

Seborrheic Dermatitis (hardinmd.lib.uiowa.edu/seborrheicdermatitis.html)

Greasy, yellow scales with or without erythematous base; common in Parkinson disease and in debilitated patients; can affect nasal labial folds, eyebrows, hairline, sideburns, posterior auriculare, and midchest

Treatment

- Hydrocortisone 1% or 2% crm▲ q12h or triamcinolone 0.1% oint q12h × 2 wk
- Scalp: shampoo containing selenium sulfide, zinc, or tar
- Ketoconazole 2% crm▲ for severe conditions if Pityrosporum orbiculare infection suspected

Skin Maceration

Erythema; abraded, excoriated skin; blisters; white and silver patches; can affect any area constantly in contact with moisture, covered by occlusive dressing or bandage; skin folds, groin, buttocks

Prevention and Treatment

- Eliminate cause of moisture.
  - Toileting program for incontinence (p 149)
  - Condom catheter
  - Indwelling catheter (reserve for most intractable conditions)
  - FI collector
- Protect skin from moisture.
  - Clean gently with mild soap after each incontinent episode.
  - Apply moisture barrier (eg, Vaseline, Proshield, Smooth and Cool, Calmoseptine).

- Use disposable briefs that wick moisture from the skin; use linen incontinence pads when disposable briefs worsen perineal dermatitis.

Urticaria (hardinmd.lib.uiowa.edu/hives.html)

Hives
- Uniform, red edematous plaques surrounded by white halos, can affect any skin surface
- Treatment
  - Identify cause
  - Oral H_1 antihistamines (**Table 114**) or oral H_2 antihistamines (**Table 57**)
  - Oral glucocorticoids (eg, prednisone 40 mg q24h)
  - Doxepin▲ (po or topical *Zonalon* 5%) for refractory cases

Angioedema
- Larger, deeper than hives; can affect lips, eyelids, tongue, larynx, GI tract
- Treatment
  - Oral H_1 antihistamines (**Table 114**)
  - Oral glucocorticoids
  - For severe reactions, epinephrine 0.3 mL of a 1:1000 dilution *(EpiPen)* SC

Cholinergic
- Round, red papular wheals; can affect any skin surface
- Treatment
  - Hot shower may relieve itching
  - Oral H_1 antihistamines (**Table 114**) 1 h before exercise

Xerosis

Dull, rough, flaky, cracked; nummular; can affect all skin surfaces

Treatment
- Increase humidity
- Avoid excess bathing, sponges, brushes, and use of bath oils, which can lead to falls from slippery feet
- Tepid water in baths or showers
- Oatmeal baths
- Apply emollient oint (eg, *Aquaphor*) or crm (eg, *Eucerin*) immediately after bathing
- Hydrocortisone 1% oint

DERMATOLOGIC MEDICATIONS

Table 44. Topical Antifungal Medications

Medication	Formulation	Dermatologic Indications	Dosing Frequency
Butenafine *(Lotrimin ultra*, Mentax)*	1% crm	*Tinea pedis, T cruris, T corpis, T versicolor*	q24h × 2–4 wk
Ciclopirox▲ *(Loprox, Penlac)*	0.77% crm, gel, lot, sus; 1% shp; 8% lacquer	*Tinea pedis, T cruris, T corpis, T versicolor;* candidiasis; scalp seborrhea; onychomycosis	2 ×/wk × 4 wk; shp 3 ×/wk; lacquer qhs

(cont.)

Table 44. Topical Antifungal Medications (cont.)

Medication	Formulation	Dermatologic Indications	Dosing Frequency
Clotrimazole▲* (*Cruex, Mycelex,* others)	1% crm, sol	Candidiasis, dermatophytoses; superficial mycoses	q12h
Econazole▲ nitrate *(Spectazole)*	1% crm▲ 1% foam	Candidiasis; *Tinea cruris, T corpis, T versicolor*	q24h × 2–4 wk
Ketoconazole▲ *(Nizoral, Nizoral A-D*)*	2% crm, foam, gel 1% and 2% shp	Candidiasis; seborrhea; *Tinea cruris, T corpis, T versicolor*	q12–24h × 2–4 wk; shp 2 ×/wk
Luliconazole *(Luzu)*	1% crm	*T pedis, T crusis*	q24h × 1–2 wk
Miconazole▲* (eg, *Micatin, Monistat-Derm*)	2% crm, lot, pwd, spr, tinc	*Tinea cruris, T corpis, T pedis*	q12h × 2–4 wk
Naftifine *(Naftin)*	1% and 2% crm, gel	*Tinea cruris, T corpis, T pedis*	Crm q24h up to 4 wk Gel q12h–24h up to 4wk
Nystatin▲ *(Mycostatin, Nilstat, Nystex)*	100,000 U/g crm, oint, pwd	Mucocutaneous candidiasis	q8–12h up to 4 wk
Oxiconazole *(Oxistat)*	1% crm, lot	*Tinea corpis, T cruris, T pedis, T versicolor*	q12–24h × 2–4 wk
Sertraconazole *(Ertaczo)*	2% crm	*Tinea pedis*	q12h × 4 wk
Sulconazole *(Exelderm)*	1% crm, sol	*Tinea corpis, T cruris*	q12–24h × 3–4 wk
Terbinafine▲ *(Lamisil, LamisilAT*)*	1% crm▲, sol, gel, spr	*Tinea cruris, T corpis, T pedis, T versicolor*	q12h × 1–4 wk
Tolnaftate▲* (*Absorbine Jr. Antifungal, Tinactin,* others)	1% crm▲, gel, S▲, pwd▲, spr	*Tinea cruris, T corpis, T pedis*	q12h × 2–4 wk
Triacetin *(Myco Nail*)*	25% sol	*Tinea pedis*	q12h, continue for 7 d after symptoms have resolved
Undecyclenic acid *(FungiNail*)*	25% sol	*Tinea pedis*, ringworm (except nails and scalp)	q12h × 4 wk

* OTC

Table 45. Topical Corticosteroids

Medication	Strength and Formulations	Frequency of Applications
Lowest Potency		
Hydrocortisone▲	0.5%*, 1%, 2.5% crm, oint, lot, sol	q6–8h
Low Potency		
Alclometasone dipropionate▲ᵃ *(Aclovate)*	0.05% crm, oint	q8–12h
Desonide▲ *(DesOwen, Tridesilon)*	0.05% crm, oint, foam, lot, gel	q6–12h

(cont.)

Table 45. Topical Corticosteroids (cont.)

Medication	Strength and Formulations	Frequency of Applications
Fluocinolone acetonide▲ *(Synalar)*	0.01% crm, sol	q6–12h
Mid-potency		
Betamethasone dipropionate▲ *(Diprosone)*	0.05% lot	q6–12h
Betamethasone valerate▲ *(Valisone)*	0.1% crm	q6–12h
Clocortolone pivalate▲ *(Cloderm)*	0.1% crm	q6–24h
Desoximetasone▲ *(Topicort)*	0.05% crm	q12h
Fluocinolone acetonide▲ *(Synalar)*	0.025% crm, oint	q6–12h
Flurandrenolide *(Cordran)*	0.05% crm, oint, lot, tape	q12–24h
Fluticasone propionate▲ *(Cutivate)*	0.05% crm, 0.005% oint	q12h
Hydrocortisone butyrate *(Locoid)*	0.1% oint	q12–24h
Hydrocortisone valerate▲ *(Westcort)*	0.2% crm, oint	q6–8h
Mometasone furoate▲ª *(Elocon)*	0.1% crm, lot, oint	q24h
Prednicarbate▲ *(Dermatop)*	0.1% crm, lot	q12h
Triamcinolone acetonide▲ *(Aristocort, Kenalog)*	0.025%, 0.1% crm, oint, lot	q8–12h
Higher Potency		
Amcinonide▲ *(Cyclocort)*	0.1%, crm, oint, lot	q8–12h
Betamethasone dipropionate▲ *(Diprolene AF)*	0.05% augmented crm	q6–12h
Betamethasone dipropionate▲ *(Diprosone)*	0.05%, crm, oint	q6–12h
Betamethasone valerate▲ *(Valisone)*	0.1% oint	q6–12h
Desoximetasone▲ *(Topicort)*	0.25% crm, oint, spr; 0.05% gel	q12h
Diflorasone diacetate▲ *(Florone, Maxiflor)*	0.05%, crm, oint	q6–12h
Fluocinonide▲ *(Lidex)*	0.05% crm, oint, gel	q6–12h
Halcinonide▲ *(Halog)*	0.1% crm, oint	q8–24h
Triamcinolone acetate▲	0.5% crm, spr	q8–12h
Super Potency		
Betamethasone dipropionate▲ *(Diprolene)*	0.05% oint, lot, gel (augmented)	q6–12h
Clobetasol propionate *(Temovate)*	0.05% crm▲, oint▲, lot, gel▲, shp, spr	q12h
Diflorasone diacetate▲ *(Psorcon)*	0.05% optimized oint	q8–24h
Halobetasol propionate▲ *(Ultravate)*	0.05% crm, oint	q12h

ª Hydrocortisone (all forms), alclometasone, and mometasone are nonfluorinated.

*OTC

HYPOTHYROIDISM
Common Causes
- Autoimmune (primary thyroid failure)
- Following tx for hyperthyroidism
- Pituitary or hypothalmic disorders (secondary thyroid failure)
- Medications, especially amiodarone (rare after first 18 mo of tx) and lithium

Screening for hypothyroidism in asymptomatic older persons is controversial

Evaluation
TSH, and if high, repeat TSH and free T_4

Pharmacotherapy
- Tx of subclinical hypothyroidism (TSH 5–10 mIU/L, normal free T_4 concentration, and no overt symptoms) is controversial and should be tailored to the individual patient based on symptoms, atherosclerotic heart disease, HF, or risk factors for these diseases.
- Levothyroxine▲ (T_4 *[Eltroxin, Levo-T, Levothroid, Synthroid]* [T: 25, 50, 75, 88, 100, 112, 125, 137, 150, 175, 200, 300 mcg]) given on empty stomach and waiting for 1 h before eating or hs (4 h after last meal), which is more potent. Start at 25–50 mcg and increase by 12- to 25-mcg intervals q4–8wk with repeat TSH testing until TSH is in normal range. Prescribe product from same manufacturer for individual patients for consistent bioavailability. If adherence is a problem, can be given weekly or twice weekly.
- Combinations of levothyroxine and L-triiodothyronine (T_3) are not recommended.
- For myxedema coma: Load T_4 400 mcg IV or 100 mcg q6–8h for 1 d, then 100 mcg/d IV (until patient can take orally) and give stress doses of corticosteroids (p 103); then start usual replacement regimen.
- Thyroid USP is not recommended. (Avoid.[BC]) To convert thyroid USP to thyroxine: 60 mg USP = 50 mcg thyroxine.
- If patients are npo and must receive IV thyroxine, dose should be half usual po dose.
- If tx has been interrupted for <6 wk and without an intercurrent cardiac event or marked weight loss, previous full replacement dose can be resumed.
- Monitor TSH level at least q12mo (ASCE/ATA) in patients on chronic thyroid replacement tx. Normal TSH ranges are higher in older persons and higher target (eg, 4–6 mIU/L) may be appropriate.

HYPERTHYROIDISM
Common Causes
- Graves' disease
- Toxic nodule
- Toxic multinodular goiter
- Medications, especially amiodarone (can occur any time during tx)

Evaluation
TSH, free T_4
- If TSH is low and free T_4 is normal, recheck TSH in 4–6 wk; if TSH is still low, check free T_3.
- If TSH is low and free T_4 or free T_3 is high, check radioactive iodine uptake and, if thyroid nodularity, thyroid scan.

Pharmacotherapy

- β-blockers (p 53) if symptomatic hyperthyroidism
- Radioactive iodine ablation is usual tx of choice for older persons, but surgery (works faster but more likely to become hypothyroid) or medical tx are options. Pretreat with methimazole and β-blockers before iodine ablation if symptomatic or if free T_4> 2–3 × normal. Monitor free T_4 and total T_3 within 1–2 mo after tx. Pretreat with methimazole and β-blockers before surgery. Give potassium iodide in immediate preoperative period. After surgery, measure calcium or intact PTH, stop antithyroid drugs, and taper β-blockers.
- Methimazole▲ *(Tapazole* [T: 5, 10]): First-line drug tx; start 5–20 mg po q8h, then adjust. If used as primary tx, continue for 12–18 mo then DC or taper if TSH is normal. Check CBC, LFTs before starting.
- Propylthiouracil (PTU [T: 50]): Use only if allergic to or intolerant of methimazole; can cause serious liver injury; start 100 mg po q8h, then adjust up to 200 mg po q8h prn. Check CBC, LFTs before starting.
- When dose has stabilized, follow TSH per hypothyroid monitoring.
- Adjunctive tx with β-blockers (**Table 29**) or calcium antagonists (**Table 29**) may improve symptoms.
- In older adults, treat both symptomatic hyperthyroidism and subclinical hyperthyroidism (low TSH and normal serum free T_4 and T_3 concentrations confirmed by repeat testing in 3–6 mo) if TSH <0.1 mIU/L or if TSH 0.1–0.5 mIU/L and underlying cardiovascular disease or low BMD.

EUTHYROID SICK SYNDROME
Definition
Abnormal thyroid function tests in nonthyroidal illness

Evaluation
- Do not assess thyroid function in acutely ill patients unless thyroid dysfunction is strongly suspected.
- Low T_3, high reverse T_3, low T_4, low or high TSH may be seen.
- If TSH is very low (<0.1 mIU/L in high sensitivity assays), then hyperthyroidism is likely.
- If TSH is very high (>20 mIU/L), then hypothyroidism is likely.
- If thyroid disease is not strongly suspected, recheck in 3–6 wk.

SOLITARY THYROID NODULE
Evaluation
- Ultrasound of thyroid
- TSH
  - If TSH is normal or high, perform fine-needle aspirate if nodule ≥1 cm. Do not perform radioclide scan.[CW]
  - If TSH is low, perform radionuclide scan; if "hot," then rarely cancer and manage as described below; if "cold," perform fine-needle aspirate.

Management
- Benign nodules: follow clinically and with ultrasound q12–24mo initially
- "Hot" nodules: radioactive iodine or surgery
- Malignant nodules, suspicious for malignancy: surgery
- Follicular neoplasm; surgery or molecular testing

- Atypical cells of undetermined significance (ACUS) or follicular lesions of undetermined significance. If low suspicion, gene expression classifier. If suspicion is high, check for molecular abnormalities.
- Nondiagnostic: repeat fine-needle aspirate with ultrasound guidance.

HYPERCALCEMIA

Common Causes
- Primary hyperparathyroidism
- Malignancy
- Thyrotoxicosis
- Increased calcium intake (rare unless also CKD or milk-alkali syndrome)
- Hypervitaminosis D
- Lithium
- Thiazide diuretics
- Granulomatous diseases

Evaluation
- Ionized calcium
- Intact PTH
  - If high, measure urinary calcium excretion. If high, then primary hyperparathyroidism. If low, then familial hypocalciuric hypercalcemia.
  - If low, measure PTHrP, 1,25(OH) Vitamin D, and 25(OH) Vitamin D. If PTHrP is high, workup for malignancy. If normal and 1,25(OH) Vitamin D is high, get CXR. If normal and 25(OH) Vitamin D is high, probably due to medications, vitamins, supplements. If all are normal, consider other causes (eg, myeloma, vitamin A toxicity).

Management
Treat underlying cause, if possible.

Nonpharmacologic
Asymptomatic mild (<12 mg/dL) or moderate (12–14 mg/dL) hypercalcemia: avoid dehydryation, bedrest, or physical inactivity

Pharmacologic
If symptomatic or >14 mg/dL:
- Isotonic saline 200–300 mL/h and then adjusted to maintain 100–150 mL/h urine output
- Calcitonin 4 (IU/kg)
- Zoledronic acid (4 mg over 15 min) or pamidronate (50–90 mg over 2 h)
- Saline and calcitonin will lower calcium within 12–48 h. Zolendronic acid/pamidronate will be effective by 48–96 h.
- Other tx (eg, denosumab, cinacalcet) are reserved for refractory hypercalcemia or specific causes.

DIABETES MELLITUS

Definition and Classification (ADA)
DM is a group of metabolic diseases characterized by hyperglycemia resulting from defects in insulin secretion, insulin action, or both.

Type 1: Caused by an absolute deficiency of insulin secretion.

Type 2: Caused by a combination of resistance to insulin action and an inadequate compensatory insulin secretory response. Type 2 DM is a progressive disorder requiring higher dosages or additional medications over time.

Screening—Screen asymptomatic older adults if BMI ≥25 kg/m² and an additional risk factor (eg, physical inactivity, first-degree relative, HTN, high-risk ethnic group, HDL ≤35 mg/dL, high triglycerides >250 mg/dL, hx gestational DM) with HbA$_{1c}$, fasting plasma glucose or OGTT if patient is likely to benefit from identification and tx based on current health and prognosis; repeat at 3-yr intervals.

Criteria for Diagnosis—One or more of the following:
- Symptoms of DM (eg, polyuria, polydipsia, unexplained weight loss) plus casual plasma glucose concentration ≥200 mg/dL
- Fasting (no caloric intake for ≥8 h) plasma glucose ≥126 mg/dL
- 2-h plasma glucose ≥200 mg/dL during an OGTT
- Unless hyperglycemia is unequivocal, diagnosis should be confirmed by repeat testing.
- HbA$_{1c}$ >6.5

Pre-diabetes—Any of the following:
- Impaired fasting glucose: defined as fasting plasma glucose ≥100 and <126 mg/dL
- Impaired glucose tolerance: 2-h plasma glucose 140–199 mg/dL
- HbA$_{1c}$ 5.7–6.4%

Prevention/Delay of Type 2 DM in Patients with Pre-diabetes
- Lifestyle modification (most effective)
  - Weight loss (target 7% loss) if overweight
  - Reduction in total and saturated dietary fat
  - High dietary fiber (14 g fiber/1000 kcal) and whole grains
  - Mediterranean diet and extra-virgin olive oil
  - Exercise (at least 150 min/wk of moderate activity, such as walking)
- Pharmacologic
  - Metformin (850 mg q12h) (less effective than lifestyle modification)
  - Valsartan (beginning 80 mg/d and increased to 160 mg/d after 2 wk as tolerated) slightly reduces risk of developing DM but does not reduce rate of cardiovascular events.
  - Acarbose (100 mg q8h) (less effective than lifestyle modification)

Management of Diabetes

Hospital and Nursing Home Settings
- Target glycemic control:
  - If critically ill, 140–180 mg/dL, which usually requires IV insulin infusion.
  - If noncritically ill, there are no clear evidence-based guidelines, but fasting <140 mg/dL and random <180 mg/dL are suggested (might be relaxed if severe comorbidities [ADA]).
  - If good nutritional intake, scheduled basal and prandial insulin doses with correction doses with rapid-acting analog (aspart, glulisine, or lispro).[BC]
    - If npo or poor oral intake, basal plus correction dose only.
  - If insulin-naive, patient can initiate insulin at total daily dose of 0.3 U/kg, half as long-acting (basal) and half as rapid-acting before each meal.
- Correction dose for older persons is 1 unit for every 40–50 mg/dL in excess of 140 mg/dL.
- Point-of-care blood glucose monitoring is used to guide insulin dosing.
- **Nursing home**: Do not use sliding-scale insulin in chronic glycemic management.[BC, CW]

Outpatient Settings

Evaluate for Comorbid Conditions (AGS, ADA): Depression (p 78), polypharmacy (p 16), cognitive impairment (p 335), UI (p 146), falls (p 113), pain (p 234) (AGS), PAD (claudication hx and assessment of pedal pulses) (p 61) (ADA). Stress test screening for CAD is of no benefit in asymptomatic patients (p 39).

Goals of Treatment (ADA, AGS):

Older adults who are functional, cognitively intact, and have significant life expectancy should receive diabetes care with goals similar to those developed for younger adults (ADA) (**Table 46**).

Patient Health	A_{1c} goal	FPG or PPG, mg/dL	Bedtime glucose, mg/dL	BP goal, mmHg	Lipid Tx
Table 46. Goals of Treatment for Older Patients with Diabetes Mellitus					
Healthy	7.0–7.5%	90–130	90–150	<140/80	Statin
Complex/intermediate[a]	7.5–8.0%	90–150	100–180	<140/80	Statin
Very complex/poor health[b]	8.5–9.0%	100–180	110–200	<150/90	Consider statin

Notes: FPG = fasting plasma glucose; PPG = post-prandial glucose.

[a] multiple (3+) coexisting chronic illness or 2+ IADL impairments or mild-to-moderate cognitive impairment

[b] LTC or end-stage chronic illnesses or moderate-to-severe cognitive impairment or 2+ ADL dependencies

Nonpharmacologic Interventions:

- Individualize medical nutrition tx to achieve tx goals (diet plus exercise is more effective than diet alone)
- Lifestyle (eg, regular exercise for ≥150 min/wk, resistance training 3×/wk if not contraindicated, alcohol and smoking cessation)
- Weight loss if overweight or obese
- Macronutrient (carbohydrate, protein, and fat) distribution should be based on individualized assessment of current eating patterns, preferences, and metabolic goals.
- Carbohydrate intake from vegetables, fruits, whole grains, legumes, and dairy products should be advised over intake from other carbohydrate sources, especially those that contain added fats, sugars, or sodium.
- Fructose consumed as "free fructose" (ie, naturally occurring in foods such as fruit) may result in better glycemic control compared to isocaloric intake of sucrose or starch, and free fructose is not likely to have detrimental effects on triglycerides as long as intake is not excessive (>12% energy).
- The amount of dietary saturated fat, cholesterol, and trans fat recommended for people with DM is the same as that recommended for the general population.
- Mediterranean diet high in monounsaturated fatty acids may be beneficial in glycemic control and cardiovascular risk reduction.
- For younger and healthier older adults with BMI >35 kg/m^2 who have type 2 DM that is difficult to control with lifestyle and pharmacotherapy, consider bariatric surgery.
- High-fiber diet (25 g insoluble and 25 g soluble/d)
- Limit alcohol intake to <1 drink/d in women and <2 drinks/d in men
- Patient and family education for self-management (reimbursed by Medicare)
- Psychosocial assessment and care

Pharmacologic Interventions for Type 2:
- Avoid using medications to achieve a HbA_{1c} <7.5% in most older adults.[CW]
- For healthy and younger people with DM with goal of <7.5%, if diet and exercise have not achieved target HbA_{1c} in 6 mo, begin drug tx.
- Management of glycemia: stepped tx* (ADA).
  Step 1: Metformin▲ (reduce dose in Stage 3 CKD; avoid in Stage 4 CKD) beginning 500 mg q12h or q24h; can titrate up q5–7d to max of 2000 mg/d if no AEs and blood glucose uncontrolled.
  Step 2: If HbA_{1c} target not achieved after 3 mo of monotherapy, add one of the following:
  ◦ Basal insulin (intermediate at bedtime or long-acting at bedtime or morning) 10 U or 0.2 U/kg; can increase by 2–4 U q3d depending on fasting blood glucose. When fasting blood glucose is at goal, recheck HbA_{1c} in 2–3 mo. If hypoglycemia or fasting blood glucose <70 mg/dL, reduce dose by 4U or 10%, whichever is greater. If above target HbA_{1c}, check pre-lunch, dinner, and bedtime blood glucose concentrations and add rapid- or intermediate-acting insulin (**Table 48**).
    ▪ Use 4-mm, 32-gauge needle if BMI <40 kg/m^2 and 8-mm, 32-gauge needle if BMI >40 kg/m^2. Inject at 90% without a pinch.
    ▪ Injection sites for human insulin: fastest onset is abdomen and slowest onset is thigh.
    ▪ Timing for prandial insulin: if blood glucose is in 100s, give 10 min before eating; if blood glucose is in 200s, give 20 min before eating; if blood glucose is in 300s, give 30 min before eating.
    ▪ If using fixed daily insulin doses, carbohydrate intake on a day-to-day basis should be consistent with respect to time and amount.
  ◦ Sulfonylurea (glipizide preferred)
  ◦ Less well-validated *Step 2* tx
    ▪ Thiazolidinediones
    ▪ DPP-4 enzyme inhibitors
    ▪ SGLT2 inhibitors
    ▪ GLP–1 receptor agonists
  Step 3: Combine *Step 2* agents. If HbA_{1c} target not achieved after 3 mo, add a third agent. D/C sulfonylureas and meglitinides when insulins are started.
  Step 4: Other agents (**Table 47**) may be appropriate for selected patients.

*Reinforce lifestyle modifications at every visit.

Table 47. Non-insulin Agents for Treating Diabetes Mellitus			
Medication	**Dosage**	**Formulations**	**Comments (Metabolism)**
Oral Agents			
Biguanide	Decrease hepatic glucose production; lower HbA_{1c} by 1.0–2.0%; do not cause hypoglycemia		
Metformin▲ *(Glucophage)*	500–2550 mg divided	T: 500, 850, 1000	Avoid in patients with CR ≥1.5 mg/dL (men) or ≥1.4 mg/dL (women) or eGFR <30 mL/1.73 m^2, HF, COPD, ↑ LFTs; hold before contrast radiologic studies; may cause weight loss (K)
(Glucophage XR)▲	1500–2000 mg/d	T: ER 500, 750	

(cont.)

Table 47. Non-insulin Agents for Treating Diabetes Mellitus (cont.)

Medication	Dosage	Formulations	Comments (Metabolism)
2nd-Generation Sulfonylureas	Increase insulin secretion; lower HbA$_{1c}$ by 1.0–2.0%; can cause hypoglycemia and weight gain; use of clarithromycin, levofloxacin, trimethoprim-sulfamethsoxazole, metronidazole, and ciprofloxacin are associated with increased risk of hypoglycemia		
✔ Glimepiride▲ *(Amaryl)*	4–8 mg once (begin 1–2 mg)	T: 1, 2, 4	Numerous drug interactions, long-acting (L, K)
✔ Glipizide▲ *(Glucotrol) (Glucotrol XL)*BC	2.5–40 mg once or divided 5–20 mg once	T: 5, 10 T: ER 2.5, 5, 10	Short-acting (L, K) Long-acting (L, K)
Glyburide▲ (generic or *Diaβeta, Micronase)*	1.25–20 mg once or divided	T: 1.25, 2.5, 5	Long-acting, ↑ risk of hypoglycemia; not recommended for use in older adults (L, K)
Micronized glyburide *(Glynase)*	1.5–12 mg once	T: 1.5, 3, 4.5, 6	Long-acting, ↑ risk of hypoglycemia; not recommended for use in older adults (L, K)
α-*Glucosidase Inhibitors*	Delay glucose absorption; lower HbA$_{1c}$ by 0.5–1%; can cause hypoglycemia and weight gain		
Acarbose▲ *(Precose)*	50–100 mg q8h, just ac; start with 25 mg/d	T: 25, 50, 100	GI AEs common, avoid if Cr >2 mg/dL, monitor LFTs (gut, K)
Miglitol *(Glyset)*	25–100 mg q8h, with 1st bite of meal; start with 25 mg/d	T: 25, 50, 100	Same as acarbose but no need to monitor LFTs (L, K)
DPP–4 Enzyme Inhibitors	Protect and enhance endogenous incretin hormones; lower HbA$_{1c}$ by 0.5–1%; do not cause hypoglycemia, weight neutral		
Alogliptin *(Nesina)*	25 mg once daily; 12.5 mg/d if CrCl 31–50 mL/min; 6.25 mg/d if CrCl 15–29 mL/min	T: 25, 12.5, 6.25	K
Linagliptin *(Tradjenta)*	5 mg	T: 5 mg	L
Sitagliptin *(Januvia)*	100 mg once daily as monotherapy or in combination with metformin or a thiazolidinedione; 50 mg/d if CrCl 31–50 mL/min; 25 mg/d if CrCl <30 mL/min	T: 25, 50, 100	
Saxagliptin *(Onglyza)*	5 mg; 2.5 mg if CrCl <50 mL/min	T: 2.5, 5	K
Meglitinides	Increase insulin secretion; lower HbA$_{1c}$ by 1.0–2.0%; can cause hypoglycemia and weight gain		
Nateglinide▲ *(Starlix)*	60–120 mg q8h	T: 60, 120	Give 30 min ac

(cont.)

Table 47. Non-insulin Agents for Treating Diabetes Mellitus (cont.)

Medication	Dosage	Formulations	Comments (Metabolism)
Repaglinide *(Prandin)*	0.5 mg q6–12h if HbA$_{1c}$ <8% or previously untreated; 1–2 mg q6–12h if HbA$_{1c}$ ≥8% or previously treated	T: 0.5, 1, 2	Give 30 min ac, adjust dosage at weekly intervals, potential for drug interactions, caution in hepatic, renal insufficiency (L)
Thiazolidinediones	Insulin resistance reducers; lower HbA$_{1c}$ by 0.5–1.5%; ↑ risk of HF; avoid if NYHA Class III or IV cardiac status; D/C if any decline in cardiac status; weight gain		
	Check LFTs at start, q2mo during 1st yr, then periodically; avoid if clinical evidence of liver disease or if serum ALT levels >2.5 times upper limit of normal; may increase risk of fractures in women (L, K)		
Pioglitazone▲ *(Actos)*	15 or 30 mg/d; max 45 mg/d as monotherapy, 30 mg/d in combination tx	T: 15, 30, 45	
Rosiglitazone *(Avandia)*	4 mg q 12–24h	T: 2, 4, 8	Prescribing and dispensing restrictions were removed in 2014.
SGLT2 Inhibitor	Decreases glucose reabsorption from kidney; lowers HbA$_{1c}$ by 0.5–1.5%; may cause ketoacidosis, genital mycotic infections, UTIs, decreased GFR		
Canagliflozin *(Invokana)*	100–300 mg/d	T: 100, 300	Initial dose 100 mg and no more than 100 mg if eGFR 45–59 mL/min/1.73 m^2; may increase fracture risk (L)
Dapaglifozin *(Farxiga)*	5–10 mg/d	T: 5, 10	Should not be used if eGFR <60 mL/min/1.73 m^2 (L)
Empagliflozin *(Jardiance)*	10–25 mg/d	T: 10, 25	Should not be used if eGRF <45 mL/min/1.73 m^2 (L)
Other			
Bromocriptine *(Cycloset)*	1.6–4.8 mg once	0.8	Start 0.8 and increase 0.8 weekly; lowers HbA$_{1c}$ by 0.5% (L)
Colesevelam *(Welchol)*	3750 mg once or 1875 mg twice	T: 625, 1875 pwd pk: 3750	Give with meals; lowers HbA$_{1c}$ by 0.5%; not absorbed (GI)
Combinations			
Glipizide and metformin▲BC *(METAGLIP)*	2.5/250 mg once; 20/2000 in 2 divided doses	T: 2.5/250, 2.5/500, 5/500	Avoid in patients >80 yr, Cr >1.5 mg/dL in men, Cr >1.4 mg/dL in women; see individual drugs (L, K)
Glyburide and metformin▲ *(Glucovance)*	1.25/250 mg initially if previously untreated; 2.5/500 mg or 5/500 mg q12h with meals; max 20/2000/d	T: 1.25/250, 2.5/500, 5/500	Starting dose should not exceed total daily dose of either drug; see individual drugs (L, K)
Pioglitazone and metformin *(ACTO plus met)*	15/850 mg q12–24h	T: 15/850	See individual drugs.

(cont.)

Table 47. Non-insulin Agents for Treating Diabetes Mellitus (cont.)

Medication	Dosage	Formulations	Comments (Metabolism)
Repaglinide and metformin (PrandiMet)	1/500 mg to 4/1000 mg twice q12h or q8h ac; max 10/2500 mg/d	T: 1/500, 2/500	See individual drugs.
Rosiglitazone and metformin (Avandamet)	2/500 mg/d or q12h; max 8/2000 mg/d	T: 2/500, 4/500, 2/1000, 4/1000	See individual drugs
Rosiglitazone and glimepiride (Avandaryl)	4/1 mg/d with first meal; max 8/4 mg/d	T: 4/1, 4/2, 4/4, 8/2, 8/4	See individual drugs
Pioglitazone and glimepiride (Duetact)	30/2 mg initially; max 45/8 mg	T: 30/2, 30/4	See individual drugs.
Saxagliptin and metformin (Kombiglyze XR)	5/1000–2000 mg once	T: ER 5/500, 5/1000, 2.5/1000	See individual drugs.
Sitagliptin and metformin (Janumet)	Begin with current doses; max 100/2000 mg in 2 divided doses	T: 50/500, 50/1000	See individual drugs.
(Janumet XR)	Begin with current doses; once a day doses	T:50/500, 50/1000, 100/1000 mg ER	
Linagliptin and metformin (Jentadueto)	Begin with current doses; twice daily with meals	T: 2.5/500, 2.5/800, 2.5/1000	See individual drugs.
Alogliptin and metformin (Kazano),	Begin with current doses	T: 12.5/500, 12.5/1000	See individual drugs.
Alogliptin and pioglitazone tablet (Oseni)	Begin with current doses	T: 25/15, 25/30, 25/45	See individual drugs.
Injectable Agents **GLP–1 Receptor Agonists**	Hypoglycemia common if combined with sulfonyl urea or insulin Lowers HbA$_{1c}$ by 0.7–1%; less likely to cause hypoglycemia than insulin or sulfonylureas; can cause weight loss. Risks include acute pancreatitis and possibly medullary thyroid cancer		
Albiglutide (Tanzeum)	30 or 50 mg SC once/wk	30, 50 mg single-dose pen	
Dulaglutide (Trulicity)	0.75 or 1.5 mg SC once/wk	0.75 mg/0.5 mL, 1.5 mg/0.5 mL single-dose pen or syringe	
Exenatide (Byetta)	5–10 mcg SC twice daily with meals	1.2-, 2.4-mL prefilled syringes	Avoid if CrCl <30 mL/min (K)
Extended release (Bydureon)	2 mg SC once/wk	2-mg prefilled syringes	Avoid if CrCl <30 mL/min (K)

(cont.)

Table 47. Non-insulin Agents for Treating Diabetes Mellitus (cont.)

Medication	Dosage	Formulations	Comments (Metabolism)
Liraglutide *(Victoza)*	0.6–1.8 mg SC once daily	0.6, 1.2, 1.8 (6 mg/mL) in prefilled, multidose "pen"	(L)
Amylin analog			
Pramlintide *(Symlin)*	60 mcg SC immediately before meals	0.6 mg/mL in 5-mL vial	Lowers HbA_{1c} by 0.4–0.7%; nausea common; reduce pre-meal dose of short-acting insulin by 50% (K)

- Management of tx-associated hypoglycemia (most common with insulin, sulfonylurea, α-glucosidase inhibitors, and meglitinides)
  ◦ If conscious, patients should have fast-acting carbohydrate (eg, glucose tabs, hard candy, paste [Instant Glucose] or instant fruit that provides 15–20 g of glucose.
  ◦ Effects may last only 15 min, so need to eat and recheck blood glucose.
  ◦ If hypoglycemia is severe (patient unconscious or cannot ingest carbohydrate), then glucagon 0.5–1 mg SC or IM.
  ◦ In medical settings, 25–50 g of D50 IV restores glucose quicker.
  ◦ If hypoglycemia unawareness or >1 episodes of severe hypoglycemia, then reevaluate regimen.
- Tx of comorbid conditions should be individualized based on life expectancy, patient preferences, and tx goals.
- Manage HTN (BP goal <140/80 mmHg; also HTN, p 50) including an ACEI or ARB. Other medications (eg, CCB, thiazide diuretic) may be needed. If patient is black, CCB or thiazide diuretic is preferred as initial tx (JNC 8).
- Treat lipid disorders (p 47).

Table 48. Insulin Preparations

Preparation	Onset	Peak	Duration	Number of Injections/d
Rapid-acting				
Insulin glulisine *(Apidra)*	20 min	0.5–1.5 h	3–4 h	3
Insulin lispro *(Humalog)*	15 min	0.5–1.5 h	3–4 h	3
Insulin aspart *(NovoLog)*	30 min	1–3 h	3–5 h	3
Inhaled (Afrezza)[a]	15 min	1 h	3–4 h	3
Regular (eg, *Humulin, Novolin*)[b]	0.5–1 h	2–3 h	5–8 h	1–3
Intermediate or long-acting				
NPH (eg, *Humulin, Novolin*)[b]	1–1.5 h	4–12 h	24 h	1–2
Insulin detemir *(Levemir)*	3–4 h	6–8 h	6–24 h depending on dose	1–2
Insulin glargine *(Lantus, Toujeo)*[c]	2–4 h	—	24 h	1

(cont.)

Table 48. Insulin Preparations (cont.)

Preparation	Onset	Peak	Duration	Number of Injections/d
Combinations				
Isophane insulin and regular insulin inj, premixed *(Novolin 70/30)*	See individual drugs	2–12 h	24 h	1–2
Insulin lispro protamine suspension and insulin lispro *(Humalog Mix 50/50; 75/25)*	See individual drugs			

[a] Available as 4-unit and 8-unit single-use cartridges administered by inhalation

[b] Also available as mixtures of NPH and regular in 50:50 proportions

[c] To convert from NPH dosing, give same number of units once a day. For patients taking NPH q12h, decrease the total daily units by 20%, and titrate on basis of response. Starting dosage in insulin-naive patients is 10 U once daily hs.

- ACEI or angiotensin II receptor blocker if albuminuria, HTN, or another cardiovascular risk factor. Check kidney function and serum potassium within 1–2 wk of initiation of tx, with each dosage increase, and at least yearly.
- ASA 75–162 mg/d if hx of heart disease but value in primary prevention is uncertain; consider using if 10-yr risk of CAD >10% (cvdrisk.nhlbi.nih.gov/calculator.asp); if allergic, clopidogrel 75 mg/d.
- Pneumococcal vaccination (PCV13 and PPSV23)
- Annual influenza vaccination
- Consider hepatitis B vaccination
- Smoking cessation

Monitoring

Initial

- Screen for PAD by checking pedal pulses and asking about claudication (p 61)
- Screen for signs and symptoms of cardiovascular autonomic neuropathy
- Comprehensive dilated eye and visual examinations by an ophthalmologist or optometrist who is experienced in management of diabetic retinopathy at time of diagnosis and at least annually if retinopathy or q2yr if not

Ongoing

- If multiple daily injections or using insulin pump, self-monitor blood glucose (SMBG) before meals and snacks, occasionally postprandially, at bedtime, before exercise, when patient suspects low blood glucose, after treating low blood glucose until patient is normoglycemic, and before critical tasks such as driving.
- The value of SMBG in type 2 DM is unclear. For older adults treated with medications that do not cause hypoglycemia, SMBG may be unnecessary and there is no consensus about the frequency of monitoring patients on medications that may cause hypoglycemia.

More frequently than annually

- BP evaluation at each visit
- HbA$_{1c}$ twice/yr in patients with stable glycemic control; quarterly, if poor control
- Insensate feet should be inspected at every visit

Annually or less frequently

- Annual comprehensive foot examination, including monofilament testing at 4 plantar sites (great toe and base of first, third, and fifth metatarsals), plus testing any one of: tuning fork, pinprick sensation, ankle reflexes, or vibration perception threshold; assessment of foot pulses; and inspection. Well-fitted walking or athletic shoes may be of benefit; refer those with sensory and structural abnormalities to foot care specialists.
- Lipid profiles may be helpful in monitoring adherence but may not be needed once stable on tx.
- Annual test for microalbuminuria by measuring albumin:Cr ratio in a random spot collection
- Annual serum Cr

ADRENAL INSUFFICIENCY

Common Causes

Secondary (more common; mineralocorticoid function is preserved, no hyperkalemia or hyperpigmentation, dehydration is less common)
- Abrupt discontinuation of chronic glucocorticoid administration
- Megestrol acetate
- Brain irradiation
- Traumatic brain injury
- Pituitary tumors

Primary (less common)
- Autoimmune
- Tuberculosis

Evaluation

- Basal (morning) plasma cortisol >18 mcg/dL excludes adrenal insufficiency, and <3 mcg/dL is diagnostic.
- ACTH stimulation test: tetracosactin *(Synacthen Depot)* 250 mcg IV; best administered in the morning; peak value at 30–60 min >18 mcg/dL is normal, <15 mcg/dL is diagnostic.
- If adrenal insufficiency is diagnosed with high ACTH (eg, >100 pg/mL), then insufficiency is primary.

Pharmacotherapy

For corticosteroid dose equivalencies, see **Table 49**. Hydrocortisone preferred for adrenal insufficiency (10–12 mg/m²/d) in 2 or 3 divided doses. If primary adrenal insufficiency, add fludrocortisone▲ to glucocorticoids.

Table 49. Corticosteroids					
Medication	**Approx Equivalent Dose (mg)**	**Relative Anti-inflammatory Potency**	**Relative Mineralo-corticoid Potency**	**Biologic Half-life (h)**	**Formulations**
Betamethasone▲ *(Celestone)*	0.6–0.75	20–30	0	36–54	T: 0.6; S: 0.6 mg/5 mL
Cortisone▲ *(Cortone)*	25	0.8	2	8–12	T: 5; S: 50 mg/mL

(cont.)

Table 49. Corticosteroids (cont.)

Medication	Approx Equivalent Dose (mg)	Relative Anti-inflammatory Potency	Relative Mineralo-corticoid Potency	Biologic Half-life (h)	Formulations
Dexamethasone▲ (Decadron, Dexone, Hexadrol)	0.75	20–30	0	36–54	T: 0.25, 0.5, 0.75, 1, 1.5, 2, 4; S: elixir 0.5 mg/5 mL; inj
Fludrocortisone▲ (Florinef)*	NA	10	4	12–36	T: 0.1
Hydrocortisone▲ (Cortef, Hydrocortone)	20	1	2	8–12	T: 5, 10, 20 S: 10 mg/5 mL; Inj
Methylprednisolone▲ (eg, Medrol, Solu-Medrol, Depo-Medrol)	4	5	0	18–36	T: 2, 4, 8, 16, 24, 32; Inj
Prednisolone▲ (eg, Delta-Cortef, Prelone Syrup, Pediapred)	5	4	1	18–36	S: 5 mg/5 mL syr 5, 15 mg/5 mL
Prednisone▲ (Deltasone, Liquid Pred, Meticorten, Orasone)	5	4	1	18–36	T: 1, 2.5, 5, 10, 20, 50 S: 5 mg/5 mL
Triamcinolone (eg, Aristocort, Kenacort, Kenalog)	4	5	0	18–36	T: 1, 2, 4, 8; S: syr 4 mg/5 mL

Note: NA = not available.

*Usually given for orthostatic hypotension at 0.1 mg q8–24h (max 1 mg/d) and at 0.05–0.2 mg/d for primary adrenal insufficiency.

Management

Stress doses of corticosteroids for patients with severe illness, injury, or undergoing surgery: In emergency situations, do not wait for test results. Give hydrocortisone 100 mg IV bolus (or if patient has not been previously diagnosed, dexamethasone 4 mg IV bolus). Also treat with IV fluids (eg, saline). For less severe stress (eg, minor illness), double or triple usual oral replacement dosage for 3 d.

- For chronic adrenal insufficiency, hydrocortisone in 2 or 3 divided doses (total dose of 10–12 mg/m²/d). Alternatives are dexamethasone or prednisone.
- For minor surgery (eg, hernia repair), hydrocortisone 25 mg/d on day of surgery and return to usual dosage on following day.
- For moderate surgical stress (eg, cholecystectomy, joint replacement), total 50–75 mg/d on the day of surgery and the first postoperative day, then usual dosage on the second postoperative day.
- For major surgical procedures (eg, cardiac bypass), total 100–150 mg/d given in divided doses for 2–3 d, then return to usual dosage.

VISUAL IMPAIRMENT

Definition

Visual acuity 20/40 or worse; severe visual impairment (legal blindness) 20/200 or worse in the better eye.

Evaluation

- Acuity testing
  - Near vision: check each eye independently with glasses using handheld Rosenbaum card at 14" or Lighthouse Near Acuity Test at 16". *Note:* Distance must be accurate.
  - Far vision: Snellen wall chart at 20'
- Visual fields (by confrontation)
- Ophthalmoscopy
- Emergent referral for acute change in vision
- Medication review for drugs associated with blurry vision (eg, amiodarone, minocycline, sildenafil, tamoxifen) and any agent with anticholinergic properties

Prevention

Biennial full eye examinations for people >65 yr old, annually for people with DM and retinopathy.

SPECIFIC CONDITIONS ASSOCIATED WITH VISUAL IMPAIRMENT

Refractive Error

The most common cause of visual impairment. Incorrect refraction may account for 20% of IADL dysfunction.

Cataracts

Lens opacity on ophthalmoscopic examination. Risk factors: age, sun exposure, smoking, corticosteroids, DM, alcohol, low vitamin intake, quetiapine. Smoking cessation reduces risk for cataract extraction.

Nonpharmacologic Treatment:

- Reduce UV light exposure.
- Surgery (American Academy of Ophthalmology criteria):
  - if visual function no longer meets the patient's needs and cataract surgery is likely to improve vision
  - when cataract coexists with lens-induced disease (eg, glaucoma) or other eye disease requiring unrestricted monitoring (eg, diabetic retinopathy)
  - The risk of bleeding is small when antithrombotic agents are continued in the perioperative period. Recommendation to hold these agents should be individualized based on both consequences of visual loss from bleeding and CV risk.
  - Do not perform preoperative medical tests for eye surgery without specific indications. Reasonable indications include an ECG in patients with heart disease, serum K^+ in patients on diuretics, and serum glucose in patients with DM.[CW]

Age-related Macular Degeneration (AMD)

Atrophy of cells in the central macular region of retinal pigmented epithelium; on ophthalmoscopic examination, white-yellow patches (drusen) or hemorrhage and scars in advanced stages. Risk factors: age, smoking, sun exposure, family hx, white race (14% of white Americans by age 80). AMD has "wet" and "dry" forms.

- Dry AMD: Accounts for ~90% of cases, is characterized by abnormalities in the retinal pigment with focal drusen, and has a natural hx of slow gradual loss of vision; may convert to the wet form.
- Wet AMD or neovascular type: Often characterized by rapid visual loss. Early intervention when the dry form converts to the wet form saves vision.

Nonpharmacologic Treatment

- Monitor daily for conversion from dry to wet form using Amsler grid.
- Patients with large drusen most at risk of conversion to wet AMD.
- Dietary modification reduces risk of progression to neovascular AMD: high intake of beta-carotene, vitamin C, zinc, n-3 long-chain polyunsaturated fatty acids, and fish.

Pharmacotherapy of Wet AMD

- Vascular endothelial growth factor (VEGF) inhibitors reduce neovascularization, eg, bevacizumab *(Avastin)* or ranibizumab *(Lucentis)* or pegaptanib *(Macugen)* intravitreal monthly or aflibercept *(Eylea, Zaltrap)* q8wk for up to 2 yr; maintains vision in the majority and improves it in a significant minority. Complications of the intraocular injections include uveitis, cataract, increased IOP, retinal detachment or endophthalmitis and visual loss in 1–2% of patients.

Pharmacotherapy of Both Wet and Dry AMD

- In intermediate or more advanced stages of dry AMD and all stages of wet AMD, zinc oxide 80 mg, cupric oxide 2 mg, lutein 10 mg, zeaxanthin 2 mg, vitamin C 500 mg, and vitamin E 400 IU taken in divided doses q12h reduces risk of progression (AREDS2 preparation).

Diabetic Retinopathy

Microaneurysms, dot and blot hemorrhages on ophthalmoscopy with proliferative retinopathy ischemia and vitreous hemorrhage. Risk factors: chronic hyperglycemia, smoking. Screen all type 2 DM at time of diagnosis, and at least annually if any retinopathy is found; if none at baseline, then rescreen every 2 yr.

Treatment

- Annual ophthalmologic evaluation determines the level of retinopathy (ie, mild, moderate, severe), whether retinopathy is proliferative or nonproliferative, and whether macular edema is present.
- The combination of these features determines the follow-up interval of 1–12 mo.
- Based on severity, laser tx may be focal, scatter, or panretinal, photocoagulation, or vitrectomy.
- The VEGF inhibitor afliberacept may be effective for macular edema.

Diabetic Management

Tailor glycemic control based on comorbidities and life expectancy (Diabetes, p 94).

Glaucoma

Characteristic optic cupping and nerve damage, and loss of peripheral visual fields. Risk factors: black race, age, family hx, increased ocular pressures. Most common cause of blindness in black Americans. Most patients need 6-mo follow-up appointments.

- Primary open-angle glaucoma is more common and asymptomatic until severe visual loss occurs. Initial tx may be either pharmacologic or laser surgery.
- Angle-closure glaucoma, while a less common disease, has both acute and chronic variants and is painful if acute, requiring emergent management.

∘ Angle-closure glaucoma is a surgical disease, although topicals are used preoperatively to control IOP.

Nonpharmacologic Treatments

- Open angle—laser trabeculoplasty is first-line nonpharmacologic tx. Surgical procedures (filtration, shunts, etc) have complications such as scarring and visual loss.
- Angle closure (both acute and chronic)—laser peripheral iridotomy

Pharmacotherapy

- Treat when there is optic nerve damage or visual field loss (**Table 50**); goal is reducing IOP. Prostaglandin analogs are often first-line tx.
- Combining drugs from different classes reduces pressure more than monotherapy.
- Patients must use proper technique both for benefit and to avoid systemic drug-related AEs, ie, instill 1 gtt under lower lid, close eye for at least 1 min to reduce systemic absorption; repeat if a second drop is needed. Systemic absorption is further reduced by teaching the patient to compress the lacrimal sac for 15–30 sec after instilling a drop. Always wait 5 min before instilling a second type of drop.

Table 50. Medications for Treating Glaucoma		
Medication	**Dosage**	**Comments (Metabolism)**
α₂-Agonists (bottles with purple caps)		*Class AEs:* low BP, fatigue, drowsiness, dry mouth, dry nose, ocular AEs, hyperemia, burning, foreign-body sensation (unknown)
Brimonidine▲ 0.1%, 0.15%, 0.2%	1 gtt q8–12h	
α-β Agonist		
Dipivefrin▲ 0.1%	1 gtt q12h	HTN, headache, tachycardia, arrhythmia (eye, L)
β-Blockers (bottles with blue or yellow caps)		*Class AEs:* hypotension, bradycardia, HF, bronchospasm, anxiety, depression, confusion, hallucination, diarrhea, nausea, cramps, lethargy, weakness, masking of hypoglycemia, sexual dysfunction. Avoid in asthma, bradycardia, COPD (L)
✓ Betaxolol▲ 0.25%, 0.5%	1–2 gtt q12h	
✓ Carteolol▲ 1%	1 gtt q12h	
✓ Levobunolol▲ 0.25%, 0.5%	1 gtt q12h	
✓ Metipranolol▲ 0.3%	1 gtt q12h	
✓ Timolol drops▲ 0.25%, 0.5%	1 gtt q12h	Not all formulations available as generic
Cholinergic Agonists (bottles with green caps)		*Class AEs:* brow ache, corneal toxicity, red eye, retinal detachment
Pilocarpine gel 4%	1/2" qhs	Systemic cholinergic effects are rare (tissues, K)
Pilocarpine▲ 0.5–6%	1 gtt q6h	
Miotic, Cholinesterase Inhibitor (bottle with green cap)		*Class AEs:* sweating, tremor, headache, salivation, confusion, high or low BP, bradycardia, bronchoconstriction, urinary frequency, GI upset (tissues, K)
Echothiophate 0.125%	1 gtt q12h	

(cont.)

Table 50. Medications for Treating Glaucoma (cont.)

Medication	Dosage	Comments (Metabolism)
Carbonic Anhydrase Inhibitors (bottles with orange caps)		
Topical		Caution in kidney failure and after corneal transplant (K)
✓Brinzolamide 1%	1 gtt q8h	
✓Dorzolamide▲ 2%	1 gtt q8h	
Oral		
Acetazolamide▲ 125–500 mg, SR 500 mg	250–500 mg q6–12h, SR 500 mg q12h	*Class AEs:* fatigue, weight loss, bitter taste, paresthesias, depression, COPD exacerbation, cramps, nausea, diarrhea, kidney failure, blood dyscrasias, hypokalemia, myopia, renal calculi acidosis; not recommended in kidney failure (K), (L, K)
Methazolamide▲ 25–50 mg	50–100 mg q8–12h	
***Prostaglandin Analogs* (bottles with turquoise caps)**		First-line tx *Class AEs:* change in eye color and periorbital tissues, hyperemia, itching
✓Bimatoprost▲ 0.03%	1 gtt qhs	(L, K, F)
✓Latanoprost▲ 0.005%	1 gtt qhs	(L)
Tafluprost* 0.0015%	1 gtt qhs	(L)
✓Travoprost 0.004%	1 gtt qhs	(L)
Combinations		
Dorzolamide/timolol▲ 0.5%/0.2%	1 gtt q12h	See individual agents (K, L)
Brimonidine/timolol 0.2%/0.5%	1 gtt q12h	See individual agents (K, L)
Brinzolamide/brimonidine 1%/0.2%	1 gtt 2×/d	See individual agents (unknown, L)

✓ = preferred for treating older adults, * = preservative-free

Note: Patients may not know names of drugs but instead refer to them by the color of the bottle cap. The usual colors are listed above.

ADDITIONAL CONSIDERATIONS IN MANAGEMENT OF EYE DISORDERS

Topical Steroid Treatment

Are prescribed for serious ocular inflammatory disorders and require monitoring by an ophthalmologist. Serious and potentially vision-threatening adverse effects can occur from chronic topical corticosteroid use. Indications for topical steroid use include:

- allergic marginal corneal ulcer
- anterior segment inflammation
- bacterial conjunctivitis
- chorioretinitis, choroiditis
- cyclitis
- endophthalmitis
- Graves' ophthalmopathy
- herpes zoster ocular infection with appropriate antiviral tx
- iritis
- nonspecific keratitis
- superficial punctate keratitis
- postoperative ocular inflammation
- optic neuritis
- sympathetic ophthalmia
- diffuse posterior uveitis
- vernal keratoconjunctivitis

Topical steroids are also used for corneal injury from thermal, chemical, or radiation burns or penetration of foreign bodies.

Low-vision Services

- Address the full range of functional visual impairment from blindness to partial sight. Refer patients with uncompensated visual loss that reduces function.
- Recommend and provide training for optical aids:
  - Electronic video magnifiers
  - Spectacle-mounted telescopes for distance vision, including driving
  - Closed-circuit television to enlarge text
  - A variety of high-technology devices are available (www.lighthouse.org).
  - iPad and iPhone apps are an inexpensive substitute for text-to-speech conversion, lighted magnifiers, big clocks, etc.
- Environmental modifications that improve function include color contrast, floor lamps to reduce glare, motion sensors to turn on lights, talking clocks, spoken medication reminders.
- Many states have "Services for the Visually Impaired" through the health department.

Dual Sensory Impairment (DSI)

- 9–21% of adults >70 yr old have loss of both vision and hearing.
- Compared with single-sensory impairment, DSI is more often associated with depression, poor self-rated health, reduced social participation, and IADL, and cognitive impairment.
- Management currently limited to vibrating devices such as alarm clocks, door bells, smoke alarms, etc.

RED EYE

The "red eye" is an eye with vascular congestion: some conditions that cause this pose a threat to vision and warrant prompt ophthalmologic referral (**Table 51**). Acute conjunctivitis and allergic conjunctivitis are common causes of red eye. Diagnosis and tx of those conditions are discussed below.

Table 51. Signs and Symptoms of Serious Conditions in Patients with Red Eye	
Red Flag Signs and Symptom	**Potentially Dangerous Condition(s)**
Lid or lacrimal sac swelling or proptosis	Orbital cellulitis, orbital tumor
Subnormal visual acuity, foreign-body sensation, severe pain, photophobia, or circumcorneal hyperemia (ciliary flush)	Keratitis, anterior uveitis; acute angle closure glaucoma; endophthalmitis, episcleritis and scleritis
Proptosis, chemosis, visual loss, and ophthalmoplegia	Cavernous sinus arteriovenous fistula

Acute Conjunctivitis

Symptoms: Red eye, foreign body sensation, discharge, photophobia

Signs: Conjunctival hyperemia and discharge

Etiology: Viral, bacterial, chlamydial

Viral Versus Bacterial:

Viral—profuse tearing, minimal exudate, preauricular adenopathy common, monocytes in stained scrapings and exudates; may be part of upper respiratory infection. Extremely contagious; wash hands frequently and use separate towels to avoid spread.

Bacterial—moderate tearing, profuse exudation, preauricular adenopathy uncommon, bacteria and polymorphonuclear cells in stained scrapings and exudates

Both—minimal itching, generalized hyperemia, occasional sore throat and fever

Treatment: Most are viral; do not treat viral infections with antibiotics; if diagnosis is uncertain, patients may be followed closely for worsening that would warrant antibiotics.[cw]

- Treat viral infections with artificial tears and cool compresses.
- If purulent discharge, suspect bacterial. Many cases resolve without antibiotics and without adverse effect on visual function. Antibiotics reduce duration of symptoms. Some recommend use of erythromycin or polymyxin/trimethropim. Avoid floxacins, which are expensive and select resistant organisms (**Table 52**). If severe, obtain culture and Gram stain, then start tx.
- If signs and symptoms do not improve in 24–48 h on tx for bacterial conjuntivitis, refer to ophthalmologist.
- If severe purulence or if patient wears contact lenses, refer to ophthalmologist immediately.

Table 52. Treatment for Acute Bacterial Conjunctivitis[a]

Medication/Formulations[b]	Comments
First Line (inexpensive, narrow spectrum)	
Erythromycin▲ 5 mg/g oint	Good if staphylococcal blepharitis is present
Trimethoprim and polymyxin▲ 1 mg/mL, 10,000 IU/mL sol	Well tolerated but some gaps in coverage
Second Line (more expensive, broad spectrum)	
Besifloxacin *(Besivance)* 0.6% sol	Very broad spectrum, a first choice in severe cases, well tolerated, expensive
Ciprofloxacin *(Ciloxan)* 0.3% sol▲, 0.3% oint	See besifloxacin
Gatifloxacin *(Tequin)* 0.3% sol	See besifloxacin
Moxifloxacin *(Avelox)* 0.5% sol	See besifloxacin
Ofloxacin▲ 0.3% sol, 0.3% oint	See besifloxacin
Tobramycin *(Tobrex)* 3 mg/g oint, 3 mg/mL sol▲	Well tolerated but more corneal toxicity

[a] Do not use steroid or steroid-antibiotic preparations in initial tx.

[b] In mild cases, solution is applied q6h and gel or oint q12h for 5–7 d. In more severe cases, solution is applied q2–3h and oint q6h; as the eye improves, solution is applied q6h and oint q12h.

Allergic Conjunctivitis

Symptoms: Prominent itching, watery discharge accompanied by nasal stuffiness (see allergic rhinitis, p 287)

Signs: Eyelid edema, conjunctival bogginess, and hyperemia (all bilateral)

Etiology: IgE–mediated hypersensitivity to airborne pollen

Treatment: Dilute and clear allergen with artificial tears. Start a nonsedating oral H_1 antihistamine (**Table 114**); if symptoms persist, add or substitute a topical H_1 antihistamine or topical mast cell stabilizer/antihistamine (**Table 53**). If these are ineffective, try topical ketorolac (**Table 53**). Nasal steroids reduce ocular symptoms to some degree (**Table 114**). If the above do not relieve symptoms, refer to an ophthalmologist (topical steroids [p 108] may be necessary but should be prescribed only by an ophthalmologist). Oral mast cell stabilizers are not used in the tx of acute ocular allergies. The OTC vasoconstrictor/antihistamines are for short-term use only (**Table 53**).

DRY EYE SYNDROME

Symptoms: Itchy or sandy eyes (foreign body sensation), visual disturbance.

Etiology: Altered tear film composition, reduced tear production, poor lid function, environment, drug-induced causes (eg, anticholinergics, estrogens, SSRIs, diuretics), or diseases such as Sjögren syndrome; refer to ophthalmology for diagnostic assistance.

Therapy:

- Artificial tear formulations (eg, *HypoTears*) administer q1–6h prn. Preservatives may cause eye irritation. Preservative-free preparations, available in single-dose vials, are expensive. Ointment preparations can be used at night or also during the day in severe cases.

- *Lacrisert* is an insert that gradually releases hydroxypropyl cellulose after placement in the inferior conjunctival sac; for moderate to severe dry eye. Apply 1–2×/d.

- Environmental strategies: room humidifiers, frequent blinking, and swim goggles or moisture chambers fit to eye glasses are all helpful.

- Cyclosporine ophthalmic emulsion 0.05% *(Restasis)* 1 gtt OU q12h. Indicated when tear production is suppressed by inflammation. May take 4–6 wk to achieve results. Does not increase tears in people using topical anti-inflammatories or punctal plugs. AEs: burning, hyperemia, discharge, pain, blurring. Patients should have a complete ophthalmologic examination before receiving a prescription.

- Temporary or permanent punctal plugs; do not place punctal plugs for mild dry eye before trying other medical tx.[CW]

Table 53. Topical Therapy for Allergic Conjunctivitis

Category/Medication	Formulation and Dosing	Adverse Events[a]
H₁ Antihistamines		
Alcaftadine *(Lastacaft)*	0.25%, 1 gtt OU q24h	*Class effects*: Itching, erythema, headache, rhinitis, dysgeusia, cold syndrome, headache, keratitis
Azelastine▲ *(Optivar)*	0.05%, 1 gtt OU q6h	
Bepotastine *(Bepreve)*	1.5%, 1 gtt OU q12h	
Emedastine *(Emadine)*	0.05%, 1 gtt OU q12h	
Epinastine *(Elestat)*	0.5%, 1 gtt OU q12h	
Ketotifen▲ *(Zaditor, Alaway)*	0.025%, 1 gtt OU q8–12h	
Olopatadine *(Patanol)*	0.1%, 1 gtt OU q12h	
Olopatadine *(Pataday)*	0.2%, 1 gtt OU q24h	
NSAID		
Ketorolac▲ *(Acular)*	0.5%, 1 gtt OU q6h	Ocular irritation, burning
Mast cell stabilizers$_b$		
Lodoxamide *(Alomide)*	0.1%, 1–2 gtt OU q6h	Ocular irritation, burning
Nedocromil *(Alocril)*	2%, 1–2 gtt OU q12h	Headache, ocular irritation, burning
Pemirolast *(Alamast)*	0.1%, 1–2 gtt OU q6h	Headache, rhinitis, flu-like symptoms, ocular irritation, burning

(cont.)

Table 53. Topical Therapy for Allergic Conjunctivitis (cont.)

Category/Medication	Formulation and Dosing	Adverse Events[a]
Vasoconstrictor/Antihistamine combinations (for short-term use only)		
Naphazoline▲ (0.03%, 0.1%, 0.13%)	OTC; 1-2 gtt q3–4h as needed for no more than a few days	*Class effects:* Caution in heart disease, HTN, BPH, narrow angle glaucoma; chronic use can cause follicular reactions or contact dermatitis
Pheniramine maleate (0.3–0.315%)/naphazoline hydrochloride (0.025–0.027%)▲	OTC; 1–2 gtt up to q6h for no more than a few days	

[a] Any may cause stinging, which can by reduced by refrigerating drops.

[b] Not used in acute allergy; use when allergen exposure can be predicted, and use well in advance of exposure.

DEFINITION

An event whereby an individual unexpectedly comes to rest on the ground or another lower level without known loss of consciousness (AGS/BGS Clinical Practice Guideline: Prevention of Falls in Older Persons, 2010). Excludes falls from major intrinsic event (eg, seizure, stroke, syncope) or overwhelming environmental hazard.

ETIOLOGY

Typically multifactorial. Composed of intrinsic (eg, poor balance, weakness, chronic illness, visual or cognitive impairment), extrinsic (eg, polypharmacy), and environmental (eg, poor lighting, no safety equipment, loose carpets) factors. Commonly a nonspecific sign for one of many acute illnesses in older adults.

RISK FACTORS

Table 54. Risk Factors and Medications Associated with Falls

Risk Factor	OR* for all fallers (those who fell at least once during follow-up)	OR for recurrent fallers (those who fell at least twice during follow-up)
Hx of falls	2.8	3.5
Parkinson disease	2.7	2.8
Gait deficit	2.1	2.2
Walking aid use	2.2	3.1
Vertigo	1.8	2.3
Depression	1.6	1.9
Fear of falling	1.6	2.5
Poor self-rated health	1.5	1.8
Rheumatic disease	1.5	1.6
Cognitive impairment	1.4	1.6
Urinary incontinence	1.4	1.7
Pain (yes/no)	1.4	1.6
Visual deficit, particularly unilateral visual loss	1.4	1.6
Comorbidity	1.2	1.5
Balance deficit	ND	ND
Hearing impairment	1.2	1.5
Impaired ADLs	ND	ND
>2 pain locations	ND	ND
Higher pain severity	ND	ND
Pain interference with activities	ND	ND

(cont.)

Table 54. Risk Factors and Medications Associated with Falls (cont.)

Risk Factor	OR* for all fallers (those who fell at least once during follow-up)	OR for recurrent fallers (those who fell at least twice during follow-up)
Medications Associated with Falls		
Sedatives (Avoid.[BC]), hypnotics (including benzodiazepines)	1.4	1.5
Anticonvulsants (Avoid unless safer alternatives are not available; avoid except if seizure disorder.[BC])	1.9	2.7
Antipsychotics (Avoid.[BC])	ND	ND
Antiarrhythmics (Class 1A)	ND	ND
Antihypertensives	ND	ND
Anxiolytics, including benzodiazepines (Avoid.[BC])	ND	ND
Diuretics	ND	ND
MAOIs, SSRIs, TCAs (Avoid.[BC])	ND	ND
Skeletal muscle relaxants (Avoid.[BC])	ND	ND
Systemic glucocorticoids	ND	ND

*Odds ratio in community dwelling older adults from Deandrea S et al. *Epidemiology* 2010;21(5):658–668.
ND: no data on OR or unable to calculate; associations noted in other studies

SCREENING

Fall risk screening or assessment is a quality measure included in the CMS Physician Quality Reporting System (PQRS), Meaningful Use Incentive Program, Medicare Annual Wellness Visit, and Accountable Care Organization programs. Tool kits available to guide screening and tailored intervention from AHRQ in nursing facilities (AHRQ 2010; www.ahrq.gov/professionals/systems/long-term-care/resources/injuries/fallspx) and in hospitals (AHRQ 2013; www.ahrq.gov/professionals/systems/hospital/fallpxtoolkit/index.html) and Stopping Elderly Accidents, Deaths and Injuries (STEADI; Stevens JA et al. *Health Promot Pract* 2013;14[5]:706–714). www.cdc.gov/Steadi/webinar.html

See **Figure 5** for recommended assessment strategies. USPSTF does not recommend multifactorial assessment, although small benefit (6% reduction in fall risk; 11% when risk factors managed).

Assessment Considerations

USPSTF recommends 3 factors to identify increased risk for falls in older adults: hx of falls, hx of mobility problems, and poor performance on the timed Get-up and Go Test.

Assess risk of falling as part of routine primary healthcare visit (at least annually). Risk of falling significantly increases as number of risk factors increases. Falling is more frequent in ambulatory residents in long-term care and in acute care settings.

- Screen for fall risk in nursing home (Morse Fall Scale, www.primaris.org/node/816).
- Screen for fall risk in acute care setting (Hendrich II Fall Risk Model, consultgerirn.org/uploads/File/trythis/try_this_8.pdf).
- Assess for risk factors (**Table 54**) using a multidisciplinary approach, including PT and OT if problems with gait, balance, or lower extremity strength identified.

Gait, Balance, and Mobility Assessment

- Functional gait: observe patient rising from chair, walking (stride length, base of gait, velocity, symmetry), turning, sitting (Get-up and Go Test)
- Balance: semi-tandem, and full tandem stance; Functional Reach test; Berg Balance Scale (especially retrieve object from floor); Short Physical Performance Battery (SPPB)

Figure 5. Assessment and Prevention of Falls

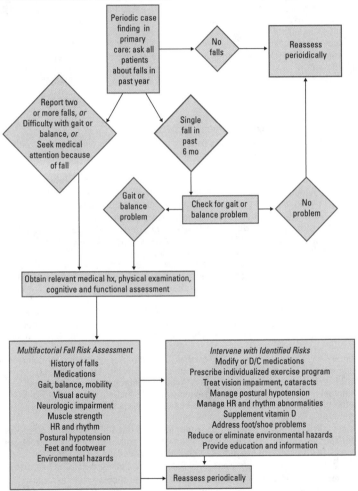

Sources: American Geriatrics Society and British Geriatrics Society. *Clinical Practice Guideline for the Prevention of Falls in Older Persons*. New York: American Geriatrics Society; 2010; www.medcats.com/FALLS/frameset.htm; and Pighills AC et al. *J Am Geriatr Soc* 2011;59:26–33.

- Mobility: observe patient's use and fit of assistive device (eg, cane, walker) or personal assistance, extent of ambulation, restraint use, footwear evaluation.
  - Cane fitting: top of the cane should be at the top of the greater trochanter or at the break of the wrist when patient stands with arms at side; when the patient holds the cane, there is approximately a 15-degree bend at the elbow. Canes are most often used to improve balance but can also be used to reduce weight-bearing on the opposite leg.
  - Walker fitting: walkers are prescribed when a cane does not offer sufficient stability. Front-wheeled walkers allow a more natural gait and are easier for cognitively impaired patients to use. Four-wheeled rolling walkers (ie, rollators) have the advantage for a smoother faster gait, but require more coordination because of the brakes; however, they are good for outside walking because the larger wheels move more easily over sidewalks.
- ADLs: complete ADL skill evaluation, including use of adaptive equipment and mobility aids as appropriate.
- Complete environmental assessment, including home safety, and mitigate identified hazards.

PREVENTION

See **Figure 5** for recommended prevention strategies.

Recommendations below are primarily based on studies of community-dwelling older adults with limited evidence from RCTs regarding single or multifactorial interventions in the long-term care setting and in cognitively impaired.

- Begin fall prevention program targeting interventions for risk factors (**Table 55**).
  - Consider balance of benefits and harms, based on prior falls circumstances, medical comorbid conditions, and patient values, in providing comprehensive intervention.
- Metaanalysis of individualized home-based exercise programs showed 16% reduction in falls in those not recently discharged from hospital but no significant differences in injurious falls or fractures. Physical activity, balance, mobility, and muscle strength improved (Hill K et al. *Maturitas.* 2015;82(1):72–84).
- Up to 3 preventive home visits that included risk assessment, home counseling, and booster showed a 37% reduction in the rate of falls in RCT with functionally impaired patients aged 80 and older, although cost-effectiveness is a concern. (Luck T et al. *Clin Interv Aging* 2013;8:697–702.)
- Exercise fall prevention programs with community-dwelling older adults reduce the rate of falls and prevent injury from falls. Estimated reduction in injuries by 37% for all injurious falls, 43% for severe injurious falls, and 61% for falls resulting in fractures (El-Khoury F et al. *BMJ* 2013;347:1–13)
- Evidence-based programs advocated by the CDC and/or Administration for Community Living. Exercise: Tai Chi: Moving for Better Balance (or similar tai chi classes), OTAGO Exercise Program, Stay Safe, Stay Active. Multifactorial evidence-based educational programs: Stepping On, Prevention of falls in the elderly trial (PROFET), A Matter of Balance. Additional evidence based programs at www.cdc.gov/homeandrecreationalsafety/Falls/compendium.html.
- Additional CDC recommendations for visually impaired (eg, VIP trial home safety program) and for specific situations such as walking on ice and snow (eg, Yaktrax Walker). See www.cdc.gov/HomeandRecreationalSafety/Falls/compendium/1.2_otago.html
- See Prevention (p 270) or Musculoskeletal Disorders (p 194) for details on exercise.
- Recent metaanalysis of RCTs in long-term care facilities showed multifactorial interventions are most effective in reducing falls in long-term care facilities and hospitals. Inconsistent evidence exists for exercise and vitamin D as single interventions in long-term care facilities. No evidence for hip protectors and medication review in long-term care facilities. (Stubbs B et al. *Maturitas* 2015;81(3):335–42).

Table 55. Preventing Falls: Selected Risk Factors and Suggested Interventions	
Factors	**Suggested Interventions (Outcome Reduction*)**
General Risk	Offer: exercise program to include combination of aerobic, resistance (strength) training, gait, and balance training
	• medical assessment before starting • tailor to individual capabilities • initiate with caution in those with limited mobility not accustomed to physical activity • prescribed by qualified healthcare provider • regular review and progression
	(↓ risk 13% [USPSTF];
	↓ risk 15%; ↓ rate 29% [Cochrane];
	Tai Chi: ↓ risk 29%, ↓ rate 22% [Cochrane])
	Education and information, CBT intervention to decrease fear of falling and activity avoidance (limited evidence [Cochrane])
	Recommend daily supplementation of vitamin D (at least 800 IU) to achieve 25-hydroxy level >30 (Osteoporosis, p 229). (↓ risk 17% [Cochrane])
Medication-related Factors	
Use of benzodiazepines, sedative-hypnotics, antidepressants, or antipsychotics	Consider agents with less risk of falls
	Avoid if hx of falls or fracture.[BC]
	Taper and D/C medications, as possible
	Address sleep problems with nonpharmacologic interventions (p 316)
	Educate regarding appropriate use of medications and monitoring for AEs
Recent change in dosage or number of prescription medications *or* use of ≥4 prescription medications *or* use of other medications associated with fall risk	Review medication profile and reduce number and dosage of all medications, as possible
	(Withdrawal of antipsychotics: no ↓ risk; ↓ rate 66% [Cochrane])
	Monitor response to medications and to dosage changes
Mobility-related Factors	
Environmental hazards (eg, improper bed height, cluttered walking surfaces, lack of railings, poor lighting)	Improve lighting, especially at night
	Remove floor barriers (eg, loose carpeting)
	Replace existing furniture with safer furniture (eg, correct height, more stable)
	Install support structures, especially in bathroom (eg, railings, grab bars, elevated toilet seats)
	Use nonslip bathmats
	(↓ risk 12%; ↓ rate 19%; more effective delivered by OT [Cochrane])
Impaired gait, balance, or transfer skills	Refer to PT for comprehensive evaluation and rehabilitation
	Refer to PT or OT for gait training, transfer skills, use of assistive devices, balancing, strengthening and resistance training, and evaluation for appropriate footwear

(cont.)

Table 55. Preventing Falls: Selected Risk Factors and Suggested Interventions (cont.)	
Factors	**Suggested Interventions (Outcome Reduction*)**
Impaired leg or arm strength or range of motion, or proprioception	Refer to PT or OT
Medical Factors	
Parkinson disease, osteoarthritis, depressive symptoms, impaired cognition, carotid sinus hypersensitivity, other conditions associated with increased falls	Optimize medical tx
	Monitor for disease progression and impact on mobility and impairments
	Determine need for assistive devices
	Use bedside commode if frequent nighttime urination
	Cardiac pacing in patients with carotid sinus hypersensitivity who experience falls due to syncope
	($\downarrow$ rate 27%, but not risk [Cochrane])
Postural hypotension: drop in SBP $\geq$20 mmHg (or $\geq$20%) with or without symptoms, within 3 min of rising from lying to standing	See orthostatic postural hypotension, p 64
Visual (Eye Disorders, p 105)	Cataract extraction (first eye cataract removal, rate $\downarrow$ 34%, but not second eye)
	Avoid wearing multifocal lenses while walking, particularly up stairs

*risk of falls = # people falling; rate of falling = # falls per person

Sources: Available evidence on rate of falling and risk for falling from Gillespie LD et al. *Cochrane Database Syst Rev.* 2012 Sep 12;9:CD007146; Moyer VA, USPSTF. *Ann Intern Med.* 2012;157(3):197–204; Bolland MJ et al. *Lancet Diabetes Endrocrinol* 2014;2(7):573–580.

EVALUATION OF FALL

Diagnose and treat underlying cause. Exclude acute illness or underlying systemic or metabolic process (eg, infection, electrolyte imbalance) as indicated by hx, examination, and laboratory studies. Determine if fall is syncopal or nonsyncopal (Syncope, p 63).

History

- Circumstances of fall (eg, activity at time of fall, location, time, footwear at time of fall, lighting)
- Associated symptoms (eg, lightheadedness, vertigo, syncope, weakness, confusion, palpitations, joint pain, joint stability, feelings of pitching [common in Parkinson disease], foot pain, ankle instability)
- Relevant comorbid conditions (eg, prior stroke, parkinsonism, cardiac disease, DM, seizure disorder, depression, anxiety, hyperplastic anemia, sensory deficit, osteoarthritis, osteoporosis, hyperthyroidism, glucocorticoid excess, GI or chronic renal disease, myeloma)
- Medication review, including OTC medications and alcohol use; note recent changes in medications (p 16)

Physical Examination

Look for:

- Vital signs: postural pulse and BP lying and 3 min after standing, temperature
- Head and neck: visual impairment (especially poor acuity, reduced contrast sensitivity, decreased visual fields, cataracts), motion-induced nystagmus (Dix-Hallpike test), bruit, nystagmus
- Musculoskeletal: arthritic changes, motion or joint limitations (especially lower extremity joint function), postural instability, skeletal deformities, podiatric problems, muscle strength
- Neurologic: slower reflexes, altered proprioception, altered mental status, focal deficits, peripheral neuropathy, gait or balance disorders, hip flexor weakness, instability, tremor, rigidity
- Cardiovascular: heart arrhythmias, cardiac valve dysfunction (peripheral vascular changes, pedal pulses)

Diagnostic Tests

- Laboratory tests for people at risk include CBC, serum electrolytes, BUN, Cr, glucose, B_{12}, thyroid function
- Bone densitometry in all women >65 yr old except those on osteoporosis tx or those who have osteopenic fragility fractures
- Cardiac workup if symptoms of syncope or presyncope (Syncope Evaluation, p 63)
- Imaging: neuroimaging if head injury or new, focal neurologic findings on examination or if a CNS process is suspected; spinal imaging to exclude cervical spondylosis or lumbar stenosis in patients with abnormal gait, neurologic examination, or lower extremity spasticity or hyperreflexia
- Drug concentrations for anticonvulsants, antiarrhythmics, TCAs, and high-dose ASA

DYSPHAGIA

See also p 260.

Types/Presentation/Patient Complaints

Table 56. Dysphagia Complaints		
Classification	Presentation and Signs	Common Causes
Oral	Inability to move food or medication from mouth to pharynx. Food deposits in cheeks	Dementia
Pharyngeal	Impaired involuntary food transport pharynx to esphogus with airway protection. Coughing, choking, or nasal regurgitation	Stroke, Parkinson disease, CNS tumor, ALS, local strictures
Esophageal	Sensation that food is stuck in the throat	Impaired esophageal motility, obstruction, medication

Evaluation

- Physical examination
  - Oral cavity, head, neck, and supraclavicular region
  - All cranial nerves with emphasis on nerves V, VII, IX, X, XI, XII
- Review medications for those that can decrease saliva production (eg, anticholinergics)
- Referral to speech-language pathologists
- Diagnostic tests (as indicated)
  - Modified barium swallow or videofluoroscopy to assess swallowing mechanism; may document aspiration
  - Fiberoptic endoscopic evaluations of swallowing (FEES) provides detailed evaluation of lesions in oropharynx, hypopharynx, larynx, and proximal esophagus; also visualizes pooled secretions or food
  - Upper endoscopy
  - Esophageal manometry often used in combination with barium radiography; more useful for assessment of esophageal dysphagia

Treatment

- Identify and treat underlying cause (eg, endoscopic dilation, cricopharyngeal myotomy, botulinum toxin injection in cricopharyngeal muscle)
- Dietary modifications based on recommendation of speech pathologist or dietitian
- Swallowing rehabilitation, eg, multiple swallows, tilt head back and place bolus on strong side, or chin tuck
- Avoid rushed or forced feeding
- Sit upright at 90 degrees
- Elevate head of the bed at least 30 degrees
- Review medications and administration for unsafe practices, eg, crushing enteric-coated or ER formulations
- Symptomatic presbyesophagus responds to esophageal dilatation
- Neuromuscular electrical stimulation (NMES)

Food Consistencies

- Pureed: thick, homogenous textures; pudding-like
- Ground/minced: easily chewed without coarse texture; excludes most raw foods except mashed bananas
- Soft or easy to chew: soft foods prepared without a blender; tender meats cut to ≤1-cm pieces; excludes nuts, tough skins, and raw, crispy, or stringy foods
- Modified general: soft textures that do not require grinding or chopping

Fluid Consistencies and Thickening Agents

- Thin: regular fluids
- Nectar-like: thin enough to be sipped through a straw or from a cup, but still spillable (eg, eggnog, buttermilk); 2–3 tsp of thickening powder to ½ cup (4 fl oz) of liquid
- Honey-like: thick enough to be eaten with a spoon, too thick for a straw, not able to independently hold its shape (eg, yogurt, tomato sauce, honey); 3–5 tsp of thickening powder to ½ cup (4 fl oz) of liquid
- Spoon-thick: pudding-like, must be eaten with a spoon (eg, thick milk pudding, thickened applesauce); 5–6 tsp of thickening powder to ½ cup (4 fl oz) of liquid
- Thickening agents are starch- or gum-based. Liquids thickened with modified starch continue to thicken or over-thicken over time. The thicker the product, the less consumed and the greater risk for dehydration.

GASTROESOPHAGEAL REFLUX DISEASE (GERD)

Evaluation and Assessment

Empiric tx is appropriate when hx is typical for uncomplicated GERD.

- Endoscopy (if symptoms are chronic or persist despite initial management, atypical presentation)
- Ambulatory pH testing

Risk Factors

- Obesity
- Hiatal hernia
- Use of estrogen, nitroglycerin, tobacco

Symptoms Suggesting Complicated GERD and Need for Evaluation

- Dysphagia
- Bleeding
- Weight loss
- Anemia
- Choking, cough, shortness of breath, hoarseness
- Chest pain
- Pain with swallowing
- Vomiting

Management

- Acid suppression with a PPI or H_2 antagonist (**Table 57**)
- Antacids
- Avoid alcohol and fatty foods
- Avoid lying down for 3 h after eating
- Avoid tight-fitting clothes
- Change diet (avoid pepper, spearmint, chocolate, spicy or acidic foods, carbonated beverages)
- Drink 6–8 oz water with all medications
- Chew gum or use oral lozenges to stimulate salivation, which neutralizes gastric acid
- Elevate head of the bed (6–8 in)
- Lose weight (if overweight)
- Stop drugs that may promote reflux or can induce esophagitis
- Stop smoking
- Consider surgery (not recommended for PPI nonresponders)

Treatment with PPIs

- Initial tx: 8 wk with once-a-day PPI with morning meal
- Maintenance tx if symptoms remain after stopping or if complicated by erosive esophagitis or Barrett esophagus

Table 57. Pharmacologic Management of GERD[a][cw]

Medication	Initial Oral Dosage	Formulations (mg) (Metabolism, Excretion)
PPIs[b]		
Dexlansoprazole *(Dexilant)*	30 mg/d × 4 wk	C: ER 30, 60 (L)
✓Esomeprazole magnesium *(Nexium)*	20 mg/d × 4 wk	C: ER 20, 40 (L)
Esomeprazole strontium	24.6 mg/d × 4 wk	C: ER 24.65, 49.3 (L)
✓Lansoprazole▲* *(Prevacid)*	15 mg/d × 8 wk	C: ER 15, 30; gran for susp: 15, 30/pk (L)
✓Omeprazole▲* *(Prilosec)*	20 mg/d × 4–8 wk	C: ER 10, 20,[c] 40; T: enteric-coated 20 (L)
✓Pantoprazole *(Protonix)*	40 mg/d × 8 wk	T: enteric-coated 20, 40; inj (L)
✓Rabeprazole *(AcipHex)*	20 mg/d × 4–8 wk; 20 mg/d maintenance, if needed	T: ER enteric-coated 20 (L)
H2 Antagonists (for less severe GERD)(Avoid.[BC])		
Cimetidine▲*d *(Tagamet HB 200)*	400 or 800 mg q12h	S: 200 mg/20 mL, 300 mg/5 mL with alcohol 2.8%; T: 100, 200[c], 300, 400, 800; inj (K, L)
✓Famotidine▲* *(Pepcid)*	20 mg q12h × 6 wk	S: oral sus 40 mg/5 mL; T: film-coated 10[c], 20, 40; ODT 20, 40; C (gel): 10[c]; ChT: 10[c]; inj (K)
✓Nizatidine▲ *(Axid)*	150 mg q12h	C:150, 300; T: 75 (K)
Ranitidine▲* *(Zantac)*	150 mg q12h	Pk: gran, effervescent (EFFERdose) 150 mg; S: syr 15 mg/mL; T: 75[c], 150, 300; T: effervescent (EFFERdose) 150; inj (K, F)
Prokinetic Agents[g]		
✓Domperidone[e]	10 mg 15–30 min ac and hs	T: 10 mg (L)
Metoclopramide▲f *(Reglan)*	5 mg q6h, ac, and hs	S: syr, sugar-free 5 mg/5 mL, conc 10 mg/mL; T: 5, 10; inj (K, F)

✓ = preferred for treating older adults

* Available OTC

[cw]Use lowest dose needed to achieve symptom control

[a] PPIs more effective than H₂ antagonists for tx and maintenance

[b] Associated with osteopenia/osteoporosis; can inhibit CYP2C19 and -3A4; prolonged exposure may increase risk of fractures, community-acquired pneumonia, *Clostridium difficile* diarrhea, hypomagnesemia; reduce vitamins C and B₁₂ concentrations, and gastric atrophy. Monitor magnesium if taken long term or with digoxin.

[c] OTC strength

[d] Inhibits CYP1A2, –2D6, –3A4

[e] Available in the United States only through an Investigational New Drug application for compassionate use in patients refractory to other tx (www.fda.gov); domperidone is approved in Canada as a tx for upper GI motility disorders associated with gastritis and diabetic gastroparesis, and for prevention of GI symptoms associated with use of dopamine-agonist anti-Parkinson agents.

f Risk of EPS high in people >65 yr old.

g No role in absence of gastroparesis.

Source: Data from Katz PO et al. *Am J Gastroenterol.* 2013;108:308–328.

PEPTIC ULCER DISEASE

Causes

Helicobacter pylori is the major cause. NSAIDs are the second most common cause.

Diagnosis of *H pylori*
- Endoscopy with biopsy
- Serology
- Urea breath test
- Fecal antigen test

Initial Treatment Options
- Empiric anti-ulcer tx for 6 wk
- Definitive diagnostic evaluation by endoscopy
- Noninvasive testing for *H pylori* and tx with antibiotics for those that test positive (see **Table 58** for regimens)
- Review patient's chronic medications for drug interactions before selecting regimen; many potential drug interactions and adverse drug events.

Table 58. Pharmacotherapeutic Management of *H pylori* Infection		
Regimen	**Duration**	**Comments**
Triple Therapy		Preferred if no previous macrolide exposure
PPI[a] q12h[b] *plus* Clarithromycin 500 mg q12h *plus* Amoxicillin 1000 mg q12h	10–14 d	Example: *PrevPac* (includes lansoprazole 30 mg)
Metronidazole 500 q12h	—	Preferred if penicillin allergy or unable to tolerate bismuth quadruple tx
Second-line Triple Therapy		
PPI[a] q24h *plus* Amoxicillin 1 g *plus* Metronidazole 500 mg q12h	7–14 d	
Quadruple Therapy		
PPI[a] q12h[b] or H_2 antagonist *plus* Bismuth subsalicylate 525 mg q6h *plus* Metronidazole 250 mg q24h *plus* Tetracycline 500 mg q24h *(Helidac)*	10–14 d	Consider if penicillin allergy or previous macrolide exposure, *or* as second-line if triple tx fails
PPI[a] q12h[b] or H_2 antagonist *plus* Bismuth subcitrate 425 mg q24h *plus* Metronidazole 250 mg q24h *plus* Tetracycline 500 mg q24h *(Plyera)*	10–12 d	

a Associated with osteopenia/osteoporosis; can inhibit CYP2C19 and -3A4; prolonged exposure may increase risk of fractures, community-acquired pneumonia, hospital-acquired *Clostridium difficile* diarrhea; reduce vitamins C and B_{12} concentrations

b Esomeprazole is dosed 40 mg q24h.

Source: Adapted from Chey WD et al. *Am J Gastroenterol.* 2007;102(8):1808–1825.

Medications

Bismuth subsalicylate▲ *(Pepto-Bismol)* (for complete information, see **Table 61**)

Antibiotics: (for complete information, see **Table 77**)

PPIs: See **Table 57**.

STRESS-ULCER PREVENTION IN HOSPITALIZED OLDER ADULTS

Risk Factors (in order of prevalence in older adults)

- Hx of GI ulceration or bleed in past year
- Sepsis
- Multiple organ failure
- Hypotension
- Mechanical ventilation for >48 h
- Kidney failure
- Major trauma, shock, or head injury
- Glasgow Coma Scale <10
- Coagulopathy (platelets <50,000/μL, INR >1.5, or PTT >2 × control)
- Burns over >25% of body surface area
- Hepatic failure/partial hepatectomy
- Intracranial HTN
- Spinal cord injury
- Quadriplegia

Prophylaxis

- H_2 antagonists (**Table 57**)
- PPIs (**Table 57**)
- Sucralfate▲
- Antacids
- Enteral feedings

Key Points

- Prophylaxis has not been shown to reduce mortality.
- No one regimen has shown superior efficacy.
- Choice of regimen depends on access to and function of GI tract and presence of nasogastric suction.
- D/C H_2 antagonists, PPIs, and other tx for stress-ulcer prevention when risk factors are eliminated, when transferred before transfer to skilled nursing facility or discharge from hospital.

IRRITABLE BOWEL SYNDROME (IBS)

Signs and Symptoms

Symptoms should be present ≥12 wk.

Consistent with IBS:

- Abdominal pain
- Bloating
- Constipation
- Diarrhea

Not Consistent with IBS:

- Weight loss
- First onset after age 50
- Nocturnal diarrhea
- Family hx of cancer or inflammatory bowel disease
- Rectal bleeding or obstruction
- Laboratory abnormalities
- Presence of fecal parasites

Diagnosis (of exclusion)

Exclude ischemia, diverticulosis, colon cancer, inflammatory bowel disease by physical examination and testing (colonoscopy, CT scan, or small-bowel series). Do not repeat CT unless major changes in clinical findings.[CW]

Treatment

- Reassurance; not life threatening; focus on relief of physical and emotional symptoms
- Dietary modification
  - Avoid foods that trigger symptoms or produce excess gas or bloating
  - Consider a trial of a lactose-free diet
- Behavioral interventions: hypnosis, biofeedback, psychotherapy have been shown to be more effective than placebo. Other interventions: increase physical activity, trials of gluten-free diet.
- Fiber supplements (**Table 59**)
  - Synthetic: polycarbophil[▲]
  - Natural: psyllium[▲]
- Antispasmodics (short-term use only; avoid unless no other alternatives)
  - Dicyclomine *(Bentyl[BC]* [C: 10[▲]; T: 20[▲]; syr: 10 mg/5 mL; inj]) 10–20 mg po q6h prn (L)
  - Hyoscyamine[▲BC] *(Anaspaz, Levsin, Levsin/SL,* others [T (sl): 0.125, 0.15; T ER, C: 0.375; inj: 125 sol]) 0.125–0.25 mg po/sl q6–8h prn (L, K)
- Antidiarrheals: may be helpful for diarrhea but not for global IBS symptoms, abdominal pain, or constipation
  - Loperamide[▲] *(Imodium A-D* [C, T: 2; sol 1 mg/5 mL]) 4 mg × 1, then 2 mg after each loose bowel movement; max 16 mg/24 h
- Antidepressants
  - TCAs and SSRIs may be beneficial for patients with diarrhea or pain. See Depression, p 78, for dosing.
- Laxative for IBS constipation
  - Linaclotide *(Linzess* [C:145, 290 mcg]): 290 mcg q24h on empty stomach
- Serotonin agent
  - Alosetron *(Lotronex* [T: 0.5, 1 mg]): serotonin 3 antagonist; tx of women with severe diarrhea-predominant IBS who have not responded to conventional tx (restricted distribution in the US); 0.5 mg po q12h × 4 wk, increase to 1 mg q12h × 4 wk, stop if no response (K, L)

CONSTIPATION

Definition

Frequency of bowel movements <2–3 times/wk, straining at defecation, hard feces, or feeling of incomplete evacuation. Clinically, large amount of feces in rectum on digital examination and/or colonic fecal loading on abdominal radiograph.

Medications That Constipate

- Analgesics—opioids
- Antacids with aluminum or calcium
- Anticholinergic drugs
- Antidepressants, lithium
- Antihypertensives
- Antipsychotics
- Barium sulfate
- Bismuth
- Calcium channel blockers
- Diuretics
- Iron

Conditions That Constipate

- Colon tumor or mechanical obstruction
- Dehydration
- Depression
- DM
- Hypercalcemia
- Hypokalemia
- Hypothyroidism
- Immobility
- Low intake of fiber
- Panhypopituitarism
- Parkinson disease
- Spinal cord injury
- Stroke
- Uremia

Management of Chronic Constipation

Step 1: Stop all constipating medications, when possible.

Step 2: Increase dietary fiber to 6–25 g/d, increase fluid intake to ≥1500 mL/d, and increase physical activity; or add bulk laxative (**Table 59**), provided fluid intake is ≥1500 mL/d. If fiber exacerbates symptoms or is not tolerated, or patient has limited mobility, go to Step 3.

Step 3: Add an osmotic (eg, 70% sorbitol sol, polyethylene glycol *[MiraLAX]*).

Step 4: Add stimulant laxative (eg, senna, bisacodyl), 2–3 times/wk. (Alternative: saline laxative, but avoid if CrCl <30 mL/min.)

Step 5: Use tap water enema or saline enema 2 times/wk.

Step 6: Use oil-retention enema for refractory constipation.

Table 59. Medications That May Relieve Constipation

Medication	Onset of Action	Starting Dosage	Site and Mechanism of Action
Bulk laxatives—not useful in managing opioid-induced constipation			
Methylcellulose▲ *(Citrucel)**	12–24 h (up to 72 h)	2–4 caplets or 1 heaping tbsp with 8 oz water q8–24h	Small and large intestine; holds water in feces; mechanical distention
Psyllium▲ *(Metamucil)**ª	12–24 h (up to 72 h)	1–2 capsules, pks, or tsp with 8 oz water or juice q8–24h	Small and large intestine; holds water in feces; mechanical distention
Polycarbophil▲ *(FiberCon*, others)ª	12–24 h (up to 72 h)	1250 mg q6–24h	Small and large intestine; holds water in feces; mechanical distention
Wheat dextrin *(Benefiber)**	24–28 h		Small and large intestine; holds water in feces; mechanical distention
Chloride channel activator			
Lubiprostone *(Amitiza)*	24–28 h	24 mcg q12h with food C: 8, 24 mcg	Enhances chloride-ion intestinal fluid secretion; does not affect serum Na+ or K+ concentrations. For idiopathic chronic constipation.
Linaclotide *(Linzess)*		145 mcg q24h without food	
Opioid antagonists			
Alvimopan *(Entereg)*	NA	Initial: 12 mg po 30 min to 5 h before surgery Maintenance: 12 mg po q12h the day after surgery × 7 d max	Hospital use only; for accelerating time to recovery after partial large- or small-bowel resection with primary anastomosis; contraindicated if >7 consecutive d of therapeutic opioids (L, K, F)

(cont.)

Table 59. Medications That May Relieve Constipation (cont.)

Medication	Onset of Action	Starting Dosage	Site and Mechanism of Action
Methylnaltrexone (Relistor)	30–60 min	Weight-based dosing: <38 kg: 0.15 mg/kg 38 to <62 kg: 8 mg 62–114 kg: 12 mg >114 kg: 0.15 mg/kg (all SC q48h); if CrCl <30 mL/min, decrease dosage 50%	Peripheral-acting opioid antagonist for the tx of opioid-induced constipation in palliative care patients who have not responded to conventional laxatives (L, K, F)
Osmotic laxatives			
Lactulose▲ (Chronulac)	24–48 h	15–30 mL q12–24h	Colon; osmotic effect
Polyethylene glycol▲ (Miralax)*	48–96 h	17 g pwd q24h (~1 tbsp) dissolved in 8 oz water	GI tract; osmotic effect
Sorbitol 70%▲*	24–48 h	15–30 mL q12–24h; max 150 mL/d	Colon; delivers osmotically active molecules to colon
Glycerin supp*	15–30 min		Colon; local irritation; hyperosmotic
Sodium, potassium, and magnesium sulfate (Suprep bowel prep kit)	24 h		Small and large intestine; hyperosmotic
Saline laxatives			
Magnesium citrate▲ (Citroma)*	30 min–3 h	120–240 mL × 1; 10 oz q24h or 5 oz q12h followed by 8 oz water × ≤5d	Small and large intestine; attracts, retains water in intestinal lumen; potential hypermagnesemia in patients with renal insufficiency
Magnesium hydroxide▲ (Milk of Magnesia)*	30 min–3 h	30 mL q12–24h 311-mg tab (130 mg magnesium); 400, 800 mg/5 mL sus	Osmotic effect and increased peristalsis in colon; potential hypermagnesemia in patients with renal insufficiency
Sodium phosphate/ biphosphate emollient enema▲ (Fleet)*	2–15 min	14.5-oz enema × 1 per 24 h	Colon; osmotic effect; potential hypermagnesemia in patients with renal insufficiency
Stimulant laxatives			
Bisacodyl tablet▲ (Dulcolax)*	6–10 h	5–15 mg × 1	Colon; increases peristalsis
Bisacodyl suppository▲ (Dulcolax)*	15 min–1 h	10 mg × 1	Colon; increases peristalsis
Senna▲ (Senokot)*	6–10 h	1–2 tabs or 1 tsp qhs	Colon; direct action on intestine; stimulates myenteric plexus; alters water and electrolyte secretion
Surfactant laxative (fecal softener)			
Docusate▲ (Colace)*	24–72 h	100 mg q12–24h	Small and large intestine; detergent activity; facilitates admixture of fat and water to soften feces (effectiveness questionable); does not increase frequency of bowel movements

*Available OTC

[a] Psyllium caplets and packets contain ≥3 g dietary fiber and 2–3 g soluble fiber each. A teaspoonful contains ~3.8 g dietary fiber and 3 g soluble fiber.

NAUSEA AND VOMITING

Causes

- CNS disorders (eg, motion sickness, intracranial lesions)
- Drugs (eg, chemotherapy, NSAIDs, opioid analgesics, antibiotics, digoxin)
- GI disorders (eg, mechanical obstruction; inflammation of stomach, intestine, or gallbladder; pseudo-obstruction; motility disorders; dyspepsia; gastroparesis)
- Infections (eg, viral or bacterial gastroenteritis, hepatitis, otitis, meningitis)
- Metabolic conditions (eg, uremia, acidosis, hyperparathyroidism, adrenal insufficiency)
- Psychiatric disorders

Evaluation

- If patient is not seriously ill or dehydrated, can probably wait 24–48 h to see if symptoms resolve spontaneously.
- If patient is seriously ill, dehydrated, or has other signs of acute illness, hospitalize for further evaluation.
- If symptoms persist, evaluate on the basis of the most likely causes.

Pharmacologic Management

- If analgesic drug is suspected, decrease dosage, consider adding antiemetic until tolerance develops, or change to a different analgesic drug.
- Drugs that are useful in the management of nausea and vomiting are listed in **Table 60**.

Table 60. Antiemetic Therapy

Class/Site of Action	Dosage (Metabolism)	Formulation
Dopamine antagonists/CTZ vomiting center		
Haloperidol▲BC	IM, po: 0.5–1 mg q6h (L, K)	p 262
Metoclopramide▲BC (Reglan)	PONV: 5–10 mg IM near the end of surgery Chemotherapy (IV): 1–2 mg/kg 30 min before and q2–4h or q4–6h (K)	T: 5, 10 S: 10 mg/mL; syr (sugar-free): 5 mg/mL Inj: 5 mg/mL
Prochlorperazine▲BC (Compazine)	IM, po: 5–10 mg q6–8 h, usual max 40 mg/d IV: 2.5–10 mg, max 10 mg/dose or 40 mg/d; may repeat q3–4h prn (L)	T: 5, 10, 25 mg C: 10, 15, 30 mg Syr: 5 mg/5 mL Inj: 5 mg/mL Sp: 2.5, 10, 25
Serotonin (5-HT$_3$) antagonists/CTZ, gut		
✓Ondansetron▲ (Zofran)	PONV: 16 mg po 1 h before anesthesia IM, IV: 4 mg immediately before anesthesia; repeat if needed (L) Radiation tx: 8 mg po 1–2 h before, then 8 mg po q8h × 1–2 d	T: 4, 8, 24 mg ODT: 4, 8 mg S: 4 mg/5 mL Inj: 2 mg/mL
Granisetron (Kytril)	PONV: 1 mg IV before anesthesia or anesthesia reversal Chemotherapy: 2 mg/d po (L, K) Radiation tx: 2 mg po 1 h before	T: 1 mg S: 2 mg/10 mL Inj: 1 mg/mL Pch: 3.1 mg/24 h
Dolasetron (Anzemet)	PONV: 100 mg po 2 h before surgery; 12.5 mg IV 15 min before stopping anesthesia (L)	T: 50, 100 mg Inj: 20 mg/mL

(cont.)

Table 60. Antiemetic Therapy (cont.)		
Class/Site of Action	Dosage (Metabolism)	Formulation
Antimuscarinic/H₁ antagonist/vestibular apparatus		
Diphenhydrinate▲ᵃ (Dramamine)*	IM, IV, po: 50–100 mg q4–6h; max 400 mg/d (L)	T, ChT: 50 mg S: 12.5 mg/4 mL, 16.62 mg/5 mL Inj: 10 mg/mL
Meclizine▲ᵃ (Antivert)*	Motion sickness: 12.5–25 mg 1 h before travel, repeat dose q12–24h if needed Vertigo: 25–100 mg/d in divided doses (L)	T: 12.5, 25, 50 mg ChT: 25 mg C: 25, 30 mg
Scopolamineᵃ (Transderm Scop)	Motion sickness: apply 1 pch behind ear ≥4 h before travel/exposure; change q3d (L)	Pch: 1.5 mg

✓ = preferred for treating older adults

*Available OTC

ᵃ Avoid unless no other alternatives.[BC]

Notes: CTZ = chemoreceptor trigger zone; PONV = postoperative nausea and vomiting. All have potential CNS toxicity. Metoclopramide associated with EPS and TD.

DIARRHEA

Causes
- Drugs (eg, antibiotics [**Table 77** and below], laxatives, colchicine)
- Fecal impaction
- GI disorders (eg, IBS, malabsorption, inflammatory bowel disease)
- Infections (eg, viral, bacterial, parasitic)
- Lactose intolerance

Evaluation
- If patient is not seriously ill or dehydrated and there is no blood in the feces, can probably wait 48 h to see if symptoms resolve spontaneously.
- If patient is seriously ill, dehydrated, or has other signs of acute illness, hospitalize for further evaluation.
- If diarrhea persists, evaluate on the basis of the most likely causes.

Pharmacologic Management
Drugs that are useful in the management of diarrhea are listed in **Table 61**.

Table 61. Antidiarrheals		
Drug	Dosage (Metabolism)	Formulations
✓ Attapulgite (Kaopectate)*	1200–1500 mg after each loose bowel movement or q2h; 15–30 mL up to 9×/d, up to 9000 mg/24 h (not absorbed)	S: oral conc 600, 750 mg/15 mL; T: 750; ChT: 300, 600
✓ Bismuth subsalicylate▲* (Pepto-Bismol)	2 tabs or 30 mL q30–60 min prn up to 8 doses/24 h (L, K)	S: 262 mg/15 mL, 525 mg/15 mL; T: 324; ChT: 262

(cont.)

Table 61. Antidiarrheals (cont.)		
Drug	Dosage (Metabolism)	Formulations
Diphenoxylate with atropine▲ (Lomotil)ᵃ	15–20 mg/d of diphenoxylate in 3–4 divided doses; maintenance 5–15 mg/d in 2–3 divided doses (L)	S: oral, diphenoxylate hydrochloride 2.5 mg + atropine sulfate 0.025 mg/5 mL; T: diphenoxylate hydrochloride 2.5 mg + atropine sulfate 0.025 mg
✓ Loperamide▲ (Imodium A-D)*	Initial: 4 mg followed by 2 mg after each loose bowel movement, up to 16 mg/d (L)	Caplet: 2; C: 2; T: 2; S: oral, 1 mg/5 mL
Rifaximin (Xifaxan)	Traveler's diarrhea: 200 mg 3×/d × 3 d	T: 200, 550

✓ = preferred for treating older adults

*Available OTC

ᵃ Anticholinergic, potential CNS toxicity

ANTIBIOTIC-ASSOCIATED DIARRHEA (AAD)

(Antibiotic-associated pseudomembranous colitis [AAPMC])

Definition

A specific form of *Clostridium difficile* pseudomembranous colitis

Risk Factors

- Almost any oral or parenteral antibiotic and several antineoplastic agents, including cyclophosphamide, doxorubicin, fluorouracil, methotrexate
- Advanced age
- Duration of hospitalization
- PPI

Prevention

The use of probiotic products to prevent primary infection remains controversial. Two systematic reviews and meta-analyses found that they significantly reduce the risk of AAD and *C difficile* diarrhea. Since their publication, the largest trial, conducted in elderly inpatients, found the combination lactobacilli and bifidobacteria did not reduce the risk of AAD or *C difficile* diarrhea. Probiotics should be used with caution by immunocompromised patients.

Presentation

- Abdominal pain, cramping
- Dehydration
- Diarrhea (can be bloody)
- Fecal leukocytes
- Fever (100–105°F)
- Hypoalbuminemia
- Hypovolemia
- Leukocytosis

Symptoms appear a few days after starting to 10 wk after discontinuing the offending agent.

Evaluation and Empiric Management

- D/C unnecessary antibiotics, and agents that can slow gastric motility such as opioids and antidiarrheal agents.
- Initiate empiric tx if severe or complicated *C difficile* suspected.

- Perform *C difficile* toxin test on 2 separate bowel movements. If suspicion remains after 2 negative tests, a third toxin test can be performed. Some laboratories perform *C difficile* A and B toxin DNA testing, which is highly sensitive; repeat testing is unnecessary unless symptoms or clinical situation change.
- Place patient in contact isolation and observe infection control procedures. Hand washing is crucial and must be done with soap and water to remove spores. Hand sanitizers do not kill or remove spores.
- Provide adequate fluid and electrolyte replacement.
- Consider empiric metronidazole (**Table 62** for dosing).

Diagnosis
- Only liquid stools should be tested for *C difficile*.
- Isolation of *C difficile* or its toxin from symptomatic patient
- Nucleic acid amplification tests (NAAT) for toxin genes are superior to toxin A + B enzyme immunoassays.
- Repeated testing is discouraged.
- Testing for a cure should not be performed.

Treatment

Table 62. Treatment of Suspected or Confirmed *Clostridium difficile* Infection

Clinical Definition	Supportive Clinical Data	Treatment
Toxin negative on 2 specimens		D/C contact isolation D/C metronidazole/vancomycin Begin antidiarrheal agent Evaluate other causes
Initial episode, mild or moderate	Leukocytosis (WBC ≤15,000 cells/μL), serum Cr <1.5 times premorbid level	Metronidazole 500 mg po q8h × 10–14 d *Fidaxomicin 200 mg po q12h × 10 d
Initial episode, severe	Leukocytosis (WBC >15,000 cells/μL), which signifies colonic inflammation; serum Cr ≥1.5 times premorbid level, which signifies dehydration	Vancomycin 125 mg po q6h × 10–14 d Oral vancomycin is available as a capsule (125, 250) or by reconstituting the powder for injection for oral administration.
Initial episode, severe, complicated	Hypotension or shock, ileus, megacolon in the absence of abdominal distention	Vancomycin 500 mg po or nasogastric tube q6h plus metronidazole IV 500 mg q8h; if complete ileus or toxic megacolon, add vancomycin 500 mg/500 mL pr is an option.
First recurrence		Same as initial episode, unless severe, then use vancomycin
Second recurrence		Vancomycin in a tapered and/or pulsed regimen

Source: Adapted from Cohen SH et al. *Infect Control Hosp Epidemiol* 2010;31(5):431–455.

*Fidaxomicin *(Dificid)* [T: 200 mg; 92% F, minimal systemic absorption]. Clinical trials did not include patients with life-threatening or fulminant *C difficile* infection, toxic megacolon, or with >1 *C difficile* infection in the previous 3 mo. Fidaxomicin is not in the guidelines of the Society for Healthcare Epidemiology of America and the Infectious Diseases Society of America (SHEA/IDSA). Cure rates between vancomycin and fidaxomicin do not differ. With both tx, age (per decade) is associated with a decreased cure rate, decrease in sustained response, and increased recurrence rate.

- Oral vancomycin is an option for patients allergic to or who cannot tolerate metronidazole.
- Fecal transplant is a promising alternative tx to antibiotics. It is not universally available, nor has its place in tx been determined.

HEMORRHOIDS

Contributing Factors
- Constipation
- Prolonged straining
- Exercise
- Gravity
- Low-fiber diet
- Pregnancy
- Increased intraabdominal pressure
- Irregular bowel habits
- Age

Classification
- External: distal to the dentate line and painful if thrombotic, itchy
- Internal: proximal to the dentate line without sensitivity to pain, touch, or temperature; mucous discharge; feeling of incomplete evacuation
  - *Grade*
    - First-degree: no prolapse, may bleed after defecation, only seen via anoscope
    - Second-degree: prolapse outside anal canal with defecation and retract spontaneously
    - Third-degree: prolapse and require manual reduction
    - Fourth-degree: prolapsed, nonreducible

Treatment

Diet and Lifestyle Changes
- High-fiber diet (20–35 g/d) or psyllium, methylcellulose, or calcium polycarbophil
- Increased fluid intake
- Avoid prolonged time on commode

Topical Treatments
- Sitz baths (40° C)
- Protectants plus vasoconstrictor, eg, light mineral oil, petrolatum, shark liver oil *plus* phenylephrine *(Preparation H*, Anucort*, Cortifoam*)*, or with hydrocortisone (oint, crm, gel, foam, supp, wipes); apply/insert up to 4 × /d.

Office-based Procedures
- Rubber band ligation: for first-, second-, or third-degree internal hemorrhoids
  - Contraindicated in patients who are anticoagulated
  - D/C antiplatelet drugs (including ASA) for 5–7 d before and after banding
- Sclerotherapy
- Bipolar diathermy
- Infrared photocoagulation

HEARING IMPAIRMENT

DEFINITION

The most common sensory impairment in old age; presbycusis affects 30–47% of the population older than 65 yr. To quantify hearing ability, the necessary intensity (decibel = dB) and frequency (Hertz) of the perceived pure-tone signal must be described.

Importance: Hearing impairment is strongly correlated with depression, decreased quality of life, poorer memory and executive function, and incident dementia.

EVALUATION

Screening and Evaluation

- Note problems during conversation.
- Ask the question: Do you feel you have hearing loss? A "yes" response should prompt referral to audiology.
- Test with handheld audioscope or whisper test. Refer patients who screen positive for audiologic evaluation.
- Whisper test: stand behind patient at arm's length from ear, cover untested ear, fully exhale, whisper a combination of 3 numbers and letters (eg, 6-K-2) and ask patient to repeat the set; if patient unable to repeat all 3, whisper a second set. Inability to repeat at least 3 of 6 is positive for impairment.

Audiometry

- Documents the dB loss across frequencies
- Determines the pattern of loss (see Classification, below)
- Determines if loss is unilateral or bilateral and assesses speech discrimination

CLASSIFICATION

See **Table 63**. Mixed hearing disorders are quite common, particularly involving features of age-related presbycusis and conductive loss. Central auditory processing disorders become clinically important when superimposed on other ear pathology.

	Sensorineural Hearing Loss	Conductive Hearing Loss	Central Auditory Processing Disorder
Pathologic process	Cochlear or retrocochlear (cranial nerve VIII) pathology	Impaired transmission to inner ear from external or middle ear pathology	CNS change interfering with ability to discriminate speech, particularly when background noise is present
Weber test findings	Lateralizes away from impaired ear	Lateralizes toward impaired ear	Normal
Rinne test findings	Normal	Abnormal in impaired ear	Normal
Audiogram/ Audiometry findings	Air and bone conduction thresholds equal	Air conduction thresholds greater than bone conduction thresholds	Normal for pure tone audiometry; impaired for speech discrimination

Table 63. Classification of Hearing Disorders

(cont.)

	Sensorineural Hearing Loss	Conductive Hearing Loss	Central Auditory Processing Disorder
Common causes	Age-related presbycusis (high frequency loss, problems with speech discrimination) most common	Cerumen impaction	Dementia
		Otosclerosis	Stroke
	Excessive noise exposure	RA	Presbycusis
	Acoustic neuroma	Paget disease	Possibly normal aging
	Ménière disease (both high- and low-frequency loss)	Psoriasis	
		Osteoma	
	Ototoxic drugs	Exostosis	
		Squamous cell cancer	

Table 63. Classification of Hearing Disorders (cont.)

MANAGEMENT

Remove Ear Wax

Ear wax causes conductive loss and further reduces hearing. Soft wax can be flushed with a syringe, removed with a cerumen scoop, or suctioned. Dry wax should be softened before removal by doing the following:

Fill ear canal with 5–10 gtt water and cover with cotton q12h × ≥4 d. Liquid must stay in contact with ear for ≥15 min. Hearing may worsen as cerumen expands. Water is as effective as commercial preparations (eg, *Debrox, Cerumenex, Colace).* Use of any of the commercial preparations for >4 d may cause ear irritation.

Table 64. Rehabilitation of Hearing Loss, by Level of Loss

Level of Loss (dB)	Difficulty Understanding	Need for Hearing Technology
16–25 (slight)	None	None
26–40 (mild)	Normal speech	Hearing aid or MEI in specific situations
41–55 (moderate)	Loud speech	Hearing aid or MEI in many situations
56–69 (moderately severe)	Anything but amplified speech	Hearing aid, MEI, or EAS for all communication
70–90 (severe)	Even amplified speech	EAS or cochlear implant
≥91 (profound)	Even amplified speech	Cochlear implant and/or speech reading, aural rehabilitation, sign language

Notes: EAS = electric acoustic stimulation; MEI = middle ear implant.

Hearing Technology

Hearing Aids: Digital devices enhance select frequencies for each ear. Amplification in both ears (binaural) provides best speech understanding; unilateral aid may be appropriate if hearing loss is asymmetrical, if hearing-aid care is challenging, or if cost is a factor. Features that enhance sound and speech quality include directional microphones, open-fit hearing aids, ear-to-ear wireless coordination, and in the canal extended-wear aids *(Lyric).*

Cochlear Implants: Bypass the middle ear, directly innervate the cochlear nerve. Results after age 65 comparable to those in younger people. Failure rate <1%, but patient selection important. Selection criteria:

- Moderate to profound bilateral sensorineural hearing loss
- <60% correct on hearing in noise test in one or both ears
- Unilateral deafness with or without severe ipsilateral tinnitus
- Benefit from aids less than that expected from implant
- No external or middle ear pathology
- No medical contraindication to general anesthesia
- No contraindication to surgical placement of device
- Family support, motivation, appropriate expectations

Electric Acoustic Stimulation: Use of a cochlear implant and hearing aid in the same ear; for patients who have ≥60 dB hearing loss at frequencies >1000 Hz, even though they may have mild to moderate hearing loss at frequencies ≤1000 Hz. Benefit patients more than either modality alone. The hearing aid amplifies residual hearing at low frequencies, while the cochlear implant provides electric stimulation to the high frequencies. Users still perform well when using the implant without the hearing aid.

Middle Ear Implants: A fully implantable ossicular stimulator; all components (including battery) are implanted under the skin; for adults who cannot wear hearing aids for medical (eg, collapsed ear canal, inability to handle device) or personal (ie, cosmetic) reasons. FDA-approved implant for severe hearing loss *(Esteem)* has limited availability, is expensive, and the reoperation rate exceeds 20%. Probably not better than external aids.

Bone-Anchored Hearing Aids: BAHA is small titanium implant inserted into the skull where it osteointegrates. A small portion of the implant protrudes through the skin to form a snap attachment point for a removable bone-conduction hearing aid. The device bypasses the external canal and middle ear. *Potential indications:* Congenital atresia of the ear canal, chronic infection of the middle or outer ear, allergic reactions to standard hearing aids, single-sided deafness (eg, after removal of an acoustic neuroma or from a viral or vascular insult). The limited evidence on benefits is through case series reports.

Hearing Assistive Technologies benefit people at all levels of hearing from normal to profound impairment. Patients who have difficulty hearing in some or many situations even with hearing aids or cochlear implants will benefit. At www.soundstrategy.com, access the *Hearing Assessment Tool.* Registering for a free account allows use of the tool to identify adaptive technology to enhance communication in 4 critical areas:
- face-to-face communication (eg, restaurants)
- enjoying electronic media (TV, radio, movie theater, concerts)
- telephone—both land lines and cell phones
- detecting important warning sounds (doorbells, telephone, smoke alarm)

The assistive technology includes hardwired body-style amplifiers, wireless (loop, FM, infrared, and digital systems), telecommunication devices, visual technology, and alerting technology. Personal pocket devices (eg, *Pocketalker)* are inexpensive, and apps are available to convert a smart phone and a headset into a pocket device.

Tips for Communication with Hearing-impaired People
- Ask the person how best to communicate
- Stand or sit 2–3 ft away
- Have the person's attention
- Have the person seated in front of a wall, which helps reflect sound
- Speak toward the better ear
- Use lower-pitched voice
- Speak slowly and distinctly; don't shout

- Rephrase rather than repeat
- Pause at the end of phrases or ideas
- Ask the person to repeat what was heard

Tips for Approaches to Patients Resistant to Acquiring/Using Hearing Aids

Set appropriate expectations, inform the patient, support and assist the patient during the period of adjustment.
- Hearing aids do not produce normal hearing; they are aids to hearing
- Hearing aids usually need adjustments over months; expect to see the audiologist often
- Report problems: hearing or understanding speech in specific situations (eg, noisy environments); difficulty operating the hearing aid; aid-associated discomfort
- Inquire how the patient feels about hearing aid appearance
- Recommend group audiologic visits of newly fitted patients, if available
- Include caregivers in the process of fitting hearing aids
- Regularly examine ears for cerumen or other pathology

Tips for Treating Hearing Loss in Older Adults with Frailty or Multiple Morbidities

- Include hearing evaluation in team-based geriatric assessment
- Assess, and when possible, improve visual function
- Assess and treat physical, cognitive, and affective disorders
- For patients with hearing aids and problems with manual dexterity, consider easier-to-use hearing aid models (eg, behind-the-ear or in-the-ear types)
- For hearing-impaired patients with advanced cognitive deficits
  - Prevent loss of hearing aid by attaching a metal loop to its body and tying a thin nylon line through the loop, fasten the other end of the line to the patient's clothing
  - Educate caregivers on proper use of hearing aids
  - Consider use of personal amplifier *(pocket-talker)* or other assistive listening device if patient is unable to use a hearing aid
- Assess for hearing deficits and correct them in patients presenting with geriatric syndromes

TINNITUS

Definition

The perception of sound in the absence of external acoustic stimulus. The patient's description of the sound helps in diagnosis of the cause. Some tinnitus is normal, typically last <5 min, <once/wk. Pathologic tinnitus last >5 min, >weekly.

Evaluation

- Examine ear canals for cerumen, otitis externa or interna; treat and reassess.
- Check medications that cause or exacerbate tinnitus, eg, NSAIDs, ASA, antibiotics (especially erythromycin), loop diuretics (especially furosemide), chemotherapy, quinine.
- Assess the severity of tinnitus by asking: Is it annoying? Have major consequences for quality of life? Interfere with work or family life? Yes to more of these questions suggests greater severity.
- Unless initial evaluation shows the likely cause to be presbycusis or a myofascial disorder, refer to otolaryngology.
- If the examiner can hear the tinnitus (objective tinnitus), refer the patient to otolaryngology.

Some of the More Common Causes of Tinnitus

- **Originating from the auditory system:** presbycusis, otosclerosis, vestibular schwannoma, Chiari malformations
- **Myofascial disorders:** temporomandibular joint (TMJ) dysfunction, whiplash injuries, craniocervical disease
- **Vascular disorders:** arterial bruits, arteriovenous shunts, paraganglioma, venous hums, high cardiac output states
- **Neurologic disorders:** Tensor tympani and/or stapedius muscle spasm, palatal muscles myoclonus
- **Patulous eustachian tube**

Treatment

- Is first directed at the underlying disorder (eg, hearing aids for the hearing impaired or tx of TMJ disorder)
- If the patient still has tinnitus that produces distress, symptom-oriented tx include:
  - CBT: improves quality of life, reduces depression, and has the best evidence supporting its use.
  - Cochlear implants for those with profound hearing loss provides long-term tinnitus suppression.

ANEMIA

Evaluation

- Hematopoietic reserve capacity declines with age (eg, slower return of Hb to normal after phlebotomy); don't perform serial blood counts in clinically stable patients.[CW] Excessive phlebotomy can lead to unnecessary transfusions.
- Evaluate people >65 yr old when Hb <13 in men and <12 in women.
- Evaluate if Hb falls >1 g/dL in 1 yr.
- Physical examination and laboratory tests for kidney or liver disease.
- Evaluate GI and GU source if iron deficient.
- Check WBC and peripheral blood smear; pursue suspected causes as appropriate.
- Combined deficiencies are common in older adults; reasonable to check B_{12}, folate, and iron in all cases. MCV is not reliable in combined deficiency states.
- Check reticulocyte count and reticulocyte index.
  - Reticulocyte count or index high: adequate response, suspect blood loss or RBC destruction (Hemolytic anemia, p 142).
  - Reticulocyte count or index normal or low: evaluate for possible B_{12} or folate deficiency (**Figure 6**), and possible iron deficiency (**Figure 7**)

Figure 6. Evaluation of Hypoproliferative Anemia Due to Possible B_{12} or Folate Deficiency

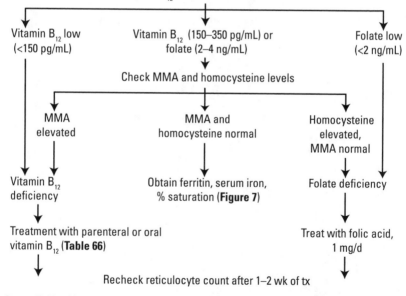

Check vitamin B_{12} and serum or RBC folate levels

Vitamin B_{12} low (<150 pg/mL)

Vitamin B_{12} (150–350 pg/mL) or folate (2–4 ng/mL)

Folate low (<2 ng/mL)

Check MMA and homocysteine levels

MMA elevated

MMA and homocysteine normal

Homocysteine elevated, MMA normal

Vitamin B_{12} deficiency

Obtain ferritin, serum iron, % saturation (**Figure 7**)

Folate deficiency

Treatment with parenteral or oral vitamin B_{12} (**Table 66**)

Treat with folic acid, 1 mg/d

Recheck reticulocyte count after 1–2 wk of tx

Source: Balducci L. *J Amer Geriatr Soc* 2003; 51(3 Suppl):S2–9. Reprinted with permission.

Figure 7. Evaluation of Possible Iron Deficiency Anemia

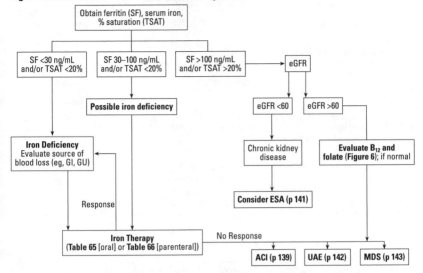

Notes: ACI = anemia of chronic inflammation; ESA = erythropoiesis-stimulating agent; MDS = myelodysplastic syndrome; UAE = undifferentiated anemia of the elderly.

Common Anemias of Later Life: Diagnosis and Treatment

Iron deficiency anemia (Figure 7)
- Serum iron and iron saturation are both low, transferrin is high, and ferritin ≤30.
- Begin tx with oral iron using the steps outlined in **Table 65**.
- If oral iron replacement is inadequate or not tolerated, use parenteral replacement (**Table 66**).
- Don't transfuse RBCs for iron deficiency without hemodynamic instability.**CW**

Anemia of chronic inflammation (ACI; also known as anemia of chronic disease)
- Most common causes in older adults:
  - Acute and chronic infection
  - Chronic inflammation
  - Malignancy
  - Protein calorie malnutrition
  - Unidentified chronic disease
- Laboratory tests: usually low iron, low or normal TIBC, ferritin >100 ng/mL
- Check erythropoietin level; if <500 mU/mL may respond to administration of recombinant human erythropoietin (**Table 67**).
- Drug-related AEs from erythropoietin tx in ACI have not been well studied.
- Restoring Hb to 10–11 g/dL improves quality of life, function, and possibly survival.

Combined iron deficiency and anemia of inflammation
- Usual laboratory values (iron, TIBC, ferritin) less reliable in presence of inflammatory conditions (**Figure 7**).

Table 65. Steps in Oral Iron Replacement

		Hb (g/dL)	Oral elemental iron total replacement dose (mg)
Step 1: Estimate iron replacement dose based on Hb		>11	5,000
		9–11	10,000
		<9	15,000

	Preparation*	Number of tablets to achieve 5000-mg elemental iron replacement
Step 2: Select an oral iron preparation (only 10% of oral iron is absorbed)	Ferrous sulfate (Elixir 2.7 mg/15 mL, 324-mg tab, 65 mg elemental iron)	75
	Ferrous gluconate (300-mg tab, 36 mg elemental iron)	140
	Ferrous fumarate (100-mg tab, 33 mg elemental iron)	150
	Iron polysaccharide (150-mg tab, 150 mg elemental iron)	33
Step 3: Decide on dosing frequency	Many patients cannot tolerate more than a single tablet daily. Iron is best absorbed on an empty stomach. Assess tolerance after 1 wk (phone call); if not tolerating, adjust dose, interval, or preparation.	
Step 4: Recheck Hb and ferritin after each 5000-mg cycle	Give additional 5000-mg cycles prn.	

*Tolerance to GI side effects improves, however cost increases going down the list of preparations.

Note: 1 unit packed RBCs replaces 500 mg iron, or approximately the same as is absorbed from a 5000-mg cycle of oral iron. Reticulocytosis should occur in 7–10 d. Lack of correction with replacement suggests nonadherence, malabsorption, or ongoing blood loss. H_2-blockers, antacids, and PPIs reduce absorption, and some patients will need parenteral replacement (**Table 66**). Enterically coated preparations are less well absorbed.

Table 66. Parenteral Iron Replacement[a]

Medication	Formulation and Dosage
Iron sucrose *(Venofer)*	200 mg IV, injected undiluted over 2–5 min on 5 different occasions within 14-d period (total cumulative dose of 1000 mg) Other recommended dosing options: • 100 mg, dilute to max of 100 mL in NS and infuse over ≥15 min • 300 mg, dilute to max of 250 mL in NS and infuse over 1.5 h • 400 mg, dilute to max of 250 mL in NS and infuse over 2.5 h
Ferumoxytol *(Feraheme)*	510 mg IV × 1 dose followed by 510 mg 3–8 d later
Ferric carboxymaltose *(Injectafer)*	750 mg IV followed by 750 mg IV 7 d later; total cumulative dose not to exceed 1500 mg elemental iron; weight less than 50 kg, 15 mg/kg IV followed by 15 mg/kg IV 7 d later
Sodium ferric gluconate complex[b] *(Ferrlecit, Nulecit)*	10 mL IV (125 mg elemental iron) in 100 mL NS, over 1 h **or** slow IV (12.5 mg/min) undiluted; usual minimum cumulative dose 1 g elemental iron over 8 consecutive dialysis sessions

[a] Parenteral iron is 100% absorbed, so estimate total dose as 10% of the oral dose in **Table 65**.

[b] Used during hemodialysis: treats iron deficiency anemia, during epoetin tx.

- Anemia often more severe than in chronic inflammation alone. Iron, transferrin, and saturation reduced. If ferritin ≤45, iron deficiency is confirmed. If 45–99, iron deficiency is possible; either treat presumed iron deficiency and evaluate response by reticulocyte count at 2 wk or check soluble transferrin receptor (sTfR). If sTfR/log ferritin >1.5, iron deficiency is confirmed.

Anemia of chronic kidney disease

- Caused by decreased erythropoietin production; check erythropoietin level, iron studies, B_{12}, and folate.
- Correct all correctable causes of anemia (iron deficiency, inflammation) before using erythropoiesis-stimulating agents (ESAs). Keep transferrin saturation 20–50% and ferritin 100–500 ng/mL. Oral iron absorption is poor in CKD; parenteral replacement often needed.
- Restoring Hb levels with ESAs decreases transfusions and fatigue but doubles stroke risk in people with DM, CKD, and anemia. Don't administer ESAs to CKD patients with Hb ≥10 g/dL without symptoms of anemia.[CW]
- Guidelines (www.kdigo.org), recommend individualized tx.
  ○ Use ESAs with caution (if at all) in patients with malignancy, hx of stroke, or hx of malignancy.
  ○ For most patients, consider ESA and iron replacement when Hb is 9–10 g/dL with the goal of avoiding Hb <9 and the need for transfusion.
  ○ Some patients will have improved quality of life with Hb above 11.5 and will accept the risk; do not let Hb exceed 13.
  ○ Begin erythropoietin based on body weight (**Table 67**); check Hb q2wk with target increase of 0.5–1 g/dL/wk, not more. Adjust erythropoietin dosage q4wk; increase or decrease by 25% to reach goal. Reduce dose or frequency of ESA when Hb exceeds target, rather than stopping.
  ○ Some patients will not respond to usual dosages, and it may be that risk of cardiovascular events are a result of high dosages. Failure to respond to ESAs in the first month of usual weight-based dosing is ESA hyporesponsiveness. In these patients do not use more than twice the weight-based dose.
  ○ Evaluate for antibody-mediated pure red cell aplasia in patients using ESAs for >8 wk if Hb declines 0.5–1 g/wk.

Table 67. Erythropoiesis-stimulating Agents		
Medication	**Formulation and Dosage**	**Comments**
Epoetin alfa *(Epogen, Procrit)*	50–150 U/kg SC or IV 3×/wk in CKD; 150 U/kgSC 3×/wk U/wk in chemotherapy	*Caution:* Raise Hb only to avoid need for transfusion; higher Hb increases cardiovascular events.
Darbepoetin alfa *(Aranesp)*	2.25mcg/kg/wk in chemotherapy; 0.45 mcg/kg/wk in CKD; dose q2–4wk when Hb stable.	*All Agents:* Monitor BP, adjust dosage q4–6wk based on response. Use in cancer patients not on chemotherapy increases risk of death. Use in patients on chemotherapy reduces need for transfusion but increases risk of thromboembolic events.
Methoxy polyethylene glycol-epoetin beta *(Mircera)*	0.6 mcg/kg IV q2wk on CKD	

Anemia of B₁₂ and folate deficiency (Figure 6)

- Laboratory tests: anemia or pancytopenia, macrocytosis
- Serum B_{12} 65–95% sensitivity for clinical deficiency if <200 pg/mL; deficiency is possible at <350 pg/mL; check serum methylmalonic acid level (MMA) to confirm deficiency.
- Borderline folate levels 2–4 ng/mL should prompt homocysteine check for deficiency. A few days of poor po intake lowers serum (but not body stores) of folate.
- Treatment:
  - B_{12} 1000 mcg IM daily × 5 d, then weekly × 4 wk, then 1000 mcg IM every mo.
  - Alternatives for maintenance replacement include: 100 mcg/d po or 2500 mcg sl once daily or nasal spr *(Nascobal)* 500 mcg intranasally in one nostril once weekly (nasal spr should be administered ≥1 h before or after ingestion of hot foods or liquids).
  - If using nonparenteral formulations, monitor levels to ensure replacement is adequate, using MMA every 1–3 yr.
  - Folate 1 mg/d po for 1–4 mo or until complete hematologic recovery.

Undifferentiated (or Unexplained) Anemia of the Elderly (UAE)

- No evidence of B_{12} or folate deficiency, iron studies all normal, CrCl >30 mL/min; hypocellular bone marrow; erythropoietin levels low for degree of anemia; inflammatory markers not elevated.
- Prevalence: <1/3 of all anemias after age 65
- May be age-related decline in hematopoietic reserve, low erythropoietin, or poor response to endogenous erythropoietin or low testosterone in men
- At follow-up, at least 25% evolve to a myelodysplastic syndrome.

Hemolytic anemia

- Hallmark is high reticulocyte count. About 2% of all anemias after age 65.
- Most common cause is autoimmune (low haptoglobin, positive direct antiglobulin) associated with chronic lymphocytic leukemia, medications, lymphoma, collagen vascular disease; idiopathic.
- Causes if not autoimmune: mechanical heart valve, other intrinsic cause.

RBC Transfusion for Anemia

Acute blood loss

- Studies support restricting transfusion until Hb is 7–8 g/dL in patients with hip fracture, those who have cardiovascular disease or risk factors, those undergoing cardiac surgery, and those in ICU. This threshold is appropriate in older patients.**ᶜᵂ**
- Improved outcomes using the 7–8 g/dL threshold include reduced risk of bacterial infection, MI, mortality, rebleeding, and pulmonary edema.
- Avoid transfusions of RBC for arbitrary hemoglobin or hematocrit thresholds and in the absence of symptoms of active coronary disease, HF, or stroke.**ᶜᵂ**

Chronic anemia

- Chronic anemia due to refractory aplastic anemia, myelodysplastic syndromes, etc, will require transfusion. For these patients the transfusion threshold is based on symptoms to generally maintain Hb >9 g/dL in men and 8 g/dL in women.
- Don't transfuse more units of blood than absolutely necessary.**ᶜᵂ** Single-unit transfusions should be the standard in stable noncardiac patients.**ᶜᵂ**

PANCYTOPENIA

Unless due to B_{12} deficiency or drug-induced (eg, chloramphenicol, NSAIDs, antithyroid drugs, corticosteroids, penicillamine, allopurinol, gold, etc), bone marrow aspirate is indicated; causes include cancer, fibrosis, myelodysplasia, and aplastic anemia.

Aplastic Anemia

- Hematopoietic stem cell failure; in 78%, cause is idiopathic but felt to be immune mediated
- Diagnosis: hypocellular bone marrow
- Treatment: 75% respond to immunosuppressive tx

Myelodysplastic Syndromes (MDS)

A group of stem cell disorders with decreased production of blood elements causing risk of symptomatic anemia, infection, and bleeding; risk of transformation to acute leukemia varies by syndrome. May be responsible for a high proportion of unexplained anemias in older patients (p 142).

Diagnosis

The diagnosis of MDS should be considered in any older patient with unexplained cytopenia(s) or monocytosis. Inspection of the peripheral blood smear and bone marrow aspirate is a next step in diagnosis. Because these alone are not diagnostic of MDS, in vitro bone marrow progenitor cultures, trephine biopsies, flow cytometry, immunohistochemical studies, and chromosome analysis are routinely needed for diagnosis.

Staging and Prognosis

- Four different classification systems are available to help estimate prognosis, but none explain most of the variability in survival.
- Classification systems stratify patients from low- to high-risk groups based on various characteristics that differ by classification system.
- In general, poorer survival occurs with: higher proportion of blast cells, complex (>3 different) karyotypes or abnormal chromosome 7, and greater number of cell lines with cytopenias (Hb <10 g/dL, absolute neutrophils <1800/μL, platelet count <100,000).
- Median survival of high-risk patients is independent of age and is under 6 mo. However, among low-risk patients, survival is substantially affected by age with mean survival for those <60 yr old about 11.8 yr, >60 yr old about 4.8 yr, and >70 yr old about 3.9 yr.
- The higher the blast count the more likely the conversion to acute myelogenous leukemia (AML); but the most common causes of death are complications of the cytopenias, not acute leukemia.

Monitoring

- Should be under the direction of a hematologist and will vary by patient age, disease stage, and prognosis and tx status.
- Monitor all patients for development of symptomatic cytopenias (anemia, infection, bleeding) and progression to AML.

Therapy

- Low-risk patients are not treated until they become transfusion dependent.
- Tx is warranted with symptomatic cytopenias, although there is no consensus regarding standard tx and patients should be encouraged to join clinical trials.
- Lower-risk patients are generally treated with low-intensity tx including growth factors, then lenalidomide, then hypomethylating agents.
- High- and intermediate-risk patients receive hypomethylating agents, stem cell transplant, or remission-induction chemotherapy.

- Only stem cell transplant holds a hope for cure; while not usually an option for patients aged >60–65 yr old, clinical trials are enrolling patients 50–75 yr old.

PRIMARY MYELOPROLIFERATIVE DISORDERS
Polycythemia Vera
- Diagnosis: elevated RBC mass with normal arterial oxygen saturation and splenomegaly
- If no splenomegaly, 2 of the following: leukocytosis, increased leukocyte alkaline phosphatase, or increased B_{12}; or genetic testing showing JAK-2
- Treatment: phlebotomy to achieve iron deficiency and hematocrit ≤45, and ASA 325 mg/d

Essential Thrombocytosis
- Platelet count >600,000/μL on 2 occasions ≥1 mo apart; Hb <13 mg/dL or normal RBC mass
- Normal iron marrow stores and no splenomegaly; exclude reactive thrombocytosis
- No Philadelphia or *bcr-abl* gene rearrangements or myelofibrosis in marrow
- Treatment: For patients at high risk of thrombohemorrhagic events, use low-dose ASA and hydroxyurea. Anagrelide is less effective at preventing thrombosis.

Chronic Myelogenous Leukemia
- Leukocytosis with early myeloid forms evenly distributed in peripheral blood
- Philadelphia chromosome in >95% of cases
- Leukocyte alkaline phosphatase score low
- Treatment: Chronic and accelerated phases—tyrosine kinase inhibitors (imatinib, nilotinib, dasatinib, bosutinib). Stem cell transplant is reserved for patients in the accelerated phase.

Myelofibrosis
- Pancytopenia, splenomegaly, and other extramedullary hematopoiesis
- Marrow fibrosis (dry tap) and peripheral blood: leukoerythroblastosis, tear-drop cells
- Acute leukemia develops in 5–20%
- Treatment: Hematopoietic stem cell transplantation (rarely an option for patients >65 yr old); ruxolitinib reduces symptoms and improves median survival for select patients.

MONOCLONAL GAMMOPATHY AND MULTIPLE MYELOMA
Monoclonal Gammopathy of Undetermined Significance (MGUS)
- Definition: monoclonal immunoglobulin concentration in serum ≤3 g/dL; no end organ damage (ie, no lytic bone lesions, anemia, hypercalcemia, or renal insufficiency); plasma cells in marrow ≤10%
- Prevalence increases with age: 3.2% at ≥50 yr; 6.6% at ≥80 yr
- Evaluation: SPEP, serum immunofixation, and serum κ:λ light-chain ratio
  - If initial monoclonal protein is <1.5 g/dL and no other risk factors (see below), repeat laboratory testing at 6 mo and q2–3 yr thereafter if stable.
  - If initial monoclonal protein is ≥1.5 g/dL or any other of the risk factor (see below) is present, obtain bone marrow biopsy and skeletal survey, and repeat laboratory testing at 6 mo and annually.
  - If monoclonal protein is IgM, obtain abdominal CT to exclude a lymphoproliferative process.
- 0.4–1%/yr progress to multiple myeloma. **Risk factors** for progression: monoclonal protein ≥1.5 g/dL, monoclonal immunoglobulin other than IgG, abnormal serum free light chain ratio (κ:λ light chains) of <0.26 or >1.65. The greater the number of factors present, the greater the risk of progression.

- Increased risk of vertebral fracture; bone turnover markers are normalized with use of bisphosphonates.

Multiple Myeloma

- Smoldering myeloma (asymptomatic stage) defined by presence of:
  - Serum monoclonal protein >3 g/dL and/or plasma cells >10% to <60%
  - No end organ damage
  - A subset of high-risk patients may benefit from tx, but should enroll in clinical trials.
- Symptomatic multiple myeloma, defined by presence of:
  - Serum or urinary monoclonal protein >3 g/dL *and*
  - Clonal plasma cells in bone marrow >10% or plasmacytoma *and*
  - Presence of end organ damage, hypercalcemia, lytic lesions, renal failure, anemia, *or* recurrent infections
  - Or >60% clonal plasma cells in bone marrow in the absence of end-organ damage
- Treat symptomatic patients. First, determine eligibility for stem cell transplant and risk based on genetic abnormalities.
  - Transplant candidates first receive induction tx; exact agents selected based on risk.
  - Nontransplant candidates receive chemotherapy based on risk.
  - Frail older adults are generally treated with reduced doses of lenalidomide and dexamethasone; higher-risk patients may receive alternate agents.
  - Zoledronic acid (not all bisphosphonates) started at the time of diagnosis reduces skeletal events and improves overall survival independent of skeletal events. This effect was seen whether patients received transplant or oral agents.
  - Adverse effects of bisphosphonates include hypocalcemia, fever, and in 1/163 osteonecrosis of the jaw. Risk of osteonecrosis of jaw is reduced with good oral hygiene. Monitor for micro-albuminuria and stop tx if this develops.
- Performance status (ie, limitation in self-care ability: ≥50% of time in bed or chair), age >70 yr old, and albumin <3 g/dL have as much prognostic value as any of the disease factors.
- Patients at all stages are at risk of venous and possibly also arterial thrombosis related to both the disease and its tx (eg, thalidomide).
- Supportive care for all patients with advanced disease
  - Anemia may require transfusion. Erythropoietin is generally reserved for patients on chemotherapy with Hb <10 g/dL.
  - IV immunoglobulins monthly for recurrent bacterial infections and hypogammaglobulinemia; administer pneumococcal but not varicella vaccine.
  - Surgical fixation and radiation tx for fractures and impending fractures.
  - Maintain hydration with at least 2 L/d and avoid NSAIDs and contrast because of renal dysfunction.
  - Provide adequate analgesia.

URINARY INCONTINENCE (UI)

UI is the complaint of involuntary leakage of urine. In older adults, it is most often multifactorial and results from some combination of lower urinary tract abnormalities, changes in neurologic control of voiding, multimorbidity, and functional impairment. Like other geriatric syndromes, effective tx requires addressing more than one factor.

Classification of UI

Transient and Functional Causes of Incontinence: UI is caused or exacerbated by factors outside the lower urinary tract (eg, comorbidities, medications, mobility). However, UI from these sources is transient only if they are recognized and addressed. These same factors are frequent contributors to UI in patients with urge, stress, and other causes of persistent UI.

Table 68. Types of Persistent Urinary Incontinence: Characteristics and Causes

Type	Characteristic	Causes
Urge	UI with compelling and often sudden need to void	Idiopathic or associated with CNS lesions or bladder irritation from infection, stones, or tumors
Stress	UI with increased intra-abdominal pressure (eg, cough or sneeze)	Due to failure of sphincter mechanisms to remain closed during bladder filling; insufficient pelvic support in women; prostate surgery in men
Mixed	UI with both urgency and increases in intra-abdominal pressure	Some of the above
Overflow (Detrusor Underactivity)	UI is continual, and postvoid residual urine is increased (typically >500 mL)	Impaired detrusor contractility from neuropathy, DM, vitamin B12 deficiency, tabes dorsalis, alcoholism, or spinal disease, or bladder outlet obstruction in men most often due to BPH, cancer, or stricture; in women due to prior incontinence surgery or a large cystocele
Detrusor Hyperactivity with Increased Capacity (DHIC)	Characteristically UI with urge symptoms, but stress-related UI may occur; postvoid residual moderately elevated 200–300 mL.	Detrusor does not contract sufficiently to empty but still has low-grade hyperactivity causing urgency. Underlying causes believed to stem from some of the same processes as urge and overflow UI.

Other (rare): Bladder-sphincter dyssynergia, fistulas, reduced detrusor compliance

Overactive Bladder: Frequency and urgency without UI; tx is the same as for urge UI.

Evaluation

History
- Determine type of UI (**Table 68**)
- Identify "red flag" symptoms including sudden onset of UI, pelvic pain (constant, worsened, or improved with voiding), and hematuria. These suggest neoplastic or neurologic disease and require prompt referral to a urologist if UTI is excluded.
- Lower urinary tract symptom review: frequency, nocturia, slow stream, hesitancy, interrupted voiding, terminal dribbling

- Medical condition status and medications used to treat them, reviewed in association with onset or worsening of UI
- Ask "How does UI affect your life?" and also ask about the presence of FI.

Physical Examination
- Functional status (eg, mobility, dexterity)
- Mental status (important for planning tx)
- Findings:
  - Bladder distention
  - Cord compression (interosseous muscle wasting, Hoffmann's or Babinski's signs)
  - Rectal mass or impaction
  - Sacral root integrity (anal sphincter tone, anal wink, perineal sensation)
  - Volume overload, edema

Male GU
Prostate consistency; symmetry; if uncircumcised, check phimosis, paraphimosis, balanitis

Female GU
Atrophic vaginitis (p 304); pelvic support (cystocele, rectocele, prolapse; p 333)

Testing
- **Bladder Diary:** Record time and volume of incontinent and continent voids, activities and time of sleep; knowing oral intake is sometimes helpful. Sample diary available at niddk. nih.gov/health-information/health-topics/urologic-disease/daily-bladder-diary/Pages/facts. aspx.
- **Postvoid Residual:** If available, bladder ultrasound after voiding is preferred to catheterization. If >200 mL, repeat; still >200 mL suggests detrusor weakness, neuropathy, medications, fecal impaction, outlet obstruction, or DHIC. Even if postvoid residual is not available, begin tx steps as shown in **Figure 8**.
- **Laboratory:** UA to check for hematuria or glycosuria; urine C&S if onset of UI or worsening of UI is acute; serum glucose and calcium if polyuric; renal function tests and B_{12} if urinary retention; urine cytology if hematuria or pain.

Figure 8. Stepwise Evaluation and Treatment of Common UI Conditions

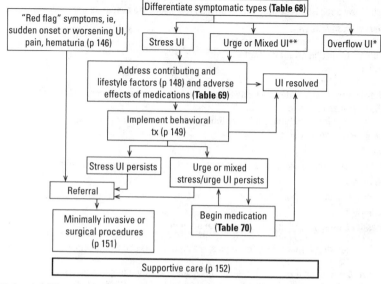

* Referral to differentiate neuropathy from obstruction (also **Table 68**)

** Treat both components of Mixed UI

- **Urodynamic Testing:** Usually not needed; indicated before corrective surgery, when diagnosis is unclear, when empiric tx is ineffective, or if postvoid residual volume >200–300 mL (possibly lower in men).
- Don't perform cystoscopy, urodynamics or renal and bladder ultrasound in work-up of uncomplicated urge UI.[cw]

Management in a Stepped Approach

Contributing Factors

- Environment: ensure adequate access
- Mentation: If the patient is cognitively impaired, recommend **Prompted toileting** (152).
- Manual dexterity: compensate for deficits, eg, by adapting clothing
- Medical conditions: optimize tx for HF, COPD, or chronic cough
- Medications: eliminate or minimize those with adverse effects (**Table 69**)
- Mobility: improve mobility or adapt environment

Lifestyle Factors

- Caffeine and diuretic (including carbonated) beverages produce rapid bladder filling
- Fluid intake: avoid extremes of fluid intake (<32 oz or >64 oz), reduce fluids after supper time to avoid nocturia
- Constipation: produces urethral obstruction or places pressure on bladder
- Weight loss: 60% UI reduction with large weight loss (≥16 kg); 30% decrease in odds for stress UI with 3.5 kg loss
- Smoking: produces chronic cough, encourage patient to quit

Behavioral Therapy

- Efficacy for behavioral tx: >35% reduction in UI; 50% greater patient perception of cure.
- Two components of bladder training for urge UI:
  1) Voiding on schedule during the day (start q2h) to keep bladder volume low. When no incontinence for 2 d, increase voiding interval by 30–60 min until voiding q3–4h.
  2) Urge suppression (**Figure 9**), which retrains the CNS and pelvic mechanisms to inhibit contractions and leakage.

Figure 9. Urge Suppression

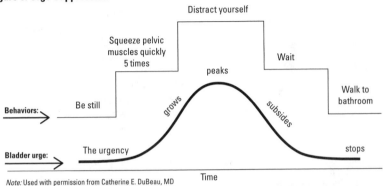

Note: Used with permission from Catherine E. DuBeau, MD

- Tx for stress UI involves timed toileting (as above) and also pelvic muscle (Kegel) exercises—isolate pelvic muscles (avoid thigh, rectal, buttocks contraction); perform slow velocity contraction, sustained for 6–8 sec. Perform 3 sets of 8–12 contractions in each set, on 3–4 d/wk (not daily) for at least 15–20 wk. Handout alone can reduce leakage by 50% (www.nlm.nih.gov/medlineplus/ ency/patientinstructions/000141.htm). Biofeedback can help with teaching; covered by Medicare if patient unsuccessful after 4 wk of conventional teaching (refer to PT).
- Tx for post-prostatectomy UI
  ○ Pelvic floor electrical stimulation and biofeedback begun soon after catheter removal in post-prostatectomy patients improves early recovery of continence.
  ○ Even for those with UI ≥1 yr after prostatectomy, pelvic floor exercises and urge control (**Figure 9**) reduces the number of incontinence episodes by more than half. Send patients to an experienced continence specialist for training (nurse practitioner or PT).
- Behavioral tx is at least as effective for overactive bladder symptoms in men on α-blocker tx as antimuscarinic tx. For benefit, patients should not have outlet obstruction (ie, postvoid residual urine not >150 mL) (also Prostate, p 275)
- DHIC is first treated with behavioral methods; may add detrusor muscle-relaxing medications but follow postvoid residual; clean intermittent self-catheterization if needed.

Pharmacotherapy

- First eliminate medications causing/exacerbating UI if possible (**Table 69**).

Table 69. Medications Commonly Associated with UI

Medication/Class	Adverse Effects/Comments
ACEIs	Cough (stress UI) or cough-induced urge UI
Alcohol	Frequency, urgency, sedation, immobility
α-Adrenergic agonists	Outlet obstruction (men)
α-Adrenergic blockers (Avoid[BC])	Stress leakage (women)
Anticholinergics (Avoid[BC])	Impaired emptying, delirium, fecal impaction
Cholinesterase inhibitors	Increased uninhibited contractions and urgency
Calcium channel blockers	Impaired detrusor contraction, edema with nocturnal diuresis
Estrogen (oral, transdermal)	Stress and mixed UI (women), avoid systemic estrogens in women with UI[BC]
GABA-ergics (gabapentin, pregabalin)	Edema, nocturnal diuresis
Loop diuretics	Polyuria, frequency, urgency
NSAIDs/thiazolidinediones	Edema, nocturnal diuresis
Sedative hypnotics	Sedation, delirium, immobility
Opioid analgesics	Constipation, sedation, delirium
TCHS and antipsychotics (Avoid[BC])	Anticholinergic effects, sedation, immobility

- Data suggesting benefit of topical postmenopausal estrogen tx in urge and possibly stress UI are limited.
- See **Table 70** for pharmacotherapy for urge and mixed UI. All have shown equal efficacy in randomized controlled clinical trials. No oral antimuscarinic is clearly superior in terms of cognitive AEs. Combining antimuscarinics and cholinesterase inhibitors should be avoided.
- Significant benefit (≥50% reduction in UI) from pharmacotherapy occurs in <20% of patients.
- Select among alternative medications based on drug-related AEs (harms) (**Table 70**).
- >50% of patients stop tx by the end of 1 yr.
- Chronic antimuscarinic use is associated with tooth loss and caries; routine dental care is important.
- Reevaluate use of these agents regularly after they are prescribed for lack of efficacy. D/C medication if not effective. Avoid use of anticholinergic agents.[BC]

Table 70. Pharmacotherapy for Urge or Mixed Urinary Incontinence

Medication	Dosage	Formulations	Adverse Events/ Comments (Metabolism)
Antimuscarinics			*Class AEs:* dry mouth, blurry vision, dry eyes, delirium/confusion/dementia, constipation
Oxybutynin (*Ditropan*▲, *Ditropan XL*▲, *Gelnique* *Oxytrol Women*[OTC])	2.5–5 mg q8–12h 5–20 mg/d 1 g gel topically q24h 3.9 mg/d (apply pch 2 × /wk)	T: 5; S: 5 mg/5 mL SR: 5, 10, 15 10% gel, unit dose (1.14 mL) Transdermal pch 39 cm²	Dry mouth and constipation less with XL and pch than immediate release pch/gel: rotate sites to reduce skin irritation (L); OTC *Oxytrol* is less expensive

(cont.)

Table 70. Pharmacotherapy for Urge or Mixed Urinary Incontinence (cont.)

Medication	Dosage	Formulations	Adverse Events/ Comments (Metabolism)
Tolterodine (Detrol, Detrol LA)	2 mg q12h 4 mg/d	T: 1, 2 C: ER 2, 4	Withdrawn from tx trials for drug-related AEs; not different from placebo; P450 interactions (L, CYP3A4 and CYP2D6)
Trospium (Sanctura, Sanctura XR)	20 mg q12–24h (on empty stomach) 60 mg/d (XR)	T: 20 C: ER 60	Dyspepsia, headache; caution in liver dysfunction; dose once daily at hs in patients ≥75 yr old or with CrCl <30 mL/min; XR formulation not recommended if CrCl <30 mL/min (L, K)
Darifenacin (Enablex)	7.5–15 mg/d	T: 7.5, 15	Gastric retention; not recommended in severe liver impairment. Withdrawal from tx trials for drug-related AEs; not different from placebo. (L, CYP3A4 and CYP2D6)
Solifenacin (VESIcare)	5–10 mg/d	T: 5, 10	Same as darifenacin; max dose 5 mg if CrCl <30 mL/min or moderate liver impairment. Women with urge UI who have taken other antimuscarinics that have failed may benefit from a trial dose of the 5-mg dose (no additional benefit at the 10-mg dose) (L, CYP3A4)
Fesoterodine (TOVIAZ)	4–8 mg/d	T: 4, 8	Max dose 4 mg if CrCl <30 mL/min (L, CYP3A4, CYP2D6)
β-3 agonist			
Mirabegron (Myrbetriq)	25–50 mg/d	T: 25, 50	Hypertension (monitor BP), nausea, headache, dizziness, tachycardia. AF; max dose 25 mg if CrCl <30 mL/min; not recommended in severe kidney or severe liver impairment; raises digoxin and reduces metoprolol levels (L, CYP2D6). Combination with antimuscarinics should be done with caution while monitoring postvoid residual urine.

Note: For prostate obstruction UI, see Benign Prostatic Hyperplasia, p 275.

Minimally Invasive Procedures

• Sacral nerve neuromodulation can be effective for refractory urge UI and urinary retention (both idiopathic and neurogenic). Electrode is implanted to stimulate S3; done as a trial before permanent device.

• Pessaries may benefit women with vaginal (p 333) or uterine prolapse who experience retention and stress or urge UI.

- Botulinum toxin is also effective for refractory urge UI (not FDA-approved for this purpose), but patients must be willing to perform self-catheterization because risk of retention is high.

Surgical Therapy
- Consider for the 50% of women whose stress UI does not respond adequately to behavioral tx and exercise.
- Type of surgery depends on type of urethral function impairment, patient-related factors, and coexisting conditions (eg, prolapse).

Supportive Care
- Pads and protective garments should be chosen on the basis of gender and volume of urine loss. Medicaid (some states) covers pads; Medicare does not.
- Because of expense, patients may not change pads frequently enough.

Causes of Nocturnal Frequency
Defined as greater than 2 voiding episodes/night
- Consider these more common causes first:

Cause	Characteristics	Therapy
Overactive bladder	Day- and nighttime frequency	**Table 70**
BPH	Elevated AUA symptom score (p 344)	Tx for BPH (p 275)
Sleep disorders	Complains of poor sleep	p 316
Sleep apnea	Snoring or observed apnea	p 319
Stasis edema	Edema accumulates through the day	Compression stockings during the day
Uncontrolled diabetes	Elevated HbA_{1c}	p 94–103
Excess PM fluid intake	Especially alcohol after supper	Restrict fluids 4h before bedtime

- Then consider these causes of nocturnal polyuria defined as >1/3 of 24-h urine output between bedtime and waking; use bladder diary with measured voided volumes.

Heart failure	Consistent hx and exam	p 42–45
Autonomic dysfunction	Orthostatic hypotension; Parkinson disease and Parkinson plus syndromes	Desmopressin[BC] 0.1–0.2 mg po at hs; monitor for hyponatremia at initiation of tx; contraindicated if liver, renal, or heart failure
Reversal of diurnal fluid excretion	Patient often describes putting out more urine through the night than during the day	Trial short-acting potent diuretic after supper (eg, bumetanide 0.5–1.5 mg) to induce a brisk diuresis; if no response consider a trial of desmopressin[BC] (as above)

UI in Special Populations

Nursing-home Residents and People with Cognitive Impairment
- Rather than bladder diaries, observe toileting patterns and UI episodes over several days.
- Trial of prompted toileting in patients who are able to state their name and transfer with assist of no more than one. Continue prompted schedule; ability to toilet at least 75% of the time during a 3-d trial is considered success.

- **Prompted toileting** consists of:
  - Asking if patient needs to void, and taking him or her to toilet starting at 2- to 3-h intervals during day; encourage patients to report continence status; praise patient when continent and responds to toileting.
  - Simply asking the patient if they need to toilet will NOT improve UI.
- Consider use of antimuscarinics in patients with urge UI who succeed with prompted toileting and still have UI episodes.
- Do not neglect evaluation for stress UI and outlet obstruction.

UI in Patients with Heart Failure

- 50% of HF patients have lower urinary tract symptoms
- If complaint is stress UI due to cough, check to see if patient is taking ACE inhibitor; if so switch to ARB
- If complaint is urge UI or nocturia:
  - Rule out HF exacerbation and treat if needed
- If pedal edema is present, reduce or eliminate CCBs and other edema-causing drugs **(Table 69)**; use compression stockings if HF is stable and elevate legs at level of the heart in late afternoon or evening
- Reduce/taper diuretics with careful follow-up of patient; avoid hs dosing
- Keep fluid intake at about 1.5 L/d and <2 L/d
- See Lifestyle and Behavioral Therapy p 149
- Caution in use of antimuscarinics, which can cause dry mouth, increase fluid intake, and exacerbate HF

Catheter Care

- Use catheter **only** for chronic urinary retention, to protect pressure ulcers, and when requested by patients or families to promote comfort (eg, at end of life).[CW]
- Leakage around catheter can be caused by large Foley balloon, too large catheter diameter, constipation, impaction.
- Bacteriuria is universal; treat only if symptoms (eg, fever, inanition, anorexia, delirium) or if bacteriuria persists after catheter removal.
- Suprapubic catheters reduce meatal and penile trauma but not infection. Condom catheters are less painful and have a somewhat lower complication rate.
- Replace catheter if symptomatic bacteriuria develops, then culture urine from new catheter.
- Nursing-facility patients with catheters should reside in separate rooms.
- For acute retention, catheterize for 7–10 d, then do voiding trial after catheter removal.

Replacing Catheter: Routine replacement not necessary. Changing q4–6wk is reasonable to prevent blockage. Patients with recurrent blockage need increased fluid intake, possibly acidification of urine, or change of catheter q7–10d.

FECAL INCONTINENCE (FI)

Definition

"Involuntary loss of liquid or solid stool that is a social or hygienic problem" (International Continence Society)

Prevalence

After age 65: 6–10% of men and 15% of community-dwelling women, 14% of hospitalized, 45% of nursing-home residents

Risk Factors

Constipation, diarrhea, age >80 yr, female sex, UI, impaired mobility, dementia, neurologic disease

Age-related Factors

Decreased strength of external sphincter and weak anal squeeze; increased rectal compliance, decreased resting tone in internal sphincter, and impaired anal sensation

Causes: FI is commonly multifactorial.
- Overflow: from colonic distention by excessive feces, causing continuous soiling
- Loose feces: caused by medications, neoplasia, colitis, lactose intolerance
- Functional incontinence: associated with poor mobility
- Dementia related: uninhibited rectal contraction, often have UI
- Anorectal incontinence: weak external sphincter (surgery, multiparity, etc)
- Comorbidity: stroke, DM (autonomic neuropathy), sacral cord dysfunction

Evaluation

History
- Ask about "red flag" symptoms/signs that signal serious disease and require prompt referral to a gastroenterologist (ie, hematochezia, anemia, unexplained weight loss, refractory constipation, new onset constipation or diarrhea, and positive family hx of colon cancer or inflammatory bowel disease)
- Description of FI (eg, diarrhea, hard feces, etc), including usual bowel habit, change in habit, usual fecal consistency
- Frequency, urgency, ability to delay, difficulty wiping, post-defecation soiling, ability to distinguish feces and flatus
- Evacuation difficulties: straining, incomplete emptying, rectal prolapse or pain
- Functional: communication of needs, need for assistance, toilet access
- Other: bowel medications, other medications, UI, prior tx (eg, pads)

Examination
- Examine/palpate abdomen for colonic distention, and visually inspect anus for fissures and hemorrhoids.
- Check for rectal prolapse while patient seated on commode; check for rectocele in women.
- Perform rectal examination for sphincter tone, volume and consistency of feces; heme test.
- Observe gait, mobility, dressing, hygiene, mental status.

Laboratory
- TSH, electrolytes, calcium

Bowel investigations
- Abdominal radiograph: may identify colonic distention by excessive feces
- Colonoscopy: only when pathology suspected (unexplained loose feces, bleeding)
- Anorectal physiology tests: not generally needed for tx and are reserved for patients who do not respond to usual tx.

Treatment: Multiple interventions may be required.

Main approach is to simulate the patient's usual bowel pattern.
- Use rectal evacuants to stimulate evacuation and to establish a bowel pattern.
- Use evacuants in the following order: glycerine Sp, bisacodyl Sp, microenemas (eg, *Enemeez*, docusate 5 mL), phosphate or tap water enemas; digital stimulation.

- Use antidiarrheals to slow an overactive bowel or to enable planned evacuation with rectal preparations.

Constipation (p 125): often plays a role; evaluate (if needed) and treat

Modify fecal consistency to achieve soft, formed feces.

- Loose feces: use fiber or loperamide titrated to effect, sometimes as little as q48h.
- Hard feces: modify diet; add MgSO or MgOH at low dosages. In poorly mobile people, bran and fiber may exacerbate constipation.

Patient education

- Respond promptly on urge to defecate.
- Take loperamide 2–4 mg 45 min before meal or social event to prevent evacuation.
- Use coffee to stimulate the gut.
- Position on toilet with back support, foot stool to achieve squat position.
- Exercise to improve bowel motility.
- Those who are able may be taught rectal sphincter exercises (tighten rectal sphincter for 10 sec 50×/d) or may use biofeedback.
- Biofeedback improves FI by strengthening pelvic floor muscles, improving the ability to sense rectal distension, and improving coordination of sensory and strength components.

Rectal evacuation and toilet training

- Following a routine improves bowel control.
- When no spontaneous bowel action, stimulate with suppositories or enemas (**Table 59**); those with incompetent sphincters may need microenemas.
- Bed pans should not be used; bedside commodes are not as good as toilets.

Nursing-home residents and very disabled older adults: FI is most often due to colonic loading and overflow. Treat as follows:

- Daily enemas until no more results.
- Add a daily osmotic laxative (**Table 59**) and follow bowel training (above).
- Fecal transit can be stimulated with abdominal massage in direction of colonic transit.

Other therapies

- Manual evacuation may be appropriate in some patients.
- Skin care: Wet wipes better than dry; commercial preparations better than soap and water; toilet tongs and bottom wipers help those with shoulder disease.
- Surgery:
  ○ Full-thickness rectal prolapse usually requires surgery using a transanal or intra-abdominal approach.
  ○ When FI is the result of sphincter injury (eg, obstetrical or fistula repair), surgical repair is often successful.
  ○ Sphincter dysfunction without an identifiable cause has a lower surgical cure rate, but may approach 50%.
  ○ Division of the external anal sphincter or anal fissure can be repaired, but long-term results are less than satisfactory.
  ○ Selected patients have improved quality of life through creation of a stoma.
- Sacral nerve stimulation for patients with both intact and defective rectal sphincters is FDA-approved for chronic FI in patients who cannot tolerate more conservative tx or in whom such tx has not been effective. Patients must show appropriate response to a trial of stimulation and must be able to operate the device.

- A perianal bulking agent *(Solesta)* is available for patients in whom other tx has failed. Gel is injected into the tissue below the anal lining to promote tissue growth. In turn, the anal opening narrows, and patients may have better bowel control. Tx is contraindicated in active inflammatory bowel disease, immunodeficiency disorders, previous pelvic radiation, and significant rectal prolapse.

ANTIMICROBIAL STEWARDSHIP: PRINCIPLES FOR PRESCRIBERS

- Collaborate with local antimicrobial stewardship teams and efforts.
- Be familiar with formulary restrictions and preauthorization requirements.
- Participate in educational offerings on antimicrobials and antimicrobial stewardship.
- Streamline or deescalate empirical antimicrobial tx based on C&S results.
- Optimize and individualize antimicrobial dose and duration of tx.
- Avoid duplicative, redundant, or overlaps in tx (eg, piperacillin/tazobactam with metronidazole or another beta-lactam)
- Switch eligible patients from IV to oral antimicrobials.

PNEUMONIA

Presentation

Can range from subtle signs such as lethargy, anorexia, dizziness, falls, and delirium to septic shock or acute respiratory distress syndrome. Pleuritic chest pain, dyspnea, productive cough, fever, chills, or rigors are not consistently present in older adults.

Evaluation and Assessment

- Physical examination: Respiratory rate >20 breaths/min; low BP; chest sounds may be minimal, absent, or consistent with HF; 20% are afebrile.
- CXR: Infiltrate may not be present on initial film if the patient is dehydrated.
- Sputum: Gram's stain and culture (optional per ATS guidelines)
- CBC with differential: Up to 50% of patients have a normal WBC count, but 95% have a left shift.
- BUN, Cr, electrolytes, glucose
- Blood culture × 2
- Oxygenation: ABG or oximetry
- Test for *Mycobacterium tuberculosis* with acid-fast bacilli stain and culture in selected patients.
- Test for *Legionella* spp in patients who are seriously ill without an alternative diagnosis, are immunocompromised, are nonresponsive to β-lactam antibiotics, have clinical features suggesting this diagnosis, or in outbreak setting. Urinary antigen testing is highly specific for serotype 1 but lacks specificity for other serotypes. Value and use vary by geographic region.
- Test for urinary antigen for pneumococcus.
- Thoracentesis (if moderate to large effusion)

Aggravating Factors (* indicates modifiable)

- Age-related changes in pulmonary reserve
- Alcoholism
- Altered mental status
- Aspiration
- Comorbid conditions that alter gag reflexes or ciliary transport
- COPD or other lung disease
- Heart disease
- Heavy sedation* or paralytic agents
- Hyperglycemia*
- Intubation, mechanical ventilation (orotracheal intubation and orogastric tubation preferred)
- Malnutrition
- Medications*: immunosuppressants, sedatives, anticholinergic or other agents that dry secretions, agents that increase gastric pH
- Nasogastric tubes
- Oral care* (manual brushing plus rinse with fluoride/chlorhexidine 0.12% × 30 sec/d)
- Poor compliance with infection control* (eg, hand disinfection)
- Supine positioning* (semirecumbent, 30–45 degrees preferred)
- Swallowing* (eat/feed upright at 90 degrees over 15–20 min)

Predominant Organisms by Setting

Community-acquired:

- *Streptococcus pneumoniae*
- *Legionella* spp
- Respiratory viruses
- *Haemophilus influenzae*
- Gram-negative bacteria
- *Chlamydia pneumoniae*
- *Moraxella catarrhalis*
- *M tuberculosis*
- Endemic fungi
- Anaerobes

Nursing-home–acquired:

- *Strep pneumoniae*
- Gram-negative bacteria
- *Staphylococcus aureus* (including MRSA)
- Anaerobes
- *H influenzae*
- Group B streptococci
- *Chlamydia pneumoniae*

Hospital-acquired:

- Gram-negative bacteria
- Anaerobes
- Gram-positive bacteria
- Fungi

Supportive Management

- Chest percussion
- Inhaled β-adrenergic agonists
- Mechanical ventilation (if indicated)
- Oxygen as indicated
- Rehydration

Empiric Antibiotic Therapy (Table 77)

The antibiotic regimen should be narrowed if the causative organism has been identified. If antibiotic tx is initiated ≥4 h post-hospitalization, increased mortality may result.

Table 71. Treatment of Community-acquired Pneumonia for Immunocompetent Patients by Clinical Circumstances or Setting[a]

Clinical Circumstances or Setting	Treatment Options
Outpatient, previously healthy and no antibiotic tx in past 3 mo	Azithromycin, clarithromycin, or erythromycin Alternative: doxycycline
Outpatient, with comorbidities[b] or antibiotic tx in past 3 mo[d]	A fluoroquinolone[c] alone *or* Azithromycin, clarithromycin, or erythromycin *plus* amoxicillin (high dose) or amoxicillin-clavulanate Alternative β-lactams: ceftriaxone, cefpodoxime, or cefuroxime Alternative to a macrolide: doxycycline
Hospitalized patient	A fluoroquinolone[c] alone *or* Azithromycin or clarithromycin *plus* cefotaxime, ceftriaxone, or ampicillin Alternative β-lactam: ertapenem Alternative to a macrolide: doxycycline
Hospitalized patient, intensive care unit	
No concern about *Pseudomonas*	Cefotaxime, ceftriaxone, or ampicillin-sulbactam *plus* azithromycin or fluoroquinolone[c]
No concern about *Pseudomonas* but β-lactam allergy	Fluoroquinolone[c] *plus* aztreonam
Concern about *Pseudomonas*	Piperacillin-tazobactam, imipenem, meropenem, or cefepime *plus* ciprofloxacin or levofloxacin; *or* Piperacillin-tazobactam, imipenem, meropenem, or cefepime *plus* an aminoglycoside *and* azithromycin, ciprofloxacin, or levofloxacin
Concern about *Pseudomonas* and β-lactam allergy	Aztreonam *plus* ciprofloxacin or levofloxacin *plus* an aminoglycoside
Nursing-home patient[e,f]	Fluoroquinolone[c,d] alone *or* Azithromycin, clarithromycin, or erythromycin *plus* amoxicillin (high dose) or amoxicillin-clavulanate

[a] Because of the geographical variability in antimicrobial resistance patterns, refer to local tx recommendations.

[b] Comorbidities: chronic heart, lung, liver, or kidney disease; DM; alcoholism; malignancies; asplenia; immunosuppressing conditions or drugs

[c] Fluoroquinolones (respiratory): moxifloxacin, levofloxacin, or gemifloxacin

[d] Choice of antibiotic should be from a different class

[e] Patients being treated in the nursing home; for tx of nursing-home patients who are hospitalized, see hospitalized patient or intensive care unit.

[f] Because of the incidence of Gram-negative and atypical bacterial pneumonia in nursing-home patients, experts in geriatric infectious disease often recommend expanded Gram-negative antibiotic coverage.

Source: Mandell LA et al. *Clin Infect Dis* 2007;44:S27–72.

Nursing-home or Hospital-acquired Pneumonia Requiring Parenteral Treatment: Alternative Recommendations

Antibiotics are indicated if:
- Temperature ≥102° F (38.9° C) + RR >25 or productive cough
- Temperature ≥100° F (37.8° C) + <102° F (38.9° C) + RR >25, pulse >100, rigors or new onset delirium
- Afebrile with COPD + new or increased cough with purulent sputum
- Afebrile without COPD + new or increased cough + RR >25 or new-onset delirium

Empiric Treatment

Antipseudomonal cephalosporin (cefepime or ceftazidime) *or*

Antipseudomonalcarbepenem (imipenem or meropenem) *or*

β-lactam/β-lactamase inhibitor (piperacillin-tazobactam)

plus

Antipseudomonal fluoroquinolone (ciprofloxacin or levofloxacin) *or*
Aminoglycoside (amikacin, gentamicin, or tobramycin)

plus

Linezolid or vancomycin (if risk factors for MRSA are present or if local incidence is high)

For both sets of empiric tx guidelines, the choice of combination depends on local bacteriologic patterns.

Source: Adapted from: ATS and IDSA Guidelines for the management of adults with hospital-acquired, ventilator-associated, and healthcare-associated pneumonia. *Am J Resp Crit Care Med* 2005;171:388–416.

Duration of Treatment

Inpatient—until clinical indicators have been reached:
- Temperature <100°F (37.8°C)
- HR <100 bpm
- Respiratory rate <25/min
- SBP >90 mmHg
- O_2 saturation >90%
- Ability to maintain oral intake

Switch from parenteral to oral antibiotics when patient is hemodynamically stable, shows clinical improvement, is afebrile for 16 h, and can tolerate oral medications; total duration of tx 7–14 d depending on clinical response. Tx courses of 7–8 d are recommended for clinically improving hospital-acquired pneumonia not caused by *Pseudomonas* spp, *Steriotrophous*, or other nonfermenting Gram-negative bacilli.

Outpatient and long-term care facility—usually 10–14 d

> *Note:* The empiric use of vancomycin should be reserved for patients with a serious allergy to β-lactam antibiotics or for patients from environments in which MRSA is known to be a problem pathogen. For all cases, antimicrobial tx should be individualized once Gram's stain or culture results are known.

URINARY TRACT INFECTION OR UROSEPSIS

Definition

Bacteriuria is the presence of a significant number of bacteria in the urine without reference to symptoms.

- **Symptomatic bacteriuria** usually has signs of dysuria and increased frequency of urination; fever, chills, nausea may be present; >10^5 cfu/mL of the same organism from a single specimen supports the diagnosis of UTI, counts ≥10^3 cfu/mL are diagnostic for specimens obtained by in and out catheterization. New onset or worsening of UI may be the only symptom.

- **Asymptomatic bacteriuria** is seen when there is an absence of symptoms, including absence of fever (<100.4°F [38°C]) plus:
  ○ the same organism(s) ($\geq 10^5$ cfu/mL) is found on 2 consecutive cultures in women
  ○ one bacterial species ($\geq 10^5$ cfu/mL) in a single clean-catch specimen in men
  ○ one bacterial species ($\geq 10^2$ cfu/mL) in a catheterized specimen in men and women
- **Complicated UTI in women**—affecting the lower or upper urinary tract and associated with underlying condition that increases risk of infection and of tx failure (eg, obstruction, anatomical abnormality, resistant organisms, or urologic dysfunction).

Risk Factors

- Abnormalities in function or anatomy of the urinary tract
- Catheterization or recent instrumentation
- Comorbid conditions (eg, DM, BPH)
- Female gender
- Limited functional status

Assessment and Evaluation

Choice is based on presenting symptoms and severity of illness.

- UA with culture (do not obtain sample from catheter bag)
- Blood culture × 2
- BUN, Cr, electrolytes
- CBC with differential

Expected Organisms

Noncatheterized Patients: Most common: *Escherichia coli, Proteus* spp, *Klebsiella* spp, *Providencia* spp, *Citrobacter* spp, *Enterobacter* spp, coagulase-negative staphylococci, *Gardnerella vaginalis*, group B streptococci, and *Pseudomonas aeruginosa* if recent antibiotic exposure, known colonization, or known institutional flora

Nursing-Home–Catheterized Patients: All of the above plus enterococci, staphylococcus aureus, and fungus (eg, candida)

Empiric Antibiotic Treatment

- Routine tx of asymptomatic bacteriuria is not recommended.[CW]
  ○ Asymptomatic bacteriuria has not been associated with adverse outcomes.
  ○ Screening and tx is recommended before a urologic procedure anticipated to result in mucosal bleeding.
- Empiric regimens should be changed based on C&S results, patient factors, and tx costs.
- Tx duration should be at least 3–7 d for women with uncomplicated UTI; 7–12 d for complicated UTI; and >14 d and up to 6 wk for men if prostatitis present.

Community-Acquired or Nursing-Home–Acquired Cystitis or Uncomplicated UTI (oral route): TMP/SMZ DS, cephalexin, ampicillin, or amoxicillin. Amoxicillin-clavulanate should be reserved for patients with sulfa allergy and for settings with known β-lactam resistance. Fluoroquinolones should be reserved for patients with allergies to sulfa or β-lactams, or for settings with known resistance.

Suspected Urosepsis (IV route): Third-generation cephalosporin plus aminoglycoside, aztreonam, or fluoroquinolone ±aminoglycoside.

Vancomycin should be reserved for patients with a serious allergy to β-lactam antibiotics.

UTI Prophylaxis

- Leads to antibiotic resistance regardless of patient's catheter status or duration of catheterization; generally not recommended. Noncatheterized women with a hx of UTI, especially if caused by *E coli*, may benefit from prophylaxis with cranberry juice (250–300 mL/d). Time to benefit may be ≥2 mo.
- Vaginal atrophy due to estrogen depletion may predispose women to recurrent UTIs. Local topical estrogen replacement may be indicated (**Table 125**).

SEPSIS AND SYSTEMIC INFLAMMATORY RESPONSE SYNDROME (SIRS)
Definitions

Sepsis—consequence of a dysregulated inflammatory response to an infection

SIRS—a clinical syndrome identical to sepsis due to either infectious or noninfectious causes

Diagnostic Criteria

Infection, documented or suspected, plus some of the following features:

- Temperature >38.3°C or <38°C
- HR >90 bpm or >2 SD above normal for age
- Tachypenea RR >20 breaths per min
- Altered mental status
- Significant edema or (+) fluid balance
- Blood glucose >140 mg/dL in nondiabetics
- WBC >12,000 or <4000
- Normal WBC with >10% immature forms
- Plasma CRP >2 SD above normal
- Plasma procalcitonin >2 SD above normal
- SBP <90 mmHg, mean arteriol pressure (MAP) <70 mmHg, or SBP decrease >40 mmHg
- Hypoxemia PaO_2/FiO_2 <300
- Acute oliguria
- Increased serum Cr >0.5 mg/dL
- INR >1.5 or activated PTT >60 sec
- Ileus
- Platelet count <100,000
- Plasma total bilirubin >4 mg/dL
- Hyperlactatemia >1 mmol/L
- Decreased capillary refill or mottling

Risk Factors

- Bacteremia
- Age ≥65 yr
- Immunosuppression
- DM or cancer
- Community-acquired pneumonia
- Genetic factors

Management

Supportive Care

- Respiratory: Oxygen and ventilator assistance as needed
- Goal-directed tx (if needed)
  - Rapidly infused bolus IV fluids defined by volume; assess before and after each bolus
  - Use pressors when IV fluids are not sufficient or lead to cardiogenic pulmonary edema
  - Reserve intropics (eg, dobutamine) for refractory patients with decreased cardiac output
  - RBC transfusion if HbA_{1c} <7 g/dL, hemorrhagic shock, or myocardial ischemia

Early Goals of Treatment

- MAP >65 mmHg

- Urine output >0.5 mL/kg/h
- Central venous pressure 8–12 mmHg
- Central venous oxygen saturation (ScvO$_2$) ≥70% or SvO$_2$ ≥65%

Infection
- Identify and remove (when possible) infection loci
- IV antibiotics within 6 h associated with decreased mortality
- Empiric: vancomycin plus 1 or 2 other antibiotics depending if *Pseudomonas sp* is suspected
- Glucocorticoids if SBP <90 mmHg (severe septic shock)

METHICILLIN-RESISTANT STAPHYLOCOCCUS AUREUS (MRSA)

Risk Factors
- Long-term-care residence
- Hemodialysis or peritoneal dialysis
- IV drug use
- DM
- Recent surgery
- Previous colonization
- Poor functional status
- Wounds
- Invasive devices, (eg, catheters, feeding tube)

Types

Community-acquired
Usually skin and soft tissue infection (SSTI) or severe necrolyzing pneumonia
Usual tx: clindamycin, doxycycline, minocycline, or TMP-SMX

Hospital-acquired
Usual tx: vancomycin +/– aminoglycoside and/or rifampin; daptomycin; or linezolid

Alternative tx for complicated SSTI: ceftaroline or telavancin

Duration of Treatment
- SSTI or pneumonia: 7–10 d
- Bacteremia, (–) valve endocarditis: 4 wk after culture negative
- Osteomyelitis or infected prosthetics: >6 wk

Decolonization with mupirocin or other antiseptics should be restricted to MRSA outbreaks and recurrent infections.

HERPES ZOSTER ("SHINGLES")

Definition
Cutaneous vesicular eruptions followed by radicular pain secondary to the recrudescence of varicella zoster virus. Recurrence may occur but rare in immunocompetent older people.

Prevention
Zoster vaccine *(Zostavax)* for individuals ≥50 yr who are immunocompetent and without contraindication to the vaccine. The USPSTF and ACIP recommend vaccination in immunocompetent persons >60 yr. Patients who have had shingles in the past can receive the vaccine to prevent future episodes. There is no specific period of time that needs to have elapsed, but the rash should have resolved before administering the vaccine (**Table 104**).

Clinical Manifestations
- Abrupt onset of pruritus or pain along a specific dermatome (**Figure 1**)

- Macular, erythematous rash that becomes vesicular and pustular (Tzanck cell test positive) after ~3 d, crusts over and clears in 10–14 d
- Complications: post-herpetic neuralgia, visual loss or blindness if ophthalmic involvement

Pharmacologic Management

When started within 72 h of the rash's appearance, antiviral tx (**Table 72**) decreases the severity and duration of the acute illness and possibly shortens the duration and reduces the risk of post-herpetic neuralgias. (See p 228 for tx of post-herpetic neuralgia.)

Table 72. Antiviral Treatments for Herpes Zoster

Medication, Route	Dosage	Formulations	Reduce dosage when
Acyclovir▲ *(Zovirax)*			
Oral	800 mg 5 ×/d for 7–10 d	T: 400, 800; C: 200; S: 200 mg/5 mL	CrCl[a] <25 mL/min
IV[b]	10 mg/kg q8h for 7 d	500 mg/10 mL	CrCl[a] <50 mL/min
Famciclovir▲ *(Famvir)*			
Oral	500 mg q8h for 7 d	T: 125, 250, 500	CrCl[a] <60 mL/min
Valacyclovir▲[c] (Valtrex)			
Oral	1000 mg q8h for 7 d	C: 500, 1000	CrCl[a] <50 mL/min

[a] The CrCl listed is the threshold below which the dosage (amount or frequency) should be reduced. See package insert for detailed dosing guidelines.

[b] Use IV for serious illness, ophthalmic infection, or patients who cannot take oral medication.

[c] Preferred to po acyclovir; prodrug of acyclovir with serum concentrations equal to those achieved with IV administration.

INFLUENZA

Vaccine Prevention (ACIP Guidelines)

Yearly vaccination is recommended for all adults ≥65 yr and all residents and staff of nursing homes, or residential or long-term care facilities. Nursing-home residents admitted during the winter months after the vaccination program has been completed should be vaccinated at admission if they have not already been vaccinated. The influenza vaccine is contraindicated in people who have an anaphylactic hypersensitivity to eggs or any other component of the vaccine. Dose: 0.5 mL IM once in the fall for those living in the northern hemisphere.

Table 73. Diagnostic Tests for Influenza

Method	Test Time	Acceptable Specimens, Detection and Differentiation
Viral cell culture (conventional)	3–10 d	NP swab, throat swab, NP or bronchial wash, nasal or endotracheal aspirate, sputum
Reverse-transcriptase-polymerase chain reaction (RT-PCR)	1–6 h	Detect and differentiate Types A and B, including subtypes NP swab, throat swab, NP or bronchial wash, nasal or endotracheal aspirate, sputum
		Detect and differentiate Types A and B, including H1N1 and avian H5N1 subtypes

(cont.)

Table 73. Diagnostic Tests for Influenza (cont.)		
Method	**Test Time**	**Acceptable Specimens, Detection and Differentiation**
Immunofluorescence, direct (DFA) or indirect (IFA) antibody staining	1–4 h	NP swab or wash, bronchial wash, nasal or endotracheal aspirate
		Detect and differentiate between Types A and B, between A/B, and other respiratory viruses
Rapid influenza diagnostic tests	<30 min	NP swab (throat swab), nasal wash, nasal aspirate
		Antigen (EIA) detects and differentiates between A and B, and detection of Type B varies with EIA

Notes: EIA = enzyme immunoassay; NP = nasopharyngeal.

Pharmacologic Prophylaxis and Treatment with Antiviral Agents

Indications:

- Prevention (during an influenza outbreak): people who are not vaccinated, are immunodeficient, or may spread the virus
- Prophylaxis: during 2 wk required to develop antibodies for people vaccinated after an outbreak of influenza A
- Reduction of symptoms, duration of illness when started within the first 48 h of symptoms
- During epidemic outbreaks in nursing homes
- Resistance to antivirals and the emergence of specific strains of influenza (eg, H1N1) have led to frequent updates of recommendations for prophylaxis and tx. Check the CDC Web site for the most current information and guidance (www.cdc.gov/flu/professionals/antivirals/).

Duration: Tx of symptoms: 3–5 d or for 24–48 h after symptoms resolve. Prophylaxis during outbreak: min 2 wk or until ~1 wk after outbreak ends.

Table 74. Antiviral Treatment of Influenza		
Agent	**Formulation**	**Dosage**
Amantadine▲ *(Symmetrel)* [a]	C: 100 mg S: 50 mg/5 mL	100 mg/d po[b]
✓ Oseltamivir *(Tamiflu)* [c]	C: 75 mg S: 12 mg/mL	Tx: 75 mg po q12h × 5d (75 mg/d po if CrCl 10–30 mL/min); not recommended if CrCl <10 mL/min
		Prophylaxis: 75 mg/d po × ≥7d up to 6 wk if immunocompetent (12 wk if not) (75 mg po q48h if CrCl 10–30 mL/min); not recommended if CrCl <10 mL/min
Rimantadine *(Flumadine)* [a]	T▲: 100 mg	100 mg/d po for adults aged ≥65 yr old including nursing-home residents
Zanamivir *(Relenza)* [c,d]	Inh: 5 mg/blister	Tx: 2 × 5-mg inhalations q12h × 5 d
		Give doses on first d ≥2 h apart
		Prophylaxis: 2 × 5-mg inhalations q24h; household setting—start 36 h after onset of signs and symptoms of initial case, duration 10 d; community—begin within 5 d of outbreak, duration 30 d.

(cont.)

Table 74. Antiviral Treatment of Influenza (cont.)		
Agent	**Formulation**	**Dosage**
Peramivir *(Rapivab)*	IV: 200 mg/20 mL	600 mg IV × 1 CrCl 30–49 mL/min: 200 mg × 1 CrCl 10–29 mL/min: 100 mg × 1 End-stage renal disease requiring intermittent hemodialysis: 100 mg × 1, administered after dialysis

✓ = preferred for treating older adults

[a] No longer recommended for prophylaxis.

[b] Dosage adjustments for kidney function, CrCl (mL/min): ≥30 = 100 mg/d; 20–29 = 200 mg 2×/wk; 10–19 = 100 mg 3×/wk; <10 = 200 mg alternating with 100 mg q7d.

[c] Must be started within 2 d of symptom onset or of contact with an infected individual.

[d] Do not use in patients with COPD or asthma.

TUBERCULOSIS (TB)

TB in older adults may be the reactivation of old disease or a new infection due to exposure to an infected individual. If a new infection is suspected or the patient has risk factors for resistant organisms, then bacterial sensitivities must be determined.

Risk or Reactivating Factors

- Chronic institutionalization
- Corticosteroid use
- DM
- Malignancy
- Malnutrition
- Kidney failure

Diagnosis

- Mantoux tuberculin skin test (TST): 0.1 mL of tuberculin PPD intradermal injection into the inner surface of the forearm
- Read 48–72 h after injection (**Table 75** for interpretation).
- Repeat ("booster") 1–2 wk after initial skin testing can be useful for nursing-home residents, healthcare workers, and others who are retested periodically to reduce the likelihood of misinterpreting a boosted reaction to subsequent TSTs.

Interferon-gamma release assays (IGRAs)
- QuantiFERON = TB Gold In-Tube test (QFT-GIT)
- T-SPOT
  (+) Patient has been infected; additional tests if latent TB or tubercular disease
  (–) Latent TB or tubercular disease not likely

Treatment

Latent Infection: See **Table 75** and **Table 76**.

Table 75. Identification of Patients at High Risk of Developing TB Who Would Benefit from Treatment of Latent Infection	
Population	**Minimum Induration Considered a Positive Test**
Considered positive in any person, including those considered low risk	15 mm
Residents and employees of hospitals, nursing homes, and long-term facilities for older adults, residential facilities for AIDS patients, and homeless shelters	10 mm

(cont.)

Table 75. Identification of Patients at High Risk of Developing TB Who Would Benefit from Treatment of Latent Infection (cont.)

Population	Minimum Induration Considered a Positive Test
Recent immigrants (<5 yr) from countries where TB prevalence is high	10 mm
Injectable-drug users	10 mm
People with silicosis; DM; chronic kidney failure; leukemia; lymphoma; carcinoma of the head, neck, or lung; weight loss of ≥10%; gastrectomy or jejunoileal bypass	10 mm
Recent contact with TB patients	5 mm
Fibrotic changes on CXR consistent with prior TB	5 mm
Immunosuppressed (receiving the equivalent of prednisone at ≥15 mg/d for ≥1 mo), organ transplant recipients, patients receiving TNF-α inhibitors	5 mm
HIV-positive patients	5 mm

Table 76. Treatment of Latent Tuberculosis in HIV(-) Adults

Self-administration	Direct Observation Treatment (DOT)
INH▲ 5 mg/kg (max 300 mg/d) × 6 or 9 mo	INH 900 mg 2/wk × 6 or 9 mo Weekly INH 15 mg/kg (rounded to the nearest 50 or 100 mg) plus rifapentine 32.1–49.9 kg = 750 mg or if ≥50.0 kg, 900 mg max

Notes: INH; no dose adjustment in renal impairment; multiple CYP effects; T: 100, 300 mg; Sol: 50 mg/mL; Inj Rifapentine: no dose adjustment in renal impairment; strong inducer of CYP2C8, 2C9, and 3A4; T: 50 mg.

Active Infection:

Refer to CDC guidelines at www.cdc.gov/mmwr/preview/mmwrhtml/rr5211a1.htm#tab2.

HUMAN IMMUNODEFICIENCY VIRUS (HIV)

Reasons for increase in HIV infection in adults ≥50 yr old:
- Increased survival of people with HIV
- Age-associated decrease in immune function with resultant increased susceptibility
- Tx for erectile dysfunction leading to more sexual activity
- Difficulty with condom use secondary to erectile dysfunction
- Less condom use by partners of postmenopausal women
- Older women with vaginal dryness and thinning
- Older adults think only the young are at risk
- Mortality old > young secondary to non-HIV-related causes

Presentation

Many symptoms that may delay diagnosis are common in older adults:
- Anorexia
- Arthralgias
- Earlier, more symptomatic menopause
- Fatigue
- Flu-like symptoms
- Forgetfulness
- Hypogonadism
- Insomnia
- Myalgias
- Pain in hands or feet (neuropathy)
- Recurrent pneumonia
- Sexual disorders
- Weight loss

Comorbidities common in older adults that can occur earlier in people with HIV:
- Cancers (eg, anal, liver, lung)
- Cirrhosis
- Cognitive deficits
- CAD

- DM
- Dyslipidemia
- HTN
- Obstructive lung disease
- Osteoporosis
- Vascular disease

Laboratory Abnormalities

- Anemia
- Leukopenia
- Persons aged ≥65 yr old have a lower CD_4 count at diagnosis
- Low cholesterol
- Transaminitis

Screening

Routine screening of adults ≥65 yr old is not recommended.
Screening is recommended regardless of age if:

- Starting tx for TB
- Treating a sexually transmitted disease
- Other HIV risk factors are present: unprotected sex and multiple partners, hazardous alcohol or illicit drug use
- Unexplained anemia
- Peripheral neuropathy
- Oral candidiasis
- Herpes zoster (widespread infection)
- Recurrent bacterial pneumonia
- Unexplained weight loss or pronounced fatigue

Treatment

Antiretroviral tx is recommended in patients aged >50 yr old, regardless of CD_4 count.

- Viral load suppression greatest in ≥60 yr old after initiating antiretroviral tx
- HIV-1 RNA suppression old > young
- CD_4 response to tx young > old

For complete guidelines on antiretroviral regimens, aidsinfo.nih.gov/contentfiles/AA_Tables.pdf.

Tx-naive patients:

- Non-nucleoside reverse transcriptase inhibitor (NNRTI) + 2 nucleoside reverse transcriptase inhibitors (NRTIs) *or*
- Protease inhibitor with ritonavir (preferred) + 2 NRTIs, *or*
- Integrase strand transfer inhibitor + 2 NRTIs

Pre-exposure prophylaxis:

The combination of emtricitabine and tenofovir *(Truvada*; T 200 mg/300 mg; K<60 mL/min) in combination with safer sex practices is approved for pre-exposure prophylaxis to reduce the risk of sexually-acquired HIV-1 in adults at high risk.

Complications of Pharmacotherapy

- Increased cholesterol (accelerated atherosclerosis)
- Glucose intolerance
- Drug-drug interactions
- Drug toxicity
- Little data on the effects of age on drug pharmacokinetics in HIV-positive patients
- Increased pill burden

Monitor

- BMD
- Kidney function
- Liver function

Table 77. Antibiotics

Antimicrobial Class, *Subclass*	Dosage	Adjust When CrCl[a] Is: (mL/min) (Elimination)	Formulations
β-Lactams Penicillins			
Amoxicillin▲ *(Amoxil)*	po: 250 mg–1 g q8h	<50 (K)	T: film coated 500, 875 C: 250, 500 ChT: 125, 200, 250, 400 S: 125, 200, 250, 400 mg/5 mL
Ampicillin▲	po: 250–500 mg q6h IM/IV: 1–2 g q4–6h	<30 (K)	C: 250, 500 S: 125, 250 mg/5 mL Inj
Penicillin G▲	IV: 3–5 × 10⁶ U q4–6h IM: 0.6–2.4 × 10⁶ U q6–12h	<30 (K, L)	Inj procaine for IM
Penicillin VK▲	po: 125–500 mg q6h	[b] (K, L)	T: 250, 500 S: 125, 250 mg/5 mL
Antipseudomonal Penicillin			
Piperacillin▲ *(Pipracil)*	IM: 1–2 g q8–12h IV: 2–4 g q6–8h	<40 (K, F)	Inj
Antistaphylococcal Penicillins			
Dicloxacillin▲ *(Dycill, Pathocil)*	po: 125–500 mg q6h	NA (K)	C: 125, 250, 500 S: 62.5 mg/5 mL
Nafcillin▲	IM: 500 mg q4–6h IV: 500 mg–2 g q4–6h	NA (L)	Inj
Oxacillin▲ *(Bactocill)*	IM, IV: 250 mg–2 g q6–12h	<10 (K)	Inj
Monobactam (antipseudomonal)			
Aztreonam *(Azactam)*	IM: 500 mg–1 g q8–12h IV: 500 mg–2 g q6–12h	<30 (K)	Inj
Carbapenems			
Doripenem *(Doribax)*	IV: 500 mg q8h	<50 (K)	Inj
Ertapenem *(Invanz)*	IM, IV: 1 g q24h × 3–14 d IM × 7 d max IV × 14 d max	<30 (K, F)	Inj
Imipenem-cilastatin *(Primaxin)*	IM: 500 mg–1 g q8–12h IV: 500 mg–2 g q6–12h	<70 (K)	Inj
Meropenem *(Merrem IV)*	IV: 1 g q8h	≤50 (K, L)	Inj
Penicillinase-resistant Penicillins			
Amoxicillin–clavulanate▲ *(Augmentin)*	po: 250 mg q8h, 500 mg q12h, 875 mg q12h	<30 (K, L)	T: 250, 500, 875 ChT: 125, 200, 250, 400 S: 125, 200, 250, 400 mg/5 mL
Ampicillin–sulbactam▲ *(Unasyn)*	IM, IV: 1–2 g q6–8h	<30 (K)	Inj

(cont.)

Table 77. Antibiotics (cont.)

Antimicrobial Class, *Subclass*	Dosage	Adjust When CrCl[a] Is: (mL/min) (Elimination)	Formulations
Penicillinase-resistant and Antipseudomonal Penicillins			
Ceftazidime-avibactam *(Avycaz)*	IV: 2.5 g q8h	<50 (K)	Inj
Piperacillin–tazobactam▲ *(Zosyn)*	IV: 3.375 g q6h	<40 (K, F)	Inj
Ticarcillin–clavulanate *(Timentin)*	IV: 3 g q4–6h	<60 (K, L)	Inj
First-generation Cephalosporins			
Cefadroxil▲ *(Duricef)*	po: 500 mg–1 g q12h	<50 (K)	C: 500 T: 1 g S: 250, 500 mg/5 mL
Cefazolin▲ *(Ancef, Kefzol)*	IM, IV: 500 mg–2 g q12h	<55 (K)	Inj
Cephalexin▲ *(Keflex)*	po: 250 mg–1 g q6h	<40 (K)	C: 250, 500 T: 250, 500, 750 S: 125, 250 mg/5 mL
Second-generation Cephalosporins			
Cefaclor▲ *(Ceclor)*	po: 250–500 mg q8h	<50 (K)	C: 250, 500 S: 125, 187, 250, 375 mg/5 mL T: ER 375, 500
Cefotetan▲ *(Cefotan)*	IM, IV: 1–3 g q12h or 1–2 g q24h (UTI)	<30 (K)	Inj
Cefoxitin▲ *(Mefoxin)*	IM, IV: 1–2 g q6–8h	<50 (K)	Inj
Cefprozil▲ *(Cefzil)*	po: 250–500 mg q12–24h	<30 (K)	T: 250, 500 S: 125, 250 mg/5 mL
Cefuroxime axetil▲ *(Ceftin)*	po: 125–500 mg q12h IM, IV: 750 mg–1.5 g q6h	<20 (K)	T: 250, 500▲ S: 125, 150 mg/5 mL Inj▲
Third-generation Cephalosporins			
Cefdinir▲ *(Omnicef)*	po: 300 mg q12h or 600 mg/d × 10 d	<30 (K)	C: 300 S: 125, 250/5 mL
Cefditoren *(Spectracef)*	po: 400 mg q12h × 10 d (bronchitis) 400 mg q12h × 14 d (pneumonia) 200 mg q12h × 10 d (soft tissue or skin)	<50 (K)	T: 200, 400
Cefixime *(Suprax)*	po: 400 mg/d	<60 (K)	C, T: 400 CT: 100, 200 S: 100, 200 mg/5 mL
Cefotaxime▲ *(Claforan)*	IM, IV: 1–2 g q6–12h	<20 (K)	Inj

(cont.)

Table 77. Antibiotics (cont.)

Antimicrobial Class, *Subclass*	Dosage	Adjust When CrCl[a] Is: (mL/min) (Elimination)	Formulations
Cefpodoxime▲ *(Vantin)*	po: 100–400 mg q12h	<30 (K)	T: 100, 200 S: 50, 100 mg/5 mL
Ceftazidime▲ *(Ceptaz, Fortaz)*	IM, IV: 500 mg–2 g q8–12h UTI: 250–500 mg q12h	<50 (K)	Inj
Ceftibuten *(Cedax)*	po: 400 mg/d	<50 (K)	C: 400 S: 90, 180 mg/5 mL
Ceftriaxone▲ *(Rocephin)*	IM, IV: 1–2 g q12–24h	NA (K)	Inj
Fourth-generation Cephalosporins			
Cefepime▲ *(Maxipime)*	IV: 500 mg–2 g q12h	<60 (K)	Inj
Fifth-generation Cephalosporin			
Ceftaroline fosamil *(Tefloro)*	400–600 mg q12h	≤50 (K)	IV: 400, 600 mg
Aminoglycosides			
Amikacin▲ *(Amikin)*	IM, IV: 15–20 mg/kg/d divided q12–24h; 15–20 mg/kg q24–48h	<60, TDM (K)	Inj
Gentamicin▲ *(Garamycin)*	IM, IV: 2–5 mg/kg/d divided q12–24h; 5–7 mg/kg q24–48h	<60, TDM (K)	Inj ophth sus, oint
Streptomycin▲	IM, IV: 10 mg/kg/d not to exceed 750 mg/d	<50 (K)	Inj
Tobramycin▲ *(Nebcin)*	IM, IV: 2–5 mg/kg/d divided q12–24h; 5–7 mg/kg q24–48h	<60, TDM (K)	Inj ophth sus, oint
Macrolides			
Azithromycin▲ *(Zithromax)*	po: 500 mg on day 1, then 250 mg/d IV: 500 mg/d	NA (L)	S: 100, 200 mg/5 mL, 1 g (single-dose pk) T: 250, 500, 600 mg Inj
Clarithromycin▲ *(Biaxin, Biaxin XL)*	po: 250–500 mg q12h ER: 1000 mg/d	<30 (L, K)	S: 125, 250 mg/5 mL T: 250, 500 ER: 500
Erythromycin▲	po: Base: 333 mg q8h Stearate or base: 250–500 mg q6–12h Ethylsuccinate: 400–800 mg q6–12h IV: 15–20 mg/kg/d divided q6h	NA (L)	Base: C, T: 250, 333, 500 Stearate: T: 250 Ethylsuccinate: S: 100, 200, 400 mg/5 mL T: 400 Inj
Fidaxomycin *(Dificid)*	po: 200 mg q12h	NA (F)	T: 200 mg
Ketolide			
Telithromycin *(Ketek)*	po: 800 mg/d × 5–10 d	<30 (L, K)	T: 300, 400

(cont.)

Table 77. Antibiotics (cont.)

Antimicrobial Class, *Subclass*	Dosage	Adjust When CrCl[a] Is: (mL/min) (Elimination)	Formulations
Quinolones			
Ciprofloxacin▲ *(Cipro)*	po: 250–750 mg q12h ophth: **Table 52**	po: <50 (L, K)	T: 100, 250, 500, 750▲ S: 250 mg/5 mL, 500 mg/5 mL Ophth sol:▲
	IV: 200–400 mg q12h	IV: <30	3.5 mg/5 mL Inj
(Cipro XR)			XR▲: 500, 1000
Gemifloxacin *(Factive)*	po: 320 mg/d	≤40 (K, L, F)	T: 320 mg
Levofloxacin▲ *(Levaquin)*	po, IV: 250–500 mg/d	<50 (K)	T: 250, 500, 750 S: 125 mg/5mL
Moxifloxacin *(Avelox)*	po: 400 mg q12h	NA (L, F, K)	Inj T: 400
Norfloxacin *(Noroxin)*	po: 400 mg q12h	<30 (K, F)	T: 400
Ofloxacin▲ *(Roxin)*	po, IV: 200–400 mg q12–24h ophth **Table 52**	<50 (K)	T: 200, 300, 400▲ Ophth: 0.3%▲
Tetracyclines			
Doxycycline▲ (eg, *Vibramycin)*	po, IV: 100–200 mg/d q12–24h	NA (K)	C, T: 50, 75, 100, 150 S: 25, 50 mg/5 mL Inj
Minocycline▲ *(Minocin)*	po, IV: 200 mg once, then 100 mg q12h	NA (K)	C: 50, 75, 100 S: 50 mg/5 mL Inj
Tetracycline▲	po, IV: 250–500 mg q6–12h	NA (K)	C: 250, 500
Glycycline			
Tigecycline *(Tygacil)*	IV: 100 mg once, then 50 mg q12h × 5–14 d	NA (K, F, L)	Inj
Other Antibiotics			
Chloramphenicol▲ *(Chloromycetin)*	po, IV: 50 mg/kg/d q6h; max: 4 g/d	NA (L)	Inj
Clindamycin▲ *(Cleocin)*	po: 150–450 mg q6–8h; max: 1.8 g/d IM, IV: 1.2–1.8 g/d q8–12h; max: 3.6 g/d	NA (L)	C: 75, 150, 300▲ S: 75 mg/5 mL▲ Inj▲
Co-trimoxazole▲ (TMP/ SMZ, *Bactrim)*	Doses based on the trimethoprim component: po: 1 double-strength tab q12h; IV: sepsis: 20 TMP/kg/d given q6h	≤30 (K, L)	T: SMZ 400, TMP 80 double-strength: SMZ 800, TMP 160 S: SMZ 200, TMP 40 mg/5 mL Inj

(cont.)

Table 77. Antibiotics (cont.)

Antimicrobial Class, *Subclass*	Dosage	Adjust When CrCl[a] Is: (mL/min) (Elimination)	Formulations
Dalbavancin *(Dalvance)*	IV: 1000 mg × 1 dose, then 500 mg × 1 dose 1 wk later	<30	Inj
Daptomycin *(Cubicin)*	IV: 4 mg/kg/d × 7–14 d	<30 (K, L)	Inj
Fosfomycin *(Monurol)*	Complicated UTI: Women— po: 3 g in 90–120 mL water × 1 dose Men—po: 3 g in 90–120 mL water q2–3d × 3 doses Prostatitis—po: 3 g in 90–120 mL water q3d × 21 d	(K, F)	pwd: 3 g/pk
Linezolid *(Zyvox)*	po: 600 mg q12h IV: 600 mg q12h	NA	T: 600 S: 100 mg/5 mL Inj
Metronidazole▲ *(Flagyl, MetroGel)*	po: 250–750 mg q6–8h	≤10 (L, K, F)	T: 250, 500▲ ER: 750 C: 375▲
	Topical: apply q12h		Topical gel: 0.75%▲ (30 g)
	Vaginal: 1 applicator full (375 mg) qhs or q12h		Vaginal gel: 0.75%▲ (70 g) Inj▲
Nitrofurantoin▲BC *(Macrobid, Macrodantin)*	po: 50–100 mg q6h	Do not use if <30 (L, K)	C: 25, 50▲, 100▲ S: 25 mg/5 mL▲
Oritavancin *(Orbactiv)*	IV: 1200 mg × 1 dose for ABSSI	(K, F)	Inj
Quinupristin-dalfopristin *(Synercid)*	Vancomycin-resistant *E faecium*: IV: 7.5 mg/kg q8h Complicated skin or skin structure infection: 7.5 mg/kg q12h	NA (L, B, F, K)	Inj
Tedizolid *(Sivextro)*	po, IV: 200 mg q24h × 6 d for BSSI	(L)	T, Inj: 200 mg
Telavancin *(Vibativ)*	IV: 10 mg/kg q24h × 1–2 wk	≤50 (K)	Inj
Vancomycin *(Vancocin)*	po: *C difficile*: 125–500 mg q6–8h IV: 500 mg–1 g q8–24h Peak: 20–40 mcg/mL Trough: 5–10 mcg/mL	<60 (K)	C: 125, 250 S: 25, 50 mg/mL Inj▲

(cont.)

Table 77. Antibiotics (cont.)			
Antimicrobial Class, *Subclass*	**Dosage**	**Adjust When CrCl[a] Is: (mL/min) (Elimination)**	**Formulations**
Antifungals (also **Table 44**)			
Amphotericin			
Amphotericin B▲ *(Fungizone)*	IV: test dose: 1 mg infused over 20–30 min; if tolerated, initial therapeutic dosage is 0.25 mg/kg; the daily dosage can be increased by 0.25-mg/kg increments on each subsequent day until the desired daily dosage is reached Maintenance dosage: IV: 0.25–1 mg/kg/d or 1.5 mg/kg q48h; do not exceed 1.5 mg/kg/d	[c] (K)	Topical: crm, lot, oint: 3% Inj
Amphotericin B Lipid Complex *(Abelcet)*	2.5–5 mg/kg/d as a single infusion	[c] (K)	Inj
Amphotericin B Liposomal *(AmBisome)*	3–6 mg/kg/d infused over 1–2 h	[c] (K)	Inj
Amphotericin B Cholestreyl Sulfate Complex *(Amphotec)*	3–4 mg/kg/d infused at 1 mg/kg/h; max dosage 7.5 mg/kg/d	[c] (K)	Inj
Azoles			
Fluconazole▲ *(Diflucan)*	po, IV: first dose 200–800 mg, then 100–400 mg q24h for 14 d–12 wk, depending on indication Vaginal candidiasis: 150 mg as a single dose	<50 (K)	T: 50, 100, 150, 200 S: 10, 40 mg/mL Inj
Itraconazole *(Sporanox)*	po: 200–400 mg/d; dosages >200 mg/d should be divided. Life-threatening infections: loading dose: 200 mg q8h should be given for the first 3 d of tx IV: 200 mg q12h × 4 d, then 200 mg/d	<30 (L)	C: 100▲ T: 200 S: 10 mg/mL Inj
Ketoconazole▲ *(Nizoral)*	po: 200–400 mg/d shp: 2/wk × 4 wk with ≥3 d between each shp Topical: apply q12–24h	NA (L, F)	T: 200 shp: 2% crm: 2%
Miconazole▲ *(Monistat IV)*	IT: 20 mg q1–2d IV: initial: 200 mg, then 1.2–3.6 g/d divided q8h for up to 2 wk	NA (L, F)	Inj

(cont.)

Table 77. Antibiotics (cont.)

Antimicrobial Class, *Subclass*	Dosage	Adjust When CrCl[a] Is: (mL/min) (Elimination)	Formulations
Posaconazole *(Noxafil)*	Candida or aspergillosis, invasive: Prophylaxis: T: 300 mg × 1 d; Maintenance: T: 300 mg q24h; Sus: 200 mg q8h; IV: 300 mg × 2 on day 1, maintenance 300 mg q24h. Duration: recovery from neutropenia or immunosuppression.	NA	T: 100 sus: 40 mg/mL Inj
	Oropharyngeal infection: Initial: 100 mg q12h × 1 d; maintenance: 100 mg q24h × 13 d.		
	Refractory oropharyngeal infection: Sus: 400 mg q12h; duration based on underlying disease and clinical response.		
Voriconazole *(VFEND)*	IV: loading dose 6 mg/kg q12h for 2 doses, then 4 mg/kg q12h po: >40 kg: 200 mg q12h; ≤ 40 kg: 100 mg q12h If on phenytoin, IV: 5 mg/kg q12h, and po: >40 kg: 400 mg q12h; ≤40 kg: 200 mg q12h	<50 (IV only) (L)	Inj TL 50, 200 mg sus: 40 mg/mL
Echinocandins			
Anidulafungin *(Eraxis)*	Esophageal candidiasis: 100 mg on day 1, then 50 mg/d × ≥13 d and 7 d after symptoms resolve	NA (L, F)	Inj
Caspofungin *(Cancidas)*	Initial: 70 mg infused over 1 h; esophageal candidiasis: 50 mg/d; dosage with concurrent enzyme inducers: 70 mg/d	NA (L, F)	Inj
Micafungin *(Mycamine)*	Esophageal candidiasis: 150 mg/d; prophylaxis in stem cell transplant: 50 mg/d	NA (L, F, K)	Inj
Other Antifungals			
Flucytosine *(Ancobon)*	po: 50–150 mg/kg/d divided q6h	<40 (K)	C: 250, 500
Griseofulvin▲ *(Fulvicin P/G, Grifulvin V)*	po: Microsize: 500–1000 mg/d in single or divided doses Ultramicrosize: 330–375 mg/d in single or divided doses Duration based on indication	NA (L)	Microsize: S: 125 mg/5 mL T: 125, 250, 500

(cont.)

Table 77. Antibiotics (cont.)

Antimicrobial Class, *Subclass*	Dosage	Adjust When CrCl[a] Is: (mL/min) (Elimination)	Formulations
Terbinafine▲ *(Lamisil)*	po: 250 mg/d × 6–12 wk for superficial mycoses; 250–500 mg/d for up to 16 mo Topical: apply q12–24h for max of 4 wk	<50 (L, K)	T: 250 mg▲ crm: 1%▲ Topical S: 1%

Notes: ABSSI = acute bacterial skin and skin structure infection; BSSI = bacterial skin and skin structure infection; NA = not applicable; TDM = adjust dose on basis of therapeutic drug monitoring principles and institutional protocols.

[a] The CrCl listed is the threshold below which the dosage (amount or frequency) should be adjusted. See package insert for detailed dosing guidelines.

[b] Dosage should not exceed 250 mg q6h in kidney impairment.

[c] Adjust dosage if decreased kidney function is due to the medication, or give every other day.

[bc]Avoid.

ACUTE KIDNEY INJURY

Definition

An acute deterioration in kidney function defined by decreased urine output or increased values of kidney function tests, or both. Oliguria (<500 mL urine output/d) has worse prognosis.

Precipitating and Aggravating Factors (Italicized type indicates most common.)

- *Acute tubular necrosis* due to hypoperfusion or nephrotoxins
- Medications (eg, aminoglycosides, radiocontrast materials, NSAIDs, ACEIs), including those causing allergic interstitial nephritis (eg, NSAIDs, penicillins and cephalosporins, sulfonamides, fluoroquinolones, allopurinol, rifampin, PPIs)
- Multiple myeloma
- Obstruction (eg, BPH)
- Vascular disease (thromboembolic, atheroembolic)
- *Volume depletion* or redistribution of ECF (eg, cirrhosis, burns)

Evaluation

- Review medication list
- Catheterize bladder, determine postvoid residual
- UA (**Table 78** for likely diagnoses)
- Renal ultrasonography
- Renal biopsy in selected cases
- If patient is not on diuretics, determine fractional excretion of sodium (FENa):

$$FENa = \left[\frac{urine\ Na/plasma\ Na}{urine\ Cr/plasma\ Cr} \right] \times 100$$

FENa <1% indicates prerenal cause; FENa >2% generally indicates acute tubular necrosis; FENa 1–2% is nondiagnostic. Some older adults who have prerenal cause may have FENa ≥1% because of age-related changes in sodium excretion.

- If patient is receiving diuretics, determine fractional excretion of urea (FEUrea):

$$FEUrea = \left[\frac{urine\ urea\ nitrogen/BUN}{urine\ Cr/plasma\ Cr} \right] \times 100$$

FEUrea ≤35% indicates prerenal azotemia; FEUrea >50% indicates acute tubular necrosis; FEUrea 36–50% is nondiagnostic.

Table 78. Likely Diagnoses Based on UA Findings

Findings	Diagnoses
Hematuria, RBC casts, heavy proteinuria	Glomerular disease or vasculitis
Granular and epithelial cell casts, free epithelial cells	Acute tubular necrosis

(cont.)

Table 78. Likely Diagnoses Based on UA Findings (cont.)	
Findings	**Diagnoses**
Pyuria, WBC casts, granular or waxy casts, little or no proteinuria	Acute interstitial nephritis, glomerulitis, vasculitis, obstruction, renal infarction
Normal UA	Prerenal disease, obstruction, hypercalcemia, myeloma, acute tubular necrosis

Urinary eosinophils are neither sensitive nor specific for acute interstitial nephritis but may be helpful in some cases.

Prevention of Radiocontrast-induced Acute Kidney Failure in High-Risk Patients (Cr >1.5 mg/dL, GFR <60 mL/min/1.73 m² body surface area)

- MRI radiocontrast is gadolinium given IV. Avoid if GFR <30 mL/min. Can cause nephrogenic systemic fibrosis.
- CT radiocontrast are iodinated agents give IV or po (diluted). Low osmolal or iso-osmolal contrast agents should be used in low doses. Brain CTs generally should be noncontrast unless evaluating for an abscess or malignancy.
- Abdomen and pelvic CT scan be noncontrast when evaluating for ureteral calculi, acute bleeding, or retroperitoneal hematoma. For all other indications, contrast is preferred, usually IV unless looking for perforation, fistula, or obstruction of bowel.
- Risk of nephrotoxicity is almost exclusively associated with IV contrast.
- Hold NSAIDs and diuretics for 24 h and metformin for 48 h before administration.
- Avoid closely spaced repeat studies (eg, <48 h apart).
- Intravenous hydration
  - 0.9% saline IV 1 mL/kg/h for 24 h beginning 2–12 h before administration and continuing 6–12 h after procedure, *or*
  - Sodium bicarbonate (154 mEq/L) 3 mL/kg/h for 1 h before procedure and 1 mL/kg/h for 6 h after procedure, especially if insufficient time for hydration before procedure
- Oral acetylcysteine *(Mucomyst)* (100, 200/mL) 1200 mg po q12h the day before and the day of procedure (controversial); does not reduce the risk in at-risk patients undergoing coronary and peripheral vascular angiography.
- Some preliminary evidence supports the use of statins for prevention.
- Repeat serum Cr 24–48 h after administration.

Treatment

- D/C medications that are possible precipitants; avoid contrast dyes.
- If prerenal pattern, treat HF (p 42) if present. Otherwise, volume repletion. Begin with fluid challenge 500–1000 mL over 30–60 min. If no response (increased urine output), give furosemide 100–400 mg IV.
- If obstructed, leave urinary catheter in place during evaluation and while specific tx is implemented.
- If acute tubular necrosis, monitor weight daily, record intake and output, and monitor electrolytes frequently. Fluid replacement should be equal to urinary output plus other drainage plus 500 mL/d for insensible losses.
- If acute interstitial nephritis (except if NSAID-induced) and does not resolve with 3–7 d, then glucocorticoids (eg, prednisone 1 mg/kg/d) for a minimum 1–2 wk and gradual taper when Cr has returned near baseline for a total duration of 2–3 mo.
- Dialysis is indicated when severe hyperkalemia, acidosis, or volume overload cannot be managed with other tx or when uremic symptoms (eg, pericarditis, coagulopathy, or encephalopathy) are present.

CHRONIC KIDNEY DISEASE

Definition

Kidney damage as evidenced by urinary albumin excretion of >30 mg/d or eGFR <60 mL/min/1.73 m^2, for 3 mo or more irrespective of the cause.

Classification (Kidney Disease Outcomes Quality Initiative)

- *Stage G1:* GFR >90 mL/min/1.73 m^2 and persistent albuminuria
- *Stage G2:* GFR 60–89 mL/min/1.73 m^2 and persistent albuminuria
- *Stage G3:* GFR 30–59 mL/min/1.73 m^2
- *Stage G4:* GFR 15–29 mL/min/1.73 m^2
- *Stage G5:* GFR <15 mL/min/1.73 m^2 or end-stage renal disease

Albumin

A1: Daily albumin excretion rate <30 mg/dL

A2: Daily albumin excretion rate 30–300 mg/dL

A3: Daily albumin excretion rate >300 mg/dL

- Cause of CKD also has prognostic value for kidney outcomes and other complications.
- Refer to a nephrologist for co-management if stages G4 A3 and all stage G5 are at very high risk of complications and need for dialysis. Stages G4 A1 and A2, and G3 A2 and A3 (if GFR <44) and A3 (if GFR 44–59) are at high risk of complications. If stage G4–G5 or additional indications of urine albumin-to-Cr ratio >300 mg/g, resistant hypertension, unexplained hematuria or cause of CKD, >30% decline in GFR in <4 mo, CKD complications (see below).

Evaluation

- Hx and physical examination: assess for DM, HTN, vascular disease, HF, NSAIDs, contrast dye exposure, angiographic procedures with possible cholesterol embolization, glomerulonephritis, myeloma, BPH or obstructive cancers, current or previous tx with a nephrotoxic drug, hereditary kidney disease (eg, polycystic)
- Blood tests (CBC, comprehensive metabolic profile, phosphorus, cholesterol, ESR, serum protein immunoelectrophoresis)
- Progression to kidney failure can be predicted by age, sex, eGFR, urine albumin:Cr ratio, serum calcium, serum phosphate, serum bicarbonate, and serum albumin using equation: www.qxmd.com/calculate-online/nephrology/kidney-failure-risk-equation.
- Estimate CrCl or GFR (p 1). CrCl is usually about 20% higher than true GFR. eGFR based on the MDRD equation and true GFR are very close when the GFR is <60 mL/min/1.73 m^2, but true GFR exceeds eGFR by a small amount when GFR is >60 mL/min/1.73 m^2. Older people with eGFR 45–59 mL/min/1.73 m^2 may have normal kidney function for their age.
- If GFR 15–59 mL/min/1.73 m^2, then measure iPTH; if iPTH >100 pg/mL, then measure serum 25-hydroxy vitamin D.
- UA and quantitative urine protein (protein:Cr ratio or 24-h urine for protein and Cr); urine immunoelectrophoresis, if indicated; at all stages, heavier proteinuria is predictive of mortality, ESRD, and doubling of serum Cr.
- Renal ultrasound (large kidneys suggest tumors, infiltrating disease, cystic disease; small kidneys suggest CKD; can also identify cysts, stones, masses, and hydronephrosis)
- Exclude renal artery stenosis with MRI angiography, spiral CT with CT angiography, or duplex Doppler ultrasound if acute rise in Cr shortly after beginning tx with ACEI or ARB
- Renal biopsy in selected cases

Treatment

- Attempt to slow progression of kidney failure
  - Control BP *most important* (target <130/80 if proteinuria [>500 mg/d] Kidney Diseases: Improving Global Outcomes [KDIGO]); <140/80 regardless of proteinuria (JNC 8). Begin with ACEI or ARB; in black patients without proteinuria, thiazide diuretic or CCB are acceptable options.
  - If DM or proteinuria, begin ACEI or ARB (**Table 25**) regardless of whether or not patient has HTN.
  - DM control (p 95)
  - Treat hyperlipidemia (p 47)
  - Moderate dietary protein restriction, 0.8–1 g/kg/d, especially if diabetic nephropathy; if stage G4 or G5 CKD, consider low-protein (0.6 g/kg/d) diet.
  - Smoking cessation
  - Reduction of proteinuria to <1 g/d, if possible and at least to <60% of baseline
  - Avoid triamterene and NSAIDs[CW] in stages 4 and 5 CKD.[BC]
- Prevent and treat symptoms and complications
  - Hyperkalemia: if present (p 185); low potassium diet <40–70 mEq/d; avoid NSAIDs.
  - Acidosis: Sodium bicarbonate (daily dosage of 0.5–1 mEq/kg) tx to maintain serum bicarbonate concentration >23 mEq/L.
  - Mineral and bone complications:
    - Normalize serum calcium with calcium carbonate▲ (500 mg elemental calcium q6–24h) or calcium acetate *(PhosLo)* (3 or 4 tabs q8h with meals); if hypocalcemia is refractory, consider calcitriol *(Rocaltrol)* 0.25 mcg/d.
    - Normalize serum phosphate (2.7–4.6 g/dL) if not on dialysis and maintain between 3.5 and 5.5 mg/dL if on dialysis; restrict dairy products and cola to phosphate intake <900 mg/d. When hyperphosphatemia is refractory, begin:
      - If serum calcium is low, calcium carbonate▲ (1250–1500 mg q8h with meals) or calcium acetate *(PhosLo)* (3 or 4 tabs q8h with meals).
      - If serum calcium is normal or calcium supplementation is ineffective:
        - Sevelamer hydrochloride *(Renagel)* [T: 400, 800; C: 403] or sevelamer carbonate *(Renvela)* [0.8 g pk, T: 800], which does not lower bicarbonate, 800–1600 mg po q8h with each meal.
        - Lanthanum carbonate *(Fosrenol)* [ChT: 250, 500] at initial dosage of 250–500 mg po q8h with each meal, then titrate in increments of 750 mg/d at intervals of 2–3 wk to max of 3750 mg/d.
  - Total elemental calcium (dietary and phosphate should be <2 g)
  - Avoid aluminum and magnesium phosphate binders
  - Treating vitamin D insufficiency improves biochemical markers but the effect on clinical outcomes is uncertain. Use vitamin D_2 (ergocalciferol) 50,000 U/mo or oral vitamin D with calcitriol 25 mcg/d if 25(OH) vitamin D is <30 ng/mL. Stop if corrected serum calcium is >10.2 mg/dL.
  - Anemia: Monitor Hb yearly if stage G3, q6mo if stages G4 or G5, and q3mo if on dialysis. Treat anemia with iron (if iron-deficient) to maintain transferrin saturation >20% and serum ferritin >100 ng/L and, if necessary, erythropoietin-darbepoetin (**Table 67**) to maintain a target Hb goal of ≤11 g/dL. Don't administer erythropoiesis-stimulating agents to patients with CKD with Hb ≥10 g/dL without signs or symptoms.[CW]
  - Cardiovascular:
    - Manage volume overload (HF, p 42).
    - HTN control: target <140/80; <130/80 if proteinuria >500 mg/d

- Prevent and treat cardiovascular disease (p 39). The value of statins for patients on maintenance dialysis is questionable.
  ○ Prevention: Immunize with *Pneumovax* and, if stage G4 or G5 CKD, hepatitis B vaccines if hepatitis B surface antigen and antibody are negative.
  ○ Prepare for dialysis or transplant. Educate patients regarding options of hemodialysis, peritoneal dialysis, and kidney transplantation. If estimated GFR <25 mL/min/1.73 m², recommend referral for arteriovenous fistula access, which takes months before it is ready to be used. If estimated GFR <20 mL/min/1.73 m², patients can be listed for cadaveric kidney transplant. Patients >65 yr old can be considered for transplantation if substantial life expectancy.
- Dialysis is indicated when severe hyperkalemia, acidosis, or volume overload cannot be managed with other tx or when uremic symptoms (eg, pericarditis, coagulopathy, or encephalopathy) are present.
- Other than transplantation, renal replacement can be by hemodialysis or peritoneal dialysis (continuous or automated, which uses short dwells and automated technology to operate at near maximum solute clearance rates). Although more older persons select hemodialysis and few switch from hemodialysis to peritoneal dialysis, differences in survival between approaches have not been demonstrated.
- Don't perform routine cancer screening for dialysis patients with limited life expectancies without signs or symptoms.[CW]

VOLUME DEPLETION (DEHYDRATION)

Definition
Losses of sodium and water that may be isotonic (eg, loss of blood) or hypotonic (eg, nasogastric suctioning)

Precipitating Factors
- Blood loss
- Diuretics
- GI losses
- Kidney or adrenal disease (eg, renal sodium wasting)
- Sequestration of fluid (eg, ileus, burns, peritonitis)
- Age-related changes (impaired thirst, sodium wasting due to hyporeninemic hypoaldosteronism, and free water wasting due to renal insensitivity to antidiuretic hormone)

Evaluation

Clinical Symptoms
- Anorexia
- Nausea and vomiting
- Orthostatic lightheadedness
- Delirium
- Weakness

Clinical Signs
- Dry tongue and axillae
- Oliguria
- Orthostatic hypotension
- Elevated HR
- Weight loss (most specific)

Laboratory Tests
- Serum electrolytes
- Urine sodium (usually <10 mEq/L) and FENa (usually <1% but may be higher because of age-related sodium wasting)
- Serum BUN and Cr (BUN:Cr ratio often >20)

Management
- Weigh daily; monitor fluid losses and serum electrolytes, BUN, Cr.
- If mild, oral rehydration of 2–4 L of water/d and 4–8 g Na diet; if poor oral intake, give IV D5W 1/2 NS with potassium as needed.
- If hemodynamically unstable, give IV 0.9% saline 1–2 L as quickly as possible until SBP ≥100 mmHg and no longer orthostatic. Then switch to D5W 1/2 NS. Monitor closely in patients with a hx of HF. Avoid hyperoncotic starch solutions, which are associated with acute kidney injury and increased mortality.

HYPERNATREMIA

Causes
- Pure water loss
  - Insensible losses due to sweating and respiration
  - Central (eg, post-traumatic, CNS tumors, meningitis) diabetes insipidus or nephrogenic (eg, hypercalcemia, lithium) diabetes insipidus
- Hypotonic sodium loss
  - Renal causes: osmotic diuresis (eg, due to hyperglycemia), postobstructive diuresis, polyuric phase of acute tubular necrosis
  - GI causes: vomiting and diarrhea, nasogastric drainage, osmotic cathartic agents (eg, lactulose)
- Hypertonic sodium gain (eg, tx with hypertonic saline)
- Impaired thirst (eg, delirious or intubated) or access to water (eg, functionally dependent) may sustain hypernatremia

Evaluation
- Measure intake and output.
- Obtain urine osmolality:
  - >800 mOsm/kg suggests extrarenal (if urine Na <25 mEq/L) or remote renal water loss or administration of hypertonic Na+ salt solutions (if urine Na >100 mEq/L).
  - <250 mOsm/kg and polyuria suggest diabetes insipidus.

Treatment
- Treat underlying causes.
- Correct slowly over at least 48–72 h using oral (can use pure water), nasogastric (can use pure water), or IV (D5W, 1/2 or 1/4 NS) fluids; correct at rate of no more than 1 mmol/L/h if acute (eg, developing over hours) and at no more than 10 mmol/L/d if of longer duration.
- Correct with NS only in cases of severe volume depletion with hemodynamic compromise; once stable, switch to hypotonic solution.
- When repleting fluids, use the following formula to estimate the effect of 1 L of any infusate on serum Na:

$$\text{Change in serum Na} = \frac{\text{infusate Na} - \text{serum Na}}{\text{total body water} + 1}$$

  - Infusate Na (mmol/L): D5W = 0; 1/4 NS = 34; 1/2 NS = 77; NS = 154
  - Calculate total body water as a fraction of body weight (0.5 kg in older men and 0.45 kg in older women).

- Divide tx goal (usually 10 mmol/L/d) by change in serum Na/L (from formula) to determine amount of solution to be given over 24 h.
- Compensate for any ongoing obligatory fluid losses, which are usually 1–1.5 L/d.
- Divide amount of solution for repletion plus amount for obligatory fluid losses by 24 to determine rate per hour.

HYPONATREMIA

Classifications

Acuity: hyperacute (within hours), acute (within 24 h), chronic (at least 48 h or unknown)

Severity: mild (130–135 mEq/L), moderate (121–129 mEq/L), severe (≤120 mEq/L)

Symptoms: absent, mild to moderate (eg, headache, nausea, vomiting, fatigue, gait disturbances, confusion), severe (eg, seizures, optimization, coma, respiratory arrest)

Causes

- With increased plasma osmolality: hyperglycemia (1.6 mEq/L decrement for each 100 mg/dL increase in plasma glucose)
- With normal plasma osmolality (pseudohyponatremia): severe hyperlipidemia, hyperproteinemia (eg, multiple myeloma)
- With decreased plasma osmolality:
  ◦ With ECF excess: kidney failure, HF, hepatic cirrhosis, nephrotic syndrome
  ◦ With decreased ECF volume: renal loss from salt-losing nephropathies, diuretics, cerebral salt wasting, osmotic diuresis; extrarenal loss due to vomiting, diarrhea, skin losses, and third-spacing (usually urine Na <20 mEq/L, FENa <1%, and uric acid >4 mg/dL)
  ◦ With normal ECF volume: primary polydipsia (urine osmolarity <100 mOsm/kg), hypothyroidism, adrenal insufficiency, SIADH (urine Na >40 mEq/L and uric acid <4 mg/dL)

Management

Treat underlying cause. Specific tx only if symptomatic (eg, altered mental status, seizures), severe acute hyponatremia (eg, <120 mEq/L), or hyperacute regardless of symptoms.

- If initial volume estimate is equivocal, give fluid challenge of 0.5–1 L of isotonic (0.9%) saline.
- If volume depletion, give saline IV (corrects ~1 mEq/L for every liter given) or oral salt tablets.
- If edematous states, SIADH, or chronic renal failure, fluid restriction to below the level of urine output is the primary tx.
- Hypovolemic hyponatremia is almost always chronic (except for cerebral salt wasting and after diuretic initiation), and hypertonic saline is seldom indicated.
- Emergent tx with hypertonic (3%) saline initially with 100 mL bolus over 10–15 min; correct 2–4 mEq/L (goal is 4–6 mEq/L) in first 2–4 h. Concurrent desmopressin (1–2 µg IV or SC q6–8h for 24–48 h) may help prevent overly rapid correction but is usually not used if HF or cirrhosis. Monitor sodium q2h. Indications include:
  ◦ severe symptoms
  ◦ acute hyponatremia (<24 h) even with mild symptoms
  ◦ hyperacute due to self-induced water intoxication
  ◦ symptomatic postoperative hyponatremia or associated with intracranial pathology
- Nonemergent tx for
  ◦ asymptomatic acute or subacute hyponatremia or chronic severe hyponatremia with mild to moderate symptoms: 3% hypertonic saline 50 mL bolus or slow infusion 15–30 mL/h

- ○ chronic moderate hyponatremia with mild to moderate symptoms
  - ▪ If edematous states, SIADH, advanced CKD, or primary polydyspsia, then fluid restriction
- Goal is <4–6 mEq/L during first 24 h and no more than 9 mEq/L in any 24 h (more rapid correction can result in central pontine myelinolysis).
- Monitor Na closely and taper tx when >120 mEq/L or symptoms resolve.
- Arginine vasopressin receptor antagonists
  - ○ Conivaptan *(Vaprisol)* is effective in euvolemic hyponatremia in hospitalized patients; 20 mg IV over 30 min once, followed by continuous infusion of 20–40 mg over 24 h for 4 d max (L) (CYP3A4 interactions).
  - ○ Tolvaptan *(Samsca)* 15–60 mg/d [T: 15, 30]: initiate in hospital and monitor blood sodium concentration closely. Not to be used for more than 30 d.

SYNDROME OF INAPPROPRIATE SECRETION OF ANTIDIURETIC HORMONE (SIADH)

Definition

Hypotonic hyponatremia (<280 mOsm/kg) with:
- Less than maximally dilute urine (usually >100 mOsm/kg)
- Elevated urine sodium (usually >40 mEq/L)
- Normal volume status
- Normal kidney, adrenal, and thyroid function

Precipitating Factors, Causes

- Medications (eg, SSRIs, SNRIs, chlorpropamide, carbamazepine, oxcarbazepine, NSAIDs, barbiturates, antipsychotics, mirtazapine. Use with caution.[BC])
- Neuropsychiatric factors (eg, neoplasm, subarachnoid hemorrhage, psychosis, meningitis)
- Postoperative state, especially if pain or nausea
- Pulmonary disease (eg, pneumonia, tuberculosis, acute asthma)
- Tumors (eg, lung, pancreas, thymus)

Evaluation

- BUN, Cr, serum cortisol, TSH
- CXR
- Review of medications
- Neurologic tests as indicated
- Urine sodium and osmolality

Management

Acute Treatment: See euvolemic hyponatremia management, p 183.

Chronic Treatment:
- D/C offending medication or treat precipitating illness.
- Restrict water intake (unless due to subarachnoid hemorrhage) to <800 mL/d with goal of Na ≥130 mEq/L.
- Liberalize salt intake or give salt tablets. Can also give IV saline but the electrolyte concentration of the fluid must be greater than the electrolyte concentration of urine. Usually, hypertonic saline, if given.
- If urinary osmolality is twice the plasma osmolality, loop diuretics (eg, furosemide 20 mg q12h) may help facilitate excess water excretion.
- Demeclocycline▲ *(Declomycin)* 150–300 mg q12h [T: 150, 300] (may be nephrotoxic in patients with liver disease) only if symptomatic and above steps do not work.
- Tolvaptan *(Samsca)* 15–60 mg/d [T:15, 30]: initiate in hospital and monitor blood sodium concentration closely only if symptomatic and above steps do not work. Risk of hepatotoxicity. Do not use for >30 d and not in patients with chronic liver diseases.

HYPERKALEMIA

Causes

- Kidney failure
- Addison disease
- Hyporeninemic hypoaldosteronism
- Renal tubular acidosis
- Acidosis
- Diabetic hyperglycemia
- Hemolysis, tumor lysis, rhabdomyolysis
- Medications (potassium-sparing diuretics, ACEIs, trimethoprim-sulfamethoxazole, β-blockers, NSAIDs, cyclosporine, tacrolimus, pentamidine, heparin, digoxin toxicity)
- Pseudohyperkalemia from extreme thrombocytosis or leukocytosis
- Transfusions of stored blood
- Constipation

Evaluation

- ECG; peaked T waves typically occur when K+ exceeds 6.5 mEq/L. ECG changes are more likely with acute increases of K+ than with chronic increases.

Treatment

Minor elevations

- K+ <6 mEq/L without ECG changes:
  - Low-potassium diet (restrict orange juice, bananas, potatoes, cantaloupe, honeydew, tomatoes)
  - Oral diuretics (eg, oral torsemide or bumetanide, combined oral loop and thiazide-like diuretics; metolazone is the most K+ wasting); avoid hypovolemia
  - Oral sodium bicarbonate (650–1300 mg q12h); not recommended as a single agent
  - Reduce or D/C medications that increase K+
- K+ 6–6.5 mEq/L without ECG changes: above tx plus sodium polystyrene sulfonate▲ *(SPS, Kayexalate)* 15–30 g po q6–24h, or prn as enema 30–50 g in 100 mL of dextrose; full effect takes 4–24 h and generally requires multiple doses over 1–5 d. Can expect approximately 1 mEg/d reduction. Other laxatives (eg, sorbitol).
- K+ 6.5 mEq/L with peaked T waves but no other ECG changes: hospitalization is decided case-by-case based on acuteness of onset, cause, and other patient factors.

Absolute indications for hospitalization

- K+ >8 mEq/L
- ECG changes other than peaked T waves (eg, prolonged PR, loss of P waves, widened QRS)
- Acute deterioration of kidney function

Inpatient management of hyperkalemia

- Antagonism of cardiac effects of hyperkalemia (most rapid-acting acute tx; use only for severe hyperkalemia with significant ECG changes when too dangerous to wait for redistribution tx to take effect)
  - 10% calcium gluconate IV infused over 2–3 min (20–30 min if on digoxin) with ECG monitoring; effect lasts 30–60 min, may repeat if needed

- Reduction of serum K+ by redistribution into cells (acute tx; can be used in combination with calcium gluconate, and different redistribution tx can be combined depending on severity of hyperkalemia)
  - Insulin (regular) 10 U in 500 mL of 10% dextrose over 30–60 min or bolus insulin (regular) 10 U IV followed by 50 mL of 50% dextrose
  - Albuterol 0.5 mg in 100 mL of 5% dextrose given over 10–15 min or nebulized 10–20 mg in 4 mL of NS over 10 min (should not be used as single agent)
  - Sodium bicarbonate if significant metabolic acidosis, but should not be used as single agent.
- Removal of potassium from body (definitive tx; work more slowly)
  - Diuretics (eg, oral torsemide or bumetanide, IV furosemide, combined oral loop and thiazide-like diuretics; metolazone is the most K+ wasting). Avoid hypovolemia.
  - Fludrocortisone▲ 0.1–0.3 mg/d
  - Sodium polystyrene sulfonate▲ *(SPS, Kayexalate)* 15–30 g po q6–24h or prn as enema 30–50 g in 100 mL of dextrose; full effect takes 4–24 h; do not use in postoperative patients, patients with ileus, receiving opiates, or with bowel obstruction. If packaged in sorbitol *(SPS)*, may cause intestinal necrosis.
  - Dialysis

DEFINITION

There is no uniformly accepted definition of malnutrition in older adults. Some commonly used definitions include those listed below.

Community-dwelling Older Adults

- ASPEN criteria for adult malnutrition (2 of the following):
  - Insufficient energy intake
  - Loss of muscle mass
  - Fluid accumulation (eg, edema)
  - Weight loss
  - Loss of subcutaneous fat
  - Diminished function by hand-grip strength
- Involuntary weight loss (eg, ≥2% over 1 mo, >10 lb over 6 mo, ≥4% over 1 yr)
- BMI <22 kg/m^2
- Hypoalbuminemia (eg, ≤3.8 g/dL)
- Hypocholesterolemia (eg, <160 mg/dL)
- Overweight (BMI 25–29.9 kg/m^2); not associated with increased mortality if >70 yr old
- Obesity (BMI ≥30 kg/m^2)
- Specific vitamin or micronutrient deficiencies (eg, vitamin B$_{12}$)
- Cancer-related anorexia/cachexia syndrome: a hypercatabolic state (increased resting energy expenditure) with high levels of tumor-activated or host-produced immune responses (eg, proinflammatory cytokines) to the tumor
- Sarcopenia age-related loss of muscle mass (eg, 2 SDs below mean for young healthy adults) with loss of strength and performance; contributors include decreased sex hormones, increased insulin resistance, increased inflammatory cytokines, decreased physical activity, inadequate protein intake, and spinal cord changes (decreased motor units)

Hospitalized Patients

- Dietary intake (eg, <50% of estimated needed caloric intake)
- Hypoalbuminemia (eg, <3.5 g/dL)
- Hypocholesterolemia (eg, <160 mg/dL)

Nursing-home Patients (Triggered by the Minimum Data Set)

- Weight loss of ≥5% in past 30 d; ≥10% in 180 d
- Dietary intake <75% of most meals

EVALUATION

Screening

Proposed screening instruments have not been adequately validated or do not demonstrate sufficient sensitivity and specificity to warrant use in clinical practice.

Multidimensional Assessment

In the absence of valid nutrition screening instruments, clinicians should focus on whether the following issues may be affecting nutritional status:

- Economic barriers to securing food
- Social isolation (eg, eating alone)
- Availability of sufficiently high-quality food
- Dental problems that preclude ingesting food

- Medical illnesses that:
  - interfere with ingestion (eg, dysphagia), digestion, or absorption of food
  - increase nutritional requirements or cause cachexia
  - require dietary restrictions (eg, low-sodium diet or npo)
- Functional disability that interferes with shopping, preparing meals, or feeding
- Food preferences or cultural beliefs that interfere with adequate food intake
- Poor appetite
- Depressive symptoms

Anthropometrics

Weight on each visit and yearly height (p 1)

Evaluation for Comorbid Medical Conditions

- CBC, ESR, and comprehensive metabolic panel (if none abnormal, then likelihood ratio for cancer is 0.2)
- CXR
- TSH

Biochemical Markers

Serum Proteins: All may drop precipitously because of trauma, sepsis, or major infection.
- Albumin (half-life 18–20 d) has prognostic value in all settings.
- Transferrin (half-life 7 d)
- Prealbumin (half-life 48 h) may be valuable in monitoring nutritional recovery.

Serum Cholesterol (Low or Falling Levels): Has prognostic value in all settings but may not be nutritionally mediated.

MANAGEMENT

Universal Recommendations

Vitamin D and Calcium

All older adults should receive calcium 1200 mg/d and vitamin D 800–1000 IU/d. The USPSTF concluded that there is insufficient evidence to recommend screening for vitamin D deficiency.

Multivitamins

- Observational data in postmenopausal women indicate no effect on breast, colorectal, endometrial, lung, or ovarian cancers, MI, stroke, VTE, or mortality.
- In clinical trials in middle-aged men, multivitamins have not been shown to decrease cardiovascular disease or mortality, but there is a small reduction in total cancer risk.
- Clinical trial data show no benefit in reducing infections in outpatient and nursing home settings.

Mediterranean Diet

- Observational data indicate improved health status and reductions in cardiovascular disease, cancer, and overall mortality, as well as lower incidences of Parkinson disease and Alzheimer disease.
- Clinical trial data demonstrate reduction in major cardiovascular events and cognitive decline with Mediterranean diet supplemented by either extra-virgin olive oil or mixed nuts.

Calculating Basic Energy (Caloric) and Fluid Requirements

- WHO energy estimates for adults 60 yr old and older:
  - Women (10.5) (weight in kg) + 596
  - Men (13.5) (weight in kg) + 487
- Harris-Benedict energy requirement equations:
  - Women: 655 + (9.6) (weight in kg) + (1.7) (height in cm) − (4.7) (age in yr)
  - Men: 66 + (13.7) (weight in kg) + (5) (height in cm) − (6.8) (age in yr)
- Fluid requirements for older adults without heart or kidney disease are ~30 mL/kg/d.

Depending on activity and physiologic stress levels, these basic requirements may need to be increased (eg, 25% for sedentary or mild, 50% for moderate, and 100% for intense or severe activity or stress).

Obesity and Overweight Management

Nonpharmacologic Treatment

- Overweight probably does not increase mortality risk; however, weight loss in obese older adults may decrease mortality risk.
- In younger overweight and obese patients, no particular combination of protein, carbohydrate, and fat in weight loss diets offers any advantage in losing weight.
- Moderate exercise at 90 min/3×/wk and a caloric prescription to produce a deficit of 500–750 calories/d can lead to weight loss of 10% and improved functional status in younger (mean age 70) obese older persons.
- Lower energy-density diet (fewer calories per volume of food) may be more effective in reducing weight regain after loss.
- Bariatric surgery (based on studies of younger persons): Increased remissions from DM and lower incidence of micro- and macrovascular complications. Reduced cardiovascular and all-cause mortality.
  - Adjustable gastric banding placed laparoscopically; 47% excess weight loss (ie, above BMI 25) at 15 yr; safest procedure
  - Sleeve gastrectomy with most of greater curvature removed; 59% excess weight loss; less effective than gastric bypass but lower rate of complications
  - Roux-en-Y gastric bypass creating pouch of stomach anastomosing jejunum; 54–66% excess weight loss
  - Biliopancreatic diversion with duodenal switch: ≥70% excessive weight loss

Pharmacologic Treatment

- Drugs to treat obesity have not been studied extensively in older persons; information below is based on studies of younger persons.
- Consider if BMI ≥30 or 27–29 if comorbidities.
- When using pharmacologic management, weight loss of 10–15% is considered a good response and >15% is considered excellent. If ≥5% weight loss is not achieved in 12 wk, stop or taper depending upon specific drug.
- Orlistat *(Xenical, Alli)* 120 mg q8h [C: 60 mg *(Alli)* OTC, 120 mg] has the longest-term data on safety and efficacy. Abdominal discomfort and flatus are the most common adverse effects. Average weight loss 3 kg; <50% of adults lose ≥5%.
- Lorcaserin 10 mg q12h *(Belviq)* [T: 10 mg]. <50% lose >5%.
- Phentermine-topiramate ER *(Qsymia)* [ER T: 3.75 mg/23 mg, 7.5 mg/46 mg, 1.25 mg/69 mg, 5 mg/92 mg]. Begin 3.75 mg/23 mg daily for 14 d, then increase; 3.75 mg/46 mg may be more effective but should not be used if cardiovascular disease or HTN. Can cause dry mouth, paresthesia, constipation, dysgeusia, cognitive changes; 70% achieve ≥5% weight loss.

- Bupropion-naltrexone *(Contrave)* [ER T: 8/90 mg]. Can cause nausea, vomiting, headache, constipation, dizziness, and dry mouth; 39–56% have ≥5% weight loss
- Liraglutide *(Saxenda)* [inj: 18 mg/3 mL]. Begin 0.6 mg daily × 7 d, then each wk increase dose by 0.6 mg/d to a total of 3 mg SC daily; adjunct to reduced calorie diet and increased physical activity. Can cause nausea, vomiting, constipation, diarrhea; 50–63% of adults lose ≥5%.
- Other drugs have limited effectiveness or high potential for adverse effects or abuse.

Undernutrition Management

- If possible, remove disease-specific (eg, for hypercholesterolemia) dietary restrictions.
- If needed, help arrange shopping, cooking, and feeding assistance, including home-delivered meals and between-meal snacks.
- Increase caloric density of foods.
- Refeeding syndrome caused by the glucose-induced acute transcellular shift of phosphate typically occurs in malnourished patients who have had poor oral intake and then receive IV glucose-containing fluids, or enteral or parenteral nutrition. Symptoms occur most commonly within 2–4 d of refeeding and include hypophosphatemia, hyperglycemia, and hyperinsulinemia, which may be accompanied by hypokalemia, hypomagnesemia, and fluid retention. Supplementing IV fluids with potassium phosphate or oral phosphate and potassium may help prevent this syndrome.
- Post-hospitalization home visits by a dietitian may be valuable.

Appetite Stimulants

- No medications are FDA approved to promote weight gain in older adults. Avoid using.[CW]
- Dronabinol and megestrol acetate (Avoid[BC]) (not covered by Medicare Part D) have been effective in promoting weight gain in younger adults with specific conditions (eg, AIDS, cancer). Small clinical trials of megestrol in select groups (eg, after hospitalization, nursing home) have shown benefit for some nutritional markers (eg, prealbumin, weight) but not for clinical outcomes. Avoid megestrol; may increase risk of thrombosis and death.[BC]
- A minority of patients receiving mirtazapine[▲] report appetite stimulation and weight gain.
- All medications used for appetite have substantial potential AEs.

Nutritional Supplements

- Protein and energy supplements in older adults at risk of malnutrition appear to have beneficial effects on weight gain and mortality, and shorten length of stay in hospitalized patients. Among those who are well nourished at baseline, the benefit is less clear. Supplements should be given between rather than with meals.
- For ICU patients, enteral nutrition is preferred over parenteral nutrition and should be started within the first 24–48 h after admission. Absence of bowel sounds and evidence of bowel function (eg, passing flatus or feces) are not contraindications to beginning tube feeding.
- Many formulas are available (**Table 79** and **Table 80**). Read the content labels and choose on the basis of calories/mL, protein, fiber, lactose, and fluid load.
  - Oral: Many (eg, *Resource Health Shake*) are milk-based and provide ~1–1.5 calories/mL.
  - Enteral: Commercial preparations have between 0.5 and 2 calories/mL; most contain no milk (lactose) products. For patients who need fluid restriction, the higher concentrated formulas may be valuable, but they may cause diarrhea. Because of reduced kidney function with aging, some recommend that protein should contribute no more than 20% of the formula's total calories. If formula is sole source of nutrition, consider one that contains fiber (25 g/d is optimal).

Table 79. Examples of Lactose-free Oral Products

Product	Kcal/mL	mOsm	Protein (g/L)	Water (mL/L)	Na (mEq/L)	K (mEq/L)	Fiber (g/L)
Routine use formulations							
Boost Original [a]	1.00	625	41.7	830	27.5	49.9	0
Boost Plus	1.50	670	59.2	780	36.8	38.9	0
Ensure [b]	1.05	500	38.0	840	33.0	40.0	4
Ensure Plus	1.50	680	54.9	740	40.4	43.2	12
Low volume (packaged as 45-mL supplement; nutrients are provided per serving)							
Benecalorie	330	NA	7.0	0	0.9	0	0
Clear liquid							
Boost Breeze	1.05	750	38.0	830	14.8	0.0	0
Ensure Clear [c]	1.01	700	35.0	840	5.5	0.0	0
Diabetes formulations							
Boost Glucose Control [c]	1.06	400	59.1	840	49.4	28.3	12.7
Glucerna shake [c]	0.93	530	41.8	840	38.5	41.1	12.7

NA = not available

[a] Also has pudding product that has 160 Kcal/5 oz and 0 g fiber

[b] Also has pudding product that has 170 Kcal/4 oz and 1.0 g fiber/serving

[c] Institutional formulation of Ensure differs slightly

Table 80. Examples of Lactose-free Enteral Products

Product	Kcal/mL	mOsm	Protein (g/L)	Water (mL/L)	Na (mEq/L)	K (mEq/L)	Fiber (g/L)
Diabetes formulations							
Diabetisource AC	1.20	450	60.0	820	46.0	40.8	15.2
Glucerna 1.0 Cal [a]	1.00	355	41.8	850	40.4	40.3	14.4
Low residue							
Isosource HN [b]	1.20	490	53.6	820	48.8	48.8	0
Osmolite 1 Cal [a]	1.06	300	44.3	840	40.5	40.1	0
Nutren 1.0 [c]	1.00	370	40.0	850	38.0	32.0	0
Low volume							
Nutren 2.0	2.00	745	78.0	700	56.4	49.2	0
TwoCal HN	2.00	725	84.0	700	63.3	62.4	5.1
High fiber							
Jevity 1 Cal [a]	1.06	300	43.9	830	40.5	40.5	14.3
Fibersource HN	1.20	490	54.0	810	52.0	48.0	10.0
Nutren 1.0 FIBER	1.00	410	40.0	840	38.0	32.0	14.0

[a] Also has 1.2- and 1.5-calorie formulations

[b] Also has 1.5-calorie formulation with 8 g fiber/L

[c] Also has 1.5-calorie formulation

Important Drug-Enteral Interactions

- Soybean formulas increase fecal elimination of thyroxine; time administration of thyroxine and enteral nutrition as far apart as possible.
- Enteral feedings reduce absorption of phenytoin, L-dopa, levofloxacin, and ciprofloxacin; administer these medications at least 2 h after a feeding and delay feeding at least 2 h after medication is administered; monitor levels (if taking phenytoin) and adjust dosages, as necessary.
- Check with pharmacy about suitability and best way to administer SR, enteric-coated, and microencapsulated products (eg, omeprazole, lansoprazole, diltiazem, fluoxetine, verapamil).

Gastrostomy/Jejunostomy Tube Feeding

- Chronic artificial nutrition and hydration is not a basic intervention and is associated with uncertain benefit and considerable risks and discomfort.
- Do not insert percutaneous feeding tubes if advanced dementia; instead offer oral assisted feedings.[cw]
- Artificial nutrition and hydration should be used only for specific medical indications, not to increase patient comfort.
- Some evidence supports the use of gastrostomy tubes in head and neck cancer.
- For dysphagia and aspiration, the evidence for gastronomy tubes is conflicting without support of randomized trials.

Tips for Successful Tube Feeding

- Tube feeding can begin 4 h after placement, though early feeding may result in increased gastric residual volumes.
- Bolster should be positioned to allow 1 to 2 cm movement.
- Gauze pads should be placed over, not underneath, the external bolster.
- Gastrostomy tube feeding may be either intermittent or continuous.
- Jejunostomy tube feedings must be continuous.
- Polyurethane tubes have less dysfunction than silicone tubes.
- Continuous tube feeding is associated with less frequent diarrhea but with higher rates of tube clogging.
- To prevent clogging and to provide additional free water, flushing with at least 30–60 mL of water q4–6h is recommended. Do not allow formula bags to run dry. Administer only liquid or crushed and dissolved medication through tubes.
- Do not give more than one medication at a time, and flush with 20 mL before and after medication administration.
- Do not administer bulk-forming laxatives (eg, methylcellulose or psyllium) through feeding tubes.
- If clogged, begin with gentle flush with warm water with 30–60 mL syringe. Allow water to sit for 5 min and repeat. Pancrelipase *(Viokase)* mixed with a bicarbonate 324-mg tab or 1/8 tsp baking soda in warm water may be helpful. Papain and chymopapain are more effective at clearing clogged tubes than sugar-free carbonated beverages or cranberry juice. Commercial devices (eg, *Clog Zapper*) may be effective.
- Diarrhea, which develops in 5–30% of people receiving enteral feeding, may be related to the osmolality of the formula, the rate of delivery, high sorbitol content in liquid medications (eg, APAP, lithium, oxybutynin, furosemide), or other patient-related factors such as antibiotic use or impaired absorption.
- To help prevent aspiration, maintain 30- to 45-degree elevation of the head of the bed during continuous feeding and for at least 2 h after bolus feedings.

- Check gastric residual volume before each bolus feeding. Gastric residual volumes in the range of 200–500 mL should raise concern and lead to the implementation of measures to reduce risk of aspiration, but automatic cessation of feeding should not occur for gastric residual volumes <500 mL in the absence of other signs of intolerance. If needed, naloxone *(Narcan)* 8 mg q6h per nasogastric tube, metoclopramide▲ *(Reglan)* 10 mg, or erythromycin 250 mg IV [5 mg/5 mL] q6h may be useful for problems with high gastric residual volume once mechanical obstruction has been excluded.
- Tubes removed inadvertently during the first 4 wk should not be reinserted blindly. Rather, they should be endoscopically, radiologically, or surgically reinserted, which can usually be through the same site.

Parenteral Nutrition
- Indicated in those with digestive dysfunction precluding enteral feeding.
- In ICU settings, if enteral nutrition is not feasible, should wait 8 d to begin parenteral nutrition.
- Delivers protein as amino acids, carbohydrate as dextrose (D5 = 170 kcal/L; D10 = 340 kcal/L), and fat as lipid emulsions (10% = 1100 kcal/L; 20% = 2200 kcal/L).
- Usually administered as total parenteral nutrition through a central catheter, which may be inserted peripherally.

NECK PAIN: DIFFERENTIAL DIAGNOSIS AND TREATMENT
Cervical Stenosis/Radiculopathy

Noncompressive: Herpes zoster, Lyme disease, lymphoma, carcinomatosis, demyelination

Compressive: Cervical spondylosis, disk herniation

Treatment: Most patients improve without specific tx. If radicular pain, paresthesias, numbness, or nonprogressive neurologic deficits, prescribe oral analgesics and avoidance of aggravating movements. If severe, short course of oral prednisone. PT when pain is tolerable. If severe or disabling persistent symptoms, then epidural steroids. Surgery if symptoms and neurologic signs, documented nerve root compression by MRI or CT, and persistence of pain for 6–12 wk or progressive motor weakness.

SHOULDER PAIN: DIFFERENTIAL DIAGNOSIS AND TREATMENT

Rotator Cuff Tendinitis, Subacromial Bursitis, or Rotator Tendon Impingement on Clavicle

Dull ache radiating to upper arm. Painful arc is characteristic. Also can be distinguished by applying resistance against active range of motion while immobilizing the neck with hand.

May cause shoulder impingement syndrome (insidious onset of anterolateral acromial pain frequently radiating to lateral mid-humerus). Pain is worse at night, exacerbated by lying on the involved shoulder or sleeping with the arm overhead. Active and passive range of motion are normal. Lidocaine injection will result in normal strength and temporary pain relief (**Table 81**).

Table 81. Use of Lidocaine Injections to Distinguish Different Shoulder Pain Syndromes[a]

Cause of shoulder pain	Response to Lidocaine Injection	
	Strength/Range of Motion	*Pain*
Tendinitis, bursitis	Normal	Temporary relief
Rotator cuff tear	Persistent weakness	Temporary relief
Frozen shoulder	No change in range of motion	

[a] Insert a 1½-inch, 22-gauge needle 1½ inches below the midpoint of the acromion to a depth of 1 to 1½ inches. The angle of entry parallels the acromion. One mL of lidocaine is injected into the deltoid, and 1–2 mL into the subacromial bursa. Dramatic relief of pain and improvement of function by injection into subacromial bursa effectively excludes glenohumeral joint process.

Most accurate bedside tests are (muscle being tested):

- Painful arc test: pain on abduction 60–120 degrees and external rotation suggests impingement or rotator cuff disorder due to compression
- Drop arm test (supraspinatus): inability to maintain the arm in an abducted 90-degree position indicates tear
- External rotation resistance test (infraspinatus): elbows flexed, thumbs up with examiner's hands outside patient's elbows; patient is asked to resist inward pressure; pain or weakness indicates tendonitis or tear
- External rotation lag test (supraspinatus and infraspinatus): elbow at 90-degree flexion and 20-degree abduction, examiner passively rotates patient's arm into full external rotation; inability to maintain this position indicates tear
- Internal rotation lag test (subscapularis): elbow at 90-degree flexion, dorsum of hand on back; hand is lifted off back by examiner; inability to maintain position indicates tear

Treatment: Identify and eliminate provocative, repetitive injury (eg, avoid overhead reaching). A brief period of rest and immobilization with a sling may be helpful. Pain control with APAP or a short course of NSAIDs (**Table 82**), home exercises or PT (especially assisted range of motion and wall walking), and corticosteroid injections (p 200) may be useful.

Rotator Cuff Tears

Mild to complete; characterized by diminished shoulder movement. Chronic full thickness tear may not have pain but have loss of range of active or passive motion. After lidocaine injection of shoulder, weakness persists despite pain relief (**Table 81**). Ultrasound (preferred test) when performed by experienced operators or MRI establishes diagnosis.

Treatment: If due to injury, a brief period of rest and immobilization with a sling may be helpful. Pain control with APAP or a short course of NSAIDs (**Table 82**), home exercises or PT (especially assisted range of motion and wall walking) may be useful. Subacromial glucocorticoid injections may provide short-term pain relief, but multiple injections may be deleterious to healthy tendons. If no improvement after 6–8 wk of conservative measures, consider surgical repair, which may improve long-term (5 yr) pain but not function.

Bicipital Tendinitis

Pain felt on anterior lateral aspect of shoulder, tenderness in the groove between greater and lesser tuberosities of the humerus. Pain is elicited on resisted flexion of shoulder, flexion of the elbow, or supination (external rotation) of the hand and wrist with the elbow flexed at the side.

Treatment: Identify and eliminate provocative, repetitive activities (eg, avoid overhead reaching). A period of rest (at least 7 d with no lifting) and corticosteroid injections (p 200) are major components of tx. After rest period, PT should focus on stretching biceps tendon (eg, putting arm on doorframe and hyperextending shoulder, with some external rotation). Tendon sheath injection with corticosteroids may be helpful.

Frozen Shoulder (Adhesive Capsulitis)

Loss of passive external (lateral) rotation, abduction, and internal rotation of the shoulder to <90 degrees. Usually follows three phases: painful (freezing) phase lasting wks to a few mo; adhesive (stiffening) phase lasting 4–12 mo; resolution phase lasting 6–24 mo. Lidocaine injection does not restore range of motion (**Table 81**).

Treatment: Avoid rest and begin with gentle home exercises for shoulder mobility including stretching the arm in flexion, horizontal adduction, and internal and external rotation. Transition to PT when patient begins to improve. Low-dose (eg, 20 mg triamcinolone) corticosteroid injections (p 200) given early may reduce pain and permit more aggressive PT. If no response after 6–12 mo, consider surgical manipulation under anesthesia or arthroscopic release.

BACK PAIN: DIFFERENTIAL DIAGNOSIS AND TREATMENT

Axial mechanical back pain is associated with osteoporotic fractures, metastatic bone lesions with or without fractures, internal disc disruption (typically in younger patients), and ligament tears.

Lateral mechanical pain can result from facet arthropathy, sacroiliac joint dysfunction, fascial strain or injury (myofascial pain), or ligament strain. These patients may present with different patterns of radiating pain, but typically the pain does not spread to below the knee. In contrast, pain from lumbar spinal stenosis typically radiates below the knee.

Do not perform imaging for lower back pain within the first 6 wk unless red flags are present (severe or progressive neurologic deficits or when serious underlying conditions are present).[CW]

Do not prescribe opioids for acute disabling low back pain before evaluation and trial of other alternatives is considered.[CW]

Acute Lumbar Strain (Low Back Pain Syndrome)

Acute pain frequently precipitated by heavy lifting or exercise. Pain may be central or more prominent on one side and may radiate to sacroiliac region and buttocks. Pain is aggravated by motion, standing, and prolonged sitting, and relieved by rest. Sciatic pain may be present even when neurologic examination is normal. In sciatica, pain radiating below the knee is more likely to represent true radiculopathy than proximal leg pain.

Treatment: Most can continue normal activities. If a patient obtains symptomatic relief from bed rest, generally 1–2 d lying in a semi-Fowler position or on side with the hips and knees flexed with pillow between legs will suffice. Do not recommend bedrest without completing an evaluation or for more than 2 days.[CW] Treat muscle spasm with the application of ice, preferably in a massage over the muscles in spasm. A short course of NSAIDs (**Table 82**) can be used to control pain. Spinal manipulation, including high-thrust osteopathic manipulation, is also effective for uncomplicated low back pain. As pain diminishes, encourage patient to begin isometric abdominal and lower-extremity exercises. Symptoms often recur. Education on back posture, lifting precautions, and abdominal muscle strengthening may help prevent recurrences.

Acute Disk Herniation

Over 90% of cases have herniation at L4–L5 or L5–S1 levels, resulting in unilateral impairment of ankle reflex, toe and ankle dorsiflexion, and pain (commonly sciatic) on straight leg raising (can be tested from sitting position by leg extension). Pain is acute in onset and varies considerably with changes in position.

Treatment: Initially same as acute lumbar strain (above). The value of epidural injections and surgery for pain without neurologic signs is controversial. Epidural injection of a combination of a long-acting corticosteroid with an epidural anesthetic may provide modest, transient relief and results in less surgery at 1 yr if symptoms unresponsive to conservative tx. Consider surgery if recurrence or neurologic signs persist beyond 6–8 wk after conservative tx. The value of epidural injections and surgery for pain without neurologic signs is controversial. Surgery for severe sciatica provides faster pain relief and perceived recovery rates but no difference in perceived recovery and disability at 1 yr compared with conservative management.

Osteoarthritis and Chronic Disk Degeneration

Characterized by aching pain aggravated by motion and relieved by rest. Occasionally, hypertrophic spurring in a facet joint may cause unilateral radiculopathy with sciatica.

Treatment: Identify and eliminate provocative activities. Education on back posture, lifting precautions, and abdominal muscle strengthening. APAP or a short course of NSAIDs, including topicals (**Table 82**). Corticosteroid injections may be useful (p 200). Acupuncture and sham acupuncture may provide benefit. Consider opioids and other pain tx modalities for chronic refractory pain (p 234).

Unstable Lumbar Spine

Severe, sudden, short-lasting, frequently recurrent pain often brought on by sudden, unguarded movements. Pain is reproduced when moving from the flexed to the erect position. Pain is usually relieved by lying supine or on side. Impingement on nerve roots by spurs from facet joints or herniated disks can cause similar complaints, although symptoms in these conditions usually worsen over time. Symptoms can mimic disk herniation or degeneration, or osteoarthritis. Lumbar flexion radiographs can be diagnostic.

Treatment: Abdominal and paraspinal exercises, lumbrosacral corset. Surgery only in severe cases.

Lumbar Spinal Stenosis

Symptoms increase on spinal extension (eg, with prolonged standing, walking downhill, lying prone) and decrease with spinal flexion (eg, sitting, bending forward while walking, lying in the flexed position). Only symptom may be fatigue or pain in buttocks, thighs, and legs when walking (neurogenic or pseudoclaudication). May have immobility of lumbar spine, pain with straight leg raises, weakness of muscles innervated by L4 through S1 (**Table 3**). Over 4 yr, 15% improve, 15% deteriorate, and 70% remain stable.

Treatment: APAP or a short course of NSAIDs (**Table 82**), PT, and exercises to reduce lumbar lordosis (eg, bicycling) are sometimes beneficial. Corticosteroid injections have not been demonstrated to have advantage beyond lidocaine-only injections. Although data are conflicting, surgical decompression (laminectomy and partial fascectomy) may be more effective than conservative tx (eg, PT) in relieving moderate or severe symptoms. If no spondylolisthesis; intraspinous spacer insertion (distraction) may be effective and is less invasive.

If spondylolithesis or scoliosis, then fusion may be better than simple decompression. Simple and complex fusion have more complications and higher costs than decompression alone. However, recurrence of pain several years after surgery is common. Depression, comorbidity influencing walking capacity, cardiovascular comorbidity, and scoliosis predict worse surgical outcome. Male gender, younger age, better walking ability and self-rated health, less comorbidity, and more pronounced canal stenosis predict better surgical outcome.

Vertebral Compression Fracture

Immediate onset of severe pain; worse with sitting or standing; sometimes relieved by lying down. CT scan can help determine instability and MRI can determine acuity of fracture.

Treatment: See Osteoporosis, p 229. Bed rest, analgesia, and mobilization as tolerated. Bracing is unproved except for traumatic vertebral fractures. Nasal calcitonin (for no longer than 2–4 wk), teriparatide or pamidronate (30 mg/d IV for 3 consecutive d) may provide symptomatic improvement. May require hospitalization to control symptoms. Although little evidence supports the effectiveness of percutaneous vertebral augmentation (vertebroplasty and kyphoplasty), some groups recommend augmentation for severe ongoing pain from a known fracture (AAOS, NICE). Vertebroplasty is easier to perform and less expensive. Avoid muscle relaxants. Pain may persist for 1 yr or longer.

Nonrheumatic Pain (eg, Tumors, Aneurysms)

Gradual onset, steadily expanding, often unrelated to position and not relieved by lying down. Night pain when lying down is characteristic. Upper motor neuron signs may be present. Involvement is usually in thoracic and upper lumbar spine.

HIP PAIN: DIFFERENTIAL DIAGNOSIS AND TREATMENT

Trochanteric Bursitis

Pain in lateral aspect of the hip that usually worsens when patient sits on a hard chair, lies on the affected side, or rises from a chair or bed; pain may improve with walking. Local tenderness over greater trochanter is often present, and pain is often reproduced on resisted abduction of the leg or internal rotation of the hip. However, trochanteric bursitis does not result in limited range of motion, pain on range of motion, pain in the groin, or radicular signs.

Treatment: Identify and eliminate provocative activities. Position pillow posterolaterally behind involved side to avoid lying on bursae while sleeping. Check for leg length discrepancy, prescribe orthotics if appropriate. Injection of a combination of a long-acting corticosteroid with an anesthetic is most effective tx.

Osteoarthritis

"Boring" quality pain in the hip, often in the groin, and sometimes referred to the back or knee with stiffness after rest. Passive motion is restricted in all directions if disease is fairly advanced. In early disease, pain in the groin on internal rotation of the hip is characteristic.

Treatment: See also Osteoarthritis, p 202. Chondroitin sulfate, glucosamine, and capsaicin are not recommended. Participation in cardiovascular, resistance, or aquatic exercises. Weight loss if overweight. Elective total hip replacement is indicated for patients who have radiographic evidence of joint damage and moderate to severe persistent pain or disability, or both, that is not substantially relieved by an extended course of nonsurgical management.

Hip Fracture

Sudden onset, usually after a fall, with inability to walk or bear weight, frequently radiating to groin or knee. If hip radiograph (Anterior-Posterior with maximal internal rotation and lateral view) is negative and index of suspicion is high, obtain MRI. Fractures are 45% femoral neck, 45% intertrochanteric, and 10% subtrochanteric.

Treatment: Tx is surgical with open reduction and internal fixation (ORIF), hemiarthroplasty, or total hip replacement (THR), depending on site of fracture and amount of displacement. Sliding hip screws may have lower complication rates than intramedullary nails for extracapsular fractures. Displaced femoral neck fractures are generally treated with hemiarthroplasty or THR. Subtrochanteric fractures can be treated with intramedullary nails.

Perioperative Care:

- Co-management of hip fracture by geriatrics and orthopedic surgery improves patient outcomes. Features of a co-management service usually include:
  - Placement of patient on orthopedic ward with daily visits by orthopedic and geriatrics services
  - Clear delineation of who writes orders for fluid management, pain management, anticoagulation, catheter care, and antibiotics
  - 24-h/d availability of geriatrics
  - Standardized order sets
  - Frequent daily communication between orthpedic and geriatrics services (eg, co-rounding)
- Timing of surgery: Early surgery (within 48 h) is associated with better outcomes but may be due to more comorbidity in those with delayed surgery.
- Treat comorbid conditions (eg, anemia, volume depletion, metabolic abnormalities, infections, HF, CAD).
- Adequate pre- and postoperative analgesia (eg, 3-in-1 femoral nerve block, intrathecal morphine).
- Regional anesthesia if possible
- Antibiotics: Perioperative antibiotics (cefazolin or vancomycin) should be given beginning within 1 h of surgery.
- Pressure-reducing rather than standard mattress; if high risk of pressure sore, use large cell, alternating pressure air mattress.
- Oximetry for at least 48 h with supplemental oxygen prn.
- Graduated compression stockings do not add benefit beyond DVT prophylaxis medications.

- Intermittent pneumatic leg compression is recommended for the duration of the hospital stay.
- DVT prophylaxis: Give preoperatively if surgery delay is expected to be >48 h; otherwise begin 12–24 h after surgery. First choices are enoxaparin and dalteparin but other agents can be used (Antithrombotic Therapy and Thromboembolic Disease, p 26, for regimens). Recommended duration is for up to 35 d but at least 10 d and probably 1 mo if patient is inactive or has comorbidities.
- Preoperative traction has no demonstrated benefit.
- Avoid indwelling urinary catheters.
- Nutritional supplements if undernourished
- Transfuse only if symptomatic or Hb <8 g/dL.
- Begin assisted ambulation within 48 h.
- Monitor for development of delirium, malnutrition, and pressure sores.
- Weightbearing: Usually as tolerated for hemiarthroplasty or THR; toe-touch if ORIF or intertrochanter fracture.
- Hip precautions: No adduction past midline; no hip flexion beyond 90%; no internal rotation (toes upright in bed).
- Treat osteoporosis regardless of BMD: Wait 2 wk before starting bisphosphonates; make sure vitamin D is replete (Osteoporosis, p 229).
- Fall prevention: See Fall Prevention, p 113.

For patients who were nonambulatory before the fracture, conservative management is an option.

Nonrheumatic Pain

Referred pain from viscera, radicular pain from the lower spine, avascular necrosis, Paget disease, metastasis. Tx based on identified etiology.

KNEE PAIN: DIFFERENTIAL DIAGNOSIS AND TREATMENT

Osteoarthritis

Pain usually related to activity (eg, climbing stairs, arising from chair, walking long distances). Morning stiffness lasts <30 min. Crepitation is common. Examination should attempt to exclude other causes of knee pain such as hip arthritis with referred knee pain (decreased hip range of motion), chondromalacia patellae (tenderness only over patellofemoral joint), iliotibial band syndrome (tenderness is lateral to the knee at site of insertion in fibular head or where courses over lateral femoral condyle), anserine bursitis (tenderness distal to knee over medial tibia), and determination of malalignment varus (bowlegged) or valgus (knock-kneed).

Treatment: See Osteoarthritis Treatment, p 202.

HAND AND WRIST PAIN: DIFFERENTIAL DIAGNOSIS AND TREATMENT
De Quervain Tendinopathy

Pain or tenderness at radial side of wrist

Treatment: Forearm-based thumb splint, NSAIDs, and, if refractory, glucocorticoid injections. If no improvement after injections, consider surgery.

Osteoarthritis

Hand pain (including hand aching or stiffness) plus ≥3 of the following 4 features (ACR):

(1) hard tissue enlargement of 2 of the following: second and third distal interphalangeal (DIP) joints, the second and third proximal interphalangeal (PIP) joints, and the first carpometacarpal (CMC) of both hands

(2) hard enlargement of 2 or more DIP joints

(3) fewer than 3 swollen metacarpophalangeal (MCP) joints

(4) deformity of at least 1 of the 10 joints above

X-ray confirmation is not necessary.

Treatment: See Osteoarthritis, p 202. Avoid opioid analgesics and intraarticular tx.

Inflammatory (Rheumatoid and Psoriatic) Arthritis

Typically MCP and PIP joints with morning stiffness often lasting >1 h

Treatment: See Rheumatoid arthritis.

Carpal Tunnel Syndrome

Painful tingling or hypoesthesia, or both, in one or both hands in distribution innervated by median nerve. Causes include:

- Repetitive activities
- DM
- Thyroid disease
- Amyloidosis
- RA
- Space-occupying lesions (eg, lymphoma)
- Trauma (eg, Colles' fracture)

Physical examination demonstrates decreased sensation in palm, thumb, index finger, middle finger, and thumb side of ring finger, weak handgrip, and tapping over median nerve at wrist causes pain to shoot from wrist to hand (Tinel's sign). An acute flexion of wrist for 60 sec (Phalen's test) should also cause pain.

Laboratory studies should include: fasting glucose, TSH, nerve conduction velocity testing (confirms diagnosis).

Treatment: (combined modalities may be effective if single modalities fail)

Nonpharmacologic

Modify work or leisure activities to avoid repetitive movement, carpal tunnel mobilization (moving bones in wrist through PT or OT), and yoga may provide some symptom relief. Splinting in neutral position, especially at night; surgery (more effective than splinting) is indicated for prolonged (usually >6 mo) of moderate to severe symptoms (pain and numbness, diminished hand function, thenar eminence atropy) after confirmation of median nerve injury by electrodiagnostic testing. Nerve and tendon gliding maneuvers have not been shown to be effective.

Pharmacologic

Injectable corticosteroids, (eg, methylprednisolone 15 mg) are more effective than oral; oral corticosteroids, (eg, prednisone 20 mg/d for 1 wk followed by 10 mg/d for a second wk).

COMMON FOOT DISORDERS

Bunion: prominent and dorsal medial eminence of the first metatarsal; associated with hallux valgus

Calluses and corns: diffuse thickening of the stratum corneum in response to repeated friction or pressure (calluses); corns are similar but have a central, often painful core and are often found at pressure points, especially caused by ill-fitting shoes or gait abnormalities

Equinus: tight Achilles tendon

Hallux valgus (ie, bunion): deviation of the tip of the great toe, or main axis of the toe, toward the outer or lateral side of the foot

Hammertoe (digiti flexus): muscle tendon imbalance causing contraction of the proximal or distal interphalangeal joint, or both

Metatarsalgia: usually 2nd and 3rd metatarsal pain (like stepping on a stone) due to collapsed transverse metatarsal heads. Tx is conservative and includes metatarsal pads to relieve distal plantar pressure. If ineffective, then customized orthotics. Surgery is last resort.

Morton neuroma: burning pain usually between 3rd and 4th distal metatarsals. Ultrasound can distinguish between bursal swelling and synovitis. Tx is conservative and includes reducing pressure on metatarsal heads using a support or padded sole insert. If not controlled, then glucocorticoid injection. Do not use alcohol injections.[CW] Surgery if symptoms persist >9–12 mo of tx.

Pes cavus: higher than normal arch that can result in excessive pressure, usually placed on the metatarsal heads, and cause pain and ulceration

Tarsal tunnel syndrome: an entrapment neuropathy of the posterior tibial nerve

Treatment:

- Calluses and corns are treated with salicylic acid plaster 40%, available OTC (eg, Mediplast, Sal-acid plaster) after paring skin with a #15 scalpel blade. Remove dead skin with metal nail file or pumice stone each night before replacing the patch. Do not use in patients with peripheral neuropathy.
- Orthoses can be placed either on the foot or into the shoe to accommodate for a foot deformity or to alter the function of the foot to relieve physical stress on a certain portion of the foot. OTC devices made of lightweight polyethylene foam, soft plastics, or silicone are available for a certain size of foot. Custom-made orthoses are constructed from an impression of a person's foot.
- If conservative methods fail, refer to podiatry or orthopedics for consideration of surgery.

PLANTAR FASCIITIS

Definition

Strain or inflammation in plantar fascia causing foot pain that is worse when beginning to walk; 80% resolve spontaneously within 1 yr.

Causes/Risk Factors

- Jumping
- Running
- Rheumatic diseases
- Obesity
- Flat feet
- Plantar spurs

Evaluation

Examiner should dorsiflex toes and then palpate plantar fascia to elicit pain points; posterior heel pain is uncommon and suggests other diagnosis.

Treatment

Nonpharmacologic

- Rest and icing
- Exercises (calf plantar fascia stretch, foot/ankle circles, toe curls); strengthening with unilateral heel raises with a towel under the toes may be superior
- Avoid walking barefoot or in slippers
- Foot (low-dye) taping may be of benefit
- Prefabricated silicone heel inserts
- Shoes (running, arch support, crepe sole)
- Short-leg walking cast
- Surgery (rarely needed) and not before trying 6 mo of non-operative care.[CW]

Pharmacologic
- NSAIDs (short duration, 2–3 wk)
- Corticosteroid (eg, methylprednisolone 20–40 mg) and analgesic (eg, 1% lidocaine) injection of fascia; use only if conservative measures fail

OSTEOARTHRITIS

Classification
- Noninflammatory: pain and disability are generally the only complaints; findings include tenderness, bony prominence, and crepitus.
- Inflammatory: may also have morning stiffness lasting >30 min and night pain; findings may include joint effusion on examination or radiograph, warmth, and synovitis on arthroscopy.

Nonpharmacologic Approaches
- Superficial heat: hot packs, heating pads, paraffin, or hot water bottles (moist heat is better)
- Deep heat: microwave, shortwave diathermy, or ultrasound
- Biofeedback and transcutaneous electrical nerve stimulation
- Exercises:
  - All programs should include isometric strengthening, stretching, range of motion.
  - Those who can tolerate basics can progress to isotonic strengthening and aerobic exercises.
  - Swimming, bicycling, walking, and Tai Chi have low joint-loading and may protect the knee. Splints may also help protect the joints.
  - Closed-chain (the limbs are stationary while the body moves) avoid joint torsion.
  - Walking and home-based quadriceps strengthening have comparable effectiveness on pain and disability for knee osteoarthritis.
  - Supervised settings have better adherence than unsupervised home-based exercise.
- PT, OT
- Weight loss: especially for low back, hip, and knee arthritis
- Splinting and orthotics: Avoid splinting for long periods (eg, >6 wk) because periarticular muscle weakness and wasting may occur. For base-of-thumb osteoarthritis, use of a custom-made neoprene splint worn only at night results in decreased pain and disability at 12 mo. Medially wedged insoles if knee lateral compartment osteoarthritis. Laterally wedged subtalar strapped insoles if medial compartment osteoarthritis. Bracing (eg, neoprene sleeves over the knee, valgus brace) to correct malalignment is often helpful.
- Assistive devices: Cane should be used in the hand contralateral to the affected knee or hip. Cane length should be to the level of the wrist crease. Use walker if moderate or severe balance impairment, bilateral weakness, or unilateral weakness requiring support of >15–20% of body weight.
- Acupuncture as an adjunct to NSAIDs or analgesics for knee osteoarthritis or chronic low back pain
- Surgical intervention (eg, debridement, meniscal repair, prosthetic joint replacement)

Pharmacologic Intervention (Figure 10)

Topical Analgesics: Liniments containing methyl salicylates (**Table 101**), capsaicin crm, lidocaine 5% pch *(Lidoderm)*, diclofenac gel or pch (**Table 82**).

Intra-articular, Bursal, and Trigger-point Injections:

- Corticosteroids (eg, methylprednisolone acetate, triamcinolone acetonide, and triamcinolone hexacetonide [longest acting]) may be particularly effective if monoarticular symptoms. Typical doses for all these drugs:
  - 40 mg for large joints (eg, knee, ankle, shoulder)
  - 30 mg for wrists, ankles, and elbows
  - 10 mg for small joints of hands and feet

Often mixed with lidocaine 1% or its equivalent (some experts recommend giving equal volume with corticosteroids, whereas others give 3–5 times the corticosteroid volume depending on size of joint) for immediate relief. Effect typically lasts 1–2 mo. Usually given no more often than 3×/yr.

- Glucocorticoid injections have also been used for back pain due to radiculopathy, spinal stenosis, and nonspecific low back pain. For spinal stenosis, they have been no more effective than lidocaine injections. Best evidence is for short-term pain relief of radiculopathy due to a herniated disc. Each injection increases the subsequent risk of vertebral fracture. Intra-disk and facet injections have not been effective and evidence on sacroiliac joint injections is inconclusive.
- Chemonucleolysis (enzymatic) injections of disc may have limited benefit.
- Etanercept, botulinum toxin, and methylene blue have not been found to be beneficial.
- Blocks and radiofrequency ablation of medial branch of the primary dorsal ramus have limited evidence of effectiveness.
- Prolotherapy (repeated injection of irritants to increase inflammation and strengthen surrounding ligaments) has little evidence of effectiveness.
- Hyaluronic acid preparations *(Euflexxa, Hyalgan, Orthovisc, Synvisc, Supartz)* 3–5 injections 1 wk apart for knee osteoarthritis. A formulation *(Synvisc-One)* is available that requires only one injection. Benefit is usually modest but may last ≥6 mo.

Nutriceuticals: Glucosamine sulfate (500 mg q8h) with chondroitin (400 mg q8h) has been effective for some patients. Results of clinical trials have been variable but a recent meta-analysis has shown a small but clinically significant benefit of chondroitin for knee osteoarthritis.

APAP: First choice for mild/moderate pain. Fewer AEs although less effective than NSAIDs.

Figure 10. Pharmacologic Management of Osteoarthritis*

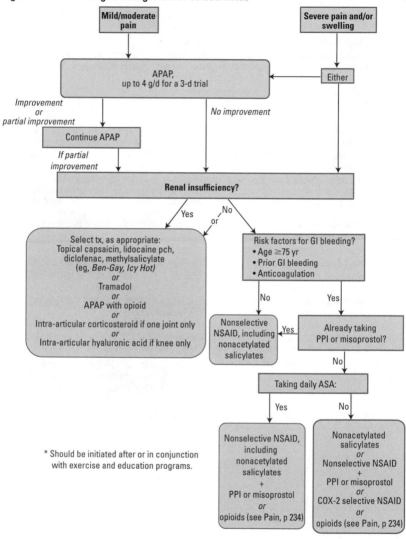

* Should be initiated after or in conjunction with exercise and education programs.

Source: Adapted from original material courtesy of Catherine MacLean, MD, PhD. Reprinted with permission.

NSAIDs: Topicals are preferred over oral in persons >75 yr old. Often provide pain relief but have higher rates of AEs than APAP (**Table 82**). Not recommended for long-term use. Combining with APAP is slightly more effective but may increase risk of bleeding. Misoprostol▲ *(Cytotec)* 100–200 mg q6h with food [T: 100, 200], or a PPI (**Table 57**) may be valuable prophylaxis against NSAID-induced ulcers in high-risk patients. Selective COX-2 inhibitors have lower likelihood of causing gastroduodenal ulcers than nonselective NSAIDs. All may increase INR in patients receiving warfarin. Avoid in individuals with HTN, HF, or CKD of all causes, including DM.[CW]

Oral Opioids: Use requires careful risk-benefit analysis.

Other:

- Tramadol for knee or hip arthritis. Begin with 25 mg [T:50] q4–6h, not to exceed 300 mg/d if age >75.
- Colchicine (0.6 mg q12h) may be of benefit in inflammatory osteoarthritis with recurrent symptoms.
- Duloxetine *(Cymbalta)* [C: 20, 30, 60], beginning at 30 mg/d and increasing to 60 mg/d after 1 wk, may have benefit in chronic low-back pain and osteoarthritis, particularly knee.

Table 82. APAP and NSAIDs

Class, Drug	Usual Dosage for Arthritis	Formulations	Metabolism, Excretion
✔APAP▲	Drug of choice for chronic musculoskeletal conditions; no anti-inflammatory properties and less effective than NSAIDs; hepatotoxic above 4 g/d; at high dosages (≥2 g/d) may increase INR in patients receiving warfarin▲; reduce dosage 50–75% if liver or kidney disease or if harmful or hazardous alcohol intake		
	650 mg q4–6h (q8h if CrCl <10 mg/mL)	T: 80, 325, 500, 650; C: 160, 325, 500; S: elixir 120/5 mL, 160/5 mL, 167/5 mL, 325/5 mL; S: 160/5 mL, 500/15 mL; Sp: 120, 325, 600	(L, K)
Extended release	1300 mg q8h	ER: 650	
ASA▲	650 mg q4–6h	T: 81, 325, 500, 650, 975; Sp: 120, 200, 300, 600	(K)
Extended release▲	1300 mg q8h or 1600–3200 mg q12h	CR: 650, 800	
Enteric-coated▲*	1000 mg q6h	T: 81, 162, 325, 500, 690, 975	

(cont.)

✔ = preferred for treating older adults
* Also OTC in a lower tab strength

Table 82. APAP and NSAIDs (cont.)

Class, Drug	Usual Dosage for Arthritis	Formulations	Metabolism, Excretion
Nonacetylated Salicylates	Do not inhibit platelet aggregation; fewer GI and renal AEs; no reaction in ASA-sensitive patients; monitor salicylate concentrations		
✔Choline magnesium salicylate▲ *(Tricosal, Trilisate, CMT)*	3 g/d in 1, 2, or 3 doses	T: 500, 750, 1000; S: 500 mg/5 mL	(K)
✔Choline salicylate *(Arthropan)*	4.8–7.2 g/d divided	T: 325, 545, 600, 650 S: 870 mg/5 mL	(L, K)
✔Magnesium salicylate▲* (eg, *Novasal*)	2 tabs q6–8h, max 4800 mg q24h	T: 467, 600, 650	Avoid in kidney failure
✔Salsalate▲	1500 mg to 4 g/d in 2 or 3 doses	T: 500, 750	(K)
Nonselective NSAIDs	Avoid chronic use without GI protection; avoid in HF.[BC]		
Diclofenac▲ *(Cataflam, Voltaren)*	50–150 mg/d in 2 or 3 doses	T: 50, 75; 50, enteric coated	(L)
(Voltaren-XR)	100 mg/d	T: ER 100	(L)
(Zipsor)	25 mg up to q6h	C: 25	(L)
(Zorvolex)	18–25 mg q8h	C: 18, 35	(L)
(Pennsaid)	apply 40 gtt per knee q6h	sol: 1.5%	(L)
✔Enteric coated			
(Arthrotec 50)	1 tab q8–12h	50 mg with 200 mcg misoprostol	(L)
(Arthrotec 75)	1 tab q12h	75 mg with 200 mcg misoprostol	(L)
✔Gel *(Voltaren Gel)*	2–4 g q6h	1%	(L)
(Solaraze)		3%	(L)
(Generic)		3%	(L)
✔Patch *(Flector)*	1 q12h	1.3%	(L)
Diflunisal▲ *(Dolobid)*	500–1000 mg/d in 2 doses	T: 500	(K)
✔Etodolac▲ *(Lodine)*	200–400 mg q6–8h	T: 400, 500; ER 400, 500, 600	Fewer GI AEs (L)
(Lodine XL)	400–1000 mg/d	C: 200, 300	
Fenoprofen▲* *(Nalfon)*	200–600 mg q6–8h	C: 200, 300; T: 600	Higher risk of GI AEs (L)
Flurbiprofen▲ *(Ansaid)*	200–300 mg/d in 2, 3, or 4 doses	T: 50, 100	(L)

(cont.)

✓ = preferred for treating older adults

* Also OTC in a lower tab strength

Table 82. **APAP and NSAIDs (cont.)**

Class, Drug	Usual Dosage for Arthritis	Formulations	Metabolism, Excretion
✔Ibuprofen▲	1200–3200 mg/d in 3 or 4 doses	T: 100, 200, 300, 400, 600, 800; ChT: 50, 100; S: 100 mg/5 mL	Fewer GI AEs (L)
with famotidine *(Duexis)*	1 tab q8h	T: 800 with 26.6 mg famotidine	
Injectable *(Caldolor)*	400–800 mg IV q6h (max 3200 mg/d)	Inj	
✔Ketoprofen▲ *(Orudis)*	50–75 mg q8h	T: 12.5; C: 50, 75	(L)
Sustained release *(Oruvail* [Canadian brand])	200 mg/d	C: 200	(L)
Ketorolac▲ *(Toradol)*	10 mg q4–6h, 15 mg IM or IV q6h	T: 10 Inj	Duration of use should be limited to 5 d (K)
Meclofenamate sodium▲	200–400 mg/d in 3 or 4 doses	C: 50, 100	High incidence of diarrhea (L)
Mefenamic acid▲ *(Ponstel)*	250 mg q6h	C: 250	(L)
✔Meloxicam▲ *(Mobic)*	7.5–15 mg/d	T: 7.5, 15 S: 7.5 mg/5 mL	Has some COX-2 selectivity; fewer GI AEs (L)
✔Nabumetone▲ *(Relafen)*	500–1000 mg q12h	T: 500, 750	Fewer GI AEs (L)
✔Naproxen▲ *(Naprosyn)*	220–500 mg q12h	T: 220, 375, 500, 750 S: 125 mg/5 mL	(L)
Delayed release *(EC-Naprosyn)*	375–500 mg q12h	T: 375, 500	(L)
Extended release *(Naprelan)*	750–1000 mg/d	T: 250, 375, 500	(L)
Naproxen sodium▲ *(Anaprox)*	275 mg or 550 mg q12h	T: 275, 550	(L)
✔Oxaprozin▲ *(Daypro)*	1200 mg/d	C: 600	(L)
Piroxicam▲ *(Feldene)*	10 mg/d	C: 10, 20	Can cause delirium (L)
Sulindac▲ *(Clinoril)*	150–200 mg q12h	T: 150, 200 C: 200	May have higher rate of renal impairment (L)
Tolmetin ▲ *(Tolectin)*	600–1800 mg/d in 3 or 4 doses	T: 200, 600 C: 400	(L)
Trolamine salicylate *(Aspercreme* and others) OTC	3–4 ×/d	10% sol	

(cont.)

✔ = preferred for treating older adults

* Also OTC in a lower tab strength

Table 82. APAP and NSAIDs (cont.)

Class, Drug	Usual Dosage for Arthritis	Formulations	Metabolism, Excretion
Selective COX-2 Inhibitor	Avoid in HF.[BC]		
✔Celecoxib *(Celebrex)*	100–200 mg q12h	C: 50, 100, 200, 400	Increased risk of MI; less GI ulceration; do not inhibit platelets; may increase INR if taking warfarin[▲]; avoid if moderate or severe hepatic insufficiency; may induce renal impairment; contraindicated if allergic to sulfonamides (L)

✔ = preferred for treating older adults

* Also OTC in a lower tab strength

RHEUMATOID ARTHRITIS
Evaluation and Diagnosis

Evaluation: RF, anti-CCP, antinuclear antibody (ANA), CBC, ESR, CRP, LFTs, BUN, Cr, eye exam (if starting hydroxychloroquine), hepatitis B screen, hepatitis C screen (if at increased risk), tuberculosis test (if starting biologic), x-rays of hands, wrists, and feet

Table 83. 2010 American College of Rheumatology/European League Against Rheumatism (ACR/EULAR) Criteria for Diagnosis of Rheumatoid Arthritis*

A. Joint involvement (any swollen or tender joint excluding first carpometacarpal, metatarsophalangeal, and distal and proximal interphalangeal joints)	
1 large joint (shoulders, elbows, hips, knees, ankles)	0
2 to 10 large joints	1
1 to 3 small joints (with or without involvement of large joints)	2
4 to 10 small joints (with or without involvement of large joints)	3
>10 joints (at least 1 small joint)	5
B. Serology (at least 1 test result is needed for classification)	
Negative RF and negative anticitrullinated protein antibody (ACPA)	0
Low-positive (<3 × upper limit of normal) RF or low-positive ACPA	2
High-positive (>3 × upper limit of normal) RF or high-positive ACPA	3
C. Acute-phase reactants (at least one test result is needed for classification)	
Normal CRP and normal ESR	0
Abnormal CRP or abnormal ESR	1
D. Duration of symptoms (by patient self-report)	
<6 wk	0
≥6 wk	1

Scoring: Add score of categories A–D; a score of ≥6/10 is needed for classification of a patient as having definite RA.

* Aimed at classifying newly presenting patients; patients with erosive disease or longstanding disease with a hx of presenting features consistent with these criteria should be classified as having RA.

Note: Adapted from Aletaha D et al. *Arthritis Rheum* 2010;62(9):2569–2581. This material is reproduced with permission of John Wiley & Sons, Inc.

Staging
- Duration: early <6 mo, intermediate 6–24 mo, late >24 mo
- Activity: low, moderate, high by various criteria; see www.rheumatology.org/Practice-Quality/Clinical-Support/Criteria
- Poor prognostic factors: functional limitation, extra-articular disease, RF positivity ± anti-CCP antibodies, and/or bony erosions by radiography

Management (co-management with rheumatology) (based on 2013 EULAR recommendations)
- Monitor q1–3 mo if active disease; if no improvement by 3 mo or target not reached by 6 mo, then adjust tx

Nonpharmacologic
- Patient education
- Exercise
- PT and OT
- Atherosclerosis risk factor modification
- Splints and orthotics
- Surgery for severe functional abnormalities due to synovitis or joint destruction
- Bone protection (see Osteoporosis, p 229)

Pharmacologic
All patients with established disease should be offered DMARDs as soon as possible; goal is to induce remission and then lower dosages to maintain remission. Tight control of disease activity is associated with better radiographic and functional outcomes.
- Analgesics (**Table 82** and Pain, p 234)
- NSAIDs (**Table 82**)
- Glucocorticoids (eg, prednisone ≤15 mg/d or equivalent) with osteoporosis prevention measures (Osteoporosis, p 229). Avoid in delirium.[BC] Low-dose prednisone (10 mg/d) has benefit as an adjunct to methotrexate.
- Methotrexate should be part of first tx strategy. Dual and triple nonbiologic DMARD combinations are also used with methotrexate as one component. Triple tx (sulfasalazine, hydroxychloroquine, and methotrexate) is as effective as etanercept plus methotrexate in patients who have active disease despite methotrexate alone. See www.rheumatology.org/Practice-Quality/Clinical-Support/Clinical-Practice-Guidelines.
- Use biologic DMARDs only after failure of nonbiologic DMARDs.[CW] When poor prognostic factors are present, consider biologicals, which may be added to methotrexate (**Table 84**). If a first biological has failed, treat with different biological. Consider tofacitinib if other biologicals have failed.
- If in persistent remission after tapering glucocorticoids, consider tapering biologicals.
- Flares can be treated with increased dose of oral or pulse intravenous glucocorticoids (eg, 3 infusions of up to 1000 mg methylprednisolone weekly).
- Frequent or severe flares should prompt consideration of escalation of dose or modification of regimen.

Table 84. Nonbiologic DMARDs

Medication	Starting/Usual Dosage	Formulations	Indications	Comments*
Hydroxy-chloroquine▲	Begin 200–400 mg/d; dose at <6.5 mg/kg/d to reduce risk of retinal toxicity	T: 200	Monotherapy for durations <24 mo, low disease activity, and without poor prognostic features	Baseline and annual eye examination; contraindicated in G6PD deficiency
Sulfasalazine▲ (Azulfidine, Azulfidine EN-tabs)	Begin at 500 mg/d to avoid GI upset; increase dosage by 500 mg every 3–4 d until taking 2–3 g/d split between 2 doses	T: 500	Monotherapy for all disease durations and all degrees of disease activity, and without poor prognostic features	Check CBC, LFTs q8wk
Methotrexate▲ (Rheumatrex, Trexall)	10–25 mg/wk, adjust dosage for renal impairment (hold if CrCl <30 mL/min)	T: 2.5 T: 2.5, 5, 7.5, 10, 15	Monotherapy for all disease durations and all degrees of disease activity, irrespective of poor prognostic features	Check for hepatitis B and C; check CBC (hold if WBC <3000/mm³), LFTs q8wk; give folic acid 1 mg/d; may cause oral ulcers, hepatotoxicity, pulmonary toxicity, cytopenias; avoid if liver disease
Leflunomide▲ (Arava)	Begin 100 mg/d × 3 d, then 20 mg/d	T: 10, 20	Monotherapy for all disease durations and all degrees of disease activity, irrespective of poor prognostic features	Check for hepatitis B and C; check CBC (hold if WBC <3000/mm³), LFTs q8wk; may cause hepatotoxicity, cytopenias; avoid if liver disease

*Check baseline CBC, LFTs, Cr for all.

○ Biologic DMARDs: Not used in early RA and only low or moderate disease activity; increased risk of serious infections and reactivation of latent infections; check PPD and make sure patient is up-to-date on all vaccinations before starting; check baseline CBC, LFTs, Cr when using any biologic. Hold tx for any infection but can start shortly after bacterial infection is successfully treated; may increase risk of skin cancers. Avoid live vaccinations while on biologics.

■ Anti-TNF-α agents: Used if inadequate response to methotrexate, if moderate disease activity and poor prognostic features, or if high activity regardless of poor prognostic features. May be added to or substituted for methotrexate. Combinations of biologic DMARDs are not recommended.

□ Adalimumab (Humira) 40 mg SC every other wk, or 40 mg SC every wk if not taking methotrexate

□ Certolizumab (Cimzia) 400 mg SC at 0, 2, and 4 wk; then 200 mg q2wk or 400 mg q4wk

□ Etanercept (Enbrel) 50 mg SC once/wk or 25 mg SC twice/wk

□ Infliximab (Remicade) 3 mg/kg IV in conjunction with methotrexate; repeat in 2–6 wk, then q8wk

□ Golimumab (Simponi) 50 mg SC every mo

■ IL-1 receptor antagonist: anakinra (Kineret) 100 mg SC daily

- Medications used when response to DMARD has been inadequate:
  - T-cell activation inhibitor: abatacept *(Orencia)* <60 kg: 500 mg; 60–100 kg: 750 mg; >100 kg: 1 g IV at 0, 2, and 4 wk, then q4wk (do not use with anti-TNF-α agents or with anakinra)
  - Anti-CD20 monoclonal antibody: rituximab *(Rituxan)* 1000 mg IV in conjunction with methotrexate; repeat in 2 wk
  - IL-6 inhibitor: tocilizumab *(Actemra)* 4 mg/kg IV over 1 h q4wk; if response is not adequate, can increase to 8 mg/kg q4wk
  - Kinase inhibitor: tofacitinib *(Xeljanz)* [T: 5 mg] 5 mg q12h; can use in combination with non-biologics

GOUT

Definition

Urate crystal disease that may be expressed as acute gouty arthritis, usually in a single joint of foot, ankle, knee, or olecranon bursa; or chronic arthritis.

Precipitating Factors

- Alcohol, heavy ingestion
- Allopurinol, stopping or starting
- Binge eating
- Dehydration
- Diuretics (except potassium-sparing)
- Fasting
- Infection
- Serum uric acid concentration, any change up or down
- Surgery

Evaluation of Acute Gouty Arthritis

Joint aspiration to remove crystals and microscopic examination to establish diagnosis; serum urate (can be normal during flare)

Management

Treatment of Acute Gouty Flare: Any of the following are appropriate first-line options (ACR):
- Intra-articular injections (p 203) if only 1 or 2 joints involved
- NSAIDs (**Table 82**); avoid ASA
- Colchicine 1.2 mg (2 tabs) for the first dose, followed 1 h later by 0.6 mg (total dose 1.8 mg) unless patient has received this regimen within the last 14 d
- Prednisone▲ 5 mg/kg/d for 5–10 d, then stop for 2–5 d at full dose, then taper 7–10 d
- If polyarticular or multiple large joint involvement or severe pain, consider combination tx of methylprednisolone 0.5–2 mg/kg po q12h with taper or ACTH 25–40 IU SC; may repeat daily for 3 d
- IL–1 inhibitors (canakinumab [*Ilaris*] and anakinra [*Kineret*]) may be useful if cannot tolerate other options

Pharmacologic anti-inflammatory prophylaxis: Colchicine 0.6 mg/d or twice daily for 2–4 wk before beginning any tx in **Table 85**.

Table 85. Medications Useful in Managing Chronic Gout

Medication	Usual Dosage	Formulations	Comments (Metabolism, Excretion)
✔Allopurinol▲ (Zyloprim, Lopurin)	100–900 mg/d in divided doses if >300 mg/d	T: 100, 300	Consider if nephrolithiasis, tophi, Cr ≥2 mg/dL, 24-h urinary uric acid >800 mg. Starting dosage should not exceed 100 mg/d and 50 mg/d in ≥stage 4 CKD. Do not initiate during flare; reduce dosage in renal or hepatic impairment; increase dose by 100 mg every 2–5 wk to normalize serum urate level; monitor CBC; rash is common; if Han Chinese or Thai, screen for HLA-B*5801 before initiating (K)
Colchicine* (Colcrys)[a]	0.5–0.6 mg/d	T: 0.5, 0.6; Inj	May also be effective in prevention of recurrent pseudogout; monitor CBC (L)
Febuxostat (Uloric)	40–80 mg/d	T: 40, 80	Begin 40 mg/d; increase to 80 mg/d if uric acid >6 mg/dL at 2 wk; not recommended if CrCl <30 mL/min (K, L)
Losartan (Cozaar)	12.5–100 mg q12–24h	T: 25, 50, 100	Modest uricosuric effect that plateaus at 50 mg/d; may be useful in patients with HTN or HF
Pegloticase (Krystexxa)	8 mg IV q2wk	8 mg/1-mL vial	Effective in reducing flares in allopurinol intolerant or refractory patients with high uric acid levels; may cause anaphylaxis, gout flares, and infusion reactions; contraindicated if G6PD deficiency (K)
Probenecid▲ * (Benemid)	500–1500 mg in 2–3 divided doses	T: 500	Contraindicated as first-line if hx of urolithiasis. Measure urinary uric acid before initiating and if >800 mg/24 h, then contraindicated. Adjust dose to normalize serum urate level or increase urine urate excretion; inhibits platelet function; may not be effective if renal impairment; (K, L)

✓ = preferred for treating older adults

* Probenecid (500 mg) and colchicine (0.5 mg) combinations (ColBenemid, Col-Probenecid, Proben-C) are available. Available as generic.

[a] No longer available as generic.

- If unable to tolerate low-dose colchicine, low-dose NSAIDs with PPI (if indicated)
- If neither of the above are tolerated, or if either are contraindicated or ineffective, low-dose prednisone or prednisolone (<10 mg/d)
- Duration of tx is:
  - 3–6 mo after achieving target urate, if not tophi
  - Until tophi resolve
  - Indefinitely if tophi persist after achieving target urate

Treatment of Hyperuricemia

Nonpharmacologic: Lifestyle modification (weight loss if overweight, decrease in saturated fats, substitute low-fat dairy products for red meat or fish, limit alcohol use, avoid organ meats high in purine content [eg, sweetbread, liver, kidney]; avoid high fructose corn syrup—sweetened sodas). D/C nonessential medications that induce hyperuricemia (eg, thiazides and loop diuretics, niacin).

Pharmacologic:

Indications for pharmacologic tx: Established diagnosis of gouty arthritis and:

- Tophus or tophi
- Frequent attacks (≥2/yr)
- CKD stage 2 or worse
- Past urolithiasis

Target is <6 mg/dL and often <5 mg/dL. First-line is either allopurinol or febuxostat. If contraindicated or not tolerated, probenicid. Fenofibrate and losartan are also uricosuric.

Pegloticase is reserved for patients with severe gout disease burden and refractory or intolerance to first-line agents.

PSEUDOGOUT

Definition

Crystal-induced arthritis (especially affecting wrists and knees) associated with calcium pyrophosphate. A small proportion have pseudo-RA (chronic crystal inflammatory arthritis) with chronic joint inflammation.

Risk Factors

- Advanced osteoarthritis
- DM
- Gout
- Hemochromatosis
- Hypercalcemia
- Hyperparathyroidism
- Hypomagnesemia
- Hypophosphatemia
- Hypothyroidism
- Neuropathic joints
- Older age

Precipitating Factors

- Acute illness
- Dehydration
- Minor trauma
- Surgery

Evaluation of Acute Arthritis

Joint aspiration and microscopic examination to establish diagnosis; radiograph indicating chondrocalcinosis (best seen in wrists, knees, shoulder, symphysis pubis)

Management of Acute Flare

If one or two joints, aspiration and intra-articular glucocorticoid may be effective. If multiple joints, see Gout, management (p 211). NSAIDs are often used first, because colchicine is less effective in pseudogout.

Prevention of Recurrence

If >3 attacks/yr, consider colchicine 0.6 mg q12h.

If chronic calcium pyrophosphate crystal inflammatory arthritis (ie, pseudo-RA), then NSAIDs +/– colchicines and, if needed, followed by methotrexate and/or hydroxychloroquine.

POLYMYALGIA RHEUMATICA, GIANT CELL (TEMPORAL) ARTERITIS

Definitions and Evaluation

Polymyalgia Rheumatica: Proximal limb and girdle stiffness usually lasting ≥30 min without tenderness but with constitutional symptoms (eg, fatigue, malaise, weight loss) for ≥1 mo and sedimentation rate elevated to >50 mm/h (7–22% will have normal sedimentation rate), and CRP; consider ultrasound to demonstrate effusions within shoulder bursae or MRI to demonstrate tenosynovitis or subacromial and subdeltoid bursitis if diagnosis is uncertain.

Provisional ACR/EULAR classification criteria include:
- required criteria: age >50 yr, bilateral shoulder aching, abnormal CRP or ESR
- morning stiffness >45 min (2 points)
- hip pain/limited range of motion (1 point)
- absence of rheumatoid factor and/or anti-citrullinated protein antibody (2 points)
- absence of peripheral joint pain (1 point)

Scores ≥4 had 68% sensitivity and 78% specificity. Specificity is higher (88%) for discriminating shoulder conditions from polymyalgia rheumatica and lower (65%) for discriminating RA from polymyalgia rheumatica. A subsequent single-site study demonstrated better test characteristics in an unselected population with early inflammatory articular disease.

Clinical usefulness of these criteria remain to be determined.

Giant Cell (Temporal) Arteritis: Medium to large vessel vasculitis that presents with symptoms of polymyalgia rheumatica, headache, unexplained fever or anemia, scalp tenderness, jaw or tongue claudication, visual disturbances, TIA or stroke, and elevated sedimentation rate and CRP. The presence of synovitis suggests an alternative diagnosis. Giant cell arteritis is confirmed by temporal artery biopsy. The value of other diagnostic tests (Doppler ultrasound, MRI, positron-emission tomography) is still unproved.

Management

Polymyalgia Rheumatica:
- Low-dosage (eg, 10–15 mg/d) prednisone or its equivalent; increase dosage if symptoms are not controlled within 1 wk. If symptoms are not controlled by 20 mg/d, then consider alternative diagnosis (eg, giant cell arteritis, paraneoplastic syndrome)
- Methylprednisolone▲ 120 mg IM q3–4 wk is also effective.
- After 2–4 wk, begin gradual taper by 10–20% every 2 wk to lowest dose that will control symptoms and CRP or sedimentation rate. Once-daily dose is 10 mg, taper in 1-mg/mo decrements.
- Some patients with milder symptoms may respond to NSAIDs alone.
- Monitor symptoms and CRP or sedimentation rate.
- Maintain tx for ≥1 yr to prevent relapse. Relapse occurs in 25–50%, and resuming previous dose that controlled symptoms or increasing steroid dosage if still on steroids is necessary.
- Consider osteoporosis prevention medication (p 230).

Giant Cell (Temporal) Arteritis:
- Tx should not be delayed while waiting for pathologic diagnosis from temporal artery biopsy. Begin prednisone (40–60 mg/d) or its equivalent while biopsy and pathology are pending.
- Adding methotrexate▲ po 7.5–15 mg/wk and folate 5–7.5 mg/d may reduce the amount of steroid needed and the risk of relapse, but the effect is moderate at best.
- After 2–4 wk, begin taper by 10 mg after 2 wk and another 10 mg prednisone/d at 4 wk, gradual taper (by 10% every 1–2 wk) over 9–12 mo. Once daily dose is 10 mg, taper in 1-mg/mo decrements. Monitor Hb, ESR, CRP before dose changes, but treat based on symptoms, not lab tests.
- High-dose parenteral steroids (eg, 1000 mg methylprednisolone IV daily for 3 d) for visual loss is controversial.
- For refractory cases, IL–6 receptor inhibitor tocilizumab *(Actemra)* beginning 4 mg/kg every 4 wk with maximum dose 800 mg or cyclophosphamide, mean dose 100 mg/d [T: 25, 50] may be helpful. Anti-TNF agents (infliximab, etanercept, and adalimumab) have not been effective.

- Use low-dosage ASA (81–100 mg/d) to reduce risk of visual loss, TIA, or stroke. Combine with PPI or misoprostol.
- Be aware of higher rates of systemic infection during first 6 mo of tx and higher rates of cardiovascular disease.
- Monitor symptoms and CRP or sedimentation rate.
- Maintain tx for ≥1 yr to prevent relapse.
- Consider osteoporosis prevention medication (p 230).
- Monitor for development of thoracic aortic aneurysm, especially ascending, with CXR yearly for up to 10 yr.

TREMORS

Table 86. Classification of Tremors

Tremor Type	Hz (cycles/sec)	Associated Conditions	Features	Treatment
Cerebellar	3–5	Cerebellar disease	Present only during movement; ↑ with intention; ↑ amplitude as target is approached	Symptomatic management
Essential	4–12	Familial in 50% of cases	Varying amplitude; common in upper extremities, head, neck; ↑ with antigravity movements, intention, stress, medications	Long-acting propranolol▲ or atenolol▲ (Table 29); or primidone *(Mysoline)* 100 mg qhs start, titrate to 0.5–1 g/d in 3–4 divided doses [T: 50, 250; S: 250 mg/5 mL]; or gabapentin▲ (Table 92)
Parkinson	3–7	Parkinson disease, parkinsonism	"Pill rolling;" present at rest; ↑ with emotional stress or when examiner calls attention to it; commonly asymmetric	See Parkinson disease (p 220)
Physiologic	8–12	Normal	Low amplitude; ↑with stress, anxiety, emotional upset, lack of sleep, fatigue, toxins, medications	Tx of exacerbating factor

DIZZINESS

- Medications commonly associated with orthostatic hypotension include:
  - Cardiac: α-blockers, β-blockers, ACEIs, diuretics, nitrates, clonidine, hydralazine, methyldopa, reserpine, dipyridamole
  - CNS: antipsychotics, opioids, medications for Parkinson disease, skeletal muscle relaxants, TCAs
  - Urologic: antimuscarinic agents for UI, PDE-5 inhibitors
- Caffeine, alcohol, nicotine, and head trauma can also cause or contribute to dizziness.

Table 87. Classification of Dizziness

Primary Symptom	Duration	Diagnosis	Management
Dizziness			
Lightheadedness 1–30 min after standing	Seconds to minutes (E)	Orthostatic hypotension	pp 64–65
Wobbly/off balance gait; impairment in >1 of the following: vision, vestibular function, spinal proprioception, cerebellum, lower-extremity peripheral nerves	Occurs with ambulation (C)	Multiple sensory impairments including peripheral neuropathy; Parkinson Disease	Correct or maximize sensory deficits; PT for balance and strength training

(cont.)

Table 87. Classification of Dizziness (cont.)			
Primary Symptom	**Duration**	**Diagnosis**	**Management**
Unsteady gait with short steps; ↑ reflexes and/or tone	Occurs with ambulation (C)	Ischemic cerebral disease	ASA▲; modification of vascular risk factors; PT
Provoked by head or neck movement; reduced neck range of motion	Seconds to minutes (E)	Cervical spondylosis	Behavior modification; reduce cervical spasm and inflammation
Drop attacks			
Provoked by head or neck movement, reduced vertebral artery flow seen on Doppler or angiography	Seconds to minutes (E)	Postural impingement of vertebral artery	Behavior modification
Vertigo			
Brought on by position change, positive Dix-Hallpike test	Seconds to minutes (E)	Benign paroxysmal positional vertigo	Epley or Semont maneuver to reposition crystalline debris*
Acute onset, nonpositional	Days	Labyrinthitis/ vestibular neuronitis	Methylprednisolone▲, 100 mg/d po × 3 d with subsequent gradual taper over 3 wk to improve vestibular function recovery; meclizine▲ (see **Table 60**) for acute symptom relief
Low-frequency sensorineural hearing loss and tinnitus, ear pain, sense of fullness in ear	Minutes to hours (E)	Ménière disease	Meclizine▲,BC (**Table 60**) for acute symptom relief; diuretics and/or salt restriction for prophylaxis
Vascular disease risk factors, cranial nerve abnormalities	10 min to several hours (E)	TIAs	ASA▲; modification of vascular risk factors

Notes: C = chronic; E = episodic.

*www.youtube.com/watch?v=nX1HU-CCg2Y or www.youtube.com/watch?v=hiP7ifVxb0Q

MANAGEMENT OF ACUTE STROKE

Examination
- Cardiac (murmurs, arrhythmias, enlargement)
- Neurologic (serial examinations)
- Optic fundi
- Vascular (carotids and other peripheral pulses)

Tests
- Bloodwork: BUN, CBC with platelet count, Cr, electrolytes, glucose, cardiac troponins, INR, PT, PTT, oxygen saturation
- Emergent brain MRI or noncontrast CT
- ECG
- The National Institutes of Health Stroke Scale (NIHSS; www.ninds.nih.gov/doctors/ NIH_Stroke_Scale.pdf) can quantify stroke severity and prognosis. NIHSS score >15

signifies major or severe stroke with high risk of death or significant permanent neurologic disability; NIHSS score <8 has a good prognosis for neurologic recovery.
- Other tests as indicated by clinical presentation:
  ○ ABG if hypoxia is suspected
  ○ Thrombin time and/or ecarin clotting time if patient is taking direct thrombin inhibitor or factor Xa inhibitor
  ○ Intracranial angiography by MRA, CT angiography, or Doppler ultrasound if intraarterial fibrinolysis or mechanical thrombectomy is being contemplated
  ○ Echocardiography (transesophageal preferred over transthoracic) for detection of cardiogenic emboli
  ○ Carotid duplex and transcranial Doppler studies for detection of carotid and vertebrobasilar embolic sources, respectively

Provide Supportive Care
- Maintain O_2 saturation >94%.
- Correct metabolic and hydration imbalances.
- Detect and treat coronary ischemia, HF, arrhythmias.
- In patients with ischemic stroke and restricted mobility, implement DVT/PE prophylaxis with UFH▲, LMWH, or fondaparinux (**Table 19**).
- Monitor and treat hyperthermia, using antipyretics (eg, APAP) for temperature >100.4°F.
- Monitor for depression.
- Refer to rehabilitation when medically stable.
- Discharge on statin drug (**Table 27** and **Table 28**).

Antithrombotic Therapy for Ischemic Stroke (AHA/American Stroke Association Guidelines)
- Consider IV thrombolysis if patient presents within 180 min of symptom onset.
  ○ Data on overall risk/benefit ratio of IV thrombolysis in adults >75 yr old are limited.
  ○ Absolute contraindications:
    ▪ BP ≥185/110 mmHg
    ▪ subarachnoid hemorrhage or hx of intracranial hemorrhage
    ▪ intracranial neoplasm, arteriovenous malformation, or aneurysm
    ▪ head trauma or stroke in past 3 mo
    ▪ GI bleed or urinary hemorrhage in past 21 d
    ▪ recent intracranial or intraspinal surgery
    ▪ active bleeding or acute trauma
    ▪ INR >1.7 or PT >15 sec
    ▪ heparin use in past 48 h with supranormal PTT
    ▪ current use of direct thrombin inhibitor or factor Xa inhibitor with elevated tests for anticoagulation (eg, PTT, INR, thrombin time, ecarin clotting time)
    ▪ platelet count <100,000 mm^3
    ▪ blood glucose <50 mg/dL
  ○ Relative contraindications (carefully consider risk/benefit of thrombolysis if 1 or more are present):
    ▪ minor or rapidly improving stroke symptoms
    ▪ seizure at stroke onset with postictal neurologic impairments
    ▪ major surgery or serious trauma in past 14 d
    ▪ GI or urinary tract hemorrhage in past 21 d
    ▪ acute MI in past 3 mo

- Use recombinant tissue plasminogen activator (tPA), 0.9 mg/kg IV, max dose 90 mg.
  - Risk of intracranial hemorrhage 3–7%; age >75 yr old and NIHSS >20 are among risk factors for intracranial hemorrhage.
- IV thrombolysis can be considered 3–4.5 h after symptom onset; additional relative exclusion criteria include age >80 yr old or NIHSS >25.
- Antiplatelet tx: use ASA▲ 162–325 mg/d (initial dose 325 mg), begun within 24–48 h of onset in patients not receiving thrombolytic tx.
- Anticoagulants are not recommended except in DVT/PE prophylactic dosages for medical patients with restricted mobility (**Table 19**).

Management of Acute Hypertension in Ischemic Stroke

- If patient is otherwise eligible for IV thrombolysis (see contraindications, p 218), attempt to lower BP to ≤185/110 mmHg so that patient may undergo reperfusion tx. Options for lowering BP are:
  - Labetalol▲ *(Normodyne, Trandate)*: 10–20 mg IV over 1–2 min, may repeat once; **or**
  - Nicardipine▲ *(Cardene)*: 5 mg/h IV, increasing by 2.5 mg/h q5–15 min to max of 15 mg/h
- If patient is ineligible or not being considered for thrombolytic tx, do not lower BP if SBP ≤220 mmHg or if DBP ≤120 mmHg; higher BP may be lowered gently, with goal of 15% reduction over first 24 h. Choice of BP-lowering agent should reflect patient's comorbidities (**Table 29**).

STROKE PREVENTION

Risk Factor Modification

- Stop smoking.
- Reduce BP to at least 140/90 mmHg.
- In patients ≥80 yr old with few cardiovascular comorbidities, 150/80 mmHg is a reasonable BP tx goal.
- Treat dyslipidemia (**Table 27** and **Table 28**).
- Start anticoagulation (**Table 19**) or antiplatelet (**Table 18**) tx for AF.
- Low-sodium (≤2–3 g/d), high-potassium (≥4.7 g/d) diet
- Exercise (≥30 min of moderate intensity activity daily)
- Weight reduction (BMI <25 kg/m^2)

Antiplatelet Therapy for Patients With Prior TIA or Stroke

- First-line tx is ASA▲ 81–325 mg/d.
- Addition of a combination form of ASA and long-acting dipyridamole *(Aggrenox)* 1 tab q12h [T: 25/200] may provide additional benefit. Watch for AE of headache.
- Clopidogrel▲ *(Plavix)* 75 mg/d [T: 75] if intolerant to ASA or ASA ineffective.
- In the absence of AF, warfarin tx is no more effective and is associated with more bleeding than ASA in preventing strokes.

		Treatment	
Presentation	**% Stenosis**	**Options**	**Comments**
Prior TIA or stroke	≥70	CA/CE[a] or MM	CE superior to medical tx only if patient is reasonable surgical risk and facility has track record of low complication rate for CE (<6%)

Table 88. Treatment Options for Carotid Stenosis in Older Adults

(cont.)

Table 88. Treatment Options for Carotid Stenosis in Older Adults (cont.)

Presentation	% Stenosis	Treatment Options	Comments
Prior TIA or stroke	50–69	CE or MM	Serial carotid Doppler testing may identify rapidly developing plaques
Prior TIA or stroke	<50	MM	CE of no proven benefit in this situation
Asymptomatic	≥70	CA/CE[a, b] or MM	CA/CE[a,b] should be considered over MM only for the most healthy
Asymptomatic	<70	MM	CE of no proven benefit in this situation

Notes: CA = carotid angioplasty with stent placement in patients with multiple comorbidities and/or at high surgical risk; CE = carotid endarterectomy; MM = medical management.

[a] Younger patients may have a greater risk of stroke with CA and a greater risk of mortality with CE, compared to older patients. Mortality risk for CA and stroke risk for CE are the same in both groups.

[b] Don't recommend CE for asymptomatic carotid stenosis unless the complication rate is low (<3%).[CW]

PARKINSON DISEASE

Diagnosis Requires:

- Bradykinesia, eg:
  - Slowness of initiation of voluntary movements (eg, glue-footedness when starting to walk)
  - Reduced speed and amplitude of repetitive movements (eg, tapping index finger and thumb together)
  - Difficulty switching from one motor program to another (eg, multiple steps to turn during gait testing)
- ***and*** one or more of the following:
  - Muscular rigidity (eg, cogwheeling)
  - 3–7 Hz resting tremor
  - Impaired righting reflex (eg, retropulsed during sternal push or shoulder pull test)
- Other clinical features of Parkinson disease:
  - Postural instability and falls
  - Hyposmia
  - Hypophonia
  - Micrographia
  - REM sleep behavior disorder
  - Constipation
  - Masked facies
  - Infrequent blinking
  - Drooling
  - Seborrhea of face and scalp
  - Festinating gait
- Neuropsychiatric conditions are also common usually later in the clinical course: anxiety, depression, dementia, visual hallucinations, dysthymia, psychosis, delirium

Table 89. Distinguishing Early Parkinson Disease From Other Parkinsonian Syndromes

Condition	Tremor	Asymmetric Involvement	Early Falls	Early Dementia	Postural Hypotension
Parkinson disease	+	+	–	–	–
Drug-induced parkinsonism	+/–	–	–	–	–
Vascular parkinsonism	–	+/–	+/–	+/–	–

(cont.)

Condition	Tremor	Asymmetric Involvement	Early Falls	Early Dementia	Postural Hypotension
Dementia with Lewy bodies	+/–	+/–	+/–	+	+/–
Progressive supranuclear palsy	–	–	+	+/–	–
Corticobasilar ganglionic degeneration	–	+	+	–	+
Multiple system atrophy	–	+/–	+/–	–	+

Notes: + = usually or always present; +/– = sometimes present; – = absent.

Source: Adapted from Christine CW, Aminoff MJ. *Am J Med* 2004;117:412–419.

Nonpharmacologic Management

- Patient education is essential, and support groups are often helpful; see p 348 for telephone numbers, Web sites.
- Monitor for orthostatic hypotension (p 64).
- PT/Exercise programs to improve physical functioning, stability, and constipation:
  ○ Regular aerobic exercise (eg, treadmill training)
  ○ Balance and flexibility exercises (eg, tai chi)
  ○ Resistance training
- OT to maximize fine-motor functioning with adaptive equipment (eg, specialized eating utensils) and to perform home safety evaluations
- Speech-language tx to improve dysarthria and hypophonia
- Diet with increased fiber and hydration to minimize constipation; adequate vitamin D and calcium as osteopenia is common

Surgical Treatment—Deep Brain Stimulation (DBS)

- DBS of the globus pallidus or subthalamic nucleus is used for tx of motor complications of Parkinson disease.
- DBS is best suited for patients who have fluctuating motor problems (tremor and other dyskinesias) despite medical tx and who have few comorbidities, especially no dementia.
- Compared with medical tx in selected patients, DBS can significantly increase motor function (several more hours per day of "on" time) and decrease troubling dyskinesias.
- Early (0–3 mo) complications include surgical site infection (~10%), symptomatic intracranial hemorrhage (~2%), death (~1%), cognitive and speech problems (10–15%), and an increased risk of falls.

Pharmacologic Treatment (Tables 90 and 91)

- Begin tx when symptoms interfere with function.
- Start at low dose and titrate upward gradually.
- Monitor orthostatic BP during titration of medications.
- Tailor tx to symptoms.

Table 90. Symptom-Directed Treatment of Parkinson Disease

Category	Symptoms	Treatment Options
Motor	Tremor, bradykinesia, rigidity	Use dopamine, dopamine agonists
	Persistent tremor despite dopamine/dopamine agonist tx	Add β-blocker or clozapine; consider DBS
	Bradykinesia, motor fluctuations, increased "off time" despite dopamine tx	Increase dopamine dose; add dopamine agonist or COMT inhibitor or MAO B inhibitor (**Table 91**); consider DBS for refractory motor fluctuations
	Postural instability or gait impairment despite dopamine tx	Add amantadine or cholinesterase inhibitor
Nonmotor	Depression	Try SSRI or SNRI; consider careful trial of TCA[BC]; consider trial of pramipexole
	Cognitive impairment/Parkinson disease/Dementia	Consider trial of cholinesterase inhibitor, monitoring carefully for exacerbation of tremor or GI side effects
	Orthostatic hypotension	See Orthostatic (Postural) Hypotension (p 64)
	REM sleep behavioral disorder	Consider careful trial of clonazepam only in healthier patients without dementia or sleep apnea at low risk of falls; try melatonin in patients for whom clonazepam is not indicated
Drug-Induced	Dyskinesias	Carefully reduce dopamine dose (if motor symptoms worsen, try adding low dose of dopamine agonist); add amantadine; consider clozapine
	Nausea	Slowly titrate dopamine dose; consider domperidone (**Table 57**); avoid metoclopramide, prochlorperazine, and promethazine[BC]
	Impulse-control disorders	Reduce or D/C dopamine agonists; consider trial of amantadine
	Hallucinations/psychosis	Exclude systemic illness; carefully reduce antiparkinsonian drugs; try quetiapine or clozapine (avoid all antipsychotics except quetiapine and clozapine[BC])

Table 91. Medications for Parkinson Disease

Class, Medication	Initial Dosage	Formulations	Comments (Metabolism, Excretion)
Dopamine			
✓Carbidopa-levodopa[▲]* (Sinemet, Parcopa)	1/2 tab of 25/100 q812h	T: 10/100, 25/100, 25/250	Mainstay of Parkinson disease tx; increase dose by 1/2–1 tab q1–2wk to achieve minimal target dose of 1 tab q8h, then titrate upward gradually prn; watch for GI AEs, orthostatic hypotension, confusion; long-term tx associated with motor fluctuations and dyskinesias (addition of dopamine agonist may attenuate these effects) (L)
✓Sustained-release carbidopa-levodopa[▲]* (Sinemet CR)	1 tab/d	T: 25/100, 50/200	Useful at daily dopamine requirement ≥300 mg; slower absorption than carbidopa-levodopa; can improve motor fluctuations (L)

(cont.)

Table 91. Medications for Parkinson Disease (cont.)

Class, Medication	Initial Dosage	Formulations	Comments (Metabolism, Excretion)
Dopamine Agonists			More CNS AEs than dopamine
Apomorphine *(Apokyn)*	2 mg SC	Inj: 10 mg/mL	Use with extreme caution; can cause severe orthostasis; indicated only for "off" episodes associated with L-dopa tx
Bromocriptine▲ *(Parlodel)*	1.25 mg q12–24h	T: 2.5 C: 5	Increase by 1.25-mg increments q2–5d, titrating to effective dosage (10–30 mg/d) (L)
✓Pramipexole▲* *(Mirapex)*	0.125 mg/d	T: 0.125, 0.25, 0.5, 1, 1.5	Increase gradually to effective dosage (0.5–1.5 mg q8h) (K)
✓Extended-release Pramipexole▲* *(Mirapex ER)*	0.375 mg/d	T: 0.375, 0.75, 1.5, 2.25, 3, 3.75, 4.5	Increase gradually to effective dosage (1.5–4.5 mg qd) (K)
✓Ropinirole* *(Requip)*	0.25 mg/d	T▲: 0.25, 0.5, 1, 2, 3, 4, 5 CR: 4, 8	Increase gradually to effective dosage (up to 1–8 mg q8h) (L)
✓Extended-release ropinirole▲* *(Requip XL)*	2 mg/d	T: 2, 4, 6, 8, 12	Increase gradually to effective dosage (up to 6–24 mg qd) (L)
Rotigotine *(Neupro)*	2 mg/24 h for early stage disease; 4 mg/24 h for advanced disease	pch: 1, 2, 3, 4, 6, 8 mg/24 h	Increase weekly to effective dosage (max 6 mg/24 h for early stage disease, 8 mg/24 h for advanced disease) (K)
Catechol *O*-Methyl-transferase (COMT) Inhibitors			Adjunctive tx with L-dopa
✓Tolcapone *(Tasmar)*	100 mg q8h	T: 100, 200	Monitor LFTs q6mo (L, K)
✓Entacapone *(Comtan)*	200 mg with each L-dopa dose	T: 200	Watch for nausea, orthostatic hypotension (K)
Anticholinergics			
Benztropine▲, BC *(Cogentin)*	0.5 mg/d	T: 0.5, 1, 2	Can cause confusion and delirium; helpful for drooling. Avoid.BC (L, K)
Trihexyphenidyl▲, BC *(Artane, Trihexy)*	1 mg/d	T: 2, 5 S: 2 mg/5 mL	Same as above. Avoid.BC (L, K)
Dopamine Reuptake Inhibitor			
Amantadine▲ *(Symmetrel)*	100 mg q12–24h	T: 100 C: 100 S: 50 mg/5 mL	Useful in early and late Parkinson disease; watch closely for CNS AEs; do not D/C abruptly (K)
Monoamine Oxidase B (MAO B) Inhibitors			
Rasagiline *(Azilect)*	0.5 mg/d	T: 0.5, 1	Interactions with numerous drugs and tyramine-rich foods; expensive (L, K)
Selegiline▲ *(Carbex, Eldepryl, Zelapar)*	5 mg qam; 1.25 mg/d for ODT	T: 5 ODT: 1.25	Use as adjunctive tx with dopamine; do not exceed a total dosage of 10 mg/d; metabolized to amphetamine derivatives (L, K)

(cont.)

Table 91. Medications for Parkinson Disease (cont.)			
Class, Medication	**Initial Dosage**	**Formulations**	**Comments (Metabolism, Excretion)**
Combination Medication			
Carbidopa-levodopa + entacapone *(Stalevo)*	1 tab/d	T: 12.5/50/200, 25/100/200, 37.5/150/200	Should be used only after individual dosages of carbidopa, L-dopa, and entacapone have been established (L, K)

✓ = preferred for treating older adults

* = first-line tx

MULTIPLE-SYSTEM ATROPHY (MSA)

Diagnosis (see also Table 89)

- Diagnosis is made on hx and physical findings.
- May have early nonmotor phase characterized by urinary and/or sexual dysfunction, orthostatic hypotension, REM sleep behavior disorder.
- Clincal hallmarks are (in varying combinations):
  - Progressive autonomic failure – erectile dysfunction, genital hyposensitivity in women, urinary dysfunction, orthostatic hypotension.
  - Parkinsonism – bradykinesia, rigidity, falls; resting pill-rolling tremor is not usually seen but may have postural action tremor.
  - Cerebellar dysfunction – wide-based gait ataxia, uncoordinated limb movements.
- Other common features include:
  - Inspiratory stridor
  - Pronounced neck flexion (antecollis)
  - Depression and/or anxiety
  - Absence of dementia and hallucinations
  - Frontal lobe executive dysfunction and attention deficits

Clinical Course

- Rapid progression of motor symptoms once they appear (about half of patients will require a walking aid within 3 yr after onset of motor manifestations).
- Progressive course over approximately 6–10 yr, culminating in death.
- Late stage characterized by frequent falls, profound bradykinesia, unintelligible speech, recurrent aspiration pneumonia

Management

- Tx is for symptom management of above conditions; there are no known disease-altering tx.
- Up to 40% of patients will respond transiently to L-dopa tx, which should be continued if there are no side effects.
- Neurorehabilition programs can be helpful for maximizing mobility, preventing falls, increasing communication ability, and preventing choking episodes.

SEIZURES

Classification

- Generalized: All areas of brain affected with alteration in consciousness
- Partial: Focal brain area affected, not necessarily with alteration in consciousness; can progress to generalized type

Initial Evaluation, Assessment

- History: neurologic disorders, trauma, drug and alcohol use
- Physical examination: general, with careful neurologic
- Routine tests: BUN, calcium, CBC, Cr, ECG, EEG, electrolytes, glucose, head CT, LFTs, magnesium
- Tests as indicated: head MRI, lumbar puncture, oxygen saturation, urine toxic or drug screen

Common Causes

- Advanced dementia
- CNS infection
- Drug or alcohol withdrawal
- Idiopathic causes
- Metabolic disorders
- Prior stroke (most common)
- Toxins
- Trauma
- Tumor

Management

- Treat underlying causes.
- Institute anticonvulsant tx (**Table 92**). Virtually all anticonvulsant medications can cause sedation and ataxia.
- Avoid the following drugs, which can lower seizure threshold: bupropion, chlorpromazine, clozapine, maprotiline, olanzapine, thioridazine, thiothixene, and tramadol.[BC]

Table 92. Anticonvulsant Therapy in Older Adults

Medication	Dosage (mg)	Target Blood Concentration (mcg/mL)	Formulations	Comments (Metabolism, Excretion)
◆Carbamazepine▲ (Tegretol, Epitol) (Tegretol XR, Carbatrol, Equetro)	200–600 q12h	4–12	T: 200▲ ChT: 100 S: 100/5 mL▲ T: 100, 200, 400▲ C: ER 100, 200, 300	Many drug interactions; mood stabilizer; may cause SIADH, thrombocytopenia, leukopenia (L, K)
◆Gabapentin▲ (Neurontin)	300–600 q8h or q12h	NA	C: 100, 300, 400 T: 600, 800 S: 250/5 mL	Used as adjunct to other agents; adjust dosage on basis of CrCl (K)
Lacosamide (VIMPAT)	50–200 q12h	NA	T: 50, 100, 150, 200 S: 10/mL	Used as adjunct to other agents for partial-onset seizures; not studied in older adults (L, K)
Lamotrigine▲ (Lamictal)	100–300 q12h	2–4	T: 25, 100, 150, 200 ChT: 2, 5, 25▲	Prolongs PR interval; risk of severe rash; when used with valproic acid, begin at 25 mg q48h, titrate to 25–100 mg q12h (L, K)

(cont.)

Table 92. Anticonvulsant Therapy in Older Adults (cont.)

Medication	Dosage (mg)	Target Blood Concentration (mcg/mL)	Formulations	Comments (Metabolism, Excretion)
Levetiracetam▲ (Keppra)	500–1500 q12h	NA	T▲: 250, 500, 750 S▲: 100/mL CR: 500, 750	Reduce dosage in renal impairment: CrCl 30–50: 250–750 q12h CrCl 10–29: 250–500 q12h CrCl <10: 500–1000 q24h
Oxcarbazepine (Trileptal)	300–1200 q12h	NA	T▲: 150, 300, 600 ChT: 2, 5, 25 S: 300/5 mL	Can cause hyponatremia, leukopenia (L)
Phenobarbital▲ (Luminal)	30–60 q8–12h	20–40	T: 15, 16, 30, 32, 60, 100 S: 20/5 mL	Many drug interactions; not recommended for use in older adults (L)
Phenytoin▲ (Dilantin)	200–300/d	5–20	C: 30, 100▲ ChT: 50 S: 125/5 mL▲	Many drug interactions; exhibits nonlinear pharmacokinetics (L)
◆Pregabalin (Lyrica)	50–200 q8–12h		C: 25, 50, 75, 100, 150, 200, 225, 300	Indicated as adjunct tx for partial-onset seizures only; not well studied in older adults (K)
Tiagabine (Gabitril Filmtabs)	2–12 q8–12h	NA	T: 2, 4, 12, 16, 20	AE profile in older adults less well described (L)
Topiramate▲ (Topamax)	25–100 q12–24h	NA	T: 25, 100, 200 C, sprinkle: 15, 25	May affect cognitive functioning at high dosages (L, K)
Extended-release topiramate▲ (Trokendi XR, Qudexy XR)	25–200/d	NA	C: 25, 50, 100, 150, 200	
Valproic acid▲ (Depacon, Depakene, Depakote)	250–750 q8–12h	50–100	T: 125, 250, 500 C: 125, 250 S: 250/5 mL	Can cause weight gain, tremor, hair loss; several drug interactions; mood stabilizer; monitor LFTs and platelets (L)
(Depakote ER)			T: 500	
Zonisamide▲ (Zonegran)	100–400/d	NA	C: 25, 100	Anorexia; contraindicated in patients with sulfonamide allergy (K)

Notes: NA = not available   ◆ = also has primary indication for neuropathic pain.

APHASIA

Table 93. Aphasias in Which Repetition Is Impaired

Type	Fluency	Auditory Comprehension	Associated Neurologic Deficits	Comments
Broca's	−	+	Right hemiparesis	Patient aware of deficit; high rate of associated depression; message board helpful for communication
Wernicke's	+	−	Often none	Patient frequently unaware of deficit; speech content usually unintelligible; tx often focuses on visually based communication
Conduction	+	+	Occasional right facial weakness	Patient usually aware of deficit; speech content usually intelligible
Global	−	−	Right hemiplegia with right field cut	Most commonly due to left middle cerebral artery thrombosis, which has a poor prognosis for meaningful speech recovery

Notes: + = present; − = absent.

PERIPHERAL NEUROPATHY

History and PE

- Time course
  - Acute (<4 wk): conditions such as vasculitis, Guillain-Barré
  - Subacute (1–3 mo): conditions such as chronic inflammatory demyelinating polyneuropathy (CIDP), drugs, toxins
  - Chronic (>3 mo): extension of subacute causes, metabolic/systemic disorders (eg, DM, kidney failure, hypothyroidism, collagen vascular disease), malignancy (eg, lung paraneoplastic syndromes, myeloma)
- Family hx: Charcot-Marie-Tooth disease is most common hereditary neuropathy
- Drug and toxin exposure hx
  - Drugs: alcohol, amiodarone, antibiotics (eg, metronidazole, dapsone), chemotherapeutic agents, phenytoin, statins
  - Toxins: solvents, heavy metals, insecticides
- Type of neurologic deficit
  - Motor: Guillain-Barré, porphyria, lead exposure
  - Sensory: hereditary sensory neuropathy, vitamin B_{12} deficiency, lung paraneoplastic syndromes
  - Mixed motor and sensory: most neuropathies are mixed
- Establish pattern of involvement
  - Focal: entrapment syndromes, compression neuropathies
  - Multifocal, asymmetric: DM vasculitis
  - Multifocal, symmetric: metabolic disorders, drugs, toxins
- If symmetric, determine location
  - Proximal: many causes, including Guillain-Barré syndrome, porphyria, CIDP, Lyme disease
  - Distal: many causes from either axonal or demyelinating processes

- Nerve conduction studies can help distinguish the more common axonal pathologies (DM, medication effects, alcohol abuse, kidney failure, malignancy) from demyelinating ones (including Guillain-Barré syndrome and CIDP)
- About 30% of cases are due to DM
- About 30% of cases are idiopathic
- Reasonable blood screening tests would include CBC, glucose, Cr, BUN, TSH, LFTs, vitamin B$_{12}$ level, ESR, SPEP

Treatment

Prevention of Complications

- Protect distal extremities from trauma—appropriate shoe size, daily foot inspections, good skin care, avoidance of barefoot walking.
- Prevent falls (p 113–119)
- Maintain appropriate glycemic control in diabetic neuropathy.

Medications for Painful Neuropathy

- Expected to achieve a 30–50% reduction in pain in roughly 1/3 of patients
- Help only pain, not other neurologic symptoms
- Should be started at low dosage and increased as needed and tolerated
- In older adults, anticonvulsants are reasonable as first-line oral agents:
  - Gabapentin▲ *(Neurontin)* can begin 100–200 mg qhs but may need up to 100–600 mg q8h or q12h if CrCl <60 mL/min [C: 100, 300, 400; T: 600, 800; S: 250/5 mL]
  - Pregabalin *(Lyrica)* 75–300 mg po q12h [C: 25, 50, 75, 100, 150, 200, 225, 300]: primary indication is for management of post-herpetic neuralgia, diabetic peripheral neuropathy, or fibromyalgia
  - Carbamazepine▲ *(Tegretol)* 200–400 mg q8h [T: 200; ChT: 100; S: 100 mg/5 mL]; *(Tegretol XR)* 200 mg q12h [T: 100, 200, 400; C: CR 200, 300]
- Other oral agents that may be effective include:
  - TCAs^BC; eg, nortriptyline▲ *(Aventyl, Pamelor)* 10–100 mg qhs [T: 10, 25, 50, 75] or desipramine▲ *(Norpramin)* 10–75 mg qam [T: 10, 25, 50, 75]; benefits often outweighed by side effects in older adults
  - Duloxetine *(Cymbalta)* 20–60 mg/d [C: 20, 30, 60]
  - SSRIs have not been shown to be as effective as TCAs (**Table 41**)
  - Lamotrigine *(Lamictal,* **Table 92**) 400–600 mg/d
  - Opioids: watch for AEs of itching, mood changes, weakness, confusion
  - Tramadol▲ *(Ultram)* 200–400 mg/d
- Topical agents that may be effective include:
  - Capsaicin crm▲ (eg, *Zostrix*) 0.075% applied q6–8h [0.025%, 0.075%]
  - Capsaicin cutaneous pch *(Qutenza)* applied by health professional, using a local anesthetic, to the most painful skin areas (max of 4 pchs). Apply for 30 min to feet, 60 min for other locations. Risk of significant rise in BP after placement; monitor patient for at least 1 h [179-mg pch].
  - Transcutaneous electrical nerve stimulation
  - Lidocaine 5% pch *(Lidoderm)* 1–3 patches covering the affected area up to 24 h/d [700-mg pch]

COMMONLY USED DEFINITIONS

- Established osteoporosis: occurrence of a minimal trauma fracture of any bone (WHO).
- Osteoporosis: a skeletal disorder characterized by compromised bone strength (bone density and bone quality) predisposing to an increased risk of fracture (NIH Consensus Development Panel. *JAMA* 2001;285 [6]:785–795.)
- Osteoporosis: BMD 2.5 SD or more below that of younger normal individuals (T score) (WHO). Scores between 1 and 2.5 SD below young normals are termed osteopenia. Some experts prefer to use Z score, which compares an individual with a population adjusted for age, sex, and race. For each SD decrement in BMD, hip fracture risk increases about 2-fold; for each SD increment in BMD, hip fracture risk is about halved.

RISK FACTORS FOR OSTEOPOROTIC FRACTURE

- Advanced age*
- Female sex*
- BMI (both low and high)*
- Previous fracture as adult*
- Parent fractured hip*
- Current smoking*
- On glucocorticoids*
- RA*
- Secondary osteoporosis*
- Alcohol (>3 drinks/d)*
- Low BMD*
- Frailty
- Dementia
- Depression
- Impaired vision
- Low physical activity
- Early menopause (<45 yr old)
- Recurrent falls
- Nocturia
- Kidney failure (GFR <45 mL/min/1.73 m²) body surface area

*indicates included in the WHO Fracture Risk Assessment Tool (FRAX)

TOXINS AND MEDICATIONS THAT CAN CAUSE OR AGGRAVATE OSTEOPOROSIS

- Alcohol (>2 drinks/d)
- ADT
- Anticonvulsants
- Antipsychotics
- Corticosteroids
- Heparin
- Lithium
- Nicotine (ie, smoking)
- Phenytoin
- PPIs (if ≥1 yr)
- SSRIs
- Thyroxine (if overreplaced or in suppressive dosage)

EVALUATION

- BMD at least once in all women after age 65 (and younger if risk is greater than or equal to that of a 65-yr-old, using FRAX calculator), insufficient evidence to support screening in men (USPSTF) but National Osteoporosis Foundation (NOF) recommends BMD in all men after age 70, and in men with prior clinical fracture after age 65 (**Table 104**). Uncertain how often to repeat. Some suggest in 3 yr for patients with osteopenia and in 5 yr for those with normal bone density. Do not routinely repeat more than once every 2 yr.[CW] Although some professional societies recommend monitoring BMD q2yr, the value of monitoring BMD in patients already receiving tx is unproved. Even patients who continue to lose BMD during tx have benefits in fracture reduction. Although NOF recommends screening with vertebral imaging (dual-energy x-ray absorptiometry or x-ray) for women ≥70 and men ≥80 with any T score ≤-1.0 and women 65–69 and men 70–79 with any T score ≤1.5, this is controversial and is not covered by Medicare.
- Serum 25-hydroxy vitamin D (treat if <30 ng/mL) expected rise is 1 ng/mL/100 IU vitamin D_3; if <20 ng/mL, consider 50,000 U vitamin D_2 (ergocalciferol) once/wk.

- Some experts recommend excluding secondary causes (serum PTH, TSH, calcium, phosphorus, albumin, alkaline phosphatase, bioavailable testosterone in men, kidney function tests, LFTs, CBC, UA, electrolytes, protein electrophoresis). Less consensus on 24-h urinary calcium excretion, cortisol, antibodies associated with gluten enteropathy.

MANAGEMENT

Universal Recommendations

- Calcium (elemental) 1200 mg/d for women >50 yr old and men >70 yr old, 1000 mg/d for men <70 yr old. For most patients, calcium carbonate is sufficient and least expensive. For patients on PPIs (**Table 104**) or who have achlorhydria, calcium citrate should be used. For patients who have difficulty swallowing calcium citrate tabs, smaller tabs of 125 mg *(Freeda Mini Cal-citrate)* and granules, 1 tsp = 760 mg *(Freeda Calcium Citrate Fine Granular)*, are available. Initiating calcium may be associated with a modest increased risk of cardiovascular events (MI or stroke) in women, and the benefits vs risks of supplementation remains to be clarified.
- Vitamin D at least 800 IU (Institute of Medicine); D_3 (cholecalciferol) is preferred form
- OTC calcium plus vitamin D preparations vary considerably in amounts of each, so ask patients to read labels (look for elemental calcium) to ensure they are getting adequate amounts.
- Avoid tobacco
- Exercise for muscle strengthening and balance training
- No more than moderate alcohol use
- Treat nocturia to lower falls risk
- Falls prevention (**Table 55**)

Pharmacologic Prevention and Treatment

- Patients with prior fragility fracture should be treated. Fragility fractures include those occurring from a fall from a standing height or less, without major trauma such as a motor vehicle accident. Fragility fractures occur particularly at the spine, hip, wrist, humerus, rib, and pelvis. Certain skeletal locations, including the skull, cervical spine, hands, feet, and ankles, are not associated with fragility fractures.
- For those who have not had prior fractures, estimated 10-yr probability of major osteoporotic or hip fracture based on risk factors with or without BMD can be calculated using FRAX (www.shef.ac.uk/FRAX/). Some countries use FRAX first and perform BMD only if tx decision is equivocal.
- The NOF has recommended initiating pharmacologic management (**Table 94**) if BMD T scores at any site are:
  - Below −2.5 in the absence of risk factors
  - −1 to −2.5 if 10-yr risk (based on FRAX) of hip fracture is >3% or 10-yr risk of major osteoporotic fracture (cervical spine, forearm, hip, or shoulder) is >20%
- Some question NOF guidelines because application would result in pharmacotherapy for 72% of white women >65 yr old and 93% of women >75 yr old compared with bone density criteria alone, which would result in pharmacotherapy of 50% of women in both age groups. Also should consider patient's expected survival and whether patient will live long enough to accrue benefit of tx.
- Bisphosphonates are first-line tx but are contraindicated in renal failure. If CrCl <35 mL/min, denosumab is alternative. However, few data supporting efficacy in Stage 4 and 5 CKD and CKD increases risk of hypocalcemia.
- IV bisphosphonates are generally used in patients with GI contraindications (eg, esophageal disorders, feeding tubes) or are unable to sit up following oral dosing.

- Begin bisphosphonate tx in patients receiving or who will receive chronic glucocorticoids (≥5 mg prednisone or equivalent for ≥3 mo) who have other fracture risk factors or if T score is less than −1.0.
- Bisphosphonate tx of patients with locally advanced or high-risk prostate cancer receiving ADT is cost-effective if osteoporosis based on BMD, prior fracture, or age >80.
- Some experts recommend using bisphosphonates that have demonstrated efficacy in reducing hip fractures and shorter-acting agents as preferred initial tx (**Table 95**).
- PPIs reduce the effectiveness of oral bisphosphonates, and some experts recommend holding the PPI the day before bisphosphonate administration and not administering the PPI until >60 min after the bisphosphonate has been taken.
- Bisphosphonates are more effective in preventing hip fracture when adherence is >80% (compared with adherence <50%). Adherence is better with weekly compared to daily regimens.
- The duration of bisphosphonate tx is uncertain. The risk of subtrochanteric or femoral shaft fractures increases with tx beyond 3 yr. An FDA analysis concluded neither clear benefit nor harm for overall osteoporotic fracture risk by continuing bisphosphonates beyond 5 yr. Once bisphosphonates have been discontinued, there are no data on whether or when to resume tx.
- Although some evidence supports the use of vitamin K supplements to prevent fractures, confirmatory studies are needed.

Table 94. Pharmacologic Prevention and Treatment of Osteoporosis[a]

Medication	Dosage	Formulations	Administration
Bisphosphonates	*Class effect:* Esophagitis; bone, joint, or muscle pain; osteonecrosis of jaw (estimated 1–28 cases/100,000 patient-yrs with oral tx)[b]; occipital inflammation; possibly atrial fibrillation); association with atypical femoral fractures rare (<9/10,000 patient-yrs). Do not use if CrCl <35 mL/min. Consider discontinuing or suspending after 5 yr.		
Alendronate▲ *(Fosamax)*	Prevention: 5 mg/d or 35 mg/wk Tx: 10 mg/d or 70 mg/wk	T: 5, 10, 35, 40, 70	Must be taken fasting with water; patient must remain upright and npo for ≥30 min after taking; do not use if CrCl <35 mL/min; relatively contraindicated in GERD
Effervescent *(Binosto)* with cholecalciferol	70 mg/wk 1 tab/wk	T: 70 T: 70/2800U; 70/5600U	
Ibandronate *(Boniva)*	Tx and prevention: po: 150 mg/mo or 2.5 mg/d IV: 3 mg q3mo	T: 2.5, 150 IV: 1 mg/mL (available in 3-mL prefilled syringes)	Must be taken fasting with water; patient must remain upright and npo for ≥60 min after taking; do not use if CrCl <30 mL/min
Risedronate▲ *(Actonel)*	Tx and prevention: 35 mg/wk, 5 mg/d, or 150 mg/mo	T: 5, 30, 35, 150	Must be taken fasting or ≥2 h after evening meal; patient must remain upright and npo for 30 min after taking; do not use if CrCl <30 mL/min
Delayed release *(Atelvia)*	35 mg/wk	T: 35 DR	
Zoledronic acid▲ *(Reclast)*	5 mg IV given over >15 min every yr for tx or q2yr for prevention	5 mg/100 mL	May cause acute renal failure in patients using diuretics

(cont.)

Medication	Dosage	Formulations	Administration
Others			
Raloxifene *(Evista)*	60 mg/d	T: 60	Used more often for prevention because of reduced risk of breast cancer; may cause hot flushes, myalgias, cramps, and limb pain
Calcitonin *(Calcimar, Cibacalcin, Miacalcin, Osteocalcin, Salmonine)*	Tx and prevention: 100 IU/d SC (human) or 200 IU intranasally (salmon) in alternate nostrils q48h	Inj: human *(Cibacalcin)* 0.5 mg/vial Intranasal▲: salmon 200 U/mL *(Miacalcin)*	May also be helpful for analgesic effect in patients with acute vertebral fracture (also p 197); rhinitis in 10–12%; increased risk of cancer
Estrogen▲	p 333		For use in select patients; for risks and benefits, see p 333
Teriparatide *(Forteo)*	Tx: 20 mcg/d for up to 24 mo	Inj: 3 mL, 28-dose disposable pen device	Contraindicated in patients with Paget disease or prior skeletal radiation tx; can cause hypercalcemia (L, K); tx for 1 yr followed by 1 yr of bisphosphonates or raloxifene can maintain 1-yr gains in BMD
Denosumab *(Prolia)*	60 mg SC q6mo	Inj: 60 mg/mL in pre-filled syringe	Skin infections, dermatitis, osteoneorosis of jaw, hypocalcemia especially if CrCl <30 mL/min and uncorrected calcium. Risk of atypical fracture is expected to be similar to bisphosphonates.
Combination			
Conjugated estrogens/ bazedoxifene *(Duavee)*	1 tab/d	T: 45/20 (conjugated estrogens/ bazedoxifene)	In clinical trials, no increase in vaginal bleeding, breast, endometrial, or ovarian cancer, VTE, or MI. Long-term risk for VTE or ischemic stroke uncertain

[a] Unless specified, medication can be used for prevention or tx.

[b] Risk factors include IV tx (little data on osteoporosis doses); cancer; dental extractions, implants, and poor-fitting dentures; glucocorticoids; smoking; and preexisting dental disease. Some experts recommend that bisphosphonates be stopped for several months before and after elective complex oral procedures (or, if procedures are emergent, that bisphosphonates be held for several months after).

Pharmacologic Treatment Regimens for Those with Prior Osteoporotic Fractures

- BMD measurement is unnecessary (**Table 94** for tx regimens).
- Combination tx (eg, estrogen plus bisphosphonate or calcitonin) is slightly more effective in improving BMD but has not been proved to affect fracture rates.
- For high-risk patients with multiple fractures who continue to fracture after 1 yr of bisphosphonate tx or who are intolerant of bisphosphonates, consider teriparatide. Although some evidence supports teriparatide to accelerate bone healing, this evidence is preliminary and use for this purpose is not standard practice.
- Denosumab is an alternative for those who are intolerant of bisphosphonates.

Osteoporosis in Men

- If symptomatic hypogonadism or a cause for hypogonadism, then testosterone replacement.
- In general, nonpharmacologic tx, indications for pharmacologic tx, and choices of drugs are the same as for women. Bisphosphonate tx has been evaluated less in men. Zoledronic acid reduces the risk of morphometric vertebral fractures.

Table 95. Bone Outcomes of Medications for Osteoporosis Based on Randomized Clinical Trials[a]

Medication	Spine BMD and Fracture	Hip BMD	Hip Fracture	All Nonspinal Fractures
Estrogen[▲]	improved	improved	reduced	reduced
Raloxifene	improved	improved	no data	reduced
Alendronate[▲]	improved	improved	reduced	reduced
Ibandronate	improved	improved	no data	no effect
Risedronate	improved	improved	reduced	reduced
Calcitonin (nasal)[b]	improved	no effect	no effect	no effect
Zoledronic acid	improved	improved	reduced	reduced
Teriparatide[c]	improved	improved	no data	reduced
Denosumab	improved	improved	reduced	reduced

[a] The populations studied, sample sizes of individual studies, and duration of follow-up vary considerably; hence, this summary must be interpreted cautiously. Moreover, several randomized clinical trials are currently in progress and new findings may appear.

[b] Based on observational data, calcitonin appears to be less effective in preventing nonspinal fractures.

[c] More effective than bisphosphonates in increasing BMD and reducing spinal fractures in patients receiving systemic glucocorticoid tx for ≥3 mo.

Table 96. Effects on Other Outcomes, Level of Evidence,[a] and Risks of Medications for Osteoporosis

Medication	CHD Risk Factors	CHD Prevention	CHD Treatment	Breast Cancer	Deep Vein Thrombosis
Estrogen[▲b]	improved (R)	↑ risk (R)	no effect (R)	↑ risk (R)	↑ risk (R)
Raloxifene	improved (R)	no effect	↓ risk (R)	↓ risk (R)	↑ risk (R)
Bisphosphonates[c]	no data	no data	no data	↓ risk (R) invasive ↑ risk of ductal carcinoma in situ (O)	no data
Calcitonin[d] (nasal)	no data	no data	no data	no data	no data

Notes: R = randomized clinical trial; O = observational study.

[a] The populations studied, sample sizes of individual studies, and duration of follow-up vary considerably; hence, this summary must be interpreted cautiously. Moreover, several RTCs are currently in progress and new findings may appear.

[b] In the Women's Health Initiative estrogen-alone trial, only stroke and PE risk were increased.

[c] Alendronate[▲], ibandronate, risedronate, zoledronic acid

[d] Risk of any cancer is increased.

DEFINITION

An unpleasant sensory and emotional experience associated with actual or potential tissue damage (International Association for Study of Pain taxonomy)

Acute Pain

Distinct onset, usually evident pathology, short duration; common causes: trauma, postsurgical pain

Persistent Pain

Pain that does not remit in the expected amount of time; due to ongoing nociceptive, neuropathic, or mixed pathophysiologic processes, often associated with functional and psychologic impairment; may occur in absence of any past injury or evident body damage; can fluctuate in character and intensity over time (**Table 97**).

Table 97. Types of Pain, Examples, and Treatment

Type of Pain and Examples	Typical Description	Effective Drug Classes and Nonpharmacologic Treatments
Peripheral Nociceptive: somatic (eg, tissue injury of bones, soft tissue, joints, muscles)		
Arthritis, acute postoperative, fracture, bone metastases	Well localized, constant; aching, stabbing, gnawing, throbbing	APAP, opioids, NSAIDs; PT and CBT
Peripheral Nociceptive: visceral		
Renal colic, constipation	Diffuse, poorly localized, referred to other sites, intermittent, paroxysmal; dull, colicky, squeezing, deep, cramping; often accompanied by nausea, vomiting, diaphoresis	Tx of underlying cause, APAP, opioids; PT and CBT
Peripheral Neuropathic: peripheral nervous system		
Cervical or lumbar radiculopathy, post-herpetic neuralgia, trigeminal neuralgia, diabetic neuropathy, phantom limb pain, post-stroke syndrome, herniated intervertebral disc, drug toxicities	Prolonged, usually constant, but can have paroxysms; sharp, burning, pricking, tingling, pins and needles, shooting electric-shock–like; associated with other sensory disturbances, eg, paresthesias and dysesthesias; allodynia, hyperalgesia, impaired motor function, atrophy, or abnormal deep tendon reflexes	TCAs, SNRIs, anticonvulsants, opioids, topical anesthetics; PT and CBT
Central, Undetermined, or Mixed		
Myofascial pain syndrome, somatoform pain disorders, fibromyalgia; post-stroke; temporomandibular joint dysfunction, tension HA	No identifiable pathologic processes or symptoms out of proportion to identifiable organic pathology; widespread musculoskeletal pain, stiffness, and weakness; fatigue, sleep disturbance; taut bands of muscles and trigger points; sensitivity to sensory stimuli	Antidepressants, antianxiety agents; PT, CBT, and psychological tx

Note: Cancer pain may present with any of the types described above

EVALUATION

Key Points, Approach

- Perform comprehensive evaluation for underlying cause of pain, pain characteristics, and impact of physical and psychosocial function. Identify multiple factors that when combined with pain can cause disability (eg, anxiety, depression, beliefs, insomnia, fear avoidance, biomechanical issues).
- Use multidisciplinary assessment and tx (eg, pharmacists, physical therapists, psychologists) when possible, particularly for persistent pain.
- For persistent pain when considering opioid tx, assess pain intensity and frequency, function and effect on ADLs, quality of life, depression, anxiety, potential misuse or abuse of opioid medication, potential adverse effects of opioids.
- Consider patient's report as the most reliable evidence of pain intensity.
- Assess for pain on each presentation (older adults may be reluctant to report pain).
- Use synonyms for pain (eg, burning, aching, soreness, discomfort).
- Use a standard pain scale (eg, Numeric Rating Scale, Verbal Descriptor Scale, or Faces Pain Scale); adapt for sensory impairments (eg, large print, written vs spoken).
- Use simple pain tools (eg, scale with none, mild, moderate, or severe pain) or questions with yes/no answers to solicit self-report of pain in persons with moderate cognitive impairment.
- Reassess regularly for improvement, deterioration, and complications/AEs, and document.

Assessment in Cognitively Impaired Patients

- Assess pain in persons with severe cognitive impairment or inability to communicate pain using the Pain Assessment algorithm (**Figure 11**), including medical hx and physical examination to identify potential pain etiologies.
- In cognitively impaired persons with behavioral disturbances/agitation suspected of an underlying pain etiology for which other causes have been ruled out and behaviors not responding to nondrug intervention, try an analgesic trial for diagnostic purposes to evaluate pain as etiology. The following is a guide to be adjusted based on individual comorbidities and/or contraindications:
  - Try APAP 1st (if no hepatic dysfunction). Order scheduled rather than prn. APAP is often effective in improving behaviors and/or function.
    - If no response to APAP and localized inflammatory pain suspected, try topical NSAIDs.
    - If no response, try oral morphine sulfate (5 mg q12h to max 10 mg q12h) or buprenorphine transdermal pch (5 mcg/h to max mcg/h).
  - If no response to APAP and neuropathic pain is suspected, try pregabalin 25 mg/d, max 300 mg/d.
- Carefully monitor response to analgesics with each change as agent and dose are titrated to achieve pain relief yet avoid undesirable AEs.
- If behavior improves with pain tx, establish pain tx plan considering risks/benefits of tx options.

History and Physical Examination

- Evaluate underlying diseases that are known to be painful in older persons (**Table 97**).
- Consider potential drug toxicities (eg, amiodarone, bortezomib, leflunomide, ixabepilone, chemotherapeutic agent neuropathy, antibiotic-induced neuropathies). Note if neuropathy is acute after starting medication, or if there is increase in existing neuropathy after adding a new medication.
- Focus on a complete examination of pain source and on musculoskeletal, peripheral vascular, and neurologic systems as well as any body part that might be source of referred pain.

- Physical exam essential to identify physical pain contributions (eg, leg length discrepancy, hip OA, myofascial pain, sacroiliac joint syndrome).
- Distinguish new illness from chronic condition.
- Analgesic hx: effectiveness and AEs, current and previous prescription drugs, OTC drugs, "natural" remedies.

Figure 11. Pain Assessment in Older Adults with Severe Cognitive Impairment

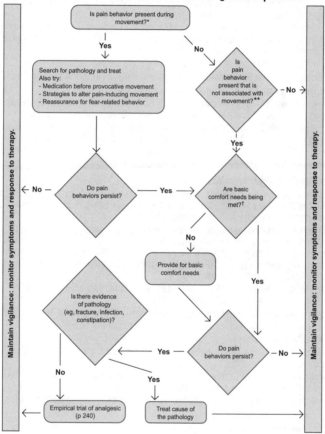

* Examples: grimacing, guarding, combativeness, groaning with movement; resisting care

** Examples: agitation, fidgeting, sleep disturbance, diminished appetite, irritability, reclusiveness, disruptive behavior, rigidity, rapid blinking

† Examples: toileting, thirst, hunger, visual or hearing impairment

Sources: American Geriatrics Society. *J Amer Geriatr Soc* 2002; 50(6, Suppl): S205–S240; and Weiner D, Herr K, Rudy T, eds. Persistent Pain in Older Adults: An Interdisciplinary Guide for Treatment, 2002, Copyright Springer Publishing Company, Inc., New York 10036.

- Assess effectiveness of prior nondrug tx.
- Laboratory and diagnostic tests to establish etiologic diagnosis. More than half of patients who report being pain-free have radiographic evidence of degenerative joint disease, thus not useful as evidence of pain etiology.
  - Avoid imaging studies (MRI, CT, or x-rays) for acute low-back pain without specific indications.^{CW}
  - Don't recommend advanced imaging (eg, MRI) of the spine within the first 6 wk in patients with nonspecific acute low-back pain in the absence of red flags (eg, trauma hx, unintentional weight loss, immunosuppression, cancer hx, IV drug use, steroid use, osteoporosis, age >50, focal neurologic deficit, and progression of symptoms).^{CW}
  - Do not use electromyography and nerve conduction studies to determine cause of axial lumbar, thoracic, or cervical spine pain.^{CW}

Characteristics of Pain Complaint

Provocative (aggravating) and Palliative (relieving) factors
Quality (eg, burning, stabbing, dull, throbbing)
Region (eg, pain map)
Severity (eg, scale of 0 for no pain to 10 for worst pain possible)
Timing (eg, when pain occurs, frequency and duration)

Psychosocial Assessment

Depression (p 338–339 for screen), anxiety, mental status (p 335 for screen). Impact on family or significant other. Enabling behaviors by others (eg, over solicitousness, codependency, reinforcing debility).

Functional Assessment

ADLs, impact on activities (p 336–337 for screens), and quality of life

Brief Pain Inventory

Use for comprehensive assessment of pain and its impact (www.geriatricscareonline.org).

MANAGEMENT

Goal: To find optimal balance in pain relief, functional improvement, and AEs. Nondrug (complementary and alternative tx) can be beneficial and considered early in tx plan, particularly in managing persistent pain problems. Combination of drug and nondrug approaches may lower dosing of analgesics and reduce drug-related AEs.

Establish patient tx goals and expectations, social and family supports, before initiating tx.

Develop a therapeutic alliance and reinforce positive outcomes at each visit.

Involve caregivers and seek out resources (eg, community-based programs) to help reinforce adherence to tx plans.

Acute Pain and Short-term Management

- Identify cause of pain and treat if possible.
- Use fixed schedule of APAP, NSAIDs (consider nonselective vs celecoxib depending on risk factors and comorbidities, **Figure 10**), or opioids (**Table 100**).
  - Do not exceed 4000 mg maximum daily dose of APAP
  - IV acetaminophen (Ofirmev; 15 mg/kg q6h or 12.5 mg/kg q4h adult dose) option if no other route available; expensive.
  - Exparel is a liposome injection of bupivacaine, an amide-type local anesthetic, indicated for administration into the surgical site to produce postsurgical analgesia (ie, one-time intraoperative injection). Caution with hepatic and renal disease. Monitoring of

cardiovascular and respiratory (adequacy of ventilation) vital signs and the patient's state of consciousness should be performed after injection of bupivacaine and other amide-containing products.

- ○ When opioids required, use should taper with healing of injury, usually no longer than 90 d at most.
- ○ Do not exceed daily opioid po MS Equiv of 100 mg.
- Refer to PT for nonpharmacologic strategies (eg, relaxation, heat or cold, TENS, joint mobilization, stabilizing exercises, assistive devices).
- ○ Do not recommend bed rest for more than 48 h when treating low-back pain.^{CW}
- Patient-controlled analgesia (PCA): Requires patient comprehension of PCA instructions
- ○ Indications
  - ▪ Acute pain (eg, postoperative pain, trauma)
  - ▪ Persistent pain in patients who are npo
- ○ Dosing strategies (**Table 98**)
  - ▪ Titrate up PCA dose 25–50% if pain still not well controlled after 12 h.
  - ▪ Unless patient is awakened by pain during sleep, continuous opioid infusion not recommended because of increased risk of opioid accumulation and toxicity.
  - ▪ If basal rate used, hourly monitoring of sedation and respiratory status is warranted. If low respiratory rate (≤8) and moderate sedation (difficulty arousing patient from sleep) after expected peak of opioid, withhold further opioid until respiratory rate rises or pain returns. If needed, a small dose of dilute naloxone can be given and repeated.
  - ▪ D/C PCA when patient able to take oral analgesics or unable to self-medicate due to altered mental status or physical limitations.

Table 98. Typical Initial Dosing of PCA for Older Adults with Severe Pain

Medication (usual concentration)	Usual Dose Range*	Usual Lockout (min)
Morphine▲ (1 mg/mL)	0.5–2.5 mg	5–10
Hydromorphone▲ (0.2 mg/mL)	0.05–0.3 mg	5–10

* For opioid-naive patients, consider lower end of dosage range.

Persistent Pain

- Identify and treat local causes of pain with local tx (eg, manipulation, massage, heat, PT, TENS), topical anesthetics, minor interventions (eg, steroid joint injection), or surgery (eg, lidocaine oint/pch or diclofenac gel/pch/gtt).
- Educate patient and promote self-management and coping. Include caregiver when possible.
- ○ Promote healthy behaviors including physical activity, weight control, and sleep.
- ○ Refer to Pain Self Management program and resources (healthinaging.org/resources/resource:-2/)
- ○ Refer to Arthritis Foundation or community resources such as senior centers (arthritis.org/living-with-arthritis/pain-management/)
- In those overweight with mild to moderate pain, start with weight loss (eg, MOVE!® Weight Management program, cardiovascular and/or resistance land-based exercises, aquatic program)
- Emphasize self-administered tx (eg, heat, cold, massage, liniments, and topical agents, distraction, relaxation, music) and self-management approaches (eg, CBT). Prescribe exercise for analgesic effects (p 274).
- Prescribe assistive devices for joint unloading.

- Combine pharmacologic and nonpharmacologic strategies.
  - Add tx taught and/or conducted by professionals (eg, coping skills, biofeedback, imagery, hypnosis) as needed.

Nonpharmacologic Treatment

Table 99. Nondrug Interventions for Persistent Pain in Older Adults		
Intervention	**Outcomes**	**Problems Studied**
Physical		
Exercise (walking, tai chi, yoga)	+	LE OA; CLBP, chronic pain
Acupuncture	+	Back, knee, shoulder, neck
TENS	+/–	Knee, back
Qigong	+/–	Back, neck
Massage	+	Back, neck
Psychosocial		
Cognitive Behavioral Training	+	Chronic pain
Guided Imagery with Progressive Muscle Relaxation	+	Chronic OA pain
Music	+	Chronic pain
Mindfulness-based Meditation	+/–	CLBP
Self-Management Education	+	Chronic pain, CLBP

Notes: Short-term efficacy, good tolerance, low risk, low cost; Best format, intensity, duration, content not established; Studies in older adults limited; No clear consensus on best. + = positive outcomes; +/– = mixed outcomes; CLBP = chronic low-back pain; LE OA = lower extremity osteoarthritis; TENS = transcutaneous electrical nerve stimulation.

Source: Park J et al. *J Am Geriatr Soc.* 2012;60(3):555–568.

- Treat comorbid psychiatric conditions associated with persistent pain including anxiety, depression, and posttraumatic stress disorder.
  - Options include psychotherapy, biofeedback, mindfulness training, counseling (relationship, social, financial, substance abuse).
- Consider therapeutic injections to treat acute and chronic pain syndromes (see Musculoskeletal chapter for specific indications).
  - Injections are rarely sole tx.
  - Diagnostic value can be determined by response to an injected local anesthetic.
  - Spinal cord stimulation may be useful for failed back syndrome (ie, post-laminectomy), complex regional pain syndrome, and neuropathic and ischemic pain.
  - Intrathecal infusions may be indicated for both cancer and noncancer pain.
- When appropriate, refer for:
  - Consult PT and OT for mechanical devices to minimize pain and facilitate activity (eg, splints), transcutaneous electrical nerve stimulation, range-of-motion and ADL programs.
  - Pain clinic with interdisciplinary team approach for complex pain syndromes with poor response to first-line tx.
  - Psychiatric pain management consult for somatization or severe mood or personality disorder.

- Anesthesia pain management consult for possible interventional tx (eg, neuroaxial analgesia, injection tx, neuromodulation) when more conservative approaches are ineffective.
- Pain or chemical dependency specialist referral for management of at-risk patients and ongoing chemical dependency, "chemical coping," aberrant drug-related behaviors, and drug withdrawal.

Pharmacologic Treatment

Approach

- Base initial choice of analgesic on the severity and type of pain and impact on function; consider cost, availability, patient preference, comorbidity, impairments, safety, and adverse outcomes (**Figure 10** and **Table 100**)
- For ongoing analgesic tx, careful risk/benefit analysis should be completed when determining appropriate drug and use.

Table 100. Principles of Analgesic Management in Older Adults	
Drug Class and Dosing	**Practical Considerations**
Step 1: Treatment of Mild Pain (Score of 1–3 and limited functional impairment)	
Acetaminophen (APAP) **(Table 82)**	APAP should be considered initial and ongoing pharmacotherapy in treating persistent mild to moderate musculoskeletal pain with maximal dose of 4 g in healthy patients and 3 g in frail older adults. Advise against alcohol use; schedule around-the-clock.
	NOT anti-inflammatory; leading cause of acute liver failure (including accidental overdose); monitor for severe liver injury and acute renal failure.
Nonacetylated salicylates (eg, salsalate, trisalicylate) **(Table 82)**	Consider if inflammatory pain. Educate regarding salicylism. Avoid in patients with advanced renal disease or hepatic impairment.
Topical analgesics, counterstimulants **(Table 101)**	Consider for localized neuropathic and/or nonneuropathic persistent pain. Lidocaine 5% pch *(Lidoderm)* 12 h on/12 h off safe, effective for postherpetic neuralgia. Limited evidence for other painful conditions. 8% capsaicin pch *(Qutenza)* for neuropathic pain. May take up to 2 wk before tx benefit. Menthol, methyl salicylate, or capsaicin available
	OTC compounded topical analgesics available, although no evidence to support use
Topical NSAIDs **(Table 82)**	As effective as oral NSAIDs with fewer systemic AE for chronic musculoskeletal pain, particularly hand and knee OA Diclofenac 1% gel, 1.5% topical sol, 1.3% pch

(cont.)

Table 100. Principles of Analgesic Management in Older Adults (cont.)	
Drug Class and Dosing	**Practical Considerations**
NSAIDs/Cox-2 anti-inflammatory drug **(Table 82)**	Avoid nonselective NSAIDs for chronic use and in patients with hx of gastric or duodenal ulcers, unless other alternatives are not effective and patient can take gastroprotective agent.[BC]
	Use NSAIDs with caution in highly selected patients for short-term use.
	Use misoprostol or PPI with nonselective NSAIDs to reduce GI bleeding risk. Avoid scheduled use of PPI for >8 wk unless for high-risk patients (eg, chronic NSAID use)[BC]
	Consider celecoxib for patients who would benefit from anti-inflammatory medication with no cardiovascular risk based on risk/benefit assessment **(Figure 10** and **Table 82)**. Long-term use not recommended.
	Avoid in HF.[BC] Avoid in renal impairment (CrCL <30 mL/min). Caution in patients with cardiovascular disease or at risk for cardiovascular disease.

Step 2: Treatment of Moderate Pain (Score 4–7 and interference with active function), pain not alleviated with medicine from Step 1, and/or if pain worsens

Short-Acting Opioids	Select patients who may benefit from low-dose opioid tx in combination with other tx (eg, specific somatic, peripheral, or neuropathic pain).
	Combination products not recommended for chronic use.
	Total dose limited by max dose for APAP; all combination products now contain ≤325 mg of APAP per unit dose, consistent with FDA guidance.
	Avoid opioids in chronic central or visceral pain syndromes such as fibromyalgia, headaches, or abdominal pain.
	Start stimulant laxative to prevent tx-related constipation.

Drug/Formulations	**MS Equiv[a] (Route)**	**Starting Dosage for Opioid-Naïve**	**Comments**
Codeine▲ T: 15, 30, 60; S: 15/5 mL; Inj	200 mg (po)	15 mg q4–6h	Not recommended due to CYP2D6 metabolism—variability in metabolism; limited analgesia
Codeine + APAP▲ T: 15/325, 30/325, 60/325, 7.5/300, 15/300, 30/300, 60/300; S: 12/120/5 mL	200 mg (po)	1–2 15/325 tabs q4–6h; if 1 tab used, add 325 mg APAP	Caution: Total APAP dosage should not exceed 4g/d
Hydrocodone + APAP▲ (eg, *Lorcet, Lortab, Norco*) T: 5/325, 10/325 S: 2.5/167/5 mL (contains 7% alcohol) (eg, *Vicodin*) T: 5/300, 7.5/300, 10/300	30 mg (po)	2.5–5 mg q4–6h	*Caution:* Total APAP dosage should not exceed 4g/d
Hydrocodone + ibuprofen▲ (eg, *Vicoprofen*) T: 7.5/200	30 mg	7.5/200	Monitor renal function and use gastric protection ER tablets without abuse-deterrent formulation

(cont.)

Table 100. Principles of Analgesic Management in Older Adults (cont.)

Drug/Formulations	MS Equiv[a] (Route)	Starting Dosage for Opioid-Naïve	Comments
Oxycodone▲ *(Oxy IR, Oxecta, Roxicodone)* T: 5, 15, 30; C: 5; S: 5 mg/mL, 20 mg/mL	20 mg (po)	2.5–5 mg q3–4h	Limited information on dosing in renal failure; use caution despite weak active metabolites
			ER abuse-deterrent products available
Oxycodone + APAP▲ *(Percocet, Tylox)* T▲: 2.5/325, 5/325, 7.5/325, 10/325 S: 5/325/5 mL	20 mg (po)	2.5–5 mg oxycodone q6h including 325 mg APAP	
(Magnacet) T: 2.5/400, 5/400, 7.5/400, 10/400	20 mg (po)	2.5–5 mg oxycodone q6h including 400 mg APAP	
Oxycodone + ASA▲ *(Percodan)* T: 2.25/325, 4.5/325	20 mg (po)	2.25–4.5 mg oxycodone q6h	Monitor renal function and use gastric protection
Oxycodone + ibuprofen▲ *(Combunox)* T: 5/400	20 mg (po)	1 tab po q6h; do not exceed 4 tabs in 24h	Monitor renal function and use gastric protection. Tx not to exceed 7 d.
Tramadol▲BC *(Ultram)* T: 50	150–300 mg (po)	25 mg q4–6h; not >300 mg for those >75 yr old	Not first-line tx; consider before starting pure opioids.
Tramadol[BC] + APAP▲ *(Ultracet)* T: 37.5/325	37.5/325 mg (po)	2 tabs q4–6h; max 8 tabs/d	Avoid in seizure disorders.[BC] Risk of seizures (↑risk with higher doses and combination with SSRI/TCA) and orthostatic hypotension; with-drawal symptoms can occur
			Risk of serotonin syndrome when combined with SSRIs.
			Risk of suicide for patients who are addiction prone, taking tranquilizers or antidepressant drugs, and at risk of overdosage. Additive effects with alcohol and other opioids.
			Caution: total APAP dosage should not exceed 4 g/d.
			When CrCl <30 mL/min, reduce dose for IR; Avoid ER.[BC]

(cont.)

Table 100. Principles of Analgesic Management in Older Adults (cont.)	
Drug Class and Dosing	**Practical Considerations**
Adjuvants (**Table 101**)	Consider adjuvant analgesics, including antidepressants and anticonvulsants, for patients with neuropathic pain or mixed pain syndromes, or refractory persistent pain.
	Tailor to pain characteristics/etiology and risk factors
	Effects may be enhanced when used in combination with other analgesics and/or nondrug strategies.
	Select agents with lowest AE profiles.
	Begin low and titrate slowly; allow adequate therapeutic trial (eg, 2–3 wk for onset of efficacy).

Step 3: Treatment of Moderate to Severe Pain (Score 4–10), pain not alleviated with nondrug interventions and medicine from Step 2, and severe enough to impact function and quality of life

Opioids	Patients with moderate to severe pain, pain-related functional impairment, or diminished quality of life due to pain should be considered for opioid tx when other recommended tx approaches prove unsuccessful. Long-term safety of opioid use in persistent pain in older adults has not been established.
	Don't prescribe opioid analgesics as long-term tx for chronic noncancer pain until the risks are considered and discussed with the patient.[CW]
	Risk of fall or fracture, increased risk of hospitalization relative to NSAIDs, constipation, and other adverse effects impact tx success. Avoid in patients with hx of falls or fractures, except for pain management due to recent fractures or joint replacement.[BC]
	Institute fall prevention when starting opioids due to increased risk of fracture in the first 2 wk of short-acting opioid tx (See Falls Prevention).
	Medications with long half-life or depot effects (eg, methadone, levorphanol, transdermal fentanyl) used and titrated cautiously, with close supervision of effects; duration of effects may exceed usual dose intervals because of reduced metabolism and clearance.
	Assess for ongoing attainment of tx goals, adverse effects, and safe and responsible medication use.
	Tx not resulting in functional improvement should be tapered or discontinued and other tx options explored.

Drug/Formulations	**MS Equiv[a] (Route)**	**Starting Dosage for Opioid-Naïve**	**Comments**
Morphine *(MSIR, Astramorph PF, Duramorph, Infumorph, Roxanol, OMS Concentrate, MS/L, RMS, MS/S)* C: 15, 30; soluble T: 15, 30; S: 10 mg/5 mL, 20 mg/5 mL, 100 mg/5 mL, 4 mg/mL, 20 mg/mL; Sp: 5, 10, 20, 30; Inj	30 mg (po), 10 mg (IV, IM, SC)	5 mg po q4h; 1–2 mg IV q3–4h; 2.5–5 mg IM, SC q4h; 5–10 mg Sp q3–4h	Not recommended in renal failure; metabolites accumulate

(cont.)

Table 100. Principles of Analgesic Management in Older Adults (cont.)

Drug/Formulations	MS Equiv[a] (Route)	Starting Dosage for Opioid-Naïve	Comments
Hydromorphone▲ *(Dilaudid, Hydrostat)* T: 2, 4, 8; S: 5 mg/5 mL; Sp: 3; Inj	7.5 mg (po), 1.5 mg (IV, IM, SC), 6 mg (rectal)	1–2 mg po q3–6h; 0.1–0.3 mg IV q2–3h; 0.4–0.5 mg IM, SC q4–6h; 3 mg Sp q4–8h	Considered safer in renal insufficiency
Oxymorphone *(Opana, Opana injectable)* T: 5, 10; Sp: 5; Inj	10 mg (po), 1 mg (IV, IM, SC)	5 mg po q4–6h; 0.5 mg IM, IV, SC q4–6h	Use carefully in renal failure and liver impairment
			ER option with abuse deterrent properties
Tapentadol *(Nucynta)* T: 50, 75, 100	20 mg (po)	50 mg q4–6h	Dual mechanism: μ agonist/ norepinephrine reuptake inhibitor
			Risk of serotonin syndrome when combined with serotonergic drugs; nausea, vomiting, constipation, dizziness, somnolence
			Maximum dose: IR 600 mg/d, ER 500 mg/d; titrate off ER formulation
			Lowest available dose may be high in opioid-naive patients in unmonitored settings; additional caution is warranted to observe for signs of excessive sedation.

Drug Class and Dosing	Practical Considerations
Extended Release and Long-Acting Opioids	FDA label indication for ER opioids for management of pain severe enough to require daily, around-the-clock, long-term opioid tx and for which alternative tx options are inadequate.
	ER formulation should ONLY be used in opioid tolerant patients (ie, those taking at least 60 mg/d of oral morphine, 25 mcg/h of transdermal fentanyl, 30 mg/d of oral oxycodone, 8 mg/d of oral hydromorphone, 25 mg/d of oral oxymorphone, or an equianalgesic dosage of another opioid for ≥1 wk.)
	Note: Conversion from any oral immediate-release opioid should be based on conversion ratios; start by administering 50% of calculated total daily dose of ER opioid, and titrate until adequate pain relief is achieved with tolerable adverse effects.

Drug/Formulations	MS Equiv[a] (Route)	Starting Dosage for Opioid-Naïve	Comments
ER Hydrocodone bitartate *(ZohydroER)* C: 10, 15, 20, 30, 40, 50	30 mg (po)	10 mg q12h[d]	For opioid-tolerant patients, calculate based on conversion factors.

(cont.)

Table 100. Principles of Analgesic Management in Older Adults (cont.)

Drug/Formulations	MS Equiv[a] (Route)	Starting Dosage for Opioid-Naïve	Comments
ER Hydromorphone (Exalgo) T: 8, 12, 16, 32	7.5 mg (po)	8 mg q24h	Starting dose for ER formulation equivalent to total daily dose of oral hydromorphone, taken q24h; titrate every 3–4 d to adequate pain relief. Tablets should be swallowed whole or can lead to rapid release and absorption of potentially fatal dose of hydromorphone.
ER Morphine▲			
(MS Contin) T: CR 15, 30, 60, 100, 200	MS Contin: 30 mg (po)	MS Contin: 20–30 mg q24h, 15 mg q12h	
(Kadian) C: ER 10, 20, 30, 50, 60, 80, 100, 200	Kadian: 30 mg (po)	Kadian: 20 mg q24h	
(Oramorph SR) T: SR 15, 30, 60, 100	Oramorph SR: 30 mg (po)	Oramorph SR: 15 mg q24h	
(Avinza) ER 30, 45, 60, 75, 90, 120	Avinza: 60 mg (po)	Avinza: 30 mg q24h	
ER Morphine/naltrexone (Embeda) C: ER 20/0.8, 30/1.2, 50/2, 60/2.4, 80/3.2, 100/4	30 mg (po)	20 mg/0.8 mg q12–24h	These products contain an opioid antagonist intended to decrease misuse/abuse. If the product is used as intended and taken whole, analgesia is not affected. If the product is altered (eg, chewed, crushed, dissolved), the opioid antagonist is released and can reverse analgesic effects.
ER Oxycodone▲ (OxyContin) T: CR 10, 20, 40, 80, 160	20–30 mg (po)	20 mg q24h, 10 mg q12h	
Oxycodone/ acetaminophen ER (Xartemis XR) T: 7.5/325	20 mg (po)	2 T q12h	Portion released immediately and remainder over dosing interval
Oxycodone/naloxone (Targiniq ER) T:10/5, 20/10, 40/20	20 mg (po)	10 mg q12h in opioid naive; adjust in opioid tolerant (see package insert)	
Oxymorphone ER▲ (Opana ER) T: 5, 10, 20, 30, 40	10 mg (po)	5 mg q12h; titrate dosage by 5-mg increments q12h	Use carefully in renal failure and liver impairment

(cont.)

Table 100. Principles of Analgesic Management in Older Adults (cont.)

Drug/Formulations	MS Equiv[a] (Route)	Starting Dosage for Opioid-Naïve	Comments
Tapentadol ER *(Nucynta ER)* T: 50, 100, 150, 200, 250	20 mg (po)	50 mg q12h	
Tramadol ER[BC] *(Ultram ER, ConZip)* T: 100, 200, 300 C: 150	150–300 mg (po)	100 mg q24h or calculate 24-h total dose for immediate-release tramadol	Avoid in seizure disorders.[BC] When CrCl <30 mL/min, reduce dose for IR; Avoid ER.[BC]
Transdermal buprenorphine *(Butrans Transdermal System CIII)* 5, 10, 15, 20 mcg/h	NA (see package insert)	5 mcg/h if <30 MS equiv for opioid-naive or if taking <30 mg oral morphine equiv; 10 mcg/h if 30–80 oral MS equiv with 1 pch × 7 d.	Indicated for severe, chronic pain requiring around-the-clock analgesia for extended time. Monitor for respiratory depression, especially within the first 24–72 h of initiation or dose escalation. Initiate dosing regimen on individual basis and consult conversion instructions; do not titrate dose until exposed continuously for 72 h at previous dose. Caution if switching from pure μ-opioid agonist. Do not exceed one 20 mcg/h. *Butrans* system due to the rise of QTc prolongation. Avoid exposing *Butrans* application site and surrounding area to direct external heat sources (eg, heating pads). Temperature-dependent increases in buprenorphine release from the system may result in overdose and death. Careful patient selection because of abuse potential—monitor for signs of misuse, abuse, and addiction. Taper dose gradually every 7 d to D/C tx.

(cont.)

Table 100. Principles of Analgesic Management in Older Adults (cont.)

Drug/Formulations	MS Equiv[a] (Route)	Starting Dosage for Opioid-Naïve	Comments
Transdermal fentanyl[▲] *(Duragesic)* 12 mcg/h, 25 mcg/h, 50 mcg/h, 75 mcg/h, 100 mcg/h	NA (see package insert)	12 mcg/h or higher q72h (if able to tolerate 60 mg oral morphine equiv/24 h)	Not recommended for tx of acute pain.
			Do not use in opioid-naive patients.
			Acceptable in renal failure; monitor carefully if using long term.
			Caution: Active ingredient accumulates in subcutaneous fat; thus, duration of action may be >17 h.
			If transitioning from IV fentanyl to pch, the hourly rate is the pch dose (eg, if patient is taking 50 mcg/h IV, start with a 50-mcg pch).
			Incomplete cross-tolerance already accounted for in conversion to fentanyl; when converting to other opioid from fentanyl, generally reduce the equianalgesic amount by 50%.
			Remove pch before MRI.
Methadone		For details on methadone prescribing and monitoring, see geriatricscareonline.org	Methadone is an option if other long-acting agents are not affordable, but should be used with extreme caution and only with expertise and monitoring ability because of highly variable half-life, risk of dose accumulation, and high interpatient variability. Associated with prolonged QTc interval.
			Acceptable in renal insufficiency.
			Consider palliative care or pain service.

Drug Class and Dosing	Practical Considerations
Rapid-acting opioids	Do not use in opioid-naïve patients. Use is for breakthrough pain in those on opioid tx.

(cont.)

Drug/Formulations	MS Equiv[a] (Route)	Starting Dosage for Opioid-Naïve	Comments
Fentanyl *(Actiq)* Loz on a stick: 200, 400, 600, 800, 1200, 1600 mcg	NA	Suck on 200 mcg loz over 15 min, effect within 10 min	
Fentanyl *(Abstral, Fentora)* sl or buccal: 100, 200, 300, 400, 600, 800 mcg	NA	100 mcg	
Fentanyl *(Lazanda)* Nasal spr: 100, 400 mcg/10 mcL	NA	100 mcg	
Fentanyl *(Subsys)* sl spr: 100, 200, 400, 600, 800 mcg	NA	100 mcg	
Fentanyl *(Onsolis)* Buccal film: 200, 400, 600, 800, 1200 mcg	NA	One 200-mcg film, titrate using multiples of the 200-mcg film until patient reaches a dose that provides adequate analgesia with tolerable AEs; do not use >4 of the 200-mcg films simultaneously	
Fentanyl HCl iontophoretic transdermal system (ITS) System pch with battery contains 80 doses of 40 mcg each	NA	40-mcg dose with 10-min lockout through electrical stimulus	

[a] MS Equiv = morphine sulfate (MS) equivalent dose: morphine equivalency = dose of opioid equivalent to 10 mg of parenteral morphine or 30 mg of oral morphine with chronic dosing.

NA = not applicable

Administration and Dosing of Opioids

Initiating

- Select least invasive route (usually oral) and fast-onset, short-acting analgesics for episodic or breakthrough pain.
- Begin with lowest dose possible, usually 25–50% adult dose, increasing slowly.
- Titrate dose on basis of persistent need for and use of medications for breakthrough pain. If using ≥3 doses/d of breakthrough pain medication, consider increased dosage of ER medication.

Changing

- Use long-acting or SR analgesics for continuous pain after stabilizing dose with short-acting opioid. Administer around-the-clock for continuous pain.

- Use morphine equivalents (MS Equiv) as a common denominator for all dose conversions to avoid errors, and titrate to effectiveness. See www.hopweb.org.
- When changing opioids, decrease equivalent analgesic dose by 25–50% because of incomplete cross-tolerance.

Tapering

- Opioid analgesics should not be discontinued abruptly. Gradual tapering is necessary to avoid withdrawal symptoms (eg, agitation, anxiety, muscle aches, runny nose/tearing, nausea, insomnia, abdominal cramps, diaphoresis, tachycardia, HTN).
- Opioid doses exceeding 100 mg of morphine sulfate equivalents may increase risk of overdose and should prompt consideration of tapering and referral to pain specialist.
- Approach to weaning off long-term opioid use can range from a slow 10% dose reduction per wk to a more rapid 25–50% reduction every 2–3 d. Decreasing the daily dosage by 10–20% each day for 10 d can wean most patients without adverse responses. Adapt based on comorbidities and withdrawal symptoms when process is begun.
- Tapering may require conversion to short-acting opioids. For patients at cardiovascular risk, a slower taper with close monitoring for sympathetic hyperactivity is recommended, and low-dose clonidine may be useful in preventing some of the physiologic (and symptomatic) stress related to opioid withdrawal.

Management of Opioid Adverse Events

- Anticipate, prevent, and vigorously treat AEs; older adults more sensitive to AEs.
- Warn about risk of APAP toxicity when using combination products and importance of including all OTC products with APAP in daily APAP total (not to exceed 4 g/d in healthy older adults).
- Monitor for dry mouth, constipation, sedation, nausea, delirium, urinary retention, and respiratory depression. Growing evidence of concerns related to cognitive impairment, sleep, endocrine dysfunction (hypogonadism), immunosuppression, and hyperalgesia.
- Tolerance can develop to most adverse effects of opioids, except constipation. Reduce dosage and/or consider adding medication to counter medication-related AEs, if troublesome, until tolerance develops.
- Warn patient about risk of sedation with opioids that gradually resolves within 1 wk.
- Begin prophylactic, osmotic, or stimulant laxative when initiating opioid tx (**Table 59**); if patient has sufficient fluid intake, cautiously increase fiber or psyllium▲; titrate laxative dose up with opioid dose.
- Instances of severe opioid-induced constipation may respond to oral naloxone 0.8–2 mg q12h, titrated to a max of 12 mg/d given in water or juice, along with routine bowel regimen.
- Opioid antagonists approved to treat opioid-induced constipation (OIC). Careful titration and observation are necessary because some patients may experience partial analgesia reversal (also p 126).
  - Methylnaltrexone bromide *(Relistor)* approved for tx OIC in adults with chronic, noncancer pain and those with advanced illness receiving palliative care SC 8 mg (38–62 kg) to 12 mg (62–114 kg) and 0.15 mg/kg for other weights with one dose q48h.
  - Oral naloxegol *(Movantik)* 25 mg po once daily is indicated for the tx of OIC in adult patients with chronic noncancer pain. D/C all maintenance laxative tx before initiating naloxegol. Laxatives can be used as needed if no response to naloxegol after 3 d.

Prevention of Opioid Misuse and Withdrawal

Opioids should be initiated as a trial, to be continued if progress is documented toward functional goals, and if there is no evidence of complications, including misuse or diversion.

An ongoing tx plan for all patients receiving opioid tx that includes the following is good practice:

- Assess for risk of opioid misuse or abuse (eg, Opioid Risk Tool [ORT]); Substance Abuse, p 323, Appendix.
  ○ Score of 8 or higher is considered high risk. Prescribe opioids only after all other tx modalities exhausted, under close supervision—ideally in consultation with a pain or addiction specialist.
  ○ In at-risk patients requiring opioid management, abuse-deterrent agents may be useful (eg, *Embeda, Targiniq ER*)
- Perform urine drug testing before initiating opioid tx and at least yearly (be aware that false-negative and -positive results are possible, so cautious interpretation is needed)
- Consider a written opioid agreement (www.aapainmanage.org/literature/Articles/OpioidAgreement.pdf).
- Consult state prescription monitoring program to evaluate multisourcing.
- Physical dependence is expected with long-term opioid use (can occur with several weeks of around-the-clock use); it is not the same as substance abuse or addiction.
- In at-risk patients, adjust prescribing boundaries (eg, weekly pickup at local pharmacy).
- Risk evaluation and mitigation strategy (REMS) requires companies to provide educational materials for patients on safe use of long-acting or extended-release opioids. Prescriber training provided but not required.
- Monitor pain and signs of misuse during ongoing opioid use (eg, Current Opioid Misuse Measure [COMM]; www.painedu.org).

Table 101. Adjuvant Medications for Pain Relief in Older Adults[a]

Class, Medication	Indications/Comments
Anticonvulsants (also **Table 94** and p 224)	Indicated for neuropathic pain, fibromyalgia If one does not work, try another. Numerous drug interactions (fewer for gabapentin and pregablin); adverse effects include sedation, dizziness, peripheral edema Avoid in hx of falls or fractures.[BC]
Carbamazepine▲ *(Tegretol)* *(Tegretol XR; Carbatrol)*	Many drug interactions; mood stabilizer; used for trigeminal or glossopharyngeal neuralgia; may cause SIADH, thrombocytopenia, leukopenia
Oxcarbazepine *(Trileptal, Oxtellar XR)*	
Gabapentin▲ *(Neurontin)* (p 228)	Recommended as first line or as co-analgesic in postherpetic neuralgia and/or dermatosis papulosa nigra. Slow titration based on analgesic response increasing every 3–7 d (may take several mo). If CrCl >15–29 mL/min: dose at 200–700 mg/d; if CrCl >30–59 mL/min, dose at 200–700 q12h; if CrCl ≤15 mL/min, dose at 100–300 mg/d
Pregabalin *(Lyrica)* (p 228)	Primary indication is for management of post-herpetic neuralgia, diabetic peripheral neuropathy, and fibromyalgia; fewer AEs and titration to analgesic effect more rapid. Start 100 mg/d in divided doses increasing to 300 mg/d over several wks. Effect in 3–4 wk.
Lamotrigine▲ *(Lamictal)*	Prolongs PR interval; risk of severe rash

(cont.)

Table 101. Adjuvant Medications for Pain Relief in Older Adults[a] (cont.)

Class, Medication	Indications/Comments
Antidepressants (Table 41)	Indicated for neuropathic pain, fibromyalgia, chronic musculoskeletal pain, including osteoarthritis and chronic low-back pain, depression. TCAs often helpful for migraine or tension headaches and arthritic conditions. Avoid tertiary amines due to increased AEs.
	Of TCAs, low-dose desipramine[▲] or nortriptyline[▲] best side effect profile, however Avoid due to anticholinergic, sedating and orthostatic hypotension.[BC]
	Older adults more sensitive to anticholinergic effects, use cautiously with comorbid disease.
	SNRIs lower anticholinergic properties.
	Data on SSRIs for pain management lacking, but may increase bleeding risk if combined with ASA or NSAIDs; taper dose before discontinuing.
Duloxetine *(Cymbalta)*	Most common AEs: nausea, dizziness, dry mouth, constipation, diarrhea, urinary hesitancy; significant drug-drug interactions
Venlafaxine[▲] *(Effexor) (Effexor* XR)	Low anticholinergic activity; minimal sedation and hypotension; may increase BP and QT_c; may be useful when somatic pain present; EPS, withdrawal symptoms, hyponatremia
Milnacipran *(Savella)*	Dual reuptake inhibitor; used to treat pain of fibromyalgia; contraindicated with MAOI or within 2 wk of MAOI discontinuation
Corticosteroids (Table 49)	Low-dose medical management may be helpful in inflammatory pain conditions. Intraarticular injection first- line tx for hip OA
Counterirritants	Use in localized musculoskeletal pain. May be effective for arthritic pain, but effect limited when pain affects multiple joints. Apply to affected area and monitor for skin injury, especially if used with heat or occlusive dressing.
✓Camphor-menthol-phenol[▲] *(Sarna)* *	lot: camphor 5%, menthol 5%, phenol 5% prn; max q6h
✓Camphor and phenol[▲] *(Campho-Phenique)**	S: camphor 5%, phenol 4.7% prn; max q8h
✓Methyl salicylate and menthol[▲]	Monitor for salicylate toxicity if used over several areas.
(*Ben-Gay* oint*, *Icy Hot* crm*)	methyl salicylate 18.3%, menthol 16% q6–8h
(*Ben-Gay* extra strength crm*)	methyl salicylate 30%, menthol 10% q6–8h
✓Trolamine salicylate[▲] (*Aspercreme* rub*)	trolamine salicylate 10% q6h or more frequently
Skeletal Muscle Relaxants	Limited evidence of effectiveness, predominantly sedating with limited analgesic effect. Recommended for short-term use to relieve acute pain associated with true spasticity (baclofen and tizanidine may be useful). Avoid or use with caution in older adults due to limited efficacy and adverse effects.[BC] Monitor for muscle weakness, urinary function, cognitive effects, sedation, orthostasis; potential for many drug-drug interactions. Avoid abrupt discontinuation because of CNS irritability.
Baclofen[▲] *(Lioresal)*	T: 10, 20; Inj 5 mg up to q8h

(cont.)

Table 101. Adjuvant Medications for Pain Relief in Older Adults[a] (cont.)	
Class, Medication	**Indications/Comments**
Tizanidine▲ *(Zanaflex)*	T: 2, 4; 2 mg up to q8h
Topical Analgesic	Temporary tx of minor pain associated with muscles and joints due to backache, strains, sprains, cramps, arthritis; pain associated with diabetic neuropathy
✓Capsaicin▲ (eg, *Capsin, Capzasin, No Pain-HP, R-Gel, Zostrix, Qutenza*) crm, lot, gel, roll-on: 0.025%, 0.075%; cutaneous pch 8% q6–8h	Only use in dermal neuropathic pain. Renders skin and joints insensitive by depleting and preventing reaccumulation of substance P in peripheral sensory neurons; may cause burning sensation (which is intolerable to some) up to 2 wk; instruct patient to wash hands after application to prevent eye contact; do not apply to open or broken skin. Pch should be applied by health professional, using a local anesthetic, to the most painful skin areas (max of 4 pch). Apply for 30 min to feet, 60 min to other locations. Risk of significant rise in BP after placement; monitor patient for at least 1 h.
✓Lidocaine *(Lidoderm)* transdermal pch 5% 12 h on, 12 h off; up to 24 h on	Used for neuropathic pain, may be helpful for low-back pain, osteoarthritis. Monitor for rash or skin irritation; potential for systemic absorption; dosing limit of 3 pch applied 12h/d
Neuromuscular Blocking Agent	Injected into muscles to treat myofascial pain syndrome resulting from skeletal muscle spasm and migraines when source is neck or facial muscles
Onabotulinumtoxin A *(Botox)*	Dosing individualized based on muscle affected, severity of muscle activity, and prior experience; not to exceed 360 U q12–16 wk
Antiemetic/Cannabinoid	
Dronabinol *(Marinol)*	Chronic pain. Limited evidence but effective in controlling cancer and noncancer persistent pain. C: 2.5, 5, 10; 10 mg 3×/d to 4×/d

✓ = preferred for treating older adults

*Available OTC

[BC]Avoid

[a] Useful for moderate and/or severe pain depending on pain etiology.

DEFINITION

"Palliative care means patient and family-centered care that optimizes quality of life by anticipating, preventing and treating suffering. Palliative care throughout the continuum of illness involves addressing physical, intellectual, emotional, social and spiritual needs to facilitate patient autonomy, access to information and choice." (From National Quality Forum's *National Framework and Preferred Practices for Palliative and Hospice Care*, 2013.)

PRINCIPLES

• Initiate palliative care at the time of diagnosis of serious or life-threatening disease.
• Support, educate, and treat both patient and family.
• Address physical, psychologic, social, and spiritual needs.
• Use comprehensive, interprofessional team (physicians, nurses, social workers, chaplain, pharmacist, physical and occupational therapists, dietitian, family and caregivers, volunteers).
• Focus on symptom management, comfort, meeting goals, completion of "life business," healing relationships, and bereavement.
• Make care available 24 h/d, 7 d/wk.
• Educate, plan, and document advance directives; final wishes; healthcare and financial proxy; family awareness of decisions.
• Coordinate care among providers. Help integrate potentially curative, disease-modifying, and palliative tx.
• Offer bereavement support.
• Provide therapeutic environment (palliation can be given in any location).
• Advocate comprehensive palliative care for all suffering patients with serious illness, especially those dying.

QUALITY OF LIFE

Ways to help patient and family enhance quality of life with chronic illness and/or at the end of life:

• Communicate, listen
• Teach stress management, coping
• Use all available resources
• Support decision making
• Encourage conflict resolution
• Help complete unfinished business
• Urge focus on non–illness-related affairs
• Urge focus on one day at a time
• Help anticipate grief, losses
• Help focus on attainable goals
• Encourage spiritual practices
• Promote physical, psychologic comfort
• Refer to PT

DECISIONS ABOUT PALLIATIVE CARE

Follow principles involved in informed decision making (**Figure 2**) to determine decisional capacity (p 10).

When to Communicate Bad News

Patients need to be alerted to the expected trajectory of their serious or life threatening disease, and advanced care planning should be initiated at the time of first diagnosis. Updates on the progression of the patient's disease along the trajectory of the illness should be communicated with the patient and their family at least annually or more frequently depending on the needs of the patient.

Communicating Bad News (SPIKES)

S=Setting: Prepare for discussion by ensuring all information/facts/data are available. Deliver in person in private area without interruptions or physical barriers. Determine individuals who patient may want involved.

P=Establish patients' perception of their illness (knowledge and understanding) by asking open-ended questions. Use vocabulary patient uses when breaking bad news.

I=Secure invitation to impart medical information. Determine what/how much patient wants to know.

K=Deliver knowledge and information in sensitive, straightforward manner; avoid technical language and euphemisms. Check for understanding after small chunks of information and clarify concepts and terms.

E=Use empathetic and exploratory responses; use active listening, encourage expression of emotions, acknowledge patient's feelings.

S=Strategize and summarize and organize an immediate tx plan addressing patient's concerns and agenda. Provide opportunity to raise important issues. Reassess understanding of condition and tx plan and determine need for further education and follow-up with patient and family.

Hospice Referral

- Patients, families, or other healthcare providers can be referred for required physician's certification of limited life expectancy (prognosis of ≤6 mo for most hospice programs [**Table 102**]) is required.
- Encourage nursing home staff to interview residents to determine goals, preferences, and palliative care needs suggestive of appropriateness for hospice. Discuss patient's wishes with primary care provider and evaluate whether patient meets hospice criteria. Fax request for hospice referral to primary care provider are effective.
- Referral is appropriate when curative tx is no longer indicated (ie, ineffective, AEs too burdensome) and life is limited to months.
- Course of disability in last year of life does not follow predictable pattern based on the condition leading to death. For advanced dementia, high levels of disability are common. However, for cancer, organ failure, frailty, sudden death, and other conditions, very low levels of disability are seen only a few months before death. Need for services to assist with ADLs is as great for persons dying from organ failure and frailty as for those with cancer and greater for those with advanced dementia.
- Hospice must be accepted by the patient or family, or both, and can be rescinded at any time.
- Hospice provides palliative medications, durable medical supplies and equipment, team member visits as needed and desired by patient and family (physician, nurses, home health aide, social worker, chaplain), and volunteer services.
- Optimal hospice care requires adequate time in the program; referral when death is imminent does not take full advantage of hospice care.
- Hospice care is usually delivered in patient's home, but it can be delivered in a nursing home or residential care facility (long-term care, assisted living) or in an inpatient setting (hospice-specific or contracted facility) if acuity or social circumstances warrant.
- Coverage of hospice services variable (eg, inpatient availability, amount of home care, sites for care), so determine and discuss with patient/family.

Table 102. Typical Trajectory and Hospice Eligibility for Selected Diseases

Disease	Typical Determinants for Hospice Eligibility*
Cancer	Clinical findings of malignancy with widespread, aggressive, or progressive disease evidenced by increasing symptoms, worsening laboratory values, and/or evidence of metastatic disease Impaired performance status with a Palliative Performance Scale (PPS; p 342) value of ≤70% Refuses further curative tx or continues to decline in spite of definitive tx
Dementia	Have all of the following characteristics • FAST Scale Stage 7 (p 343) Have had 1 of the following in the past 12 mo: • aspiration pneumonia • pyelonephritis or other upper UTI • decubitus ulcer (multiple, stage 3–4) • fever (recurrent after antibiotics) • inability to maintain sufficient fluid and calorie intake with 10% weight loss during previous 6 mo, or serum albumin < 2.5 g/dL • septicemia
Failure to thrive**	BMI <22 kg/m² and either declining enteral/parenteral nutritional support or not responding to such support, despite adequate caloric intake Karnofsky score ≤40 or PPS value ≤40% (p 341) Must have chronic disease diagnosis (eg, HF, COPD)
End-stage heart disease	Optimally treated for HD or either not candidates for surgical procedures or who decline those procedures (optimally treated: not on vasodilators have a medical reason for refusing [eg, hypotension or renal disease]) *and* Significant symptoms of recurrent HF at rest and classified as NYHA Class IV (ie, unable to carry on any physical activity without symptoms, symptoms present at rest, symptoms increase if any physical activity is undertaken) Documentation of following will support eligibility but not required: • tx-resistant symptomatic supraventricular or ventricular arrhythmia • hx of cardiac arrest or resuscitation or unexplained syncope • brain embolism of cardiac origin • concomitant HIV disease • documented ejection fraction of ≤20%
End-stage liver disease	Prothrombin time >5 sec longer than control, or INR >1.5 *and* serum albumin <2.5 g/dL At least one of the following: ascites, refractory to tx or patient noncompliant; spontaneous bacterial peritonitis; hepatorenal syndrome (elevated Cr and BUN with oliguria [<400 mL/d]) and urine sodium concentration <10 mEq/L; hepatic encephalopathy, refractory to tx, or patient noncompliant; recurrent variceal bleeding despite intensive tx Documentation of the following will support eligibility, but not required: • progressive malnutrition • muscle wasting with reduced strength and endurance • continued active alcoholism (ethanol intake >80 g/d) • hepatocellular carcinoma; hepatitis B positivity (HBsAg) • hepatitis C refractory to interferon tx Awaiting liver transplant may be certified for Medicare hospice benefit, but if donor organ is procured, patient should be discharged from hospice

(cont.)

Table 102. Typical Trajectory and Hospice Eligibility for Selected Diseases (cont.)

Disease	Typical Determinants for Hospice Eligibility*
End-stage pulmonary disease	Disabling dyspnea at rest, poorly or unresponsive to bronchodilators, resulting in decreased functional capacity, eg, bed to chair existence, fatigue, and cough (documentation of FEV_1, after bronchodilator, <30% of predicted is objective evidence for disabling dyspnea, but is not necessary to obtain) **and** Progression of end-stage pulmonary disease, as evidenced by *prior* increased visits to emergency department or *prior* hospitalization for pulmonary infections and/or respiratory failure or increasing physician home visits before initial certification (documentation of serial decrease of FEV_1 >40 mL/yr is objective evidence for disease progression, but is not necessary to obtain) **and** Hypoxemia at rest on room air, as evidenced by pO_2 ≤55 mmHg or O_2 sat ≤88% or hypercapnia, as evidenced by $PaCO_2$ ≥50 mmHg. Values may be obtained from MR within 3 mo. Documentation of the following will support eligibility, but not required: right HF secondary to pulmonary disease (cor pulmonale), unintentional progressive weight loss of >10% of body weight over preceding 6 mo, resting tachycardia >100 bpm
Acute renal failure	Not seeking dialysis or renal transplant or discontinuing dialysis **and** CrCl <10 mL/min (<15 mL/min for DM) **or** Serum Cr >8 mg/dL (>6 mg/dL for DM) Documentation of the following will support eligibility, but not required: • mechanical ventilation • chronic lung disease • advanced liver disease • immunosuppression/AIDS • cachexia • disseminated intravascular coagulopathy • malignancy (other organ system) • advanced cardiac disease • sepsis • albumin <3.5 g/dL • platelet count <25,000 • GI bleeding
Chronic renal failure	Not seeking dialysis or renal transplant or discontinuing dialysis **and** CrCl <10 mL/min (<15 mL/min for DM) **or** Serum Cr >8 mg/dL (>6 mg/dL for DM) (<15 mL/min with comorbid CHF; <20 mL/min for diabetics) Documentation of the following signs and symptoms of renal failure lend support for eligibility: • uremia • intractable hyperkalemia (>7) not responsive to tx • hepatorenal syndrome • oliguria (<400 mL/d) • uremic pericarditis • intractable fluid overload not responsive to tx

(cont.)

Table 102. Typical Trajectory and Hospice Eligibility for Selected Diseases (cont.)

Disease	Typical Determinants for Hospice Eligibility*

Amyotrophic lateral sclerosis (ALS)	Considered terminal stage of ALS (life expectancy 6 mo or less) if patient meets one of the following criteria (characteristics occurring within the 12 mo before initial hospice certification):
	1. Critically impaired breathing capacity evidenced by all the following:
	  • Vital Capacity (VC) <30% of normal
	  • Significant dyspnea at rest
	  • Requires supplemental oxygen at rest
	  • Patient declines artificial ventilation; external ventilation for comfort only
	2. Rapid progression of ALS and critical nutritional impairment
	  a. Rapid progression of ALS evidenced by all the following:
	    • Progression from independent ambulation to wheelchair or bedbound status
	    • Progression from normal to barely intelligible or unintelligible speech
	    • Progression from normal to pureed diet
	    • Progression from independence in most or all ADLs to needing major assistance by caretaker in all ADLs
	  b. Critical nutritional impairment evidenced by all the following:
	    • Oral intake insufficient
	    • Continuing weight loss
	    • Dehydration or hypovolemia
	    • Absence of artificial feeding methods
	3. Rapid progression of ALS (see 2a above) and life-threatening complications:
	  a. Rapid progression of ALS (see 2 above)
	  b. Life-threating complications as demonstrated by one of the following:
	    • Recurrent aspiration pneumonia (with or without tube feedings)
	    • Upper urinary tract infection (pyelonephritis)
	    • Sepsis
	    • Recurrent fever after antibiotic tx
	    • Stage 3 or 4 decubitus ulcer(s)
	May determine life expectancy of 6 mo or less even if the above findings are not present. Comorbidities also support eligibility for hospice care.

Stroke/Coma	Considered in terminal stage of stroke if the meet the following criteria:
	  • Karnofsky Performance Status (KPS) or PPS of 40% or less
	  • Inability to maintain hydration and calorie intake with one of the following:
	    ○ Weight loss >10% in last 6 mo or >7.5% in last 3 mo
	    ○ Serum albumin <2.5 g/dL
	  • Current hx of pulmonary aspiration not responsive to speech language pathology intervention
	  • Sequential calorie counts documenting inadequate caloric/fluid intake;
	  • Dysphagia, which prevents sufficient intake of food and fluids to sustain life in a patient who declines or does not receive artificial nutrition and hydration
	Considered in terminal stage of coma (any etiology) with any 3 of the following on day 3 of the coma:
	  • Abnormal brain stem response
	  • Absent verbal response
	  • Absent withdrawal response to pain
	  • Serum Cr >1.5 mg/dL
	Documentation of the following factors will support eligibility for hospice care:
	  • Medical complications, in the context of progressive clinical decline, within previous 12 mo
	    ○ Aspiration pneumonia
	    ○ Upper UTI (pyelonephritis)
	    ○ Sepsis
	    ○ Refractory stage 3–4 decubitus ulcers
	    ○ Fever recurrent after antibiotics
	  • Diagnostic imaging factors will support poor prognosis after stroke

* May vary depending on fiscal intermediary; additional supportive indications available for most
diagnoses. Source: Adapted from www.montgomeryhospice.org/health-professionals/end-stage-
indicators (extracted from CMS documentation LCD for Hospice-Determining Terminal Status
[L13653]).

** Adult failure to thrive can be used to determine hospice eligibility, but should not be listed as principal
diagnosis.

Advance Directives and Living Wills

- Designed to respect patient's autonomy and determine his/her wishes about future life-sustaining medical tx if unable to indicate wishes. (See Assessment regarding Informed Decision-making and Patient Preferences for Life-sustaining Care, p 10.)
- Written by the patient and documented, although not accepted by emergency medical services as legally valid forms; vary from state to state.

Oral Statements

- Conversations with relatives, friends, and clinicians are most common form; should be thoroughly documented in medical record for later reference.
- Properly verified oral statements carry same ethical and legal weight as those recorded in writing.

Instructional Advance Directives (DNR Orders, Living Wills, POLST, MOLST)

- Do-Not-Resuscitate (DNR) orders written by the physician based on the wishes previously expressed by the individual in his or her advanced directive or living will.
- Physician Orders for Life-Sustaining Treatment (POLST) or Medical Orders for Life-Sustaining Treatment (MOLST) include written instructions about the initiation, continuation, withholding, or withdrawal of particular forms of life-sustaining medical tx.
- POLST documents differ from state to state, but are designed to be recognizable (eg, bright pink; posted on refrigerator), used by first responders, and transferred across settings.
- Clinicians who comply with such directives are provided legal immunity for such actions.
- POLST form can be very useful in formalizing patient preferences (www.polst.org). May be revoked or altered at any time by the patient.
- Key elements of POLST Plan of Care address: cardiopulmonary resuscitation; level of medical intervention desired in the event of an emergency (comfort only, limited tx, or full tx); and use of artificial nutrition and hydration. Some states include use of antibiotics, hospitalization, and mechanical ventilation.
- To determine whether POLST should be completed, ask "Would I be surprised if this person died in the next year?" If no, the POLST is appropriate.

Durable Power of Attorney for Healthcare or Healthcare Proxy

A written document that enables a capable person to appoint someone else to make future medical tx choices for him or her in the event of decisional incapacity (**Figure 2**).

Key Interventions, Treatment Decisions to Include in Advance Directives

- Resuscitation procedures
- Mechanical respiration
- Chemotherapy, radiation tx
- Dialysis
- Simple diagnostic tests
- Pain control
- Blood products, transfusions
- Intentional deep sedation
- ICD and pacemakers

Withholding or Withdrawing Therapy

- There is no ethical or legal difference between withholding an intervention (not starting it) and withdrawing life-sustaining medical tx (stopping it after it has been started).

- Beginning a tx does not preclude stopping it later; a time-limited trial may be appropriate.
- Palliative care should not be limited, even if life-sustaining tx are withdrawn or withheld.
- Decisions on artificial feeding should be based on the same criteria applied to use of ventilators and other medical tx.
- Initiate discussion about pacemaker deactivation only if there is a potential patient benefit; consider the potential negative effects of deactivation before disabling the pacemaker. *Note*: Pacemaker is not a resuscitative device and usually does not keep palliative-care patients alive.
- Reanalyze risk-to-benefit ratio of ICD tx in patients with terminal illness. Life-prolonging tx may no longer be desired.

Euthanasia

- Active euthanasia: direct intervention, such as lethal injection, intended to hasten a patient's death; a criminal act of homicide.
- Passive euthanasia: withdrawal or withholding of unwanted or unduly burdensome life-sustaining tx; appropriate in certain circumstances.
- Assisted suicide: the patient's intentional, willful ending of his or her own life with the assistance of another; a criminal offense in most states.

Death Certificate Completion (see Assessment and Approach chapter, p 13)

- Certification of death at the end of life should be completed by the hospice medical director and provides personal information about the decedent and about circumstances and cause of death.
- Information is important for settlement of estate and provides family members closure, peace of mind, and documentation of the cause of death.

MANAGEMENT OF COMMON END-OF-LIFE SYMPTOMS
Pain

- Primary goal: to alleviate suffering at end of life. See Pain chapter (p 234) for assessment and interventions.
- The most distressing symptom for patients and caregivers
- Placement of Foley catheters, limited repositioning to prevent increased pain are acceptable for comfort measures at the end of life.
- If intent is to relieve suffering, the risk that sufficient medication appropriately titrated will produce an unintended effect (hastening death) is morally acceptable (double effect).
- Alternate routes may be needed, eg, transdermal, transmucosal, rectal, vaginal, topical, epidural, and IT.
- Recommend expert pain management consult if pain not adequately relieved with standard analgesic guidelines and interventions.
- Additional tx may include:
  ◦ radionuclides and bisphosphonates (for metastatic bone pain)
  ◦ radiation tx or chemotherapy directed at source of pain
- Pain crisis: Palliative sedation for intractable pain and suffering is an important option to discuss with patients. Ketamine▲ *(Ketalar)* 0.1 mg/kg IV bolus. Repeat prn q5min. Follow with infusion of 0.015 mg/kg/min IV (if IV access not available, SC at 0.3–0.5 mg/kg). Decrease opioid dosage by 50%. Benzodiazepines may be used to induce sleep state in the event of excruciating pain unrelieved by other options. Observe for problems with increased secretions and treat (p 261).

Weakness, Fatigue

Nonpharmacologic
- Modify environment to decrease energy expenditure (eg, placement of phone, bedside commode, drinks).
- Adjust room temperature to patient's comfort.
- Teach reordering tasks to conserve energy (eg, eating first, resting, then bathing).
- Modify daily procedures (eg, sitting while showering rather than standing).

Pharmacologic
- Treat remediable causes such as pain, medication toxicity, insomnia, anemia, and depression.
- Consider psychostimulants (eg, dextroamphetamine▲ *[Dexedrine]* [Avoid[BC]] 2.5 mg po qam or q12h, methylphenidate▲ *[Ritalin]* 2.5 mg po qam or q12h to start titrate upward to 3×/d or 4×/d prn, or modafinil *[Provigil]* 200 mg qam); monitor for signs of psychosis, agitation, or sleep disturbance. Avoid in insomnia.[BC]

Dysphagia (also p 120)

Nonpharmacologic
- Feed small, frequent amounts of pureed or soft foods.
- Avoid spicy, salty, acidic, sticky, and extremely hot or cold foods.
- Keep head of bed elevated for 30 min after eating. If possible, feed patient sitting upright.
- Instruct patient to wear dentures and to chew thoroughly.
- Use suction machine when necessary.
- Have speech therapist do a bedside swallowing assessment to develop techniques for mouth positioning, swallowing techniques, assistive equipment, and correct consistency of food and beverages.
- For painful mucositis: Do not use magic mouthwash.[CW] Use frequent and consistent oral hygiene; salt or soda mouth rinses.

Pharmacologic
- For oral candidiasis: clotrimazole 10-mg troches▲, 5 doses/d, *or* fluconazole▲ 150 mg po followed by 100 mg/d po × 5 d.
- For severe halitosis: antimicrobial mouthwash; fastidious oral and dental care; treat putative respiratory tract infection with broad-spectrum antibiotics.

Dyspnea (p 286)

Nonpharmacologic
- Teach positions to facilitate breathing, elevate head of bed or sitting position leaning on table, pursed lips breathing with COPD.
- Teach relaxation techniques.
- Eliminate smoke and allergens.
- Ensure brisk air circulation (facial breeze) with a room fan; oxygen is indicated only for symptomatic hypoxemia (ie, SaO_2 <90% by pulse oximetry) or if comfort perceived by patient.
- Do not administer supplemental oxygen to relieve dyspnea in patients with cancer who do not have hypoxia.[CW]
- Use olive oil or swabs, and humidified oxygen, for dry mouth.

Pharmacologic

- Opioids: oral morphine▲ concentration (20 mg/mL: 1/4 to 1/2 mL sl, po; repeat in 15–30 min prn) *or* morphine tabs 5–10 mg po q2h; if oral route not tolerated, nebulized morphine 2.5 mg in 2–4 mL NS *or* fentanyl 25–50 mcg in 2–4 mL NS; *or* IV morphine 1 mg or equivalent opioid q5–10min.
- Bronchodilators (**Table 120**).
- Diuretics, if evidence of volume overload (**Table 29**).
- Anxiolytics (eg, lorazepam▲ po, sl, SC 0.5–2 mg q2–4h or prn); titrate slowly to effect.
- Guaifenesin *(Robitussin)* or nebulized saline to loosen thick secretions.

Constipation (p 125)

- Most common cause: adverse effects of opioids, medications with anticholinergic adverse effects. Use stimulant or osmotic laxative (**Table 59**). Consider enema if no bowel movement for 4 d. Evaluate for bowel obstruction or fecal impaction.
- Opioid-induced constipation not responsive to laxative tx: methylnaltrexone bromide *(Relistor)* SC 8 mg (38–62 kg) to 12 mg (62–114 kg) and 0.15 mg/kg for other weights with 1 dose q48h; also newly approved oral naloxegol *(Movantik)* (**Table 59**).

Bowel Obstruction

Indications for Radiographic Evaluation

- To differentiate between constipation and mechanical obstruction
- To confirm the obstruction, determine site and nature if surgery is being considered

Nonpharmacologic Management

- Nasogastric intubation: only if surgery is being considered, for high-level obstructions, and poor response to pharmacotherapy
- Percutaneous venting gastrostomy: for high-level obstructions and profuse vomiting not responsive to antiemetics
- Palliative surgery
- Hydration: IV or hypodermoclysis

Pharmacologic Management (aimed at specific symptoms)

- Nausea and vomiting: haloperidol▲ *(Haldol)* po, IM 0.5–5 mg (≤10 mg) q4–8h prn; ondansetron▲ *(Zofran)* IV (over 2–5 min) 4 mg q12h, po 8 mg q12h [inj; T: 4, 8, 24; S: 4 mg/5 mL] (**Table 60**).
- Spasm, pain, and vomiting: scopolamine▲ IM, IV, SC 0.3–0.65 mg q4–6h prn; po 0.4–0.8 mg q4–8h prn; transdermal 2.5 cm² pch applied behind the ear q3d [inj; T: 0.4; pch 1.5 mg] *or* hyoscyamine▲ *(Levsin/SL)* sl [T: 0.125; S: 0.125 mg/mL] 0.125–0.25 q6–8h.
- Diarrhea and excessive secretions: loperamide▲ *(Imodium A-D)* (**Table 61**); octreotide▲ *(Sandostatin)* SC 0.15–0.3 mg q12h [inj], very expensive.
- Pain: **Table 100**.
- Inflammation due to malignant obstruction: dexamethasone▲ *(Decadron)* po 4 mg q6h × 5–7 d.

Excessive Secretions

Nonpharmacologic: Positioning and suctioning, prn

Pharmacologic: Glycopyrrolate▲ 0.1–0.4 mg IV, SC q4h prn *or* scopolamine▲ 0.3–0.6 mg SC prn *or* transdermal scopolamine pch q72h *or* atropine▲ 0.3–0.5 mg SC, sl, nebulized q4h prn

Cough (p 285)

Nausea, Vomiting (p 128)

Determine cause to select appropriate antiemetic based on pathway-mediating symptoms and neurotransmitter involved (**Table 60**). For refractory nausea and vomiting (ie, not amenable to other tx), a trial of dexamethasone (2 mg q8h) can be tried; risks are dyspepsia, altered mental status

Do not use topical lorazepam *(Ativan)*, diphenhydramine *(Benadryl)*, haloperidol *(Haldol)* ("ABH") gel for nausea.[CW]

Anorexia, Cachexia, Dehydration

See also Malnutrition (p 187) and volume depletion (p 181). Universal symptom of patients with serious and life-threatening illness.

Note: Percutaneous feeding tubes are not recommended in patients with dementia; instead offer oral assisted feeding.[CW]

Reassure patient and caregivers that appetite abates with age and dehydration is not uncomfortable.

Nonpharmacologic

- Educate patient and family on effects of disease progression resulting in lack of appetite and weight loss.
- Promote interest, enjoyment in meals (eg, alcoholic beverage if desired, involve patient in meal planning, small frequent feedings, cold or semi-frozen nutritional drinks).
- Good oral care is important.
- Alleviate dry mouth with ice chips, popsicles, moist compresses, or artificial saliva.

Pharmacologic

- Corticosteroids: dexamethasone▲ 1–2 mg po q8h; methylprednisolone▲ 1–2 mg po q12h; prednisone▲ 5 mg po q8h. Systematic review finds beneficial in palliative care patients with cancer, but no evidence for use in end-stage nonmalignant disease. Insufficient evidence to recommend any particular corticosteroid or dosing regimen.

Source: Miller S et al. *J Palliat Med* 2014;17(4):482–485.

Note: Avoid prescription appetite stimulants or high-calorie supplements for tx of anorexia or cachexia in older adults; instead, optimize social supports, provide feeding assistance, and clarify patient goals and expectations.[CW]

Altered Mental Status, Delirium (Delirium, p 66)

Anxiety, Depression

- Provide opportunity to discuss feelings, fears, existential concerns
- Referral to appropriate team members (spiritual, nursing)
- Medicate (Anxiety, p 36, and Depression, p 78)

Skin Failure

An event in which the skin and underlying tissue die due to hypoperfusion that occurs concurrent with severe dysfunction or failure of other organs (Langemo DK et al. *Adv Skin Wound Care* 2006;19[4]:206–211).

See Skin Ulcers (p 305) for Chronic Wound Assessment.

Management

- Interdisciplinary approach focused on resident-centered and caregiver-centered outcomes

- Engage in frank discussions regarding prognosis, tx of symptoms, and goals of care
- Manage pain determining if acute pain associated with debridement, associated with care routines, or chronic
- Repositioning to off-load pressure
- Dietary consultation regarding amount of calories and fluid to promote healing, if healing is considered possible
- Avoid wet-to-dry dressings, which can increase bacterial burden and infection
- Recommended dressings: nonadhesive, absorptive, and odor-controlling that prevent dessication of wound bed, protect periwound from maceration, and can be left in place for longer periods (eg, hydrogels, foams, polymeric membrane foams, silicones, alginates)
- Control odor by removing necrotic debris and using antimicrobials, activated charcoals, and external odor absorbers

Source: Fine P. *The Hospice Companion: Best Practices for Interdisciplinary Assessment and Care of Common Problems During the Last Phase of Life*, 2nd edition. Oxford University Press; 2012.

PREOPERATIVE CARE

Surgical Decision-Making

- With the prospect of potential surgery, the patient's tx goals should be determined before surgical consultation.
- Goal setting is predicated on decision-making capacity, patient preferences, and life expectancy (see *Goal-Oriented Care, Life Expectancy, and Medical Decision-Making and Informed Decision-Making and Patient Preferences for Life-Sustaining Care,* p 9–10).
- Cognitive impairment, functional dependence, malnutrition, and frailty are risk factors for adverse outcomes of surgery (eg, mortality, functional decline, institutionalization)
- If surgery is determined to be a potential option that is in accordance with tx goals, additional assessments should be conducted to further estimate surgical risk (see next 3 sections).

Cardiac Risk Assessment in Noncardiac Surgery (2014 ACC/AHA Guidelines)

- Risk of perioperative cardiac complications (eg, MI, death) is related to patient characteristics and type of surgery.
  - Major patient-related risk factors include active HF, LV dysfunction, CAD, and valvular disease.
  - Other patient-related factors include age, renal dysfunction, DM, and poor functional status.
  - Surgeries conferring increased risk include open aortic or other vascular, cardiac, intrathoracic, intraabdominal, major orthopedic, and major GU procedures.
  - Low-risk surgeries (<1% perioperative risk of MI or death) include cataract, endoscopic, breast, dermatologic, and superficial procedures.
- Several tools are available for formal assessment of cardiac risk, including:
  - Revised Cardiac Risk Index (RCRI): score 1 point each for: Cr ≥2 mg/dL, HF, DM, hx of stroke or TIA, CAD, and undergoing intrathoracic, intraabdominal, or suprainguinal vascular surgery. Total score ≥2 confers increased risk.
  - Two risk calculators from the American College of Surgeons are available at www.riskcalculator.facs.org and www.surgicalriskcalculator.com/miorcardiacarrest.
- **Figure 12** shows a suggested algorithm for assessment of cardiac risk.
- Obtain a preoperative ECG for patients with known CAD, arrhythmia, PAD, prior stroke or TIA, or other structural heart disease. ECG is not indicated in patients undergoing low-risk surgery.

Choosing Wisely Recommendations for Preoperative Cardiac Assessment

- Don't perform stress cardiac imaging or advanced noninvasive imaging as a preoperative assessment in patients scheduled to undergo low-risk noncardiac surgery.[CW]
- Patients who have no cardiac hx and good functional status do not require preoperative stress testing before noncardiac thoracic surgery.[CW]
- Don't perform preoperative medical tests for eye surgery unless there are specific medical indications.[CW]

Figure 12. Assessing Cardiac Risk in Noncardiac Surgery

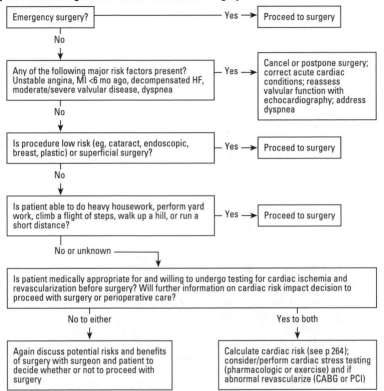

Source: Adapted from Fleisher LA et al. *J Am Coll Cardiol* 2014;pii: S0735–1097(14)05536–3.

- Avoid echocardiograms for preoperative/perioperative assessment of patients with no hx or symptoms of heart disease.[CW]
- Don't order coronary artery calcium scoring for preoperative evaluation for any surgery, irrespective of patient risk.[CW]
- Don't initiate routine evaluation of carotid artery disease before cardiac surgery in the absence of symptoms or other high-risk criteria.[CW]

Pulmonary Risk Assessment

Major risk factors for postoperative pulmonary complications:
- COPD
- ASA Class II – V (I – healthy; II – mild systemic disease; III – moderate/severe systemic disease; IV – life-threatening systemic disease; V – moribund)
- ADL dependence
- HF

- Prolonged (>3 h) surgery; abdominal, thoracic, neurologic, head and neck, or vascular surgery; AAA repair; emergency surgery
- General anesthesia
- Serum albumin <3.5 mg/dL

Minor risk factors:
- Confusion/delirium
- Weight loss >10% in previous 6 mo
- BUN >21 mg/dL or Cr >1.5 mg/dL
- Alcohol use
- Current cigarette use
- Sleep apnea
- Pulmonary hypertension

Reducing risk of postoperative pulmonary complications:
- Smoking cessation 6–8 wk before surgery
- Before cardiac surgery, there is no need for pulmonary function testing in the absence of respiratory symptoms.[CW]
- Preoperative training in incentive spirometry, active-cycle breathing techniques, and forced-expiration techniques
- Postoperative incentive spirometry, chest PT, coughing, postural drainage, percussion and vibration, suctioning and ambulation, intermittent positive-pressure breathing, and/or CPAP
- Nasogastric tube use for patients with postoperative nausea or vomiting, inability to tolerate oral intake, or symptomatic abdominal distention

Other Preoperative Assessments

Screen for Conditions Associated with Postoperative Complications:
- Cognitive impairment: Mini-Cog (p 335)
- Depression: PHQ-2 (p 338)
- Delirium risk factors: p 66
- Alcohol and substance abuse: CAGE questionnaire (p 324)
- Functional impairment: ADLs, IADLs
- Malnutrition: BMI <18.5 kg/m^2, >10% unintentional weight loss in past 6 mo, serum albumin <3.0 g/dL
- Frailty syndrome: at least 3 of the following: ≥10 lb unintentional weight loss in past year (shrinkage), decreased grip strength (weakness), self-reported poor energy and endurance (exhaustion), low weekly energy expenditure (low physical activity), slow walking (slowness)

Routine Laboratory Tests
- Recommended: Hb, Cr, BUN, albumin, or basic metabolic panel if it includes these tests and is cheaper
- Not routinely recommended as should be obtained selectively according to the patient's conditions: electrolytes, CBC, platelets, ABG, PT, PTT
- Don't obtain preoperative chest radiography in the absence of clinical suspicion for intrathoracic pathology.[CW]

Cataract Surgery:
Routine laboratory testing or cardiopulmonary risk assessment is unneccessary for cataract surgery performed under local anesthesia. If patient is on anticoagulation tx, it should not be interrupted. Use of α_1-blockers for BPH (p 275) within 14 d

of cataract surgery is associated with increased risk of complications (intraoperative floppy iris syndrome), but it is unknown if cessation of α_1-blockers before surgery lowers risk.

Antiplatelet Therapy: If surgery poses high bleeding risk (eg, CABG, intracranial surgery, prostate surgery), D/C antiplatelet tx 5–9 d before procedure.

Patients With Bare Metal Stents (BMS) or Drug-Eluting Stents (DES) on Dual Antiplatelet Therapy:

- If possible, postpone surgery until 30 d after BMS were placed and 12 mo after DES were placed.
- If surgery cannot be delayed until 30 d after BMS or 12 mo after DES placement:
  - For most surgeries, which are at low risk of bleeding, continue dual antiplatelet tx.
  - Continue dual antiplatelet tx during the first 6 wk after placement of stent unless risk of bleeding is judged to be higher than benefit of stent thrombosis prevention.
  - For surgeries at intermediate risk of bleeding in patients with DES placement >12 mo previous, D/C clopidogrel or prasugrel 5–7 d before procedure and maintain ASA tx. Because the platelet inhibition of ticagrelor is reversible, it should be stopped 1 d before procedure.
  - For surgeries at high risk of catastrophic bleeding (intracranial, spinal canal, or posterior chamber eye surgery), D/C clopidogrel or prasugrel 5 d before procedure, D/C ticagrelor 1 d before procedure, and consider D/C of ASA 5 d before procedure. Stopping ASA is an individual decision based on patient's risk factors for stent thrombosis and on assessed bleeding risk.
  - If both antiplatelet agents need to be stopped, consider bridging tx (requires admitting patient 2–4 d before surgery) with tirofiban or eptifibatide (**Tables 13** and **19**) in patients felt to be at very high risk of stent thrombosis (consult with cardiology).
  - If antiplatelet tx is discontinued, resume it the day of the surgical procedure.

Anticoagulation:

- For procedures at minimal risk of bleeding (eg, cataract surgery, dermatologic procedures), maintain anticoagulation before surgery.
- Cessation of oral anticoagulation tx before surgery that is assessed to be of significant bleeding risk (eg, abdominal, thoracic, or orthopedic surgery, spinal puncture, liver or kidney biopsy, TURP, or placement of spinal or epidural catheter/port):
  - Stop warfarin 5 d before surgery.
  - Bridging tx with LMWH is based on VTE risk (**Table 103**)
  - DVT tx doses of LMWH (**Table 19**) should be used for bridging tx. Begin LMWH 3 d before surgery; give last preoperative LMWH dose at one-half of total daily dose 24 h before surgery.
  - Stop dabigatran 1–3 d before surgery (2–4 d if CrCl <50 mL/min) and stop apixaban or rivaroxaban 1–2 d before surgery.
- Resumption of anticoagulation tx after surgery:
  - If bridging, resume LMWH 24 h after surgery, longer (48–72 h) with major surgical procedures or difficulty with hemostasis.
  - Resume warfarin, apixaban, rivaroxaban, or dabigatran 12–24 h after surgery if adequate hemostasis.
- Minor dental procedures: stop warfarin 2–3 d before procedure and recommend administration of prohemostatic agent (eg, tranexamic acid) by dentist.

Table 103. Indications for Perioperative Anticoagulation Bridging Therapy (ACCP Guidelines)

Thromboembolic Risk	Patient Conditions Determining Risk	Recommendations for LMWH Bridging Therapy
Low	• No VTE in past 12 mo • AF without prior TIA/stroke and 0–2 SRF • Bileaflet mechanical aortic valve without AF, prior TIA/stroke, or SRF	Not recommended
Intermediate	• VTE in past 3–12 mo • Recurrent VTE • Active malignancy • AF without prior TIA/stroke and with 3–4 SRF • Bileaflet mechanical aortic valve with AF, prior TIA/stroke, or any SRF	Optional according to individual thrombotic and bleeding risk
High	• VTE within past 3 mo • TIA/stroke within 3 mo • Rheumatic heart disease • AF with prior TIA/stroke and 3–4 SRF • Mechanical mitral valve or ball/cage mechanical aortic valve	Recommended

Notes: SRF = stroke risk factors: age ≥75 yr, HTN, DM, HF.

Diuretics and Hypoglycemic Agents: Withhold on day of surgery.

SSRIs: SSRIs increase risk of bleeding with surgery, but discontinuing them before surgery is not recommended unless routine medication review indicates no therapeutic need.

Advance Directives: Establish or update.

Reducing Cardiovascular Complications of Surgery (MI, Ischemia, Death, Infection)

• **β-blockers**: if chronically stable on β-blocker, continue perioperatively at usual dose. In patients with intermediate- or high-risk myocardial ischemia found on stress testing or with RCRI score >3 (p 264), consider initiating long-acting β-blocker days to weeks before surgery (target HR=60) and continuing throughout postoperative period.

• **Statins**: continue as usual dosage for patients already on a statin. Strongly consider prescribing a statin for all patients undergoing vascular surgery or for patients with multiple cardiac risk factors undergoing non–low-risk surgery.

• **Antiplatelets**: before CABG and other high-risk procedures for bleeding (p 272), D/C ASA, clopidogrel, or prasugrel 5 d before surgery and D/C ticagrelor 1 d before surgery. Resume antiplatelets as soon as possible after surgery, within 24 h after CABG.

• **Anticoagulants**: for VTE prophylaxis see **Tables 14 and 15**. For patients already on an anticoagulant, see **Table 103** for management guidelines.

• **Antibiotics**: for endocarditis prophylaxis, see p 272.

POSTOPERATIVE DELIRIUM (also **DELIRIUM**, p 66)

Epidemiology and Risk Factors

• Occurs after 15–50% of surgeries depending on type of procedure.
• Most episodes occur in first 2 postoperative days.
• Occurrences after postoperative day 2 are usually due to surgical complications or alcohol/sedative withdrawal.
• Major risk factors:
  ◦ age ≥80
  ◦ dementia

- recent or unresolved delirium
  - major cardiac, open vascular, major abdominal surgery
  - emergency surgery
  - major surgical complication (eg, cardiogenic shock, prolonged intubation)
  - postoperative ICU stay ≥2 d
- Minor risk factors:
  - age 70–79
  - mild cognitive impairment
  - hx of stroke
  - poor functional status
  - significant comorbidity
  - alcohol or sedative use
  - depressive symptoms
  - abdominal, orthopedic, ENT, gynecologic, urologic surgery
  - general anesthesia
  - regional anesthesia with IV sedation
  - minor surgical complication (eg, infection, minor bleeding)
  - poorly controlled pain
  - exposure to opiates or sedatives
  - postoperative ICU stay <2 d

Diagnosis and Management

- Systematic **preoperative** assessment and risk-lowering interventions have been shown to reduce the rate of postoperative delirium. This can be accomplished through proactive geriatrics team consultation/co-management, nurse-run programs to detect and prevent delirium, and the Hospital Elder Life Program (HELP) intervention (www.hospitalelderlifeprogram.org).
- See pp 66–69 for delirium diagnosis (Confusion Assessment Method or CAM) and management.

PREVENTIVE TESTS AND PROCEDURES

Table 104. Recommended Primary and Secondary Disease Prevention for People Aged 65 and Older

Preventive Strategy	Frequency
USPSTF or CDC[a] Recommendations for Primary Prevention	
ASA to prevent MI and/or stroke[b]	daily in men aged 45–79, and in women aged 55–79 in whom benefit of stroke risk reduction outweighs risk of GI bleeding
BMD (women)	at least once after age 65
BP screening	yearly
Counseling for healthy diet and physical activity	At least once in overweight/obese adults with CVD risk factors
DM screening	every 3 yr in people with BP >135/80 mmHg
Exercise, vitamin D supplementation	adults aged ≥65 at increased risk of falls
Hepatitis A vaccination	at least once in adults at high risk (Section 12 of www.cdc.gov/vaccines/schedules/hcp/imz/adult-conditions.html)
Hepatitis B vaccination	at least once in adults at high risk (Section 13 of www.cdc.gov/vaccines/schedules/hcp/imz/adult-conditions.html)
Herpes zoster vaccination	once after age 60 in immunocompetent people[c]
HIV screening	at least once in person ≥65 with risk factors for HIV
Influenza vaccination	yearly
Lipid disorder screening	every 5 yr, more often in CAD, DM, PAD, prior stroke
Obesity (height and weight)	yearly
Pneumonia vaccination	once at age 65 with PCV13 pneumococcal conjugate vaccine, followed 6–12 mo later by dose of PPSV23 pneumococcal polysaccharide vaccine[d]
Smoking cessation	at every office visit
Tetanus vaccination	every 10 yr
USPSTF[a] Recommendations for Secondary Prevention	
AAA ultrasonography	once between age 65–75 in men who have ever smoked
Alcohol abuse screening	unspecified but should be done periodically
Depression screening	yearly
FOBT/sigmoidoscopy/colonoscopy[cw]	yearly/every 5 yr/every 10 yr from age 50 to age 75[e]
Hepatitis B screening	at least once in adults at high risk (www.uspreventiveservicestaskforce.org/Page/Document/UpdateSummaryFinal/hepatitis-b-virus-screening-2014
Hepatitis C screening	at least once in adults at high risk (www.uspreventiveservicestaskforce.org/Page/Document/UpdateSummaryFinal/hepatitis-c-screening)
Low-dose CT scanning for lung cancer	yearly in persons aged 55–80 with ≥30 pack-yrs of smoking and currently smoke or have quit in the past 15 yr

(cont.)

Table 104. Recommended Primary and Secondary Disease Prevention for People Aged 65 and Older (cont.)

Preventive Strategy	Frequency
Mammography[f]	every 2 yr in women aged 50–74

Other[g] Recommendations for Primary Prevention

BMD (men)	at least once after age 70
Calcium (1200 mg) and vitamin D (≥800 IU) to prevent osteoporosis	daily
Measurement of serum CRP	at least once in people with one CAD risk factor
Omega-3 fatty acids to prevent MI, stroke	at least 2 ×/wk (see MI care, p 41)

Other[g] Recommendations for Secondary Prevention

Skin examination	yearly
Cognitive impairment screening	yearly
Glaucoma screening	yearly
Hearing impairment screening	yearly
Inquiry about falls	yearly
TSH, especially in women	yearly
Visual impairment screening	yearly

[a] US Preventive Services Task Force (www.uspreventiveservicestaskforce.org/Home/GetFileByID/989); Centers for Disease Control and Prevention (www.cdc.gov/vaccines/schedules/hcp/adult.html)

[b] Use with caution in adults ≥80 yr old.[BC]

[c] May vaccinate patients 1 yr after zoster infection; patients on chronic acyclovir, famciclovir, or valacyclovir tx should D/C the medication 24 h before zoster vaccination and resume the medication 14 d after vaccination.

[d] Adults >65 yr old who have already received PPSV23 should receive a dose of PCV13 at least 1 yr after PPSV23 vaccination.

[e] Do not repeat colorectal cancer screening (by any method) for 10 yr after a high-quality colonoscopy is negative in average-risk individuals.[CW]

[f] Mammograms to age 70 are almost universally recommended; many organizations recommend that mammography should be continued in women over 70 who have a reasonable life expectancy.

[g] Not endorsed by USPSTF/CDC for all older adults, but recommended in selected patients or by other professional organizations.

For individualized age- and sex-specific USPSTF prevention recommendations (www.ahrq.gov/professionals/clinicians-providers/guidelines-recommendations/guide)

The USPSTF recommends **against** screening for:
- Asymptomatic bacteriuria with UA
- Bladder cancer with hematuria detection, bladder tumor antigen measurement, NMP22 urinary enzyme immunoassay, or urine cytology
- CAD with ECG, exercise treadmill test, or electron-beam CT in people with few or no CAD risk factors
- Carotid artery stenosis with duplex ultrasonography

- Cervical cancer in women aged ≥65 who have had adequate prior screening or who have had a hysterectomy for benign disease
- Colon cancer with FOBT/sigmoidoscopy/colonoscopy in people ≥85 yr old. Screening may be modestly beneficial in people 76–85 yr old with long life expectancy and no or few comorbidities.
- COPD with spirometry
- Ovarian cancer with transvaginal ultrasonography or CA-125 measurement
- PAD with measurement of ABI
- Pancreatic cancer with ultrasonography or serologic markers
- Prostate cancer with PSA and/or digital rectal examination
- Don't use PET/CT for cancer screening in healthy individuals.[CW]

CANCER SCREENING AND MEDICAL DECISION MAKING

- Many decisions about whether or not to perform preventive activities are based on the estimated life expectancy of the patient. Refer to **Table 7** for life expectancy data by age and sex.
- Most cancer screening tests do not realize a survival benefit for the patient until after 10 yr from the time of the test. Cancer screening should be discouraged or very carefully considered in patients with ≤10 yr of estimated life expectancy.
- Don't recommend screening for breast or colorectal cancer, or prostate cancer (with the PSA test), without considering life expectancy and the risks of testing, overdiagnosis, and overtreatment.[CW]

ENDOCARDITIS PROPHYLAXIS (AHA GUIDELINES)
Antibiotic Regimens Recommended (Table 77)

Table 105. Endocarditis Prophylaxis Regimens	
Situation	**Regimen (Single Dose 30–60 Min Before Procedure)***
Oral	Amoxicillin[▲] 2 g po
Unable to take oral medication	Ampicillin[▲] 2 g, cefazolin[▲] 1 g, or ceftriaxone[▲] 1 g IM or IV
Allergic to penicillins or ampicillin	Cephalexin[▲] 2 g, clindamycin[▲] 600 mg, azithromycin[▲] 500 mg, or clarithromycin[▲] 500 mg po
Allergic to penicillins or ampicillin and unable to take oral medication	Cefazolin[▲] 1 g, ceftriaxone[▲] 1 g, or clindamycin[▲] 600 mg IM or IV

* For patients undergoing invasive respiratory tract procedures to treat an infection known to be caused by *Staph aureus*, or for patients undergoing surgery for infected skin, skin structures, or musculoskeletal tissue, regimen should include an antistaphylococcal penicillin or cephalosporin.

Source: Wilson W et al. *Circulation* (online) 2007: circ.ahajournals.org/content/116/15/1736.full.pdf.

Cardiac Conditions Requiring Prophylaxis

- Prosthetic cardiac valve
- Previous infective endocarditis
- Cardiac transplant recipients who develop cardiac valvulopathy
- Unrepaired cyanotic congenital heart disease
- Repaired congenital heart disease with residual defects at the site or adjacent to the site of a prosthetic patch or device
- Congenital heart disease completely repaired with prosthetic material or device (prophylaxis needed for only the first 6 mo after repair procedure)

Cardiac Conditions Not Requiring Prophylaxis

All cardiac conditions or procedures not listed above.

Procedures Warranting Prophylaxis (only in patients with cardiac conditions listed above)

- Dental procedures requiring manipulation of gingival tissue, manipulation of the periapical region of teeth, or perforation of the oral mucosa (includes extractions, implants, reimplants, root canals, teeth cleaning during which bleeding is expected)
- Invasive procedures of the respiratory tract involving incision or biopsy of respiratory tract mucosa
- Surgical procedures involving infected skin, skin structures, or musculoskeletal tissue

Procedures Not Warranting Prophylaxis

- All dental procedures not listed above
- All noninvasive respiratory procedures
- All GI and GU procedures

ANTIBIOTIC PROPHYLAXIS FOR PATIENTS WITH TOTAL JOINT REPLACEMENTS (TJR)

Procedures/Conditions Prompting Consideration of Antibiotic Prophylaxis

- The American Academy of Orthopedic Surgeons in conjunction with the American Dental Association recommend that clinicians consider discontinuing the practice of routine antibiotic prophylaxis in patients with prior TJR who are undergoing dental procedures (www.orthoguidelines.org/topic?id=1002).
  - Bacteremias are produced not just by dental procedures, but also by common daily activities such as tooth brushing.
  - While antibiotic prophylaxis reduces bacteremia after dental procedures, there is no evidence that withholding antibiotics or dental procedures themselves are associated with prosthetic knee or hip infections.
- Antibiotic prophylaxis should be considered for patients with prior TJR, regardless of when joint was replaced, who are undergoing ophthalmic, orthopedic, vascular, GI, head and neck, gynecologic, or GU procedures.
- Additional risk factors for considering prophylaxis in patients with prior TJR: immunocompromised state; disease-, radiation-, or drug-induced immunosuppression; inflammatory arthropathies; malnourishment; hemophilia; HIV infection; type 1 DM; malignancy; megaprostheses; comorbidities (eg, DM, obesity, smoking)
- Conditions not requiring prophylaxis: patients with pins, plates, or screws

Suggested Prophylactic Regimens

- Dental procedures (see those listed on p 272 for endocarditis): amoxicillin[▲], cephalexin[▲], or cephradine[▲] 2 g po 1 h before procedure
- Prophylactic antibiotic recommendations for other types of procedures vary by procedure (Antimicrobial Prophylaxis for Surgery. *The Medical Letter, Treatment Guidelines* 2006;4[52]:83–88).

Sources: Prevention of Orthopaedic Implant Infection in Patients Undergoing Dental Procedures, the American Academy of Orthopaedic Surgeons & American Dental Association (see entire statement at www.orthoguidelines.org/topic?id=1002) and Antibiotic Prophylaxis for Bacteremia in Patients with Joint Replacements, American Academy of Orthopaedic Surgeons Information Statement, February 2009).

EXERCISE PRESCRIPTION
Before Giving an Exercise Prescription

Screen patient for:
- Musculoskeletal problems: decreased flexibility, muscular rigidity, weakness, pain, ill-fitting shoes
- Cardiac disease: consider stress test if older adult is beginning a vigorous exercise program and is sedentary with symptoms of active CVD (eg, angina, HF, PAD), DM, end-stage renal disease, or chronic lung disease.

Individualize the Prescription

Initiating low-intensity (rated 1–4 on a 10-point scale by the patient) to moderate-intensity (rated 5–6 on a 10-point scale) exercise is generally safe in older adults with multiple chronic conditions. Guidelines below should be adjusted according to patient's ability to tolerate each activity. Specify short- and long-term goals; include the following components (CDC and American College of Sports Medicine/AHA recommendations):

Endurance: Moderate-intensity activity, ≥30 min ≥5×/wk
- Moderate-intensity activities such as brisk walking are those that increase HR and would be rated 5–6 on a 10-point intensity scale by the patient.
- It is never too late to start exercising. Brisk walking in previously sedentary older adults significantly lowers risk of disability.
- Using pedometers to record the number of steps in a walking program has been demonstrated to increase physical activity, lower BMI, and lower BP.

Strength: Weight (resistance) training at least 2×/wk, 10 exercises on major muscle groups, 10–15 repetitions per exercise

Flexibility: Static stretching, at least 2×/wk for ≥10 min of flexibility exercises, 10–30 sec per stretch, 3–4 repetitions of major muscle/tendon groups

Balance: Balance exercises are recommended for people with mobility problems or who fall frequently.

Patient information: See go4life.nia.nih.gov.
See also Assessment and Management of Falls, **Figure 5**.

BENIGN PROSTATIC HYPERPLASIA (BPH)

Lower urinary tract symptoms (LUTS; increased frequency of urination, nocturia, hesitancy, urgency, and weak urinary stream) may or may not be associated with enlarged prostate gland, bladder outlet obstruction (eg, urinary retention, recurrent infection, renal insufficiency), or histological BPH.

Evaluation

Evaluation of severity of symptoms (AUA Symptom Index for BPH, p 344): Detailed medical hx focusing on physical exam of the urinary tract, including abdominal exam, digital rectal exam, and a focused neurologic exam; UA and culture if pyuria or hematuria. Postvoid residual (PVR) if neurologic disease or prior procedure that can affect bladder or sphincter function, UI, or reports of incomplete emptying. PVR should be performed before initiating antimuscarinic tx (below). Measurement of PSA is controversial, but should not be measured if life expectancy is <10 yr. Don't order Cr or upper tract imaging if only lower urinary tract symptoms.[CW]

Management

Mild Symptoms: (eg, AUA/International Prostate Symptom Score [IPSS] <8; p 344) watchful waiting

Moderate to Severe Symptoms: (eg, AUA score ≥8) watchful waiting, medical or surgical tx

Nonpharmacologic Treatment: Avoid fluids before bedtime, reduce mild diuretics (eg, caffeine, alcohol), double voiding to empty bladder completely, voiding in sitting position (if LUTS).

Pharmacologic Treatment: Combining drugs from different classes may have better long-term effectiveness than single-agent tx. Because of immediate onset of benefit, many recommend beginning with α-adrenergic blockers. If overactive bladder symptoms without evidence of bladder outlet obstruction or high PVR, consider beginning with antimuscarinics or combination α blocker and antimuscarinic.

If large prostate (eg, >30 g) or severe symptoms, consider beginning with combined tx (α-adrenergic blockers and 5-α reductase inhibitors). No dietary supplements have been demonstrated to be effective.

- **α₁-Blockers** reduce dynamic component by relaxing prostatic and bladder detrusor smooth muscle. Nonselective and selective agents are equally effective. Do not start in men with planned cataract surgery until after surgery is completed. First-generation drugs appear to have lower rates of intraoperative floppy iris syndrome. Use of PDE5 inhibitors (sildenafil, tadalafil, vardenafil) with α₁-blockers can potentiate hypotensive effect.
  - **First-generation** (can cause orthostatic hypotension and dizziness, which may be potentiated by sildenafil [*Viagra*], vardenafil [*LEVITRA*], and perhaps tadalafil [*Cialis*])
    - Terazosin▲ *(Hytrin)* increase dosage as tolerated: days 1–3, 1 mg/d hs; days 4–7, 2 mg; days 8–14, 5 mg; day 15 and beyond, 10 mg [T: 1, 2, 5, 10]. Avoid use as antihypertensive or in patients with syncope.[BC]
    - Doxazosin▲ *(Cardura)* start 0.5 mg with max of 16 mg/d [T: 1, 2, 4, 8]. Avoid use as antihypertensive or in patients with syncope.[BC]
  - **Second-generation** (less likely to cause hypotension or syncope, also benefits hematuria; more likely to cause ejaculatory dysfunction)
    - Tamsulosin▲ *(Flomax)* 0.4 mg 30 min after the same meal each day and increase to 0.8 mg if no response in 2–4 wk [T: 0.4]; decreases ejaculate volume; increases risk of retinal

detachment, lost lens or lens fragment, or endophthalmitis if taken within 14 d before cataract surgery

- Silodosin *(Rapaflo)* 8 mg/d, 4 mg/d in moderate kidney impairment; not recommended in severe kidney or liver impairment [C: 4, 8]; decreases ejaculate volume; retrograde ejaculation in ~30%
- Alfuzosin ER▲ *(Uroxatral)* 10 mg after the same meal every day [T: 10]

• **5-α Reductase inhibitors** (reduce prostate size and are more effective with large [>30 g] glands; do not use in absence of prostate enlargement; tx for 6–12 mo may be needed before symptoms improve) may help prostate-related bleeding and can decrease libido, ejaculation, and erectile function. Both finasteride and dutasteride reduce the incidence of prostate cancer but may lead to higher incidence of high-grade tumors in later years.
  ◦ Finasteride▲ *(Proscar)* 5 mg/d [T: 5]
  ◦ Dutasteride *(Avodart)* 0.5 mg/d [C: 0.5]

• **Antimuscarinic agents** (bladder relaxants) may have additional benefit beyond α_1-blockers on urinary frequency and urgency (**Table 70**) but use with caution if PVR >250–300 mL.

• **Phosphodiesterase-5 (PDE-5) inhibitors** (**Table 123**) may improve symptoms of BPH/lower urinary tract symptoms in men with or without erectile dysfunction but do not improve flow rates. Do not use daily if CrCl <30 mL/min.

Surgical Management: Indicated if recurrent UTI, recurrent or persistent gross hematuria, bladder stones, hydronephrosis, or renal insufficiency are clearly secondary to BPH or as indicated by severe symptoms (AUA score >16), patient preference, or ineffectiveness of medical tx. For men with moderate symptoms (AUA scores 8–15), surgical tx is more effective than watchful waiting, but the latter is a reasonable alternative.

Surgical options include:

Large Prostate
• Transurethral resection of the prostate (TURP), increasingly bipolar is used; standard tx, best long-term outcome data; 1% risk of UI and no increased risk of sexual dysfunction.
• Open prostatectomy for large glands (>50 g), usually longer hospital stay and more blood loss
• Transurethral plasma vaporization of the prostate ("button" procedure) is associated with less bleeding and hyponatremia (TURP syndrome) but higher rates of postoperative irritative voiding symptoms, dysuria, urinary retention, recatheratization, and repeat surgery. Also no tissue available for pathology.
• Laser photoselective vaporization (PVP) or laser enucleation (HoLEP, ThuLEP) using laser as a knife

Small Prostate with Bladder Outlet Obstruction
• Transurethral incision of the prostate (TUIP), which is limited to prostates with estimated resected tissue weight (if done by TURP) of ≤30 g
• Transuretral (TUMT) or transrectal microwave thermotherapy (TRMT) is the least operator-dependent but has inconsistent results

High-Risk Patients
• Laser photoselective vaporization (PVP)
• Transurethral radiofrequency ablation is less effective than TURP but may be an option for men with substantial comorbidity who are poor surgical candidates.
• Radiofrequency ablation
• TUIP

- Prostatic urethral lift (sutures that hold the prostate away from the urethra) has evidence for short-term benefit and preserves sexual function (up to 12 mo)
- Botulinum toxin may be effective but requires further study before it can be recommended.

PROSTATE CANCER

Screening is not recommended for older men.

Evaluation

Predicting extent of disease:
- PSA (p 272)
- Biopsy (Gleason primary and secondary grade)
- Digital rectal examination
- If life expectancy ≤5 yr and asymptomatic, no further workup
- CT or MRI abdomen and pelvis if life expectancy >5 yr or symptomatic, T3 or T4 disease, and nomogram-predicted probability of lymph node involvement >10% **or**
- Bone scan (if symptomatic or at increased risk for bone metastases (serum PSA >20 ng/mL, or serum PSA >10 ng/mL with a T2 tumor, or a Gleason ≥8 lesion, or stage T3 or T4)

Do not perform PET, CT, and radionuclide bone scan in the staging of early prostate cancer at low risk of metastasis.[CW]

Histology

- Gleason score ≤6 has low 15–20 yr morbidity and mortality; watchful waiting usually appropriate.
- Gleason score ≥7, higher PSA and younger age associated with higher morbidity and mortality; best tx strategy (surgery, radiation tx, ADT, etc) is not known.

Staging

T1 = Clinically inapparent tumor, neither palpable nor visible by imaging

   a. Incidental finding <5% of tissue

   b. Incidental finding >5% of tissue

   c. Identified by needle biopsy (eg, because of increased PSA)

T2 = Tumor confined within prostate

   a. <1/2 of 1 lobe

   b. >1 lobe

   c. Both lobes

T3 = Tumor extends through the prostate capsule

   a. Unilateral or bilateral extracapuslar extension

   b. Invading seminal vesicle

T4 = Tumor is fixed or invades adjacent structures other than seminal vesicles

N = Regional nodes indicating Stage IV disease

M = Distal metastasis indicating Stage IV disease

Initial Treatment of Early Prostate Cancer

- Based on aggressiveness risk of cancer (National Comprehensive Cancer Network www.nccn.org/professionals/physician_gls/f_guidelines.asp#prostate):
  - **Very low risk:** T1c, Gleason score <6, <3 positive biopsy cores, <50% cancer in each core, PSA <10 ng/mL, and PSA density 0.15 ng/mL

  If ≥20 yr expected survival, active surveillance (ie, tx if progression) or treat with

prostatectomy, brachytherapy, or external beam radiation tx (EBRT) with short-term androgen-deprivation therapy (ADT).

If 10–20 yr expected survival, treat with active surveillance.

If <10 yr expected survival, observation.

- **Low risk:** Stage T1 *or* T2a, Gleason score ≤6, PSA <10 ng/mL
  If >10 yr expected survival, active surveillance, EBRT, or brachytherapy, or radical prostatectomy ± pelvic lymph node dissection. If <10 yr expected survival, observation.

- **Intermediate risk:** Stage T2b–c *or* PSA 10–20 ng/mL *or* Gleason score 7
  If <10 yr expected survival, observation.
  If ≥10 yr expected survival, radical prostatectomy with pelvic lymph node dissection, EBRT ± short-term ADT ± brachytherapy, or brachytherapy alone. If PSA is still detectable, evaluate for distant metastasis and if present see below (Therapy for PSA-only Recurrence and Therapy for Metastatic Bone Disease).

- **High risk:** T3a *or* Gleason score 8–10, PSA >20 ng/mL
  Treat with radical prostatectomy + pelvic lymph node dissection or EBRT+ brachytherapy ± ADT (2–3 yr). At 24 mo, sexual dysfunction rates are similar with prostatectomy, EBRT, or brachytherapy.

- **Very high risk:** T3b–T4
  Same as for high risk or ADT for patients who are not candidates for definitive tx.

Therapy for Metastatic Disease

- For metastasis in regional nodes, ADT or EBRT + ADT.
- For distant metastatic disease, ADT.

Treatment Modalities

- Radical prostatectomy reduced short- and long-term overall and disease-specific mortality, metastasis, and local progression compared with watchful waiting in men <65 yr old with early disease, regardless of histology and PSA, including those who are at low risk. UI is more common but treatable (tx for post-prostatectomy UI, p 149) and may gradually improve.
- Radiation tx may cause transient PSA increase that does not reflect cancer recurrence. Irritative or obstructive urinary symptoms and bowel frequency and urgency are more common.
  - EBRT
  - Brachytherapy (radioactive seed implantation) has greater effect on prostate than EBRT.
- Proton-beam tx is controversial and remains unproved.
- Hormonal tx is reserved for locally advanced or metastatic disease.
- Monotherapy can be either bilateral orchiectomy or a GnRH agonist.
- Combined androgen blockade (GnRH agonist plus antiandrogen) is used to avoid "flare" phenomenon (ie, increased symptoms early in tx), but survival benefit is uncertain and side effects are greater than with monotherapy.
- In case of relapse without evidence of metastasis, sequential hormonal manipulations are often used first:
  - Withdrawal of antiandrogen may induce remission.
  - Patients often respond when changed to a second antiandrogen.
  - When antiandrogens no longer control disease, adrenal suppression with aminoglutethimide or ketoconazole and hydrocortisone replacement may be effective.
- If castration-recurrent metastatic disease, maintain castrate levels of testosterone and chemotherapy or autologous cellular immunotherapy. (www.nccn.org/professionals/physician_gls/f_guidelines.asp#prostate)

Monitoring

After surgery or radiation tx, PSA should be <0.1 ng/mL or undetectable. Monitor PSA every 6–12 mo for 5 yr (every 3 mo if high risk), then every year. Digital rectal exam yearly but may be omitted if PSA undetectable. If nodal or metastatic disease, physical exam and PSA q3–6 mo. If undetectable PSA after radical prostatectomy and subsequent detectable PSA that increases on ≥2 determinations, then workup for distant metastasis. A PSA doubling time of 3–12 mo in the absence of clinical recurrence indicates a higher risk of development of systemic disease and cancer-specific death.

Therapy for PSA-only Recurrence (no evidence of other disease)

If after radical prostatectomy, EBRT ± ADT or observation.

If after radiation tx, ADT or observation.

Therapy for Metastatic Bone Disease

In men receiving long-term ADT or HT for cancer and in those with bone metastasis, zoledronic acid 5 mg IV annually or denosumab 120 mg SC q4wk reduces the proportion of patients with skeletal-related events or fracture.

Table 106. Common Medications for Prostate Cancer Therapy			
Class, Medication	**Dosage**	**Metabolism**	**Adverse Events/ Comments**
GnRH Agonists	*Class AEs:* certain symptoms (urinary obstruction, spinal cord compression, bone pain) may be exacerbated early in tx; risk is less when combined with antiandrogens		
Goserelin acetate implant *(Zoladex)*	3.6 mg SC q28d or 10.8 mg q3mo	Rapid urinary and hepatic excretion, no dosage adjustment in renal impairment	Hot flushes (60%), breast swelling, libido change, impotence, nausea
Leuprolide acetate▲ *(Lupron Depot)*	7.5 mg IM qmo or 22.5 mg q3mo or 30 mg q4mo	Unknown; active metabolites for 4–12 wk, dose-dependent	Hot flushes (60%), edema (12%), pain (7%), nausea, vomiting, impotence, dyspnea, asthenia (all 5%), thrombosis, PE, MI (all 1%); headache as high as 32%
Triptorelin *(Trelstar Depot, Trelstar LA)*	Depot: 37.5 mg q28d IM LA: 11.25 mg q84d	Hepatic metabolism and renal excretion (42% as intact peptide)	Hot flushes, ↑ glucose, ↓ Hb, ↓ RBC, ↑ alkaline phosphatase, ↑ ALT or AST, skeletal pain, ↑ BUN
Histrelin acetate *(Vantas)*	50-mg SC implant q12mo	Hepatic metabolism	Hot flushes, fatigue, headaches, nausea, mild renal impairment
Antiandrogens (most often used in combination with GnRH agonists)	*Class AEs:* nausea, hot flushes, breast pain, gynecomastia, hematuria, diarrhea, liver enzyme elevations, galactorrhea		
Bicalutamide▲ *(Casodex)*	50 mg/d po [T: 50]	Metabolized in liver, excreted in urine; half-life 10 d at steady state	

(cont.)

Table 106. **Common Medications for Prostate Cancer Therapy (cont.)**

Class, Medication	Dosage	Metabolism	Adverse Events/ Comments
Flutamide▲ *(Eulexin)*	250 mg po q8h [C: 125]	Renal excretion; half-life 5–6 h	Greatest GI toxicity in the class; severe liver dysfunction reported
Nilutamide *(Nilandron)*	300 mg/d po for 30 d, then 150 mg/d po [T: 50]	80% protein bound; liver metabolism, renal excretion; half-life 40–60 h	Delayed light adaptation
GnRH Antagonist			
Degarelix *(Firmagon)*	240 mg SC, then 80 mg SC q28d	Liver 70–80%, Renal 20–30%	Prolonged QT interval, hot flushes, weight gain, fatigue, ↑AST and ALT

PROSTATITIS

Definition

Acute or chronic inflammation of the prostate secondary to bacterial (usually Gram-negative organisms) and nonbacterial causes

Symptoms and Diagnosis

Acute: fever; chills; dysuria; obstructive symptoms; tender, tense, or boggy on examination (examination should be minimal to avoid bacteremia); Gram stain and culture of urine

Chronic: recurrent UTIs, especially with same organism; obstructive or irritative symptoms with voiding, perineal pain (may include chronic pelvic pain syndrome). Examination often indicates hypertrophy, tenderness, edema, or nodularity, but may be normal. Compare first void or midstream urine with prostatic secretion or postmassage urine: bacterial if leukocytosis and bacteria in expressed sample, nonbacterial if sample sterile with leukocytosis

Treatment (Table 77)

Antibiotic tx should be based on Gram stain and culture. Begin tx for acute prostatitis empirically to cover likely organisms (gram negative) while culture is pending. Do not insert Foley catheter in acute prostatitis. If urinary retention, consult a urologist.

Acute prostatitis (recommend tx for 4–6 wk)
- Co-trimoxazole▲ DS 1 po q12h, *or*
- Ciprofloxacin▲ 500 mg po or 400 mg IV q12h, *or*
- Ofloxacin▲ 400 mg po once, then 300 mg q12h, *or*
- 3rd-generation cephalosporin▲ or aminoglycoside▲ IV
- If patient is toxic, then combine aminoglycoside with fluoroquinolone.

Chronic prostatitis (fluoroquinolones have good penetration of inflamed prostate and are generally considered first choice)
- Co-trimoxazole▲ DS 1 po q12h × 2–4 mo, *or*
- Ciprofloxacin▲ 500 mg po q12h × at least 6 wk, *or*
- Levofloxacin 500 mg po q24h × at least 6 wk, *or*
- Ofloxacin▲ 200 mg q12h × 3 mo

α-blockers may help chronic prostatitis in combination with antibiotics. Less consistent benefits have been demonstrated with anti-inflammatory agents and finasteride.

DIFFERENTIAL DIAGNOSIS
- Bipolar affective disorder
- Delirium
- Dementia
- Medications/drugs: eg, antiparkinsonian agents, anticholinergics, benzodiazepines or alcohol (including withdrawal), stimulants, corticosteroids, cardiac medications (eg, digitalis), opioid analgesics
- Late-life delusional (paranoid) disorder
- Major depression
- Physical disorders: hypo- or hyperglycemia, hypo- or hyperthyroidism, sodium or potassium imbalance, Cushing syndrome, Parkinson disease, B_{12} deficiency, sleep deprivation, AIDS
- Pain, untreated
- Schizophrenia
- Structural brain lesions: tumor or stroke
- Seizure disorder: eg, temporal lobe

Risk Factors for Psychotic Symptoms in Older Adults: chronic bed rest, cognitive impairment, female gender, sensory impairment, social isolation

MANAGEMENT
- Establish a trusting therapeutic relationship with the patient; focus on empathizing with the distress that symptoms cause rather than reality orientation.
- Encourage patients to maintain significant, supportive relationships.
- Alleviate underlying physical causes.
- Address identifiable psychosocial triggers.
- Before using an antipsychotic to treat behavioral symptoms of dementia, carefully assess for possible psychotic features (ie, delusions and hallucinations) and if psychotic symptoms are severe, frightening, or may affect safety.
- For *DSM–5*, rate presence and severity (most severe in last 7 d) of psychotic symptoms (eg, hallucinations, delusions, disorganized speech) on a 5-point scale ranging from 0 (not present) to 4 (present and severe).
- Aripiprazole, olanzapine, quetiapine, risperidone▲ are first choice because of fewer AEs (TD extremely high in older adults taking first-generation antipsychotics). See **Table 108** and **Table 109** for AEs of second-generation antipsychotics.
- Caution if hx of falls and fractures
- All antipsychotics are associated with increased mortality in older adults.

Table 107. Representative Medications for Treatment of Psychosis

Class, Medication	Dosage*	Formulations	Comments (Metabolism)
Second-generation Antipsychotics			Avoid for behavioral problems of dementia
✓Aripiprazole *(Abilify)*	2–5 (1) initially; max 30/d	T: 2, 5, 10, 15, 20, 30 ODT: 10, 15 IM: 9.75 mg/1.3 mL S: 1 mg/mL	Wait 2 wk between dosage changes (CYP2D6, -3A4) (L)
Asenapine *(Saphris)*	5–10 mg q12h	SL: 5, 10	Do not swallow (L)
Clozapine▲ *(Clozaril)*	25–150 (1)	T: 25, 100 ODT: 12.5, 25, 100	May be useful for parkinsonism and TD; significant risk of neutropenia and agranulocytosis; weekly CBCs × 6 mo, then biweekly (L)
Iloperidone *(Fanapta)*	Initial: 1 mg q12h, increase by ≤2 mg q12h daily to 6–12 mg q12h; max 24 mg/d	T: 1, 2, 4, 6, 8, 10, 12	Very limited geriatric data (CYP2D6), inhibits 2C19 and 3A4 (L)
Lurasidone *(Latuda)*	40 mg	T: 40–80	Very limited geriatric data
✓Olanzapine▲ *(Zyprexa)*	2.5–10 (1)	T: 2.5, 5, 7.5, 10, 15, 20 ODT: 5, 10, 15, 20 IM: 5 mg/mL	Weight gain (L)
Paliperidone *(Invega)*	3–12 (1)	T: ER 3, 6, 9	CrCl 51–80 mL/min, max 6 mg/d; CrCl ≤50 mL/min, max 3 mg/d; very limited geriatric data (K)
✓Quetiapine▲ *(Seroquel)*	25–800 (1–2)	T: 25, 100, 200, 300 T: ER 50, 150, 200, 300, 400	Ophthalmic examination recommended q6mo (L, K)
✓Risperidone▲ *(Risperdal)*	0.25–1 (1–2)	T: 0.25, 0.5, 1, 2, 3, 4 ODT: 0.5, 1, 2, 3, 4 S: 1 mg/mL IM long-acting: 25, 37.5, and 50 mg/2 mL	Dose-related EPS; IM not for acute tx; do not exceed 6 mg (L, K)
Ziprasidone *(Geodon)*	20–80 (1–2)	C: 20, 40, 60, 80 IM: 20 mg/mL	May increase QT_c; very limited geriatric data (L)
Low Potency First Generation			
Thioridazine▲ (eg, *Mellaril*)	25–200 (1–3)	T: 10, 15, 25, 50, 100, 150, 200 S: 30 mg/mL	Substantial anticholinergic effects, orthostasis, QT_c prolongation, sedation, TD; for acute use only. Avoid.[BC] (L, K)
Intermediate Potency First Generation			
Perphenazine▲ *(Trilafon)*	2–32 (1–2)	T: 2, 4, 8, 16	Risk of TD with long-term use. Avoid.[BC] (L, K)

(cont.)

Table 107. Representative Medications for Treatment of Psychosis (cont.)

Class, Medication	Dosage*	Formulations	Comments (Metabolism)
High Potency First Generation			Avoid.[BC]
Haloperidol▲ *(Haldol)*	0.5–2 (1–3); depot 25–200 mg IM q4wk	T: 0.5, 1, 2, 5, 10, 20 S: conc 2 mg/mL Inj: 5 mg/mL (lactate)	EPS, TD; for acute use only (L, K) Depot form is for chronic use; monitor for TD and D/C if signs appear
Fluphenazine	1–2.5 mg/d (max 5 mg/d) (1)	T: 1, 2.5, 5, 10 S: conc 5 mg/mL IM: 2.5 mg/mL (decanoate)	EPS, TD, akathisia (L, K)

✓ = preferred for treating older adults but does not imply low risk; mortality may be increased in patients with dementia.

* Total mg/d (frequency/d)

Table 108. Adverse Events of Preferred Second-generation Antipsychotics

	Aripiprazole	Olanzapine	Quetiapine	Risperidone
Level of Evidence	CR	RCT	RCT	RCT
Cardiovascular				
Hypotension	?	+	+++	+
QT$_c$ prolongation[a]	?	+	+	+
Endocrine/Metabolic				
Weight gain	?	+++	++	++
DM	?	+++	++	++
Hypertriglyceridemia	0	+	0	?
Hyperprolactinemia	?	?	?	+++
Gastrointestinal				
Nausea, vomiting, constipation	0	0	?	?
Neurologic				
EPS	++	+	+	+++
Seizures	?	?	?	ND
Sedation	?	+	+	+
Systemic				
Anticholinergic	0	++	+	0
Neuroleptic malignant syndrome	ND	ND	ND	+

Notes: CR = case reports; RCT = randomized clinical trials; ND = no data; ? = uncertain effect; 0 = no effect; + = mild effect; ++ = moderate effect; +++ = severe effect

[a] QT$_c$ upper limit of normal = 440 millisec

Table 109. Management of Adverse Events of Antipsychotic Medications

AE	Treatment	Comment
Drug-induced parkinsonism	Reduce dosage or change drug or drug class	Often dose related; avoid anticholinergic agents
Akathisia (motor restlessness)	Consider adding β-blocker (eg, propranolol▲ [Inderal] 20–40 mg/d) or low-dose benzodiazepine (eg, lorazepam▲ 0.5 mg q12h)	Also seen with second-generation antipsychotics; more likely with traditional agents
Hypotension	Slow titration; reduce dosage; change drug class	More common with low-potency agents
Sedation	Reduce dosage; give hs; change drug class	More common with low-potency agents
TD	Stop drug (if possible); consider second-generation antipsychotic (eg, aripiprazole, quetiapine) with lower potential for EPS	Increased risk in older adults; may be irreversible

Note: Periodic (q4mo) reevaluation of antipsychotic dosage and ongoing need is important (see CMS guidance on unnecessary drugs in the nursing home: www.cms.gov/transmittals/downloads/R22SOMA.pdf). Older adults are particularly sensitive to AEs of antipsychotic drugs. They are also at higher risk of developing TD. Periodic use of an AE scale such as the AIMS is highly recommended

COUGH

Among the most common symptoms in office practice; consider likely diagnosis based on duration of symptoms and treat the specific disorder (**Table 110**). **Table 111** lists agents sometimes used in symptomatic management of cough.

Table 110. Diagnosis and Treatment of Cough by Duration of Symptoms	
Cause	**Preferred Treatment**
Acute cough: duration up to 3 wk	
Acute rhinosinusitis (the common cold)	Sinus irrigation or nasal ipratropium (*Atrovent NS 0.06%*, **Table 114**). Not recommended: sedating antihistamines (dry mouth, urinary retention, confusion); oral pseudoephedrine[BC] (HTN, tachycardia, urinary retention). Don't routinely treat uncomplicated illness with antibiotics.[CW]
Allergic rhinitis	p 288
Bacterial sinusitis	Oxymetazoline[▲] nasal spr (eg, *Afrin*) × 5 d; antibiotic against *Haemophilus influenzae* and streptococcal pneumonia × 2 wk
Pertussis	Macrolide or trimethoprim-sulfa antibiotic × 2 wk
Other: pneumonia, HF, asthma, COPD exacerbation	Pneumonia, p 157; HF, p 42; asthma, p 293; COPD, p 290
Subacute cough: duration 3–8 wk*	
Postinfectious	Inhaled ipratropium (*Atrovent*); systemic steroids tapered over 2–3 wk; if protracted, dextromethorphan with codeine; use bronchodilators if there is bronchospasm (**Table 120**)
Subacute bacterial sinusitis	As for acute bacterial sinusitis, but treat for 3 wk
Asthma	p 42
Pertussis	Macrolide or trimethoprim-sulfa antibiotic × 2 wk; may need to treat as above for postinfectious cough
Chronic cough: duration >8 wk*	(25% of patients have more than 1 cause requiring concurrent tx)
Perennial rhinitis *or* postnasal drainage	p 287. Tx for 2–4 wk for reduction/resolution
Chronic bacterial sinusitis	Same as for subacute bacterial sinusitis but also cover mouth anaerobes × 3 wk; may need follow-up course of nasal steroids
Asthma or cough variant asthma	p 42. Tx for 6–8 wk for reduction/resolution
Other: ACEIs, reflux esophagitis	Stop ACEI (cough may persist for 4 wk); treat reflux for 6–8 wk for reduction/resolution using a PPI
Aspiration	Dysphagia, p 120. Evaluate with modified barium swallow
Sleep Apnea	May present as cough that is also present at night
Nonasthmatic eosinophilic bronchitis	Eosinophils in sputum, but no reversible airway obstruction on spirometry; treat with inhaled glucocorticoids (p 297) for 3–4 wk
Smoking	Cessation of smoking for 4 wk
Idiopathic	A proportion of patients do not have identified cause

*Obtain chest radiograph, spirometry, sputums to exclude malignancy, TB; obtain eosinophil count, etc.

Management

- Do not suppress cough in stable COPD.
- For symptomatic relief, **Table 111**

Table 111. Antitussives and Expectorants

Medication	Dosage and Formulations	Adverse Events (Metabolism)
Benzonatate[▲a] (Tessalon Perles)	100 mg po q8h (max: 600 mg/d) C: 100, 200	CNS stimulation or depression, headache, dizziness, hallucination, constipation (L)
Dextromethorphan[▲a] (eg, Robitussin DM)	10–30 mL po q4–8h C: 30 S: 10 mg/5 mL	Mild drowsiness, fatigue; interacts with SSRIs and SNRIs; combination may cause serotonin syndrome (L)
Guaifenesin[▲b] (eg, Robitussin)	5–20 mL po q4h S: 100 mg/5 mL	None at low dosages; high dosages cause nausea, vomiting, diarrhea, drowsiness, abdominal pain (L)
Codeine phosphate/ Guaifenesin[▲c]	S: 10 mg/5 mL/100 mg/5 mL; 10 mg/5 mL/300 mg/5 mL T: 10 mg/300 mg	Sedation, constipation (L)
Hydrocodone/Homatropine[▲a] (Hycodan)	5 mL po q4–6h S: 5 mg/5 mL/1.5 mg/mL T: 5 mg/1.5 mg	Sedation, constipation, confusion (L)

[a] Antitussive

[b] Expectorant

[c] Antitussive and expectorant

DYSPNEA

Definition

A subjective experience of breathing discomfort that consists of qualitatively distinct sensations that vary in intensity (ATS)

Characteristics

- >65 yr: occurs in 17% at rest at least occasionally; in 38% when hurrying on level ground or on slight hill
- Hx: consider if level of dyspnea is appropriate to level of exertion (vs suggests pathology)
  - Consider age, peers, usual activities, level of fitness
  - Ask, "What activities have you stopped doing?"
- Associated symptoms: cough, sputum, wheezing, chest pain, orthopnea, paroxysmal nocturnal dyspnea

Evaluation

Hx and physical examination should suggest organ system; then evaluate for cause (**Table 112**).

Table 112. Diagnosis of Dyspnea

Suspected System	Diagnostic Strategy	Diagnosis
Cardiac	Chest radiograph, ECG, echocardiogram, radionuclide imaging, BNP (p 43)	Ischemic or other form of heart disease

(cont.)

Table 112. Diagnosis of Dyspnea (cont.)		
Suspected System	**Diagnostic Strategy**	**Diagnosis**
Lung	Spirometry	Asthma, COPD, or restriction
	Diffusing capacity	Emphysema or interstitial lung disease
	Echocardiogram	Pulmonary HTN
Respiratory muscle dysfunction	Inspiratory and expiratory mouth pressures	Neuromuscular disease
Deconditioning/ obesity vs psychological disorders	Cardiopulmonary exercise test	Deconditioning shows decreased maximal oxygen consumption but normal cardiorespiratory exercise responses.

Therapy

Nonpharmacologic

- Exercise reduces dyspnea and improves fitness in almost all older adults regardless of cause; physical conditioning reduces dyspnea during ADLs and exercise, and is primary tx for deconditioning.
  - Use low-impact, indoor activity
  - Base intensity on HR or symptom of dyspnea
  - Recommend 20–30 min on most days
- Indications for pulmonary rehabilitation include the following:
  - Dyspnea during rest or exertion
  - Hypoxemia, hypercapnia
  - Reduced exercise tolerance or a decline in ADLs
  - Worsening dyspnea and a reduced but stable exercise tolerance level
  - Pre- or postoperative lung resection, transplantation, or volume reduction
  - Chronic respiratory failure and the need to initiate mechanical ventilation
  - Ventilator dependence
  - Increasing need for emergency department visits, hospitalization, and unscheduled office visits

Pharmacologic: See specific diseases elsewhere in this chapter.

ALLERGIC RHINITIS

Description

- The most common atopic disorder
- Symptoms include rhinorrhea, sneezing, and irritated eyes (Allergic Conjunctivitis, p 110), nose, and mucous membranes.
- May be seasonal, but in older adults is more often perennial.
- Postnasal drip, mainly from chronic rhinitis, is the most common cause of chronic cough.

Therapy

Nonpharmacologic: Avoid allergens, eliminate pets and their dander, dehumidify to reduce molds; saline and sodium bicarbonate nasal irrigation (eg, Sinu*Cleanse*) are helpful as primary or adjunctive tx; reduce outdoor exposures during pollen season; reduce house dust mites by encasing pillows and mattresses. Arachnocides reduce mites.

Pharmacologic: Target tx to symptoms and on whether symptoms are seasonal or perennial; **Table 113** and **Table 114**.

Stepped tx: For mild or intermittent symptoms, begin with an oral second-generation antihistamine or nasal steroid; for moderate or severe symptoms, begin maximum dose of a nasal steroid; if symptoms uncontrolled, add a nasal or an oral antihistamine; if still uncontrolled, add or substitute a leukotriene modifier for one of the other agents.

Refractory symptoms: Consider other causes of chronic rhinosinusitis, refer to otolaryngologist; if allergy likely, refer to allergist/immunologist.

Ocular symptoms: Oral H_1 antihistamine or topical ophthalmic H_1 antihistamine are drugs of choice (allergic conjunctivitis, p 110 and **Table 113**).

Table 113. Choosing Medication for Allergic Rhinitis or Conjunctivitis

Medication or Class	Rhinitis	Sneezing	Pruritus	Congestion	Eye Symptoms
Nasal steroids[a]	+++	+++	++	++	++
Ipratropium, nasal[a]	++	0	0	0	0
Antihistamines[b,c]	++	++	++	+	+++
Pseudoephedrine, nasal[d]	0	0	0	++++	0
Cromolyn, nasal[c]	+	+	+	+	0
Leukotriene modifiers	+	+	+	+	++

Note: 0 = drug is not effective; the number of "+'s" grades the drug's effectiveness.

[a] Effective in seasonal, perennial, and vasomotor rhinitis.

[b] Better in seasonal than in perennial rhinitis; nasal, ocular, and oral forms; ocular form effective only for eye symptoms, but nasal form may help ocular symptoms.

[c] Start before allergy season.

[d] Topical tx rapid in onset but results in rebound if used for more than a few days; enhances effectiveness of nasal steroids and improves sleep during severe attacks.

Table 114. Medications for Allergic Rhinitis

Type, Medication	Geriatric Dosage	Formulations	Adverse Events/Comments
H_1-Receptor Antagonists or Antihistamines		*Class AEs:* bitter taste, nasal burning, sneezing (nasal preparations); eye burning, stinging, injection (ocular preparations)	
Oral			
✓Cetirizine▲*	5 mg/d (max)	T: 5, 10▲; syr 5 mg/5 mL	
✓Desloratadine (Clarinex)	5 mg/d	T: 5	
✓Fexofenadine▲*,ª	60 mg po q12h; q24h if CrCl <40 mL/min	T▲: 30, 60, 180; C: 60 ODT: 30 S▲: 30/5 mL	Least sedating in the class; fruit juice reduces absorption, so take 4 h before or 1–2 h after ingestion of juice
Levocetirizine (Xyzal)	2.5 mg/d po if CrCl 50–80 mL/min; q48h if CrCl 30–50; 2×/wk if CrCl 10–30. Not recommended if CrCl <10 mL/min.	T: 5 mg S: 0.5 mg/mL	Somnolence, pharyngitis, fatigue

(cont.)

Table 114. Medications for Allergic Rhinitis (cont.)

Type, Medication	Geriatric Dosage	Formulations	Adverse Events/Comments
✓Loratadine▲*, a	5–10 mg/d	T: 10; rapid disintegrating tab 10 mg; syr 1 mg/mL	
Nasal			
✓Azelastine▲	1–2 spr q12h[b]	137 mcg/ actuation, 0.15%	
✓Olopatadine (Patanase)	2 spr q12h	0.6%	Epistaxis
Decongestant			
Pseudoephedrine▲,BC (also in combination preparations*)	60 mg po q4–6h	T: 30, 60; SR: 120; S: elixir 30 mg/5 mL	Arrhythmia, insomnia, anxiety, restlessness, elevated BP, urinary retention in men
Nasal Steroids			
Second generation (systemic bioavailability < 1% or undetectable)			
✓Fluticasone propionate▲, *	2 spr/d[b] or 1 spr 2×/d	120 spr	*Class AEs:* nasal burning, sneezing, bleeding; septal perforation (rare); fungal overgrowth (rare)
Fluticasone furoate (Veramyst)	2 spr/d[b] ,1spr/d maintenance	120 spr	
Mometasone (Nasonex)	2 spr/d[b]	120 spr	
Ciclesonide (Omnaris) (Zetonna)	2 spr/d[b] 1 spr/d[b]	250 spr	
First generation (systemic bioavailability 10–50%)			
Beclomethasone (Beconase AQ) (Qnasl)	1–2 spr q12h[b] 2 spr/d	80 spr	*As above* PLUS: systemic ADEs from absorbed steroids.
Triamcinolone (Nasacort Allergy 24)* (Nasacort AQ)	2 spr/d[b]	100 spr	
Budesonide (Rhinocort-Aqua)	1 spr/d[b]	200 spr	
Flunisolide▲	2 spr 2×/d	200 spr	
Mast Cell Stabilizer			
Cromolyn▲ (NasalCrom)	1 spr q6–8h[b]; begin 1–2 wk before exposure to allergen	2%, 4%	Nasal irritation, headache, itching of throat
Leukotriene Modifiers (p 298)			Less effective than nasal steroids
Other			
Ipratropium▲ (Atrovent NS)	2 spr q6–12h[b]	0.03, 0.06%[c] sol	Epistaxis, nasal irritation, upper respiratory infection; sore throat, nausea Caution: Do not spray in eyes

✓ = preferred for treating older adults; *OTC; BC Avoid.

Allegra-D and *Claritin-D*, also available as *Allegra-D 24 Hour* and *Claritin-D 24 Hour*, are not recommended; all contain pseudoephedrine. Contraindicated in narrow angle glaucoma, urinary retention, MAOI use within 14 d, severe HTN, or CAD. May cause headache, nausea, insomnia.
b Spr per nares
c Use 0.06% for tx of viral upper respiratory infection.

CHRONIC OBSTRUCTIVE PULMONARY DISEASE

Diagnosis

Consider COPD if any of these factors are present in an individual over 40 yr old. The greater the number of factors, the more likely is the diagnosis.
- **Dyspnea:** that is progressive, worse with exercise, and persistent
- **Chronic cough:** with or without sputum production
- **Hx of exposure to risk factors:** tobacco smoke, smoke from heating fuels, occupational dust, and chemicals
- **Family hx of COPD**

Spirometry is required to establish a diagnosis. Assess airflow limitation based on spirometry measures after bronchodilators. COPD is diagnosed when FEV_1/FVC <0.70 or perhaps 0.65 (in patients over age 65) or FEV_1/FEV_6 <0.70 in patients over 65 or those with severe disease.

Therapy

- Should be based on 3 factors: symptoms, airflow limitation, and frequency of exacerbations
- Assess **symptoms** using quantitative scale, eg, The Modified Medical Research Council Dyspnea Scale (MMRC) shown below:
  0 "I only get breathless with strenuous exercise"
  1 "I get short of breath when hurrying on the level or walking up a slight hill"
  2 "I walk slower than people of the same age on the level because of breathlessness or have to stop for breath when walking at my own pace on the level"
  3 "I stopped for breath after walking about 100 yards or after a few minutes on the level"
  4 "I am too breathless to leave the house" or "I am breathless when dressing"

MMRC 0–1, indicates fewer symptoms; MMRC ≥2, indicates more symptoms
- Then determine stage of **airflow limitation** by FEV_1 as follows:

Stage	% predicted
Mild	FEV_1 ≥80%
Moderate	50% FEV_1 <80%
Severe	30% FEV_1 <50%
Very Severe	FEV_1 <30%

- Finally, classify frequency of **exacerbations** as follows: low risk ≤1 exacerbation/yr and no hospitalization, high risk ≥2 exacerbations/yr or ≥1 exacerbation/yr with one or more hospitalizations.
- Use **Table 115** to classify patients by type which determines tx.

Table 115. Combined Assessment of COPD

Patient Type	Characteristic	Risk* Spirometric Classification	Risk* Exacerbations per year	Symptom Score (eg, mMRC)
A	low risk, fewer symptoms	mild/moderate	≤1	Low 0–1
B	low risk, more symptoms	mild/moderate	≤1	High ≥2
C	high risk, fewer symptoms	severe/very severe	≥2 or ≥1 with ≥1 hospitalization	Low 0–1
D	high risk, more symptoms	severe/very severe	≥2 or ≥1 with ≥1 hospitalization	High ≥2

* Where assessment of risk is based on the highest risk according to either spirometry or exacerbation hx.

Source: Adapted from www.goldcopd.org.

• The goal of tx is to minimize both symptoms and number of exacerbations. The degree of airflow limitation and risk of exacerbation influences but should not be the sole determinant of tx.

Stepped Approach: Add agents when symptoms or exacerbations are inadequately controlled; D/C medication if no improvement. Assess improvement in symptoms, ADLs, exercise capacity, rapidity of symptom relief (**Tables 121** and **120**) Long-term tx with long-acting anticholinergics (eg, tiotropium), long-acting β-agonists, and inhaled steroids slows the loss of FEV$_1$ and reduces the number of exacerbations and/or hospitalization. For acute exacerbations, see **Table 117**.

Table 116. Pharmacotherapy for Stable COPD[a]

Patient Group	First Choice	Second Choice	Alternate Choice[c]
A	Short-acting anticholinergic prn **or** Short-acting β$_2$-agonist prn	Long-acting anticholinergic **or** Long-acting β$_2$-agonist **or** Short-acting β$_2$-agonist and short-acting anticholinergic	Theophylline[d]
B	Long-acting anticholinergic **or** Long-acting β$_2$-agonist	Long-acting anticholinergic **and** Long-acting β$_2$-agonist	Short-acting β$_2$-agonist **and/or** short-acting anticholinergic Theophylline[d]
C	ICS[b] + Long-acting β$_2$-agonist **or** Long-acting anticholinergic	Long-acting anticholinergic **and** Long-acting β$_2$-agonist **or** Long-acting anticholinergic and PDE4 inhibitor **or** Long-acting β$_2$-agonist and PDE4 inhibitor	Short-acting β$_2$-agonist **and/or** short-acting anticholinergic Theophylline[d]

(cont.)

Table 116. Pharmacotherapy for Stable COPD[a] (cont.)

Patient Group	First Choice	Second Choice	Alternate Choice[c]
D	ICS[b] + Long-acting β_2-agonist **and/or** Long-acting anticholinergic	ICS[b] + Long-acting β_2-agonist and Long-acting anticholinergic **or** ICS[b] + Long-acting β_2-agonist and PDE4 inhibitor **or** Long-acting anticholinergic and Long-acting β_2-agonist **or** Long-acting anticholinergic and PDE4 inhibitor	Short-acting β_2-agonist **and/or** short-acting anticholinergic Theophylline[d]

Notes: ICS, inhaled corticosteroids. Source: Adapted from www.goldcopd.org.

[a] Medications are mentioned in alphabetical order; not necessarily in order of preference.

[b] Consider osteoporosis prophylaxis.

[c] Medications in this column can be used alone or in combination with other options in the First and Second Choice columns.

[d] Avoid in insomia[BC]; caution in patients taking other medications.

Table 117. COPD Exacerbation: Diagnosis and Therapy

Stage	Treatment
COPD Exacerbation (assess cardinal symptoms: increased dyspnea, sputum volume, and sputum purulence)	
Mild exacerbation (1 cardinal symptom)	Increase dosage and/or frequency of β_2-agonist; no antibiotics; monitor for worsening
Moderate or severe exacerbation (2 or 3 cardinal symptoms)	Add steroid (eg, prednisone 40 mg po every day for 5 d) Add respiratory fluoroquinolone (moxifloxacin, levofloxacin, or gemifloxacin) or amoxicillin-clavulanate; if at risk of *Pseudomonas*, consider ciprofloxacin and obtain sputum culture; if antibiotics in last 3 mo, use alternative class CBC, CXR, ECG, ABG; titrate O_2 to 88–92% sat and recheck ABG. If 1 or more of severe dyspnea, signs of respiratory muscle fatigue, or PCO_2 ≥45 or pH <7.35, then noninvasive positive-pressure ventilation reduces risk of ventilator use, mortality, and length of hospital stay. Hospitalized patients should have thromboprophylaxis.

Other Considerations for Controlling COPD Symptoms

Smoking Cessation: Essential at any age (p 325).

Anxiety or Major Depression: Seen in up to 40% of patients and should be treated.

Mucolytic Therapy: Not recommended in stable COPD. Consider for patients with chronic productive cough; continue if reduced cough and sputum during a trial. Example tx: guaifenesin[▲] long-acting 600 mg po q12h

Rehabilitation and Nutritional Support: Patients at all stages benefit from exercise training, ie, increased exercise tolerance results in decreased dyspnea and fatigue (p 274). Nutritional support promotes weight gain and fat free mass.

Long-term Oxygen Therapy: For indications, see **Table 118**. Assess patients with FEV$_1$ <30%, cyanosis, edema, HF, resting O$_2$ sats <92%.

Table 118. Indications for Long-term Oxygen Therapy[a,c]

PaO$_2$ Level	SaO$_2$ Level	Other
≤55 mmHg	≤88%	>15 h/d for benefit[a], greater if 20 h/d[b]
55–59 mmHg	≥89%	Signs of tissue hypoxia (eg, cor pulmonale by ECG, HF, hematocrit >55%); or nocturnal desaturation, sats <90% for >30% of the time
≥60 mmHg	≥90%	Desaturation with exercise Desaturation with sleep apnea not corrected by CPAP

[a] Titrate O$_2$ saturation to ~90%.

[b] Improves survival, hemodynamics, polycythemia, exercise capacity, lung mechanics, and cognition.

[c] For patients recently discharged home on supplemental oxygen after hospitalization for acute illness, don't renew oxygen without reassessing need.[CW]

Source: www.goldcopd.org

Other Considerations in Severe COPD

Patients should be given the opportunity to discuss palliative and end-of-life care. In particular, if the patient should become critically ill, is ICU care consistent with goals of care and are they willing to accept the burdens of such care?

ASTHMA

Definition

- A heterogenous disease usually characterized by airway inflammation. It is defined by the hx of respiratory symptoms such as wheezing, shortness of breath, chest tightness, and cough that vary over time and intensity together with variable airflow limitation.

Diagnosis in Older Adults

- Half of older people with asthma have not been diagnosed.
- Diagnosis is based on symptoms and requires spirometry.[CW]
  - Aging reduces FEV$_1$/FVC and may result in overdiagnosis of COPD. For this reason, some older adults with asthma are misdiagnosed with COPD.
  - If FEV$_1$/FVC is ≤0.65 and the diffusing capacity of carbon dioxide is reduced, then COPD is likely. The diffusing capacity of carbon dioxide is normal in asthma.
  - If a short-acting β$_2$-agonist does not reverse airflow obstruction during pulmonary function tests (asthma is not excluded), do one of the following:
    - Perform bronchial provocative testing (induce obstruction), *or*
    - Repeat testing after 2 wk of oral steroids to determine if obstruction seen in the initial test is reversible.
  - Over half of people >65 yr old with airflow obstruction have both COPD and asthma ("overlap" syndrome); inhaled glucocorticoids must be part of the treatment.

Additional Considerations

- Age of onset: Some older adults have had asthma from a young age; others develop asthma for the first time after 65 yr. Second peak in incidence after 65 yr; 5–10% after 65 yr are affected and account for two-thirds of asthma deaths.
- Those with long-standing asthma develop fixed obstruction (reduced FEV_1/FVC that is not reversed by bronchodilators) as an effect of both the disease and aging.
- Cough is a common presentation for asthma in those >65 yr old.
- Symptoms may be confused with those of HF, COPD, GERD, chronic aspiration.
- Typical triggers: aeroallergens, irritants (eg, smoke, paint, household aerosols), viral upper respiratory infection, GERD, allergic rhinitis, metabisulfate ingestion (eg, wine, beer, food preservatives), medications (eg, ASA, NSAIDs, β-blockers).
- About 95% of patients with asthma also have perennial rhinitis and tx of both improves asthma outcomes.

Therapy

Nonpharmacologic

Avoid triggers; educate patients on disease management. Peak flow meters are less helpful in monitoring older adults; aging decreases peak flow and increases variability.

Pharmacologic

Good evidence on best tx for older adults with asthma is lacking because most clinical trials exclude people >65 yr old and those with comorbidities or a hx of smoking >10 pack-years.

Stepped approach:

- The **number of the following symptoms** that were present in **the last 4 wk** determines the level of symptom control:
  - Daytime symptoms >2×/wk?
  - Limitations of activities due to asthma?
  - Nighttime waking due to asthma?
  - Reliever needed more than 2×/wk?
- Asthma is: "Well Controlled" if 0 (zero) symptoms; "Partly Controlled" with 1–2 symptoms; and "Uncontrolled" with 3–4 symptoms.
- Any exacerbation should prompt review of maintenance tx to ensure that it is adequate.
- By definition, an exacerbation in any week makes that an uncontrolled asthma week.
- If control not achieved, step up, but first review medication technique, adherence, and avoidance of triggers (**Table 119**)
- When symptoms controlled for 3 mo, try stepwise reduction, eg, step down from twice-daily steroid and long-acting β-agonist combination to once daily.
- Long-acting β-agonists should not be used unless given in combination with an inhaled steroid. Long-acting β-agonists as monotherapy are associated with increased mortality and are contraindicated as monotherapy.

Use separate AeroChamber for steroids; wash AeroChamber monthly.

Table 119. Asthma Therapy for Older Adults

Step[a]	Preferred	Other Options
Step 1	Inhaled short-acting β-agonist prn	Consider low-dose inhaled corticosteroid (ICS)
Step 2	Low-dose ICS	Leukotriene modifier or low-dose theophylline[b, BC]
Step 3	Low-dose ICS + long-acting β-agonist	Medium-/high-dose ICS *or* low-dose ICS + leukotriene modifier (or SR-theophylline[b, BC])
Step 4	Medium/high-dose ICS + long-acting β-agonist	Add tiotropium or high-dose ICS + leukotriene modifier (*or* SR + theophylline[b, BC])
Step 5	Refer for add-on tx (eg, anti-IgE tx)	Add tiotropium, or add low-dose oral corticosteroid

[a]Go to next step if symptoms not controlled; prn short-acting β-agonist at all steps. After 3 mo of stability, try reduction but do not stop ICS.

[b]Many drug interactions with theophylline limit its use in older people; CNS stimulant.[BC]

Source: Adapted from: www.ginasthma.org

"Therapy of Acute Exacerbations"

Mild attacks: reduction in peak flow <20%, nocturnal awakening, and increased use of short acting β-agonist can usually be managed at home.

Moderate attacks may require and severe attacks usually require care in clinic or hospital.

- Begin short-acting β-agonist 2–4 puffs by MDI or nebulizer with ipratropium every 20 min × 1 h, then 2–4 puffs every 3–4 h (mild) and 6–10 puffs every 2 h (moderate and severe)
- Oral glucocorticoids (0.5–1.0 mg/kg prednisolone) in moderate/severe attacks
- If hypoxemic, titrate O_2 to 95% saturation
- Combined β-agonist/anticholinergic reduces need for hospitalization
- Do not use theophylline with high doses of β-agonists
- Severe attacks unresponsive to oral steroids and bronchodilators; give 2 g magnesium sulfate IV; DO NOT give: sedatives, mucolytics, chest PT, vigorous hydration, antibiotics, or epinephrine.

DELIVERY DEVICES FOR ASTHMA AND COPD

Metered-dose inhalers (MDIs): prescribed as number of puffs. Spacers (require a separate prescription) improve drug delivery and should be used for essentially all older patients. Use separate spacers for steroids. Wash spacer monthly.

Dry powder inhalers (DPIs): prescribed as caps or inhalations; require moderate to high inspiratory flow. DPIs are not used correctly by 40% of people >60 yr old and 60% of those >80 yr old. Instructions should be repeated and reinforced for proper use and effective tx.

Soft mist inhalers (SMIs): prescribed as inhalations. Less dependent on inspiratory flow rates. Drug delivery to lung similar to MDI with spacer, however proper technique can be complex for patients.

Nebulizers: prescribed as milligrams or milliliters of solution. Consider for patients with disabling or distressing breathlessness on maximal tx with inhalers. Often the best choice for patients with cognitive impairment or when patients cannot manage DPIs or MDIs. Caution when patients with glaucoma use nebulized anticholinergics; the mask should fit well, or a T-type delivery device should be used. Ultrasonic and jet nebulizers are available; the latter can be used with supplemental oxygen.

Table 120. Asthma and COPD Medications

Medication Class/Agent)	Dosage	Adverse Events (Metabolism, Excretion)
Short-acting Anticholinergics		
✓ Ipratropium *(Atrovent)*	2–6 puffs q6h or 0.5 mg by nebulizer▲ q6h	Dry mouth, urinary retention, possible increase in cardiovascular mortality (lung, poorly absorbed; F)
Long-acting Anticholinergics		
Aclidinium *(Tudorza Pressair)*	1 inhalation (400 mcg) q12h	Broncospasm, nasopharyngitis, cough, diarrhea, and drug-related AEs seen with ipratropium (lung, poorly absorbed; F)
Tiotropium *(Spiriva)*	1 inhalation cap (18 mcg) daily (inhale twice from cap)	Same as ipratropium except good data on cardiovascular safety (14% K, 86% F)
(Spiriva Respimat Spray)	2 inhalations (5 mcg) daily	
Umeclidinium *(Incruse Ellipta)*	1 inhalation (62.5 mcg)/d	Nasopharangitis, upper respiratory infection, cough, arthralgia, AF <1% in trials
Short-acting β 2-Agonists (SABA)[a]	*Class AEs:* tremor, nervousness, headache, palpitations, tachycardia, cough, hypokalemia. Caution: use half-doses in patients with known or suspected coronary disease (L)	
✓ Albuterol *(Ventolin)*	2 puffs q4–6h, max 12 puffs/d or 2.5 mg by nebulizer q6h;▲ T: 2, 4 po q6–8h; ER 4–8 mg po q12h▲	AEs more common with oral formulation
(Ventolin Rotacaps)	1–2 caps q4–6h; 200 mcg/cap	
Levalbuterol *(Xopenex)*	0.31, 0.63, 1.25 mg q6–8h by nebulizer; inhaler 2 puffs q4–6h	Expensive; no advantage over racemic albuterol (intestine, L)
Pirbuterol *(Maxair)*	2–3 puffs q4–6h	Mechanism may be difficult for older adults to trigger (L, K)
Long-acting β-Agonists	*Class AEs:* tremor, nervousness, headache, palpitations, tachycardia, cough, hypokalemia	
Arformoterol *(Brovana)*	2 mL q12h by nebulizer	Caution: use half-doses in patients with known or suspected coronary disease; not for acute exacerbation. These agents should not be used in asthma without an inhaled steroid. (L)
✓ Salmeterol *(Serevent Diskus)*	1 cap q12h; 50 mcg/cap	
✓ Formoterol *(Foradil)*	1 cap q12h; 20 mcg/2 mL q12h per nebulizer	Onset of action 1–3 min (L, K)

(cont.)

Table 120. **Asthma and COPD Medications (cont.)**

Medication Class/Agent	Dosage	Adverse Events (Metabolism, Excretion)
Indacaterol *(Arcapta)*	1 cap q24hr (75 mcg/cap)	NOT indicated for asthma; greater bronchodilator effect than other long-acting β-agonists, also greater risk of cough after inhalation
Corticosteroids: Inhaled	*Class AEs:* nausea, vomiting, diarrhea, abdominal pain; oropharyngeal thrush; dysphonia; dosages >1 mg/d may cause adrenal suppression, reduce calcium absorption and bone density, and cause bruising (L)	
✓ Beclomethasone *(QVAR)*	2–4 puffs q6–12h [40, 80 mcg/puff, max 640 mcg/d]	
✓ Budesonide▲	180–720 mcg q12h [90, 180 mcg/inhalation]	
Budesonide inhalation solution▲	0.25, 0.5, 1.0 mg/2 mL q12h	
Ciclesonide *(Alvesco)*	80–320 mcg q12h [80, 160 mcg/inhalation]	
✓ Flunisolide▲	80–320 mcg q12h [80 mcg/inhalation]	
✓ Fluticasone propionate▲	88–880 mcg q12h [44, 110, 220 mcg/puff]	
✓ Fluticasone furoate *(Arnuity Ellipta)*	1 inhalation/d [100, 200 mcg/inhalation]	
Mometasone *(Asmanex HFA)*	1–2 inhalation q12h [100, 200 mcg]	
(Asmanex Twisthaler)	1 inhalation q12h [110, 220 mcg/inhalation]	
Corticosteroids: Oral		
Prednisone▲	20 mg po q12h [T: 1, 2.5, 5, 10, 20, 50; elixir 5 mg/5 mL]	Leukocytosis, thrombocytosis, sodium retention, euphoria, depression, hallucination, cognitive dysfunction; other effects with long-term use (L)
Methylxanthines Long-acting theophyllines▲,BC		*Class AEs:* atrial arrhythmias, seizures, increased gastric acid secretion, ulcer, reflux, diuresis; clearance ↓ by 30% after 65 yr; initial dosage ≤400 mg/d, titrate using blood levels; 16-fold greater risk of life-threatening events or death after age 75 at comparable blood levels (L)
(eg, *Theo-Dur, Slo-Bid*)	100–200 mg po q12h [T: 100, 200, 300, 450]	
(eg, *Theo-24*)	400 mg/d po [C: 100, 200, 300, T: 400, 600]	

(cont.)

Table 120. Asthma and COPD Medications (cont.)

Medication Class/Agent	Dosage	Adverse Events (Metabolism, Excretion)
Leukotriene Modifiers		
Montelukast *(Singulair)*	10 mg po in AM [T: 10; ChT: 4, 5]	Headache, drowsiness, fatigue, dyspepsia; minimal data in older adults; leukotriene-receptor antagonist (L)
Zafirlukast *(Accolate)*	20 mg po q12h 1 h ac or 2 h pc [T: 10, 20]	Headache, somnolence, dizziness, nausea, diarrhea, abdominal pain, fever; monitor LFTs; monitor coumarin anticoagulants; leukotriene-receptor antagonist (L, reduced by 50% if >65 yr)
Zileuton *(Zyflo)*	600 mg po q6h [T: 600]	Dizziness, insomnia, nausea, abdominal pain, abnormal LFTs, myalgia; monitor coumarin anticoagulants; other drug interactions; inhibits synthesis of leukotrienes (L)
PDE4 Inhibitor		
Roflumilast *(Daliresp)*	500 mcg/d po, for use in severe COPD (FEV$_1$ <50%) associated with chronic bronchitis but not emphysema [T: 500 mcg]	Weight loss, nausea, headache, back pain, influenza, insomnia; do not use if acute bronchospasm or moderate or greater liver impairment, caution in patients with depression (suicidality); inhibits CYP3A4 and - 1A2 (eg, erythromycin) (L)
Combinations and Other Medications		
✓ Albuterol-Ipratropium *(Duoneb)*	0.09/0.018 mg/puff, 2–3 puffs q6h; 3 mg/0.5 mg by nebulizer▲ q6h	Same as individual agents (L, K)
✓ *Combivent Respimat*	100/20 mcg 1 inhalation q6h (not to exceed 6 inhalations in 24 h)	
✓ Budesonide-Formoterol *(Symbicort)*	2 inhalations q12h (80 mcg, 160 mcg/4.5 mcg)	Same as individual agents (L, K)
Cromolyn sodium (eg, *Intal*)	2 mL (10 mg/mL) q6h by nebulizer	Cough, throat irritation (L, K)
✓ Formoterol-Mometasone *(Dulera)*	1–2 inhalations (5 mcg/100, 200 mcg per inhalation)	Nasopharyngitis, sinusitis, headache
Omalizumab *(Xolair)*	150–375 mg SC q2–4wk based on body weight and pre-tx IgE level	Malignancy, rare anaphylaxis; half-life 26 d (L, bile); expensive ($6,000–$25,000/yr)
✓ Salmeterol-Fluticasone combination *(Advair Diskus)*	1 inhalation q12h (50 mcg/100, 250, or 500 mcg/cap)	Same as long-acting β-agonists and inhaled steroids
Tiotropium-Olodaterol *(Stiolto Respimat)*	2 inhalations q24h (2.5/2.5 mcg per inhalation)	Same as long-acting β-agonists and tioropium

(cont.)

Table 120. Asthma and COPD Medications (cont.)

Medication Class/Agent	Dosage	Adverse Events (Metabolism, Excretion)
Umeclidium-vilanterol (Anoro Ellipta)	1 inhalation q24h (62.5 mcg/25 mcg)	Same as long-acting β-agonists; see also Umeclindinium. Not for use in asthma.
Vilanterol-Fluticasone (Breo Ellipta)	1 inhalation q24h (25 mcg/100 mcg)	Same as long-acting β-agonists and inhaled steroids

✓ = preferred for treating older adults

[a] Older nonselective β_2-agonists such as isoproterenol, metaproterenol, or epinephrine are not recommended and are more toxic.

RESTRICTIVE LUNG DISEASE (RLD)

- Up to 11% of people over age 75 meet criteria for RLD. In old age, RLD is often due to disorders outside of the lung itself. RLD can be disabling, progressive, and sometimes treatable.
- RLD is more likely to produce ADL disability (RR = 9.0; 95% CI: 3.1–26.6) than is moderate COPD (RR = 2.3; 95% CI: 0.7–4.5).
- These disorders are characterized by reduced total lung capacity (TLC). However, TLC is not part of routine pulmonary function tests (PFTs). In practice, FVC is used as a surrogate for TLC.

Diagnosis and Staging

- Patients present with exertional dyspnea which often has insidious onset. PFTs show decreased lung volumes (FVC <80% of the lower limit of normal [LLN]), a FEV_1/FVC ratio >85–90%, and flow volume curve shows a complex profile.
- Disease severity is based on the degree of reduction of FVC; FVC 60–80% of LLN = mild, 50–60% = moderate, <50% = severe

Differential Diagnosis

The many disorders that cause RLD can be grouped as shown in **Table 121** along with differentiating characteristics and some common causes in the older population.

Table 121. Common Causes of Restrictive Lung Diseases in Older Adults		
Category (Mechanism)	**Differentiating PFT Findings**	**Common Causes**
Intrinsic lung diseases (inflammation or scarring of the lung tissue)	Abnormal DLCO	Idiopathic pulmonary fibrosis Post-inflammatory lung fibrosis Radiation Drug induced Connective tissue diseases (RA, etc) Chronic HF
Extrinsic disorders (mechanical compression of lungs or limitation of expansion)	Normal DLCO	Kyphosis/Kyphoscoliosis Obesity
Neuromuscular disorders (decreased ability of the respiratory muscles to inflate/ deflate lungs)	Normal DLCO Reduced maximal inspiratory and/or expiratory pressures	Amyotrophic lateral sclerosis Thyroid and adrenal disorders Vitamin D deficiency Post-polio syndrome

(cont.)

Table 121. Common Causes of Restrictive Lung Diseases in Older Adults (cont.)		
Category (Mechanism)	**Differentiating PFT Findings**	**Common Causes**
CNS disorders	Normal DLCO	Parkinson disease Multisystemic atrophy Progressive supranuclear palsy Multiple sclerosis

Note: DLCO = diffusing capacity of the lung for carbon monoxide.

Therapy

Follows the underlying cause. Because many of these disorders are outside of the lung itself, diagnosis and management often falls to geriatric healthcare providers.

IMPOTENCE (ERECTILE DYSFUNCTION OR ED)

Definition

Inability to achieve sufficient erection for intercourse. Prevalence nearly 70% by age 70.

Causes

Often multifactorial; >50% of cases arterial, venous, or mixed vascular cause (**Table 122**).

Table 122. Causes of Erectile Dysfunction (ED) in Older Men

Causes (in order of frequency)	Associated Findings/Risk Factors	Onset
Vascular	Vascular risk factors; femoral bruits; poor pedal pulses. Venous vascular disease suggested by penile plaques (Peyronie disease).	Gradual
Neuropathic	DM; hx of pelvic trauma, surgery, irradiation; spinal injury or surgery; Parkinson disease, multiple sclerosis; alcoholism; loss of bulbocavernosus reflex or orthostatic BP changes	Gradual
Drug induced (p 305)	Loss of sleep-associated erections	Sudden
Psychogenic, including bereavement	Sleep-associated erections or erections with masturbation are intact	Sudden
Hypogonadism[a]	Decreased libido >ED; low testosterone, small testes, gynecomastia	Gradual
Thyroid or adrenal disorders or hyperprolactinemia	Rare <5% of cases; other associated symptoms of the underlying problem	Gradual

[a] Don't prescribe testosterone for men with ED and normal testosterone levels.[CW]

Therapy

An at-home trial of a PDE5 inhibitor (**Table 123**) is both diagnostic and therapeutic for the common causes of ED (vascular, neuropathic, mixed); these agents are also effective for ED after prostate cancer tx. Alternate tx (devices, injections) are included in **Table 123**.

Table 123. Management of Erectile Dysfunction

Therapy	Dose	Formulation	Comments
PDE5 Inhibitors			
Avanafil *(Stendra)*	start 50 mg 30 min before sexual activity	50, 100, 200	*All Agents*: Effective in 60–70% of men with ED of various etiologies. Contraindicated with use of nitrates and nonischemic optic neuropathy. PDE5 inhibitors potentiate the hypotensive effects of α-blockers. Potent CYP3A4 inhibitors reduce metabolism of all PDE5 inhibitors and increase risk of toxicity. *Common tx-related AEs*: headache, flushing, rhinitis, dyspepsia *Other tx-related AEs*: priapism, low back pain, bluish discoloration of vision
Sildenafil *(Viagra)*	start 25 mg 1 h before sexual activity	25, 50, 100	*Other AEs*: increased sensitivity to light, blurred vision

(cont.)

Table 123. Management of Erectile Dysfunction

Therapy	Dose	Formulation	Comments
Vardenafil *(LEVITRA)*	start 2.5 mg 1 h before sexual activity	2.5, 5, 10, 20	*Other AEs:* Avoid using in congenital or acquired QT prolongation and in patients taking class IA or III antiarrhythmics.
Tadalafil *(Cialis)*	start 5 mg 30–60 min before sexual activity; lasts 24 h	2.5, 5, 10, 20	*Other AEs:* myalgia, pain in limbs; 2.5 mg/d may be as effective as taking higher doses prn.
Devices			
Vacuum tumescence devices (eg, *Osbon-Erec Aid*)	N/A	N/A	*Rare:* ecchymosis, reduced ejaculation, coolness of penile tip. Good acceptance in older population; intercourse successful in 70–90% of cases.
Penile prosthesis	N/A	N/A	*Complications:* infection, mechanical failure, penile fibrosis
Prostaglandin E			
Alprostadil	Intracavernosal 5–40 mcg *or* intraurethral 125–1000 mcg	Intracavernosal: 5, 10, 20, 40 mcg *or* intraurethral: 125, 250, 500, 1000 mcg	*Risks:* hypotension, bruising, bleeding, priapism; erection >4 h requires emergency tx; intraurethral safer and more acceptable. Rarely used since PDE5 inhibitors became available. 50% of patients stop tx within 1 yr due to discomfort or inconvenience.

Diagnosis of Hypogonadism in Middle-aged and Older Men

- Hypogonadism is more closely associated with libido than with ED.
- Diagnose testosterone deficiency only in men with consistent symptoms and unequivocally low testosterone levels.
- Morning total testosterone level <320 ng/dL (11 nmol/L) that remains <320 ng/dL on repeat testing and a free testosterone level of <640 pg/dL (<220 pmol/L) using a reliable assay suggests deficiency.
- Ask the following questions from the European Male Aging Study Sexual Function Questionnaire. If the answer to **all 3 questions** is the response in **bold**, hypogonadism is likely present.
  - How often did you think about sex? This includes times of just being interested in sex, day dreaming, or fantasizing about sex, as well as times when you wanted to have sex.
    - **2 or 3 times or less in the last month**
    - Once/wk or more often
  - It is common for men to experience erectile problems. This may mean that one is not always able to get or keep an erection that is rigid enough for satisfactory activity (including sexual intercourse and masturbation). In the last *month*, are you:
    - Always able to keep an erection that would be good enough for sexual intercourse, or usually able to get and keep an erection that would be good enough for sexual intercourse
    - **Sometimes or never able to get and keep an erection that would be good enough for sexual intercourse**
  - How frequently do you awaken with full erection?
    - **Once in the last month or less often**
    - 2 or 3 times or more often in the last month

Therapy for Hypogonadism

- Prescribe testosterone only when there is clear evidence of deficiency.[CW]
- Testosterone possibly increases cardiovascular events in men with cardiovascular risk.
- Testosterone is not recommended with breast or prostate cancer, prostate nodule or induration, PSA >3 ng/dL, or significant prostate obstructive symptoms.
- Testosterone is not recommended if hematocrit >50%, untreated sleep apnea, or HF.
- Avoid testosterone/methyltestosterone unless for moderate to severe hypogonadism.[BC]
- Monitor AEs and response q3mo. *AEs:* polycythemia, fluid retention, liver dysfunction.
- During tx, check serum testosterone concentration and adjust dose to achieve concentration in midrange of normal; check midway between injections (except undecanoate, check before next injection); all other preparations check manufacturer's recommendation for monitoring levels and adjusting dose.
- Probably effective in the tx of opioid-induced androgen deficiency.

Table 124. Management of Hypogonadism with Testosterone Replacement

Testosterone Preparation	Starting Dose	Formulation
Injectable		
Testosterone enanthate▲	50–200 mg IM q2–4wk	200 mg/mL
Testosterone cypionate▲	50–400 mg IMq2–4wk	100, 200 mg/mL
Testosterone undecanoate *(Aveed)*	750mg IM at 0 and 4 wk then q10 wk	250 mg/mL
Transdermal		
Androderm	4 mg/d	2, 4 mg/24-h pch
AndroGel metered-dose pump	4 pumps/d 2 pumps/d	1%: 12.5 mg/pump 1.62%: 20.25 mg/pump
Androgel transdermal gel	50 mg qd 40.5 mg qd	1%: 25, 50 mg/pk 1.6%: 20.25, 40.5 mg/pk
Fortesta	4 spr/d	60-g canister (10 mg/spr)
Testim	1 tube/d	5-g tube (50-mg)
Buccal		
Striant	1 tab q12h	T: 30 mg
Intranasal		
Natesto	1 pump each nares 3×/d	5.5 mg/pump

FEMALE SEXUAL DYSFUNCTION

Definitions

Dyspareunia: pain with intercourse

Female Sexual Interest/Arousal Disorder *(FSIAD):* absence or significantly reduced sexual interest/arousal for at least 6 mo that causes clinically significant distress

Evaluation

- Ask about sexual problems (eg, changes in libido, partner's function, and health issues).
- Screen for depression.
- Perform pelvic examination for vulvovaginitis, vaginal atrophy, conization (decreased distensibility and narrowing of the vaginal canal), scarring, pelvic inflammatory disease, cystocele, and rectocele.

- Factors Aggravating Dyspareunia
  - Anticholinergic medications (vaginal dryness)
  - Gynecologic tumors
  - Interstitial cystitis
  - Myalgia from overexertion during Kegel exercises
  - Pelvic fractures
  - Retroverted uterus
  - Sacral nerve root compression
  - Vaginal atrophy from estrogen deprivation
  - Osteoarthritis
  - Vulvar or vaginal infection
- DSM-5 Criteria for FSAID (in addition to the above) must have at least 3 of the following:
  - Absent/reduced interest in sexual activity
  - Absent/reduced sexual/erotic thoughts or fantasies
  - No/reduced initiation of sexual activity; unresponsive to partner's attempt to initiate sexual activity
  - Absent/reduced sexual excitement/pleasure during sexual activity in at least 75% of encounters
  - Absent/reduced sexual interest/arousal in response to any internal or external cues (eg, written, verbal, visual)
  - Absent/reduced genital or nongenital sensations during sexual activity in at least 75% of sexual encounters

Management

Dyspareunia
- Identify and treat clinical pathology.
- Water-soluble lubricants (eg, *Replens*) are highly effective as monotherapy for dyspareunia in those who cannot or will not use hormones, or as a supplement to estrogen.
- For vaginismus (vaginal muscle spasm), trial cessation of intercourse and gradual vaginal dilation may help.
- Topical estrogens (**Table 125**) treat dyspareunia with minimal systemic levels when used in 0.5–1 g 2–3×/wk.
- Moderate to severe atrophic vaginitis may also be treated with the selective estrogen-receptor modulator, ospemifene 60 mg orally once daily with food for the shortest duration necessary; in women with a uterus, consider concomitant progestin tx. Contraindications: stroke, MI, DVT, or PE, estrogen-dependent neoplasia, and genital bleeding.

FSIAD
- The OTC botanical massage oil *Zestra* appears to improve desire and arousal in women with mixed desire/interest/arousal/orgasm disorders but can cause vaginal burning.
- Studies of sildenafil have not consistently shown effectiveness.
- Flibanserin (*Addyi*, a postsynaptic 5-HT1A agonist 5-HT2A antagonist) 100 mg qhs studied in premenopausal women; Dizziness was the most common AE (also somnolence, nausea, fatigue). No postmenopausal women were enrolled in the studies submitted for FDA approval.
- Short-term use of androgens provides modest but meaningful improvement (not approved in the United States).

Table 125. Topical Estrogens Without Systemic Effects	
Estrogen	**Dosage**
Estrogen cream *(Premarin, Ogen, Estrace)*	Use minimum dose (0.5 g[a] for *Premarin*, 2 g[b] for *Ogen* and *Estrace*) daily × 2 wk, then 1–3×/wk thereafter
Estradiol vaginal ring *(Estring)*	Insert intravaginally and change q90d
Estradiol vaginal tablets *(Vagifem)*	Insert 25 mcg intravaginally daily × 2 wk, then twice/wk

[a]A "dime" size amount is an easy way to describe to patients.
[b]About 4 times the "dime" size amount is needed.

DRUG-INDUCED SEXUAL DYSFUNCTION

Agents Associated with Sexual Dysfunction in both Men and Women

The following drugs and drug classes are believed to sometimes cause sexual dysfunction. In cases of suspected drug-induced sexual dysfunction, improvement after drug withdrawal provides the best evidence for the adverse effect. Tx with a drug from an alternative class to treat an underlying condition may be necessary.

* Antidepressants: SSRIs (see below) reduce libido and delay orgasm; lithium causes ED, MAOIs may cause ED or anorgasmia.
* Antipsychotics: olanzapine produces less loss of libido/ED than risperidone, clozapine, and oral and depot first-generation agents.
* Antihypertensives: any agent may cause ED related to reduced genital blood flow.
  ○ Spironolactone has antiandrogen effect.
  ○ Centrally acting sympatholytics (eg, clonidine) produce relatively high rates of sexual dysfunction (ED and loss of libido).
  ○ Peripherally acting sympatholytics, eg, reserpine (ED and loss of libido).
* Digoxin: possibly related to reduced testosterone levels
* Lipid-lowering agents: fibrates (gynecomastia and ED) and many statins (eg, lovastatin, pravastatin, simvastatin, atorvastatin) are the subject of case reports of both ED and gynecomastia. Statins affect the substrate for sex hormones and have been shown to reduce total and sometimes also bioavailable testosterone.
* Acid-suppressing drugs: The histamine$_2$-blockers cimetidine and more rarely ranitidine cause gynecomastia. Famotidine has caused hyperprolactinemia and galactorrhea. The PPI omeprazole has caused gynecomastia.
* Metoclopramide: induces hyperprolactinemia
* Anticonvulsants: phenobarbital, phenytoin, carbamazepine, primidone; all increase metabolism of androgen.
* Anticholinergics and antihistamines produce vaginal dryness.
* Alcohol: high dosages reduce libido.
* Opioids: reduce libido and produce anorgasmia related to reduced testosterone.

Management of SSRI-Induced Sexual Dysfunction

* Wait for tolerance to develop (4–6 mo of tx may be needed).
* Pharmacologic management:
  ○ For escitalopram and sertraline (not other SSRIs), reducing dosage or "drug holidays" (skip or reduce weekend dose) may help, but may result in relapse and nonadherence.
  ○ In both men and women, sildenafil 50–100 mg po improved sexual function in prospective, parallel-group, randomized, double-blind, placebo-controlled clinical trials.
  ○ Consider change in tx to bupropion, mirtazapine, nefazodone, or vilazodone.
  ○ Adding bupropion to SSRI reduces sexual dysfunction.

CHRONIC WOUND ASSESSMENT AND TREATMENT
Wound Assessment

Evaluation of chronic wounds should include the following (**Table 126** for wound characteristics specific to ulcer type):

• Location
• Wound size and shape: length, width, depth, stage (pressure ulcer), grade (diabetic foot ulcer)
• Wound bed: color, presence of slough, necrotic tissue, granulation tissue, epithelial tissue, undermining or tunneling
• Exudate: purulent vs nonpurulent (serous, serosanguineous)
• Wound edges: distinct, diffuse, rolled under
• Periwound skin and soft tissue: erythema, edema, induration, temperature
• Presence of pain at rest and with wound care procedures
• Signs of wound infection:
  ◦ Increased necrotic tissue
  ◦ Foul odor
  ◦ Purulent exudate
  ◦ Halo of erythema at wound edges
  ◦ Wound breakdown
  ◦ Increasing pain
  ◦ Marked edema
  ◦ Friable granulation tissue
  ◦ Serous exudate with nonspecific inflammation
  ◦ Nonhealing, new tunneling, or enlarged wound
  ◦ Heat

Table 126. Typical Wound Characteristics by Ulcer Type

	Arterial	Diabetic	Pressure	Venous
Location	Tips of toes or between toes, on pressure points of foot (eg, heel or lateral foot), or in areas of trauma	Plantar surface of foot, especially over metatarsal heads, toes, and heel	Over bony prominences (eg, trochanter, coccyx, ankle)	Gaiter area, particularly medial malleolus
Size and shape	Shallow, well-defined borders	Wound margins with callus	Variable length, width, depth depending on stage (staging system, p 311)	Edges may be irregular with depth limited to dermis or shallow subcutaneous tissue
Wound bed	Pale or necrotic	Granular tissue unless PAD present	Varies from bright red, shallow crater to deeper crater with slough and necrotic tissue; tunneling and undermining	Ruddy red; yellow slough may be present; undermining or tunneling uncommon
Exudate	Minimal amount due to poor blood flow	Variable amount; serous unless infection present	May be purulent, becoming serous as healing progresses; foul odor with infection	Copious; serous unless infection present

(cont.)

Table 126. Typical Wound Characteristics by Ulcer Type (cont.)

	Arterial	Diabetic	Pressure	Venous
Surrounding skin	Halo of erythema or slight fluctuance indicates infection	Normal; may be calloused	May be distinct, diffuse, rolled under; erythema, edema, induration if infected	May appear macerated, crusted, or scaly; presence of stasis dermatitis, hyperpigmentation
Pain	Cramping or constant deep aching	Variable intensity; none with advanced neuropathy	Painful, unless sensory function impaired or with deep, extensive tissue necrosis	Variable; may be severe, dull, aching, or bursting in character

- Swab culture of wound surface exudates is of no value in diagnosing infection due to wound contamination. Educate staff not to collect cultures of wound slough or pus; encourage use of Levine's technique.
  - Levine's technique (cleanse with NS followed by rotating a swab over a 1-cm square area of viable wound tissue [not necrotic] with sufficient pressure to express fluid from the wound tissue beneath the wound surface)

Principles of Wound Treatment

- Remove debris from wound surface.
  - Cleanse using NS or Lactated Ringer's with each dressing change. Avoid antiseptics because of cytotoxicity.
  - Irrigate using 4–15 psi to cleanse adherent debris. Use 8 mmHg pressure (19-gauge catheter and 35-mL syringe) when wound is deep, tunneled, or undermined.
- Remove necrotic tissue. Consider combining autolytic or topical enzyme debridement methods with sharp debridement to facilitate more rapid removal of necrotic tissue, by experienced clinician or licensed podiatrist.
  - Sharp debridement
  - Autolytic methods (eg, moisture-retaining dressings or hydrogels)
  - Mechanical (eg, wet-to-dry dressings)
  - Chemical (eg, topical enzymes such as *Accuzyme, Santyl*)
- Pack dead space (tunnels, undermining) loosely with moistened gauze dressings or strips of calcium alginate.
- Control pain associated with wound care procedures by offering pain medication 30 min before procedure.
  - Gauze-based negative pressure wound tx (TPWT), rather than foam, less painful in older adults, those with bone and tendon exposition wounds
  - For moderate to severe pain not managed by oral medications or with dose-limiting AEs, topical opioids may be used, eg, mixture of 10 mg morphine sulfate injectable combined with 8 g of neutral water-based gel applied 2×/d. Can titrate up to 10 mg morphine sulfate injectable with 5 g neutral water-based gel applied 2–3×/d.
  - High intensity TENS may help moderate to severe pain during wound care procedures.
- Control bacterial burden/infection.
  - Monitor for signs of infection.
  - Debride all necrotic tissue *(except* in lower extremity with arterial insufficiency).
  - If infection is suspected, assess type and quantity of bacteria by validated quantitative swab or tissue biopsy. Suspect infection if epithelialization from margin is not progressing

within 2 wk of debridement and initiation of offloading (use of cast, splint, or special shoe to shift pressure from wound to surrounding support structure).

○ For ulcers with ≥1 million CFU/g of tissue or any tissue level of β-hemolytic streptococci, use a topical antimicrobial (eg, *Silvadene* or dressings with bioavailable silver, cadexomer iodine at concentrations up to 0.45%; p 312). Limit duration of use of topical antimicrobials to avoid cytotoxicity or bacterial resistance.

○ Consider 2-wk trial of topical antibiotic for clean ulcers that are not healing after 2–4 wk optimal care; antibiotic spectrum should include Gram-negative, Gram-positive, and anaerobic organisms.

○ Use systemic antibiotics if obvious signs of localized infection, cellulitis, osteomyelitis, or systemic inflammatory response (**Table 127**).

Table 127. Empiric Antibiotic Therapy to Treat Infections in Chronic Wounds

Severity of Infection	Clinical Features	Medication Options	Duration of Treatment
Mild	Superficial, localized signs of inflammation/infection, without signs of a systemic response or osteomyelitis, and ambulatory management planned	Cephalexin Clindamycin Amoxicillin/clavulanate Clindamycin plus ciprofloxacin, moxifloxacin, or linezolid (for MRSA)	2 wk
Moderate	Superficial to deep tissue involvement, a systemic response, no osteomyelitis, and either planned ambulatory or inpatient management	Clindamycin plus ciprofloxacin Clindamycin po plus ceftriaxone Vancomycin (for MRSA) Linezolid (for MRSA)	2–4 wk
Severe	Deep tissue with a systemic response, presence of osteomyelitis, or is life-/limb-threatening, and requires inpatient care	Clindamycin po plus ceftriaxone Piperacillin/tazobactam Clindamycin po plus gentamicin Imipenem Meropenem Vancomycin (for MRSA) Linezolid (for MRSA)	2–12 wk (Bone and joint involvement requires prolonged oral tx after IV tx completed.)

Source: Adapted from Landis, SJ. *Advances in Skin and Wound Care* 2008;21:531–540.

○ Treat cellulitis surrounding ulcer with a systemic Gram-positive bactericidal antibiotic (cellulitis, p 85) unless Gram-negative organisms are suspected and require aggressive IV tx.

○ If osteomyelitis is suspected, evaluate with radiographs, MRI, CT, or radionuclide scan.

○ Referral for surgical evaluation is warranted.

• Provide moist wound environment and control exudates.

○ Dressings (p 312)

• Adjunctive tx to support wound healing process

○ Negative-pressure wound tx (ie, vacuum-assisted closure [VAC])

▪ Indications: Stage III and IV pressure ulcers, neuropathic ulcers, venous ulcers, dehisced incisions with trapping of third-space fluid around wound

▪ Contraindications: Presence of *any* nonviable, necrotic tissue in wound; untreated osteomyelitis; malignancy in or surrounding wound

▪ Avoid use in frail elderly patients on anticoagulants (eg, *Coumadin*, heparin, etc)

▪ Guidelines for use:

○ Negative pressure = 75–125 mmHg depending on wound characteristics

- Dressing change regimen: 48 h after placement, then every other day
  - Cycle: continuous for initial 48 h, then intermittent (5 min negative pressure followed by 2 min of no pressure) for remainder of tx
  - Specialized training in application and monitoring of tx essential for successful outcome
  - Electrical stimulation
    - Indications: Stage III and IV pressure ulcers, arterial ulcers, diabetic foot ulcers, and venous ulcers if no evidence of measurable improvement after ≥30 d of standard wound care
    - Contraindications: presence of cardiac pacemaker, malignancy, osteomyelitis
    - Precautions: avoid placement of electrodes over topical substances containing metal ions, tangential to the heart, or over the carotid sinus
    - Guidelines for use:
      - Refer to PT for stimulation parameters
      - Predominant type of current used is pulsed current (either low- or high-voltage)
      - Electrode placement—two options:
        - One electrode placed directly in contact with saline-moistened gauze on wound surface and second electrode 15–30 cm from wound edge
        - Electrodes placed on skin at wound edges on opposite sides of wound
      - Pulse frequency: 100 pulses/sec with current sufficient to produce tingling sensation
      - Tx administered for 1 h, 5–7 d/wk, continued as long as wound is progressing toward closure
  - Growth factor tx
    - *Regranex*, a recombinant platelet-derived growth factor, applied topically in thin layer to a clean wound bed for 12 h followed by 12 h of saline-moistened gauze dressing
    - Indications: Currently for diabetic foot ulcers but may have benefit in other nonhealing wounds.
    - Contraindications: Not recommended for use in patients with known malignancies.
    - Guidelines for use:
      - Must be used in conjunction with offloading of pressure on foot, regular sharp debridement, absence of necrotic tissue, and maintenance of uninfected status.
      - If wound closure is not ≥30% in 10 wk or complete in 20 wk, reevaluate tx plan and consider surgical intervention (especially if osteomyelitis is present).
- Prevent further injury
  - Use pressure-reducing mattresses or chair cushions and float the heels (pillows under the calf and knee) and device to keep covers off toes
  - Reposition q2h and avoid any pressure on the wound
- Support repair process
  - Protein (1.25–1.5 g/kg/d) and calories (30–35/kg/d) unless contraindicated because of impaired renal function
  - Correct deficiencies of vitamin C and zinc if suspected
  - Avoid exposure to cold; vasoconstriction reduces blood flow to wound
  - Avoid smoking to prevent vasoconstriction that reduces blood flow to wound
  - Ensure adequate hydration with oral or parenteral fluids
- If ulcer does not show signs of healing over 2-wk period of optimal tx, reevaluate wound management strategies and factors affecting healing.

ARTERIAL ULCERS

Definition

Any lesion caused by severe tissue ischemia secondary to atherosclerosis and progressive arterial occlusion

Wound Assessment

- See Chronic Wound Assessment (p 306).
- Assess ABI: If ABI <0.5, wound healing unlikely without revascularization.

Management (also PAD, p 61, Diabetes, p 94, Chronic Heart Failure, p 42, and Renal Failure, p 177)

Protect from Injury

- Avoid compression of arterial wounds when ABI is <0.8.
- Avoid friction and pressure by using lamb's wool or foam between toes.
- Float the heels (pillows under the calf and knee) and use suitable device to keep covers off toes.
- Use positioning devices to avoid pressure on feet (eg, heel protectors).

Local Wound Care

Tx dictated by adequacy of perfusion and status of wound bed:

- Avoid debridement of necrotic tissue until perfusion status is determined.
- Assess vascular perfusion and refer for surgical intervention if consistent with overall goals of care.
- If wound is infected, revascularization procedures, surgical removal of necrotic tissue, and systemic antibiotics are tx of choice.
- Topical antibiotics should not be used solely to treat infected ischemic wounds and may cause sensitivity reactions.
- If wound is uninfected and dry eschar is present, maintain dry intact eschar as a barrier to bacteria. Application of an antiseptic may decrease bacterial burden on wound surface although evidence is lacking.
- If wound is uninfected and soft slough and necrotic tissue are present, apply moisture-retaining dressings that allow frequent inspection of wound for signs of infection.

DIABETIC (NEUROPATHIC FOOT) ULCERS

Definition

Any lesion on the plantar surface of the foot caused by neuropathy and repetitive pressure on foot.

Wound Assessment

- See Chronic Wound Assessment (p 306).
- Assess for specific diabetes-related signs of infection:
  - Sudden increase in blood glucose
  - Wound can be probed to the bone—highly sensitive indicator of osteomyelitis
  - Exclude gross arterial disease by assessment for palpable pedal pulses, toe:brachial index >0.7 (or ABI >0.9), a transcutaneous oxygen pressure of >30 mmHg, or normal Doppler-derived wave form.
- Determine grade of ulcer (Wagner Classification)
  Grade 0: Preulcerative lesions; healed ulcers present; bony deformity present
  Grade 1: Superficial ulcer without subcutaneous tissue involvement

Grade 2: Penetration through subcutaneous tissue
Grade 3: Osteitis, abscess, or osteomyelitis
Grade 4: Gangrene of digit
Grade 5: Gangrene of foot requiring disarticulation

Management (also Diabetes, p 94)

Local Wound Care

In addition to recommendations under Chronic Wound Treatment (p 307):

- Debride devitalized tissue and callus: surgical debridement is method of choice for effective, rapid removal of nonviable tissue
- Avoid occlusive dressings to reduce risk of wound infection
- Offload pressure and stress from foot
  ○ Avoidance of pressure on foot essential to management of diabetic foot ulcer
  ○ Use orthotic that redistributes weight on plantar surface of foot when ambulating (eg, total contact cast, *DH Pressure Relief Walker*)
- If ulcer does not reduce in size by ≥50% after 4 wk of tx, reassess tx and consider alternative options (eg, negative-pressure wound tx, growth factor tx, skin substitutes, extracellular matrix, hyperbaric oxygen tx).
  ○ Skin substitutes *(Apligraf, Dermagraft, OrCel, TransCyte)* containing growth factors present in the skin may stimulate healing and decrease time to wound closure. Wound must be granular to be effective.
  ○ Hyperbaric oxygen tx effective in promoting healing of complicated chronic diabetic foot ulcers is covered by Medicare and some insurance companies. Caution in patients with HF, advanced COPD, and those treated with anticancer drugs. Tx applied in chamber for 1.5–2 h/d for 20–40 d.

PRESSURE ULCERS

Definition

Any lesion caused by unrelieved pressure resulting in damage of underlying tissue; usually develops over bony prominence

Wound Assessment

- See Chronic Wound Assessment (p 306).
- Determine level of tissue injury by using Pressure Ulcer Staging System:
  ○ **Stage I:** An observable pressure-related alteration of intact skin that, as compared with an adjacent or opposite area on the body, may include changes in one or more of the following: skin temperature (warmth or coolness), tissue consistency (firm or boggy feel), and/or sensation (pain, itching). The ulcer appears as a defined area of persistent redness in lightly pigmented skin, whereas in darker skin tones, it may appear with persistent red, blue, or purple hues.
  ○ **Stage II:** Partial-thickness skin loss involving epidermis and/or dermis; presents as abrasion, blister, or shallow crater.
  ○ **Stage III:** Full-thickness skin loss involving damage or necrosis of subcutaneous tissue that may extend down to, but not through, underlying fascia; presents as deep crater with or without undermining of adjacent tissue.
  ○ **Stage IV:** Full-thickness skin loss with extensive destruction; tissue necrosis; or damage to muscle, bone, or supporting structures. May have associated undermining of sinus tracts. *Note:* eschar-covered ulcers cannot be staged until eschar is removed.
  ○ **Suspected Deep Tissue Injury:** Localized area of purple or maroon discoloration of intact skin or blood-filled blister indicating underlying soft-tissue injury due to pressure and/or

shear. May be preceded by pain, tissue firmness, mushiness, or bogginess; and cooler or warmer temperature than adjacent tissue.

○ **Unstageable:** Covered with eschar or necrotic tissue.

Management

Local Wound Care: Common Dressings for Pressure Ulcer Treatment

Transparent film

Brand names: *Bioclusive, 3M Tegaderm, Blisterfilm, ClearSite, Comfeel Film, CarraSmart Film, DermaView, Mepore, Opsite, Polyskin II*

Indications and Use: Stages I and II, protection from friction, superficial scrape, autolytic debridement of slough; apply skin prep to intact skin to protect from adhesive

Contraindications: Draining ulcers, suspicion of skin infection or fungus

Foam

Brand names: *Allevyn, Lyofoam, COPA, ComfortFoam, DermaFoam, Flexzan, Mepilex, Mitraflex, 3M Tegaderm Foam, Polyderm, PolyMem, Tielle, VigiFoam*

Indications and Use: Stages II and III, light to moderate exudate; leave in place 3–5 d, can apply as window to secure transparent film

Contraindications: Excessive exudate; dry, crusted wound; dry eschar; periwound maceration likely if not changed appropriately

Foam with silver

Brand names: *Allevyn Ag Foam, Aquacel Ag Foam, Bordered Foam/Ag, HydraFoam/Ag, PolyMem Silver, Optifoam AG, Contreet Foam*

Indications and Use: Infected Stage II and III ulcers; highly colonized ulcer

Contraindications: Sensitivity to silver; excessive exudate; dry, crusted wound; dry eschar; exudate must be present for silver to be released; inactivates enzymatic debriding agents; periwound maceration likely if not changed appropriately

Hydrocolloids

Brand names: *DuoDERM, Extra Thin DuoDERM, DuoDERM CGF, DuoDERM Signal, 3M Tegasorb, 3M Tegasorb Thin, RepliCare, RepliCare Thin, Comfeel Plus, Nu-DERM, Cutinova Hydro, Hydrocol II, Restore, Restore CX, Restore Plus, Ultec, Ultec Pro, DermaFilm, Exuderm, Exuderm LP, SignaDRESS, MPM Excel, ProCol, Odor Shield*

Indications and Use: Stages II and III; light to moderate drainage; reduces wound pain; autolytic debridement of slough; preventive for high-risk friction areas; leave in place 3–7 d; can apply as window to secure transparent film or under-taping; can apply over alginate to control drainage; must control maceration; apply skin prep to intact skin to protect from adhesive

Contraindications: Fragile skin; infected ulcers; heavily draining wounds, sinus tracts

Hydrocolloid with silver

Brand names: *Contreet*

Indications and Use: Infected ulcer; highly colonized ulcer; antimicrobial; leave in place up to 7 d

Contraindications: Sensitivity to silver; ionic silver released only in presence of exudate; inactivates enzymatic debriding agents; fragile skin; heavily draining wounds, sinus tracts

Hydrogel (amorphous gels)

Brand names: Intrasite Gel, AquaSite Hydrogel, Aquasorb, Biolex, CarraDres, Curasol Gel, Restore Hydrogel, SAF-Gel, SoloSite Wound Gel, 3M Tegaderm Hydrogel, Dermagran, DuoDERM Hydroactive Gel, Normlgel, Nu-Gel, Purilon Gel, Skintegrity Hydrogel, SAF-Gel, Viniferamine Wound Hydrogel, Cutimed Gel

Indications and Use: Stages II, III, and IV; dermabrasion; skin tears; necrotic ulcers; reduces ulcer pain; rehydrates ulcer bed; softens and loosens slough and necrosis; use in place of saline gauze for packing cavities, tunnels, and undermining; stays moist longer than saline gauze; leave in place 1–3 d depending on type of gel; may require secondary dressing

Contraindications: Avoid use with heavily draining wounds; may cause periwound maceration

Hydrogel with silver

Brand names: SilvaSorb Gel, SilvrSTAT, Silver-Sept Wound Gel, Vinieramine Wound Hydrogel AG, Silver-Sept Silver Antimicrobial Skin & Wound Gel, Gentell Hydrogel AG

Indications and Use: Infected ulcers; highly colonized ulcers; antimicrobial; rehydrates ulcer bed; Leave in place maximum of 3 d

Contraindications: Sensitivity to silver; avoid use with topical medications; inactivates enzymatic debriding agents; avoid use with heavily draining wounds; may cause periwound maceration; signs of systemic side effects, especially erythema multiforme; fungal proliferation

Hydrogel sheets

Brand names: Vigilon, AquaClear, AquaDerm, AquaSite, Comfort-Aid, Curasol, Elasto-Gel, FLEXIGEL, Hydrogel, Spand-Gel, Aquasorb, Nugel, Curagel, Derma-Gel, FlexiGel

Indications and Use: Stage II; needs to be held in place with topper dressing

Contraindications: Avoid use in macerated areas; wounds with moderate to heavy exudate

Calcium alginate

Brand names: Sorbsan, Kaltostat, Algiderm, DU-DERM Alginate, 3M Tegagen HI & HG Alginate, Cutimed, ALGICELL, ALGISITE M, DermaGinate, Gentell, Melgisorb, NU-DERM, Sorbalgon, CalciCare, SeaSorb

Indications and Use: Stages III and IV; excessive drainage; sinus tracts, tunnels, or cavities; apply dressing within wound borders; must use skin prep to protect periwound skin; requires secondary dressing; change q24–48h

Contraindications: Dry or minimally draining wound; dry eschar; superficial wounds with maceration; may produce odor during dressing change; can macerate periwound skin

Calcium alginate with silver

Brand names: Algidex Ag Alginate, 3M Tegaderm Alginate AG, SofSorb AG, ALGICELL Ag, DermaSyn/Ag, SILVERCEL, McKesson Calcium Alginate with Silver

Indications and Use: Infected Stage III and IV ulcers with or without sinus tracts, tunnels, or cavities or excessive drainage; highly colonized ulcer; apply dressing within wound borders; must use skin prep to protect periwound skin; requires secondary dressing; change q24–48h

Contraindications: Sensitivity to silver; exudate must be present for silver to be released; inactivates enzymatic debriding agents; dry or minimally draining wound; dry eschar; superficial wounds with maceration; may produce odor with dressing change; can macerate periwound skin

Gauze packing ▲ (moistened with saline)

Brand names: Kendall Fluff Kerlix, Curity, Johnson & Johnson (eg, square 2 × 2s/4 × 4s)

Indications and Use: Stages III and IV; moderate to heavy exudate; wounds with depth, especially those with tunnels, undermining; must be remoistened at least q4h to maintain moist wound environment

Contraindications: May macerate periwound skin; may be painful to remove; can traumatize tissue when removed

Composites (2 or more physically distinct dressing products combined as a single dressing)

Brand names: 3M Tegaderm, Alldress, CombiDERM, Comfortell, COVRSITE plus, DermaDress, DuDress, Gentell Comfortell, Covaderm Plus, Epigard, Medipore, Viasorb, McKesson Super Absorbent Dressing

Indications and Use: Stages I, II, III, and IV; light, moderate, or heavy exudate; conform to skin surface shape; designed with adhesive border; easy application and removal; dressing change frequency dependent on wound type (follow package insert)

Contraindications: Caution with fragile skin; adhesive may injure skin; some types may be contraindicated with Stage IV ulcers (refer to package insert); may not maintain moist wound environment

Collagen

Brand names: CellerateRX Gel/Powder, Fibracol, Kollagen Medifil Particles/Gel/Pads, Kollagen-Skin Temp II, Promogran Matrix, Stimulen, ColActive Plus, DermaCol, BIOSTEP matrix dressing, BGC Matrix, CollaSorb, Endoform Dermal Template, Excellagen, Helicoll, Puracol Plus, Simpurity collagen pad, Triple Helix Collagen

Indications and Use: Stage III and selected Stage IV (refer to package insert); light, moderate, or heavy exudate; chronic, nonhealing ulcers; nonadherent, absorbent, biodegradable gel; accommodates to wound surface; may be combined with topical agents; change dressing q1–3d

Contraindications: Sensitivity to collagen or bovine products; avoid use with necrotic ulcers; rehydration may be needed

Collagen with silver

Brand names: ColActive Plus AG, Prisma Matrix, SilvaKollagen Gel, DermaCol AG, BIOSTEP Ag, PROMOGRAN PRISMA, Puracol Plus AG, SilvaKollagen Gel

Indications and Use: Infected Stage III and selected Stage IV ulcers; highly colonized ulcers; light, moderate, or heavy exudate; antibacterial; leave in place maximum of 7 d

Contraindications: Sensitivity to collagen, bovine products, or silver; inactivates enzymatic debriding agents

Adapted from: Copyright 2016 by Rita Frantz. Used with permission.

Surgical Repair

Surgical referral is warranted for Stage IV pressure ulcers and for severely undermined or tunneled wounds.

VENOUS ULCERS

Definition

Any lesion caused by venous insufficiency precipitated by venous HTN

Wound Assessment

- See Chronic Wound Assessment (p 306).
- Assess lower-extremity edema.
- Assess pedal pulses to exclude ischemic ulcers.

Management

Compression Therapy

- Essential component of venous ulcer tx decreases healing time and pain
- Provides externally applied pressure to lower extremity to facilitate normal venous return
- Therapeutic level of compression is 30–40 mmHg at ankle, decreasing toward knee
- Avoid compression tx when ABI ≤0.8
- Types of compression tx:
  - Static compression device
    - Layered compression wraps *(Profore, ProGuide, Dynapress)*
    - Short-stretch wraps *(Comprilan)*
    - Paste-containing bandages *(Unna's boot, Duke boot)*
      - Preferable for actively ambulating patient; support compression of calf muscle "pump"
  - Dynamic compression devices (indicated when static compression not feasible)
    - Pneumatic compression device (intermittent pneumatic pumps)
    - Powered devices that propel venous blood upward when applied to lower leg
  - Compression tx for long-term maintenance
    - Therapeutic compression stockings *(Jobst, Juzo, Sigvaris, Medi-Strumpf, Therapress Duo)*

Local Wound Care

In addition to recommendations under Chronic Wound Treatment (p 307):

- Use exudate-absorbing dressings (eg, calcium alginate dressings, foam dressings). *Note:* A recent review indicates no benefit of alginate dressing over hydrocolloid or plain nonadherent dressings.
- Use skin sealant to protect skin around wound from exudates.
- Skin substitutes (eg, *Apligraf, Dermagraft, GammaGraft, OrCel, TransCyte*) containing growth factors present in skin may decrease wound healing time and decrease pain. Wound must be granular to be effective.
- Infected venous ulcers should be treated with systemic antibiotics because of development of resistant organisms with topical antibiotics.

Surgical Intervention

If manifestations of chronic venous insufficiency and ulceration are resistant to more conservative tx or if venous obstruction is present, surgical repair (eg, skin graft) is tx of choice.

CLASSIFICATION

- Circadian rhythm disorders (eg, jet lag)
- **Insomnia** (difficulty initiating or maintaining sleep, or poor quality sleep)
- Parasomnias (disorders of arousal, partial arousal, and sleep stage transition)
- Hypersomnia of central origin (eg, narcolepsy)
- **Sleep-related breathing disorders** (central and obstructive sleep apnea and sleep-related hypoventilation-hypoxia syndromes)
- **Sleep-related movement disorders** (eg, RLS, periodic limb movement disorder)

Bolded disorders are covered here. Others are covered in *JAGS* 2009;57:761–789.

INSOMNIA

Risk Factors and Aggravating Factors

Treatable Associated Medical and Psychiatric Conditions: adjustment disorders, anxiety, bereavement, cough, depression, dyspnea (cardiac or pulmonary), GERD, nocturia, pain, paresthesias, Parkinson disease, stress, stroke

Medications That Cause or Aggravate Sleep Problems: alcohol, antidepressants, β-blockers, bronchodilators, caffeine, clonidine, corticosteroids, diuretics, L-dopa, methyldopa, nicotine, phenytoin, progesterone, quinidine, reserpine, sedatives, sympathomimetics including decongestants

Management

- For most patients, behavioral tx should be initial tx. Medications are usually not the best solution.[CW] Despite benefits of hypnotics on sleep quality, total sleep time, and frequency of nighttime awakening, these are small compared to the risk of adverse cognitive or psychomotor events. Combined behavioral tx and pharmacotherapy is more effective than either alone.
- Sleep improvements are better sustained over time with behavioral tx, including discontinuing pharmacotherapy after acute tx.

Nonpharmacologic

- Stimulus control
  Measures recommended to improve sleep hygiene:
  - During the daytime:
    - Get out of bed at the same time each morning regardless of how much you slept the night before.
    - Exercise daily but not within 2 h of bedtime.
    - Get adequate exposure to bright light during the day.
    - Decrease or eliminate naps, unless necessary part of sleeping schedule.
    - Limit or eliminate alcohol, caffeine, and nicotine, especially before bedtime.
  - At bedtime:
    - If hungry, have a light snack before bed (unless there are symptoms of GERD or it is otherwise medically contraindicated), but avoid heavy meals at bedtime.
    - Don't use bedtime as worry time. Write down worries for next day and then don't think about them.
    - Sleep only in your bedroom.

- Control nighttime environment, ie, comfortable temperature, quiet, dark.
  - Wear comfortable bedclothes.
  - If it helps, use soothing noise (eg, a fan or other appliance or a "white noise" machine).
  - Remove or cover the clock.
  - No television watching in the bedroom.
  - Avoid reading e-books or tablets with light-emitting device. Standard Kindle doesn't emit light.
  - Maintain a regular sleeping time, but don't go to bed unless sleepy.
  - Develop a sleep ritual (eg, hot bath 90 min before bedtime followed by preparing for bed for 20–30 min, followed by 30–40 min of relaxation, meditation, or reading).
  - If unable to fall asleep within 15–20 min, get out of bed and perform soothing activity, such as listening to soft music or reading (but avoid exposure to bright light or computer screens).
- CBT combines multiple behavioral approaches (eg, sleep restriction, stimulus control, cognitive tx); preliminary evidence supports that this also can be delivered either by telephone or via the Internet. More effective than tai chi.
- Sleep restriction: reduce time in bed to estimated total sleep time (min 5 h) and increase by 15 min/wk when ratio of time asleep to time in bed is ≥90%. During the period of sleep restriction, daytime sleepiness may be increased and reaction time may be slower. Effect size is comparable to CBT.
- Relaxation techniques—physical (progressive muscle relaxation, biofeedback); mental (imagery training, mindfulness meditation, hypnosis)
- Bright light: 10,000 lux for 30 min/d upon awakening for difficulty initiating sleep; 2,500 lux for 2 h/d in evening for difficulty maintaining sleep

Pharmacologic—Principles of Prescribing Medications for Sleep Disorders

- Combine with behavior tx rather than give medication alone.
- Use lowest effective dose.
- All increase risk of falls.
- Do not use OTC antihistamines to treat insomnia in older adults.
- For patients with anxiety at bedtime, consider SSRIs or buspirone.
- For sleep-onset insomnia, use a shorter-acting agent (eg, zolpidem, zaleplon). For sleep-maintenance insomnia, use a longer-acting agent (eg, eszopiclone, zolpidem ER, doxepin).
- Use intermittent dosing (2–4×/wk).
- Prescribe medications for short-term use (no more than 3–4 wk).
- D/C medication gradually.
- Be alert for rebound insomnia after discontinuation.

Table 128. Useful Medications for Sleep Disorders in Older Adults

Class, Medication	Usual Dose	Formulations	Half-life	Comments (Metabolism, Excretion)
Antidepressant, sedating				
Trazodone▲ (Desyrel)	25–50 mg	T: 50, 100, 150, 300	12 h	Moderate orthostatic effects; effective for insomnia with or without depression (L)
Doxepin (Silenor)	3 mg	T: 3, 6	15.3 h	May cause next-day sedation; many potential drug interactions

(cont.)

Table 128. Useful Medications for Sleep Disorders in Older Adults (cont.)

Class, Medication	Usual Dose	Formulations	Half-life	Comments (Metabolism, Excretion)
Benzodiazepines, intermediate-acting[a,BC]				May impair next-day performance, including driving; may cause aggressive behavior
Estazolam▲ (ProSom)	0.5–1 mg	T: 1, 2	12–18 h	Rapidly absorbed, effective in initiating sleep; slightly active metabolites that may accumulate (K)
Lorazepam▲ (Ativan)	0.25–2 mg	T: 0.5, 1, 2	8–12 h	Effective in initiating and maintaining sleep; associated with falls, memory loss, rebound insomnia (K)
Temazepam▲ (Restoril)	7.5–15 mg	C: 7.5, 15, 30	8–10 h[b]	Daytime drowsiness may occur with repeated use; effective for sleep maintenance; delayed onset of effect (K)
Nonbenzodiazepines [a,BC]				May impair next-day performance, including driving; may increase the risk of infections
Eszopiclone (Lunesta)	1 mg	T: 1, 2, 3	5–6 h	CYP3A4 interactions; avoid administration with high-fat meal; not for tx of anxiety (L)
Zaleplon▲ (Sonata)	5 mg	C: 5, 10	1 h	Avoid taking with alcohol or food (L)
Zolpidem▲ (Ambien)	5 mg	T: 5, 10	1.5–4.5 h[c]	CYP3A4 interactions; confusion and agitation may occur but are rare (L)
(Edluar)	5 mg	T: 5, 10 (sl)	2.8 h	
(Ambien CR)	6.25 mg	T: 6.25, 12.5	1.6–5.5 h	Do not divide, crush, or chew
(Zolpimist)	5 mg	Spr: 5 mg/spr	2–3 h	Spray over tongue; absorption more rapid
(Intermezzo)	1.75 mg	SL: 1.75, 3.5	2.4 h	SL: For middle-of-the-night insomnia
Orexin Receptor Agonist				
Suvorexant (Belsomra)	10–20 mg	T: 5, 10, 15, 20	12 h	Metabolized by CYP34A; can impair next-day driving
Hormone and Hormone Receptor Agonists				
Melatonin▲	0.3–5 mg	Various	1 h	May be best taken 3–5 h before bedtime; not regulated by FDA
Ramelteon (Rozerem)	8 mg within 30 min of bedtime	T: 8	Ramelteon: 1–2.6 h; active metabolite: 2–5 h	Do not administer with or immediately after high-fat meal (L, K)
Tasimelteon (Hetlioz)	20 mg hs	T: 20		Indicated for non-24-h sleep-wake disturbance; very expensive (L)

[a] May cause severe allergic reactions and complex sleep-related behavioral disturbances

[b] Can be as long as 30 h in older adults

[c] 3 h in older adults; 10 h in those with hepatic cirrhosis

SLEEP APNEA
Definition
Repeated episodes of apnea (cessation of airflow for ≥10 sec) or hypopnea (transient reduction [≥30% decrease in thoracoabdominal movement or airflow and with ≥4% oxygen desaturation, or an arousal] of airflow for ≥10 sec) during sleep with excessive daytime sleepiness or altered cardiopulmonary function. Predicts future strokes and cognitive impairment. HF (in men), and all-cause mortality (if severe).

Classification
Obstructive (OSA) (90% of cases): Airflow cessation as a result of upper airway closure in spite of adequate respiratory muscle effort
- Mild Apnea-Hypopnea Index (AHI): 5–15
- Moderate: AHI 15–30
- Severe: AHI: >30

Central (CSA): Cessation of respiratory effort

Mixed: Features of both obstructive and central

Associated Risk Factors
Family hx, increased neck circumference, male gender, Asian ethnicity, hx of hypothyroidism (in women), obesity, smoking, upper airway structural abnormalities (eg, soft palate, tonsils), HTN, HF, atrial fibrillation, stroke, chronic lung diseases, including asthma

Clinical Features
Excessive daytime sleepiness, snoring, choking or gasping on awakening, morning headache, nocturia

Evaluation
- Epworth Sleepiness Scale (www.ummidtown.org/~/media/systemhospitals/midtown/pdfs/centers/sleep/epworth_sleepiness_scale.pdf) is useful for documenting and monitoring daytime sleepiness.
- Full night's sleep study (polysomnography) in sleep laboratory is indicated for those who habitually snore and either report daytime sleepiness or have observed apnea.
- "Out-of-center" sleep testing can be used if high pre-test probability of moderate-to-severe OSA but should not be used if patients have comorbid conditions (eg, HF) that predispose to a sleep-related breathing disorder or another sleep disorder
- Results are reported as AHI, which is the number of episodes of apneas and hypopneas per hour of sleep.
- Medicare reimbursement threshold for CPAP based on a minimum of 2 h sleep by polysomnography is AHI (1) ≥15 or (2) ≥5 and ≤14 with documented symptoms of excessive daytime sleepiness, impaired cognition, mood disorders, or insomnia, or documented HTN, ischemic heart disease, or hx of stroke.
- No need for re-titration if asymptomatic, adherent patients with stable weight.[CW]

Management
Nonpharmacologic
- Patient education including information about increased risk of motor vehicle crashes
- Weight loss (eg, using very low-calorie diet) with active lifestyle counseling is effective in mild and moderate OSA. Benefit is less in severe OSA.
- Avoidance of alcohol or sedatives

- Lying in lateral rather than supine position (if normalization of AHI in non-supine position is confirmed by sleep study); may be facilitated by soft foam ball in a backpack or devices that use vibratory feedback.
- Exercise (eg, 150 min/wk [4 d/wk] moderate intensity aerobic exercise, even in the absence of weight loss, can improve symptoms.
- Oral appliances that keep the tongue in an anterior position during sleep or keep the mandible forward; less effective than CPAP in reducing AHI score but may be better tolerated. Generally used in mild to moderate OSA (AHI <30) for patients who do not want CPAP.
- For moderate sleep apnea (>15 and <30 AHI), oropharyngeal exercises, including tongue, soft palate, and lateral pharyngeal wall, performed daily improves symptoms and reduces AHI score.
- Positive airway pressure (PAP) is initial tx for clinically important sleep apnea. PAP may also improve the metabolic syndrome associated with OSA. PAP can be delivered through several modes:
  ○ Continuous (CPAP) by nasal mask, nasal prongs, or mask that covers the nose and mouth is the simplest and best studied. Other modes have not been shown to be superior. A short course (14 d) of eszopiclone may facilitate adherence when initiating CPAP.
  ○ Bilevel (BPAP) uses 2 present (inspiratory and expiratory) levels of pressure.
  ○ Autotitrating (APAP) changes PAP in response to change in air flow, circuit pressure, or vibratory snore.
  ○ Nasal (NPAP) *(Provent)* is a 1-way valve inserted into each nostril that creates resistance during exhalation.
- Bariatric surgery improves but does not cure moderate or severe OSA.

Pharmacologic (Should not be used as primary tx)
- Modafinil *(Provigil)* 200 mg qam for excessive daytime sleepiness (CYP3A4 inducer and CYP2C19 inhibitor) [T: 100, 200]; use in addition to (not instead of) CPAP

Surgical
- Palatal implants (for mild to moderate OSA)
- Tracheostomy (indicated for patients with severe apnea who cannot tolerate positive pressure or when other interventions are ineffective)
- Uvulopalatopharyngoplasty (curative in fewer than 50% of cases). Less invasive alternatives include laser-assisted uvulopalatoplasty, radiofrequency ablation, and maxillomandibular advancement. All decrease the AHI but have not been demonstrated to be superior to medical management.
- Hypoglossal nerve stimulation with an implantable neurostimulator device
- Maxillofacial surgery (rare cases)

SLEEP-RELATED MOVEMENT DISORDERS
Nocturnal Leg Cramps

Stretches of the calf and hamstrings (24 inches from wall, lean forward to wall, heels on floor, hold for 10–30 sec, repeat 5×) nightly before bedtime may help. Avoid dehydration. Despite evidence of effectiveness, quinine is not recommended for nocturnal leg cramps because of the potential for serious though uncommon AEs. Small studies have supported the use of vitamin B complex, verapamil, and diltiazem. Gabapentin has been used but with little evidence to support its effectiveness. There is no evidence to support the effectiveness of magnesium.

Restless Legs Syndrome (RLS; the majority will also have periodic limb movement disorder)

Diagnostic Criteria
- A compelling urge to move the limbs, usually associated with paresthesias or dysesthesias
- Motor restlessness (eg, floor pacing, tossing and turning in bed, rubbing legs)
- Vague discomfort, usually bilateral, most commonly in calves
- Symptoms occur while awake and are exacerbated by rest, especially at night
- Symptoms relieved by movement—jerking, stretching, or shaking of limbs; pacing

Secondary Causes: Iron deficiency, spinal cord and peripheral nerve lesions, uremia, diabetes, Parkinson disease, venous insufficiency, medications/drugs (eg, TCAs, SSRIs, lithium, dopamine antagonists, caffeine)

Nonpharmacologic Treatment
- Sleep hygiene measures (p 316).
- Avoid alcohol, caffeine, nicotine.
- Rub limbs.
- Use hot or cold baths, whirlpools.
- Vibrating pad *(Relaxis)* available by prescription only (FDA approved)

Pharmacologic Treatment
- Exclude or treat iron deficiency (treat if ferritin <75 mcg/L), peripheral neuropathy.
- If possible, avoid SSRIs, TCAs, lithium, and dopamine antagonists.

Start at low dosage, increase as needed. AASM recommendations:
- Standard medications (best benefit/burden and higher quality of evidence): Dopamine agonists pramipexole (begin at 0.125 mg) or ropinirole (begin at 0.25 mg) 1 h before time of usual onset of symptoms (**Table 91**).
- Guideline medications (less favorable benefit/burden or lower quality of evidence)
  - Carbidopa-levodopa *(Sinemet)* 25/100 mg, 1–2 h before bedtime. Symptom augmentation may develop earlier in the day (eg, afternoon instead of evening) and may be more severe with carbidopa-levodopa; tx may require reducing dosage or switching to dopamine agonist
  - Gabapentin ER formulation, gabapentin enacarbil *(Horizant)* 600 mg [T: 600] daily at 5 PM, has been FDA approved for RLS
  - Pregabalin *(Lyrica)* 300 mg/d [C: 25, 50, 75, 100, 150, 200, 225, 300]
  - Low-dose opioids
  - Cabergoline *(Dostinex)* beginning 0.25 mg twice per wk; [T: 0.5] may also be effective but has potential for causing valvular heart disease.
- Optional medications (lower quality of evidence): carbamazepine (**Table 92**), clonidine, and for patients with low ferritin levels, iron supplementation.
- If refractory, can use combination tx.
- If symptoms worsen with long-term tx (augmentation), switch tx regimen.

Periodic Limb Movement Disorder (a minority will also have RLS)

Diagnostic Criteria
- Insomnia or excessive sleepiness
- Repetitive, highly stereotyped limb muscle movements (eg, extension of big toes with partial flexion of ankle, knee, and sometimes hip) that occur during nonREM sleep
- Polysomnographic monitoring showing >15 episodes of muscle contractions per hour and associated arousals or awakenings

- No evidence of a medical, mental, or other sleep disorder that can account for symptoms

Treatment: Indicated for clinically significant sleep disruption or frequent arousals documented on a sleep study.
- Nonpharmacologic: See sleep hygiene measures, p 316.
- Pharmacologic: See RLS, Pharmacologic Treatment, above.

Rapid-Eye Movement (REM) Sleep Behavior Disorder

- Loss of atonia during REM sleep (ranging from simple limb twitches to acting out dreams), exaggeration of features of REM sleep (eg, nightmares), and intrusion of aspects of REM sleep into wakefulness (eg, sleep paralysis)
- High risk of developing neurodegenerative disorder (eg, Parkinson disease, multisystem atrophy, Lewy body dementia)

Evaluation: If needed, in-laboratory video polysomnography

Non-pharmacologic Treatment: change sleeping environment to reduce risk of injury

Pharmacologic Treatment: clonazepam 0.25–1 mg hs, high-dose melatonin 3–6 mg; if associated with Parkinson disease, L-dopa, or pramipexole

SLEEP DISORDERS IN LONG-TERM CARE FACILITIES
Risk Factors
- Medical and medication factors (Insomnia, p 316)
- Environmental factors (eg, little physical activity, infrequent daytime bright light exposure, extended periods in bed, nighttime noise and light interruptions)

Nonpharmacologic Treatment
- Morning bright light tx
- Exercise (eg, stationary bicycle, Tai Chi) and physical activity
- Reduction of nighttime noise and light interruptions
- Multicomponent interventions combining the above and a bedtime routine

Pharmacologic

One small study in a long-term care facility demonstrated benefit of a supplement (5 mg melatonin, 225 mg magnesium, and 11.25 mg zinc, mixed with 100 g of pear pulp) 1 h before bedtime.

SUBSTANCE USE DISORDERS

SCOPE OF THE PROBLEM
- Alcohol causes the primary substance use disorder in people ≥50 yr old.
- Baby boomers are likely to maintain higher alcohol consumption and have more frequent use of ilicit drugs, particularly marijuana and cocaine, than the current cohort of older people.
- 10% of people >65 yr old (12% of men, 8% of women) are current smokers.
- Prescription drug misuse/dependence is an important problem in the older population; in particular opioids and benzodiazepines are a growing problem.

DSM-5 SUBSTANCE USE AND ADDICTIVE DISORDERS

Evaluation and Classification
DSM-5 consolidates substance abuse with substance dependence and addresses each substance-related disorder (alcohol, opioid, tobacco, and sedative, hypnotic, anxiolytic) as a separate disorder but uses 11 overarching criteria (see below) for diagnosis. The number of criteria met determines the severity of the disorder.

DSM-5 Criteria/Symptoms for Substance Use Disorders
- Continuing to use a substance despite negative consequences.
- Repeated inability to carry out roles (at work, home) on account of use.
- Recurrent use in physically hazardous situations.
- Continued use despite recurrent/persistent social/interpersonal problems during use.
- Tolerance, needing increased dose to achieve effect/diminished effect with same amount.
- Withdrawal syndrome or use of the drug to avoid withdrawal.
- Using more substance or using for a longer period than intended.
- Persistent desire to cut down use or unsuccessful attempts to control use.
- Spending a lot of time obtaining, using, or recovering from use.
- Stopping/reducing important occupational, social, or recreational activities due to use.
- Craving or strong desire to use.

DSM-5 Criteria for Diagnosis and Classification of Substance Related Disorder
Two or more symptoms (above) indicate a substance-related disorder; severity is determined by the number of symptoms.
- Mild use disorder: 2–3 symptoms
- Moderate use disorder: 4–5 symptoms
- Severe use disorder: 6 or more symptoms

ALCOHOL USE DISORDERS (AUDS)

Evaluation and Classification
AUDs are often missed in older adults because of reduced social and occupational functioning; signs more often are poor self-care, malnutrition, and medical illness. Because these disorders occur along a spectrum, it is recommended that all adults are screened for use with validated questionnaires that include the following:
- How many days per week?
- How many drinks on those days?
- Maximal intake on any one day?

- What type (ie, beer, wine, or liquor)?
- What is in "a drink"?

Hazardous or At-Risk Drinking

- Will probably eventually cause harm
- No current alcohol problems
- The National Institute on Alcohol Abuse and Alcoholism (NIAAA) defines at-risk drinking for men as 15 or more drinks/wk or 5 or more on one occasion and for women and anyone >65 yr old as >7 drinks/wk or >3 drinks on one occasion.
- A standard drink is 12 oz beer, 5 oz of wine, or 1.5 oz of 80-proof liquor.

DSM-5 Criteria for AUDs (see above DSM-5 Substance-related and Addictive Disorders)

Alcohol Misuse Screening: CAGE questionnaire has been validated in the older population.

C Have you ever felt you should **C**ut down?

A Does others' criticism of your drinking **A**nnoy you?

G Have you ever felt **G**uilty about drinking?

E Have you ever had an "**E**ye opener" to steady your nerves or get rid of a hangover?

(Positive response to any suggests problem drinking.)

Aggravating Factors

Alcohol and Aging: Higher blood concentrations per amount consumed due to decreased lean body mass and total body water; concomitant medications may interact with alcohol. Abstain if cognitively impaired, on medications that interact, or comorbidities or disability are present.

Age-related Diseases: Cognitive impairment, HTN

Medications: Many drug interactions, eg, APAP, anesthetics, antihypertensives, antihistamines, antipsychotics, narcotic analgesics, NSAIDs, sedatives, antidepressants, anticonvulsant medications, nitrates, β-blockers, oral hypoglycemic agents, anticoagulants

Management of Alcohol Use Disorders

Psychosocial Interventions

- Have proven benefit across the spectrum from at-risk drinking through the spectrum of AUDs and include:
  - Motivational Interviewing is a counseling technique for eliciting behavior change by exploring and resolving the patient's ambivalence about change.
  - Cognitive-behavioral therapy (CBT)
  - Screening and brief intervention are effective for at-risk alcohol use in primary care; educate patient on effects of current drinking, point out current AEs, specify safe drinking limits (<7 drinks/wk, <3 on any 1 occasion). Patients who cannot moderate should abstain.
  - Self-help groups (eg, Alcoholics Anonymous)
- Therapeutic communities either inpatient or outpatient
- Medicare pays for annual screening and up to 4 brief counseling sessions for patients with at-risk drinking who are not yet experiencing adverse effects to their mental or emotional health. No copay or deductible when provided by a primary care provider who accepts assignment.
- The NIAAA provides an online resource: Helping Patients Who Drink Too Much: A Clinician's Guide (www.niaaa.nih.gov/guide)

Drug Therapy is probably underutilized.
- **First line**
  - Naltrexone▲ 25 mg × 2 d po, then 50 mg/d [T: 50]; Depot naltrexone *(Vivitrol)* 380 mg IM monthly; monitor LFTs, avoid in kidney failure, hepatitis, cirrhosis, and with opioid use; ~10% get nausea, headache (L, K). Risk of injection site abscess with depot naltrexone.
  - Acamprosate *(Campral)* 666 mg q8h po, reduce dosage to 333 mg q8h if CrCl 30–50 mL/min or weight <132 lb (60 kg) [T: 333]; contraindicated if CrCl <30 mL/min; diarrhea is most common drug-related AE (K). Large US trials have not shown efficacy.
- **Second line**
  - Topiramate▲ 300 mg/d po is effective at reducing relapse. The magnitude of the effect is equal to naltrexone. Drug-related AEs: cognitive impairment, paresthesias, weight loss, dizziness, depression.
  - SSRIs and other antidepressants reduce intake when alcohol dependence and depression co-occur; more favorable in later onset AUDs and with high psychosocial morbidity.
- The duration of drug tx should be at least 3 mo, or up to 12 mo, which is the period when relapse is highest.
- Combining these agents does not improve effectiveness.
- If significant depression persists after 1 wk of abstinence, tx for depression improves outcomes.

Acute Alcohol Withdrawal
- Symptoms begin 6–24 h after last alcohol and are treated with as needed benzodiazepines (p 38).
- Symptoms and signs: tremors, agitation, nausea, sweating, vomiting, hallucinations, insomnia, tachycardia, hypertension, delirium, seizures
- Assess severity of withdrawal symptoms using a validated instrument (Sullivan JT et al. *Br J Addict* 1989;84[11]:1357 or Elholm B et al. *Alcohol* 2010;45[4]:362).
- Severity of symptoms dictate whether inpatient or outpatient management is appropriate.

TOBACCO USE DISORDERS AND SMOKING CESSATION
Approach

What Health Providers Should Do
Ask about tobacco use at every visit. **Advise** all users to quit. **Assess** willingness to quit. **Assist** the patient with a quit plan, education, pharmacotherapy.

Making the Decision to Quit
Patients are more likely to stop smoking if they believe they could get a smoking-related disease and can make an honest attempt at quitting, that the benefits of quitting outweigh the benefits of continued smoking, or if they know someone who has had health problems as a result of smoking.

Setting a Quit Date and Deciding on a Plan
Pick a specific day within the next month (gives time to develop a plan). Will pharmacotherapy be used? Discuss available supports (eg, class, counseling, quit line). On quit day, get rid of all cigarettes and related items.

Treatment
- **Pharmacotherapy (Table 129)** doubles or triples quit rates compared to placebo. Combining different agents improves long-term abstinence for many patients, as does long-term nicotine replacement.

- For example, nicotine replacement with both a pch for >14 wk and ad lib gum or spray or high-dose nicotine patch (>25 mg on tapering schedule or long-term maintenance) or verenicline with a 14 mg pch
  - Nicotine replacement is contraindicated with recent MI, uncontrolled high BP, arrhythmias, severe angina, gastric ulcer
- May not be needed if patient smokes fewer than 10 cigarettes/d
- E-cigarettes: a newer form of nicotine replacement, have small and inconclusive studies on safety and effectiveness; may deliver variable (even toxic) amounts of drug; are likely to be regulated as tobacco products
- Bupropion in combination with nicotine pch is better than either alone
- Antidepressants (paroxetine, venlafaxine, nortriptyline[BC]) combined with nicotine pch
- Varenicline in trials achieved the highest quit rate of any single agent

Table 129. Pharmacotherapy for Tobacco Abuse

Drug	Dosage	Formulations	Comments (Metabolism, Excretion)
Tobacco Abuse			
Bupropion SR▲ (Wellbutrin SR, Zyban)	150 mg q12h × 7–12 wk	SR: 100, 150	Contraindicated with seizure disorders (L)
Varenicline (Chantix)[a]	0.5 mg × 3 d, 0.5 mg q12h × 4 d, then 1 mg q12h × 12–24 wk or longer	0.5, 1	AEs: nausea, vivid dreams, constipation, depression, suicide, small increased risk of cardiovascular events (L, K); reduce dosage if CrCl <30 mL/min
Nicotine Replacement			
Transdermal patches▲	15, 21, 22, 25 mg/d × 4–8 wk 10, 11, 14, 15 mg/d × 2–6 wk 5, 7, 10, 11 mg/d × 2–8 wk	5, 7, 11, 14, 15, 21, 22	Apply to clean, nonhairy skin on upper torso, rotate sites; start 10–15 mg/d with cardiovascular disease or body weight <100 lb or if smoking <10 cigarettes/d (L)
Polacrilex gum▲ (eg, Nicorette)	9–12 pieces/d	2, 4	Chew 1 piece when urge to smoke; usual 10–12/d, max 30/d; 4 mg if smoking >21 cigarettes/d (L)
Nasal spray (Nicotrol NS)	1 spr each nostril q30–60min	0.5 mg/spr	Do not exceed 5 applications/h or 40 in 24 h (L)
Inhaler (Nicotrol Inhaler)	6–16 cartridges/d	4 mg delivered/ cartridge	Max 16 cartridges/d with gradual reduction after 6–12 wk (L)
Lozenge▲	1 po prn	2, 4	Do not exceed 20/d; do not bite or chew; wean over 12 wk

[a] Partial nicotine agonist that eases withdrawal and blocks effects of nicotine if patients resume smoking.

- **Psychological**
  - Avoid people and places where tempted to smoke.
  - Alter habits: (1) switch to juices or water instead of alcohol or coffee, (2) take a walk instead of a coffee break, (3) use oral substitutions (eg, sugarless gum or hard candy).
  - Effective interventions include advice from healthcare provider to quit, self-help materials, proactive telephone counseling, group counseling, individual counseling, intra-tx social support (from a clinician), extra-tx social support (family, friends, coworkers, and smoke-free home).

- Programs that include counseling in person or by telephone increase quit rates by 10–25% when combined with pharmacotherapy.
- Medicare pays for up to 8 face-to-face visits/yr focused on counseling for smoking cessation. If there is no smoking-related disease, there is no copay.

Maintaining Smoking Cessation: Use the same methods that helped during withdrawal.

PRESCRIPTION DRUG USE DISORDERS

Common Prescription Medications Associated with Use Disorders

According to the National Institute on Drug Abuse, the following 3 classes most commonly:
- Opioids—usually prescribed to treat pain
- CNS depressants—used to treat anxiety and sleep disorders
- Stimulants—prescribed to treat attention deficit hyperactivity disorder and narcolepsy
- Diagnosis of Prescription Medication-Related Use Disorders—see DSM-5 criteria (p 323)

Adverse Events
- Benzodiazepines: falls, mobility and ADL disability, cognitive impairment, motor vehicle accidents, pressure ulcers, UI
- Nonbenzodiazepine sedatives: anxiety, depression, nervousness, hallucinations, dizziness, headache, sleep-related behavioral disturbances
- Opioids: falls and fractures
- If there is a hx or current IV drug abuse, check for hepatitis C infection.

Assessing for Risk of Medication Misuse/Abuse
- Patient education on avoiding misuse is enhanced by a standard patient-prescriber agreement (eg, www.tirfremsaccess.com/TirfUI/rems/pdf/ppaf-form.pdf).
- General risk factors include use of a psychoactive drug with abuse potential, use of other substances (alcohol, tobacco, etc), female gender, possibly social isolation, and hx of mental health disorder.
- Addiction to opioids is uncommon in those without hx of substance abuse and in those being treated for pain.
- Screen for risk of opioid misuse/abuse with the Opioid Risk Tool (p 345); this instrument differentiates low-risk from high-risk patients.

Detection of Medication Misuse/Abuse
- Detection relies on clinical judgment; monitor at-risk patients when prescribing benzodiazepines, stimulants, and opioid analgesics.
- Observe for behavior that may suggest nonadherence to prescribed medication schedule (eg, early fill request, frequent lost prescriptions).
- Record any suspicious drug-seeking or other aberrant behaviors observed or reported by others, along with actions taken.
- Document evaluation process, rationale for long-term tx, and periodic review of patient status.
- Ask about purchases of medication over the Internet. Controlled substances can readily be purchased through illegitimate Internet-based pharmacies.

Treatment for Prescription Drug Abuse/Misuse/Dependence

- Opioids
  - May need to undergo medically supervised detoxification
  - Gradual tapering of opioids is necessary (Adjustment of Dosage, p 248).
  - Behavioral tx, usually combined with medications (methadone, buprenorphine), *is* effective.
  - Opioid abuse-deterrent products (eg, *Embeda*) may reduce diversion. These agents do not have street value because they release naltrexone if not used as intended.
- CNS depressants or stimulants (general rules)
  - Primary provider encouragement to reduce use
  - Short-term substitution of other medications (eg, trazodone) for sleep
  - Gradual slow tapering of the drug
- Benzodiazepine dependence
  - Studies show supervised gradual withdrawal to be most effective
  - CBT is directed at the symptom for which the benzodiazepine was originally prescribed, most often insomnia or anxiety; for sleep-specific CBT, see p 316; may be less effective in older adults
  - Gradual withdrawal can be scheduled reduction (eg, 12.5–25% of the daily dose every 1–2 wk), or guided by symptoms where withdrawal programs have ranged from 4 wk to >1 yr.

Medical Marijuana

- Effects of short-term use: impaired short-term memory (learning), impaired coordination (eg, reduced driving skills), altered judgment; in high doses, paranoia and psychosis
- Effects of long-term use: addiction (about 9% of users overall), cognitive impairment, decreased life satisfaction and attainment, chronic bronchitis, and psychosis
- Marijuana (cannabis sitiva) contains 60 cannabinoids, 2 of which, tetrahydrocannabinol (THC) and cannabidiol (CBD), have been considered for medicinal uses. Purified and synthetic preparations of THC, CBD, and several other cannabinoids are under study for many chronic conditions (**Table 130**).
- Marijuana remains a federally designated Schedule I controlled substance. Certain states have legalized medical marijuana. In those states, healthcare providers authorize use and that authorization has been viewed by federal courts as protected physician-patient communication. **Table 130** summarizes available evidence for conditions studied in randomized clinical trials. Caution: many of the trials are small and many are of low quality.

Table 130. Common Medical Reasons Why Patients May Want to Use Marijuana

Condition	How Administered	Number of RCTs/Control	Other Evidence	Outcome of RCTs
Chemotherapy induced nausea and vomiting	Smoked	6 trials: placebo, or thiethylperazine, or oral THC	2 single-arm trials	3 positive; 3 negative
	Nabilone po Dronabinol po Nabiximols po THC po	31 trials: 8 placebo; 23 active comparator		All studies favor cannabinoid, but not all statistically significant
Pain	Smoked (6); Vaporized (2)	8 trials: all placebo	N/A	All positive; 1 with %THC dose-dependent effect
	Nabiximols po	7 trials: all placebo		Meta-analysis favors tx
Appetite and weight loss	Smoked	2 trials: 1 placebo, 1 oral THC and placebo	2 double-dummy 1 cross-sectional	Both positive; 1 oral THC equal to smoked
Crohn's disease	Smoked	1 trial (N=23): placebo	N/A	Positive
Spasticity in multiple sclerosis	Smoked	2 trials: placebo	N/A	Mixed; 1 positive; 1 negative
	Nabiximols po	6 trials: placebo		Meta-analysis including smoked favors tx, but did not reach statistical significance
	Dronabinol po	3 trials: placebo		
	THC/CBD po	4 trials: placebo		
	Nabilone po	1 trial		

Notes: N/A = not applicable.

COMMON DISORDERS

Breast Cancer

- Screen with mammography (**Table 104**) until age 70–74, perhaps longer in women with life expectancy >10 yr.[CW]

Evaluation of Patients over age 65 with newly diagnosed breast cancer should consist of:

- Hx and physical exam
- Diagnostic bilateral mammography and ultrasound if indicated
- CBC, LFTs, serum alkaline phosphatase
- Assessment of:
  - life expectancy (**Table 7**, p 9)
  - comorbidity (eg, Charlson Index); calculators available online
  - function (ADL and IADL, p 336–337 appendix)
- Considering life expectancy, comorbidity, and functional status, discuss goals of care with the patient.
- If the goal of care is cure or life prolongation, the next steps in evaluation are resection of the tumor and possibly sentinel lymph node (SLN) biopsy.
- Older women with clinically negative axillary exams, small (<2-cm tumors), and who will be treated with adjuvant HT may be managed without axillary surgery. Don't perform axillary lymph node (ALN) dissection for clinical stage I and II without attempting SLN biopsy.[CW]
- If a SLN biopsy is positive, ALN dissection is necessary for full staging. Older women are more likely to experience lymphedema after ALN dissection.
- Further evaluation depends on the stage of the disease as follows:
  - At Stage I and II, no additional evaluation for metastatic disease is needed.
    - Stage I (tumor ≤2 cm), negative nodes (N0), or no more than microscopic (0.2 cm) disease
    - Stage II (tumor >2 and ≤5 cm) with either N0 or N1; or tumor >5 cm and N0. N1 has more than microscopic disease, and mobile nodes (not matted or fixed).
  - At Stage III, patients need imaging for bone, liver, and pulmonary metastases.
    - Stage III (tumor >5 cm) or tumor of any size with fixed or matted lymph nodes on clinical exam or tumor of any size that extends directly to the chest wall or skin.
  - Stage IV is tumor with metastasis.
- Obtain tumor markers
  - In women over 65 yr old, 85% of tumors are positive for estrogen receptor (ER) and/or progesterone receptor (PR), which predicts response to adjuvant HT.
  - Among women over 85 yr old, ER/PR expression shows a decreased frequency of PR and an increase in androgen receptor positivity.
  - HER2/*neu* overexpression is less common in the tumors of older women, but when present has the same adverse prognosis.
- Don't perform PET, CT, and radionulide bone scans in staging early breast cancer at low risk for metastases.[CW]
- Patients with limited life expectancy and those who are too ill or frail to undergo surgery for the primary tumor, and whose tumors are ER-positive can be offered tx with tamoxifen or an aromatase inhibitor.

Monitoring Women with a History of Breast Cancer
- Hx, physical examination q3–6mo for 3 yr, then every 6–12 mo for 2 yr
- Increase surveillance for second primary in breasts, ovaries, colon, and rectum
- Annual mammography
- Annual pelvic examination for all patients, especially those on tamoxifen (higher risk of uterine cancer)

Adjuvant Therapy for Breast Cancer

Oral Hormone Adjuvant Therapy: Postmenopausal women with ER- or PR-positive tumors at high risk of recurrence (tumors >1 cm, or positive nodes) should be treated with oral adjuvant tx. Tx should be with an aromatase inhibitor for 2–5 yr (**Table 131**). If an aromatase inhibitor is discontinued in the first 5 yr, it is reasonable to switch to tamoxifen for at least 2 yr. For women who have completed 5 yr of tamoxifen, an additional 5 yr of aromatase inhibitors is recommended.

Table 131. Oral Agents for Breast Cancer Treatment

Class, Medication	Dosage and Formulations	Monitoring	Adverse Events, Interactions (Metabolism)
Antiestrogen Drugs			
Fulvestrant (Faslodex)	250 mg/mo IM in 1 or 2 injections Inj: 250 mg/ 5 mL; 125 mg/2.5 mL	Blood chemistry, lipids	Metabolized through CYP3A4; GI reactions, anesthesia, pain (back, pelvic, headache), hot flushes (L)
Tamoxifen▲a (Nolvadex)	20 mg/d po T: 10, 20	Annual eye examination; endometrial cancer screening	Avoid fluoxetine, paroxetine, bupropion, duloxetine, and other potent CYPD26 inhibitors that reduce tamoxifen activity; ↑ risk of thrombosis (L)
Toremifene (Fareston)	60 mg/d po T: 60	CBC, Ca, LFTs, BUN, Cr	Drug interactions: CYP3A4–6 inhibitors and inducers; ↑ warfarin effect (L)
Aromatase Inhibitors			
Anastrozole▲ (Arimidex)	1 mg/d po T: 1	Periodic CBC, lipids, serum chemistry profile	Common: arthritis, arthralgia, bone pain, asthenia, cough, dyspnea, pharyngitis, depression, headache, nausea, rash, edema. Less common: anemia, leukopenia, thromboembolism, thrombophlebitis, hypercholesterolemia, fractures, vaginal hemorrhage (L)
Exemestane▲ (Aromasin)	25 mg/d po T: 25	Periodic WBC count with differential, lipids, serum chemistry profile	Common: anxiety, depression, fatigue, insomnia, dyspnea, hot flushes, weight gain, nausea, pain at tumor site. Rare: MI (L)
Letrozole▲ (Femara)	2.5 mg/d po T: 2.5	Periodic CBC, LFTs, TSH	Common: arthralgia, back pain, bone pain, dyspnea, hot flushes, nausea. Less common: fracture, MI or ischemia, pancytopenia, thromboembolism, pleural effusion, PE. Metabolized by CYP3A4, CYP2A6; strongly inhibits CYP2A6 and moderately inhibits CYP2C19 (L)

a Reduce dosage if CrCl <10 mL/min

Adjuvant Chemotherapy: Is used after resection. Reduces risk of recurrence and improves survival, especially when risk of recurrence is >10% at 10 yr. Recurrence is reduced by 30–50% with greater benefit in ER-poor or -absent breast cancer.

Bisphosphonates: Are commonly used in postmenopausal women on other adjuvant tx for breast cancer. Five yr of zoledronic acid improves invasive disease-free survival in postmenopausal but not premenopausal women.

Therapy for Metastatic Bone Disease: Pamidronate or zoledronic acid reduces morbidity and delays time to onset of bone symptoms.

Vulvar Diseases

Non-neoplastic

- Lichen sclerosus—Common on vulva of middle-aged and older women; porcelain white appearance over the labia and may extend to the perirectal area in a classic hourglass distribution. May be asymptomatic or cause itching, soreness, or dyspareunia. When clinical diagnosis is straight forward, tx: with a high-potency steroid (eg, clobetasol propionate 0.05% q12–24h for 8–12 wk; then taper gradually to zero or continue 2–3×/wk based on symptoms). Biopsy if diagnosis is in doubt, failure to respond to clobetasol, or if there are any suspicious areas. Lichen sclerosus is associated with a small risk of squamous cell cancer; examine the vulva at least yearly, biopsy all suspicious lesions. Also ask patients to look at the skin and search for lumps or nonhealing sores monthly.
- Squamous hyperplasia—Raised white keratinized lesions difficult to distinguish from VIN; must biopsy to exclude malignancy. Tx: betamethasone dipropionate 0.05% for 6–8 wk, then 1% hydrocortisone if symptoms persist. Long-term follow-up advised.

Neoplastic

- VIN may be asymptomatic or may cause pruritus or dysuria; hypo- or hyperpigmented keratinized plaques; often multifocal; inspection ± colposcopy of the entire vulva with biopsy of most worrisome lesions; lesions graded on degree of atypia. Tx: surgical or laser ablative tx.
- Vulvar malignancy—Half of cases are in women >70 yr old; 80% are squamous cell, with melanoma, sarcoma, basal cell, and adenocarcinoma <20%; biopsy any suspicious lesion. Tx: vulvectomy, radical local excision, or 3-incision surgical techniques.

Postmenopausal Bleeding

Defined as bleeding after 1 yr of amenorrhea:

- Exclude malignancy, identify source (vagina, cervix, vulva, uterus, bladder, bowel), treat symptoms.
- Examine genitalia, perineum, rectum.
- If endometrial source, use endometrial biopsy or vaginal probe ultrasound to assess endometrial thickness (<5 mm virtually excludes malignancy).
- D&C when endometrium not otherwise adequately assessed.
- Evaluation is needed for:
  - Women on combination continual estrogen and progesterone who bleed after 12 mo.
  - Women on cyclic replacement with bleeding at unexpected times (ie, bleeding other than during the second wk of progesterone tx).
  - Women on unopposed estrogen who bleed at any time.

Vaginal Prolapse

- Child-bearing and other causes of increased intra-abdominal pressure weaken connective tissue and muscles supporting the genital organs, leading to prolapse.
- Symptoms include pelvic pressure, back pain, FI or UI, difficulty evacuating the rectum. Symptoms may be present even with mild prolapse.
- The degree of prolapse and organs involved dictate tx; no tx if asymptomatic.
- Estrogen and Kegel exercises (p 149) may help in mild cases.
- Pessary or surgery indicated with increase in symptoms. Don't exclude pessaries as an option for prolapse.[CW] Surgery needed for fourth-degree symptomatic prolapse.
- Precise anatomic defect(s) dictates the surgical approach. Surgical closure of the vagina (colpocleisis) is a simple option for frail patients who are not sexually active.
- A common classification (ACOG) for degrees of prolapse:
  ◦ First degree—extension to mid-vagina
  ◦ Second degree—approaching hymenal ring
  ◦ Third degree—at hymenal ring
  ◦ Fourth degree—beyond hymenal ring

HORMONE THERAPY

Symptoms Associated with the Postmenopausal State

- Hot flushes and night sweats
- Vaginal dryness and dyspareunia
- Sleep disturbances
- Depression
- Insufficient evidence exists to link the following commonly reported symptoms to the postmenopausal state: cognitive disturbances, fatigue, sexual dysfunction.

Therapy for Menopausal Symptoms

- Vasomotor and vaginal symptoms respond to estrogen in a dose-response fashion; start at low dosage (eg, oral conjugated or esterified estrogen 0.3 mg/d, which should be combined with medroxyprogesterone in women with an intact uterus), titrate to effect. Dyspareunia and vaginal dryness respond to topical estrogen (**Table 125** [Sexual Dysfunction chapter]).
- Conjugated estrogens 0.45 mg/bazedoxifene 20 mg *(Duavee)* po, qd treats menopausal symptoms without apparent drug-related AEs on breast or uterus. Long-term risk for thromboembolism and ischemic stroke uncertain.
- "Bioidentical hormone therapy" refers to the use of naturally occurring (rather than synthetic or animal-derived) forms of progesterone, estradiol, and estriol. These preparations are compounded by pharmacies and readily available over the Internet but are not FDA approved. The FDA and the Endocrine Society believe there is insufficient evidence to evaluate the safety and efficacy of these agents relative to FDA-approved HT.

Risk of Hormone Therapy

- Risks associated with HT use may vary based on the length of time between menopause and initiation of HT. For information on the risks and benefits of HT initiated within the first 5 yr after menopause, see the position statement of the North American Menopause Society (www.menopause.org/docs/default-document-library/psht12.pdf).
- Beginning HT in women 10 or more years after menopause is not recommended due to increase risk of MI, DVT, PE, stroke, kidney stones, dementia, and ovarian cancer.
- Older women can get hot flushes if estrogen is discontinued suddenly. Tapering (eg, q48h for 1–2 mo and then q72h for a few months) may be better tolerated.
- The fracture-protective effect from HT is lost rapidly after discontinuation; women at risk of fracture should be evaluated and treated with alternative tx (Osteoporosis, p 229).

Contraindications to Hormone Therapy

- Undiagnosed vaginal bleeding
- Thromboembolic disease
- Breast cancer
- Prior stroke or TIA
- Endometrial cancer more advanced than Stage 1
- Possibly gallbladder disease
- CHD

Intolerable Vasomotor Symptoms

- 10% of women continue with vasomotor symptoms 12yr after menopause.
- HT (estrogen and/or progesterone) is the most effective tx.
- Note contraindications above.
- Assess risk of VTE and cardiovascular disease:
  - VTE risk increased by hx of VTE, malignancy/myeloproliferative disorder, leg immobilization, or both smoking and obesity
  - Cardiovascular disease risk increased by known CAD, PAD, AAA, carotid artery disease, DM, or risk factors that confer a 10-yr risk of coronary disease >20% (cvdrisk.nhlbi.nih.gov/)
- If increased cardiovascular or VTE risk, then oral standard dosage estrogen-progestin should not be used.
- If increased cardiovascular risk (but not VTE risk), attempt to control symptoms with transdermal estrogen.
- If risk of VTE is increased and risk of cardiovascular disease is usual and patient has no uterus, transdermal estrogen may be appropriate; if patient has uterus, adding a progestin raises additional concerns.
- If neither VTE nor cardiovascular disease risk is increased, estrogen (0.3–0.625 mg po daily for women who have had a hysterectomy) or estrogen-progestin (0.45/1.5 mg or 0.625/2.5 mg po daily, for those with an intact uterus) or transdermally at lowest dosage to control symptoms may be appropriate.
- Continue to advocate tapering (p 333) at 2-yr intervals.
- If estrogen cannot be taken or if risks exceed benefits, try one of these alternatives. Expert opinion based on double-blind randomized trials and demonstrated safety and effectiveness suggests considering agents in the following sequence:
  - First, antidepressants: SSRIs: citalopram 10–20 mg/d; paroxetine 7.5–25 mg/d. Avoid SSRIs if patients are receiving tamoxifen; tamoxifen levels will be subtherapeutic. SNRIs: venlafaxine 75 mg/d; desvenlafaxine 50–200 mg/d
  - Second, anticonvulsants: gabapentin 900–2700 mg/d; pregabalin 75–300 mg/d
  - Third, α_2-Adrenergic agonists: clonidine 0.5–1.5 mg/d (Avoid in HTN[BC]); watch for orthostatic hypotension and rebound increase in BP if used intermittently. Common drug-related AEs: dry mouth, constipation, sedation.

Some assessment instruments commonly used in geriatrics practice are included on the following pages. These instruments, as well as some additional ones, are available on the *Geriatrics At Your Fingertips* Web site (see www.geriatricscareonline.org).

MINI-COG™ SCREEN FOR DEMENTIA

Step 1: Three Word Registration

Look directly at person and say, "Please listen carefully. I am going to say three words that I want you to repeat back to me now and try to remember. The words are [select a list of words from the versions below]. Please say them for me now." If the person is unable to repeat the words after three attempts, move on to Step 2 (clock drawing).

The following and other word lists have been used in one or more clinical studies. For repeated administrations, use of an alternative word list is recommended.

Version 1	Version 2	Version 3	Version 4	Version 5	Version 6
Banana	Leader	Village	River	Captain	Daughter
Sunrise	Season	Kitchen	Nation	Garden	Heaven
Chair	Table	Baby	Finger	Picture	Mountain

Step 2: Clock Drawing

Say: "Next, I want you to draw a clock for me. First, put in all of the numbers where they go." When that is completed, say: "Now, set the hands to 10 past 11."

Use preprinted circle (see mini-cog.com) for this exercise. Repeat instructions as needed as this is not a memory test. Move to Step 3 if the clock is not complete within three minutes.

Step 3: Clock Drawing

Ask the person to recall the three words you stated in Step 1. Say: "What were the three words I asked you to remember?" Record the word list version number and the person's answers.

Scoring

Word Recall: 0–3 points	1 point for each word spontaneously recalled without cueing.
Clock Draw: 0 or 2 points	Normal clock = 2 points. A normal clock has all numbers placed in the correct sequence and approximately correct position (e.g., 12, 3, 6 and 9 are in anchor positions) with no missing or duplicate numbers. Hands are pointing to the 11 and 2 (11:10). Hand length is not scored. Inability or refusal to draw a clock (abnormal) = 0 points.
Total Score: 0–5 points	Total score = Word Recall score + Clock Draw score.
	A cut point of <3 on the Mini-Cog™ has been validated for dementia screening, but many individuals with clinically meaningful cognitive impairment will score higher. When greater sensitivity is desired, a cut point of <4 is recommended as it may indicate a need for further evaluation of cognitive status.

PHYSICAL SELF-MAINTENANCE SCALE (ACTIVITIES OF DAILY LIVING, OR ADLS)

In each category, circle the item that most closely describes the person's highest level of functioning and record the score assigned to that level (either 1 or 0) in the blank at the beginning of the category.

A. Toilet _____
1. Care for self at toilet completely; no incontinence 1
2. Needs to be reminded, or needs help in cleaning self, or has rare (weekly at most) accidents 0
3. Soiling or wetting while asleep more than once a week...............................0
4. Soiling or wetting while awake more than once a week...............................0
5. No control of bowels or bladder...0

B. Feeding _____
1. Eats without assistance...1
2. Eats with minor assistance at meal times and/or with special preparation of food, or help in cleaning up after meals 0
3. Feeds self with moderate assistance and is untidy 0
4. Requires extensive assistance for all meals 0
5. Does not feed self at all and resists efforts of others to feed him or her 0

C. Dressing _____
1. Dresses, undresses, and selects clothes from own wardrobe.......................1
2. Dresses and undresses self with minor assistance 0
3. Needs moderate assistance in dressing and selection of clothes.................0
4. Needs major assistance in dressing but cooperates with efforts of others to help 0
5. Completely unable to dress self and resists efforts of others to help 0

D. Grooming (neatness, hair, nails, hands, face, clothing) _____
1. Always neatly dressed and well-groomed without assistance 1
2. Grooms self adequately with occasional minor assistance, eg, with shaving....................0
3. Needs moderate and regular assistance or supervision with grooming 0
4. Needs total grooming care but can remain well-groomed after help from others 0
5. Actively negates all efforts of others to maintain grooming 0

E. Physical Ambulation _____
1. Goes about grounds or city...1
2. Ambulates within residence on or about one block distant 0
3. Ambulates with assistance of (check one)
   a ( ) another person, b ( ) railing, c ( ) cane, d ( ) walker, e ( ) wheelchair........................0
   1.___Gets in and out without help. 2.___Needs help getting in and out
4. Sits unsupported in chair or wheelchair but cannot propel self without help....................0
5. Bedridden more than half the time..0

F. Bathing _____
1. Bathes self (tub, shower, sponge bath) without help...................................1
2. Bathes self with help getting in and out of tub..0
3. Washes face and hands only but cannot bathe rest of body 0
4. Does not wash self but is cooperative with those who bathe him or her.......................0
5. Does not try to wash self and resists efforts to keep him or her clean. 0

For scoring interpretation and source, see note after the next instrument.

INSTRUMENTAL ACTIVITIES OF DAILY LIVING SCALE (IADLS)

In each category, circle the item that most closely describes the person's highest level of functioning and record the score assigned to that level (either 1 or 0) in the blank at the beginning of the category.

A. Ability to Use Telephone _____
1. Operates telephone on own initiative; looks up and dials numbers. 1
2. Dials a few well-known numbers. 1
3. Answers telephone but does not dial. 1
4. Does not use telephone at all. 0

B. Shopping _____
1. Takes care of all shopping needs independently. 1
2. Shops independently for small purchases. 0
3. Needs to be accompanied on any shopping trip. 0
4. Completely unable to shop. 0

C. Food Preparation _____
1. Plans, prepares, and serves adequate meals independently. 1
2. Prepares adequate meals if supplied with ingredients. 0
3. Heats and serves prepared meals or prepares meals but does not maintain adequate diet. 0
4. Needs to have meals prepared and served. 0

D. Housekeeping _____
1. Maintains house alone or with occasional assistance (eg, domestic help for heavy work). 1
2. Performs light daily tasks such as dishwashing, bedmaking. 1
3. Performs light daily tasks but cannot maintain acceptable level of cleanliness. 1
4. Needs help with all home maintenance tasks. 1
5. Does not participate in any housekeeping tasks. 0

E. Laundry _____
1. Does personal laundry completely. 1
2. Launders small items; rinses socks, stockings, etc. 1
3. All laundry must be done by others. 0

F. Mode of Transportation _____
1. Travels independently on public transportation or drives own car. 1
2. Arranges own travel via taxi but does not otherwise use public transportation. 1
3. Travels on public transportation when assisted or accompanied by another. 1
4. Travel limited to taxi or automobile with assistance of another. 0
5. Does not travel at all. 0

G. Responsibility for Own Medications _____
1. Is responsible for taking medication in correct dosages at correct time. 1
2. Takes responsibility if medication is prepared in advance in separate dosages. 0
3. Is not capable of dispensing own medication. 0

H. Ability to Handle Finances _____
1. Manages financial matters independently (budgets, writes checks, pays rent and bills, goes to bank); collects and keeps track of income. 1
2. Manages day-to-day purchases but needs help with banking, major purchases, etc. 1
3. Incapable of handling money. 0

Scoring Interpretation: For ADLs, the total score ranges from 0 to 6, and for IADLs, from 0 to 8. In some categories, only the highest level of function receives a 1; in others, two or more levels have scores of 1 because each describes competence at some minimal level of function. These screens are useful for indicating specifically how a person is performing at the present time. When they are also used over time, they serve as documentation of a person's functional improvement or deterioration.

Sources: Lawton MP, Brody EM. *Gerontologist* 1969, 9:179–186. Copyright by the Gerontological Society of America. Reproduced by permission of the Gerontological Society of America.

PHQ-9 AND PHQ-2 QUICK DEPRESSION ASSESSMENT

PHQ-9 Instructions For Use: *for doctor or healthcare professional use only*

For initial diagnosis:

1. Patient completes PHQ-9 Quick Depression Assessment.
2. If there are at least 4 ✓s in the two right columns (including Questions #1 and #2), consider a depressive disorder. Add score to determine severity.
3. ***Consider Major Depressive Disorder***

   • if there are at least 5 ✓s in the two right columns (one of which corresponds to Question #1 or #2).

   Consider Other Depressive Disorder

   • if there are 2 to 4 ✓s in the two right columns (one of which corresponds to Question #1 or #2).

Note: Since the questionnaire relies on patient self-report, all responses should be verified by the clinician, and a definitive diagnosis is made on clinical grounds, taking into account how well the patient understood the questionnaire, as well as other relevant information from the patient. Diagnoses of Major Depressive Disorder or Other Depressive Disorder also require impairment of social, occupational, or other important areas of functioning and ruling out normal bereavement, a history of a Manic Episode (Bipolar Disorder), and a physical disorder, medication, or other drug as the biological cause of the depressive symptoms.

To monitor severity over time for newly diagnosed patients or patients in current treatment for depression:

4. Patients may complete questionnaires at baseline and at regular intervals (eg, q2wk) at home and bring them in at their next appointment for scoring, or they may complete the questionnaire during each scheduled appointment.
5. Add up ✓s by column. For every ✓:
   "Several days" = 1   "More than half the days" = 2   "Nearly every day" = 3
6. Add together column scores to get a TOTAL score.
7. Refer to PHQ-9 Scoring to interpret the TOTAL score.
8. Results may be included in patients' files to assist you in setting up a treatment goal, determining degree of response, as well as guiding treatment intervention.

PHQ-9 Scoring For Severity Determination
for healthcare professional use only

Scoring—add up all checked boxes on PHQ-9

For every ✓: Not at all = 0; Several days = 1; More than half the days = 2; Nearly every day = 3

Interpretation of Total Score

Total Score	Depression Severity
0–4	None
5–9	Mild
10–14	Moderate
15–19	Moderately severe
20–27	Severe

PATIENT HEALTH QUESTIONNAIRE-9

Comments

Only the patient (subject) should enter information onto this questionnaire.

Over the *last 2 weeks*, how often have you been bothered by any of the following problems?	Not at all	Several days	More than half the days	Nearly every day
1. Little interest or pleasure in doing things*	0	1	2	3
2. Feeling down, depressed, or hopeless*	0	1	2	3
3. Trouble falling or staying asleep, or sleeping too much	0	1	2	3
4. Feeling tired or having little energy	0	1	2	3
5. Poor appetite or overeating	0	1	2	3
6. Feeling bad about yourself — or that you are a failure or have let yourself or your family down	0	1	2	3
7. Trouble concentrating on things, such as reading the newspaper or watching television	0	1	2	3
8. Moving or speaking so slowly that other people could have noticed? Or the opposite — being so fidgety or restless that you have been moving around a lot more than usual	0	1	2	3
9. Thoughts that you would be better off dead or of hurting yourself in some way	0	1	2	3

SCORING FOR USE BY STUDY PERSONNEL ONLY

   _0_ + _____ + _____ + _____

   =Total Score: _____

If you checked off *any* problems, how *difficult* have these problems made it for you to do your work, take care of things at home, or get along with other people?

Not difficult at all	Somewhat difficult	Very difficult	Extremely difficult
☐	☐	☐	☐

* indicates questions of the PHQ-2

I confirm this information is accurate.	Patient's/Subject's initials:	Date:

PHQ-2 Instructions For Use: *for doctor or healthcare professional use only*

The first two questions of the PHQ-9 are often referred to as the PHQ-2. These questions are scored in the same way as the PHQ-9, but are used as an initial screening tool to get a sense of depressed mood and anhedonia over the last 2 wk. The PHQ-2 is not designed to establish a diagnosis of depression, but is used to determine whether the rest of the questions in the PHQ-9 are to be asked. PHQ-2 scores range from 0 to 6, with 3 as the typical score to trigger asking the remaining questions of the PHQ-9.

RAPID ESTIMATE OF ADULT LITERACY IN MEDICINE—SHORT FORM (REALM-SF)

The Rapid Estimate of Adult Literacy in Medicine—Short Form (REALM-SF) is a 7-item word recognition test to provide clinicians with a valid quick assessment of patient health literacy. The REALM-SF has been validated and field tested in diverse research setting, and has excellent agreement with the 66-item REALM instrument in terms of grade-level assignments.

REALM-SF Form

Patient name _____ Date of birth _____ Reading level _____

Date _____ Examiner _____ Grade completed _____

Menopause	☐
Antibiotics	☐
Exercise	☐
Jaundice	☐
Rectal	☐
Anemia	☐
Behavior	☐

Instructions for Administering the REALM-SF

1. Give the patient a laminated copy of the REALM-SF form and score answers on an unlaminated copy that is attached to a clipboard. Hold the clipboard at an angle so that the patient is not distracted by your scoring. Say:

   "I want to hear you read as many words as you can from this list. Begin with the first word and read aloud. When you come to a word you cannot read, do the best you can or say, 'blank' and go onto the next word."

2. If the patient takes more than five seconds on a word, say 'blank' and point to the next word, if necessary, to move the patient along. If the patient begins to miss every word, have him or her pronounce only known words.

Scores and Grade Equivalents for the REALM-SF

Score   Grade range

Score	Grade range
0	Third grade and below; will not be able to read most low-literacy materials; will need repeated oral instructions, materials composed primarily of illustrations, or audio or video tapes.
1–3	Fourth to sixth grade; will need low-literacy materials, may not be able to read prescription labels.
4–6	Seventh to eighth grade; will struggle with most patient education materials; will not be offended by low-literacy materials.
7	High school; will be able to read most patient education materials.

Health Literacy Measurement Tools. January 2009. Agency for Healthcare Research and Quality, Rockville, MD. http://www.ahrq.gov/populations/sahlsatool.htm

KARNOFSKY SCALE

This 10-point scale is a quick and easy way to indicate how a person is feeling on a given day, without going through several multiple-choice questions or symptom surveys.

Score	Description
100	Able to work; normal, no complaints, no evidence of disease
90	Able to work; able to carry on normal activity, minor symptoms
80	Able to work; normal activity with effort, some symptoms
70	Unable to work or carry on normal activity, cares for self independently
60	Mildly disabled, dependent; requires occasional assistance, cares for most needs
50	Moderately disabled, dependent; requires considerable assistance and frequent care
40	Severely disabled, dependent; requires special care and assistance
30	Severely disabled; hospitalized, death not imminent
20	Very sick; active supportive treatment needed
10	Moribund; fatal processes rapidly progressing

Source: Karnofsky DA, Burchenal JH. The clinical evaluation of chemotherapeutic agents in cancer. In: MacLeon CM, ed. *Evaluation of Chemotherapeutic Agents.* Columbia University Press; 1949:196.

PALLIATIVE PERFORMANCE SCALE, VERSION 2 (PPSv2)

PPS Level (%)	Ambulation	Activity and Evidence of Disease	Self-care	Intake	Conscious Level
100	Full	Normal activity and work, no evidence of disease	Full	Normal	Full
90	Full	Normal activity and work, some evidence of disease	Full	Normal	Full
80	Full	Normal activity with effort, some evidence of disease	Full	Normal or reduced	Full
70	Reduced	Unable to do normal job or work, significant disease	Full	Normal or reduced	Full
60	Reduced	Unable to do hobby or housework, significant disease	Occasional assistance required	Normal or reduced	Full or confusion
50	Mainly sit/lie	Unable to do any work, extensive disease	Considerable assistance required	Normal or reduced	Full or confusion
40	Mainly in bed	Unable to do most activity, extensive disease	Mainly assistance	Normal or reduced	Full or drowsy, ± confusion
30	Totally bed bound	Unable to do any activity, extensive disease	Total care	Normal or reduced	Full or drowsy, ± confusion
20	Totally bed bound	Unable to do any activity, extensive disease	Total care	Minimal to sips	Full or drowsy, ± confusion
10	Totally bed bound	Unable to do any activity, extensive disease	Total care	Mouth care only	Drowsy or coma, ± confusion
0	Death	—	—	—	—

Instructions: PPS level is determined by reading left to right to find a 'best horizontal fit.' Begin at left column reading downwards until current ambulation is determined, then read across to next and downwards until each column is determined. Thus, 'leftward' columns take precedence over 'rightward' columns. Also, see 'definitions of terms' for interpretation of PPSv2 and complete instructions at www.victoriahospice.org. Victoria Hospice Society©

Palliative Performance Scale, Version 2 (PPSv2). *Medical Care of the Dying, 4th ed.* Victoria, BC, Canada: Victoria Hospice Society; 2006:120-121. Reprinted with permission.

REISBERG FUNCTIONAL ASSESSMENT STAGING (FAST) SCALE

This 16-item scale is designed to parallel the progressive activity limitations associated with AD. Stage 7 identifies the threshold of activity limitation that would support a prognosis of ≤6 mo remaining life expectancy.

FAST Scale Item	Activity Limitation Associated with AD
Stage 1	No difficulty, either subjectively or objectively
Stage 2	Complains of forgetting location of objects; subjective work difficulties
Stage 3	Decreased job functioning evident to coworkers; difficulty in traveling to new locations
Stage 4	Decreased ability to perform complex tasks (eg, planning dinner for guests, handling finances)
Stage 5	Requires assistance in choosing proper clothing
Stage 6	Decreased ability to dress, bathe, and toilet independently
Substage 6a	Difficulty putting clothing on properly
Substage 6b	Unable to bathe properly, may develop fear of bathing
Substage 6c	Inability to handle mechanics of toileting (ie, forgets to flush, does not wipe properly)
Substage 6d	Urinary incontinence
Substage 6e	Fecal incontinence
Stage 7	Loss of speech, locomotion, and consciousness
Substage 7a	Ability to speak limited (1–5 words a day)
Substage 7b	All intelligible vocabulary lost
Substage 7c	Nonambulatory
Substage 7d	Unable to smile
Substage 7e	Unable to hold head up

Source: Reisberg, B., *Psychopharmacol Bull* 1988;24(4):653–659.

AUA INTERNATIONAL PROSTATE SYMPTOM SCORE (IPSS) SYMPTOM INDEX FOR BPH

Questions to be answered (circle one number on each line)	Not at all	Less than 1 time in 5	Less than half the time	About half the time	More than half the time	Almost always
1. Over the past month or so, how often have you had a sensation of not emptying your bladder completely after you finished urinating?	0	1	2	3	4	5
2. Over the past month or so, how often have you had to urinate again less than 2 hours after you finished urinating?	0	1	2	3	4	5
3. Over the past month or so, how often have you found you stopped and started again several times when you urinated?	0	1	2	3	4	5
4. Over the past month or so, how often have you found it difficult to postpone urination?	0	1	2	3	4	5
5. Over the past month or so, how often have you had a weak urinary stream?	0	1	2	3	4	5
6. Over the past month or so, how often have you had to push or strain to begin urination?	0	1	2	3	4	5
7. Over the last month, how many times did you most typically get up to urinate from the time you went to bed at night until the time you got up in the morning?	none	1 time	2 times	3 times	4 times	>5 times

AUA Symptom Score = sum of responses to questions 1–7 =____. For interpretation, see p 275.

Source: Barry MJ, et al. *J Urol* 1992;148(5):1549–1557. Reprinted with permission.

OPIOID RISK TOOL*

Factor	Score** Women	Score** Men
Family hx of substance abuse		
Alcohol	1	3
Illegal drugs	2	3
Prescription drugs	4	4
Personal hx of substance abuse		
Alcohol	3	3
Illegal drugs	4	4
Prescription drugs	5	5
Age (if between 16 and 45)	1	1
Hx of preadolescent sexual abuse	3	0
Psychological disease		
Attention-deficit disorder, obsessive-compulsive disorder, bipolar, schizophrenia	2	2
Depression	1	1
TOTAL		

*Main drawback is susceptibility to deception.

**Scoring: 0–3 = low risk, 4–7 = moderate risk, ≥8 = high risk

Note: Adapted from Webster LR, et al. *Pain Med* 2005;6:432–442.

CODING IN GERIATRICS

Source: Peter Hollmann, MD, AGSF, 2/16/16

Geriatricians Geriatricians focus on Medicare, but private payers including Medicare Advantage plans may use other valid CPT and HCPCS codes. Every procedure code (CPT or HCPCS) must be accompanied with a diagnosis code (ICD-9, to be replaced with ICD-10 in the future). These codes are particularly relevant for services performed by geriatrics healthcare professionals.

Common Procedure Codes		
Procedure Code	**Description**	**Reference/Notes**
Evaluation and Management		Documentation Guidelines available at: http://www.cms.gov/Outreach-and-Education/Medicare-Learning-Network-MLN/MLNEdWebGuide/EMDOC.html
99201-99215	Office/Outpatient Visits	Also used for Office/Outpatient Consultations when reporting to Medicare
99217-99220 99224-99226 99234-99236	Observation Services	Consultations in Observation are Office/Outpatient codes when reporting to Medicare
99221-99223 99231-99233 99238-99239	Hospital Inpatient Services	Also use for Inpatient Consultations when reporting to Medicare
99241-99245 99251-99255	Consultations	Invalid for Medicare, may be used by other payers
99291-99292	Critical Care	Used in all settings of care, geriatrician relevant
99304-99318	Nursing facility Services	
99324-99327	Domiciliary Care (eg ALF)	
99341-99350	Home Services	
99354-99357	Prolonged Services	Time based codes, track and time as it is needed for coding
99387, 99397	Comprehensive Preventive Medicine	Non-covered Medicare (see Medicare Preventive Services), may be used by other payers such as Medicare Advantage plans
99406, 99407	Tobacco Counseling	For Medicare: use is for those with illness, prevention is G code.
99490	Chronic Care Management	2015 code 20+ minutes of care coordination by qualified practice, per calendar month. 99487 and 99489 are not paid by Medicare. https://www.cms.gov/Outreach-and-Education/Medicare-Learning-Network-MLN/MLNProducts/MLN-Publications-Items/ICN909188.html
99495, 99496	Transitional Care Management Services	http://www.cms.gov/Outreach-and-Education/Medicare-Learning-Network-MLN/MLNProducts/Downloads/Transitional-Care-Management-Services-Fact-Sheet-ICN908628.pdf
99497, 99498	Advance Care Planning (new 2016)	Codes for discussion of advance directives paid by Medicare beginning 2016. https://www.cms.gov/Outreach-and-Education/Medicare-Learning-Network-MLN/MLNMattersArticles/Downloads/MM9271.pdf

(cont.)

Medicare Preventive Services		http://www.cms.gov/Outreach-and-Education/Medicare-Learning-Network-MLN/MLNProducts/PreventiveServices.html https://www.cms.gov/Medicare/Prevention/PrevntionGenInfo/Downloads/MPS_QuickReferenceChart_1.pdf
G0008, G0009	Flu and Pneumonia Vaccination	Use CPT and Q codes for vaccine supply
G0402	IPPE "Welcome to Medicare" Preventive Exam	http://www.cms.gov/Outreach-and-Education/Medicare-Learning-Network-MLN/MLNProducts/downloads/MPS_QRI_IPPE001a.pdf
G0438, G0439	Annual Wellness Visits	http://www.cms.gov/Outreach-and-Education/Medicare-Learning-Network-MLN/MLNProducts/Downloads/AWV_Chart_ICN905706.pdf
G0436, G0437	Tobacco Counseling	http://www.cms.gov/Outreach-and-Education/Medicare-Learning-Network-MLN/MLNMattersArticles/downloads/MM7133.pdf
G0442, G0443	Alcohol Screening/Counseling	http://www.cms.gov/Outreach-and-Education/Medicare-Learning-Network-MLN/MLNMattersArticles/downloads/MM7633.pdf
G0444	Depression Screen	
G0445	STI Counseling	Screening lab codes also covered (see Preventive Services publications link)
G0446	Intensive Behavioral Therapy for CVD	
G0447	Intensive Behavioral Therapy for Obesity	http://www.cms.gov/Outreach-and-Education/Medicare-Learning-Network-MLN/MLNMattersArticles/downloads/MM7641.pdf
Other Important Procedure Codes		
G0179, G0180	Home Care Certification	
G0181, G0182	Home/Hospice Care Plan Oversight	
HCPCS "J" codes	Code range within HCPCS for drugs administered eg steroid injection	

Many other codes are relevant to practice (eg EKG), but not listed for brevity. Geriatric Mental Health and Neuropsychological Testing codes not listed- see CPT.

General Information on Aging

AARP	www.aarp.org	888-OUR-AARP (888-687-2277)
AGS Foundation for Health in Aging	www.healthinaging.org	800-563-4916
Administration on Aging	www.aoa.gov	202-619-0724
American Geriatrics Society	www.americangeriatrics.org	800-247-4779
American Medical Directors Association	www.amda.com	800-876-2632
American Society of Consultant Pharmacists	www.ascp.com	800-355-2727
Argentum (formerly Assisted Living Federation of America)	www.alfa.org	703-894-1805
CDC National Prevention Information Network	www.cdcnpin.org	800-CDC-INFO (800-232-4636)
Family Caregiver Alliance	www.caregiver.org	800-445-8106
Medicare Hotline	www.medicare.gov	800-MEDICARE (800-633-4227) TTY: 877-486-2048
National Adult Day Services Association	www.nadsa.org	877-745-1440
National Council on the Aging	www.ncoa.org	202-479-1200
National Institute on Aging	www.nia.nih.gov	800-222-2225 TTY: 800-222-4225

End-of-Life

National Hospice and Palliative Care Organization	www.nhpco.org	800-646-6460 877-658-8896 (multilingual helpline)

Mistreatment of Older Adults

National Center on Elder Abuse	www.ncea.aoa.gov	855-500-3537 800-677-1116 (help hotline)

Smoking Cessation

CDC National Center for Chronic Disease Prevention and Health Promotion	www.cdc.gov/nccdphp	800-CDC-INFO (800-232-4636) TTY: 888-232-6348
National Cancer Institute	www.smokefree.gov	800-QUITNOW (800-784-8669) TTY: 800-332-8615

Specific Health Problems

Alzheimer's Association	www.alz.org	800-272-3900 TDD: 866-403-3073
Alzheimer's Disease Education and Referral Center	www.nia.nih.gov/alzheimers	800-438-4380
American Academy of Ophthalmology	www.aao.org	877-887-6327
American Association for Geriatric Psychiatry	www.aagponline.org	703-556-9222
American Cancer Society	www.cancer.org	800-ACS-2345 (800-227-2345) TTY: 866-228-4327
American College of Obstetricians and Gynecologists	www.acog.org	800-673-8444

American Diabetes Association	www.diabetes.org	800-DIABETES (800-342-2383)
American Foundation for the Blind	www.afb.org	800-AFB-LINE (800-232-5463)
American Heart Association	www.heart.org	800-AHA-USA1 (800-242-8721)
American Lung Association	www.lung.org	800-LUNG-USA (800-586-4872)
American Pain Society	www.ampainsoc.org	847-375-4715
American Parkinson Disease Association	www.apdaparkinson.org	800-223-2732
American Stroke Association	www.strokeassociation.org	888-4-STROKE (888-478-7653)
American Urological Association	www.auanet.org	866-746-4282
Arthritis Foundation	www.arthritis.org	800-283-7800
Better Hearing Institute	www.betterhearing.org	800-EAR-WELL (800-327-9355)
Endocrine Society and Hormone Foundation (obesity)	www.obesityinamerica.org	888-363-6274
Geriatric Mental Health Foundation	www.gmhfonline.org	703-556-9222
Hearing Loss Association of America	www.hearingloss.org	301-657-2248
Lighthouse International	www.lighthouse.org	800-284-4422 TTY: 212-821-9713
Meals On Wheels Association of America	www.mowaa.org	888-998-6325
National Association for Continence	www.nafc.org	800-BLADDER (800-252-3337)
National Diabetes Information Clearinghouse	www.diabetes.niddk.nih.gov	800-860-8747 TTY: 866-569-1162
National Digestive Diseases Information Clearinghouse	www.digestive.niddk.nih.gov	800-860-8747 TTY: 866-569-1162
National Eye Institute	www.nei.nih.gov	301-496-5248
National Heart, Lung, and Blood Institute	www.nhlbi.nih.gov	301-592-8573 TTY: 240-629-3255
National Institute of Arthritis and Musculoskeletal and Skin Diseases	www.niams.nih.gov	877-22-NIAMS (877-226-4267) TTY: 301-565-2966
National Institute of Mental Health	www.nimh.nih.gov	866-615-NIMH (866-615-6464) TTY: 866-415-8051
National Institute of Neurological Disorders and Stroke	www.ninds.nih.gov	800-352-9424 TTY: 301-468-5981
National Institute on Deafness and Other Communication Disorders	www.nidcd.nih.gov	800-241-1044 TTY: 800-241-1055
National Kidney and Urologic Diseases Information Clearinghouse	www.kidney.niddk.nih.gov	800-860-8747 TTY: 866-569-1162
National Osteoporosis Foundation	www.nof.org	800-231-4222
National Parkinson Foundation	www.parkinson.org	800-473-4636 (helpline)
Sexuality Information and Education Council of the US	www.siecus.org	202-265-2405
The Simon Foundation for Continence	www.simonfoundation.org	800-23-SIMON (800-237-4666)

Index

Page references followed by *t* and *f* indicate tables and figures, respectively.
Trade names are in *italics*.

A

AAA (abdominal aortic aneurysm), 61, 270*t*
AAPMC (antibiotic-associated
    pseudomembranous colitis), 130
Abandonment, 12*t*
Abatacept *(Orencia),* 211
Abbreviations, iii–vi
Abciximab *(ReoPro),* 26*t,* 34*t*
Abdominal aortic aneurysm (AAA), 61, 270*t*
Abdominal exercises, 197
Abdominal massage, 155
Abdominal pain, 241*t*
Abdominal radiography, 154
Abdominopelvic surgery, 27*t*
Abelcet (amphotericin B lipid complex), 174*t*
ABI (ankle-brachial index), 61, 62*t,* 310
Abilify, 76*t,* 282*t. See also* Aripiprazole
Absorbine Jr. Antifungal (tolnaftate), 90*t*
Abstral, 248*t. See also* Fentanyl
Abuse
    alcohol, 266, 270*t,* 323–325
    drug, 266, 327–329
    older adults, 10–12, 12*t*–13*t,* 348
    opioid misuse and withdrawal, 249–250
    prescription drug misuse, 323, 327–329,
        328
    substance use, 266, 323–329
    tobacco, 325–327, 326*t*
Acamprosate *(Campral),* 325
Acarbose *(Precose),* 95, 98*t*
ACC/AHA heart failure staging, 43*t*
Accolate (zafirlukast), 298*t*
Accountable Care Organization programs,
    114
Accupril, 55*t. See also* Quinapril
Accuzyme, 307
Acebutolol *(Sectral),* 53*t*
ACEIs (angiotensin-converting enzyme
        inhibitors)
    for ACS, 40
    for chronic angina, 41

for CKD, 180
and coexisting conditions, 56*t,* 57*t*
for cough, 285*t*
for DM type 2, 101, 102
drug interactions, 20*t*
for HF, 43*t,* 44, 44*t,* 45
for HTN, 51, 55*t*
and orthostatic hypotension, 216
for PAD, 62
for RAS, 50
and UI, 150*t*
Aceon, 55*t. See also* Perindopril
Acetaminophen. *See* APAP
Acetazolamide, 108*t*
Acetylcysteine *(Mucomyst),* 178
Acetylsalicylic acid. *See* Aspirin (ASA)
Acidosis, 180
Acid-suppressing drugs, 305
ACIP (Advisory Committee on Immunization
        Practices) guidelines, 164
AcipHex (rabeprazole), 122*t*
Aclidinium *(Tudorza Pressair),* 296*t*
Aclovate (alclometasone dipropionate), 90*t*
Acoustic neuroma, 134*t*
Acquired immune deficiency syndrome
        (AIDS), 281
Acral lentiginous melanoma, 86
ACR/EULAR criteria for rheumatoid arthritis,
        208*t*
ACS. *See* Acute coronary syndrome
Actemra (tocilizumab), 211, 214
ACTH (adrenocorticotropic hormone), 211
ACTH stimulation test, 103
Actinic keratosis, 84
Actiq, 248*t. See also* Fentanyl
Activities of daily living (ADLs)
    assessment of, 116
    in COPD therapy, 291
    Instrumental (IADLs), 337
    for pain management, 239
    Physical Self-Maintenance Scale, 336

Activities of daily living (ADLs) *continued*
   preoperative, 266
ACTO plus met (metformin and pioglitazone), 99*t*
Actonel, 231*t. See also* Risedronate
Actos (pioglitazone), 99*t*
Acuity testing, 105
Acular, 111*t. See also* Ketorolac
Acupuncture, 196, 202, 239*t*
ACUS (atypical cells of undetermined symptoms), 94
Acute bacterial conjunctivitis, 110–111, 110*t*
Acute blood loss, 142
Acute care, 7*t,* 114
Acute coronary syndrome (ACS), 39–41
   anticoagulant agents for, 32*t,* 33*t,* 34*t*
   antiplatelet agents for, 31*t*
   antithrombotic medications for, 26*t*
Acute interstitial nephritis, 177, 177*t,* 178
Acute kidney injury, 177–178, 177*t*–178*t,* 256*t*
Acute pain syndromes, 239
Acute rhinosinusitis, 285*t*
Acute tubular necrosis, 177, 177*t,* 178
Acyclovir *(Zovirax),* 164*t*
AD. *See* Alzheimer disease
Adalat CC (nifedipine SR), 55*t*
Adalimumab *(Humira),* 210, 214
Adaptive equipment, 68*t,* 221
Addiction, 323
Addyi (flibanserin), 304
Adempas (riociguat), 58
Adenocarcinoma, vulvar, 332
Adenosine stress test, 39
Adhesive capsulitis, 195
ADLs. *See* Activities of daily living
Adrenal disorders, 301*t*
Adrenal insufficiency, 103–104, 103*t*–104*t,* 183
Adrenergic agonists. *See* α-Adrenergic agonists; β-Adrenergic agonists
Adrenergic inhibitors, 53*t*–54*t. See also* α-blockers; β-blockers
Adrenocorticotropic hormone (ACTH), 211
Adrenocorticotropic hormone (ACTH) stimulation test, 103
ADT. *See* Androgen deprivation therapy

Adult Protective Services, 12
Advair Diskus (salmeterol-fluticasone), 298*t*
Advance directives, 253
   instructional, 258
   palliative care, 258
   preoperative care, 268
Advance practice nurses, 6*t*
Advicor (lovastatin with niacin), 49*t*
Advisory Committee on Immunization Practices (ACIP) guidelines, 164
Aerobic exercise. *See* Exercise
AeroChambers, 294
AF. *See* Atrial fibrillation
Aflibercept *(Eylea, Zaltrap),* 106
Afrezza (inhaled insulin), 101*t*
Afrin (oxymetazoline), 285*t*
Agency for Healthcare Research and Quality (AHRQ), 17, 114, 340
Age-related loss of muscle mass, 187
Age-related macular degeneration (AMD), 105–106
Aggrastat, 34*t. See also* Tirofiban
Aggrenox (ASA and dipyridamole), 31*t,* 219
Aggression
   in delirium, 68–69
   in dementia, 73
   sexual, 77*t*
   treatment of, 76*t*
Agitation
   in delirium, 68–69
   in dementia, 73
   and pain assessment, 235
   treatment of, 76, 76*t*–77*t*
AHI (apnea-hypopnea index), 319
AHRQ (Agency for Healthcare Research and Quality), 17, 114, 340
AIDS (acquired immune deficiency syndrome), 281
AIDS-related dementia, 69
Akathisia, 284*t*
Alamast (pemirolast), 111*t*
Alaway (ketotifen), 111*t*
Albiglutide *(Tanzeum),* 100*t*
Albumin, 188
Albuminuria, 102

Albuterol *(Ventolin, Ventolin Rotacaps),* 186, 296*t*

Albuterol-ipratropium *(Combivent Respimat, Duoneb),* 298*t*

Alcaftadine *(Lastacaft),* 111*t*

Alclometasone dipropionate *(Aclovate),* 90*t*

Alcohol
    and aging, 324
    delirium secondary to, 69
    and dizziness, 216
    drug interactions, 34, 242*t,* 324
    and osteoporosis, 229
    and sexual dysfunction, 305
    and sleep problems, 316
    and UI, 150*t*

Alcohol misuse/abuse, 266, 270*t,* 323–325

Alcohol restriction, 96

Alcohol screening/counseling, 347*t*

Alcohol Use Disorders (AUDs), 323–325

Alcohol withdrawal, 69, 325

Alcoholism, 255*t*

Aldactone, 45, 52*t. See also* Spironolactone

Aldara (imiquimod), 84, 85

Aldomet, 53*t. See also* Methyldopa

Aldosterone antagonists
    for ACS, 40
    and coexisting conditions, 56*t,* 57*t*
    for HF, 45
    for HTN, 52*t*

Alendronate *(Fosamax),* 231*t,* 233*t*

Alendronate effervescent *(Binosto),* 231*t*

Alfuzosin ER *(Uroxatral),* 276

ALGICELL, 313. *See also* Calcium alginate dressings

ALGICELL Ag, 313–314

Algiderm, 313. *See also* Calcium alginate dressings

Algidex Ag Alginate, 313–314

ALGISITE M, 313. *See also* Calcium alginate dressings

Alirocumab *(Praluent),* 49*t*

Aliskiren *(Tekturna),* 56*t*

Alldress, 314

Allegra-D (fexofenadine), 290*t*

Allegra-D 24 Hour (fexofenadine), 290*t*

Allergic conjunctivitis, 110, 111*t*–112*t,* 288*t*

Allergic rhinitis, 287–288, 288*t*–290*t*

Allevyn, 312. *See also* Foam island dressings

Allevyn Ag Foam, 312

Alli (orlistat), 189

Allopurinol *(Zyloprim, Lopurin),* 212*t,* 213

ALN (axillary lymph node) dissection, 330

Alocril (nedocromil), 111*t*

Alogliptin *(Nesina),* 98*t*

Alogliptin with metformin *(Kazano),* 100*t*

Alogliptin with pioglitazone *(Oseni),* 100*t*

Alomide (lodoxamide), 111*t*

Alosetron *(Lotronex),* 125

α-adrenergic agonists
    combined α- and β-agonists, 107*t*
    for glaucoma, 107*t*
    herbal medicine interactions, 25
    for HTN, 53*t*
    for menopausal symptoms, 334
    and UI, 150*t*

α-blockers (α-adrenergic inhibitors)
    for BPH, 275–276
    and coexisting conditions, 57*t*
    combined α- and β-blockers, 54*t,* 56*t,* 57*t*
    drug interactions, 21*t,* 275, 301*t*
    for HTN, 53*t*
    and orthostatic hypotension, 216
    for prostatitis, 280
    and UI, 150*t*

α-glucosidase inhibitors, 98*t,* 101

Alprostadil (prostaglandin E), 302*t*

ALS (amyotrophic lateral sclerosis), 257*t*

Altabax (retapamulin), 85

Altace, 55*t. See also* Ramipril

Altered mental status, 66–69

Alternative medications, 21–25

Altoprev, 48*t. See also* Lovastatin

Aluminum, 16, 19

Alveolar-arterial oxygen gradient, 1

Alvesco, 297*t. See also* Ciclesonide

Alvimopan *(Entereg),* 126*t*

Alzheimer Association, 77, 348

Alzheimer disease (AD). *See also* Dementia
    clinical features of, 70
    cognitive decline in, 69
    pharmacologic treatment of, 74–75
    progression of, 71–72

Alzheimer disease (AD) *continued*
  resources for, 348, 349
Amantadine *(Symmetrel),* 165*t,* 222*t,* 223*t*
Amaryl (glimepiride), 98*t*
Ambien, 38, 318*t. See also* Zolpidem
Ambien CR, 318*t. See also* Zolpidem
AmBisome (amphotericin B liposomal), 174*t*
Ambrisentan *(Letairis),* 58
Ambulation, 26*t*
Ambulatory BP monitoring, 50
Amcinonide *(Cyclocort),* 91*t*
AMD (age-related macular degeneration),
  105–106
American College of Rheumatology/
  European League Against Rheumatism
  (ACR/EULAR) Criteria, 208*t*
American College of Surgeons risk
  calculators, 264
American Urological Association (AUA),
  344
Amikacin *(Amikin),* 160, 171*t*
Amikin, 171*t. See also* Amikacin
Amiloride *(Midamor),* 19*t,* 20*t,* 52*t*
Aminoglutethimide, 278
Aminoglycosides
  for infectious diseases, 171*t*
  for MRSA, 163
  for pneumonia, 159*t,* 160
  for prostatitis, 280
  for urosepsis, 161
Aminolevulinic acid *(Levulan Kerastick),* 84
Aminosalicylic acid, 45
Amiodarone *(Cordarone, Pacerone)*
  for AF, 58, 59*t*
  drug interactions, 21*t,* 34, 45
  QT_c interval interactions, 21*t*
Amitiza (lubiprostone), 126*t*
Amitriptyline *(Elavil),* 67*t,* 81
Amlodipine *(Norvasc),* 55*t*
Amoxapine *(Asendin),* 67*t,* 81
Amoxicillin *(Amoxil)*
  for antibiotic prophylaxis, 272*t,* 273
  for cystitis or UTI, 161
  for *H pylori* infection, 123*t*
  for infectious diseases, 169*t*
  for pneumonia, 159*t*

Amoxicillin with clarithromycin and
  lansoprazole *(Prevpac),* 123*t*
Amoxicillin-clavulanate *(Augmentin)*
  for cellulitis, 85
  for COPD exacerbation, 292*t*
  for cystitis or UTI, 161
  for folliculitis, 85
  for infections in chronic wounds, 308*t*
  for infectious diseases, 169*t*
  for pneumonia, 159*t*
Amoxil, 169*t. See also* Amoxicillin
Amphotec (amphotericin B cholesteryl
  sulfate complex), 174*t*
Amphotericin, 174*t*
Amphotericin B *(Fungizone),* 174*t*
Amphotericin B cholesteryl sulfate complex
  (Amphotec), 174*t*
Amphotericin B lipid complex *(Abelcet),* 174*t*
Amphotericin B liposomal *(AmBisome),* 174*t*
Ampicillin
  for cystitis or UTI, 161
  for endocarditis prophylaxis, 272*t*
  for infectious diseases, 169*t*
  for pneumonia, 159*t*
Ampicillin-sulbactam *(Unasyn),* 159*t,* 169*t*
Amsler grid, 106
Amylin analogs, 101*t*
Amyotrophic lateral sclerosis (ALS), 257*t*
Amyvid (florbetapin F18), 71
Anagrelide, 144
Anakinra *(Kineret),* 210, 211
Analgesics. *See also* APAP; Aspirin
  for acute vertebral fracture, 232*t*
  adverse events, 249
  for arthritis, 203, 204*f,* 205*t*–208*t,* 209
  for cervical stenosis/radiculopathy, 194
  for hip fracture surgery, 198
  for multiple myeloma, 145
  opioids, 21*t,* 241*t*–247*t,* 248–249, 324
  for pain, 235, 238, 238*t,* 240, 240*t*–248*t,* 248,
    249
  patient-controlled, 238, 238*t*
  for plantar fasciitis, 202
  QT_c interval interactions, 21*t*
  selection of agents, 240
  topical, 240*t,* 252*t*

Analgesics *continued*
  and UI, 150*t*
Anaprox (naproxen sodium), 207*t*
Anaspaz, 125. *See also* Hyoscyamine
Anastrozole (Arimidex), 331*t*
Ancef, 170*t*. *See also* Cefazolin
Ancobon (flucytosine), 175*t*
Androderm (testosterone), 303*t*
AndroGel (testosterone), 303*t*
Androgen deficiency, opioid-induced, 303
Androgen deprivation therapy (ADT), 229,
  278, 279
Androgens, 304
Anemia, 138–142
  aplastic, 143
  of B_{12} and folate deficiency, 142
  chronic, 142
  of chronic disease, 139
  of chronic inflammation, 139
  of CKD, 141, 180
  combined iron deficiency and anemia of
    inflammation, 139–141
  hemolytic, 142
  hypoproliferative, 138*f*
  hypotension secondary to, 65
  of inflammation, 139
  iron deficiency, 139, 139*f*
  undifferentiated (or unexplained), 142
Anesthetics
  alcohol interactions, 324
  for pain, 198, 234*t*, 238, 240, 252*t*
Aneurysm, abdominal aortic (AAA), 61, 270*t*
Angina
  antihypertensive therapy and, 56*t*
  chronic, 41–42
  unstable, 39, 40, 41
Anginal chest pain or equivalent, 39
Angioedema, 89
Angiography
  in acute stroke, 218
  cardiac CT angiography, 39
  in HF, 43
  in PAD, 62*t*
Angiomax, 33*t*. *See also* Bivalirudin
Angioplasty, carotid, 219*t*–220*t*
Angiotensin II receptor blockers. *See* ARBs

Angiotensin-converting enzyme inhibitors.
  See ACEIs
Anidulafungin *(Eraxis)*, 175*t*
Ankle-brachial index (ABI), 61, 62*t*, 310
Annual Wellness Visit (AWV)
  fall prevention, 114
  procedure codes, 347*t*
  required elements, 5
  screening for cognitive impairment, 70
Annucort, 132
Anorectal physiology tests, 154
Anorexia, 187, 262
Anorgasmia, 305
Anoro Ellipta (umeclidinium-vilanterol), 299*t*
Ansaid (flurbiprofen), 206*t*
Anserine bursitis, 199
Antacids
  digoxin interactions, 45
  formulation differences, 16
  for GERD, 121
  iron interactions, 140*t*
  for stress-ulcer prevention, 124
Antara, 48*t*. *See also* Fenofibrate
Anthralin, 87
Anthropometrics, 188
Antiallergy (seasonal) medications, 17
Antiandrogens, 278, 279*t*–280*t*
Antianxiety agents, 234*t*
Antiarrhythmics
  AF refractory to, 60
  drug interactions, 302*t*
  fall risks, 114*t*
  for HF, 45
Antibiotic-associated diarrhea, 130–132
Antibiotic-associated pseudomembranous
  colitis (AAPMC), 130
Antibiotics
  for acute conjunctivitis, 110
  antimicrobial stewardship, 157
  for arterial ulcer infection, 310
  for bacterial sinusitis, 285*t*
  drug-food or -nutrient interactions, 19
  for endocarditis prophylaxis, 272*t*, 273
  for folliculitis, 85
  for *H pylori*, 123
  for halitosis at end of life, 260

Antibiotics *continued*
  for hip fracture surgery, 198
  for infections in chronic wounds, 308*t*
  for infectious diseases, 169*t*–176*t*
  for peptic ulcer disease, 124
  perioperative use, 268
  for pneumonia, 158, 159*t*
  for prostatitis, 280
  for sepsis and SIRS, 163
  for skin failure, 263
  for skin ulcer infection, 308
  and tinnitus, 136
  for UTIs, 161
  for venous ulcer infection, 315
  warfarin interactions, 34
Anti-CD20 monoclonal antibody, 211
Anticholinergics
  antidiarrheals, 130*t*
  for asthma, 295, 296*t*
  for COPD, 291, 291*t*–292*t*, 296*t*
  and dementia, 73
  drug interactions, 20*t*
  drugs with strong properties, 67*t*
  and dyspareunia, 304
  long-acting, 291, 291*t*–292*t*
  medication-induced delirium, 67*t*
  for Parkinson disease, 223*t*
  and sexual dysfunction, 305
  short-acting, 291*t*–292*t*
  and UI, 150, 150*t*
Anticoagulation. *See also* Heparin; Warfarin
  for ACS, 40, 41
  for AF, 58, 59*t*, 60
  alcohol interactions, 324
  for antithrombotic therapy, 26*t*
  cessation before surgery, 267
  for dental procedures, 267
  herbal medicine interactions, 22, 23, 24, 25
  indications for, 26*t*
  for ischemic stroke, 219
  new oral anticoagulants vs warfarin, 60*t*
  perioperative therapy, 268, 268*t*
  prescribing information, 32*t*–34*t*
  resumption after surgery, 267
  for stroke prevention, 219

Anticonvulsants
  alcohol interactions, 324
  fall risks, 114*t*
  herbal medicine interactions, 24
  for menopausal symptoms, 334
  and osteoporosis, 229
  for pain, 234*t*, 243*t*, 250*t*
  for painful neuropathy, 228
  prescribing information, 225*t*–226*t*
  for seizures, 225
  and sexual dysfunction, 305
Antidepressants. *See also* MAOIs; SSRIs; TCAs
  alcohol interactions, 324
  anticholinergic properties, 67*t*
  for AUDs, 325
  for bipolar disorders, 83*t*
  choosing, 79
  contraindicated in older adults, 81
  de-prescribing, 17
  for depression, 79, 79*t*–81*t*
  drug interactions, 20*t*, 242*t*
  food interactions, 20
  herbal medicine interactions, 24
  for IBS, 125
  for menopausal symptoms, 334
  for pain, 234*t*, 243*t*, 251*t*
  preventing falls with, 117*t*
  QT_c interval interactions, 21*t*
  and sexual dysfunction, 305
  for sleep disorders, 317*t*
  and sleep problems, 316
  for smoking cessation, 326
Antidiabetic agents, 24
Antidiarrheals
  for *C difficile* infection, 131*t*
  for fecal incontinence, 155
  for IBS, 125
  prescribing information, 129*t*–130*t*
Antidiuretic hormone, 181
Anti-embolism stockings, 46
Antiemetics
  for nausea and vomiting, 128
  for pain relief, 252*t*
  prescribing information, 128*t*–129*t*
  QT_c interval interactions, 21*t*

Antiestrogen drugs, 331*t*
Antifungals
　for candidiasis, 85
　for infectious diseases, 174*t*, 175*t*–176*t*
　for intertrigo, 86
　prescribing information, 89*t*–90*t*
　topical, 89*t*–90*t*
Antihistamines
　alcohol interactions, 324
　for allergic conjunctivitis, 110, 111*t*, 112*t*, 288*t*
　for allergic rhinitis, 288, 288*t*, 288*t*–289*t*
　for angioedema, 89
　anticholinergic properties, 67*t*
　for cholinergic reactions, 89
　de-prescribing, 17
　food interactions, 20
　for hives, 89
　and sexual dysfunction, 305
Antihypertensives
　alcohol interactions, 324
　and coexisting conditions, 56*t*–57*t*
　for emergencies and urgencies, 51
　fall risks, 114*t*
　herbal medicine interactions, 22, 24
　for HTN, 51
　oral agents, 52*t*–56*t*
　for RAS, 50
　and sexual dysfunction, 305
　that cause leg edema, 46
Anti-infectives, 21*t*
Anti-inflammatory agents, 211–212, 241*t*, 280.
　　See also NSAIDs
Antimicrobial stewardship, 157
Antimuscarinics
　anticholinergic properties, 67*t*
　for BPH, 275, 276
　for nausea and vomiting, 129*t*
　and orthostatic hypotension, 216
　for UI, 150, 150*t*–151*t*, 153
Antineoplastics, 45
Antiparkinson agents, 67*t*
Antiplatelet therapy
　for ACS, 40
　for antithrombotic therapy, 26*t*
　bridging therapy, 267

　cessation before surgery, 267
　dual antiplatelet therapy, 267
　herbal medicine interactions, 22, 23, 24, 25
　indications for, 26*t*
　for ischemic stroke, 219
　for PAD, 62, 62*t*
　perioperative use, 268
　prescribing information, 31*t*
　resumption after surgery, 267
　for stroke prevention, 219
　for VTE prophylaxis, 27*t*
Antipseudomonal agents
　for infectious diseases, 169*t*, 170*t*
　for pneumonia, 159*t*, 160
Antipsychotics
　adverse events, 281, 283*t*
　for agitation, 76, 77*t*
　alcohol interactions, 324
　anticholinergic properties, 67*t*
　atypical, 83*t*
　for bipolar disorders, 83*t*
　for delirium, 68, 69
　de-prescribing, 17
　drug interactions, 20*t*, 21*t*
　fall risks, 114*t*
　food interactions, 20
　and orthostatic hypotension, 216
　and osteoporosis, 229
　for Parkinson disease, 222*t*
　prescribing information, 282*t*–283*t*
　preventing falls with, 117*t*
　for psychotic disorders, 281
　QT$_c$ interval interactions, 21*t*
　second-generation, 38, 69, 76, 77*t*, 282*t*, 283*t*
　and sexual dysfunction, 305
　toolkit for reducing use, 74
　and UI, 150*t*
Antipyretics, 218
Antiretrovirals, 168
Antiseptics, 310
Antispasmodics, 67*t*, 125
Antistaphylococcal penicillins, 85, 169*t*, 272*t*
Antithrombotic therapy, 26–35
　for AF, 58, 59*t*, 60
　for cataract surgery, 105

Antithrombotic therapy *continued*
  indications for, 26*t*
  for ischemic stroke, 218–219
  risk instruments to guide, 59*t*
  for VTE, 27*t*, 30*t*
Anti-TNF agents, 214
Anti-TNF-α agents, 210
Antitussives, 286*t*
Antivert, 129*t. See also* Meclizine
Antiviral therapy
  for herpes zoster, 164, 164*t*
  for influenza, 165, 165*t*–166*t*
Anxiety, 36–38
  agitation treatment guidelines, 76*t*
  at bedtime, 317
  benzodiazepines for, 38, 38*t*
  buspirone management of, 38
  in COPD, 292
  at end of life, 262
  with pain, 239
Anxiolytics, 114*t*, 261
Anzemet (dolasetron), 128*t*
Aortic stenosis (AS), 60–61
Aortic valve replacement (AVR), 35*t*, 61
APAP (acetaminophen)
  for acute pain, 237–238
  for acute stroke, 218
  adverse events, 249
  alcohol interactions, 324
  for arthritis, 196, 203, 204*f*, 205*t*
  for back pain, 196
  for chronic disk degeneration, 196
  with codeine, 241*t*
  for lumbar spinal stenosis, 197
  for mild pain, 240*t*
  for moderate pain, 241*t*
  with opioids, 204*f*
  for pain, 234*t*, 235, 237–238, 242*t*
  for shoulder pain, 195
  warfarin interactions, 34
APAP (autotitrating positive airway
    pressure), 320
APAP (acetaminophen), intravenous
    (Ofirmev), 237
APAP (acetaminophen) ER, with oxycodone
    (Xartemis XR), 245*t*

APAP (acetaminophen) with hydrocodone
    (Lorcet, Lortab, Norco, Vicodin), 241*t*
APAP (acetaminophen) with oxycodone
    (Percocet, Tylox, Magnacet), 242*t*
APAP (acetaminophen) with tramadol
    (Ultracet), 242*t*
Apathy, 73, 76
Aphasia, 227*t*
Apidra, 101*t. See also* Insulin glulisine
Apixaban *(Eliquis)*
  for ACS, 41
  for AF, 59*t*, 60*t*
  for anticoagulation, 32*t*, 35*t*, 60*t*
  for antithrombotic therapy, 26*t*
  avoid use, 19*t*
  cessation before surgery, 267
  resumption after surgery, 267
  for VTE prophylaxis, 27*t*
Aplastic anemia, 143
Apligraf, 311, 315
Apnea-hypopnea index (AHI), 319
Apokyn (apomorphine), 223*t*
Apomorphine *(Apokyn),* 223*t*
Appetite loss, 19–20, 329*t. See also*
    Malnutrition
Appetite stimulants, 190
Apresoline, 54*t. See also* Hydralazine
Aquacel Ag Foam, 312
AquaClear, 313
AquaDerm, 313
Aquaphor, 89
AquaSite, 313
AquaSite Hydrogel, 313
Aquasorb, 313
Arachnocides, 287
Aranesp (darbepoetin alfa), 141*t*
Arava (leflunomide), 210*t*
ARBs (angiotensin II receptor blockers)
  for ACS, 40
  for CKD, 180
  and coexisting conditions, 56*t*, 57*t*
  for DM type 2, 101, 102
  for HF, 43*t*, 44, 44*t*
  for HTN, 51, 56*t*
  for RAS, 50
Arcapta (indacaterol), 297*t*

Arctic root, 24
AREDS2 preparation, 106
Arformoterol *(Brovana)*, 296*t*
Argatroban, 26*t*, 33*t*
Arginine vasopressin receptor antagonists, 184
Aricept, 75*t. See also* Donepezil
Arimidex (anastrozole), 331*t*
Aripiprazole *(Abilify)*
  for acute mania, 82
  adverse events, 283*t*
  for agitation, 76*t*
  for bipolar disorders, 83*t*
  for depression, 79
  for psychotic disorders, 281, 282*t*
  for tardive dyskinesia, 284*t*
Aristocort, 91*t,* 104*t. See also* Triamcinolone
Arixtra, 33*t. See also* Fondaparinux
Arnuity Ellipta, 297*t. See also* Fluticasone furoate
Aromasin (exemestane), 331*t*
Aromatase inhibitors, 331, 331*t*
Artane, 223*t. See also* Trihexyphenidyl
Arterial blood gases, 1
Arterial disease, peripheral. *See* Peripheral arterial disease (PAD)
Arterial oxygen, 1, 2
Arterial ulcers, 306*t*–307*t*, 310
Arteriovenous fistula access, 181
Arteritis, giant cell (temporal), 213–215
Arthritis. *See also* Osteoarthritis
  acute arthritis, 213
  acute gouty arthritis, 211
  acute gouty flare, 211
  APAP and NSAIDs for, 205*t*–208*t*
  chronic, 211
  chronic calcium pyrophosphate crystal inflammatory arthritis, 213
  chronic crystal inflammatory arthritis, 213
  crystal-induced, 213
  inflammatory, 200
  pain relief, 251*t*
  pseudogout, 212*t,* 213
  pseudo-RA, 213
  psoriatic, 200
  resources for, 349

rheumatoid, 200, 208–211, 208*t*
Arthritis Foundation, 238
Arthropan (choline salicylate), 206*t*
Arthrotec (enteric coated diclofenac), 206*t*
Artificial nutrition, 192, 259
Artificial tears, 110, 111
AS (aortic stenosis), 60–61
ASA. *See* Aspirin
Asenapine *(Saphris),* 282*t*
Asendin, 81. *See also* Amoxapine
Asmanex HFA, 297*t. See also* Mometasone
Asmanex Twisthaler, 297*t. See also* Mometasone
Aspercreme (trolamine salicylate), 207*t,* 251*t*
Aspergillosis, 175*t*
Aspiration, 192, 285*t. See also* Dysphagia
Aspirin (ASA)
  for ACS, 40
  for AF, 59, 59*t*
  for antithrombotic therapy, 26*t*
  for arthritis, 205*t*
  cessation before surgery, 267, 268
  for chronic angina, 41
  for dizziness, 217*t*
  for DM type 2, 102
  drug interactions, 251*t*
  enteric-coated, 205*t*
  for essential thrombocytosis, 144
  for giant cell arteritis, 215
  herbal medicine interactions, 24
  for ischemic stroke, 219
  for MI prevention, 270*t*
  for PAD, 62
  for polycythemia vera, 144
  prescribing information, 31*t*
  for preventing adverse events, 49*t*
  for stroke prevention, 219
  and tinnitus, 136
  for vertigo, 217*t*
  for VTE, 27*t,* 30
  for warfarin anticoagulation, 35*t*
Aspirin (ASA) with dipyridamole *(Aggrenox),* 26*t,* 31*t,* 219
Aspirin (ASA) with oxycodone *(Percodan),* 242*t*

Aspirin (ASA) with pravastatin *(Pravigard PAC)*, 48t
Assessment, 4–5
    ADLs, 336
    balance, 5t, 115
    cardiac risk, 264, 265f
    cognitive status, 4t, 70, 74, 335
    dentition, 4t
    depression, 338–339
    dimensions, 4t–5t
    emotional status, 4t
    environmental, 116
    environmental hazards, 5t
    fall prevention, 5t, 114–116, 115f
    financial status, 5t
    functional, 4t, 70, 115, 237, 336, 337, 343
    gait, 5t, 115
    health literacy, 17, 340
    hearing, 4t
    Instrumental ADLs (IADLs), 337
    instruments, 335–345
    Karnofsky Scale, 341
    medication review, 4t
    mobility, 116
    multidisciplinary, 235
    nutritional, 4t, 187–188
    pain, 4t, 236f
    Palliative Performance Scale, version 2 (PPSv2), 342
    preferences of care, 5t
    preoperative, 264–268, 265–266
    psychosocial, 237
    pulmonary risk, 265–266
    social status, 5t
    spiritual status, 4t
    UI, 4t
    vision testing, 4t
    wound, 306–307
Assisted feeding, 192, 262
Assisted living, 7t
Assisted suicide, 259
Assistive devices
    functional assessment, 116
    for hearing loss, 135, 136
    optical aids, 109
    for osteoarthritis, 202
    for pain management, 238
    for preventing falls, 117t
Asthma, 293–295, 295t, 296t–299t
Astramorph PF, 243t. *See also* Morphine
Atacand, 56t. *See also* Candesartan
Atelvia (risedronate), 231t
Atenolol *(Tenormin)*, 53t, 216t
Ativan, 38t, 318t. *See also* Lorazepam
Atorvastatin *(Lipitor)*, 48t, 305
Atrial fibrillation (AF), 58–60
    anticoagulant agents for, 32t, 33t, 35t
    antihypertensive therapy and, 56t
    antiplatelet agents for, 31t
    antithrombotic medications for, 26t, 59t
    rhythm control drugs for, 59t
    warfarin anticoagulation for, 35t
Atrial tachycardia, 56t
At-risk drinking, 324
Atropine, 67t, 261
Atropine with diphenoxylate *(Lomotil)*, 130t
Atrovent, 285t, 296t. *See also* Ipratropium
Atrovent NS, 285t, 289t. *See also* Ipratropium
Attapulgite *(Kaopectate)*, 129t
Atypical cells of undetermined symptoms (ACUS), 94
AUA IPSS Symptom Index for BPH, 344
Audiologists, 6t
Audiometry, 133
AUDs (Alcohol Use Disorders), 323–325
Augmentin, 169t. *See also* Amoxicillin-clavulanate
Autologous cellular immunotherapy, 278
Autolytic debridement, 307
Autonomic dysregulation, 64
Autotitrating positive airway pressure (APAP), 320
Avanafil *(Stendra)*, 301t
Avandamet (rosiglitazone and metformin), 100t
Avandaryl (rosiglitazone and glimepiride), 100t
Avandia (rosiglitazone), 99t
Avapro (irbesartan), 56t
Avastin (bevacizumab), 106
Aveed (testosterone), 303t
Avelox, 110t, 172t. *See also* Moxifloxacin

Aventyl, 81*t*, 228. *See also* Nortriptyline
Avibactam-ceftazidime *(Avycaz),* 170*t*
Avinza (morphine), 245*t*
Avodart (dutasteride), 276
AVR (aortic valve replacement), 35*t*, 61
Avycaz (ceftazidime-avibactam), 170*t*
AWV. *See* Annual Wellness Visit
Axid, 122*t*. *See also* Nizatidine
Axillary lymph node (ALN) dissection, 330
Axona (medium-chain triglyceride), 76
Azactam, 169*t*. *See also* Aztreonam
Azelaic acid *(Azelex, Finacea, Finevin),* 87
Azelastine *(Optivar),* 111*t*, 289*t*
Azelex (azelaic acid), 87
Azilect (rasagilene), 223*t*
Azilsartan *(Edarbi),* 56*t*
Azithromycin *(Zithromax)*
   for endocarditis prophylaxis, 272*t*
   for infectious diseases, 171*t*
   for pneumonia, 159*t*
   QT$_c$ interval interactions, 21*t*
   for rosacea, 88
Azoles, 174*t*–175*t*
Aztreonam *(Azactam),* 159*t*, 161, 169*t*
Azulfidine, 210*t*. *See also* Sulfasalazine

B

Back pain, 195–197
   adjuvant medications for pain relief, 252*t*
   low back pain, 196, 202, 203, 252*t*
   nondrug interventions for, 239*t*
Baclofen *(Lioresal),* 251*t*
Bacterial conjunctivitis, acute, 110–111, 110*t*
Bacterial sinusitis, 285*t*
Bacteriuria, 153, 160–161, 271
Bactocill (oxacillin), 169*t*
Bactrim, 172*t*. *See also* Co-trimoxazole
Bactroban, 85. *See also* Mupirocin
BAHAs (bone-anchored hearing aids), 135
Balance assessment, 5*t*, 115
Balance exercises, 117*t*, 221, 274
Balance impairment, 113*t*, 117*t*, 202
Bariatric surgery, 96, 189, 320
Barium swallow, 120
Basal cell carcinoma, 84–85, 332
Basic energy (caloric) requirements, 189

Bazedoxifene with estrogen *(Duavee),* 232*t*, 333
Beclomethasone *(Beconase AQ, Qnasl, QVAR),* 289*t*, 297*t*
Beconase AQ, 289*t*. *See also* Beclomethasone
Bed rest, 238
Bedside swallowing assessment, 260
Bedtime glucose, 96*t*
Behavioral disturbances/agitation, 235
Behavioral therapy. *See also* CBT (cognitive-behavioral therapy)
   for anxiety, 37
   for dementia, 74
   for DHIC, 149
   for dizziness, 217*t*
   for drop attacks, 217*t*
   for IBS, 125
   for insomnia, 316
   for opioid abuse/misuse/dependence, 328
   for overactive bladder, 149
   for preventing falls, 118*t*
   procedure codes, 347*t*
   for sleep disorders, 317
   for smoking cessation, 326–327
   for UI, 148*f*, 149
Belladonna alkaloids, 67*t*
Belsomra (suvorexant), 318*t*
Belviq (lorcaserin), 189
Benazepril *(Lotensin),* 44*t*, 55*t*
Benecalorie, 191*t*
Benecol, 47
Benefiber (wheat dextrin), 126*t*
Benemid, 212*t*. *See also* Probenecid
Ben-Gay (methylsalicylate and menthol), 204*f*, 251*t*
Benicar (olmesartan), 56*t*
Benign paroxysmal positional vertigo, 217*t*
Benign prostatic hyperplasia (BPH), 57*t*, 275–277, 344
Bentyl, 125. *See also* Dicyclomine
Benzodiazepine dependence, 328
Benzodiazepine withdrawal, 69
Benzodiazepines
   adverse events, 327
   for akathisia, 284*t*

Benzodiazepines *continued*
  for anxiety, 38, 38*t*
  avoid use, 38
  for delirium, 69
  drug interactions, 20*t*, 21*t*
  fall risks, 114*t*
  herbal medicine interactions, 24, 25
  for pain at end of life, 259
  preventing falls with, 117*t*
  for sleep disorders, 318*t*
Benzonatate *(Tessalon Perles)*, 286*t*
Benzoyl peroxide, 87
Benztropine *(Cogentin)*, 67*t*, 73, 223*t*
Bepotastine *(Bepreve)*, 111*t*
Bepreve (bepotastine), 111*t*
Bereavement, 301*t*
Berg Balance Scale, 115
Besifloxacin *(Besivance)*, 110*t*
Besivance (besifloxacin), 110*t*
β-adrenergic agonists
  for asthma, 294–295, 295*t*, 296*t*–297*t*
  combined α- and β-agonists, 107*t*
  for COPD, 291, 291*t*–292*t*, 292*t*, 296*t*–297*t*
  long-acting, 291, 291*t*–292*t*, 294, 295*t*,
    296*t*–297*t*
  for pneumonia, 158
  short-acting, 291*t*–292*t*, 295, 295*t*, 296*t*
  for UI, 151*t*
β-blockers (β-adrenergic inhibitors)
  for ACS, 40, 41
  for AF, 58
  for akathisia, 284*t*
  alcohol interactions, 324
  for anxiety disorders, 38
  for chronic angina, 41
  and coexisting conditions, 56*t*, 57*t*
  combined α- and β-blockers, 54*t*, 56*t*
  for glaucoma, 107*t*
  for HF, 43*t*, 44, 44*t*
  for HTN, 51, 53*t*–54*t*
  for hyperthyroidism, 93
  and leg edema, 46
  and orthostatic hypotension, 216
  for Parkinson disease, 222*t*
  perioperative use, 268
  and sleep problems, 316

β-carotene, 106
β-lactams/β-lactamase inhibitors, 159*t*, 160,
  169*t*
Betamethasone *(Celestone)*, 103*t*
Betamethasone dipropionate *(Diprolene,*
  Diprolene AF, Diprosone), 91*t*, 332
Betamethasone valerate *(Valisone)*, 91*t*
Betapace, 59*t*. See also Sotalol
Betapace AF, 59*t*. See also Sotalol
Betaxolol *(Kerlone)*, 53*t*, 107*t*
Bevacizumab *(Avastin)*, 106
BGC Matrix, 314
Biaxin, 171*t*. See also Clarithromycin
Biaxin XL, 171*t*. See also Clarithromycin
Bicalutamide *(Casodex)*, 279*t*
Bicarbonate, 192
Bicipital tendinitis, 195
BiDil, 45. See also Isosorbide dinitrate and
  hydralazine
Biguanides, 97*t*
Bile acid sequestrants, 48*t*, 49*t*
Bilevel positive airway pressure (BPAP),
  320
Biliopancreatic diversion, 189
Billing codes, 346–347
Bimatoprost, 108*t*
Binosto (alendronate), 231*t*
Bioclusive, 312
Biofeedback
  for fecal incontinence, 155
  for IBS, 125
  for insomnia, 317
  for osteoarthritis, 202
  for pain, 239
  for UI, 149
Bioidentical hormone therapy, 333
Biolex, 313
Biologic DMARDs, 209, 210
Biological agents, 87
Bioprosthetic heart valves, 35*t*
Biopsy, sentinel lymph node (SLN), 330
BIOSTEP, 314
BIOSTEP Ag, 314
Bipolar diathermy, 132
Bipolar disorders, 82, 83*t*, 281
Bisacodyl *(Dulcolax)*, 126, 127*t*, 154

Bismuth subsalicylate *(Pepto-Bismol),* 123*t,* 124, 129*t*
Bisoprolol *(Zebeta),* 44*t,* 53*t*
Bisphosphonates
adverse effects of, 145
for breast cancer, 332
de-prescribing, 17
effects on other outcomes, level of evidence, and risks of, 233*t*
with estrogen, 232
for metastatic bone pain, 259
for multiple myeloma, 145
for osteoporosis, 199, 230–231, 231*t,* 232, 233
Bivalirudin *(Angiomax),* 26*t,* 33*t*
Biventricular pacing, 43*t*
Bladder cancer, 271
Bladder diary, 147
Bladder outlet obstruction
causes of, 146*t*
evaluation of, 147
in nursing-home residents, 153
small prostate with, 276
Bladder training, 149
Bladder-sphincter dyssynergia, 146
Bleeding, postmenopausal, 332
Blepharitis, 110*t*
Blindness. *See* Visual impairment
BlisterFilm, 312
Blocadren (timolol), 54*t*
Blood gases, arterial, 1
Blood glucose monitoring, 102
Blood loss, acute, 142
Blood pressure
goals of treatment, 96*t*
high, 50–51, 57–58
home monitoring, 51
low, 104*t,* 118*t,* 216*t,* 283*t,* 284*t*
management in CKD, 180
management in ischemic stroke, 219
management in PAD, 62
management in stroke prevention, 219
screening, 270*t*
Blood urea nitrogen (BUN):creatinine ratio, 181
BMD (bone mineral density), 229, 233*t*

BMI (body mass index), 1, 42, 51
BNP (brain natriuretic peptide), 43
Board-and-care facilities, 7*t*
Body mass index (BMI), 1, 42, 51
Body water, total, 182
Body weight, ideal, 1
Bone densitometry (men), 271*t*
Bone densitometry (women), 119, 270*t*
Bone disease, metastatic
in breast cancer, 332
pain relief, 259
in prostate cancer, 277, 278, 279
Bone mineral density (BMD), 229, 233*t*
Bone-anchored hearing aids (BAHAs), 135
Boniva, 231*t. See also* Ibandronate
Boost Drink, 191*t*
Boost Glucose Control, 191*t*
Boost Plus, 191*t*
Bordered Foam/Ag, 312
Bosentan *(Tracleer),* 58
Bosutinib, 144
Botox (onabotulinumtoxin A), 252*t*
Botulinum toxin
for BPH, 277
for dysphagia, 120
for pain, 252*t*
for UI, 152
Bowel obstruction, 261
Bowel training, 155
BPAP (bilevel positive airway pressure), 320
BPH (benign prostatic hyperplasia), 57*t,* 275–277, 344
Brachytherapy, 278
Bracing, 197, 202
Bradykinesia, 220, 222*t*
Brain natriuretic peptide (BNP), 43
Brain tumor, 281
Breast cancer, 330–331
adjuvant therapy, 331–332
medications for osteoporosis and, 233*t*
oral agents for, 331*t*
recommendations for prevention, 271*t*
screening for, 272
Breathing disorders, sleep-related, 316
Breo Ellipta (vilanterol-fluticasone), 299*t*
Brief Pain Inventory, 237

Bright light. *See* Light therapy
Brilinta, 31*t*. *See also* Ticagrelor
Brimonidine *(Mirvasol),* 87, 107*t*
Brimonidine/brinzolamide, 108*t*
Brimonidine/timolol, 108*t*
Brintellix (vortioxetine), 80*t*
Brinzolamide, 108*t*
Brinzolamide/brimonidine, 108*t*
Broca's aphasia, 227*t*
Bromocriptine *(Cycloset, Parlodel),* 99*t*, 223*t*
Brompheniramine, 67*t*
Bronchial provocative testing, 293
Bronchitis, 170*t*, 285*t*
Bronchodilators, 261, 316
Bronchospasm, 56*t*
Brovana (arformoterol), 296*t*
Buccal testosterone *(Striant),* 303*t*
Budesonide *(Rhinocort-Aqua),* 289*t*, 297*t*
Budesonide-formoterol *(Symbicort),* 298*t*
Bumetanide *(Bumex)*
    for HTN, 52*t*
    for hyperkalemia, 185, 186
    for nocturnal polyuria, 152
Bumex, 52*t*. *See also* Bumetanide
BUN:creatinine ratio, 181
Bunion, 200
Bupivacaine *(Exparel),* 237–238
Buprenorphine, 328
Buprenorphine, transdermal *(Butrans Transdermal System CIII),* 235, 246*t*
Bupropion *(Wellbutrin, Wellbutrin XL)*
    for depression, 79, 80*t*
    and seizures, 225
    for smoking cessation, 326
    for SSRI-induced sexual dysfunction, 305
    tamoxifen interactions, 331*t*
Bupropion SR *(Wellbutrin SR, Zyban),* 80*t*, 326*t*
Bupropion-naltrexone *(Contrave),* 190
Bursal injections, 203
Bursitis
    anserine, 199
    response to lidocaine injection, 194*t*
    subacromial, 194–195, 213
    subdeltoid, 213
    trochanteric, 197–198

BuSpar, 38, 76*t*. *See also* Buspirone
Buspirone *(BuSpar)*
    for agitation, 76*t*
    for anxiety, 38, 317
    for depression, 79
Butenafine *(Lotrimin Ultra, Mentax),* 16, 89*t*
Butrans Transdermal System CIII, 246*t*. *See also* Transdermal buprenorphine
Bydureon (exenatide), 100*t*
Byetta (exenatide), 100*t*
Bypass surgery, 40, 189
Bystolic, 53*t*. *See also* Nebivolol

C
Cabergoline *(Dostinex),* 321
CABG (coronary artery bypass grafting), 40
Cachexia, 187, 262
CAD. *See* Coronary artery disease
Cadexomer iodine, 308
Caffeine
    and dizziness, 216
    for fecal incontinence, 155
    for orthostatic (postural) hypotension, 64
    for postprandial hypotension, 64
    and sleep problems, 316
    for UI, 148
CAGE questionnaire, 266, 324
Calan SR (verapamil SR), 55*t*
CalciCare, 313. *See also* Calcium alginate dressings
Calcimar, 232*t*. *See also* Calcitonin
Calcipotriene, 87
Calcitonin *(Calcimar, Cibacalcin, Miacalcin, Osteocalcin, Salmonine)*
    bone outcomes, 233*t*
    effects on other outcomes, level of evidence, and risks of, 233*t*
    with estrogen, 232
    for hypercalcemia, 94
    for osteoporosis, 232, 232*t*
    for vertebral compression fracture, 197
Calcitriol *(Rocaltrol),* 180
Calcium
    drug interactions, 19
    for HTN, 51
    for hypocalcemia, 180

Calcium *continued*
   for malnutrition, 188
   for osteoporosis, 230, 271*t*
   for Parkinson disease, 221
   with vitamin D, 230
Calcium acetate *(PhosLo)*, 180
Calcium alginate dressings *(Algiderm,*
    Curasorb Polymem Alginate, Cutimed,
    ALGICELL, ALGISITE M, DermaGinate,
    Gentell, Melgisorb, NU-DERM,
    Kaltostat, DU-DERM Alginate, SeaSorb,
Calcium alginate with silver dressings
    (Algidex Ag Alginate, 3M Tegaderm
    Alginate AG, SofSorb AG, ALGICELL Ag,
    DermaSyn/Ag, SILVERCEL, McKesson
    Calcum Alginate with Silver), 313–314
Calcium antagonists. *See* Calcium-channel
    blockers (CCBs)
Calcium carbonate, 16, 180, 230
Calcium citrate *(Freeda Mini Cal-citrate,*
    Freeda Calcium Citrate Fine Granular),
    230
Calcium gluconate, 185
Calcium polycarbophil, 132
Calcium pyrophosphate, 213
Calcium-channel blockers (CCBs)
   for ACS, 41
   for AF, 58
   for chronic angina, 41
   for CKD, 180
   and coexisting conditions, 56*t*, 57*t*
   for DM type 2, 101
   for HF, 45
   for HTN, 51, 54*t*–55*t*
   for hyperthyroidism, 93
   and leg edema, 46
   for PAH, 57
   and UI, 150*t*
Caldolor (ibuprofen), 207*t*
Calluses and corns, 200, 201
Calmoseptine, 88
Caloric requirements, 189, 309
CAM (Confusion Assessment Method), 66,
   269
CAM (Confusion Assessment Method)-ICU,
   66

CAM (Confusion Assessment Method)-S, 66
Campho-Phenique (camphor and phenol),
   251*t*
Camphor and phenol *(Campho-Phenique)*,
   251*t*
Camphor-menthol-phenol *(Sarna)*, 251*t*
Campral (acamprosate), 325
Canagliflozin *(Invokana)*, 99*t*
Canakinumab *(Ilaris)*, 211
Cancer
   bladder, 271
   breast, 233*t*, 271*t*, 272, 330–331, 331–332,
    331*t*
   cervical, 272
   colon, 272
   colorectal, 272
   decision making, 272
   determinants for hospice eligibility, 255*t*
   head and neck, 192
   hospice referral, 254
   lung, 270*t*
   medications for osteoporosis and, 233*t*
   metastatic bone disease, 259, 279, 332
   ovarian, 272
   pancreatic, 272
   prostate, 231, 272, 277–279, 279*t*–280*t*
   resources for, 348, 349
   screening, 270*t*, 272
   vulvar, 332
Cancer pain, 234*t*, 239, 252*t*
Cancer-related anorexia/cachexia
    syndrome, 187
Cancidas (caspofungin), 175*t*
Candesartan *(Atacand)*, 44*t*, 56*t*
Candidiasis, 85
   antibiotics for, 174*t*, 175*t*
   at end of life, 260
   esophageal, 175*t*
   topical antifungals for, 89*t*, 90*t*
   UTI or urosepsis, 161
   vaginal, 174*t*
Cane fitting, 116, 202
Cannabidiol (CBD), 329*t*
Cannabinoids, 252*t*
Cannabis sitiva (marijuana), 328
Capoten, 55*t*. *See also* Captopril

Capsaicin *(Capsin, Capzasin, No Pain-HP, Qutenza, R-Gel, Zostrix)*
  for osteoarthritis, 203, 204*f*
  for pain, 240*t*, 252*t*
  for painful neuropathy, 228
Capsin, 252*t. See also* Capsaicin
Capsulitis, adhesive, 195
Captopril *(Capoten),* 20, 44*t*, 55*t*
Capzasin, 252*t. See also* Capsaicin
Carac, 84. *See also* 5-Fluorouracil
Carbamazepine *(Epitol, Equetro, Carbatrol, Tegretol, Tegretol XR, Carbatrol)*
  for agitation, 76*t*
  for bipolar disorders, 83*t*
  for pain relief, 250*t*
  for painful neuropathy, 228
  for restless legs syndrome, 321
  for seizures, 225*t*
  and sexual dysfunction, 305
  warfarin interactions, 34
Carbamide peroxide *(Cerumenex, Debrox),* 134
Carbapenems, 160, 169*t*
Carbatrol, 225*t*, 250*t. See also* Carbamazepine
Carbex (selegiline), 223*t*
Carbidopa-levodopa *(Sinemet, Parcopa),* 222*t*, 321
Carbidopa-levodopa + entacapone *(Stalevo),* 224*t*
Carbidopa-levodopa SR *(Sinemet CR),* 222*t*
Carbinoxamine, 67*t*
Carbohydrates, 96, 101
Carbonic anhydrase inhibitors, 108*t*
Cardene (nicardipine), 55*t*, 219
Cardene SR (nicardipine), 55*t*
Cardiac catheterization, 39
Cardiac conduction, 20
Cardiac CT angiography, 39
Cardiac diagnostic tests, 39
Cardiac enzymes, 40
Cardiac pacing, 118*t*
Cardiac risk assessment, preoperative, 264–265, 265*f*
Cardiac risk factors, 50
Cardiac syncope, 63, 63*t*, 64

Cardiac troponins, 40
Cardiomyopathy, 65
Cardiovascular diseases, 39–65
  behavioral therapy for, 347*t*
  and CKD, 180–181
  determinants for hospice eligibility, 255*t*
  drug-induced changes in cardiac conduction, 20
  drug-QT$_c$ interval interactions, 21*t*
  endocarditis prophylaxis, 272
  exercise prescription, 274
  and intolerable vasomotor symptoms, 334
  prevention of, 26*t*, 31*t*
  resources for, 349
  risks with surgery, 265
Cardiovascular examination, 119
Cardioversion, 58, 60
Cardizem CD (diltiazem), 54*t*
Cardizem SR (diltiazem), 54*t*
Cardura (doxazosin), 53*t*, 275
Care preferences assessment, 5*t*
Care Transitions Program, 8
Caregiving. *See also* Mistreatment of older adults
  caregiver issues, 74, 77
  resources for, 348
  risk factors for inadequate or abusive caregiving, 10–11
Carisoprodol, 67*t*
β-Carotene, 106
Carotid angioplasty, 219*t*–220*t*
Carotid artery stenosis, 219*t*–220*t*, 271
Carotid endarterectomy, 219*t*–220*t*
Carotid sinus hypersensitivity, 118*t*
Carpal tunnel syndrome, 200
CarraDres, 313
CarraSmart Film, 312
Carteolol, 107*t*
Carvedilol *(Coreg),* 44*t*, 54*t*
Carvedilol CR *(Coreg CR),* 44*t*, 54*t*
Casodex (bicalutamide), 279*t*
Caspofungin *(Cancidas),* 175*t*
Cataflam, 206*t. See also* Diclofenac
Catapres, 53*t. See also* Clonidine
Catapres-TTS, 53*t. See also* Clonidine
Cataracts, 105, 118*t*, 266–267

Catechol *O*-methyltransferase (COMT) inhibitors, 223*t*
Catheter ablation, 60
Catheterization, cardiac, 39
Catheters, 153, 259
CBD (cannabidiol), 329*t*
CBT (cognitive-behavioral therapy)
    for anxiety, 37
    for AUDs, 324
    for benzodiazepine dependence, 328
    for depression, 79
    for insomnia, 317
    for persistent pain, 234*t*, 238, 239*t*
    for preventing falls, 117*t*
    for tinnitus, 137
CCBs. *See* Calcium-channel blockers
CDR (Clinical Dementia Rating), 70
Ceclor (cefaclor), 170*t*
Cedax (ceftibuten), 171*t*
Cefaclor *(Ceclor)*, 170*t*
Cefadroxil *(Duricef)*, 170*t*
Cefazolin *(Ancef, Kefzol)*, 170*t*, 198, 272*t*
Cefdinir *(Omnicef)*, 170*t*
Cefditoren *(Spectracef)*, 170*t*
Cefepime *(Maxipime)*, 159*t*, 160, 171*t*
Cefixime *(Suprax)*, 170*t*
Cefotan (cefotetan), 170*t*
Cefotaxime *(Claforan)*, 159*t*, 170*t*
Cefotetan *(Cefotan)*, 170*t*
Cefoxitin *(Mefoxin)*, 170*t*
Cefpodoxime *(Vantin)*, 159*t*, 171*t*
Cefprozil *(Cefzil)*, 170*t*
Ceftaroline fosamil *(Tefloro)*, 163, 171*t*
Ceftazidime *(Ceptaz, Fortaz)*, 160, 171*t*
Ceftazidime-avibactam *(Avycaz)*, 170*t*
Ceftibuten *(Cedax)*, 171*t*
Ceftin, 170*t*. *See also* Cefuroxime axetil
Ceftriaxone *(Rocephin)*
    for endocarditis prophylaxis, 272*t*
    for infections in chronic wounds, 308*t*
    for infectious diseases, 171*t*
    for pneumonia, 159*t*
Cefuroxime axetil *(Ceftin)*, 159*t*, 170*t*
Cefzil (cefprozil), 170*t*
Celebrex, 208*t*. *See also* Celecoxib
Celecoxib *(Celebrex)*
    for arthritis, 208*t*
    for pain, 237, 241*t*
    warfarin interactions, 34
Celestone (betamethasone), 103*t*
Celexa, 76*t*, 79*t*. *See also* Citalopram
CellerateRX Gel/Powder, 314
Cellular immunotherapy, autologous, 278
Cellulitis, 85, 109*t*, 308
Centers for Disease Control and Prevention (CDC), 116
Central auditory processing disorder, 133*t*–134*t*
Central sleep apnea (CSA), 319
Cephalexin *(Keflex)*
    for cellulitis, 85
    for cystitis or UTI, 161
    for endocarditis prophylaxis, 272*t*, 273
    for infections in chronic wounds, 308*t*
    for infectious diseases, 170*t*
Cephalosporins
    for cellulitis, 85
    for endocarditis prophylaxis, 272*t*
    for erysipelas, 85
    for impetigo, 85
    for infectious diseases, 170*t*, 170*t*–171*t*
    for pneumonia, 160
    for prostatitis, 280
    for urosepsis, 161
Cephradine, 273
Ceptaz, 171*t*. *See also* Ceftazidime
Cerebellar disease, 216*t*
Cerebellar tremor, 216*t*
Cerebral venous sinus thrombosis, 35*t*
Certolizumab *(Cimzia)*, 210
Cerumen removal, 68*t*, 134
Cerumenex (carbamide peroxide), 134
Cervical cancer, 272
Cervical spondylosis, 217*t*
Cervical stenosis/radiculopathy, 194
Cetirizine, 288*t*
CHA$_2$DS$_2$-VASc scoring, 58, 59*t*
CHADS$_2$ scoring, 35*t*, 58, 59*t*
Chantix, 326*t*. *See also* Varenicline
Chemical coping, 240
Chemical dependency, 240
Chemical peels, 84

Chemical skin ulcer debridement, 307
Chemonucleolysis (enzymatic) injections, 203
Chemotherapy
  antiemetic therapy for, 128*t*
  for breast cancer, 332
  for MDS, 143
  for multiple myeloma, 145
  for pain at end of life, 259
  and tinnitus, 136
Chest pain, 39
Chest percussion, 158
Chest x-ray, 57, 60, 285*t*
Chlamydia pneumoniae, 158
Chloramphenicol *(Chloromycetin)*, 172*t*
Chlordiazepoxide, 38
Chlorhexidine/fluoride, 158
Chloride channel activators, 126*t*
Chloromycetin (chloramphenicol), 172*t*
Chlorothiazide *(Diuril)*, 52*t*
Chlorpheniramine, 67*t*
Chlorpromazine, 21*t*, 67*t*, 225
Chlorthalidone *(Hygroton)*, 52*t*
Cholecalciferol, 230, 231*t*
Cholesterol, serum, 188
Cholesterol absorption inhibitors, 48*t*
Cholesterol screening. *See* Dyslipidemia
Cholesterol-lowering diet, 47
Cholesterol-lowering margarines, 47
Cholestyramine, 34, 45
Choline magnesium salicylate *(Tricosal, Trilisate, CMT)*, 206*t*
Choline salicylate *(Arthropan)*, 206*t*
Cholinergic agonists, 107*t*
Cholinergic urticaria, 89
Cholinesterase inhibitors
  for apathy, 76
  cognitive enhancers, 74–75, 75*t*
  de-prescribing, 17
  for glaucoma, 107*t*
  for Parkinson disease, 222*t*
  QT$_c$ interval interactions, 21*t*
  and UI, 150*t*
Chondrocalcinosis, 213
Chondroitin, 203
Chondroitin/glucosamine, 21–22

Chondromalacia patellae, 199
Chronic calcium pyrophosphate crystal inflammatory arthritis, 213
Chronic care, 7*t*
Chronic crystal inflammatory arthritis, 213
Chronic disk degeneration, 196
Chronic kidney disease (CKD), 179–181
  anemia of, 141
  antihypertensive therapy and, 56*t*
  determinants for hospice eligibility, 256*t*
Chronic low back pain
  adjuvant medications for pain relief, 251*t*, 252*t*
  nonpharmacologic approaches to, 202
  pharmacologic intervention for, 203
Chronic musculoskeletal pain, 240*t*, 251*t*
Chronic myelogenous leukemia, 144
Chronic obstructive pulmonary disease (COPD), 290–293
  assessment of, 291*t*
  with asthma, 293
  exacerbation, 292*t*
  preoperative risk assessment, 265
  resources for, 348, 349
  screening for, 272
  therapy for, 291*t*–292*t*, 292*t*, 296*t*–299*t*
Chronic pain
  medications for, 239, 241*t*, 252*t*
  nondrug interventions for, 239*t*
Chronic wounds, 306–309, 306*t*–307*t*, 308*t*
Chronulac (lactulose), 127*t*
Chymopapain, 192
Cialis (tadalafil), 275, 302*t*
Cibacalcin, 232*t*. *See also* Calcitonin
Ciclesonide *(Alvesco, Omnaris, Zetonna)*, 289*t*, 297*t*
Ciclopirox *(Loprox, Penlac)*, 87, 89*t*
Cilastatin-imipenem *(Primaxin)*, 169*t*
Cilostazol *(Pletal)*, 21*t*, 34, 62
Ciloxan, 110*t*. *See also* Ciprofloxacin
Cimetidine *(Tagamet HB 200)*
  drug interactions, 21*t*
  for GERD, 122*t*
  reduce dosage, 19*t*
  and sexual dysfunction, 305
Cimzia (certolizumab), 210

Cinacalcet, 94
Cipro, 172*t. See also* Ciprofloxacin
Cipro XR (ciprofloxacin), 172*t*
Ciprofloxacin *(Ciloxan, Cipro)*
    for acute bacterial conjunctivitis, 110*t*
    for COPD exacerbation, 292*t*
    enteral nutrition interactions, 192
    for infections in chronic wounds, 308*t*
    for infectious diseases, 172*t*
    for pneumonia, 159*t,* 160
    for prostatitis, 280
    QT$_c$ interval interactions, 21*t*
    warfarin interactions, 34
Ciprofloxacin ER *(Cipro XR),* 172*t*
Circadian rhythm disorders, 316
Cirrhosis, hepatic, 183
Citalopram *(Celexa)*
    for agitation, 76*t*
    for depression, 79*t*
    for menopausal symptoms, 334
    QT$_c$ interval interactions, 21*t*
Citrobacter, 161
Citroma (magnesium citrate), 127*t*
Citrucel, 126*t. See also* Methylcellulose
CKD (chronic kidney disease), 179–181
    anemia of, 141
    antihypertensive therapy and, 56*t*
    determinants for hospice eligibility, 256*t*
Claforan, 170*t. See also* Cefotaxime
Clarinex (desloratadine), 288*t*
Clarithromycin *(Biaxin, Biaxin XL)*
    for endocarditis prophylaxis, 272*t*
    food interactions, 20
    for *H pylori* infection, 123*t*
    for infectious disease, 171*t*
    for pneumonia, 159*t*
    QT$_c$ interval interactions, 21*t*
    for rosacea, 88
Clarithromycin with lansoprazole and
        amoxicillin *(Prevpac),* 123*t*
Claritin-D (loratadine), 290*t*
Claritin-D 24 Hour (loratadine), 290*t*
Claudication therapy, 62, 62*t*
Clavicle: rotator tendon impingement on,
        194–195
Clavulanate-amoxicillin *(Augmentin)*
    for cellulitis, 85
    for COPD exacerbation, 292*t*
    for cystitis or UTI, 161
    for folliculitis, 85
    for infections in chronic wounds, 308*t*
    for infectious diseases, 169*t*
    for pneumonia, 159*t*
Clavulanate-ticarcillin *(Timentin),* 170*t*
ClearSite, 312
Clemastine, 67*t*
Clenia (sodium sulfacetamide), 87
Cleocin, 172*t. See also* Clindamycin
Clindamycin *(Cleocin)*
    for endocarditis prophylaxis, 272*t*
    for erysipelas, 85
    for folliculitis, 85
    for infections in chronic wounds, 308*t*
    for infectious diseases, 172*t*
    for MRSA, 85, 163
Clinical Dementia Rating (CDR), 70
Clinoril, 207*t. See also* Sulindac
Clobetasol propionate *(Temovate),* 91*t,* 332
Clocortolone pivalate *(Cloderm),* 91*t*
Cloderm (clocortolone pivalate), 91*t*
Clofibrate, 34
Clog-Zapper, 192
Clomipramine, 67*t*
Clonazepam, 222*t,* 322
Clonidine *(Catapres, Catapres-TTS)*
    food interactions, 20
    for HTN, 53*t*
    and leg edema, 46
    for menopausal symptoms, 334
    and orthostatic hypotension, 216
    for restless legs syndrome, 321
    and sexual dysfunction, 305
    and sleep problems, 316
Clopidogrel *(Plavix)*
    for ACS, 40
    for AF, 59
    for antithrombotic therapy, 26*t*
    cessation before surgery, 267, 268
    for chronic angina, 41
    for DM type 2, 102
    herbal medicine interactions, 24
    for PAD, 62

Clopidogrel *(Plavix) continued*
  prescribing information, 31*t*
  for stroke prevention, 219
Clostridium difficile
  diagnosis of, 131
  pseudomembranous colitis, 130
  treatment of, 131*t*, 173*t*
Clotrimazole *(Cruex, Gyne-Lotrimin, Lotrimin,*
    Lotrimin AF for Her, Mycelex), 16, 90*t*,
    260
Clozapine *(Clozaril)*
  anticholinergic property, 67*t*
  and dementia, 73
  for Parkinson disease, 222*t*
  for psychosis, 282*t*
  and seizures, 225
  and sexual dysfunction, 305
Clozaril, 282*t. See also* Clozapine
CMS guidance on unnecessary drugs, 18
CMS Physician Quality Reporting System
    (PQRS), 114
CMT (choline magnesium salicylate), 206*t*
CNS depressants
  abuse/misuse/dependence, 327, 328
  herbal medicine interactions, 24, 25
CNS tumors, 120*t*
Cochlear implants, 134–135, 134*t*, 137
Cockcroft-Gault formula, 1
Codeine, 241*t*, 286*t*
Codeine phosphate, 286*t*
Coding, 346–347
Coenzyme Q$_{10}$, 22
Cogentin, 223*t. See also* Benztropine
Cognitive enhancers, 75, 75*t*, 76
Cognitive impairment
  in AD, 69
  in delirium, 66
  and depression, 79
  and falls, 113*t*, 116, 118*t*
  mild (MCI), 71, 73–74, 74–75
  and pain assessment, 235, 236*f*
  and Parkinson disease, 222*t*
  preventive measures for delirium, 68*t*
  progression of, 71–72
  screening for, 266, 271*t*
  treatment of, 74–76, 222*t*

UI and, 148, 152–153
Cognitive status assessment
  in cognitive dysfunction, 74
  in dementia, 70
  Mini-Cog™ screen for dementia, 335
  screening assessment, 4*t*
Cognitive-behavioral therapy (CBT). *See*
  CBT
Colace, 127*t*, 134. *See also* Docusate
ColActive Plus, 314
ColActive Plus AG, 314
ColBenemid (probenecid with colchicine),
  212*t*
Colchicine *(Colcrys)*
  for anti-inflammatory prophylaxis, 211
  for gout, 211, 212*t*
  for inflammatory osteoarthritis, 205
  for pseudogout, 213
  reduce dosage, 19*t*
Colchicine with probenecid *(ColBenemid,*
    Col-Probenecid, Proben-C), 212*t*
Colcrys, 212*t. See also* Colchicine
Cold, common, 285*t*
Cold therapy, 238
Colesevelam *(WelChol)*, 49*t*, 99*t*
Colestid, 49*t. See also* Colestipol
Colestid Tablets, 49*t. See also* Colestipol
Colestipol *(Colestid, Colestid Tablets)*, 45, 49*t*
Colitis, antibiotic-associated
  pseudomembranous, 130
Collagen dressings *(CellerateRX* Gel/
    Powder, *Fibracol, Kollagen-Medifil*
    Particles/Gels/Pads, *Kollagen-Skin*
    Temp II, Promogran Matrix, Stimulen,
    ColActive Plus, DermaCol, BIOSTEP
    matrix dressing, *BGC Matrix, CollaSorb,*
    Endoform Dermal Template, Excellagen,
    Helicoll, Puracol Plus, Simpurity
    collagen pad, *Triple Helix Collagen)*, 314
Collagen with silver dressings *(ColActive*
    Plus AG, Prisma Matrix, SilvaKollagen
    Gel, DermaCol AG, BIOSTEP Ag,
    PROMOGRAN PRISMA, Puracol Plus
    AG), 314
CollaSorb, 314
Colon cancer, 272

Colonoscopy, 154, 270*t*
Colorectal cancer, 272
Colpocleisis, 333
Colposcopy, 332
Col-Probenecid (probenecid with
    colchicine), 212*t*
Coma, 92, 257*t*
Co-management, 198
CombiDERM, 314
Combivent Respimat (albuterol-ipratropium),
    298*t*
Combunox (oxycodone + ibuprofen), 242*t*
Comfeel Film, 312
Comfeel Plus, 312. *See also* Hydrocolloids
Comfort-Aid, 313
Comfortell, 314
ComfortFoam, 312
Communicating bad news, 253–254
Communication with hearing-impaired
    people, 135–136
Community-acquired cystitis, 161
Community-acquired pneumonia, 158, 159*t*
Compazine, 128*t. See also* Prochlorperazine
Complex regional pain syndrome, 240
Compression, intermittent pneumatic
    for DVT/PE prophylaxis, 26*t*, 27*t*
    for hip fracture surgery, 199
    for venous insufficiency, 46
Compression devices, 315
Compression fractures, vertebral, 197
Compression stockings
    for hip fracture, 198
    for orthostatic (postural) hypotension, 64
    prescribing information, 46*t*
    for stasis edema, 152
    for venous insufficiency, 46
    for venous ulcers, 315
Compression therapy, 64, 315
Compression wraps, 46, 315
Comprilan wrap, 315
Computed tomography. *See* CT
COMT (catechol *O*-methyltransferase)
    inhibitors, 222*t*, 223*t*
Comtan (entacapone), 223*t*
Conduction aphasia, 227*t*
Conduction disorders, drug-induced, 20

Conductive hearing loss, 133*t*–134*t*
Confusion Assessment Method (CAM), 66,
    269
Confusion Assessment Method (CAM)-ICU,
    66
Confusion Assessment Method (CAM)-S, 66
Congestion, nasal, 288*t*
Congestive heart failure. *See* Heart failure
Congestive heart failure, Hypertension, Age,
    Diabetes, Stroke (CHADS). *See* CHADS$_2$
    scoring
Conivaptan *(Vaprisol),* 184
Conjunctival hyperemia, 110
Conjunctivitis, 110–111
    acute bacterial conjunctivitis, 110*t*
    allergic, 110, 111*t*–112*t*, 288*t*
Constipation, 125–126
    drug-induced, 283*t*
    at end of life, 261
    and fecal incontinence, 155
    medications for, 126*t*–127*t*
    opioid-induced, 249, 251*t*
    and UI, 148
Continuing care retirement communities, 7*t*
Continuous positive airway pressure (CPAP),
    319, 320
Contrave (bupropion-naltrexone), 190
Contreet, 312–313
Contreet Foam, 312
ConZip (tramadol ER), 246*t*
COPA, 312. *See also* Foam island dressings
COPD. *See* Chronic obstructive pulmonary
    disease
Coping, chemical, 240
Coping skills, 238, 239
Cordarone, 59*t. See also* Amiodarone
Cordran (flurandrenolide), 91*t*
Coreg, 54*t. See also* Carvedilol
Coreg CR, 54*t. See also* Carvedilol CR
Corgard (nadolol), 53*t*
Corlanor (ivabradine), 45
Corns, 200, 201
Coronary angiography, 43
Coronary artery bypass grafting (CABG), 40
Coronary artery disease (CAD), 39–41
    ICD placement for, 65

Coronary artery disease (CAD) *continued*
  medications for osteoporosis and, 233*t*
  screening for, 39, 271
Coronary risk assessment, preoperative, 265*f*
Cortef, 104*t. See also* Hydrocortisone
Corticosteroids. *See also* Glucocorticoids
  for acute bacterial conjunctivitis, 110*t*
  for acute disk herniation, 196
  for adrenal insufficiency, 103, 103*t*–104*t*, 104
  for allergic conjunctivitis, 110, 288*t*, 289*t*
  for allergic rhinitis, 288, 288*t*, 289*t*
  for anorexia, cachexia, dehydration, 262
  for asthma, 294, 297*t*
  for back pain, 196
  for bicipital tendinitis, 195
  for cachexia, 262
  for carpal tunnel syndrome, 200
  for cervical stenosis/radiculopathy, 194
  for chronic disk degeneration, 196
  for COPD, 291, 291*t*–292*t*, 297*t*
  for dehydration, 262
  drug interactions, 20*t*
  for frozen shoulder (adhesive capsulitis), 195
  for giant cell arteritis, 214
  inhaled, 291*t*–292*t*, 295*t*
  and leg edema, 46
  for lumbar spinal stenosis, 197
  for myxedema coma, 92
  for neurodermatitis, 86
  for ocular inflammatory disease, 108–109
  for osteoarthritis, 196, 203, 204*f*
  and osteoporosis, 229
  for pain, 238, 251*t*
  for plantar fasciitis, 202
  for psoriasis, 87
  for scabies, 88
  for shoulder pain, 195
  and sleep problems, 316
  topical, 90*t*–91*t*, 108–109
  for trochanteric bursitis, 198
Cortifoam, 132
Cortisone *(Cortone),* 103*t*
Cortone (cortisone), 103*t*

Co-trimoxazole *(Bactrim),* 172*t*, 280
Cough, 285–286
  antitussives and expectorants, 286*t*
  with asthma, 294
  chronic, 290, 292
  diagnosis and treatment by duration of symptoms, 285*t*
Coumadin, 34. *See also* Warfarin
Counseling
  for healthy diet and physical activity, 270*t*
  for pain management, 239
  procedure codes, 346*t*, 347*t*
  for sleep apnea, 319
  for smoking cessation, 326, 327
  telephone counseling, 326, 327
Counterirritants, 251*t*
Counterstimulants, 240*t*
Covaderm Plus, 314
Covera-HS (verapamil), 55*t*
COVRSITE plus, 314
COX-2 inhibitors
  for arthritis, 204*f*, 205, 208*t*
  avoid use, 44
  for pain, 241*t*
Cozaar, 56*t*, 212*t. See also* Losartan
CPAP (continuous positive airway pressure), 319, 320
Cr (creatinine), 181
Cramps, 252*t*, 320
Cranberry juice, 162
CrCl (creatinine clearance), 1
C-reactive protein (CRP), 271*t*
Creatinine (Cr), 181
Creatinine clearance (CrCl), 1
Crestor (rosuvastatin), 48*t*
Cricopharyngeal myotomy, 120
Crohn's disease, 329*t*
Cromolyn *(NasalCrom),* 288*t*, 289*t*
Cromolyn sodium *(Intal),* 298*t*
Cross-cultural geriatrics, 13
Crotamiton *(Eurax),* 88
CRP (C-reactive protein), 271*t*
Cruex, 90*t. See also* Clotrimazole
Cryosurgery, 84, 85
Crystal-induced arthritis, 213
CSA (central sleep apnea), 319

CT (computed tomography)
    cardiac CT angiography, 39
    electron-beam, 271
    intracranial angiography, 218
    low-dose, 270*t*
    single-photon emission CT (SPECT), 39
Cubicin, 173*t. See also* Daptomycin
Cultural identity, 13
Cupric oxide, 106
Curagel, 313
Curasol, 313
Curasol Gel, 313
Curettage, 84, 85, 332
Curity, 314. *See also* Gauze packing
Cushing syndrome, 281
Cutaneous capsaicin patches *(Qutenza),*
    228, 240*t*, 252*t*
Cutimed, 313. *See also* Calcium alginate
    dressings
Cutimed Gel, 313
Cutinova Hydro, 312. *See also* Hydrocolloids
Cutivate, 91*t. See also* Fluticasone
    propionate
Cyclobenzaprine, 67*t*
Cyclocort (amcinonide), 91*t*
Cyclophosphamide, 214
Cycloset, 99*t. See also* Bromocriptine
Cyclosporine, 24, 87
Cyclosporine ophthalmic emulsion
    (Restasis), 111
Cymbalta. See also Duloxetine
    for depression, 81*t*
    for osteoarthritis, 205
    for pain, 251*t*
    for painful neuropathy, 228
CYP substrates, inducers, and inhibitors
    drug interactions, 122*t*, 301*t*
    herbal medicine interactions, 22, 24, 25
Cyproheptadine, 67*t*
Cystitis, 161
Cytochrome P-450. *See* CYP substrates,
    inducers, and inhibitors
Cytotec, 205. *See also* Misoprostol

D
Dabigatran *(Pradaxa)*
    for ACS, 41
    for AF, 59*t*, 60*t*
    for anticoagulation, 33*t*, 35*t*, 60*t*
    for antithrombotic therapy, 26*t*
    avoid use, 19*t*
    cessation before surgery, 267
    resumption after surgery, 267
    for VTE, 27*t*, 30*t*
Dalbavancin *(Dalvance),* 173*t*
Dalfopristin-quinupristin *(Synercid),* 173*t*
Daliresp (roflumilast), 298*t*
Dalteparin *(Fragmin)*
    for anticoagulation, 32*t*
    for antithrombotic therapy, 26*t*
    for DVT prophylaxis, 199
    for VTE, 27*t*, 30*t*
Dalvance (dalbavancin), 173*t*
Danaparoid *(Orgaran),* 27*t*, 32*t*
Dapaglifozin *(Farxiga),* 99*t*
Daptomycin *(Cubicin),* 163, 173*t*
Darbepoetin alfa *(Aranesp),* 141*t*
Darifenacin *(Enablex),* 67*t*, 151*t*
Dasatinib, 144
DASH (Dietary Approaches to Stop
    Hypertension), 42
Daypro (oxaprozin), 207*t*
DBS (deep brain stimulation), 221, 222*t*
D&C (dilation and curettage), 332
D-dimer test, 2, 28
De Quervain tendinopathy, 199
Deafness. *See* Hearing impairment
Death certificates, 13–14, 259
Debridement, 307, 309, 311
Debrox (carbamide peroxide), 134
Decadron, 104*t*, 261. *See also*
    Dexamethasone
Decision making, informed, 11*f*
    cancer screening, 272
    goal-oriented care, 9–10
    life-sustaining care, 10
    surgical, 264
Decisional capacity, 10, 11*f*
Declomycin (demeclocycline), 184
Decongestants, 289*t*, 316
Deep brain stimulation (DBS), 221, 222*t*
Deep tissue injury, 311–312

Deep-vein thrombosis (DVT)
    diagnosis of, 28
    leg edema, 45
    management of, 30
    medications for, 27*t*, 32*t*, 233*t*
    prophylaxis of, 27*t*, 199
Defibrillators, 42, 43*t*
    placement, 65
    withholding or withdrawing therapy, 259
Degarelix *(Firmagon)*, 280*t*
Dehydration, 68*t*, 181–182, 262. *See also*
        Hydration
Delirium, 66–69
    differential diagnosis, 281
    medication-induced, 67*t*
    postoperative, 268–269
    preventive measures, 68*t*
Delta-Cortef, 104*t*. *See also* Prednisolone
Deltasone, 104*t*. *See also* Prednisone
Delusional (paranoid) disorder, late-life, 281
Delusions, 72
Demadex, 52*t*. *See also* Torsemide
Demeclocycline *(Declomycin)*, 184
Dementia, 70–77
    AIDS-related dementia, 69
    assisted feedings, 192
    and delirium, 66
    dementia syndrome, 70
    and depression, 79
    determinants for hospice eligibility, 255*t*
    differential diagnosis, 281
    distinguishing early Parkinson disease
        from other parkinsonian syndromes,
        220*t*–221*t*
    dysphagia complaints, 120*t*
    Lewy body dementia, 69, 221*t*
    management of, 281
    Mini-Cog™ screen for dementia, 335
    and Parkinson disease, 222*t*
    risk and protective factors, 73
    treatment options, 222*t*
Denosumab *(Prolia)*
    bone outcomes, 233*t*
    for hypercalcemia, 94
    for metastatic bone disease, 279
    for osteoporosis, 230, 232, 232*t*

Dental care, 150, 262
Dental procedures
    anticoagulation for, 267
    endocarditis prophylaxis for, 273
Dentists, 6*t*
Dentition assessment, 4*t*
Depacon, 83*t*, 226*t*. *See also* Valproic acid
Depakene, 83*t*, 226*t*. *See also* Valproic acid
Depakote (divalproex sodium), 76*t*, 83*t*, 226*t*.
        See also Valproic acid
Depakote ER (divalproex sodium), 226*t*
Dependency, 240, 250, 328
Depo-Medrol, 104*t*. *See also*
        Methylprednisolone
Depo-Provera, 77*t*. *See also*
        Medroxyprogesterone
Depot naltrexone *(Vivitrol)*, 325
De-prescribing medications, 17
Depression, 78–83
    agitation treatment guidelines, 76*t*
    apathy treatment, 76
    in bipolar disorder, 82
    in COPD, 292
    in dementia, 73
    differential diagnosis, 281
    at end of life, 262
    and falls, 113*t*, 118*t*
    management of, 83*t*, 222*t*
    with pain, 239
    and Parkinson disease, 82
    PHQ-2 Quick Depression Assessment, 339
    PHQ-9 Quick Depression Assessment,
        338–339
    postmenopausal, 333
    psychotic, 79, 82
    screening for, 266, 270*t*, 347*t*
    seasonal, 79
    subsyndromal, 78
    and tinnitus, 137
Dermabrasion, 84
DermaCol, 314
DermaCol AG, 314
DermaDress, 314
DermaFilm, 312. *See also* Hydrocolloids
DermaFoam, 312. *See also* Foam island
        dressings

Derma-Gel, 313
DermaGinate, 313. *See also* Calcium alginate dressings
Dermagraft, 311, 315
Dermagran, 313
DermaSyn/Ag, 313–314
Dermatitis, seborrheic, 88, 89*t*, 90*t*
Dermatologic conditions, 84–91, 349
Dermatomes, 3*f*
Dermatop (prednicarbate), 91*t*
Dermatophytoses, 90*t*
Dermatosis papulosa nigra, 250*t*
DermaView, 312
DES (drug-eluting stents), 267
Desensitization, 37
Desipramine *(Norpramin)*
  anticholinergic property, 67*t*
  for depression, 81*t*
  for pain relief, 251*t*
  for painful neuropathy, 228
Desirudin *(Iprivask),* 27*t*, 33*t*
Desloratadine *(Clarinex),* 288*t*
Desmopressin, 152, 183
Desonide *(DesOwen, Tridesilon),* 90*t*
DesOwen (desonide), 90*t*
Desoximetasone *(Topicort),* 91*t*
Desvenlafaxine *(Pristiq),* 81*t*, 334
Desyrel, 76*t*, 317*t*. *See also* Trazodone
Detrol, 151*t. See also* Tolterodine
Detrol LA (tolterodine), 151*t*
Detrusor hyperactivity with impaired contractility (DHIC), 146*t*, 147, 149
Detrusor muscle-relaxing drugs, 149
Detrusor underactivity, 146*t*
Dexamethasone *(Decadron, Dexone, Hexadrol)*
  for adrenal insufficiency, 104, 104*t*
  for anorexia, cachexia, dehydration, 262
  for inflammation due to malignant obstruction, 261
  for nausea, vomiting, 262
Dexedrine (dextroamphetamine), 260
Dexilant (dexlansoprazole), 122*t*
Dexlansoprazole *(Dexilant),* 122*t*
Dexone, 104*t. See also* Dexamethasone
Dextroamphetamine *(Dexedrine),* 260

Dextromethorphan *(Robitussin DM),* 286*t*
Dextrose solution, 185, 186, 193
DH Pressure Relief Walker, 311
DHIC (detrusor hyperactivity with impaired contractility), 146*t*, 147, 149
Diaβeta (glyburide), 98*t*
Diabetes control, 42, 180
Diabetes insipidus, 182
Diabetes mellitus (DM), 94–103
  antihypertensive therapy and, 56*t*
  drug-induced, 283*t*
  eye examinations, 105
  goals of treatment, 96*t*
  insulin preparations for, 101*t*–102*t*
  lactose-free products for, 191*t*
  non-insulin agents for, 97*t*–101*t*
  and PAD, 62
  post MI, 42
  resources for, 349
  screening for, 270*t*
Diabetic peripheral neuropathy, 228, 252*t*
Diabetic retinopathy, 106
Diabetic ulcers, 306*t*–307*t*, 310–311
Diabetisource AC, 191*t*
Dialysis, 178, 181, 186
Diarrhea, 129
  antibiotic-associated, 130–132
  antidiarrheals, 129*t*–130*t*
  at end of life, 261
  with enteral feedings, 192
  and hyponatremia, 183
Diastolic dysfunction, 42
Diathermy, 202
Diazepam, 38
Diclofenac *(Cataflam, Pennsaid, Voltaren, Voltaren-XR, Zipsor, Zorvolex),* 206*t*, 238, 240*t*
Diclofenac, enteric coated *(Arthrotec),* 206*t*
Diclofenac gel *(Voltaren Gel, Solaraze)*
  for arthritis, 203, 206*t*
  for pain, 238, 240*t*
Diclofenac patch *(Flector)*
  for arthritis, 203, 206*t*
  for pain, 238, 240*t*
Dicloxacillin *(Dycill, Pathocil),* 34, 169*t*
Dicyclomine *(Bentyl),* 67*t*, 125

Dietary Approaches to Stop Hypertension (DASH), 42
Dietary modification
  for AMD, 106
  for brain health, 73
  cholesterol-lowering diet, 47
  for CKD, 180
  for constipation, 126
  counseling for, 270*t*
  for DM, 95, 96
  for dyslipidemia, 47
  for dysphagia, 120
  for fecal incontinence, 155
  for GERD, 121
  gluten-free diet, 125
  for hemorrhoids, 132
  high-fiber diet, 95, 96, 132
  high-potassium diet, 219
  for HTN, 51
  for hyperkalemia, 185
  for hyperuricemia, 212
  for IBS, 125
  lactose-free diet, 125
  low-potassium diet, 180, 185
  low-protein diet, 180
  low-sodium diet, 219
  Mediterranean diet, 42, 73, 96, 188
  for orthostatic (postural) hypotension, 64
  for Parkinson disease, 221
  post MI, 41
  for skin failure, 263
  for sleep apnea, 319
  for stroke prevention, 219
  weight loss diets, 189
Dietary supplements, 21
Dietitians, 6*t*
Dificid (fidaxomicin), 131*t*, 171*t*
Diflorasone diacetate *(Florone, Maxiflor, Psorcon)*, 91*t*
Diflucan, 87, 174*t. See also* Fluconazole
Diflunisal *(Dolobid)*, 206*t*
Digital rectal examination (DRE), 277, 279
Digital stimulation, 154
Digiti flexus (hammertoe), 201
Digoxin *(Lanoxin, Lanoxicaps)*
  for AF, 58

drug interactions, 45
  herbal medicine interactions, 24
  for HF, 45
  and sexual dysfunction, 305
Dihydropyridines, 55*t*
Dilacor XR (diltiazem), 54*t*
Dilantin, 226*t. See also* Phenytoin
Dilation and curettage (D&C), 332
Dilatrate SR (isosorbide dinitrate SR), 41*t*
Dilaudid, 244*t. See also* Hydromorphone
Diltiazem
  for AF, 58
  digoxin interactions, 45
  enteral nutrition interactions, 192
  for nocturnal leg cramps, 320
Diltiazem SR *(Cardizem CD, Cardizem SR, Dilacor XR, Tiazac)*, 54*t*
Dimenhydrinate, 67*t*
Diovan, 56*t. See also* Valsartan
Diphenhydramine, 67*t*, 73
Diphenhydrinate *(Dramamine)*, 129*t*
Diphenoxylate with atropine *(Lomotil)*, 130*t*
Dipivefrin, 107*t*
Diprolene, 91*t. See also* Betamethasone dipropionate
Diprolene AF, 91*t. See also* Betamethasone dipropionate
Diprosone, 91*t. See also* Betamethasone dipropionate
Dipyridamole, 24, 39, 216
Dipyridamole with ASA *(Aggrenox)*, 26*t*, 31*t*, 219
Direct thrombin inhibitors
  for antithrombotic therapy, 26*t*
  prescribing information, 33*t*
  for VTE, 27*t*, 30*t*
Discharge planning, 8
Discharge summary, 8
Discontinuing medications, 17
Disease-modifying antirheumatoid drugs (DMARDs), 209, 210, 210*t*
Disk degeneration, chronic, 196
Disk herniation, acute, 196
Dispyramide, 21*t*
Distraction, 238
Ditropan, 150*t. See also* Oxybutynin

Ditropan XL, 150*t. See also* Oxybutynin
Diuretics
  and BPH, 275
  for CKD, 180
  and coexisting conditions, 56*t,* 57*t*
  for DM type 2, 101
  drug interactions, 21*t,* 231*t*
  for dyspnea, 261
  fall risks, 114*t*
  food interactions, 20
  for HF, 44, 45
  for HTN, 51, 52*t*
  for hyperkalemia, 185, 186
  for hypertensive emergencies and
    urgencies, 51
  and hyponatremia, 183
  for nocturnal polyuria, 152
  and orthostatic hypotension, 216
  for PAH, 57
  preoperative care, 268
  for SIADH, 184
  and sleep problems, 316
  and tinnitus, 136
  and UI, 148, 150*t*
  for venous insufficiency, 46
  for vertigo, 217*t*
Diuril (chlorothiazide), 52*t*
Divalproex *(Depakote, Epival),* 76*t,* 77*t*
Dix-Hallpike test, 119
Dizziness, 216, 216*t*–217*t*
DM. *See* Diabetes mellitus
DMARDs (disease-modifying antirheumatoid
    drugs), 209, 210*t*
DNR (do-not-resuscitate) Orders, 258
Dobutamine stress test, 39
Docusate *(Colace),* 127*t,* 134, 154
Dofetilide, 21*t*
Dolasetron *(Anzemet),* 128*t*
Dolobid (diflunisal), 206*t*
Domperidone, 122*t*
Donepezil *(Aricept),* 21*t,* 74, 75*t*
Do-not-resuscitate (DNR) Orders, 258
Dopamine, 222*t*
Dopamine agonists, 222*t,* 223*t,* 321
Dopamine antagonists, 128*t,* 321
Dopamine reuptake inhibitors, 223*t*

Doppler ultrasound, 42, 62*t,* 218
Doribax (doripenem), 169*t*
Doripenem *(Doribax),* 169*t*
Dorzolamide, 108*t*
Dorzolamide/timolol, 108*t*
Dostinex (cabergoline), 321
Doxazosin *(Cardura),* 53*t,* 275
Doxepin *(Silenor, Sinequan, Zonalon)*
  anticholinergic property, 67*t*
  avoid use, 81
  for hives, 89
  for sleep disorders, 317*t*
Doxycycline *(Vibramycin)*
  for infectious diseases, 172*t*
  for MRSA, 85, 163
  for pneumonia, 159*t*
  for rosacea, 88
DPIs (dry powder inhalers), 295
DPP-4 enzyme inhibitors, 97, 98*t*
Dramamine (diphenhydrinate), 129*t*
DRE (digital rectal examination), 277
Dressings
  for arterial ulcers, 310
  for diabetic foot ulcers, 311
  for pressure ulcers, 312–314
  for skin failure, 263
  for skin ulcers, 308
  for venous ulcers, 315
Dronabinol *(Marinol),* 190, 252*t,* 329*t*
Dronederone, 21*t*
Drop arm test, 194
Drop attacks, 217*t*
Droxidopa *(Northera),* 64
Drug abuse, 327–329
  commonly abused prescription drugs, 327
  preoperative screening for, 266
  prevention of opioid misuse and
    withdrawal, 249–250
  scope of the problem, 323
Drug interactions
  alcohol interactions, 324
  drug-drug interactions, 20, 20*t*–21*t*
  drug-food or -nutrient interactions, 19–20
  drug-induced changes in cardiac
    conduction, 20
  QT_c interval interactions, 21*t*

Drug prescribing. *See* Pharmacotherapy
Drug-eluting stents (DES), 267
Dry AMD (age-related macular degeneration), 106
Dry eye syndrome, 111
Dry mouth, 259, 262
Dry powder inhalers (DPIs), 295
DSI (dual sensory impairment), 109
DSM-5, 281, 323
Dual antiplatelet therapy, 267
Dual sensory impairment (DSI), 109
Duavee (estrogen with bazedoxifene), 232*t,* 333
DU-DERM Alginate, 313. *See also* Calcium alginate dressings
DuDress, 314
Duetact (pioglitazone and glimepiride), 100*t*
Duexis (ibuprofen and famotidine), 207*t*
Duke boot, 315
Dulaglutide *(Trulicity),* 100*t*
Dulcolax, 127*t. See also* Bisacodyl
Dulera (formoterol-mometasone), 298*t*
Duloxetine *(Cymbalta)*
　for anxiety disorders, 38
　avoid use, 19*t*
　for depression, 79, 81*t*
　drug interactions, 34, 331*t*
　for osteoarthritis, 205
　for pain relief, 251*t*
　for painful neuropathy, 228
DuoDERM, 312. *See also* Hydrocolloids
DuoDERM CGF, 312
DuoDERM Hydroactive Gel, 313
DuoDERM Signal, 312
Duoneb (albuterol-ipratropium), 298*t*
Durable power of attorney for health care, 10, 258
Duragesic, 247*t. See also* Fentanyl, transdermal
Duramorph, 243*t. See also* Morphine
Duricef (cefadroxil), 170*t*
Dutasteride *(Avodart),* 276
DVT. *See* Deep-vein thrombosis
Dycill, 169*t. See also* Dicloxacillin
DynaCirc CR (isradipine SR), 55*t*

Dynapress wrap, 315. *See also* Compression wraps
Dyrenium, 52*t. See also* Triamterene
Dysgeusia, 19, 20
Dyskinesia, 222*t*
Dyslipidemia, 47–48
　antihypertensive therapy and, 56*t*
　in DM, 101
　post MI, 42
　screening for, 270*t*
　in stroke prevention, 219
　treatment of, 48*t*–49*t*
Dyspareunia, 303, 304, 333
Dysphagia, 120–121
　at end of life, 259
　gastrostumy tubes for, 192
　types/presentation/patient complaints, 120*t*
Dyspnea, 286–287
　with COPD, 290, 292*t*
　diagnosis of, 286*t*–287*t*
　at end of life, 260–261
　exertional, 299
　with HF, 43
　Modified Medical Research Council Dyspnea Scale (MMRC), 290
Dyssynergia, 146

E

E faecium, vancomycin-resistant, 173*t*
Ear wax removal, 134
EAS (electric acoustic stimulation), 134*t,* 135
EBRT (external beam radiation therapy), 278, 279
ECG (electrocardiography)
　absolute indications for hospitalization, 185
　in AS, 60
　in PAH, 57
　preoperative, 264
Echinacea, 22
Echinocandins, 175*t*
Echocardiography
　in acute stroke, 218
　in AF, 60
　in AS, 60

Echocardiography *continued*
  in CAD, 39
  in HF, 42
Echothiophate, 107*t*
E-cigarettes, 326
EC-Naprosyn (naproxen), 207*t*
Econazole nitrate *(Spectazole)*, 90*t*
ECT (electroconvulsive therapy), 79, 81–82
Edarbi (azilsartan), 56*t*
Edema
  angioedema, 89
  leg, 45–47
  lymphedema, 47
  macular, 106
  myxedema coma, 92
  stasis, 152
Edluar, 318*t*. *See also* Zolpidem
Edoxaban *(Savaysa)*
  for ACS, 41
  for AF, 59*t*, 60*t*
  for anticoagulation, 33*t*, 35*t*, 60*t*
  avoid use, 19*t*
  reduce dosage, 19*t*
Effexor, 81*t*, 251*t*. *See also* Venlafaxine
Effexor XR, 81*t*, 251*t*. *See also* Venlafaxine
Effient, 31*t*. *See also* Prasugrel
Efinaconazole *(Jubila)*, 87
Efudex, 84. *See also* 5-Fluorouracil
EIA (enzyme immunoassay), 165*t*
Elasto-Gel, 313
Elavil, 81. *See also* Amitriptyline
Eldepryl (selegiline), 223*t*
Electric acoustic stimulation (EAS), 134*t*, 135
Electrical stimulation, 120, 149, 309
Electrocardiography (ECG)
  absolute indications for hospitalization,
    185
  in AS, 60
  in PAH, 57
  preoperative, 264
Electroconvulsive therapy (ECT), 79, 81–82
Electrodessication, 85
Electrolyte abnormalities, 20
Electron-beam computed tomography, 271
Electrosurgery, 84
Elestat (epinastine), 111*t*

Elidel (pimeclorimus), 87
Elimite (permethrin), 88
Eliquis, 32*t*. *See also* Apixaban
Elocon, 91*t*. *See also* Mometasone furoate
Eltroxin, 92. *See also* Levothyroxine
Emadine (emedastine), 111*t*
Embeda (ER morphine/naltrexone
    hydrochloride), 245*t*, 250, 328
Embolism. *See* Pulmonary embolism (PE)
Emedastine *(Emadine)*, 111*t*
Emotional status assessment, 4*t*
Empagliflozin *(Jardiance)*, 99*t*
Emtricitabine, 168
Enablex, 151*t*. *See also* Darifenacin
Enalapril *(Vasotec)*, 44*t*, 51, 55*t*
Enbrel, 210. *See also* Etanercept
Endocarditis prophylaxis, 268, 272–273, 272*t*
Endocrine disorders, 92–104
End-of-life care, 253–263
  planning, 65
  resources for, 348
  in severe COPD, 293
Endoform Dermal Template, 314
Endothelial receptor antagonists, 58
Endovascular repair, 61, 62*t*
Endurance training, 274
Enemas
  for constipation, 126, 127*t*, 261
  for fecal incontinence, 154, 155
  for hyperkalemia, 185, 186
  for rectal evacuation, 154
Enemeez, 154
Energy requirements, 189
Energy supplements, 190
Enoxaparin *(Lovenox)*
  for anticoagulation, 32*t*
  for antithrombotic therapy, 26*t*
  for DVT prophylaxis, 199
  reduce dosage, 19*t*
  for VTE, 27*t*, 30*t*
Ensure, 191*t*
Ensure Clear, 191*t*
Ensure Plus, 191*t*
Entacapone *(Comtan)*, 223*t*, 224*t*
Enteral nutrition
  drug interactions, 192

for ICU patients, 190
lactose-free products, 191*t*
for malnutrition, 190
for stress-ulcer prevention, 124
Entereg (alvimopan), 126*t*
Enterobacter, 161
Enterococci, 161
Enterococcus faecium, vancomycin-
resistant, 173*t*
Environmental assessment, 116
Environmental hazards assessment, 5*t*
Environmental modification
for dry eye syndrome, 111
in end-of-life care, 260
for insomnia, 317
for preventing falls, 117*t*
for sleep disorders, 322
for UI, 148
for visual impairment, 109
Enzymatic (chemonucleolysis) injections,
203
Enzyme immunoassay (EIA), 165*t*
Epigard, 314
Epinastine *(Elestat),* 111*t*
Epinephrine *(EpiPen),* 89, 299*t*
EpiPen, 89. *See also* Epinephrine
Episcleritis, 109*t*
Epitol, 225*t. See also* Carbamazepine
Epival, 76*t. See also* Divalproex
Eplerenone *(Inspra),* 40, 45, 52*t*
Epley maneuver, 217*t*
Epoetin alfa *(Epogen, Procrit),* 141*t*
Epogen (epoetin alfa), 141*t*
Epoprostenol *(Flolan),* 57
e-Prescribing, 17
Eprosartan *(Teveten),* 56*t*
EPS (extrapyramidal symptoms), drug-
induced, 69, 283*t*
Eptifibatide *(Integrilin),* 26*t,* 34*t,* 267
Epworth Sleepiness Scale, 319
Equetro, 225*t. See also* Carbamazepine
Equinus, 200
Eraxis (anidulafungin), 175*t*
Erectile dysfunction, 301–303, 301*t*–302*t*
Ergocalciferol (vitamin D₂), 180, 229
Erivedge (vismodegib), 85

Ertaczo (sertraconazole), 90*t*
Ertapenem *(Invanz),* 159*t,* 169*t*
Erysipelas, 85
Erythrocyte sedimentation rate (ESR), 2
Erythromycin, 110*t*
for cellulitis, 85
for conjunctivitis, 110
drug interactions, 34, 45
for erysipelas, 85
for folliculitis, 85
for high gastric residual volume problems,
193
for impetigo, 85
for pneumonia, 159*t*
prescribing information, 171*t*
QT_c interval interactions, 21*t*
for rosacea, 87, 88
and tinnitus, 136
Erythropoiesis-stimulating agents (ESAs),
141, 141*t,* 180
Erythropoietin
for anemia, 139, 141
for hypotension secondary to anemia, 65
for multiple myeloma, 145
Erythropoietin-darbopoetin, 180
ESAs (erythropoiesis-stimulating agents),
141, 141*t,* 180
Escherichia coli, 161
Escitalopram *(Lexapro)*
for anxiety disorders, 38
for depression, 79*t*
QT_c interval interactions, 21*t*
SSRI-induced sexual dysfunction, 305
Eskalith, 83*t. See also* Lithium
Eskalith CR, 83*t. See also* Lithium
Esmolol, 45
Esomeprazole magnesium *(Nexium),* 122*t,*
123*t*
Esomeprazole strontium, 122*t*
Esophageal candidiasis, 175*t*
Esophageal dysphagia, 120, 120*t*
Esophageal manometry, 120
Esophagitis, reflux, 285*t*
ESR (erythrocyte sedimentation rate), 2
Essential thrombocytosis, 144
Essential tremor, 56*t,* 216*t*

Estazolam *(ProSom),* 318t
Esteem, 135
Estrace, 305t. *See also* Estradiol
Estradiol *(Estrace),* 333
Estradiol vaginal ring *(Estring),* 305t
Estradiol vaginal tablets *(Vagifem),* 305t
Estring (estradiol vaginal ring), 305t
Estriol, 333
Estrogen
   with bisphosphonate or calcitonin, 232
   with progesterone, 332
   with progestin, 334
   and UI, 150t
Estrogen therapy
   for agitation, 77t
   bone outcomes, 233t
   for dyspareunia, 304
   effects on other outcomes, level of
      evidence, and risks of, 233t
   for menopausal symptoms, 333, 334
   for osteoporosis, 232, 232t
   in postmenopausal bleeding, 332
   risks, 333
   for sexual aggression, impulse-control
      symptoms in men, 77t
   topical, 304, 305t
   transdermal, 334
   for UI, 150
   for UTI prophylaxis, 162
   for vaginal prolapse, 333
Estrogen with bazedoxifene *(Duavee),* 232t,
   333
Eszopiclone *(Lunesta),* 38, 317, 318t
Etanercept *(Enbrel),* 209, 210, 214
Ethnic groups, 13
Etodolac *(Lodine),* 206t
Etodolac ER *(Lodine XL),* 206t
Etretinate, 87
Eucerin, 89
Euflexxa, 203. *See also* Hyaluronic acid
Eulexin (flutamide), 280t
Eurax (crotamiton), 88
Euthanasia, 259
Euthyroid sick syndrome, 93
Euvolemic hyponatremia, 184
Evista, 232t. *See also* Raloxifene

Evolocumab *(Repatha),* 49t
Exalgo (ER hydromorphone), 245t
Excellagen, 314
Exelderm (sulconazole), 90t
Exelon (rivastigmine), 75t
Exemestane *(Aromasin),* 331t
Exenatide *(Byetta),* 100t
Exenatide ER *(Bydureon),* 100t
Exercise(s)
   for back pain, 196
   for brain health, 73
   for chronic angina, 42
   for COPD, 293
   for DM, 96
   for dyspnea, 287
   for fecal incontinence, 155
   for HF, 43t
   for hip pain, 198
   for HTN, 51
   for low back pain syndrome, 196
   for lumbar spinal stenosis, 197
   oropharyngeal, 320
   for osteoarthritis, 198, 202
   for PAD, 62
   for pain, 238, 239t
   for Parkinson disease, 221
   pelvic muscle (Kegel), 149, 149f, 333
   for plantar fasciitis, 201
   prescription, 274
   for preventing DM, 95
   for preventing falls, 73, 116, 117t
   for preventing stroke, 219
   for prevention, 270t
   for problem behaviors, 74
   rectal sphincter, 155
   for rheumatoid arthritis, 209
   for shoulder pain, 195
   for sleep apnea, 320
   for sleep disorders, 322
   for sleep hygiene, 316
   for unstable lumbar spine, 197
   for vaginal prolapse, 333
   for weight loss, 189
Exercise treadmill test, 39, 62t
Exparel (bupivacaine), 237–238
Expectorants, 286t

Exploitation, 12t
External beam radiation therapy (EBRT), 278, 279
External rotation lag test, 194
External rotation resistance test, 194
Extra Thin DuoDERM, 312
Extracellular matrix, 311
Extrapyramidal symptoms (EPS), drug-induced, 69, 283t
Exuderm, 312. *See also* Hydrocolloids
Exuderm LP, 312
Eye disorders, 105–112
Eye examinations, 105
Eye symptoms, 288t
Eylea (aflibercept), 106
Ezetimibe *(Zetia),* 48t
Ezetimibe with simvastatin *(Vytorin),* 49t

F

Facial weakness, 227t
Factive, 172t. *See also* Gemifloxacin
Factor Xa inhibitors
    for antithrombotic therapy, 26t
    prescribing information, 32t–33t
    for VTE, 27t, 30t
Failed back syndrome, 240
Failure to thrive, 255t
Falls, 113–119
    assessment and prevention, 4, 5t, 115f
    distinguishing early Parkinson disease from other parkinsonian syndromes, 220t–221t
    general prevention, 73
    in osteoporosis, 230
    in pain management, 243t
    recommendations, 271t
    risk factors and interventions, 117t–118t
    risk factors and medications, 113t–114t
Famciclovir *(Famvir),* 164t
Familial hypercholesterolemia, homozygous, 49t
Family Caregiver Alliance, 77
Family education, 96
Family presence, 74
Famotidine *(Pepcid),* 19t, 122t, 305
Famotidine with ibuprofen *(Duexis),* 207t

Famvir (famciclovir), 164t
Fanapta (iloperidone), 279t, 282t
Far vision testing, 105
Fareston (toremifene), 331t
Farxiga (dapagliflozin), 99t
Faslodex (fulvestrant), 331t
FAST (Functional Assessment Staging) scale, 70, 343
Fasting glucose, impaired, 95
Fasting plasma glucose (FPG), 96t
Fatigue, 260
Fatty acid. *See* Omega-3 fatty acids; Polyunsaturated fatty acids
FDG-PET scans, 71
Febuxostat *(Uloric),* 212t, 213
Fecal impaction, 147
Fecal incontinence (FI), 153–156
Fecal occult blood test (FOBT), 270t
Fecal softeners, 127t
Fecal transplant, 132
Feeding, 19, 192–193, 262
FEES (fiberoptic endoscopic evaluations of swallowing), 120
Feldene (piroxicam), 207t
Felodipine *(Plendil),* 55t
Female sexual dysfunction, 303–305
Female sexual interest/arousal disorder (FSIAD), 303, 304
Femara (letrozole), 331t
FENa (fractional excretion of sodium), 177, 181
Fenofibrate *(Tricor, Lofibra, Antara),* 48t, 213
Fenofibrate delayed-release *(Trilipix),* 48t
Fenoprofen *(Nalfon),* 206t
Fentanyl *(Abstral, Actiq, Fentora, Lazanda, Onsolis, Subsys),* 248t, 261
Fentanyl, transdermal *(Duragesic),* 243t, 247t
Fentanyl HCl iontophoric transdermal system (ITS), 248t
Fentora, 248t. *See also* Fentanyl
Feraheme (ferumoxytol), 140t
Ferric carboxymaltose *(Injectafer),* 140t
Ferrlecit (sodium ferric gluconate complex), 140t
Ferumoxytol *(Feraheme),* 140t
Fesoterodine *(TOVIAZ),* 67t, 151t

Fetzima (levomilnacipran), 80*t*
FEUrea (fractional excretion of urea), 177
Feverfew, 22
Fexofenadine *(Allegra, Allegra-D, Allegra-D 24 Hour)*, 288*t*
FI (fecal incontinence), 153–156
Fiber supplements, 125
FiberCon, 126*t. See also* Polycarbophil
Fiberoptic endoscopic evaluations of swallowing (FEES), 120
Fibersource HN, 191*t*
Fibracol, 314
Fibrates, 48*t*, 305
Fibric acid derivatives, 48*t*
Fibrillation, atrial. *See* Atrial fibrillation (AF)
Fibrillation, ventricular (VF), 65
Fibromyalgia, 228, 241*t*, 251*t*
Fidaxomicin *(Dificid),* 131*t*, 171*t*
Finacea (azelaic acid), 87
Financial status assessment, 5*t*
Finasteride *(Proscar),* 25, 276, 280
Fine-needle aspiration, 94
Finevin (azelaic acid), 87
Firmagon (degarelix), 280*t*
Fish oil, 22
5-Fluorouracil *(Carac, Efudex, Fluoroplex),* 84, 85
Flagyl, 173*t. See also* Metronidazole
Flavoxate, 67*t*
Flaxseed, 23
Flaxseed oil, 23
Flector, 206*t. See also* Diclofenac patch
Fleet (sodium phosphate/biphosphate emollient enema), 127*t*
Flexibility, 221, 274
FlexiGel, 313
FLEXIGEL, 313
Flexzan, 312. *See also* Foam island dressings
Flibanserin *(Addyi),* 304
Flolan (epoprostenol), 57
Flomax (tamsulosin), 275–276
Florbetapin F18 *(Amyvid),* 71
Florinef, 104*t. See also* Fludrocortisone
Florone, 91*t. See also* Diflorasone diacetate
Flu vaccine
    ACIP guidelines, 164

    for DM, 102
    procedure codes, 346*t*
    warfarin interactions, 34
Fluconazole *(Diflucan)*
    for candidiasis, 260
    for infectious diseases, 174*t*
    for onychomycosis, 87
    QT_c interval interactions, 21*t*
    warfarin interactions, 34
Flucytosine *(Ancobon),* 175*t*
Fludrocortisone *(Florinef)*
    for adrenal insufficiency, 103, 104*t*
    for hyperkalemia, 186
    for orthostatic (postural) hypotension, 64
Fluid challenge, 178, 183
Fluid consistencies, 121
Fluid replacement, 126, 178, 182–183
Fluid requirements, 189
Fluid restriction, 152, 183, 184
Flumadine (rimantadine), 165*t*
Flunisolide, 289*t*, 297*t*
Fluocinolone acetonide *(Synalar),* 91*t*
Fluocinonide *(Lidex),* 91*t*
Fluoride/chlorhexidine, 158
Fluoroplex, 84. *See also* 5-Fluorouracil
Fluoroquinolones. *See also* Quinolones
    for COPD exacerbation, 292*t*
    for cystitis or UTI, 161
    for pneumonia, 159*t*, 160
    for prostatitis, 280
    for urosepsis, 161
5-Fluorouracil *(Carac, Efudex, Fluoroplex),* 84, 85
Fluoxetine *(Prozac)*
    for depression, 80*t*
    drug interactions, 286*t*, 331*t*
    enteral nutrition interactions, 192
Fluphenazine, 67*t*, 283*t*
Flurandrenolide *(Cordran),* 91*t*
Flurazepam, 38
Flurbiprofen *(Ansaid),* 206*t*
Flutamide *(Eulexin),* 280*t*
Fluticasone, 297*t*
Fluticasone furoate *(Arnuity Ellipta, Veramyst),* 289*t*, 297*t*

Fluticasone propionate *(Cutivate)*, 91*t*, 289*t*, 297*t*
Fluticasone-salmeterol *(Advair Diskus)*, 298*t*
Fluticasone-vilanterol *(Breo Ellipta)*, 299*t*
Fluvastatin *(Lescol, Lescol XL)*, 48*t*
Fluvoxamine *(Luvox)*, 80*t*
Foam island dressings *(Allevyn, Lyofoam, COPA, ComfortFoam, DermaFoam, Flexzan, Mepilex, Mitraflex, 3M Tegaderm Foam, Polyderm, PolyMem, Tielle, VigiFoam)*, 312, 315
Foam with silver dressings *(Allevyn Ag Foam, Aquacel Ag Foam, Bordered Foam/Ag, HydraFoam/Ag, PolyMem Silver, Optifoam AG, Contreet Foam)*, 312
FOBT (fecal occult blood test), 270*t*
Folate, 142, 214
Folate deficiency, 138*f*, 142
Foley catheters, 259
Folic acid, 138*f*
Follicular neoplasm, 93
Folliculitis, 85
Fondaparinux *(Arixtra)*
    for anticoagulation, 33*t*
    for antithrombotic therapy, 26*t*
    avoid use, 19*t*
    for DVT/PE prophylaxis, 218
    for VTE, 27*t*, 30*t*
Food consistencies, 121
Food-drug interactions, 19–20
Foot disorders, 200–201
Foot examination, 103
Foot pain, 201
Foot ulcers, diabetic (neuropathic), 310–311
Footwear, 118*t*, 201
Foradil (formoterol), 296*t*
Forced vital capacity (FVC), 299
Formoterol *(Foradil)*, 296*t*
Formoterol-budesonide *(Symbicort)*, 298*t*
Formoterol-mometasone *(Dulera)*, 298*t*
Formulas, 1–2, 1*t*
Fortaz, 171*t*. *See also* Ceftazidime
Forteo, 232*t*. *See also* Teriparatide
Fortesta (testosterone), 303*t*
Fosamax, 231*t*. *See also* Alendronate

Fosfomycin *(Monurol)*, 173*t*
Fosinopril *(Monopril)*, 44*t*, 55*t*
Fosrenol (lanthanum carbonate), 180
4AT, 66
FPG (fasting plasma glucose), 96*t*
Fractional excretion of sodium (FENa), 177, 181
Fractional excretion of urea (FEUrea), 177
Fracture Risk Assessment Tool (FRAX), 229, 230
Fractures
    fragility, 230
    hip, 198–199
    medications for osteoporosis and, 233*t*
    osteoporotic, 229
    prevention of, 231
    risk assessment, 229, 230
    spine, 233*t*
    vertebral, 197, 232*t*
Fragility fractures, 230
Fragmin, 32*t*. *See also* Dalteparin
Frailty
    hospice referral, 254
    multiple myeloma treatment in, 145
    pain management in, 240*t*
    preoperative screening, 266
    tips for treating hearing loss with, 136
Frailty syndrome, 266
FRAX (Fracture Risk Assessment Tool), 229, 230
Free fructose, 96
Freeda Calcium Citrate Fine Granular (calcium citrate), 230
Freeda Mini Cal-citrate (calcium citrate), 230
Frontotemporal dementia, 70, 74, 76
Frozen shoulder, 194*t*, 195
Fructose, free, 96
FSIAD (female sexual interest/arousal disorder), 303, 304
Fulvestrant *(Faslodex)*, 331*t*
Fulvicin P/G (griseofulvin), 175*t*
Functional assessment
    ADLs, 336
    Instrumental ADLs (IADLs), 337
    in pain, 237
    preoperative, 266
    screening assessment, 4*t*

Functional Assessment Staging (FAST) scale, 70, 343
Functional gait assessment, 115
Functional Reach test, 115
Fungal infections, 86–87, 158, 161
Fungi-Nail (undecylenic acid), 87, 90*t*
Fungizone (amphotericin B), 174*t*
Furosemide *(Lasix)*
  for acute kidney injury, 178
  for HTN, 51, 52*t*
  for hyperkalemia, 186
  for SIADH, 184
  and tinnitus, 136
FVC (forced vital capacity), 299

G
GABA-ergics, 150*t*
Gabapentin *(Neurontin)*
  for menopausal symptoms, 334
  for nocturnal leg cramps, 320
  for pain, 250*t*
  for painful neuropathy, 228
  reduce dosage, 19*t*
  for restless legs syndrome, 321
  for seizures, 225*t*
  for tremor, 216*t*
  and UI, 150*t*
Gabapentin enacarbil *(Horizant),* 321
Gabitril Filmtabs (tiagabine), 226*t*
GAD (generalized anxiety disorder), 36, 37, 38
GAD-7 (Generalized Anxiety Disorder 7-item scale), 36
Gait assessment, 5*t,* 115
Gait impairment, 113*t,* 117*t,* 222*t*
Gait training, 117*t*
Galactorrhea, 305
Galantamine *(Razadyne),* 75*t*
Galantamine ER *(Razadyne ER),* 75*t*
GammaGraft, 315. *See also* Skin substitutes
Garamycin, 171*t. See also* Gentamicin
Gardnerella vaginalis, 161
Garlic, 23
Gastric banding, 189
Gastric bypass, 189
Gastroesophageal reflux disease (GERD), 121–123, 122*t*

Gastrointestinal (GI) diseases, 120–132, 120*t*
Gastrostomy, percutaneous venting, 261
Gastrostomy tube feeding, 192–193
Gatifloxacin *(Tequin),* 110*t*
Gauze packing *(Curity, Johnson & Johnson, Kendall Fluff Kerlix),* 307, 309, 314
Gauze-based negative-pressure wound therapy, 307
Gelnique, 150*t. See also* Oxybutynin
Gemfibrozil *(Lopid),* 48*t*
Gemifloxacin *(Factive),* 159*t,* 172*t,* 292*t*
General Practitioner Assessment of Cognition (GPCOG), 70
Generalized anxiety disorder (GAD), 36, 37, 38
Generalized Anxiety Disorder 7-item scale (GAD-7), 36
Gentamicin *(Garamycin),* 160, 171*t,* 308*t*
Gentell, 313. *See also* Calcium alginate dressings
Gentell Comfortell, 314
Gentell Hydrogel AG, 313
Geodon, 282*t. See also* Ziprasidone
GERD (gastroesophageal reflux disease), 121–123, 122*t*
Get-up and Go Test, 114, 115
GI (gastrointestinal) diseases, 120–132, 120*t*
Giant cell (temporal) arteritis, 213–215
Ginger, 23
Ginkgo biloba, 23, 75
Ginseng, 23
Glaucoma, 106–107
  asthma with, 295
  medications for, 107*t*–108*t*
  screening for, 271*t*
  signs and symptoms of, 109*t*
Glaucoma surgery, 107
Glimepiride *(Amaryl),* 98*t*
Glimepiride with pioglitazone *(Duetact),* 100*t*
Glimepiride with rosiglitazone *(Avandaryl),* 100*t*
Glipizide *(Glucotrol, Glucotrol XL),* 97, 98*t*
Glipizide with metformin *(METAGLIP),* 99*t*
Global aphasia, 227*t*
Glomerular disease or vasculitis, 177*t*
Glomerular filtration rate, estimated (eGFR), 1

Glomerulitis, 177*t*
GLP-1 (glucagon-like peptide-1) receptor
     agonists, 97, 100*t*–101*t*
Glucagon, 101
Glucagon-like peptide-1 (GLP-1) receptor
     agonists, 97, 100*t*–101*t*
Glucerna 1.0 Cal, 191*t*
Glucerna shake, 191*t*
Glucocorticoids. *See also* Corticosteroids
   for acute interstitial nephritis, 178
   for adrenal insufficiency, 103
   for angioedema, 89
   for arthritis, 203, 209
   for asthma, 293, 295
   for COPD, 293
   for de Quervain tendinopathy, 199
   fall risks, 114*t*
   for hives, 89
   medications for osteoporosis and, 233*t*
   for Morton neuroma, 201
   for nonasthmatic eosinophilic bronchitis,
     285*t*
   for pseudogout, 213
   for rotator cuff tears, 195
   for sepsis and SIRS, 163
Glucophage, 97*t. See also* Metformin
Glucophage XR, 97*t. See also* Metformin
Glucosamine, 21–22, 203, 204*f*
Glucose, 95, 96*t,* 102
α-Glucosidase inhibitors, 98*t,* 101
Glucotrol, 98*t. See also* Glipizide
Glucotrol XL, 98*t. See also* Glipizide
Glucovance (glyburide and metformin), 99*t*
Gluten-free diet, 125
Glyburide *(Diaβeta, Micronase),* 98*t*
Glyburide, micronized *(Glynase),* 98*t*
Glyburide with metformin *(Glucovance),* 99*t*
Glycemic control
   for diabetic management, 96, 97
   for diabetic retinopathy, 106
   for PAD, 62
Glycerin suppository, 127*t,* 154
Glycoprotein IIb/IIIa inhibitors, 26*t,* 34*t,* 40
Glycopyrrolate, 261
Glycycline, 172*t*
Glynase (glyburide), 98*t*

Glyset (miglitol), 98*t*
GnRH agonists, 278, 279*t*
GnRH antagonists, 280*t*
Goal-oriented care, 9–10
Golden root, 24
Golimumab *(Simponi),* 210
Gonadotropin-releasing hormone (GnRH)
     agonists, 278, 279*t*
Gonadotropin-releasing hormone (GnRH)
     antagonists, 280*t*
Goserelin acetate implant *(Zoladex),* 279*t*
Gout, 56*t,* 211–213, 212*t*
GPCOG (General Practitioner Assessment of
     Cognition), 70
Granisetron *(Kytril),* 128*t*
Grifulvin V (griseofulvin), 175*t*
Griseofulvin *(Fulvicin P/G, Grifulvin V),* 175*t*
Group B streptococci, 158, 161
Growth factor therapy, 143, 309, 311
Guaifenesin *(Robitussin),* 261, 286*t,* 292
Guanfacine *(Tenex),* 53*t*
Guanylate cyclase stimulators, 58
Guided imagery, 239*t*
Gynecomastia, 305
Gyne-lotrimin, 16

H
H₁ receptor antagonists
   for allergic conjunctivitis, 110, 111*t*
   for allergic rhinitis, 288, 288*t*–289*t*
   for angioedema, 89
   for cholinergic reactions, 89
   for hives, 89
   for nausea and vomiting, 129*t*
H₂ receptor antagonists
   de-prescribing, 17
   for GERD, 121, 122*t*
   for *H pylori* infection, 123*t*
   for hives, 89
   iron interactions, 140*t*
   and sexual dysfunction, 305
   for stress-ulcer prevention, 124
HAs. *See* Hearing aids
Haemophilus influenzae, 158
Halcinonide *(Halog),* 91*t*
Haldol, 69, 261, 283*t. See also* Haloperidol

Halitosis, 260
Hallucinations, 73, 222*t*
Hallux valgus, 201
Halobetasol propionate *(Ultravate),* 91*t*
Halog (halcinonide), 91*t*
Haloperidol *(Haldol)*
    for delirium, 68, 69
    for nausea and vomiting, 128*t*, 261
    for psychosis, 283*t*
    QT$_c$ interval interactions, 21*t*
Hammertoe (digiti flexus), 201
Han Chinese, 212*t*
Hand pain, 199–200, 240*t*
Hand washing, 131
Harris-Benedict energy requirement
    equations, 189
HAS-BLED scoring, 58, 59*t*
Hazardous drinking, 324
HCTZ (hydrochlorothiazide), 52*t*
Head and neck cancer, 192
Head and neck examination, 119
Head trauma, 216
Headache, 241*t*, 252*t*
Health care proxy, 258
Health literacy assessment, 17, 340
Hearing aids (HAs)
    bone-anchored (BAHAs), 135
    for hearing impairment, 134, 136
    need for, 134*t*
    for tinnitus, 137
Hearing assessment, 4*t*
Hearing Assessment Tool, 135
Hearing assistive technologies, 135
Hearing impairment, 133–137
    classification of, 133*t*–134*t*
    dual sensory impairment (DSI), 109
    effects and rehabilitation, 134*t*
    fall risks, 113*t*
    preventive measures for delirium, 68*t*
    resources for, 349
    screening, 271*t*
Hearing technology, 134–135
Heart disease. *See also* Cardiovascular
        diseases; Heart failure (HF)
    determinants for hospice eligibility, 255*t*
    end-stage, 255*t*

ICD placement for, 65
    resources for, 349
    valvular, 26*t*, 31*t*, 35*t*, 60–61
Heart failure (HF), 42–45
    antihypertensive therapy and, 56*t*
    drugs useful in treating, 52*t*–56*t*
    and hyponatremia, 183
    ICD placement for, 65
    management of, 43*t*
    preventive measures for delirium, 68*t*
    staging, 43*t*
    target dosages of ACEIs, ARBs, and
        β-blockers, 44*t*
    warfarin anticoagulation for, 35*t*
Heat therapy, 202, 238
Heel inserts, 201
Heel pain, 201
Heel protectors, 310
Helicobacter pylori infection, 123–124, 123*t*
Helicoll, 314
Helidac, 123*t. See also* Tetracycline
HELP (Hospital Elder Life Program), 269
Hematologic disorders, 138–145
Hemiarthroplasty, 198, 199
Hemiparesis, 227*t*
Hemiplegia, 227*t*
Hemodialysis, 181
Hemolytic anemia, 142
Hemorrhoids, 132
Hendrich II Fall Risk Model, 114
Heparin. *See also* Anticoagulation
    for anticoagulation, 32*t*
    for antithrombotic therapy, 26*t*
    bridging therapy, 267, 268*t*
    LMWH, 26*t*, 27*t*, 30*t*, 32*t*, 218, 267, 268*t*
    and osteoporosis, 229
    UFH, 26*t*, 27*t*, 30*t*, 32*t*, 40, 218
    for VTE, 27*t*, 30*t*
Heparin-induced thrombocytopenia (HIT),
        26*t*, 33*t*
Heparinoids, 27*t*, 32*t*
Hepatic cirrhosis, 183
Hepatitis A vaccination, 270*t*
Hepatitis B screening, 270*t*
Hepatitis B vaccination, 102, 181, 270*t*
Hepatitis C screening, 270*t*

Hepatorenal syndrome, 255*t*
Hep-Lock, 32*t*
Herbal medications, 21–25, 68*t*
Herpes zoster ("shingles"), 163–164
  antiviral treatments, 164*t*
  post-herpetic neuralgia, 164, 228, 240*t*, 250*t*
  vaccination against, 270*t*
Hetlioz (tasimelteon), 318*t*
Hexadrol, 104*t. See also* Dexamethasone
HF. *See* Heart failure
High-fiber diet, 95, 96, 132
Hip arthroplasty, 27*t*
Hip fracture, 198–199
  medications for osteoporosis and, 233*t*
  prevention of, 231
  RBC transfusion for anemia and, 142
  risk assessment, 229
Hip fracture surgery
  anticoagulant agents for, 32*t*, 35*t*
  antiplatelet agents for, 31*t*
  antithrombotic medications for, 27*t*
  DVT/PE prophylaxis for, 27*t*
  hip fracture treatment, 198–199
Hip osteoarthritis, 198
  nonpharmacologic approaches to, 202
  pain relief for, 248*t*
  pharmacologic interventions for, 205
Hip pain, 197–199
Hip replacement
  anticoagulant agents for, 32*t*, 33*t*, 35*t*
  antiplatelet agents for, 31*t*
  antithrombotic medications for, 27*t*
  DVT/PE prophylaxis for, 27*t*
  for hip fracture, 198–199
  for osteoarthritis, 198
Histrelin acetate *(Vantas),* 279*t*
HIT (heparin-induced thrombocytopenia), 26*t*, 33*t*
HIV (human immunodeficiency virus) infection, 167–168, 255*t*, 270*t*
Hives, 89
HMG-CoA reductase inhibitors, 48*t. See also* Statin therapy
HoLEP (holmium laser enucleation of the prostate), 276

Homatropine, 67*t*
Homatropine/hydrocodone *(Hycodan),* 286*t*
Home care
  preventive visits, 116
  procedure codes, 346*t*, 347*t*
  sites of care, 7*t*
Home safety evaluations, 221
Homozygous familial hypercholesterolemia, 49*t*
Horizant (gabapentin enacarbil), 321
Hormone receptor agonists, 318*t*
Hormone therapy, 333–334
  bioidentical, 333
  for breast cancer, 331
  for dyspareunia, 305
  estrogen therapy, 150, 162, 232, 232*t*, 233*t*, 333
  GnRH agonists, 278, 279*t*
  for menopausal symptoms, 333
  for osteoporosis, 232, 232*t*
  for prostate cancer, 278
  risks, 333
  for sleep disorders, 318*t*
  that causes leg edema, 46
  for UI, 150
Hospice, 253–263, 254
  determinants for eligibility, 255*t*–257*t*
  for HF, 43*t*
  procedure codes, 347*t*
  resources for, 348
  sites of care, 7*t*
Hospital care, 8, 346*t*
Hospital Elder Life Program (HELP), 269
Hospital sites of care, 7*t*
Hospital-acquired pneumonia, 158, 160
Hot flushes, 333
HTN. *See* Hypertension
Humalog, 101*t. See also* Insulin lispro
Humalog Mix (insulin lispro protamine), 102*t*
Human immunodeficiency virus (HIV) infection, 167–168, 255*t*, 270*t*
Humira, 210. *See also* Adalimumab
Humulin (regular insulin), 101*t*
Hyalgan, 203. *See also* Hyaluronic acid
Hyaluronic acid *(Euflexxa, Hyalgan, Orthovisc, Synvisc, Supartz),* 203, 204*f*

Hycodan (hydrocodone/homatropine), 286*t*
HydraFoam/Ag, 312
Hydralazine *(Apresoline)*, 46, 54*t*, 216
Hydralazine and isosorbide dinitrate *(BiDil)*, 44, 45
Hydration, 145, 178, 261. *See also* Dehydration
Hydrochlorothiazide (HCTZ), 52*t*
Hydrocodone bitartate ER *(Zohydro ER)*, 244*t*
Hydrocodone with APAP *(Lorcet, Lortab, Norco, Vicodin)*, 241*t*
Hydrocodone with homatropine *(Hycodan)*, 286*t*
Hydrocodone with ibuprofen *(Vicoprofen)*, 241*t*
Hydrocol II, 312. *See also* Hydrocolloids
Hydrocolloid with silver *(Contreet)*, 312–313
Hydrocolloids *(Comfeel Plus, Cutinova Hydro, DermaFilm, DuoDERM, Exuderm, Hydrocol II, MPM Excel, Nu-DERM, Odor Shield, ProCol, RepliCare, Restore, SignaDRESS, 3M Tegasorb, Ultec, Ultec Pro)*, 312–313, 315
Hydrocortisone *(Cortef, Hydrocortone)*
  for adrenal insufficiency, 103, 104, 104*t*
  for dermatologic conditions, 90*t*, 91*t*
  for hemorrhoids, 132
  for intertrigo, 86
  for prostate cancer, 278
  for seborrheic dermatitis, 88
  for squamous hyperplasia, 332
  for xerosis, 89
Hydrocortisone butyrate *(Locoid)*, 91*t*
Hydrocortisone valerate *(Westcort)*, 91*t*
Hydrocortone, 104*t*. *See also* Hydrocortisone
Hydrogel, 313
Hydrogel dressings *(AquaSite Hydrogel, Aquasorb, Biolex, CarraDres, Curasol Gel, Curagel, Intrasite Gel, Restore Hydrogel, SAF-Gel, SoloSite Wound Gel, 3M Tegaderm Hydrogel, Dermagran, DuoDERM Hydroactive Gel, Normlgel, Nu-Gel, Purilon Gel, Skintegrity Hydrogel, Viniferamine Wound Hydrogel, Cutimed Gel)*, 307, 313

Hydrogel sheets *(AquaClear, AquaDerm, AquaSite, Aquasorb, ClearSite, Comfort-Aid, Curagel, Curasol, Derma-Gel, Elasto-Gel, FLEXIGEL, Hydrogel, Nugel, Spand-Gel, FlexiGel, Vigilon)*, 313
Hydrogel with silver dressings *(SilvaSorb Gel, SilvrSTAT, Silver-Sept Wound Gel, Viniferamine Wound Hydrogel AG, Silver-Sept Silver Antimicrobial Skin & Wound Gel, Gentell Hydrogel AG)*, 313
Hydromorphone *(Dilaudid, Hydrostat)*, 238*t*, 244*t*, 245*t*
Hydromorphone ER *(Exalgo)*, 245*t*
Hydrostat, 244*t*. *See also* Hydromorphone
25-Hydroxy vitamin D, 188. *See also* Vitamin D
25-Hydroxy vitamin D deficiency, 229
Hydroxychloroquine, 209, 210*t*, 213
Hydroxypropylcellulose *(Lacrisert)*, 111
Hydroxyurea, 144
Hydroxyzine, 67*t*, 73
Hygroton (chlorthalidone), 52*t*
Hyoscyamine *(Anaspaz, Levsin, Levsin/SL)*, 67*t*, 125, 261
Hyperalgesia, 249
Hyperbaric oxygen therapy, 311
Hypercalcemia, 94, 177*t*
Hypercholesterolemia, homozygous familial, 49*t*
Hyperemia, conjunctival, 110
Hyperglycemia, 158, 183, 281
Hypericum perforatum. *See* St. John's wort
Hyperkalemia, 180, 185–186
Hyperlipidemia, 183. *See also* Dyslipidemia
Hypernatremia, 182–183
Hyperphosphatemia, 180
Hyperprolactinemia, 283*t*, 301*t*, 305
Hyperproteinemia, 183
Hypersensitivity, carotid sinus, 118*t*
Hypersomnia, 316
Hypertension (HTN), 50–51
  acute, in ischemic stroke, 219
  in CKD, 180
  in DM type 2, 101, 102
  PAH, 57–58
  post MI, 42

Hyperthermia, 218
Hyperthyroidism, 56*t*, 92–93, 281
Hypertonic sodium gain, 182
Hypertriglyceridemia, 48, 283*t*
Hyperuricemia, 212–213
Hypnosis, 125, 239, 317
Hypnotics
    for anxiety, 38
    drug interactions, 20*t*, 21*t*
    and falls, 114*t*, 117*t*
    nonbenzodiazepine, 20*t*, 21*t*, 38
    and UI, 150*t*
Hypoalbuminemia, 187
Hypoaldosteronism, hyporeninemic, 181
Hypocalcemia, 180
Hypocholesterolemia, 187
Hypodermoclysis, 261
Hypogammaglobulinemia, 145
Hypoglossal nerve stimulation, 320
Hypoglycemia, 101, 281
Hypoglycemics, 23, 268, 324
Hypogonadism
    associated findings/risk factors, 301*t*
    diagnosis of, 302
    with long-term opioid use, 249
    testosterone replacement for, 233*t*,
        303*t*
    therapy for, 303
Hypomethylating agents, 143
Hyponatremia, 183–184
Hypoproliferative anemia, 138*f*
Hyporeninemic hypoaldosteronism, 181
HypoTears, 111
Hypotension
    drug-induced, 283*t*, 284*t*
    orthostatic (postural), 64–65, 104*t*, 118*t*,
        216, 216*t*, 220*t*–221*t*, 222*t*
    postprandial, 64
    secondary to anemia, 65
Hypothyroidism, 92, 183, 281
Hypotonic hyponatremia, 184
Hypotonic sodium loss, 182
Hypovolemic hyponatremia, 183
Hypoxemia, 57, 259
Hypoxia, 68*t*
Hytrin (terazosin), 53*t*, 275

I

IADLs (Instrumental Activities of Daily
        Living) Scale, 266, 337
Ibandronate *(Boniva),* 231*t*, 233*t*
IBS (irritable bowel syndrome), 124–125
Ibuprofen, 45, 207*t*
Ibuprofen, injectable *(Caldolor),* 207*t*
Ibuprofen with famotidine *(Duexis),* 207*t*
Ibuprofen with hydrocodone *(Vicoprofen),*
        241*t*
Ibuprofen with oxycodone *(Combunox),* 242*t*
ICDs (implantable cardiac defibrillators),
        42, 43*t*
    placement, 65
    withholding or withdrawing therapy, 259
ICS (inhaled corticosteroids), 291*t*–292*t*, 295*t*
ICU patients, 142, 190, 193
Icy Hot (methylsalicylate and menthol), 204*f*,
        251*t*
Ideal body weight, 1
IGRAs (interferon-gamma release assays), 166
IL-1 (interleukin-1) inhibitors, 210, 211
IL-6 (interleukin-6) inhibitors, 211, 214
Ilaris (canakinumab), 211
Iliotibial band syndrome, 199
Iloperidone *(Fanapta),* 282*t*
Iloprost *(Ventavis),* 57
Imagery, 239, 239*t*, 317
Imatinib, 23, 144
Imdur (isosorbide mononitrate SR), 41*t*
Imipenem, 159*t*, 160, 308*t*
Imipenem-cilastatin *(Primaxin),* 169*t*
Imipramine *(Tofranil),* 67*t*, 81
Imiquimod *(Aldara, Zyclara),* 84, 85
Immobility, 68*t*
Immunofluorescence antibody staining, 165*t*
Immunoglobulins, 145
Immunosuppressants, 22, 24, 143
Immunotherapy, autologous cellular, 278
Imodium A-D, 125, 130*t*, 261. *See also*
        Loperamide
Impetigo, 85
Implantable cardiac defibrillators (ICDs),
        42, 43*t*
    placement, 65
    withholding or withdrawing therapy, 259

Impotence, 301–303, 301*t*–302*t*, 305
Impulse-control disorders, 222*t*
Impulse-control symptoms in men, 77*t*
Incontinence, fecal (FI), 153–156
Incontinence, urinary. *See* Urinary
    incontinence (UI)
Incruse Ellipta (umeclidinium), 296*t*
Indacaterol *(Arcapta),* 297*t*
Indapamide *(Lozol),* 52*t*
Inderal (propranolol), 54*t*, 284*t*
Inderal LA, 54*t. See also* Propranolol LA
Infections
    antibiotics for, 169*t*–176*t*, 308*t*
    arterial ulcers, 310
    C difficile, 130, 131, 131*t*, 173*t*
    in chronic wounds, 308*t*
    diabetic foot ulcers, 310–311
    fungal, 86–87, 158
    H pylori, 123–124, 123*t*
    hepatitis A, 270*t*
    hepatitis B, 102, 181, 270*t*
    hepatitis C, 270*t*
    herpes zoster ("shingles"), 163–164, 164*t*,
        228, 240*t*, 250*t*, 270*t*
    influenza, 164–165, 164*t*–165*t*, 165*t*–166*t*,
        270*t*
    MRSA (methicillin-resistant *S aureus*), 85,
        158, 160, 163, 308*t*
    oropharyngeal, 175*t*
    pneumonia, 157–160, 170*t*, 270*t*, 346*t*
    preventive measures for, 68*t*
    prostate, 173*t*
    sepsis and SIRS, 163
    skin and soft tissue, 163, 170*t*, 173*t*
    skin ulcers, 307–308
    STI counseling, 347*t*
    tetanus, 270*t*
    tuberculosis, 166–167, 166*t*–167*t*
    urinary tract, 160–162, 171*t*, 173*t*
    venous ulcers, 315
    wound, 306, 310
Infectious diseases, 157–176, 169*t*–176*t*
Inflammation, 139–141, 261
Inflammatory arthritis, 200, 213
Inflammatory disease, ocular, 108–109
Inflammatory osteoarthritis, 202, 205

Inflammatory pain, 240*t*, 251*t*
Inflammatory response, systemic, 162–163,
    308
Infliximab *(Remicade),* 210, 214
Influenza, 164–165, 164*t*–165*t*, 165*t*–166*t*
Influenza vaccination
    ACIP guidelines, 164
    for DM, 102
    recommendations, 270*t*
    warfarin interactions, 34
Informant Questionnaire on Cognitive
    Decline in the Elderly (IQCODE), 70
Informed consent, 10
Informed decision making, 11*f*
    cancer screening, 272
    goal-oriented care, 9–10
    life-sustaining care, 10
    surgical, 264
Infrared photocoagulation, 132
Infumorph, 243*t. See also* Morphine
Ingenol mebatate *(Picato),* 84
INH. *See* Isoniazid
Inhaled corticosteroids (ICS), 291*t*–292*t*, 295*t*
Inhaled insulin *(Afrezza),* 101*t*
Inhalers, 295, 326*t*
Injectafer (ferric carboxymaltose), 140*t*
Injection therapy
    for acute disk herniation, 196
    for acute gouty flare, 211
    for carpal tunnel syndrome, 200
    for de Quervain tendinopathy, 199
    for DM, 97, 100*t*–101*t*
    for hypogonadism, 303*t*
    for lumbar spinal stenosis, 197
    for osteoarthritis, 203, 204*f*
    for pain, 239
    for plantar fasciitis, 202
    for trochanteric bursitis, 198
Innohep, 32*t. See also* Tinzaparin
Insomnia, 316–317
Inspra (eplerenone), 45, 52*t*
Instant fruit, 101
Instant Glucose, 101
Instructional advance directives, 258
Instrumental Activities of Daily Living
    (IADLs) Scale, 266, 337

Insulin
    adverse events, 101
    for DM, 96, 97
    drug interactions, 100*t*
    herbal medicine interactions, 23
    for hyperkalemia, 186
    preparations, 101*t*–102*t*
Insulin, inhaled *(Afrezza),* 101*t*
Insulin, isophane *(Novolin 70/30),* 102*t*
Insulin, regular *(Humulin, Novolin),* 101*t*
Insulin aspart *(NovoLog),* 95, 101*t*
Insulin detemir *(Levemir),* 101*t*
Insulin glargine *(Lantus),* 101*t*
Insulin glulisine *(Apidra),* 95, 101*t*
Insulin lispro *(Humalog),* 95, 101*t*
Insulin lispro protamine *(Humalog Mix),*
    102*t*
Insulin resistance reducers, 99*t*
Intal (cromolyn sodium), 298*t*
Integrase strand transfer inhibitors, 168
Integrilin, 34*t. See also* Eptifibatide
Interfacility transfer forms, 8
Interferon-gamma release assays (IGRAs),
    166
Interleukin-1 (IL-1) inhibitors, 210, 211
Interleukin-6 (IL-6) inhibitors, 211, 214
Intermezzo, 318*t. See also* Zolpidem
Intermittent pneumatic compression
    for DVT/PE prophylaxis, 26*t*, 27*t*
    for hip fracture surgery, 199
    for venous insufficiency, 46
Intermittent pneumatic pumps, 315
Internal rotation lag test, 194
International Prostate Symptom Score
    (IPSS) Symptom Index for BPH, 344
Internet-based pharmacies, 327
Interpersonal therapy, 79
Interprofessional geriatric team, 5, 6*t*
Intestinal obstruction, 261
Intra-articular injections
    for acute gouty flare, 211
    for osteoarthritis, 203, 204*f*
    for pseudogout, 213
Intracardiac thrombosis, 35*t*
Intracranial angiography, 218
Intrasite Gel, 313

Intraspinous spacer insertion (distraction),
    197
Intubation, nasogastric, 261
Invanz, 169*t. See also* Ertapenem
Invega (paliperidone), 282*t*
Invokana (Canagliflozin), 99*t*
Iodine, radioactive, 93
Iontophoric transdermal system (ITS), 248*t*
Ipratropium *(Atrovent, Atrovent NS)*
    for allergic rhinitis or conjunctivitis, 288*t*
    for asthma, 295, 296*t*
    for COPD, 296*t*
    for rhinosinusitis, 285*t*, 289*t*
    for subacute cough, 285*t*
Ipratropium-albuterol *(Combivent Respimat,
    Duoneb),* 298*t*
Iprivask, 33*t. See also* Desirudin
IPSS (International Prostate Symptom
    Score) Symptom Index for BPH, 344
IQCODE (Informant Questionnaire on
    Cognitive Decline in the Elderly), 70
Irbesartan *(Avapro),* 56*t*
Iridotomy, laser, 107
Iron deficiency, 45, 139–142, 321
Iron deficiency anemia, 139, 139*f*, 180
Iron replacement, 140*t*, 141
Iron sucrose *(Venofer),* 140*t*
Iron supplements, 321
Iron therapy
    for anemia, 139, 139*f*
    de-prescribing, 17
    for restless legs syndrome, 321
Iron-drug interactions, 19
Irritable bowel syndrome (IBS), 124–125
Ischemic pain, 239
ISMO (isosorbide mononitrate), 41*t*
Isoniazid (INH), 23, 34, 167*t*
Isoproterenol, 299*t*
Isoptin SR (verapamil), 55*t*
Isordil (isosorbide dinitrate), 41*t*
Isosorbide dinitrate *(Isordil, Sorbitrate),* 41*t*
Isosorbide dinitrate and hydralazine *(BiDil),*
    44, 45
Isosorbide dinitrate SR *(Dilatrate SR),* 41*t*
Isosorbide mononitrate *(ISMO, Monoket),*
    41*t*

Isosorbide mononitrate SR *(Imdur)*, 41*t*
Isosource, 191*t*
Isradipine SR *(DynaCirc CR)*, 55*t*
Itraconazole *(Sporanox)*, 34, 86–87, 174*t*
ITS (iontophoric transdermal system), 248*t*
Ivabradine *(Corlanor)*, 45
Ivermectin *(Soolantra, Stromectol)*, 87, 88

J
Janumet (sitagliptin and metformin), 100*t*
Janumet XR (sitagliptin and metformin), 100*t*
Januvia (sitagliptin), 98*t*
Jardiance (empagliflozin), 99*t*
Jejunostomy tube feeding, 192–193
Jentadueto (linagliptin with metformin), 100*t*
Jet lag, 316
Jevity 1 Cal, 191*t*
Jobst stockings, 64, 315
Johnson & Johnson, 314. *See also* Gauze
    packing
Joint arthroscopy, 27*t*
Joint replacement, total (TJR), 198, 243*t*, 273
Jubila (efinaconazole), 87
Juzo stockings, 315

K
Kadian (morphine), 245*t*
Kaltostat, 313. *See also* Calcium alginate
    dressings
Kaolin pectin, 45
Kaopectate (attapulgite), 129*t*
Karnofsky Scale, 341
Kava kava, 24
Kayexalate (sodium polystyrene sulfonate),
    185, 186
Kazano (alogliptin with metformin), 100*t*
Keflex, 170*t. See also* Cephalexin
Kefzol, 170*t. See also* Cefazolin
Kegel exercises, 149, 149*f*, 333
Kenacort, 104*t. See also* Triamcinolone
Kenalog, 91*t*, 104*t. See also* Triamcinolone
Kendall Fluff Kerlix, 314. *See also* Gauze
    packing
Keppra, 226*t. See also* Levetiracetam
Kerlone, 53*t. See also* Betaxolol
Ketalar (ketamine), 259

Ketamine *(Ketalar)*, 259
Ketek (telithromycin), 171*t*
Ketoconazole *(Nizoral, Nizoral A-D)*
    for dermatologic conditions, 90*t*
    for infectious diseases, 174*t*
    for prostate cancer, 278
    for seborrheic dermatitis, 88
    warfarin interactions, 34
Ketolides, 171*t*
Ketoprofen *(Orudis)*, 207*t*
Ketoprofen SR *(Oruvail)*, 207*t*
Ketorolac *(Acular, Toradol)*, 110, 111*t*, 207*t*
Ketotifen *(Alaway, Zaditor)*, 111*t*
Kidney disorders, 176–185
    acute kidney injury, 177–178, 177*t*–178*t*,
        256*t*
    chronic kidney disease (CKD), 56*t*, 141,
        179–181, 256*t*
    and hyponatremia, 183, 184
    kidney failure definition, 229
    kidney failure risk equation, 178
    medications that should be avoided or
        dosage reduced in, 19*t*
    pain management, 241*t*
    resources for, 349
Kidney transplantation, 181
Kinase inhibitors, 211
Kineret (anakinra), 210, 211
Klebsiella, 161
Knee arthroplasty, 27*t*
Knee osteoarthritis, 199
    nonpharmacologic approaches to, 202
    pharmacologic interventions for, 203, 205
Knee pain, 199, 239*t*, 240*t*
Knee replacement
    anticoagulant agents for, 32*t*, 33*t*
    antiplatelet agents for, 31*t*
    antithrombotic medications for, 27*t*
    DVT/PE prophylaxis for, 27*t*
Knee surgery, 27*t*, 35*t*
Kollagen-Medifil Particles/Gels/Pads, 314
Kollagen-Skin Temp II, 314
Kombiglyze XR (saxagliptin and metformin),
    100*t*
Krystexxa, 212*t. See also* Pegloticase
K-well (lindane), 88

Kyphoplasty, 197
Kytril (granisetron), 128*t*

L

Labetalol *(Normodyne, Trandate),* 51, 54*t*, 219
Laboratory tests, 119, 266
Labyrinthitis, 217*t*
Lacosamide *(VIMPAT),* 225*t*
Lacrisert (hydroxypropylcellulose), 111
β-Lactam/β-lactamase inhibitors, 159*t*, 160,
    169*t*
Lactose-free diet, 125
Lactose-free enteral products, 191*t*
Lactose-free oral products, 191*t*
Lactulose *(Chronulac),* 127*t*
Lamictal. See also Lamotrigine
    for bipolar disorders, 83*t*
    for pain relief, 250*t*
    for painful neuropathy, 228
    for seizures, 225*t*
Laminectomy, 240
Lamisil (terbinafine), 87, 90*t*, 176*t*
Lamisil AT, 90*t. See also* Terbinafine
Lamotrigine *(Lamictal)*
    for bipolar disorders, 83*t*
    for depression, 82
    for pain relief, 250*t*
    for painful neuropathy, 228
    for seizures, 225*t*
Lanoxicaps, 45. *See also* Digoxin
Lanoxin, 45. *See also* Digoxin
Lansoprazole *(Prevacid),* 122*t*, 123*t*, 192
Lansoprazole with clarithromycin and
        amoxicillin *(Prevpac),* 123*t*
Lanthanum carbonate *(Fosrenol),* 180
Lantus (insulin glargine), 101*t*
Laparoscopic procedures, 27*t*
Laser enucleation, 276
Laser peripheral iridotomy, 107
Laser photocoagulation, 106
Laser trabeculoplasty, 107
Laser treatment
    for actinic keratosis, 84
    for diabetic retinopathy, 106
    for glaucoma, 107
    for onychomycosis, 87

Lasix, 52*t. See also* Furosemide
Lastacaft (alcaftadine), 111*t*
Latanoprost, 108*t*
Late-life delusional (paranoid) disorder, 281
Latuda, 282*t. See also* Lurasidone
Laxatives
    for constipation, 125, 126, 126*t*, 127*t*, 249,
        261
    for fecal incontinence, 155
    for hyperkalemia, 185
    tube feeding, 192
Lazanda, 248*t. See also* Fentanyl
LDL (low-density lipoprotein), 47
L-dopa. *See* Levodopa
Leflunomide *(Arava),* 210*t*
Left ventricular thrombosis, 41
Leg compression, pneumatic, 199
Leg cramps, nocturnal, 320
Leg edema, 45–47
Leg fracture surgery, 27*t*
Legal blindness, 105
Legionella, 157, 158
Lenalidomide, 143
Lens correction, 118*t*
Lentigo maligna, 86
Lepirudin *(Refludan),* 26*t*, 33*t*
Lescol (fluvastatin), 48*t*
Lescol XL (fluvastatin), 48*t*
Letairis (ambrisentan), 58
Letrozole *(Femara),* 331*t*
Leukemia, chronic myelogenous, 144
Leukotriene modifiers
    for allergic rhinitis, 288, 288*t*, 289*t*
    for asthma, 295*t*, 298*t*
    for conjunctivitis, 288*t*, 289*t*
    for COPD, 298*t*
Leuprolide acetate *(Lupron Depot),* 77*t*, 279*t*
Levalbuterol *(Xopenex),* 296*t*
Levaquin, 172*t. See also* Levofloxacin
Levatol (penbutolol), 54*t*
Levemir (insulin detemir), 101*t*
Levetiracetam *(Keppra),* 19*t*, 226*t*
Levine's technique, 307
LEVITRA (vardenafil), 275, 302*t*
Levobunolol, 107*t*
Levocetirizine *(Xyzal),* 288*t*

Levodopa (L-dopa)
  carbidopa-levodopa *(Sinemet, Parcopa)*, 222*t*, 321
  carbidopa-levodopa + entacapone *(Stalevo)*, 224*t*
  enteral nutrition interactions, 192
  herbal medicine interactions, 24
  for MSA, 224
  for Parkinson disease, 223*t*
  and sleep problems, 316, 322
Levofloxacin *(Levaquin)*
  for COPD exacerbation, 292*t*
  enteral nutrition interactions, 192
  for infectious diseases, 172*t*
  for pneumonia, 159*t*, 160
  for prostatitis, 280
  QT$_c$ interval interactions, 21*t*
Levomilnacipran *(Fetzima)*, 80*t*
Levorphanol, 243*t*
Levo-T, 92. *See also* Levothyroxine
Levothroid, 92. *See also* Levothyroxine
Levothyroxine *(Eltroxin, Levo-T, Levothroid, Synthroid)*, 19, 92
Levsin, 125. *See also* Hyoscyamine
Levsin/SL, 125, 261. *See also* Hyoscyamine
Levulan Kerastick (aminolevulinic acid), 84
Lewy body dementia. *See also* Dementia
  clinical features, 70
  distinguishing early Parkinson disease from other parkinsonian syndromes, 221*t*
  pharmacologic management of, 69, 74
Lexapro, 79*t*. *See also* Escitalopram
Libido problems, drug-induced, 305
Lichen sclerosus, 332
Lidex (fluocinonide), 91*t*
Lidocaine *(Lidoderm)*
  to distinguish shoulder pain syndromes, 194*t*
  for frozen shoulder (adhesive capsulitis), 195
  for lumbar spinal stenosis, 197
  for osteoarthritis, 203, 204*f*
  for pain, 238, 240*t*, 252*t*
  for painful neuropathy, 228
  for plantar fasciitis, 202
  for rotator cuff problems, 194*t*, 195
Lidoderm. See also Lidocaine
  for osteoarthritis, 203, 204*f*
  for pain, 240*t*, 252*t*
  for painful neuropathy, 228
Life expectancy, 9–10, 9*t*
Lifestyle modifications
  for DM, 95, 96
  for hemorrhoids, 132
  for hyperuricemia, 212
  for sleep apnea, 319
  for UI, 148, 148*f*
Life-sustaining care preferences, 5*t*, 10
Light therapy
  for insomnia, 317
  for problem behaviors, 74
  for seasonal depression, 79
  for sleep disorders, 316, 322
Lighthouse Near Acuity Test, 105
Linaclotide *(Linzess)*, 125, 126*t*
Linagliptin (*Tradjent*a), 98*t*
Linagliptin with metformin *(Jentadueto)*, 100*t*
Lindane *(K-well, Scabene)*, 88
Linezolid *(Zyvox)*
  drug interactions, 79*t*
  for erysipelas, 85
  for infections in chronic wounds, 308*t*
  for infectious diseases, 173*t*
  for MRSA, 85, 163
  for pneumonia, 160
Liniments, 203, 238
Linzess (linaclotide), 125, 126*t*
Lioresal (baclofen), 251*t*
Lipid disorders, 101, 270*t*
Lipid emulsions, 193
Lipidemia. *See* Dyslipidemia
Lipid-lowering therapy
  for ACS, 41
  for dyslipidemia, 47, 48*t*–49*t*
  for PAD, 62
  and sexual dysfunction, 305
Lipitor, 48*t*. *See also* Atorvastatin
Liquid conversions, 1*t*
Liquid Pred, 104*t*. *See also* Prednisone
Liraglutide *(Saxenda, Victoza)*, 101*t*, 190
Lisinopril *(Prinivil, Zestril)*, 44*t*, 55*t*

Lithium *(Eskalith, Eskalith CR, Lithobid)*
  for bipolar disorders, 83*t*
  drug interactions, 20*t*, 21*t*
  herbal medicine interactions, 23
  and osteoporosis, 229
  and restless legs syndrome, 321
  and sexual dysfunction, 305
Lithobid, 83*t. See also* Lithium
Livalo (pitavastatin), 48*t*
Liver disease, 255*t*
Living wills, 10, 258
LMWH. *See* Low-molecular-weight heparin
Locoid (hydrocortisone butyrate), 91*t*
Lodine (etodolac), 206*t*
Lodine XL (etodolac), 206*t*
Lodoxamide *(Alomide),* 111*t*
Lofibra, 48*t. See also* Fenofibrate
Lomotil (diphenoxylate with atropine), 130*t*
Long-term care, 7*t*, 116, 322
Loniten (minoxidil), 54*t*
Loop diuretics
  and coexisting conditions, 56*t*, 57*t*
  drug interactions, 21*t*
  for HF, 45
  for HTN, 52*t*
  for hyperkalemia, 185, 186
  for SIADH, 184
  and tinnitus, 136
  and UI, 150*t*
Loperamide *(Imodium A-D)*
  for diarrhea, 130*t*, 261
  for fecal incontinence, 155
  for IBS, 125
Lopid (gemfibrozil), 48*t*
Lopressor, 53*t. See also* Metoprolol
Loprox (ciclopirox), 87, 89*t*
Lopurin, 212*t. See also* Allopurinol
Loratadine *(Claritin-D, Claritin-D 24 Hour),*
  67*t*, 289*t*
Lorazepam *(Ativan)*
  for akathisia, 284*t*
  for anxiety, 38*t*
  for delirium, 69
  for dyspnea, 261
  for sleep disorders, 318*t*
Lorcaserin *(Belviq),* 189

Lorcet (hydrocodone + APAP), 241*t*
Lortab (hydrocodone + APAP), 241*t*
Losartan *(Cozaar)*
  for chronic gout, 212*t*
  for HF, 44*t*
  for HTN, 56*t*
  for hyperuricemia, 213
Lotensin, 55*t. See also* Benazepril
Lotrimin AF, 16. *See also* Miconazole
Lotrimin AF for Her, 16
Lotrimin Ultra (butenafine), 16, 89*t*
Lotronex (alosetron), 125
Lovastatin *(Mevacor, Altoprev)*
  common herbal and alternative
    medications, 24
  drug interactions, 49*t*
  for dyslipidemia, 48*t*
  and sexual dysfunction, 305
Lovastatin with niacin *(Advicor),* 49*t*
Lovaza, 22, 49*t. See also* Omega-3 fatty acids
Lovenox, 32*t. See also* Enoxaparin
Low back pain
  adjuvant medications for, 251*t*, 252*t*
  chronic, 202, 203, 204
  nondrug interventions for, 239*t*
Low back pain syndrome, 196
Low-density lipoprotein (LDL), 47
Low-molecular-weight heparin (LMWH)
  for antithrombotic therapy, 26*t*
  bridging therapy, 267, 268*t*
  for DVT/PE prophylaxis, 218
  prescribing information, 32*t*
  resumption after surgery, 267
  for VTE, 27*t*, 30*t*
Low-vision services, 109
Loxapine, 67*t*
Lozol (indapamide), 52*t*
Lubiprostone *(Amitiza),* 126*t*
Lubricants, water-soluble *(Replens),* 305
Lucentis (ranibizumab), 106
Ludiomil, 81. *See also* Maprotiline
Luliconazole *(Luzu),* 90*t*
Lumbar spinal stenosis, 197
Lumbar spine, unstable, 196–197
Lumbar strain, acute, 196
Lumbosacral corset, 197

Lumbosacral nerve root compression, 2*t*
Luminal, 226*t. See also* Phenobarbital
Lunesta, 38, 318*t. See also* Eszopiclone
Lung cancer, 270*t*
Lung disease
 chronic obstructive. *See* Chronic
  obstructive pulmonary disease (COPD)
 determinants for hospice eligibility, 256*t*
 end-stage, 256*t*
 restrictive (RLD), 299–300, 299*t*–300*t*
Lupron Depot (leuprolide acetate), 77*t*, 279*t*
Lurasidone *(Latuda),* 82, 83*t*, 282*t*
Lutein, 106
Luvox (fluvoxamine), 80*t*
Luzu (luliconazole), 90*t*
Lymphedema, 47
Lyofoam, 312. *See also* Foam island
  dressings
Lyric hearing aids, 134
Lyrica. See also Pregabalin
 for pain, 250*t*
 for painful neuropathy, 228
 for restless legs syndrome, 321
 for seizures, 226*t*

M
Macitentan *(Opsumit),* 58
Macrobid (nitrofurantoin), 173*t*
Macrodantin (nitrofurantoin), 173*t*
Macrolides, 171*t*
 for cellulitis, 85
 for community-acquired pneumonia, 159*t*
 for pertussis, 285*t*
Macugen (pegaptanib), 106
Macular degeneration, age-related (AMD),
  105–106
Macular edema, 106
Magnacet (oxycodone + APAP), 242*t*
Magnesium
 drug interactions, 19
 for HTN, 51
 for nocturnal leg cramps, 320
 for sleep disorders, 322
Magnesium citrate *(Citroma),* 127*t*
Magnesium hydroxide, 16, 127*t*
Magnesium salicylate *(Novasal),* 206*t*

Magnesium sulfate, 295
Magnesium sulfate, sodium, and potassium
  (Suprep bowel prep kit), 127*t*
Major neurocognitive disorder, 70
Malalignment valgus, 199
Malalignment varus, 199
Malnutrition, 187–193, 266
Mammography, 271*t*, 330, 331
Mania, 82, 83*t*
MAO B (monoamine oxidase B) inhibitors,
  222*t*, 223*t*
MAOIs (monoamine oxidase inhibitors), 23,
  114*t*, 305
Maprotiline *(Ludiomil),* 81, 225
Marijuana *(cannabis sitiva),* 328
Marijuana, medical, 328, 329*t*
Marinol, 252*t. See also* Dronabinol
Massage
 abdominal, 155
 for delirium prevention, 68*t*
 for pain, 238, 239*t*
Mast cell stabilizers, 110, 111*t*, 289*t*
Matter of Balance program, 116
Mavik, 55*t. See also* Trandolapril
Maxair (pirbuterol), 296*t*
Maxiflor, 91*t. See also* Diflorasone diacetate
Maxillofacial surgery, 320
Maxipime, 171*t. See also* Cefepime
MCI (mild cognitive impairment), 71, 73–74,
  74–75
McKesson Calcium Alginate with Silver,
  313–314
McKesson Super Absorbent Dressing, 314
MDIs (metered-dose inhalers), 295
MDS (myelodysplastic syndromes), 143–144
Meaningful Use Incentive Program, 114
Mechanical heart valve, 35*t*
Mechanical skin ulcer debridement, 307
Mechanical ventilation, 158
Meclizine *(Antivert),* 129*t*, 217*t*
Meclofenamate sodium, 207*t*
Medicaid, 7*t*, 152
Medical decision making, 9–10, 272
Medical marijuana, 328
Medical Orders for Life-Sustaining
  Treatment (MOLST), 258

Medicare
    alcohol abuse screening and counseling
        benefits, 324
    ambulatory BP monitoring benefits, 50
    Annual Wellness Visit (AWV), 5, 70, 114,
        347*t*
    biofeedback benefits, 149
    decompression physiotherapy benefits, 47
    education benefits, 96
    hospice benefits, 255*t*–257*t*
    Part A, 7*t*
    Part B, 7*t*, 16, 46
    procedure codes, 346*t*–347*t*
    reimbursement threshold for CPAP, 319
    smoking cessation counseling benefits,
        327
Medication history, 16
Medication review
    assessment, 4*t*
    evaluation for falls, 118
    evaluation for PAD, 63
    evaluation for visual impairment, 105
Mediplast, 201
Medipore, 314
Medi-Strumpf stockings, 315
Meditation
    for depression, 79
    for insomnia, 317
    for pain, 239, 239*t*
Mediterranean diet
    for dementia, 73
    for DM, 96
    for malnutrition, 188
    post MI, 42
Medrol, 104*t. See also* Methylprednisolone
Medroxyprogesterone *(Cycrin, Depo-*
        Provera, Provera), 77*t,* 333
Mefenamic acid *(Ponstel),* 207*t*
Mefoxin (cefoxitin), 170*t*
Megestrol acetate, 190
Meglitinides, 98*t*–99*t,* 101
MEIs (middle ear implants), 134*t,* 135
Melanoma, 86, 332
Melatonin, 24
    for delirium prevention, 68*t*
    for Parkinson disease, 222*t*

for sleep disorders, 318*t,* 322
Melgisorb, 313. *See also* Calcium alginate
        dressings
Mellaril, 282*t. See also* Thioridazine
Meloxicam *(Mobic),* 207*t*
Memantine *(Namenda, Namzaric)*
    for agitation, 76
    for cognitive enhancement, 75, 75*t*
    de-prescribing, 17
Memantine ER *(Namenda XR),* 75*t*
Memory impairment. *See* Cognitive
        impairment; Dementia
Memory Impairment Screen (MIS), 70
Ménière disease, 134*t,* 217*t*
Menopause, 229, 333, 334
Men's health
    bone densitometry, 271*t*
    BPH, 57*t,* 275–277, 344
    energy (caloric) and fluid requirements,
        189
    erectile dysfunction, 301–303, 301*t*–302*t*
    hypogonadism, 302
    impulse-control symptoms, 77*t*
    osteoporosis, 233
    prostate cancer, 277–279, 279*t*–280*t*
    prostate disorders, 275–280
    prostate infection, 173*t*
    prostatitis, 280
Mental status, altered, 66–69
Mentax (butenafine), 89*t. See also*
        Butenafine
Menthol, 240*t*
Menthol with methyl salicylate *(Ben-Gay,*
        Icy Hot), 251*t*
Mentholatum *(Vicks VapoRub),* 87
Menthol-camphor-phenol *(Sarna),* 251*t*
Mepilex, 312
Mepore, 312
Meropenem *(Merrem IV)*
    for infections in chronic wounds, 308*t*
    for infectious diseases, 169*t*
    for pneumonia, 159*t,* 160
Merrem IV, 169*t. See also* Meropenem
Mestinon (pyridostigmine), 64
METAGLIP (glipizide and metformin), 99*t*
Metamucil, 126*t. See also* Psyllium

Metastatic bone disease
  in breast cancer, 332
    pain relief, 259
  in prostate cancer, 277, 278, 279
Metatarsal pads, 201
Metatarsalgia, 201
Metered-dose inhalers (MDIs), 295
Metformin *(Glucophage, Glucophage XR),*
  95, 97, 97*t*
Metformin with alogliptin *(Kazano),* 100*t*
Metformin with glipizide *(METAGLIP),* 99*t*
Metformin with glyburide *(Glucovance),* 99*t*
Metformin with linagliptin *(Jentadueto),* 100*t*
Metformin with pioglitazone *(ACTO plus
  met),* 99*t*
Metformin with repaglinide *(PrandiMet),*
  100*t*
Metformin with rosiglitazone *(Avandamet),*
  100*t*
Metformin with saxagliptin *(Kombiglyze XR),*
  100*t*
Metformin with sitagliptin *(Janumet),* 100*t*
Methadone
  for opioid abuse/misuse/dependence, 328
  for pain management, 243*t,* 247*t*
  QT$_c$ interval interactions, 21*t*
Methazolamide, 108*t*
Methicillin-resistant *S aureus. See* MRSA
Methimazole *(Tapazole),* 93
Methotrexate *(Rheumatrex, Trexall)*
  for giant cell arteritis, 214
  for pseudogout, 213
  for psoriasis, 87
  for rheumatoid arthritis, 209, 210, 210*t,* 211
Methoxy polyethylene glycol-epoetin beta
  (Mircera), 141*t*
Methyl salicylates, 203, 240*t*
Methyl sulfonyl methane (MSM), 24
Methylcellulose *(Citrucel),* 126*t,* 132, 192
Methyldopa *(Aldomet),* 53*t,* 216, 316
Methylnaltrexone bromide *(Relistor),* 127*t,*
  249, 261
Methylphenidate *(Ritalin),* 76, 80*t,* 260
Methylprednisolone *(Medrol, Solu-Medrol,
  Depo-Medrol)*
  for acute gouty flare, 211
    for adrenal insufficiency, 104*t*
    for anorexia, cachexia, dehydration,
      262
    for carpal tunnel syndrome, 200
    for giant cell arteritis, 214
    for plantar fasciitis, 202
    for polymyalgia rheumatica, 214
    for rheumatoid arthritis, 209
    for vertigo, 217*t*
Methylprednisolone acetate, 203
Methylsalicylate and menthol *(Ben-Gay, Icy
  Hot),* 204*f,* 251*t*
Methylxanthines, 297*t*
Meticorten, 104*t. See also* Prednisone
Metipranolol, 107*t*
Metoclopramide *(Reglan)*
    digoxin interactions, 45
    for GERD, 122*t*
    for high gastric residual volume problems,
      193
    for nausea and vomiting, 128*t,* 129*t*
    and Parkinson disease, 222*t*
    and sexual dysfunction, 305
Metolazone *(Mykrox, Zaroxolyn),* 52*t,* 185,
  186
Metoprolol *(Lopressor),* 44*t,* 53*t,* 58
Metoprolol, long-acting *(Toprol XL),* 53*t*
Metoproterenol, 299*t*
MetroCream, 87. *See also* Metronidazole
MetroGel, 87, 173*t. See also* Metronidazole
Metronidazole *(Flagyl, MetroCream,
  MetroGel, Noritate)*
    for *C difficile* infection, 131*t,* 132
    for *H pylori* infection, 123*t*
    for infectious diseases, 173*t*
    for rosacea, 87, 88
    warfarin interactions, 34
Mevacor, 48*t. See also* Lovastatin
Mevinolin, 24
MGUS (monoclonal gammopathy of
  undetermined significance), 144–145
MI. *See* Myocardial infarction
Miacalcin, 232*t. See also* Calcitonin
Micafungin *(Mycamine),* 175*t*
Micardis (telmisartan), 56*t*
Micatin, 90*t. See also* Miconazole

Miconazole *(Lotrimin AF, Micatin, Monistat-Derm, Monistat IV)*
   for dermatologic conditions, 90*t*
   formulation differences, 16
   for infectious diseases, 174*t*
   warfarin interactions, 34
Microalbuminuria, 103, 145
Micronase (glyburide), 98*t*
Microwave therapy, 204, 276
Midamor (amiloride), 52*t*
Midazolam, 23
Middle ear implants (MEIs), 134*t*, 135
Midodrine *(ProAmantine)*, 64
Miglitol *(Glyset)*, 98*t*
Migraine, 252*t*
Mild cognitive impairment (MCI), 71, 73–74, 74–75
Milk of Magnesia, 127*t. See also* Magnesium hydroxide
Milnacipran *(Savella)*, 251*t*
Mindfulness meditation
   for depression, 79
   for insomnia, 317
   for pain, 239, 239*t*
Mini-Cog™ screen for dementia
   assessment instrument, 335
   in cognitive dysfunction, 75
   in dementia, 70
   preoperative, 266
Mini–Mental State Examination (MMSE), 70, 71–72, 75
Minipress, 53*t. See also* Prazosin
Minocin, 172*t. See also* Minocycline
Minocycline *(Minocin)*
   for infectious diseases, 172*t*
   for MRSA, 85, 163
   for rosacea, 88
Minoxidil *(Loniten)*, 54*t*
Miotics, 107*t*
Mirabegran *(Myrbetiq)*, 151*t*
MiraLAX (polyethylene glycol, PEG), 126, 127*t*
Mirapex, 223*t. See also* Pramipexole
Mirapex ER (pramipexole ER), 217*t*
Mircera (methoxy polyethylene glycol-epoetin beta), 141*t*

Mirtazapine *(Remeron)*
   for depression, 79, 80*t*
   for malnutrition, 190
   for SSRI-induced sexual dysfunction, 305
Mirvasol, 87. *See also* Brimonidine
MIS (Memory Impairment Screen), 70
Misoprostol *(Cytotec)*, 204*f*, 205, 215
Misoprostol with diclofenac *(Arthrotec)*, 206*t*
Mistreatment of older adults, 10–12, 12*t*–13*t*, 348
Mitraflex, 312
Mitral valve prolapse, 35*t*
Mitral valve replacement surgery, 35*t*
Mitral valvular disease, rheumatic, 35*t*
MMRC (Modified Medical Research Council Dyspnea Scale), 290
MMSE (Mini–Mental State Examination), 70, 71–72, 75
Mobic (meloxicam), 207*t*
Mobility assessment, 116
MoCA (Montreal Cognitive Assessment), 70
Modafinil *(Provigil)*, 260, 320
Modified Medical Research Council Dyspnea Scale (MMRC), 290
Moexipril *(Univasc)*, 55*t*
Mohs micrographic surgery, 85
Moisture-retaining dressings, 307, 310
MOLST (Medical Orders for Life-Sustaining Treatment), 258
Mometasone *(Asmanex HFA, Asmanex Twisthaler, Nasonex)*, 289*t*, 297*t*
Mometasone furoate *(Elocon)*, 91*t*
Mometasone-formoterol *(Dulera)*, 298*t*
Monascus purpureus (red yeast rice), 24
Monistat IV, 174*t. See also* Miconazole
Monistat-Derm, 90*t. See also* Miconazole
Monoamine oxidase B (MAO B) inhibitors, 222*t*, 223*t*
Monoamine oxidase inhibitors (MAOIs), 114*t*, 305
Monobactam, 169*t*
Monoclonal gammopathy of undetermined significance (MGUS), 144–145
Monofilament testing, 103
Monoket (isosorbide mononitrate), 41*t*
Monopril, 55*t. See also* Fosinopril

Montelukast *(Singulair),* 298*t*
Montreal Cognitive Assessment (MoCA), 70
Monurol (fosfomycin), 173*t*
Mood disorder, 239
Mood stabilizers, 83*t*
Moraxella catarrhalis, 158
Morphine *(Astramorph PF, Duramorph, Infumorph, MSIR, MS/L, MS/S, OMS Concentrate, RMS, Roxanol)*
  for dyspnea, 261
  for hip fracture surgery, 198
  for pain, 238*t,* 243*t*
Morphine equivalents, 248*t,* 249
Morphine ER *(Avinza, Kadian, MS Contin, Oramorph SR),* 245*t,* 250, 328
Morphine sulfate, 40, 235, 307
Morse Fall Scale, 114
Morton neuroma, 201
Motion sickness, 129*t*
Motivational interviewing, 324
Motor function, 2*t*
Motor restlessness (akathisia), 284*t*
Movantik (naloxegol), 249, 261
MOVE!® Weight Management program, 238
Movement behavior, 64
Movement disorders, 316, 320–322
Moving for Better Balance, 116
Moxifloxacin *(Avelox)*
  for acute bacterial conjunctivitis, 110*t*
  for COPD, 292*t*
  for infections in chronic wounds, 308*t*
  for infectious diseases, 172*t*
  for pneumonia, 159*t*
  QT$_c$ interval interactions, 21*t*
  warfarin interactions, 34
MPM Excel, 312. *See also* Hydrocolloids
MRSA (methicillin-resistant *S aureus*), 163
  in cellulitis, 85
  in chronic wounds, 308*t*
  empiric antibiotic therapy against, 160, 308*t*
  in pneumonia, 158
MS Contin (morphine), 245*t*
MSA (multiple-system atrophy), 221*t,* 224
MSIR, 243*t. See also* Morphine
MS/L, 243*t. See also* Morphine

MSM (methyl sulfonyl methane), 24
MS/S, 243*t. See also* Morphine
Mucolytic therapy, 292
Mucomyst (acetylcysteine), 178
Mucositis, painful, 260
Multidisciplinary assessment, 235
Multimorbidity, 14, 15*f,* 136
Multiple myeloma, 145
Multiple-system atrophy (MSA), 221*t,* 224
Multivitamins, 188
Mupirocin *(Bactroban),* 85, 163
Muscle mass, loss of, 187
Musculoskeletal disorders, 194–215, 274, 349
Musculoskeletal examination, 119
Musculoskeletal pain, 240*t,* 251*t*
Music therapy
  for delirium prevention, 68*t*
  for insomnia, 317
  for pain, 238, 239*t*
  for problem behaviors, 74
Mycamine (micafungin), 175*t*
Mycelex, 90*t. See also* Clotrimazole
Mycobacterium tuberculosis, 157, 158
Myco-Nail (triacetin), 90*t*
Mycoses, superficial, 90*t,* 176*t*
Mycostatin (nystatin), 90*t*
Myelodysplastic syndromes (MDS), 143–144
Myelofibrosis, 144
Myeloma, 145, 177*t*
Myeloproliferative disorders, primary, 144
Mykrox, 52*t. See also* Metolazone
Mylanta, 16
Mylanta Supreme, 16
Mylanta Ultimate Strength, 16
Myocardial infarction (MI)
  in ACS, 39
  antihypertensive therapy and, 57*t*
  non-ST segment (NSTEMI), 39, 40
  ongoing hospital management of, 40, 41
  prevention of, 268, 271*t*
  ST segment (STEMI), 35*t,* 39, 40
  warfarin anticoagulation for, 35*t*
Myofascial pain syndrome, 252*t*
Myrbetiq (mirabegran), 151*t*
Mysoline, 216*t. See also* Primidone
Myxedema coma, 92

N

NAAT (nucleic acid amplification tests), 131
Nabilone, 329*t*
Nabiximols, 329*t*
Nabumetone *(Relafen)*, 207*t*
Nadolol *(Corgard)*, 53*t*
Nafcillin, 34, 169*t*
Naftifine *(Naftin)*, 90*t*
Naftin (naftifine), 90*t*
Nalfon (fenoprofen), 206*t*
Naloxegol *(Movantik)*, 249, 261
Naloxone *(Narcan)*, 193, 238, 249
Naloxone with oxycodone *(Targiniq ER)*,
    245*t*, 250
Naltrel (naltrexone), 325
Naltrexone, 325
Naltrexone depot *(Vivitrol)*, 325
Naltrexone with morphine *(Embeda)*, 245*t*,
    250, 328
Naltrexone-bupropion *(Contrave)*, 190
Namenda, 75, 75*t. See also* Memantine
Namenda XR, 75*t*
Namzaric, 75*t. See also* Memantine
Naphazoline, 112*t*
Naphazoline hydrochloride/pheniramine
    maleate, 112*t*
Naprelan (naproxen ER), 207*t*
Naprosyn, 207*t. See also* Naproxen
Naproxen *(Aleve, Naprosyn)*, 34, 207*t*
Naproxen delayed-release *(EC-Naprosyn)*,
    207*t*
Naproxen ER *(Naprelan)*, 207*t*
Naproxen sodium *(Anaprox)*, 207*t*
Narcan, 193. *See also* Naloxone
Narcolepsy, 316
Narcotics. *See* Opioids
Nasacort Allergy 24, 289*t. See also*
    Triamcinolone
Nasacort AQ, 289*t. See also* Triamcinolone
Nasal positive airway pressure (NPAP), 320
Nasal steroids
    for allergic conjunctivitis, 110, 288*t*, 289*t*
    for allergic rhinitis, 288, 288*t*, 289*t*
NasalCrom, 289*t. See also* Cromolyn
Nascobal, 142
Nasogastric intubation, 261

Nasonex, 289*t. See also* Mometasone
Nateglinide *(Starlix)*, 98*t*
Natesto (testosterone), 303*t*
National Institutes of Health Stroke Scale
    (NIHSS), 217–218
Nausea and vomiting, 128
    with bowel obstruction, 261
    drug-induced, 283*t*
    at end of life, 261, 262
    postoperative, 128*t*
    spasm, pain, and vomiting, 261
    treatment of, 128*t*–129*t*, 222*t*, 329*t*
Near vision testing, 105
Nebcin, 171*t. See also* Tobramycin
Nebivolol *(Bystolic)*, 44*t*, 53*t*
Nebulizers, 295
Neck pain, 194, 239*t*
Nedocromil *(Alocril)*, 111*t*
Nefazodone, 305
Negative-pressure wound therapy, 307,
    308–309, 311
Neglect, older adults, 10–11, 12*t*
Nephrotic syndrome, 183
Nerve block, 198, 204
Nerve conduction studies, 228
Nerve roots, 2*t*
Nesina (alogliptin), 98*t*
Neupro (rotigotine), 223*t*
Neuralgia
    post-herpetic, 164, 228, 240*t*, 250*t*
    trigeminal or glossopharyngeal, 250*t*
Neuroaxial analgesia, 240
Neurocognitive disorder, major, 70
Neurodermatitis, 86
Neuroimaging, 71
Neuroleptic malignant syndrome, 67*t*, 283*t*
Neuroleptics. *See* Antipsychotics
Neurologic disorders, 216–228
Neurologic examination, 119
Neuromodulation, 240
Neuromuscular blocking agents, 252*t*
Neuromuscular electrical stimulation
    (NMES), 120
Neurontin, 225*t*, 228, 250*t. See also*
    Gabapentin
Neuropathic erectile dysfunction, 301, 301*t*

Neuropathic foot ulcers, 306*t*–307*t*, 310–311
Neuropathic pain
    adjuvant medications for, 243*t*, 251*t*, 252*t*
    treatment of, 234*t*, 235, 239, 240*t*
Neuropathy
    painful, 228
    peripheral, 216*t*, 227–228, 252*t*
    with UI, 147
Neurorehabilitation, 224
New York Heart Association (NYHA) heart
        failure staging, 43*t*
Nexium, 122*t. See also* Esomeprazole
        magnesium
Niacin, 24, 48*t*, 49*t*
Niacin ER *(Niaspan),* 49*t*
Niacin with lovastatin *(Advicor),* 49*t*
Niacin with simvastatin *(Simcor),* 49*t*
Niaspan (niacin ER), 49*t*
Nicardipine *(Cardene),* 55*t*, 219
Nicardipine SR *(Cardene SR),* 55*t*
Nicorette (polacrilex gum), 326*t*
Nicotine, 216, 229, 316
Nicotine lozenges, 326*t*
Nicotine replacement therapy, 325–326, 326*t*
Nicotinic acid, 49*t*
Nicotrol Inhaler (nicotine replacement), 326*t*
Nicotrol NS (nicotine replacement), 326*t*
Nifedipine SR *(Adalat CC, Procardia XL),* 55*t*
Nightmares, 38
NIHSS (National Institutes of Health Stroke
        Scale), 217–218
Nilandron (nilutamide), 280*t*
Nilotinib, 144
Nilstat (nystatin), 90*t*
Nilutamide *(Nilandron),* 280*t*
Nipride (sodium nitroprusside), 51
Nisoldipine *(Sular),* 55*t*
Nitrates
    for ACS, 41
    alcohol interactions, 324
    for chronic angina, 41
    dosages and formulations, 41*t*
    drug interactions, 301*t*
    and orthostatic hypotension, 216
Nitro-Bid, 41*t. See also* Nitroglycerin

Nitrofurantoin *(Macrobid, Macrodantin),*
        173*t*
Nitroglycerin *(Nitro-Bid, Nitrol, Nitrolingual,*
        NitroMist, Nitrostat)
    for ACS, 40, 41
    for acute angina, 42
    dosage and formulations, 41*t*
    for HF, 45
Nitrol, 41*t. See also* Nitroglycerin
Nitrolingual, 41*t. See also* Nitroglycerin
NitroMist, 41*t. See also* Nitroglycerin
Nitrostat, 41*t. See also* Nitroglycerin
Nizatidine *(Axid),* 19*t*, 122*t*
Nizoral, 90*t*, 174*t. See also* Ketoconazole
Nizoral A-D, 90*t. See also* Ketoconazole
NMDA antagonists, 75*t*
NMES (neuromuscular electrical
        stimulation), 120
NNRTIs (non-nucleoside reverse
        transcriptase inhibitors), 23, 168
No Pain-HP, 252*t. See also* Capsaicin
Nociceptive pain, 234*t*
Nocturnal frequency, 152
Nocturnal leg cramps, 320
Nocturnal polyuria, 152
Nodular melanoma, 86
Nodules, thyroid, 93–94
Noise reduction, 68*t*, 322
Nolvadex, 331*t. See also* Tamoxifen
Non-nucleoside reverse transcriptase
        inhibitors (NNRTIs), 23, 168
Nonsteroidal anti-inflammatory drugs. *See*
        NSAIDs
Norco (hydrocodone + APAP), 241*t*
Norfloxacin *(Noroxin),* 172*t*
Noritate, 87. *See also* Metronidazole
Normlgel, 313
Normodyne, 54*t*, 219. *See also* Labetalol
Noroxin (norfloxacin), 172*t*
Norpramin, 81*t*, 228. *See also* Desipramine
Northera (droxidopa), 64
Nortriptyline *(Aventyl, Pamelor)*
    anticholinergic property, 67*t*
    for depression, 81*t*, 82
    for pain relief, 251*t*
    for painful neuropathy, 228

Nortriptyline *continued*
    for Parkinson disease, 82
    for smoking cessation, 326
Norvasc (amlodipine), 55*t*
Novasal (magnesium salicylate), 206*t*
Novolin (regular insulin), 101*t*
Novolin 70/30 (isophane insulin), 102*t*
NovoLog, 101*t. See also* Insulin aspart
Noxafil (posaconazole), 175*t*
NPAP (nasal positive airway pressure), 320
NRTIs (nucleoside reverse transcriptase
    inhibitors), 168
NSAIDs (nonsteroidal anti-inflammatory
    drugs)
    for acute gouty flare, 211
    for acute lumbar strain, 196
    adverse effects of, 241*t*
    alcohol interactions, 324
    for allergic conjunctivitis, 111*t*
    for anti-inflammatory prophylaxis, 212
    for arthritis, 196, 204*f*, 205, 205*t*–208*t*, 209
    avoid use, 44
    for back pain, 196
    for chronic disk degeneration, 196
    and CKD, 180
    for de Quervain tendinopathy, 199
    drug interactions, 20*t*, 21*t*, 251*t*
    herbal medicine interactions, 22, 23, 24, 25
    and leg edema, 46
    for low back pain syndrome, 196
    for lumbar spinal stenosis, 197
    nonselective, 204*f*, 205, 206*t*–207*t*
    for pain, 234*t*, 235, 237–238, 240*t*, 241*t*
    for plantar fasciitis, 202
    for polymyalgia rheumatica, 214
    for pseudogout, 213
    for shoulder pain, 195
    and tinnitus, 136
    topical, 240*t*
    and UI, 150*t*
NT-proBNP (N-terminal prohormone brain
    natriuretic peptide), 43
Nucleic acid amplification tests (NAAT), 131
Nucleoside reverse transcriptase inhibitors
    (NRTIs), 168
Nucynta (tapentadol), 244*t*

Nucynta ER (tapentadol ER), 246*t*
Nu-DERM, 312, 313. *See also* Hydrocolloids
Nugel, 313
Nu-Gel, 313
Nulecit (sodium ferric gluconate complex),
    140*t*
Nurses, interprofessional team, 6*t*
Nursing-home patients
    advanced dementia in, 72
    catheter care for, 153
    CMS guidance on unnecessary drugs
      for, 18
    community-acquired pneumonia in, 159*t*
    diabetic management in, 95
    fecal incontinence treatment for, 155
    influenza treatment for, 166
    influenza vaccination for, 164
    malnutrition in, 187
    procedure codes, 346*t*
    resources for, 348–349
    scheduled visit checklist for, 8
    sites of care, 7*t*
    sleep disorders in, 322
    UI in, 152–153
Nursing-home–acquired cystitis, 161
Nursing-home–acquired pneumonia, 158, 160
Nutren 1.0, 191*t*
Nutren 1.0 Fiber, 191*t*
Nutren 2.0, 191*t*
Nutriceuticals, 203
Nutrient-drug interactions, 19
Nutrition
    artificial, 192, 259
    enteral, 124, 190, 191*t,* 192
    oral, 190, 191*t*
    parenteral, 193
Nutritional assessment, 4*t,* 187–188
Nutritional supplements, 190, 199
Nutritional support
    for COPD, 293
    lactose-free products, 191*t*
    for malnutrition, 190
    for skin ulcers, 309
NYHA (New York Heart Association) heart
    failure staging, 43*t*
Nystatin *(Mycostatin, Nilstat, Nystex),* 90*t*

Nystex (nystatin), 90*t*

O

Oatmeal baths, 88, 89
Obesity, 189–190
   behavioral therapy for, 347*t*
   definition of, 187
   management of HTN, 51
   post MI, 42
   resources for, 349
   screening for, 270*t*
Obstruction
   bladder outlet, 146*t*, 147
   bowel, 261
   renal, 177*t*
Obstructive pulmonary disease, chronic.
    See Chronic obstructive pulmonary
    disease (COPD)
Obstructive sleep apnea (OSA), 319
Occupational therapy (OT)
   for carpal tunnel syndrome, 200
   interprofessional team, 6*t*
   for osteoarthritis, 202
   for pain management, 239
   for Parkinson disease, 221
   for preventing falls, 114, 117*t*, 118*t*
   for rheumatoid arthritis, 209
Octreotide *(Sandostatin)*, 261
Ocular inflammatory disease, 108–109
Ocular symptoms, 288
Odor absorbers, 263
Odor Shield, 312. *See also* Hydrocolloids
Ofirmev (acetaminophen), 237
Ofloxacin *(Roxin)*, 110*t*, 172*t*, 280
Ogen (estropipate), 305*t*
Olanzapine *(Zyprexa, Zydis)*
   for acute mania, 82
   adverse events, 283*t*
   for agitation, 76, 76*t*
   anticholinergic property, 67*t*
   for bipolar disorders, 83*t*
   for psychotic depression, 82
   for psychotic disorders, 281, 282*t*
   and seizures, 225
   and sexual dysfunction, 305
Olanzapine IM *(Zyprexa IntraMuscular)*, 77*t*

Oliguria, 177
Olmesartan *(Benicar)*, 56*t*
Olodaterol-tiotropium *(Stiolto Respimat)*,
   298*t*
Olopatadine *(Patanol, Pataday, Patanase)*,
   111*t*, 289*t*
Omacor, 49*t*. *See also* Omega-3 fatty acids
Omalizumab *(Xolair)*, 298*t*
Omega-3 fatty acids *(Omacor, Lovaza)*, 22
   for dyslipidemia, 48*t*, 49*t*
   for HF, 45
   for MI, stroke prevention, 271*t*
Omeprazole *(Prilosec)*, 122*t*, 192, 305
Omnaris, 289*t*. *See also* Ciclesonide
Omnicef (cefdinir), 170*t*
OMS Concentrate, 243*t*. *See also* Morphine
Onabotulinumtoxin A *(Botox)*, 252*t*
Ondansetron *(Zofran)*, 21*t*, 128*t*, 261
Onglyza (saxagliptin), 98*t*
Onsolis, 248*t*. *See also* Fentanyl
Onychomycosis, 86–87, 89*t*
Opana, 244*t*. *See also* Oxymorphone
Opana ER (oxymorphone ER), 245*t*
Open reduction and internal fixation (ORIF),
   198
Opioid abuse-deterrent products, 328
Opioid agreements, 250
Opioid antagonists, 126*t*–127*t*, 245*t*
Opioid Risk Tool (ORT), 250, 327, 345
Opioids
   abuse/misuse/dependence, 327, 328
   with acetaminophen, 204*f*
   administration and dosing, 248–249
   adverse events, 249, 327
   alcohol interactions, 324
   for back pain, 196
   drug interactions, 20*t*, 21*t*, 242*t*
   for dyspnea, 261
   extended-release, 244*t*–247*t*
   long-acting, 244*t*–247*t*
   for opioid-tolerant patients, 244*t*–247*t*
   and orthostatic hypotension, 216
   for osteoarthritis, 204*f*, 205
   for pain, 234*t*, 238, 241*t*–248*t*, 248–249,
     259, 307
   for painful neuropathy, 228

Opioids *continued*
  prevention of misuse and withdrawal, 249–250
  rapid-acting, 247t–248t
  for restless legs syndrome, 321
  risk evaluation and mitigation strategy (REMS), 250
  and sexual dysfunction, 305
  short-acting, 241t–242t
  and UI, 150t
Opsite, 312
Opsumit (macitentan), 58
Optical aids, 109
Optifoam AG, 312
Optivar, 111t. *See also* Azelastine
Oral appliances, 320
Oral care, 158, 262
Oral dysphagia, 120t
Oral hypoglycemics, 324
Oral nutrition, 190, 191t
Oral procedures, 272, 272t, 273
Oral statements, 258
Oramorph SR (morphine), 245t
Orasone, 104t. *See also* Prednisone
Orbactiv (oritavancin), 173t
OrCel, 311, 315
Orchiectomy, 278
Orencia (abatacept), 211
Orexin receptor antagonists, 318t
Orgaran, 32t. *See also* Danaparoid
Orientation protocols, 68t
ORIF (open reduction and internal fixation), 198
Oritavancin *(Orbactiv),* 173t
Orlistat *(Xenica, Alli),* 189
Oropharyngeal exercises, 320
Oropharyngeal infection, 175t
Orphenadrine, 67t
ORT (Opioid Risk Tool), 250, 327
Orthoses, 201
Orthostatic (postural) hypotension, 64–65
  corticosteroids for, 104t
  distinguishing early Parkinson disease from other parkinsonian syndromes, 220t–221t
  dizziness in, 216t
  medications associated with, 216
  preventing falls with, 118t
  treatment options, 222t
Orthostatic syncope, 63, 63t, 64
Orthotics, 201
  for arthritis, 202, 209
  for diabetic foot ulcers, 311
  for trochanteric bursitis, 198
Orthovisc, 203. *See also* Hyaluronic acid
Orudis (ketoprofen), 207t
Oruvail (ketoprofen SR), 207t
OSA (obstructive sleep apnea), 319
Osbon-Erec Aid (vacuum tumescence device), 302t
Oseltamivir *(Tamiflu),* 165t
Oseni (alogliptin with pioglitazone), 100t
Osmolality, 1, 182
Osmolite 1 Cal, 191t
Osmotics, 126, 127t
Ospemifene, 304
Osteoarthritis, 202–205
  APAP and NSAIDs for, 206t–208t
  in back, 196
  base-of-thumb, 202
  and falls, 118t
  in hand and wrist, 199–200
  in hip, 198, 202, 205, 248t
  in knee, 199, 202, 203, 205
  pain relief, 239t, 251t, 252t
  pharmacologic management of, 204f
  resources for, 349
Osteocalcin, 232t. *See also* Calcitonin
Osteomyelitis, 308, 309, 311
Osteopenia, 229
Osteoporosis, 229–233
  antihypertensive therapy and, 57t
  bone outcomes of medications for, 233t
  effects on other outcomes, level of evidence, and risks of medications for, 233t
  prevention and treatment of, 199, 231t–232t, 271t
  resources for, 349
OT. *See* Occupational therapy
OTAGO exercise program, 116
Ovarian cancer, 272

Overactive bladder, 146, 149
Overflow incontinence, 146*t. See also*
    Urinary incontinence
Overweight, 187, 189–190, 238
Oxacillin *(Bactocill)*, 169*t*
Oxaprozin *(Daypro)*, 207*t*
Oxazepam *(Serax)*, 38*t*
Oxcarbazepine *(Trileptal)*, 226*t*, 250*t*
Oxcarbazepine ER *(Oxtellar XR)*, 250*t*
Oxecta (oxycodone), 242*t*
Oxiconazole *(Oxistat)*, 90*t*
Oximetry, 198
Oxistat (oxiconazole), 90*t*
Oxtellar XR (oxcarbazepine), 250*t*
Oxy IR (oxycodone), 242*t*
Oxybutynin *(Ditropan, Ditropan XL, Gelnique,*
    Oxytrol for Women), 67*t*, 73, 150*t*
Oxycodone *(Oxy IR, Oxecta, Roxicodone)*,
    242*t*
Oxycodone ER *(OxyContin)*, 245*t*
Oxycodone with APAP *(Percocet, Tylox,*
    Magnacet), 242*t*
Oxycodone with APAP ER *(Xartemis XR)*,
    245*t*
Oxycodone with ASA *(Percodan)*, 242*t*
Oxycodone with ibuprofen *(Combunox)*,
    242*t*
Oxycodone with naloxone *(Targiniq ER)*,
    245*t*, 250
OxyContin (oxycodone ER), 245*t*
Oxygen, 1, 2
Oxygen therapy
    for ACS, 40
    for acute stroke, 218
    for diabetic foot ulcers, 311
    for dyspnea, 260
    for hip fracture, 198
    long-term, 293, 293*t*
    for PAH, 57
    for pneumonia, 158
    for sepsis and SIRS, 162
Oxymetazoline *(Afrin)*, 285*t*
Oxymorphone *(Opana)*, 244*t*
Oxymorphone ER (*Opana* ER), 245*t*
Oxytrol for Women, 150*t. See also*
    Oxybutynin

P
Pacemakers, 43*t*, 58, 259
Pacerone, 59*t. See also* Amiodarone
PAD. *See* Peripheral arterial disease
PAH (pulmonary arterial hypertension),
    57–58
Pain, 234–252
    abdominal, 241*t*
    acute, 234, 237–238, 239
    adjuvant medications for, 243*t*, 250*t*–252*t*
    analgesic management of, 240*t*–248*t*
    arthritic, 203–205, 204*f*, 206*t*–208*t*
    assessment of, 4*t*, 236*f*
    back, 195–197
    bowel obstruction, 261
    cancer, 234*t*, 239, 252*t*
    carpal tunnel syndrome, 200
    central, undetermined or mixed, 234*t*
    chest, 39
    chronic, 239, 239*t*, 241*t*, 252*t*
    differential diagnosis of, 281
    at end of life, 259
    fall risks, 113*t*
    foot, 201
    hand and wrist pain, 199–200
    heel, 201
    hip, 197–199
    inflammatory, 240*t*, 251*t*
    in intercourse, 303
    ischemic, 239
    knee, 199
    low back, 202, 203, 252*t*
    marijuana for, 329*t*
    metastatic bone, 259
    metatarsal, 201
    Morton neuroma, 201
    musculoskeletal, 240*t*, 251*t*
    myofascial pain syndrome, 252*t*
    neck, 194
    neuropathic, 234*t*, 235, 239, 240*t*, 243*t*, 251*t*,
        252*t*
    nondrug interventions for, 239*t*
    nonrheumatic, 197, 199
    opioids for, 248–249
    peripheral neuropathic, 234*t*
    peripheral nociceptive, 234*t*

Pain *continued*
  persistent, 234, 238–239, 239–240, 239*t*, 240*t*, 243*t*
  pharmacologic treatment of, 240–250
  preventive measures for delirium, 68*t*
  resources for, 349
  shoulder, 194–195
  stepwise analgesic trial for, 235
  types, examples, and treatment of, 234*t*
  wrist, 199–200
Pain crisis, 259
Painful arc test, 194
Painful neuropathy, 228, 234*t*
Palatal implants, 320
Paliperidone *(Invega)*, 282*t*
Palliative care, 253–263, 293, 348
Palliative Performance Scale, version 2 (PPSv2), 342
Pamelor, 81*t*, 228. *See also* Nortriptyline
Pamidronate, 94, 197, 332
Pancreatic cancer, 272
Pancrelipase *(Viokase)*, 192
Pancytopenia, 143–144
Panic attack, 37
Panic disorder, 37, 38
Pantoprazole *(Protonix)*, 122*t*
PaO$_2$ (partial pressure of oxygen, arterial), 2
PAP (positive airway pressure), 320
Papain, 192
Paranoid delusions, 72
Paranoid (delusional) disorder, late-life, 281
Parasomnias, 316
Parcopa, 222*t. See also* Carbidopa-levodopa
Parenteral iron replacement, 140*t*
Parenteral nutrition, 193
Parkinson disease, 220–221
  classification of, 216*t*
  dementia associated with, 74
  depression and, 82
  differential diagnosis of, 281
  distinguishing early Parkinson disease from other parkinsonian syndromes, 220*t*–221*t*
  dysphagia complaints, 120*t*
  and falls, 113*t*, 118*t*
  medications for, 222*t*–224*t*

  pharmacologic management of delirium, 69
  resources for, 349
  treatment of, 222*t*
Parkinsonism, 216*t*, 220*t*, 284*t*
Parlodel, 223*t. See also* Bromocriptine
Paroxetine *(Paxil, Paxil CR)*
  anticholinergic property, 67*t*
  for depression, 80*t*
  drug interactions, 286*t*, 331*t*
  for menopausal symptoms, 334
  for smoking cessation, 326
Partial pressure of oxygen, arterial (PaO$_2$), 2
Paste-containing bandages, 315
Pataday, 111*t. See also* Olopatadine
Patanase, 289*t. See also* Olopatadine
Patanol, 111*t. See also* Olopatadine
PATH (problem adaptive therapy), 79
Pathocil, 169*t. See also* Dicloxacillin
Patient education
  communicating bad news, 253–254
  communication with hearing-impaired people, 135–136
  for DM management, 96
  for fecal incontinence, 155
  about medications, 17
  for orthostatic (postural) hypotension, 64
  for pain management, 196, 238, 239*t*
  for Parkinson disease, 221
  for preventing falls, 116, 117*t*
  for rheumatoid arthritis, 209
  self-management education, 239*t*
  for sleep apnea, 319
Patient Health Questionnaire-2 (PHQ-2) Quick Depression Assessment, 339
Patient Health Questionnaire-9 (PHQ-9) Quick Depression Assessment, 338–339
Patient preferences for life-sustaining care, 5*t*, 10
Patient-controlled analgesia (PCA), 238, 238*t*
Paxil, 80*t. See also* Paroxetine
Paxil CR, 80*t. See also* Paroxetine
PCA (patient-controlled analgesia), 238, 238*t*
PCC (prothrombin complex concentrate), 32*t*, 35*t*
PCI (percutaneous cardiac intervention), 40

PCSK9 (proprotein convertase subtilisin kexin type 9) inhibitors, 49t
PDE-4 (phosphodiesterase-4) inhibitors, 291t–292t, 298t
PDE-5 (phosphodiesterase-5) inhibitors
  for BPH, 276
  drug interactions, 275, 301t
  for erectile dysfunction, 301, 301t–302t
  and orthostatic hypotension, 216
PE. *See* Pulmonary embolism
Peak flow meters, 294
Pear pulp, 322
Pedal pulse, 311
Pediapred, 104t. *See also* Prednisolone
Pedometers, 274
PEG (polyethylene glycol) *(MiraLAX),* 126, 127t
Pegaptanib *(Macugen),* 106
Pegloticase *(Krystexxa),* 212t, 213
Pelvic examination, 331
Pelvic floor electrical stimulation, 149
Pelvic fracture surgery, 27t
Pelvic lymph node dissection, 278
Pelvic muscle (Kegel) exercises, 149, 149f, 333
Pemirolast *(Alamast),* 111t
Penbutolol *(Levatol),* 54t
Penicillin G, 169t
Penicillin VK, 169t
Penicillinase-resistant penicillins, 169t, 170t
Penicillins
  antipseudomonal, 169t, 170t
  antistaphylococcal, 169t
  for cellulitis, 85
  endocarditis prophylaxis regimens, 272t
  for erysipelas, 85
  for folliculitis, 85
  for impetigo, 85
  for infectious diseases, 169t, 170t
  penicillinase-resistant, 169t, 170t
Penile prosthesis, 302t
Penlac (ciclopirox), 87, 89t
Pennsaid, 206t. *See also* Diclofenac
Pentoxifylline *(Trental),* 62
Pepcid, 122t. *See also* Famotidine
Peptic ulcer disease, 123–124

Pepto-Bismol (bismuth subsalicylate), 124, 129t
Peramivir *(Rapivab),* 166t
Percocet (oxycodone + APAP), 242t
Percodan (oxycodone + ASA), 242t
Percutaneous cardiac intervention (PCI), 40
Percutaneous venting gastrostomy, 261
Percutaneous vertebral augmentation, 197
Perennial rhinitis, 287, 288t, 294
Perianal bulking agents, 156
Perindopril *(Aceon),* 44t, 55t
Periodic limb movement disorder, 321–322
Peripheral arterial disease (PAD), 61–62
  antiplatelet agents for, 26t, 31t
  antithrombotic medications for, 26t
  management of, 62t
  screening for, 102, 272
  warfarin anticoagulation for, 35t
Peripheral neuropathy, 227–228
  dizziness in, 216t
  examples and treatment of, 234t
  pain relief, 252t
  and restless legs syndrome, 321
Peripheral nociceptive pain, 234t
Peritoneal dialysis, 181
Permethrin *(Elimite),* 88
Perphenazine *(Trilafon),* 67t, 282t
Personal pocket devices, 135
Personality disorder, 239
Pertussis, 285t
Pes cavus, 201
Pessaries, 151, 333
Pet therapy, 74
Petrolatum, 132
Peyronie disease, 301t
Phalen's test, 200
Pharmacists, 6t
Pharmacodynamics, 18t
Pharmacokinetics, 18t
Pharmacotherapy, 16–17
  antimicrobial stewardship, 157
  CMS guidance on unnecessary drugs, 18
  de-prescribing medications, 17
  drug-drug interactions, 20
  drug-food or -nutrient interactions, 19–20
  enteral nutrition interactions, 192

Pharmacotherapy *continued*
  fall risks, 114*t*
  misuse of prescription drugs, 327–328
  for preventing falls, 117*t*
  prevention of opioid misuse and
      withdrawal, 249–250
  QT_c interval interactions, 21*t*
Pharyngeal dysphagia, 120*t*
Pheniramine maleate/naphazoline
    hydrochloride, 112*t*
Phenobarbital *(Luminal),* 226*t,* 305
Phenol and camphor *(Campho-Phenique),*
    251*t*
Phenol-camphor-menthol *(Sarna),* 251*t*
Phentermine-topiramate *(Qsymia),* 189
Phenylephrine, 132
Phenytoin *(Dilantin)*
  drug-food or -nutrient interactions, 19
  enteral nutrition interactions, 192
  and osteoporosis, 229
  for seizures, 226*t*
  and sexual dysfunction, 305
  and sleep problems, 316
Phlebotomy, 144
Phobia, 37, 38
PhosLo (calcium acetate), 180
Phosphate, 190
Phosphodiesterase-4 (PDE-4) inhibitors,
    291*t*–292*t,* 298*t*
Phosphodiesterase-5 inhibitors. *See* PDE-5
    inhibitors
Photocoagulation, 106, 132
Photodynamic therapy, 85
Photoselective vaporization (PVP), 276
PHQ-2 Quick Depression Assessment, 339
PHQ-9 Quick Depression Assessment,
    338–339
Physical abuse, 12*t*
Physical activity
  for constipation, 126
  counseling for, 270*t*
  for IBS, 125
  for pain, 238
  for sleep disorders, 322
Physical restraints, 68
Physical self-maintenance scale, 336

Physical therapy (PT)
  for arthritis, 202, 209
  for balance and strength training, 216*t,*
    217*t*
  for bicipital tendinitis, 195
  for carpal tunnel syndrome, 200
  for cervical stenosis/radiculopathy, 194
  decompression physiotherapy, 47
  for dizziness, 216*t,* 217*t*
  for frozen shoulder (adhesive capsulitis),
    195
  interprofessional team, 6*t*
  for lumbar spinal stenosis, 197
  for pain, 234*t,* 238, 239
  for Parkinson disease, 221
  for preventing falls, 114, 117*t,* 118*t*
  for rotator cuff problems, 195
  for UI, 149
Physician assistants, 6*t*
Physician Orders for Life-Sustaining
    Treatment (POLST), 10, 258
Physician Quality Reporting System (PQRS),
    114
Physicians, interprofessional team, 6*t*
Picato (ingenol mebatate), 84
Pill cards, 17
Pilocarpine, 107*t*
Pimeclorimus *(Elidel),* 87
Pimozide, 21*t,* 67*t*
Pindolol *(Visken),* 54*t*
Pioglitazone *(Actos),* 99*t*
Pioglitazone with alogliptin *(Oseni),* 100*t*
Pioglitazone with glimepiride *(Duetact),* 100*t*
Pioglitazone with metformin *(ACTO plus
    met),* 99*t*
Piperacillin *(Pipracil),* 169*t*
Piperacillin-tazobactam *(Zosyn)*
  for infections in chronic wounds, 308*t*
  for infectious diseases, 170*t*
  for pneumonia, 159*t,* 160
Pipracil (piperacillin), 169*t*
Pirbuterol *(Maxair),* 296*t*
Piroxicam *(Feldene),* 207*t*
Pitavastatin *(Livalo),* 48*t*
Pityrosporum orbiculare, 88
Plantar fasciitis, 201–202

Platelet-derived growth factors, 309
Plavix, 31*t,* 62, 219. *See also* Clopidogrel
Plendil (felodipine), 55*t*
Pletal, 62. *See also* Cilostazol
Pneumatic compression
   for DVT/PE prophylaxis, 27*t*
   for hip fracture surgery, 199
   for venous insufficiency, 46
   for venous ulcers, 315
Pneumococcal vaccination, 102
Pneumococcus, 157
Pneumonia, 157–160
   treatment of, 159*t,* 170*t*
   vaccination against, 270*t,* 346*t*
Pneumovax, 181
Pocket Talker, 135, 136
Polacrilex gum *(Nicorette),* 326*t*
POLST (Physician Orders for Life-Sustaining
   Treatment), 10, 258
Polycarbophil *(FiberCon),* 125, 126*t,* 132
Polycythemia vera, 144
Polyderm, 312. *See also* Foam island
   dressings
Polydipsia, 183, 184
Polyethylene glycol (PEG) *(MiraLAX),* 126,
   127*t*
PolyMem, 312. *See also* Foam island
   dressings
PolyMem Silver, 312
Polymyalgia rheumatica, 213–215
Polymyxin with trimethoprim, 110, 110*t*
Polyskin II, 312
Polysomnography, 319
Polythiazide *(Renese),* 52*t*
Polyunsaturated fatty acids, 45, 106
Polyuria, nocturnal, 152
Ponstel (mefenamic acid), 207*t*
Posaconazole *(Noxafil),* 175*t*
Positioning devices, 310
Positive airway pressure (PAP), 320
Positive-pressure ventilation, 292*t*
Post-herpetic neuralgia
   pain management, 240*t,* 250*t*
   pharmacologic management, 164, 228
Postmenopausal bleeding, 332
Postmenopausal state, 333

Post-prandial glucose (PPG), 96*t*
Post-prandial hypotension, 64
Post-traumatic stress disorder (PTSD), 37,
   38, 239
Postural hypotension. *See* Orthostatic
   hypotension
Postural impingement of vertebral artery,
   217*t*
Postural instability, 222*t*
Postvoid residual (PVR), 275
Potassium
   for dehydration, 182
   for HTN, 51
   low-potassium diet, 180, 185
   for refeeding syndrome prevention, 190
Potassium, sodium, and magnesium sulfate
   (Suprep bowel prep kit), 127*t*
Potassium imbalance, 281
Potassium iodide, 93
Potassium phosphate, 190
Potassium supplements, 51
Potassium-sparing drugs, 52*t*
Power of attorney for health care, 10, 258
PPG (post-prandial glucose), 96*t*
PPIs. *See* Proton-pump inhibitors
PPSv2 (Palliative Performance Scale,
   version 2), 342
PQRS (Physician Quality Reporting System),
   114
Pradaxa, 33*t. See also* Dabigatran
Praluent (alirocumab), 49*t*
Pramipexole *(Mirapex)*
   for depression, 82
   for Parkinson disease, 82, 222*t,* 223*t*
   for REM sleep behavior disorder, 322
   for restless legs syndrome, 321
Pramipexole ER *(Mirapex ER),* 217*t*
Pramlintide *(Symlin),* 101*t*
PrandiMet (repaglinide and metformin), 100*t*
Prandin (repaglinide), 99*t*
Prasugrel *(Effient)*
   for ACS, 40
   for antithrombotic therapy, 26*t*
   cessation before surgery, 267, 268
   for chronic angina, 41
   prescribing information, 31*t*

Pravachol, 48t. *See also* Pravastatin
Pravastatin *(Pravachol)*, 48t, 305
Pravastatin/ASA *(Pravigard PAC)*, 48t
Pravigard PAC (ASA/pravastatin), 48t
Prazosin *(Minipress)*, 38, 53t
Prealbumin, 188
Precose, 98t. *See also* Acarbose
Pre-diabetes, 95
Prednicarbate *(Dermatop)*, 91t
Prednisolone *(Delta-Cortef, Prelone Syrup,
    Pediapred)*
  for acute asthma exacerbation, 295
  for acute gouty flare, 211
  for adrenal insufficiency, 104t
  for anti-inflammatory prophylaxis, 212
Prednisone *(Deltasone, Liquid Pred,
    Meticorten, Orasone)*
  for acute gouty flare, 211
  for acute interstitial nephritis, 178
  for adrenal insufficiency, 104t
  for anorexia, cachexia, dehydration, 262
  for anti-inflammatory prophylaxis, 212
  for asthma, 297t
  for carpal tunnel syndrome, 200
  for cervical stenosis/radiculopathy, 194
  for chronic adrenal insufficiency, 104
  for COPD, 292t, 297t
  for giant cell arteritis, 214
  for hives, 89
  for polymyalgia rheumatica, 214
  for rheumatoid arthritis, 209
Pregabalin *(Lyrica)*
  for anxiety disorders, 38
  for menopausal symptoms, 334
  for pain, 235, 250t
  for painful neuropathy, 228
  reduce dosage, 19t
  for restless legs syndrome, 321
  for seizures, 226t
  and UI, 150t
Prelone Syrup, 104t. *See also* Prednisolone
Premarin, 77t, 305t. *See also* Estrogen
    therapy
Preoperative care, 264–268, 265f
Preparation H, 132
Prerenal disease, 177, 177t, 178

Presbycusis, 133, 134t
Presbyesophagus, 120
Prescription drug misuse, 323, 327–329
Prescription drugs, 16–17, 327. *See also*
    Pharmacotherapy
Pressure stockings, 315. *See also*
    Compression stockings
Pressure ulcers, 306t–307t, 311–314
Pressure-reducing mattresses, 198, 309
Prevacid, 122t. *See also* Lansoprazole
Prevention, 270–274
  cardiovascular disease, 26t
  delirium, 68t
  DVT, 27t, 199
  endocarditis, 272–273, 272t
  falls, 113–119, 115f, 117t–118t
  home visits, 116
  influenza, 164, 166
  MI, 268
  osteoporosis, 231t–232t
  PE, 27t
  procedure codes, 346t–347t
  recommendations, 270t–271t, 271–272
  stress ulcer, 124
  stroke, 31t, 219, 271t
  tests, 270t–271t
  UTI, 162
  visual impairment, 105
  VTE, 26–30
Prevention of falls in the elderly trial
    (PROFET), 116
Prevpac (lansoprazole + clarithromycin +
    amoxicillin), 123t
Prilosec, 122t. *See also* Omeprazole
Primaxin (imipenem-cilastatin), 169t
Primidone *(Mysoline)*, 216t, 305
Prinivil, 55t. *See also* Lisinopril
Prisma Matrix, 314
Pristiq, 81t. *See also* Desvenlafaxine
ProAmantine (midodrine), 64
Proben-C (probenecid with colchicine), 212t
Probenecid *(Benemid)*, 19t, 212t, 213
Probenecid with colchicine *(ColBenemid,
    Col-Probenecid)*, 212t
Probiotic products, 130
Problem adaptive therapy (PATH), 79

Problem-solving therapy, 79
Procaine, 169*t*
Procardia XL (nifedipine SR), 55*t*
Procedure codes, 346*t*–347*t*
Prochlorperazine *(Compazine)*, 67*t*, 128*t*, 222*t*
ProCol, 312. *See also* Hydrocolloids
Procrit (epoetin alfa), 141*t*
PROFET (Prevention of falls in the elderly
    trial), 116
Profore wrap, 315. *See also* Compression
    wraps
Progesterone
    with estrogen, 332, 333, 334
    for menopausal symptoms, 333, 334
    and sleep problems, 316
Progestin, 304, 334
Progressive muscle relaxation, 239*t*, 317
Progressive supranuclear palsy, 221*t*
ProGuide wrap, 315. *See also* Compression
    wraps
Prokinetic agents, 122*t*
Prolia, 232*t*. *See also* Denosumab
Prolotherapy, 204
Promethazine, 67*t*, 222*t*
Promogran Matrix, 314
PROMOGRAN PRISMA, 314
Prompted toileting, 153
Propafenone *(Rythmol)*, 59*t*
Propafenone SR *(Rythmol SR)*, 59*t*
Propantheline, 67*t*
Propranolol *(Inderal)*, 54*t*, 284*t*
Propranolol LA *(Inderal LA)*, 54*t*, 216*t*
Proprotein convertase subtilisin kexin type 9
    (PCSK9) inhibitors, 49*t*
Propylthiouracil (PTU), 93
Proscar, 276. *See also* Finasteride
Proshield, 88
ProSom (estazolam), 318*t*
Prostacyclins, 57
Prostaglandin analogs, 107, 108*t*
Prostaglandin E *(Alprostadil)*, 302*t*
Prostate cancer, 277–279
    medications for, 279*t*–280*t*
    osteoporosis prevention in, 231
    screening for, 272
Prostate disorders, 275–280

Prostate infections, 173*t*
Prostatectomy, 149, 276, 278
Prostate-specific antigen (PSA), 279
Prostatic hyperplasia, benign (BPH), 57*t*,
    275–277, 344
Prostatic urethral lift, 277
Prostatitis, 280
Prosthesis, penile, 302*t*
Prosthetic heart valves, 35*t*
Protease inhibitors, 23, 168
Protein requirements, 309
Protein restriction, 180
Protein supplements, 190
Proteins, serum, 188
Proteinuria, 180
Proteus, 161
Prothrombin complex concentrate (PCC),
    32*t*, 35*t*
Proton-beam therapy, 278
Protonix (pantoprazole), 122*t*
Proton-pump inhibitors (PPIs)
    for anti-inflammatory prophylaxis, 212
    de-prescribing, 17
    drug interactions, 231
    for GERD, 121, 122, 122*t*
    for giant cell arteritis, 215
    for *H pylori* infection, 123*t*
    iron interactions, 140*t*
    for osteoarthritis, 204*f*, 205
    for peptic ulcer disease, 124
    and sexual dysfunction, 305
    for stress-ulcer prevention, 124
Protriptyline *(Vivactil)*, 67*t*, 81
Provent (nasal PAP, NPAP), 320
Providencia, 161
Provigil (modafinil), 260, 320
Prozac, 80*t*. *See also* Fluoxetine
Pruritus, 288*t*
PSA (prostate-specific antigen), 279
Pseudoephedrine, 288*t*, 289*t*
Pseudogout, 212*t*, 213
Pseudohyponatremia, 183
Pseudomembranous colitis, antibiotic-
    associated, 130
Pseudomonas, 163, 292*t*
Pseudomonas aeruginosa, 159*t*, 161

Pseudo-rheumatoid arthritis, 213
Psoralen plus ultraviolet light (PUVA), 87
Psorcon, 91*t. See also* Diflorasone diacetate
Psoriasis, 87
Psoriatic arthritis, 200
Psychiatric resources, 349
Psychogenic male sexual dysfunction, 301*t*
Psychological abuse, 13*t*
Psychosis/psychotic disorders, 281–284
   agitation treatment guidelines, 76*t*
   in dementia, 72
   and Parkinson disease, 222*t*
   psychotic depression, 79, 82
   treatment of, 222*t*, 282*t*–283*t*
Psychosocial assessment, 96, 237
Psychostimulants, 260
Psychotherapy, 125, 234*t*, 239
Psychotic depression, 79, 82
Psyllium *(Metamucil)*
   for constipation, 126*t*, 127*t*, 249
   digoxin interactions, 45
   for hemorrhoids, 132
   for IBS, 125
   tube feeding, 192
PT. *See* Physical therapy
PTSD (post-traumatic stress disorder), 37, 38, 239
PTU (propylthiouracil), 93
Pulmonary arterial hypertension (PAH), 57–58
Pulmonary disease
   chronic obstructive. *See* Chronic obstructive pulmonary disease (COPD)
   determinants for hospice eligibility, 256*t*
   end-stage, 256*t*
   restrictive lung disease (RLD), 299–300, 299*t*–300*t*
Pulmonary embolism (PE)
   acute massive PE, 30
   clinical decision rule, 29*t*
   diagnosis of, 28
   evaluation algorithm, 29*f*
   medications for osteoporosis and, 233*t*
   prophylaxis of, 27*t*
   submassive, 30
Pulmonary rehabilitation, 287

Pulmonary risk assessment, preoperative, 265–266
Pulse therapy, 86–87, 131*t*, 209
Punctal plugs, 111
Puracol Plus, 314
Puracol Plus AG, 314
Purilon Gel, 313
PUVA (psoralen plus ultraviolet light), 87
PVP (photoselective vaporization), 276
PVR (postvoid residual), 275
Pylera, 123*t. See also* Tetracycline
Pyridostigmine *(Mestinon),* 64

Q
Qigong, 239*t*
Qnasl, 289*t. See also* Beclomethasone
Qsymia (phentermine-topiramate), 189
QT_c interval interactions, 20, 21*t*
Quality of life, 253
QuantiFERON assay, 166
Qudexy XR (topiramate), 226*t*
Quetiapine *(Seroquel)*
   for acute mania, 82
   adverse events, 283*t*
   for agitation, 76, 76*t*
   for bipolar disorders, 83*t*
   for delirium, 69
   for depression, 79
   for Parkinson disease, 222*t*
   for psychosis, 282*t*
   for psychotic disorders, 281
   for tardive dyskinesia, 284*t*
Quinapril *(Accupril),* 44*t*, 55*t*
Quinidine, 21*t*, 316
Quinine, 136
Quinolones, 19, 172*t. See also* Fluoroquinolones
Quinupristin-dalfopristin *(Synercid),* 173*t*
Qutenza, 228, 240*t*, 252*t. See also* Capsaicin
QVAR, 297*t. See also* Beclomethasone

R
Rabeprazole *(AcipHex),* 122*t*
Radiation therapy
   antiemetic therapy for, 128*t*
   for basal cell carcinoma, 85

Radiation therapy *continued*
  for multiple myeloma, 145
  for pain at end of life, 259
  for prostate cancer, 278, 279
Radioactive iodine ablation, 93
Radiocontrast-induced acute kidney failure, 178
Radiofrequency ablation, 203, 276
Radiography
  abdominal, 154
  chest, 57, 60, 285*t*
Radionuclide ventriculography, 43
Radionuclides, 259
Raloxifene *(Evista),* 232*t,* 233*t*
Ramelteon *(Rozerem),* 38, 68*t,* 318*t*
Ramipril *(Altace),* 44*t,* 55*t*
Ranexa (ranolazine), 41–42
Range-of-motion programs, 239
Ranibizumab *(Lucentis),* 106
Ranitidine *(Zantac),* 19*t,* 122*t,* 305
Ranolazine *(Ranexa),* 41–42
Rapaflo (silodosin), 276
Rapid Estimate of Adult Literacy in Medicine
  – Short Form (REALM-SF), 17, 340
Rapid-eye movement (REM) sleep behavior
  disorder, 222*t,* 322
Rapivab (peramivir), 166*t*
RAS (renal artery stenosis), 50
Rasagilene *(Azilect),* 223*t*
Razadyne (galantamine), 75*t*
Razadyne ER (galantamine), 75*t*
RBC (red blood cell) transfusion, 142, 162
RCRI (Revised Cardiac Risk Index), 264
REALM-SF (Rapid Estimate of Adult Literacy
  in Medicine – Short Form), 17, 340
Reclast, 231*t. See also* Zoledronic acid
Rectal evacuants, 154
Rectal sphincter exercises, 155
Red blood cell (RBC) transfusion, 142, 162
Red eye, 109–110, 109*t*
RED (Re-Engineered Discharge) project, 8
Red yeast rice (*Monascus purpureus,* Xue
  Zhi Kang), 24
Reductase inhibitors, 48*t,* 275, 276
Re-Engineered Discharge (RED) project, 8
Refeeding syndrome, 190

Refludan, 33*t. See also* Lepirudin
Reflux, gastroesophageal (GERD), 121–123,
  122*t*
Reflux esophagitis, 285*t*
Refractive error, 105
Reglan, 122*t,* 128*t,* 193. *See also*
  Metoclopramide
Regranex, 309
Rehabilitation
  in acute stroke, 218
  for COPD, 293
  of hearing loss, 134*t*
  hospital care, 8
  inpatient, 7*t*
  neurorehabilitation, 224
  pulmonary, 287
  short stay, 7*t*
  swallowing, 120
Rehydration, 158, 178, 182
Reisberg Functional Assessment Staging
  (FAST) scale, 70, 343
Relafen (nabumetone), 207*t*
Relaxation therapy, 238, 260, 317
Relaxis (vibrating pad), 321
Relenza (zanamivir), 165*t*
Relistor (methylnaltrexone bromide), 127*t,*
  249, 261
REM (rapid-eye movement) sleep behavior
  disorder, 222*t,* 322
Remeron, 80*t. See also* Mirtazapine
Remicade, 210. *See also* Infliximab
Remodulin (treprostinil), 57
REMS (risk evaluation and mitigation
  strategy), 250
Renagel (sevelamer hydrochloride),
  180
Renal artery stenosis (RAS), 50
Renal artery stenting, 50
Renal dialysis, 178
Renal infarction, 177*t*
Renese (polythiazide), 52*t*
Renin inhibitors, 56*t*
Renvela (sevelamer carbonate), 180
ReoPro, 34*t. See also* Abciximab
Reordering tasks, 260
Repaglinide *(Prandin),* 99*t*

Repaglinide with metformin *(PrandiMet)*, 100*t*
Repatha (evolocumab), 49*t*
Repetitive transcranial magnetic stimulation (rTMS), 79, 82
Replens (water-soluble lubricant), 304
RepliCare, 312. *See also* Hydrocolloids
RepliCare Thin, 312. *See also* Hydrocolloids
Requip, 223*t. See also* Ropinirole
Requip XL (ropinirole ER), 223*t*
Reserpine *(Serpasil)*
   for HTN, 53*t*
   and orthostatic hypotension, 216
   and sexual dysfunction, 305
   and sleep problems, 316
Residential care, 7*t*
Resistance (strength) training
   for dizziness, 216*t*
   for DM, 96
   exercise prescription, 274
   for Parkinson disease, 221
   for plantar fasciitis, 201, 202
   for preventing falls, 117*t*
Resource Breeze, 191*t*
Resource Health Shake, 190
Respiratory diseases, 285–300
Respiratory tract procedures, 273
Respiratory viruses, 158
Restasis (cyclosporine ophthalmic emulsion), 111
Restless legs syndrome, 321
Restore, 312. *See also* Hydrocolloids
Restore CX, 312
Restore Hydrogel, 313
Restore Plus, 312
Restoril (temazepam), 318*t*
Restrictive lung disease (RLD), 299–300, 299*t*–300*t*
Retapamulin *(Altabax),* 85
Retinopathy, diabetic, 106
Retirement communities, continuing care, 7*t*
Revascularization, 310
Revatio, 58. *See also* Sildenafil
Reverse-transcriptase polymerase chain reaction (RT-PCR), 164*t*
Revised Cardiac Risk Index (RCRI), 264

R-Gel, 252*t. See also* Capsaicin
Rheumatic mitral valvular disease, 35*t,* 113*t*
Rheumatoid arthritis, 208–211
   ACR/EULAR criteria for, 208*t*
   in hand and wrist, 200
   pseudo-RA, 213
Rheumatrex, 210*t. See also* Methotrexate
Rhinitis, 287–288
   medications for, 288*t*–290*t*
   perennial, 287, 288*t,* 294
   seasonal, 287, 288*t*
Rhinocort-Aqua, 289*t. See also* Budesonide
Rhinosinusitis, acute, 285*t*
Rhodiola rosea, 24
Rhythm control drugs, 59*t,* 60
Rifampin, 34, 163
Rifapentine, 167*t*
Rifaximin *(Xifaxan),* 130*t*
Righting reflex, 220
Rigidity, 222*t*
Rimantadine *(Flumadine),* 165*t*
Ringworm, 90*t*
Riociguat *(Adempas),* 58
Risedronate *(Actonel),* 231*t,* 233*t*
Risedronate, delayed-release *(Atelvia),* 231*t*
Risk evaluation and mitigation strategy (REMS), 250
Risperdal, 76*t,* 282*t. See also* Risperidone
Risperidone *(Risperdal)*
   for acute mania, 82
   adverse events, 283*t*
   for agitation, 76, 76*t*
   for psychotic disorders, 281, 282*t*
   and sexual dysfunction, 305
Ritalin, 80*t,* 260. *See also* Methylphenidate
Ritonavir, 168
Rituxam (rituximab), 211
Rituximab *(Rituxam),* 211
Rivaroxaban *(Xarelto)*
   for ACS, 41
   for AF, 59*t,* 60*t*
   for anticoagulation, 33*t,* 35*t,* 60*t*
   for antithrombotic therapy, 26*t*
   avoid use, 19*t*
   cessation before surgery, 267
   reduce dosage, 19*t*

Rivaroxaban *(Xarelto) continued*
  resumption after surgery, 267
  for VTE, 27*t*, 30*t*
Rivastigmine *(Exelon)*, 75*t*
RLD (restrictive lung disease), 299–300, 299*t*–300*t*
RMS, 243*t. See also* Morphine
Robitussin, 261, 286*t. See also* Guaifenesin
Robitussin DM (dextromethorphan), 286*t*
Rocaltrol, 180. *See also* Calcitriol
Rocephin, 171*t. See also* Ceftriaxone
Roflumilast *(Daliresp),* 298*t*
Rolling walkers (rollators), 116
Ropinirole *(Requip),* 223*t*, 321
Ropinirole ER *(Requip XL),* 223*t*
Rosacea, 87–88
Rosenbaum card testing for near vision, 105
Rosiglitazone *(Avandia),* 99*t*
Rosiglitazone with glimepiride *(Avandaryl),* 100*t*
Rosiglitazone with metformin *(Avandamet),* 100*t*
Rosula (sodium sulfacetamide), 87
Rosuvastatin *(Crestor),* 48*t*
Rotator cuff tears, 194*t*, 195
Rotator cuff tendinitis, 194–195
Rotator tendon impingement on clavicle, 194–195
Rotigotine *(Neupro),* 223*t*
Roux-en-Y gastric bypass, 189
Roxanol, 243*t. See also* Morphine
Roxicodone (oxycodone), 242*t*
Roxin, 172*t. See also* Ofloxacin
Rozerem (ramelteon), 38, 318*t*
rTMS (repetitive transcranial magnetic stimulation), 79, 82
RT-PCR (reverse-transcriptase polymerase chain reaction), 164*t*
Rubber band ligation, 132
Ruxolitinib, 144
Rythmol (propafenone), 59*t*
Rythmol SR (propafenone), 59*t*

S
Sacral nerve stimulation, 151, 155
Safe sex practices, 168

SAF-Gel, 313
Saint Louis University Mental Status (SLUMS) Examination, 70
Sal-acid plaster, 201
Salicylates, nonacetylated, 206*t*, 240*t*
Salicylic acid, 87
Salicylic acid plaster, 201
Saline and sodium bicarbonate (Sinu*Cleanse*), 287
Saline solution, 94
Salmeterol *(Serevent Diskus),* 296*t*
Salmeterol-fluticasone *(Advair Diskus),* 298*t*
Salmonine, 232*t. See also* Calcitonin
Salsalate, 206*t*, 240*t*
Salt restriction, 43*t*, 217*t*
Salt tablets, 183, 184
SAMe (S-adenosylmethionine), 24
Samsca (tolvaptan), 184
Sanctura, 151*t. See also* Trospium
Sanctura XR, 151*t. See also* Trospium
Sandostatin (octreotide), 261
Santyl, 307
Saphris (asenapine), 282*t*
Sarcoma, vulvar, 332
Sarcopenia, 187
Sarna (camphor-menthol-phenol), 251*t*
Savaysa, 33*t. See also* Edoxaban
Savella (milnacipran), 251*t*
Saw palmetto, 25
Saxagliptin *(Onglyza),* 98*t*
Saxagliptin with metformin *(Kombiglyze XR),* 100*t*
Saxenda, 190. *See also* Liraglutide
Scabene (lindane), 88
Scabies, 88
Schizophrenia, 281
Sciatica, 196
Sclerotherapy, 132
Scopolamine, 67*t*, 129*t*, 261
Seasonal depression, 79
Seasonal (antiallergy) medications, 17
Seasonal rhinitis, 287, 288*t*
SeaSorb, 313. *See also* Calcium alginate dressings
Seborrheic dermatitis, 88, 89*t*, 90*t*
Secretions, excessive, 261

Sectral (acebutolol), 53*t*
Sedation, 259, 283*t*, 284*t*
Sedatives
  adverse events, 327
  alcohol interactions, 324
  and falls, 114*t*, 117*t*
  and sleep problems, 316, 317*t*
  and UI, 150*t*
Segmental pressure measurement, 62*t*
Seizures, 224–225, 281, 283*t*
Selective estrogen-receptor modulators, 304
Selective serotonin-reuptake inhibitors. *See* SSRIs
Selegiline *(Carbex, Eldepryl, Zelapar),* 223*t*
Selenium sulfide, 88
Self-help groups, 324
Self-help materials, 326
Self-maintenance physical scale (ADLs), 336
Self-management education, 239*t*
Self-monitor blood glucose (SMBG), 102
Semont maneuver, 217*t*
Senior citizen housing, 7*t*
Senna *(Senokot),* 126, 127*t*
Senokot, 127*t. See also* Senna
Sensorineural hearing loss, 133*t*–134*t*
Sensory impairments, 68*t*, 216*t*
Sentinel lymph node (SLN) biopsy, 330
Sepsis, 160–162, 162–163, 172*t*
Septic shock, severe, 163
Serax (oxazepam), 38*t*
Serevent Diskus (salmeterol), 296*t*
Seroquel, 76*t*, 282*t. See also* Quetiapine
Serotonin agents, 125
Serotonin antagonists, 125, 128*t*
Serotonin norepinephrine-reuptake inhibitors. *See* SNRIs
Serotonin 1A partial agonists, 38
Serotonin syndrome, 38, 67*t*
Serpasil, 53*t. See also* Reserpine
Sertraconazole *(Ertaczo),* 90*t*
Sertraline *(Zoloft)*
  for anxiety, 38
  for depression, 79, 80*t*, 82
  for panic disorder, 38
  for PTSD, 38

for social phobia, 38
SSRI-induced sexual dysfunction, 305
Sevelamer carbonate *(Renvela),* 180
Sevelamer hydrochloride *(Renagel),* 180
Sex practices, safe, 168
Sexual aggression, 77*t*
Sexual dysfunction, 301–305
Sexually transmitted infection (STI) counseling, 347*t*
SGLT2 (sodium-glucose cotransporter-2) inhibitors, 97, 99*t*
Shark liver oil, 132
Sharp debridement, 307, 311
Shingles. *See* Herpes zoster
Shock, septic, 163
Shoes, 118*t*, 201
Short Physical Performance Battery (SPPB), 115
Shoulder impingement syndrome, 194
Shoulder pain, 194–195, 194*t*, 239*t*
Shunts, 107
SIADH (syndrome of inappropriate secretion of antidiuretic hormone), 183, 184
Sigmoidoscopy, 270*t*
SignaDRESS, 312. *See also* Hydrocolloids
Sigvaris stockings, 315
Sildenafil *(Revatio, Viagra)*
  α_1-blocker interactions, 275
  for PAH, 58
  for sexual dysfunction, 301*t*, 305
Silenor, 317*t. See also* Doxepin
Silodosin *(Rapaflo),* 276
Silvadene, 308
SilvaKollagen Gel, 314
SilvaSorb Gel, 313
Silver dressings, 308
Silver with calcium alginate dressings *(Algidex Ag Alginate, 3M Tegaderm Alginate AG, SofSorb AG, ALGICELL Ag, DermaSyn/Ag, SILVERCEL, McKesson Calcum Alginate with Silver),* 313–314
Silver with collagen dressings *(ColActive Plus AG, Prisma Matrix, SilvaKollagen Gel, DermaCol AG, BIOSTEP Ag, PROMOGRAN PRISMA, Puracol Plus AG),* 314

Silver with foam dressings *(Allevyn Ag Foam, Aquacel Ag Foam, Bordered Foam/Ag, HydraFoam/Ag, PolyMem Silver, Optifoam AG, Contreet Foam)*, 312

Silver with hydrocolloid *(Contreet)*, 312–313

Silver with hydrogel dressings *(SilvaSorb Gel, SilvrSTAT, Silver-Sept Wound Gel, Viniferamine Wound Hydrogel AG, Silver-Sept Silver Antimicrobial Skin & Wound Gel, Gentell Hydrogel AG)*, 313

SILVERCEL, 313–314

Silver-Sept Silver Antimicrobial Skin & Wound Gel, 313

Silver-Sept Wound Gel, 313

SilvrSTAT, 313

Simcor (simvastatin with niacin), 49*t*

Simethicone, 16

Simponi (golimumab), 210

Simpurity collagen pad, 314

Simvastatin *(Zocor)*, 48*t*, 305

Simvastatin with ezetimibe *(Vytorin)*, 49*t*

Simvastatin with niacin *(Simcor)*, 49*t*

Sinemet (carbidopa-levodopa), 222*t*, 321

Sinemet CR (carbidopa-levodopa), 222*t*

Sinequan, 81. *See also* Doxepin

Single-photon emission computed tomography (SPECT), 39

Singulair (montelukast), 298*t*

Sinu*Cleanse* (saline and sodium bicarbonate), 287

Sinus irrigation, 285*t*

Sinusitis, 285*t*

SIRS (systemic inflammatory response syndrome), 162–163, 308

Sitagliptin *(Januvia)*, 98*t*

Sitagliptin with metformin *(Janumet)*, 100*t*

Sites of care, 7*t*

Sitz baths, 132

Sivextro (tedizolid), 173*t*

Skeletal muscle relaxants
   anticholinergic properties, 67*t*
   drug interactions, 251*t*
   fall risks, 114*t*
   and orthostatic hypotension, 216
   for pain relief, 251*t*–252*t*

Skeletal muscle spasms, 252*t*

Skilled nursing facilities, 7*t*

Skin and soft tissue infection (SSTI), 163, 170*t*, 173*t*

Skin care, 46, 155, 228

Skin examination, 271*t*

Skin failure, 262–263

Skin graft, 315

Skin losses, 86, 183, 311

Skin maceration, 88–89

Skin substitutes *(Apligraf, DermaGraft, GammaGraft, OrCel, TransCyte)*, 311, 315

Skin ulcers, 306–315, 306*t*–307*t*

Skintegrity Hydrogel, 313

Sleep, 238

Sleep apnea, 285*t*, 319–320

Sleep deprivation, 68*t*, 281

Sleep disorders, 316–322
   medications for, 317*t*–318*t*
   postmenopausal, 333
   REM sleep behavior disorder, 222*t*, 322

Sleep hygiene measures, 316–317, 321

Sleep restriction, 317

Sleep rituals, 317

Sleeve gastrectomy, 189

SLN (sentinel lymph node) biopsy, 330

Slo-Bid, 297*t*. *See also* Theophylline-SR

SLUMS (Saint Louis University Mental Status) Examination, 70

SMBG (self-monitor blood glucose), 102

SMIs (soft mist inhalers), 295

Smoking, 229, 323

Smoking cessation, 325–327
   for angina, 42
   for cataract treatment, 105
   for CKD, 180
   for COPD, 292
   for cough, 285*t*
   for DM, 96, 102
   for GERD, 121
   for HTN, 51
   for PAD, 62
   post MI, 41
   preoperative, 266
   for prevention, 219, 270*t*
   resources for, 348
   for UI, 148

Smoldering myeloma, 145
Smooth and Cool, 88
Sneezing, 288*t*
Snellen wall chart, 105
SNRIs (serotonin norepinephrine-reuptake
    inhibitors)
  for anxiety, 38
  for depression, 81*t*
  drug interactions, 251*t*
  for menopausal symptoms, 334
  for pain, 234*t*
  for Parkinson disease, 222*t*
Social phobia, 38
Social status assessment, 5*t*
Social support, 326
Social workers, 6*t*
Sodium, fractional excretion of (FENa), 177,
    181
Sodium, potassium, and magnesium sulfate
    (*Suprep* bowel prep kit), 127*t*
Sodium, urine, 181, 184
Sodium bicarbonate
  for acidosis, 180
  for CKD, 180
  for hyperkalemia, 185, 186
  for prevention of radiocontrast-induced
    acute kidney injury, 178
Sodium bicarbonate and saline
    (Sinu*Cleanse*), 287
Sodium disorders, 182–183, 183–184
Sodium ferric gluconate complex *(Ferrlecit,*
    Nulecit), 140*t*
Sodium imbalance, 281
Sodium nitroprusside *(Nipride),* 51
Sodium phosphate/biphosphate emollient
    enema *(Fleet),* 127*t*
Sodium polystyrene sulfonate (SPS,
    Kayexalate), 185, 186
Sodium sulfacetamide *(Clenia, Rosula),* 87
Sodium-glucose cotransporter-2 (SGLT2)
    inhibitors, 97, 99*t*
SofSorb AG, 313–314
Soft mist inhalers (SMIs), 295
Soft tissue or skin infections, 163, 170*t,* 173*t*
Solaraze, 206*t. See also* Diclofenac gel
Solesta, 156

Solifenacin *(VESIcare),* 67*t,* 151*t*
SoloSite Wound Gel, 313
Solu-Medrol, 104*t. See also*
    Methylprednisolone
Somatic pain
  adjuvant medications for, 251*t*
  antidepressants for, 81*t*
  management of, 234*t,* 241*t*
Somatization, 239
Sonata, 38, 318*t. See also* Zaleplon
Soolantra, 87. *See also* Ivermectin
Sorbalgon, 313. *See also* Calcium alginate
    dressings
Sorbitol
  for constipation, 126, 127*t*
  for hyperkalemia, 185, 186
Sorbitrate (isosorbide dinitrate), 41*t*
Sorbsan, 313. *See also* Calcium alginate
    dressings
Sorine, 59*t. See also* Sotalol
Sotalol *(Betapace, Betapace AF, Sorine),*
    21*t,* 59*t*
Soybean formulas, 192
Spand-Gel, 313
Spasm, pain, and vomiting, 261
Spasms, muscular, 196, 252*t*
Spasticity, 329*t*
SPECT (single-photon emission computed
    tomography), 39
Spectazole (econazole nitrate), 90*t*
Spectracef (cefditoren), 170*t*
Speech therapists, 6*t,* 260
SPIKES (communicating bad news), 254
Spinal cord injury, 27*t*
Spinal cord stimulation, 239
Spinal manipulation, 196
Spinal stenosis, 203
Spine fractures, 233*t*
Spine surgery, 27*t*
Spiritual care professionals, 6*t*
Spiritual status assessment, 4*t*
Spiriva, 296*t. See also* Tiotropium
Spiriva Respimat Spray, 296*t*
Spirometry, 285*t,* 290
Spironolactone *(Aldactone)*
  for ACS, 40

Spironolactone *(Aldactone) continued*
    avoid use, 19*t*
    digoxin interactions, 45
    for HF, 45
    for HTN, 52*t*
    and sexual dysfunction, 305
Splinting
    for carpal tunnel syndrome, 200
    for de Quervain tendinopathy, 199
    for osteoarthritis, 202
    for pain, 239
    for rheumatoid arthritis, 209
Sporanox, 86–87, 174*t. See also* Itraconazole
SPPB (Short Physical Performance Battery),
    115
Sprains, 252*t*
Squamous cell carcinoma, vulvar, 332
Squamous hyperplasia, 332
SSRIs (selective serotonin-reuptake
    inhibitors)
    for agitation, 76, 76*t*
    for anxiety, 38, 317
    for AUDs, 325
    for bipolar disorders, 83*t*
    for depression, 79, 79*t*–80*t*
    drug interactions, 20*t,* 21*t,* 251*t*
    fall risks, 114*t*
    for IBS, 125
    for menopausal symptoms, 334
    and osteoporosis, 229
    for pain, 242*t,* 251*t*
    for painful neuropathy, 228
    for Parkinson disease, 222*t*
    preoperative care, 268
    and restless legs syndrome, 321
    for sexual aggression, impulse-control
        symptoms in men, 77*t*
    and sexual dysfunction, 305
SSTI (skin and soft tissue infection), 163,
    170*t,* 173*t*
St. John's wort *(Hypericum perforatum),* 25
    avoid use, 81
    digoxin interactions, 45
    herbal medication interactions, 24
Stalevo (carbidopa-levodopa + entacapone),
    224*t*

Staphylococcal blepharitis, 110*t*
Staphylococcus aureus
    endocarditis prophylaxis regimens, 272*t*
    methicillin-resistant (MRSA), 85, 158, 160,
        163, 308*t*
    in nursing-home–acquired pneumonia,
        158
    in UTI or urosepsis, 161
Starch solutions, 182
Starlix (nateglinide), 98*t*
Stasis edema, 152
Statin therapy
    for ACS, 41
    for acute stroke, 218
    adverse events, 49*t*
    and dialysis, 181
    for DM, 96*t*
    for dyslipidemia, 42, 47, 48*t,* 48*t*–49*t*
    herbal medicine interactions, 24
    perioperative use, 268
    prescribing information, 47–48
    for prevention of acute kidney failure, 178
    and sexual dysfunction, 305
Stay Safe, Stay Active, 116
STEADI (Stopping Elderly Accidents, Deaths
    and Injuries), 114
Stem cell transplantation
    antibiotics for, 175*t*
    for chronic myelogenous leukemia, 144
    for MDS, 143, 144
    for multiple myeloma, 145
    for myelofibrosis, 144
Stendra (avanafil), 301*t*
Stents, 50, 267
Stepping On program, 116
Steroids. *See* Corticosteroids;
    Glucocorticoids
STI (sexually transmitted infection)
    counseling, 347*t*
Stimulants, 327, 328
Stimulen, 314
Stiolto Respimat (tiotropium-olodaterol), 298*t*
Stockings, pressure, 315. *See also*
    Compression stockings
Stopping Elderly Accidents, Deaths and
    Injuries (STEADI), 114

Strains, 252*t*
Strength training
  for dizziness, 216*t*
  for DM, 96
  exercise prescription, 274
  for Parkinson disease, 221
  for plantar fasciitis, 201, 202
  for preventing falls, 117*t*
Streptococcus pneumoniae, 158
Streptomycin, 171*t*
Stress, post-traumatic, 37, 38, 239
Stress incontinence. *See also* Urinary
    incontinence
  characteristics and causes, 146*t*
  in nursing-home residents, 153
  therapy for, 148*f*, 149, 150, 152
Stress reduction, 73
Stress testing, 39, 44
Stress ulcers, 124
Stretching exercises, 274
  for bicipital tendinitis, 195
  for frozen shoulder (adhesive capsulitis),
    195
  for nocturnal leg cramps, 320
  for osteoarthritis, 202
  for plantar fasciitis, 201
Striant (testosterone), 303*t*
Stroke
  acute, 27*t*, 217–219
  determinants for hospice eligibility, 257*t*
  differential diagnosis, 281
  gastrointestinal complaints, 120*t*
  medications for, 26*t*, 233*t*
  prevention of, 31*t*, 219, 271*t*
  resources for, 349
  risk instruments, 59*t*
Stromectol, 88. *See also* Ivermectin
Subacromial bursitis, 194–195, 213
Subdeltoid bursitis, 213
Substance related disorder, 323
Substance use disorders, 266, 323–329
Subsyndromal depression, 78
Subsys, 248*t. See also* Fentanyl
Sucralfate, 124
Sular (nisoldipine), 55*t*
Sulbactam-ampicillin *(Unasyn),* 159*t*, 169*t*

Sulconazole *(Exelderm),* 90*t*
Sulfamethoxazole, 34
Sulfasalazine *(Azulfidine)*
  digoxin interactions, 45
  for psoriasis, 87
  for rheumatoid arthritis, 209, 210*t*
Sulfonylureas, 97, 98*t*, 101
Sulindac *(Clinoril),* 34, 207*t*
Sunscreens, 84, 86, 87
Supartz, 203. *See also* Hyaluronic acid
Superficial mycoses, 90*t*, 176*t*
Suppositories, 127*t*, 154, 155
Suprax (cefixime), 170*t*
Suprep bowel prep kit (sodium, potassium,
    and magnesium sulfate), 127*t*
Surgery
  abdominopelvic, 27*t*
  for acute disk herniation, 196
  adrenal insufficiency management, 104
  for AF, 60
  anticoagulant agents for, 32*t*, 33*t*
  antithrombotic medications for, 27*t*
  aortic valve replacement (AVR), 35*t*, 61
  for arterial ulcers, 310
  for AS, 61
  for back pain, 196
  bariatric, 96, 189, 320
  for basal cell carcinoma, 85
  for bowel obstruction, 261
  for BPH, 275, 276–277
  CABG, 40
  cardiac risk assessment for, 264
  for carpal tunnel syndrome, 200
  for cataract, 105, 266–267
  for cervical stenosis/radiculopathy, 194
  cessation of anticoagulation before, 267
  cryosurgery, 84, 85
  for de Quervain tendinopathy, 199
  decision-making, 264
  dental procedures, 267
  for diabetic foot ulcers, 311
  for DM, 96
  DVT/PE prophylaxis, 27*t*
  electrosurgery, 84
  endocarditis prophylaxis, 272–273, 272*t*
  for fecal incontinence, 155

Surgery *continued*
  for follicular neoplasm, 93
  for foot disorders, 201
  for frozen shoulder (adhesive capsulitis), 195
  for GERD, 121
  for glaucoma, 107
  for hip fracture, 27*t*, 31*t*, 32*t*, 35*t*, 198
  hip replacement, 27*t*, 31*t*, 32*t*, 33*t*, 35*t*
  for hyperthyroidism, 93
  ICD placement, 65
  knee, 27*t*, 31*t*, 32*t*, 33*t*, 35*t*
  for leg fracture, 27*t*
  for lumbar spinal stenosis, 197
  maxillofacial, 320
  for melanoma, 86
  for metatarsalgia, 201
  mitral valve replacement, 35*t*
  Mohs micrographic surgery, 85
  for Morton neuroma, 201
  for multiple myeloma, 145
  for osteoarthritis, 202
  for PAD, 62*t*
  for pain management, 238
  for Parkinson disease, 221
  for pelvic fracture, 27*t*
  for plantar fasciitis, 201
  postoperative delirium, 268–269
  postoperative nausea and vomiting, 128*t*
  postoperative pain, 243*t*
  preoperative care, 264–268, 265*f*
  for pressure ulcers, 314
  prophylactic regimens for, 273
  pulmonary risk assessment for, 265–266
  RBC transfusion for anemia and, 142
  reducing cardiovascular complications of, 268
  resumption of anticoagulation after, 267
  for rheumatoid arthritis, 209
  risk calculators, 264
  for rotator cuff tears, 195
  for sleep apnea, 320
  for spinal cord injury, 27*t*
  spine, 27*t*
  thoracic, 27*t*
  for thyroid nodules, 93
  for UI, 148*f*, 152
  for unstable lumbar spine, 197
  urologic procedures, 27*t*
  for vaginal prolapse, 333
  vascular, 27*t*
  for venous ulcers, 315
  for VIN, 332
  for vulvar malignancy, 332
Surmontil, 81. *See also* Trimipramine
Suvorexant *(Belsomra)*, 318*t*
Swallowing assessment, 260
Swallowing rehabilitation, 120
Symbicort (budesonide-formoterol), 298*t*
Symlin (pramlintide), 101*t*
Symmetrel (amantadine), 165*t*, 223*t*
Sympathomimetics, 316
Synacthen Depot (tetracosactin), 103
Synalar (fluocinolone acetonide), 91*t*
Syncope, 63–64, 63*t*, 65
Syndrome of inappropriate secretion of antidiuretic hormone (SIADH), 183, 184
Synercid (quinupristin-dalfopristin), 173*t*
Synthroid, 92. *See also* Levothyroxine
Synvisc, 203. *See also* Hyaluronic acid
Synvisc-One, 203
Systemic inflammatory response syndrome (SIRS), 162–163, 308
Systolic dysfunction, 42

T
T scores, 229
T_3 (triiodothyronine), 92
T_4 (thyroxine), 92, 192, 229
Tachycardia, 56*t*, 65
Tacrolimus, 87
Tadalafil *(Cialis)*, 275, 302*t*
Tafluprost, 108*t*
Tagamet HB 200, 122*t. See also* Cimetidine
Tai Chi
  for osteoarthritis, 202
  for pain, 239*t*
  for Parkinson disease, 221
  for preventing falls, 116, 117*t*
  for sleep disorders, 322
Take Control, 47
Tamiflu (oseltamivir), 165*t*

Tamoxifen *(Nolvadex)*
   for breast cancer, 331, 331*t*
   drug interactions, 34, 334
Tamsulosin *(Flomax),* 275–276
Tanzeum (albiglutide), 100*t*
Tapazole (methimazole), 93
Tapentadol *(Nucynta),* 244*t*
Tapentadol ER (*Nucynta* ER), 246*t*
Tar, 87, 88
Tardive dyskinesia (TD), 284*t*
Targiniq ER (oxycodone with naloxone), 245*t*, 250
Tarsal tunnel syndrome, 201
Tasimelteon *(Hetlioz),* 318*t*
Tasmar (tolcapone), 223*t*
TAVR (transcatheter aortic valve replacement), 61
Tazarotene gel, 87
Tazobactam-piperacillin *(Zosyn)*
   for infections in chronic wounds, 308*t*
   for infectious diseases, 170*t*
   for pneumonia, 159*t,* 160
TB (tuberculosis), 166–167, 166*t*–167*t*
TCAs (tricyclic antidepressants)
   for bipolar disorders, 83*t*
   and dementia, 73
   for depression, 81*t*
   drug interactions, 20*t*, 21*t*, 242*t*
   fall risks, 114*t*
   for IBS, 125
   and orthostatic hypotension, 216
   for pain, 234*t,* 251*t*
   for painful neuropathy, 228
   for Parkinson disease, 222*t*
   and restless legs syndrome, 321
   and UI, 150*t*
T-cell activation inhibitors, 211
TD (tardive dyskinesia), 284*t*
Team care, 5, 6*t*
Tedizolid *(Sivextro),* 173*t*
T.E.D.™, 46
Tefloro, 171*t. See also* Ceftaroline fosamil
Tegretol. See also Carbamazepine
   for agitation, 76*t*
   for bipolar disorders, 83*t*
   for pain relief, 250*t*

   for painful neuropathy, 228
   for seizures, 225*t*
Tegretol XR. See also Carbamazepine
   for bipolar disorders, 83*t*
   for pain relief, 250*t*
   for painful neuropathy, 228
   for seizures, 225*t*
Tekturna (aliskiren), 56*t*
Telavancin *(Vibativ),* 163, 173*t*
Telephone counseling, 326, 327
Telephone translation services, 13
Telithromycin *(Ketek),* 171*t*
Telmisartan *(Micardis),* 56*t*
Temazepam *(Restoril),* 318*t*
Temovate, 91*t. See also* Clobetasol propionate
Temperature conversions, 1*t*
Temporal (giant cell) arteritis, 213–215
Tendinitis, 194–195, 194*t*
Tendinopathy, de Quervain, 199
Tenex (guanfacine), 53*t*
Tenofovir *(Truvada),* 168
Tenormin, 53*t. See also* Atenolol
Tenosynovitis, 213
TENS. *See* Transcutaneous electrical nerve stimulation
Tequin (gatifloxacin), 110*t*
Terazosin *(Hytrin),* 53*t*, 275
Terbinafine *(Lamisil, Lamisil AT),* 87, 90*t*, 176*t*
Teriparatide *(Forteo)*
   bone outcomes, 233*t*
   for osteoporosis, 232, 232*t*
   for vertebral compression fracture, 197
Tessalon Perles (benzonatate), 286*t*
Testim (testosterone), 303*t*
Testosterone, 303, 303*t*
Testosterone, buccal *(Striant),* 303*t*
Testosterone, intranasal *(Natesto),* 303*t*
Testosterone, transdermal *(Androderm, AndroGel, Fortesta, Testim),* 303*t*
Testosterone cypionate, 303*t*
Testosterone deficiency, 302
Testosterone enanthate, 303*t*
Testosterone replacement, 233, 303*t*
Testosterone undecanoate *(Aveed),* 303*t*
Tetanus vaccination, 270*t*

Tetracosactin *(Synacthen Depot)*, 103
Tetracycline *(Achromycin, Helidac, Pylera, Sumycin)*
  for cellulitis, 85
  digoxin interactions, 45
  for *H pylori* infection, 123*t*
  for infectious diseases, 172*t*
  for rosacea, 88
Tetrahydrocannabinol (THC), 329*t*
Teveten (eprosartan), 56*t*
Thai, 212*t*
Thalidomide, 145
THC (tetrahydrocannabinol), 329*t*
Theo-24, 297*t. See also* Theophylline-SR
Theo-Dur, 297*t. See also* Theophylline-SR
Theophylline, 21*t*, 291*t*–292*t*, 295*t*
Theophylline-SR *(Slo-Bid, Theo-24, Theo-Dur)*, 295*t*, 297*t*
Therapeutic communities, 324
Therapress Duo stockings, 315
Thiamine, 69
Thiazide diuretics
  for CKD, 180
  and coexisting conditions, 56*t*, 57*t*
  for HTN, 51, 52*t*, 101
  for hyperkalemia, 185, 186
Thiazolidinediones
  avoid use, 44
  for DM, 97, 99*t*
  and UI, 150*t*
Thickening agents, 121
Thienopyradines, 31*t*
Thioridazine *(Mellaril)*
  anticholinergic property, 67*t*
  and dementia, 73
  for psychosis, 282*t*
  QT_c interval interactions, 21*t*
  and seizures, 225
Thiothixene, 67*t*, 225
Third-spacing, 183
Thirst, impaired, 182
Thoracic surgery, 27*t*
3M Tegaderm, 312, 314
3M Tegaderm Alginate AG, 313–314
3M Tegaderm Foam, 312
3M Tegaderm Hydrogel, 313

3M Tegagen HI & HG Alginate, 313. *See also* Calcium alginate dressings
3M Tegasorb, 312. *See also* Hydrocolloids
3M Tegasorb Thin, 312
Thrombin inhibitors. *See* Direct thrombin inhibitors
Thrombocytopenia, heparin-induced (HIT), 26*t*, 33*t*
Thrombocytosis, essential, 144
Thromboembolism, 26–35, 27*t*, 30*t*, 32*t*, 33*t*, 35*t*, 334
Thrombolytic therapy, 40, 218–219
Thrombosis
  cerebral venous sinus, 35*t*
  deep vein (DVT), 27*t*, 28, 30, 32*t*, 45, 199, 233*t*
  intracardiac, 35*t*
  left ventricular thrombosis, 41
ThuLEP, 276
Thyroid disorders, 301*t*
Thyroid nodules, 93–94
Thyroid-stimulating hormone (TSH), 271*t*
Thyroxine (T_4), 92, 192, 229
TIA (transient ischemic attack), 26*t*, 217*t*
Tiagabine *(Gabitril Filmtabs)*, 226*t*
Tiazac (diltiazem), 54*t*
Ticagrelor *(Brilinta)*
  for ACS, 40
  for angina, 41
  for antithrombotic therapy, 26*t*
  cessation before surgery, 267, 268
  prescribing information, 31*t*
Ticarcillin-clavulanate *(Timentin)*, 170*t*
Ticlopidine, 24
Tielle, 312. *See also* Foam island dressings
Tigecycline *(Tygacil)*, 172*t*
Timed toileting, 149
Timentin (ticarcillin-clavulanate), 170*t*
Timolol *(Blocadren)*, 54*t*
Timolol drops, 107*t*
Timolol/brimonidine, 108*t*
Timolol/dorzolamide, 108*t*
Tinactin (tolnaftate), 90*t*
Tinea corpis, 89*t*, 90*t*
Tinea cruris, 89*t*, 90*t*
Tinea pedis, 89*t*, 90*t*

Tinea unguium, 86
Tinea versicolor, 89t, 90t
Tinel's sign, 200
Tinnitus, 136–137
Tinzaparin *(Innohep),* 30t, 32t
Tiotropium *(Spiriva),* 291, 295t, 296t
Tiotropium-olodaterol *(Stiolto Respimat),* 298t
Tirofiban *(Aggrastat),* 26t, 34t, 267
Tissue doppler imaging, 42
Tissue plasminogen activator (tPA), 219
Titanium, 87
Tizanidine *(Zanaflex),* 67t, 251t, 252t
TJR (total joint replacement), 198, 273
TLC (total lung capacity), 299
TMP/SMZ (trimethoprim/sulfamethoxazole)
    double strength (DS), 161, 172t
    for infectious diseases, 172t
    for MRSA, 85, 163
TMS (transcranial magnetic stimulation),
    repetitive, 79, 82
Tobacco abuse, 325–327, 326t. *See also*
    Smoking
Tobacco counseling, 346t, 347t
Tobramycin *(Nebcin, Tobrex),* 110t, 160, 171t
Tobrex, 110t. *See also* Tobramycin
Tocilizumab *(Actemra),* 211, 214
Tofacitinib *(Xeljanz),* 209, 211
Tofranil, 81. *See also* Imipramine
Toilet training, 155
Toileting, 149, 153
Tolcapone *(Tasmar),* 223t
Tolectin (tolmetin), 207t
Tolmetin *(Tolectin),* 207t
Tolnaftate *(Absorbine Jr. Antifungal, Tinactin),* 90t
Tolterodine *(Detrol, Detrol LA),* 67t, 151t
Tolvaptan *(Samsca),* 184
Topamax, 226t. *See also* Topiramate
Topicort (desoximetasone), 91t
Topiramate *(Topamax),* 226t, 325
Topiramate ER *(Trokendi XR, Qudexy XR),* 226t
Topiramate with phentermine *(Qsymia),* 189
Toprol XL (metoprolol, long-acting), 53t

Toradol, 207t. *See also* Ketorolac
Toremifene *(Fareston),* 331t
Torsemide *(Demadex),* 52t, 185, 186
Total body water, 182
Total joint replacement (TJR), 198, 273
Total lung capacity (TLC), 299
TOVIAZ, 151t. *See also* Fesoterodine
Trabeculoplasty, 107
Tracheostomy, 320
Tracleer (bosentan), 58
Tradjenta (linagliptin), 98t
Tramadol *(Ultram)*
    for osteoarthritis, 204f, 205
    for pain, 242t
    for painful neuropathy, 228
    reduce dosage, 19t
    and seizures, 225
Tramadol ER *(Ultram* ER, *ConZip),* 246t
Tramadol with APAP *(Ultracet),* 242t
Trandate, 54t, 219. *See also* Labetalol
Trandolapril *(Mavik),* 44t, 55t
Tranexamic acid, 267
Transcatheter aortic valve replacement
    (TAVR), 61
Transcranial magnetic stimulation, repetitive
    (rTMS), 79, 82
Transcutaneous electrical nerve stimulation
    (TENS)
    for osteoarthritis, 202
    for pain, 238, 239t, 307
    for painful neuropathy, 228
TransCyte, 311, 315
Transderm Scop, 129t. *See also* Transdermal
    scopolamine
Transdermal buprenorphine *(Butrans
    Transdermal System CIII),* 235, 246t
Transdermal estrogen *(Alora, Climara,
    Divigel, Elestrin, Estraderm, Estrogel,
    Evamist, Fempatch, Vivelle),* 334
Transdermal fentanyl *(Duragesic),* 243t, 247t, 248t
Transdermal lidocaine *(Lidoderm)*
    for osteoarthritis, 204f
    for pain, 240t, 252t
    for painful neuropathy, 228
Transdermal nicotine, 326t

Transdermal scopolamine *(Transderm Scop),* 129*t,* 261

Transdermal testosterone *(Androderm, AndroGel, Fortesta, Testim),* 303*t*

Transesophageal echocardiography, 60, 218

Transferrin, 188

Transferrin receptor, soluble (sTfR), 141

Transfusion therapy, 142, 145

Transient ischemic attack (TIA), 26*t,* 217*t*

Transitional care, 7*t,* 346*t*

Transitional Care Model, 8

Translation services, 13

Transparent film *(Bioclusive, 3M Tegaderm, BlisterFilm, ClearSite, Comfeel Film, CarraSmart Film, DermaView, Mepore, Opsite, Polyskin II),* 312

Transplantation
  fecal, 132
  kidney, 181
  stem cell, 143, 144, 145, 175*t*

Transrectal microwave thermotherapy (TRMT), 276

Transthoracic echocardiography, 218

Transurethral incision of the prostate (TUIP), 276

Transurethral microwave thermotherapy (TUMT), 276

Transurethral plasma vaporization, 276

Transurethral procedures, 27*t*

Transurethral radiofrequency ablation, 276

Transurethral resection of the prostate (TURP), 276

Travoprost, 108*t*

Trazodone *(Desyrel),* 76*t,* 317*t,* 328

Trelstar Depot (triptorelin), 279*t*

Trelstar LA (triptorelin), 279*t*

Tremors
  antihypertensive therapy and, 56*t*
  cerebellar, 216*t*
  classification of, 216*t*
  distinguishing early Parkinson disease from other parkinsonian syndromes, 220*t*–221*t*
  essential tremor, 56*t,* 216*t*
  physiologic, 216*t*
  treatment options, 222*t*

Trental (pentoxifylline), 62

Treprostinil *(Remodulin),* 57

Tretinoin, 87

Trexall, 210*t. See also* Methotrexate

Triacetin *(Myco-Nail),* 90*t*

Triamcinolone acetonide *(Aristocort, Kenacort, Kenalog, Nasacort Allergy 24, Nasacort AQ)*
  for adrenal insufficiency, 104*t*
  for allergic rhinitis or conjunctivitis, 289*t*
  for dermatologic conditions, 91*t*
  for intertrigo, 86
  for osteoarthritis, 203
  for seborrheic dermatitis, 88
  for shoulder pain, 195

Triamterene *(Dyrenium),* 20*t,* 52*t,* 180

Tricor, 48*t. See also* Fenofibrate

Tricosal (choline magnesium salicylate), 206*t*

Tricyclic antidepressants. *See* TCAs

Tridesilon (desonide), 90*t*

Trifluoperazine, 67*t*

Trigger-point injections, 203

Trihexy, 223*t. See also* Trihexyphenidyl

Trihexyphenidyl *(Artane, Trihexy),* 67*t,* 223*t*

Triiodothyronine (T_3), 92

Trilafon, 282*t. See also* Perphenazine

Trileptal (oxcarbazepine), 226*t,* 250*t*

Trilipix (fenofibrate), 48*t*

Trilisate (choline magnesium salicylate), 206*t*

Trimethoprim, 34, 110, 110*t*

Trimethoprim and sulfamethoxazole. *See* TMP/SMZ

Trimipramine *(Surmontil),* 67*t,* 81

Triple Helix Collagen, 314

Triptorelin *(Trelstar Depot, Trelstar LA),* 279*t*

Trisalicylate, 240*t*

TRMT (transrectal microwave thermotherapy), 276

Trochanteric bursitis, 197–198

Trokendi XR (topiramate), 226*t*

Trolamine salicylate *(Aspercreme),* 207*t,* 251*t*

Troponins, cardiac, 40

Trospium *(Sanctura, Sanctura XR),* 67*t,* 151*t*

Trulicity (dulaglutide), 100*t*

Truvada (tenofovir), 168

TSH (thyroid-stimulating hormone), 271*t*

T-SPOT assay, 166
TST (tuberculin skin test), 166
Tube feeding, 19, 192–193
Tuberculin skin test (TST), 166
Tuberculosis (TB), 166–167, 166*t*–167*t*
Tubular necrosis, acute, 177, 177*t*, 178
Tudorza Pressair (aclidinium), 296*t*
TUIP (transurethral incision of the prostate), 276
TUMT (transurethral microwave thermotherapy), 276
TURP (transurethral resection of the prostate), 276
TURP syndrome, 276
25-Hydroxy vitamin D, 188. *See also* Vitamin D
25-Hydroxy vitamin D deficiency, 229
TwoCal HN, 191*t*
Tygacil (tigecycline), 172*t*
Tylox (oxycodone + APAP), 242*t*
Tyrosine kinase inhibitors, 144

U
UAE (undifferentiated or unexplained anemia of the elderly), 142
Ubiquinol (coenzyme Q_{10}), 22
UCLA Alzheimers and Dementia Care Program, 74
UFH. *See* Unfractionated heparin
UI. *See* Urinary incontinence
Ulcers
    arterial, 306*t*–307*t*, 310
    diabetic, 306*t*–307*t*, 310–311
    H pylori-induced, 123*t*
    peptic, 123–124
    pressure, 306*t*–307*t*, 311–314, 312–314
    skin, 306–315, 306*t*–307*t*
    stress, 124
    venous, 306*t*–307*t*, 315
Uloric, 212*t*. *See also* Febuxostat
Ultec, 312. *See also* Hydrocolloids
Ultec Pro, 312
Ultracet (tramadol + APAP), 242*t*
Ultram, 228, 242*t*. *See also* Tramadol
Ultram ER (tramadol), 246*t*
Ultrasonography

abdominal aortic aneurysm, 61, 270*t*
    for osteoarthritis, 202
    for thyroid nodules, 93, 94
Ultravate (halobetasol propionate), 91*t*
Umeclidinium *(Incruse Ellipta),* 296*t*
Umeclidinium-vilanterol *(Anoro Ellipta),* 299*t*
Unasyn, 169*t*. *See also* Ampicillin-sulbactam
Undecylenic acid *(Fungi-Nail),* 87, 90*t*
Undernutrition, 190
Undifferentiated (or unexplained) anemia of the elderly (UAE), 142
Unfractionated heparin (UFH)
    for ACS, 40
    for anticoagulation, 32*t*
    for antithrombotic therapy, 26*t*
    for DVT/PE prophylaxis, 218
    for VTE, 27*t*, 30*t*
Univasc (moexipril), 55*t*
Unna's boot, 315
Urea, fractional excretion of (FEUrea), 177
Urge incontinence. *See also* Urinary incontinence
    antihypertensive therapy and, 57*t*
    characteristics and causes, 146*t*
    in nursing-home residents, 153
    therapy for, 148*f*, 149, 150, 150*t*–151*t*, 151, 152
Urge suppression, 149*f*
Urinary incontinence (UI), 146–153
    antihypertensive therapy and, 57*t*
    assessment of, 4*t*
    classification of, 146
    estrogen for, 150
    fall risks, 113*t*
    medications associated with, 150*t*
    mixed, 146*t*, 148*f*, 150, 150*t*–151*t*
    nocturnal frequency, 152
    in nursing-home residents, 152–153
    overflow, 146*t*
    resources for, 349
    stepwise evaluation and treatment of, 148*f*
    stress, 146*t*, 148*f*, 149, 150, 150*t*, 152, 153
    types of persistent UI, 146*t*
    urge, 57*t*, 146*t*, 148*f*, 149, 150, 150*t*–151*t*, 151, 152, 153
Urinary retention, 151

Urinary tract infection (UTI), 160–162, 171*t*, 173*t*

Urine osmolality, 182

Urine sodium, 181, 184

Urodynamic testing, 148

Urologic procedures, 27*t*

Urosepsis, 160–162

Uroxatral (alfuzosin ER), 276

Urticaria, 89

USPSTF, 70, 114

UTI (urinary tract infection), 160–162, 171*t*, 173*t*

UV light, 87

Uvulopalatopharyngoplasty, 320

V

VAC (vacuum-assisted closure), 308

Vaccines
hepatitis A, 270*t*
hepatitis B, 102, 181, 270*t*
herpes zoster, 270*t*
influenza, 34, 102, 164, 270*t*
pneumococcal, 102
pneumonia, 270*t*, 346*t*
tetanus, 270*t*
zoster vaccine live *(Zostavax)*, 163

Vacuum tumescence devices *(Osbon-Erec Aid)*, 302*t*

Vacuum-assisted closure (VAC), 308

Vagifem (estradiol vaginal tablets), 305*t*

Vaginal candidiasis, 174*t*

Vaginal prolapse, 333

Vaginismus, 304

Vaginitis, atrophic, 304

Valacyclovir *(Valtrex)*, 164*t*

Valerian, 25

Valisone (betamethasone valerate), 91*t*

Valproic acid *(Depacon, Depakene, Depakote)*, 83*t*, 226*t*

Valproic acid ER *(Depakote ER)*, 226*t*

Valsartan *(Diovan)*, 44*t*, 56*t*, 95

Valtrex (valacyclovir), 164*t*

Valvular heart disease (VD)
antiplatelet agents for, 31*t*
antithrombotic medications for, 26*t*
aortic stenosis, 60–61

warfarin anticoagulation for, 35*t*

Vancocin, 173*t*. *See also* Vancomycin

Vancomycin *(Vancocin)*
for *C difficile* infection, 131*t*, 132
empiric use, 160
for hip fracture surgery, 198
for infections in chronic wounds, 308*t*
for infectious diseases, 173*t*
for MRSA, 163
for pneumonia, 160
for sepsis and SIRS, 163
for UTI or urosepsis, 161

Vancomycin-resistant *E faecium*, 173*t*

Vantas (histrelin acetate), 279*t*

Vantin, 171*t*. *See also* Cefpodoxime

Vaprisol (conivaptan), 184

Vardenafil *(LEVITRA)*, 275, 302*t*

Varenicline *(Chantix)*, 326, 326*t*

Vascular dementia, 70, 74

Vascular endothelial growth factor (VEGF) inhibitors, 106

Vascular erectile dysfunction, 301, 301*t*

Vascular parkinsonism, 220*t*

Vascular surgery, 27*t*

Vasculitis, 177*t*–178*t*

Vaseline, 88

Vasoconstrictors, 110, 112*t*, 132

Vasodilators, 45, 54*t*, 61

Vasomotor rhinitis, 288*t*

Vasotec, 55*t*. *See also* Enalapril

Vasovagal syncope, 63, 63*t*, 64

VD. *See* Valvular heart disease

VEGF (vascular endothelial growth factor) inhibitors, 106

Venlafaxine *(Effexor, Effexor XR)*
for anxiety, 38
for depression, 79, 81*t*
for menopausal symptoms, 334
for pain, 251*t*
for smoking cessation, 326
for social phobia, 38

Venofer (iron sucrose), 140*t*

Venous insufficiency, 46

Venous thromboembolism (VTE), 26–30
acute, 30, 30*t*, 32*t*, 33*t*
and intolerable vasomotor symptoms, 334

Venous thromboembolism (VTE) *continued*
   long-term, 30*t*, 32*t*
   management of, 30*t*, 33*t*
   prophylaxis of, 27*t*, 32*t*, 33*t*
   warfarin anticoagulation for, 35*t*
Venous ulcers, 306*t*–307*t*, 315
Ventavis (iloprost), 57
Ventilation, 158, 162, 292*t*
Ventolin, 296*t*. *See also* Albuterol
Ventolin Rotacaps, 296*t*. *See also* Albuterol
Veramyst, 289*t*. *See also* Fluticasone furoate
Verapamil
   for AF, 58
   digoxin interactions, 45
   enteral nutrition interactions, 192
   for nocturnal leg cramps, 320
Verapamil SR *(Calan SR, Covera-HS, Isoptin
     SR, Verelan PM),* 55*t*
Verelan PM (verapamil), 55*t*
Vertebral artery impingement, 217*t*
Vertebral augmentation, percutaneous, 197
Vertebral fracture, 197, 232*t*
Vertebroplasty, 197
Vertigo, 113*t*, 129*t*, 217*t*
VESIcare, 151*t*. *See also* Solifenacin
Vestibular neuronitis, 217*t*
VF (ventricular fibrillation), 65
VFEND (voriconazole), 175*t*
Viagra, 58, 275, 301*t*. *See also* Sildenafil
Viasorb, 314
Vibativ, 173*t*. *See also* Telavancin
Vibramycin, 172*t*. *See also* Doxycycline
Vibrating pad *(Relaxis),* 321
Vicks VapoRub (mentholatum), 87
Vicodin (hydrocodone + APAP), 241*t*
Vicoprofen (hydrocodone + ibuprofen), 241*t*
Victoza, 101*t*. *See also* Liraglutide
Videofluoroscopy, 120
VigiFoam, 312. *See also* Foam island
    dressings
Vigilon, 313
Viibryd, 80*t*. *See also* Vilazodone
Vilanterol-fluticasone *(Breo Ellipta),* 299*t*
Vilanterol-umeclidinium *(Anoro Ellipta),* 299*t*

Vilazodone *(Viibryd),* 80*t*, 305
VIMPAT (lacosamide), 225*t*
VIN (vulvar intraepithelial neoplasia), 332
Viniferamine Wound Hydrogel, 313
Viniferamine Wound Hydrogel AG, 313
Viokase (pancrelipase), 192
VIP trial home safety program, 116
Viral conjunctivitis, 110–111
Visceral pain, 234*t*
Vision testing, 4, 105
Visken (pindolol), 54*t*
Vismodegib *(Erivedge),* 85
Visual aids, 68*t*
Visual impairment, 105–107
   dual sensory impairment (DSI), 109
   and falls, 113*t*, 116, 118*t*
   preventive measures for delirium, 68*t*
   resources for, 349
   screening for, 271*t*
Vital signs, 119
Vitamin B complex, 320
Vitamin B_{12}, 122*t*, 138*f*, 142
Vitamin B_{12} deficiency, 138*f*, 142, 281
Vitamin C, 106, 122*t*
Vitamin C deficiency, 309
Vitamin D (ergocalciferol)
   with calcitriol, 180
   with calcium, 230
   for malnutrition, 188
   for osteoporosis, 199, 229, 230, 271*t*
   for Parkinson disease, 221
   for preventing falls, 117*t*
   for vitamin D insufficiency, 180, 229
Vitamin D insufficiency, 180, 229
Vitamin D supplementation, 270*t*
Vitamin E, 73, 106
Vitamin K
   drug interactions, 19, 34
   for prevention of fractures, 231
   for warfarin overdose, 35*t*
Vitamin K antagonists, 26*t*, 27*t*, 30*t*
Vitrectomy, 106
Vivactil, 81. *See also* Protriptyline
Vivitrol (naltrexone), 325
Voltaren, 206*t*. *See also* Diclofenac
Voltaren Gel, 206*t*. *See also* Diclofenac gel

Voltaren-XR, 206t. *See also* Diclofenac
Volume depletion, 181–182
Volume overload, 181
Vomiting, 128
    antiemetic therapy, 128t–129t
    with bowel obstruction, 261
    drug-induced, 283t
    at end of life, 261, 262
    and hyponatremia, 183
    postoperative, 128t
Voriconazole *(VFEND),* 175t
Vortioxetine *(Brintellix),* 80t
VT (ventricular tachycardia), 65
VTE. *See* Venous thromboembolism
Vulvar diseases, 332
Vulvar intraepithelial neoplasia (VIN), 332
Vulvectomy, 332
Vytorin (ezetimibe/simvastatin), 49t

W
Walkers, 116, 202
Walking, 274
    for angina, 42
    for claudication therapy, 62
    for DM prevention/delay, 95
    for osteoarthritis, 202
    for pain, 239t
    for problem behaviors, 74
Walking aids, 113t
Walking cast, 201
Warfarin *(Coumadin),* 34. *See also*
        Anticoagulation
    for ACS, 41
    for AF, 59t
    cessation before dental procedures, 267
    cessation before surgery, 267
    COX-2 inhibitor interactions, 208t
    drug interactions, 19, 21t, 34, 59t, 331t
    herbal medicine interactions, 22, 24
    indications for anticoagulation, 35t
    indications for antithrombosis, 26t
    overdose, 35t
    for PAH, 57
    resumption after surgery, 267
    for stroke prevention, 219
    for VTE, 27t, 30, 30t

Water loss, pure, 182
Weakness, 202, 227t, 260
Weight control, 238
Weight conversions, 1t
Weight gain, drug-induced, 283t
Weight loss. *See also* Malnutrition
    for DM, 95, 96
    for GERD, 121
    for HTN, 51
    for hyperuricemia, 212
    marijuana for, 329t
    for obesity, 189
    for osteoarthritis, 198, 202
    for pain, 238
    post MI, 42
    for sleep apnea, 319
    for stroke prevention, 219
    for UI, 148
Weight loss diets, 189
Weight measurement, 43t
Weight training, 274
WelChol (colesevelam), 49t, 99t
Wellbutrin, 80t. *See also* Bupropion
Wellbutrin SR, 80t, 326t. *See also* Bupropion
Wellbutrin XL, 80t. *See also* Bupropion
Wellness visits. *See* Annual Wellness Visit
        (AWV)
Wernicke's aphasia, 227t
Westcort (hydrocortisone valerate), 91t
Westergren sedimentation rate, 2
Wet AMD (age-related macular
        degeneration), 106
Wheat dextrin *(Benefiber),* 126t
Whisper test, 133
"White coat" HTN, 50
White noise, 74, 317
Withholding or withdrawing therapy,
        258–259
Women's health, 330–334
    bone densitometry, 270t
    breast cancer, 233t, 271t, 272, 330–331,
        331–332, 331t
    complicated UTI, 161, 173t
    diarrhea-predominant IBS, 125
    dyspareunia, 303, 304, 333
    early menopause, 229

Women's health *continued*
   energy (caloric) and fluid requirements, 189
   hormone therapy, 333–334
   intolerable vasomotor symptoms, 334
   irritable bowel syndrome, 125
   mammography recommendations, 271*t*
   menopausal symptoms, 333
   osteoporosis, 57*t*, 229–233, 233*t*, 349
   postmenopausal bleeding, 332
   postmenopausal symptoms, 333
   resources for, 348, 349
   sexual dysfunction, 303–305
   TSH, 271*t*
   UTI prophylaxis, 162
   vaginal prolapse, 333
   vulvar diseases, 332
World Health Organization Fracture Risk Assessment Tool (FRAX), 229, 230
Wound assessment and treatment, 306–309
   arterial ulcers, 310
   diabetic foot ulcers, 310–311
   empiric antibiotic therapy for, 308*t*
   pressure ulcers, 311–314
   venous ulcers, 315
   wound characteristics, 306*t*–307*t*
Wrist pain, 199–200

X

Xarelto, 33*t*. *See also* Rivaroxaban
Xartemis XR (oxycodone/acetaminophen ER), 245*t*
Xeljanz, 211. *See also* Tofacitinib
Xenical (orlistat), 189
Xerosis, 89
Xerostomia, 19, 20
Xifaxan (rifaximin), 130*t*
Xolair (omalizumab), 298*t*
Xopenex (levalbuterol), 296*t*
Xue Zhi Kang (red yeast rice), 24
Xyzal (levocetirizine), 288*t*

Y

Yaktrax Walker, 116
Yoga, 200, 239*t*

Z

Z scores, 229
Zaditor (ketotifen), 111*t*
Zafirlukast *(Accolate)*, 298*t*
Zaleplon *(Sonata)*, 38, 317, 318*t*
Zaltrap (aflibercept), 106
Zanaflex, 252*t*. *See also* Tizanidine
Zanamivir *(Relenza)*, 165*t*
Zantac, 122*t*. *See also* Ranitidine
Zaroxolyn, 52*t*. *See also* Metolazone
Zeaxanthin, 106
Zebeta, 53*t*. *See also* Bisoprolol
Zelapar (selegiline), 223*t*
Zestra, 304
Zestril, 55*t*. *See also* Lisinopril
Zetia, 48*t*. *See also* Ezetimibe
Zetonna, 289*t*. *See also* Ciclesonide
Zileuton *(Zyflo)*, 298*t*
Zinc
   for AMD, 106
   drug interactions, 19
   for seborrheic dermatitis, 88
   for sleep disorders, 322
Zinc deficiency, 309
Zinc oxide, 87, 106
Ziprasidone *(Geodon)*, 82, 282*t*
Zipsor, 206*t*. *See also* Diclofenac
Zithromax, 171*t*. *See also* Azithromycin
Zocor, 48*t*. *See also* Simvastatin
Zofran, 128*t*, 261. *See also* Ondansetron
Zohydro ER (hydrocodone bitartate ER), 244*t*
Zoladex (goserelin acetate implant), 279*t*
Zoledronic acid *(Reclast)*
   bone outcomes, 233*t*
   for breast cancer, 332
   effects on other outcomes, level of evidence, and risks of, 233*t*
   for hypercalcemia, 94
   for metastatic bone disease, 279, 332
   for multiple myeloma, 145
   for osteoporosis, 231*t*, 233
Zoloft, 80*t*. *See also* Sertraline
Zolpidem *(Ambien, Ambien CR, Edluar, Intermezzo, Zolpimist)*, 38, 317, 318*t*
Zolpimist, 318*t*. *See also* Zolpidem
Zonalon, 89. *See also* Doxepin

Zonegran (zonisamide), 226*t*
Zonisamide *(Zonegran),* 226*t*
Zorvolex, 206*t. See also* Diclofenac
Zostavax (zoster vaccine live), 163
Zoster ("shingles"). *See* Herpes zoster
Zoster vaccine live *(Zostavax),* 163
Zostrix, 228, 252*t. See also* Capsaicin
Zosyn, 170*t. See also* Piperacillin-
    tazobactam

Zovirax (acyclovir), 164*t*
Zyban (bupropion SR), 80*t,* 326*t*
Zyclara, 84. *See also* Imiquimod
Zydis, 76*t. See also* Olanzapine
Zyflo (zileuton), 298*t*
Zyloprim, 212*t. See also* Allopurinol
Zyprexa, 76*t,* 282*t. See also* Olanzapine
Zyprexa IntraMuscular (olanzapine IM), 77*t*
Zyvox, 173*t. See also* Linezolid